AutoCAD® for Architectural Drawing

AutoCAD® for Architectural Drawing

For Release 14

BEVERLY L. KIRKPATRICK
Adjunct Faculty, Eastfield College

JAMES M. KIRKPATRICK
Eastfield College

Prentice Hall
Upper Saddle River, New Jersey   Columbus, Ohio

Library of Congress Cataloging-in-Publication Data

Kirkpatrick, Beverly L.
    AutoCAD for architectural drawing / Beverly L. Kirkpatrick, James M. Kirkpatrick
        p. cm.
    Includes index.
    ISBN 0-13-080263-8
    1. Architectural drawing—Computer-assisted instruction.
2. AutoCAD (Computer file) I. Kirkpatrick, James M. II. Title
NA2728.K57 1999
720′.28′402855369—dc21   98-40827
                                                                                                               CIP

Cover art: Gilber Gorski, Gorski & Associates, P.C.
Editor: Stephen Helba
Production Coordinator: Karen Fortgang, bookworks
Design Coordinator: Karrie Converse-Jones
Cover Designer: Jason Moore
Production Manager: Deidra M. Schwartz
Marketing Manager: Frank Mortimer, Jr.

This book was set in Times Roman by STELLARViSIONs and was printed and bound by
Courier/Kendallville, Inc. The cover was printed by Phoenix Color Corp.

 © 1999 by Prentice-Hall, Inc.
Simon & Schuster/A Viacom Company
Upper Saddle River, New Jersey 07458

Printed in the United States of America

10 9 8 7 6 5 4 3 2 1

ISBN: 0-13-080263-8

Prentice-Hall International (UK) Limited, *London*
Prentice-Hall of Australia Pty. Limited, *Sydney*
Prentice-Hall of Canada, Inc., *Toronto*
Prentice-Hall of Hispanoamericana, S. A., *Mexico*
Prentice-Hall of India Private Limited, *New Delhi*
Prentice-Hall of Japan, Inc., *Tokyo*
Simon & Schuster Asia Pte. Ltd., *Singapore*
Editora Prentice-Hall do Brasil, Ltda., *Rio de Janeiro*

Preface

AutoCAD has become the industry standard graphics program for architecture; it is used to complete the many drawings that make up a design project. Many architectural firms have adopted AutoCAD as their standard because:

☐ it saves time
☐ affiliated professions use it, and these firms need to be able to exhange disks in order to work on the same drawing
☐ their competitors are using it, and
☐ their clients expect it.

To be successful in architectural drafting today, students must be proficient in the use of AutoCAD. This need for a specific AutoCAD textbook is what led us to write *Auto-CAD for Architectural Drawing.*

This text, for AutoCAD Release 14, is divided into four parts:

☐ Part I: Preparing to Draw with AutoCAD (Chapters 1–3)
☐ Part II: Two-Dimensional AutoCAD (Chapters 4–14)
☐ Part III: Special Topics (Chapters 15–17)
☐ Part IV: Three-Dimensional AutoCAD (Chapters 18–19)

This new text includes many features designed to help the reader master AutoCAD Release 14.

☐ A Prompt/Response format leads the reader through each new AutoCAD command to avoid confusion and frustration.
☐ Exercises are geared to architects and space planners, providing students the opportunity to work with real-world situations.
☐ Chapters 2 and 3 are introductory chapters for using AutoCAD Release 14. Material in Chapters 4 through 19 progresses from basic to complex in a step-by-step learning process for users of Release 14.
☐ Over 400 figures (many printed to scale) support the text and reinforce the material.
☐ Illustrations located in the margins help the user locate AutoCAD commands within the AutoCAD menus and toolbars. (Margins also contain notes, tips, and warnings that give students additional support and information.)
☐ Chapters 9–15 follow the graphic development of a design project called the Tenant Space project; each chapter contains step-by-step instructions for drawing each stage of the project.
☐ Four other projects are included in the text as practice exercises.
☐ Practice exercises in every chapter review the commands learned.
☐ Learning objectives and review questions in every chapter reinforce the learning process.
☐ An *Instructor's Manual* is available to support the text.

Most importantly, this text was written to help you, the reader, master the AutoCAD program, which will be a valuable tool in your professional career.

We would like to acknowledge the following people, who contributed ideas and drawings: Mary Peyton, IALD, IES, Lighting Consultant; Roy Peyton, John Sample, Katherine Broadwell, Curran C. Redman, S. Vic Jones, W. M. Stevens, John Brooks, Bill Sorrells, and the CAD students at Eastfield College. Finally, we would like to thank Autodesk, Inc.

B.L.K.
J.M.K.

Contents

PART IV   THREE-DIMENSIONAL AUTOCAD   423

AutoCAD® for Architectural Drawing

1 Introduction

AUTOCAD FOR ARCHITECTURAL DRAWING

This book is written for students of architecture who want to learn the AutoCAD program in the most effective and efficient manner–by drawing with it. AutoCAD commands are introduced in tutorial exercises and thoroughly explained. The tutorial exercises specifically cover architectural drawings.

Nothing in AutoCAD is difficult to learn. AutoCAD is a very powerful program, however, and you can produce any type of graphics with it. As a result there are many details that must be clearly understood. This book presents these details in a manner that allows them to be easily understood. It can also be used as a reference when you forget a detail.

Chapters 1 through 5 introduce the AutoCAD program and basic two-dimensional AutoCAD commands. Chapter 6 describes the new commands used to insert raster images (like photographs) into AutoCAD drawings. Chapter 10 describes dimensioning and includes the new dimensioning elements of Release 14; Chapter 16 describes how to develop client presentations using AutoCAD. Chapter 17 describes how to customize toolbars and menus. Chapter 19 describes three-dimensional drawing and includes the solid modeling capabilities of Release 14.

BENEFITS OF USING AUTOCAD

When you become an experienced AutoCAD user you will be able to:

☐ Produce clear, precise, and impressive drawings by printing or plotting your drawings.
☐ Draw with precision so that you can measure exact distances.
☐ Change your drawings easily and quickly.
☐ Store your drawings on disks.
☐ Interchange drawings with other professionals.
☐ Use the AutoCAD presentation capabilities for client presentations, either printed or on the display screen.
☐ Be in the mainstream of today's technology.

TYPES OF DRAWINGS COMPLETED IN THE CHAPTER EXERCISES

The following are the types of drawings that are completed in the chapter exercises.

Two-Dimensional Drawings

Figure 1–1 is the first formal drawing that is completed in Chapter 5, a conference room floor plan with furniture. Chapters 9 thorough 13 follow the graphic development of five design projects. Each chapter contains step-by-step descriptions of commands used to draw the progressive stages of the first project, a Tenant Space project. Those commands can then be applied to drawing the same stage of the remaining four projects without a tutorial explanation.

Figure 1–2 shows the first stage of the tutorial project completed in Chapter 9. The Tenant Space project begins with drawing the floor plan (exterior and interior walls, doors and windows). Figure 1–3 shows the Tenant Space floor plan that is fully dimensioned in Chapter 10. Figure 1–4 shows an elevation, section, and detail that are part of a typical design package (Chapter 11). Figure 1–5 is the Tenant Space furniture plan with furniture specifications (Chapter 12). Figure 1–6 is the Tenant Space reflected ceiling plan (Chapter 13). Figure 1–7 is the Tenant Space power plan (Chapter 13). Figure 1–8 is a plat drawn in Chapter 14.

Isometric Drawings

Figure 1–9 shows an isometric drawing of the Tenant Space reception desk, which is completed in Chapter 14.

FIGURE 1–1
Conference Room Floor Plan

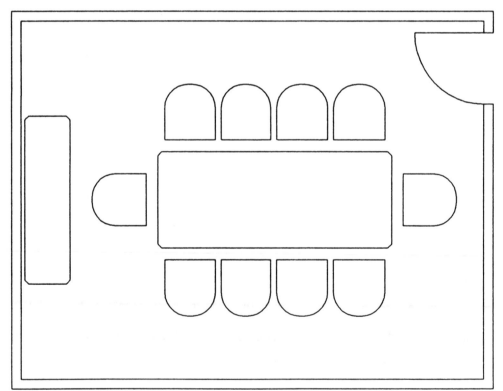

Part I: Preparing to Draw with AutoCAD

FIGURE 1–2
Tenant Space Floor Plan

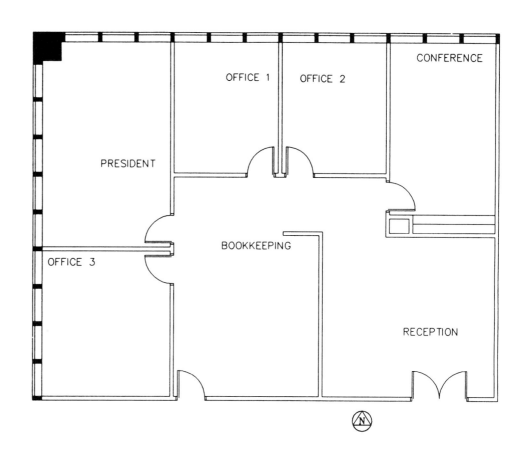

FIGURE 1–3
Dimensioned Tenant Space
Floor Plan

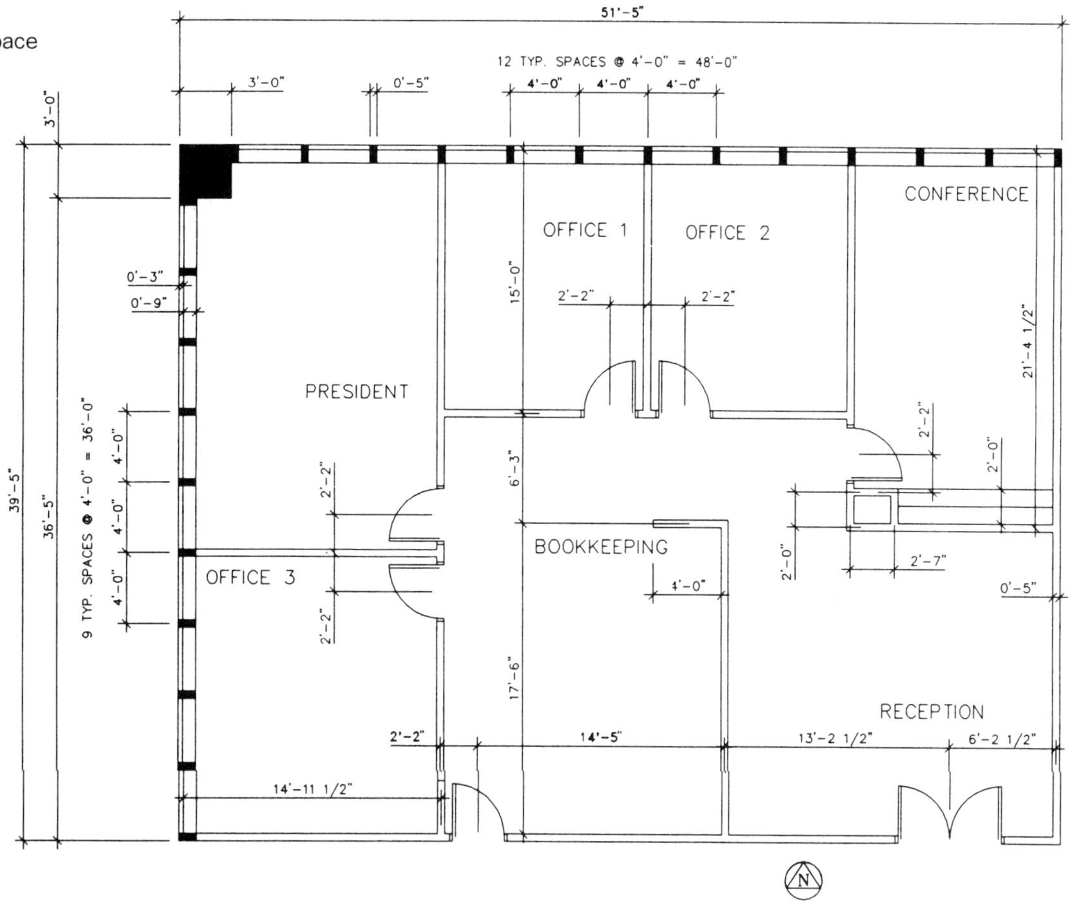

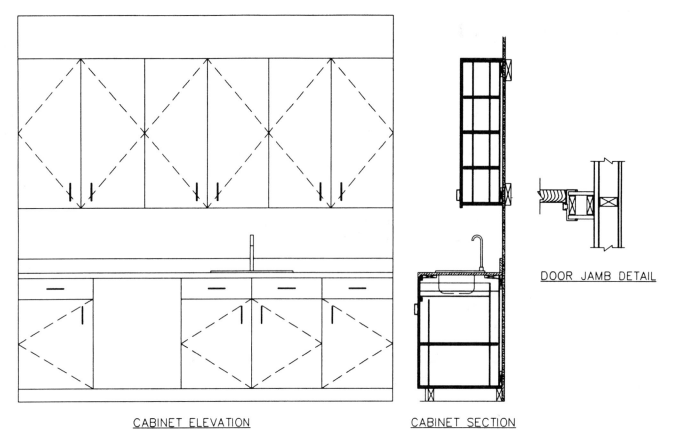

CABINET ELEVATION

CABINET SECTION

DOOR JAMB DETAIL

FIGURE 1–4
Tenant Space Elevation, Section, and Detail

FIGURE 1–5
Tenant Space Furniture Plan with
Furniture Specifications

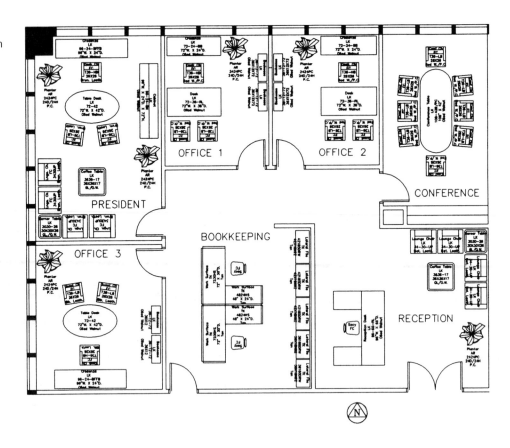

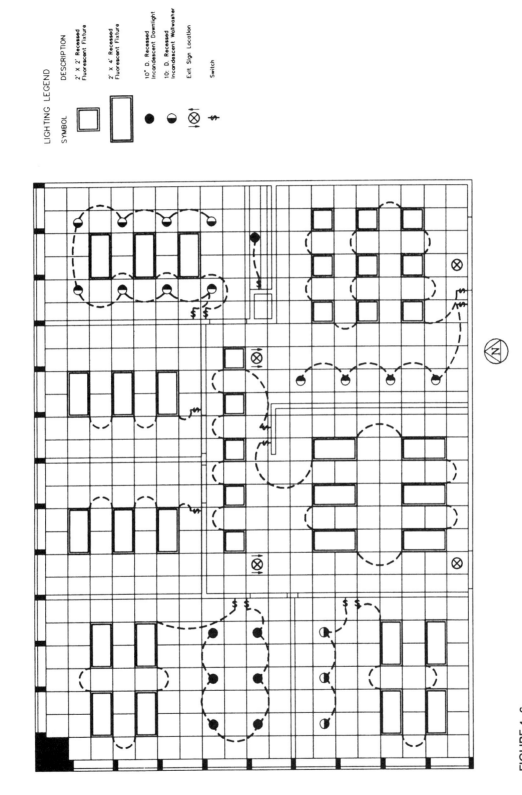

LIGHTING LEGEND

SYMBOL	DESCRIPTION
□	2' X 2' Recessed Fluorescent Fixture
▭	2' X 4' Recessed Fluorescent Fixture
●	10" D. Recessed Incandescent Downlight
◐	10: D. Recessed Incandescent Wallwasher
⊗	Exit Sign Location
$	Switch

FIGURE 1-6
Tenant Space Reflected Ceiling Plan

FIGURE 1–7
Tenant Space Power Plan

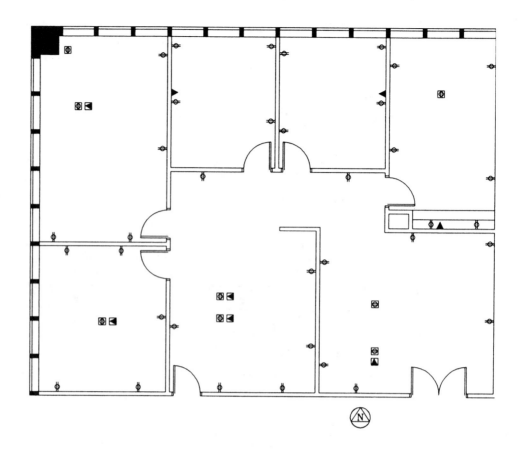

FIGURE 1–8
Plat

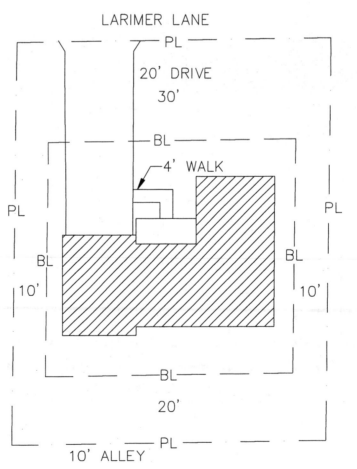

FIGURE 1–9
Tenant Space Reception Desk in
Isometric

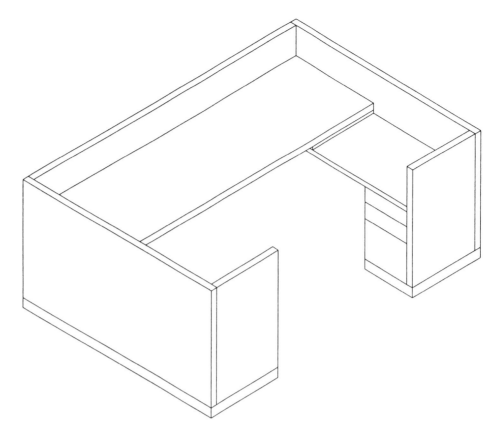

Presentation Drawings

Figure 1–10 shows a Tenant Space project presentation drawing, completed in Chapter 16. The presentation drawing uses drawings completed in the previous chapters. Details of developing slide shows and other effective presentations are also presented in Chapter 16.

Three-Dimensional Models

Figure 1–11 is a typical three-dimensional model. Basic three-dimensional commands are used to draw the Tenant Space reception desk 3D model completed in Chapter 18. Figure 1–12 shows a complex three-dimensional model of an elaborate patio area developed with solid modeling commands and completed in Chapter 19.

ADDITIONAL TOPICS DESCRIBED IN THE CHAPTER EXERCISES

Additional topics that are described in this book are:

□ The personal computer and the AutoCAD program for Windows (Chapter 2).
□ How to set up your first drawing (Chapter 3).
□ Using raster images in AutoCAD drawings (Chapter 6).
□ Adding text to your drawings (Chapter 7).
□ Printing and plotting drawings (Chapter 8).
□ Customizing AutoCAD menus and toolbars and creating macros (Chapter 17).

AutoCAD is by far the most commonly used CAD program. The time you spend learning to use AutoCAD will give you skills that you can use and develop for the rest of your career. This book has a rich variety of exercises that we hope are fun as well as educational.

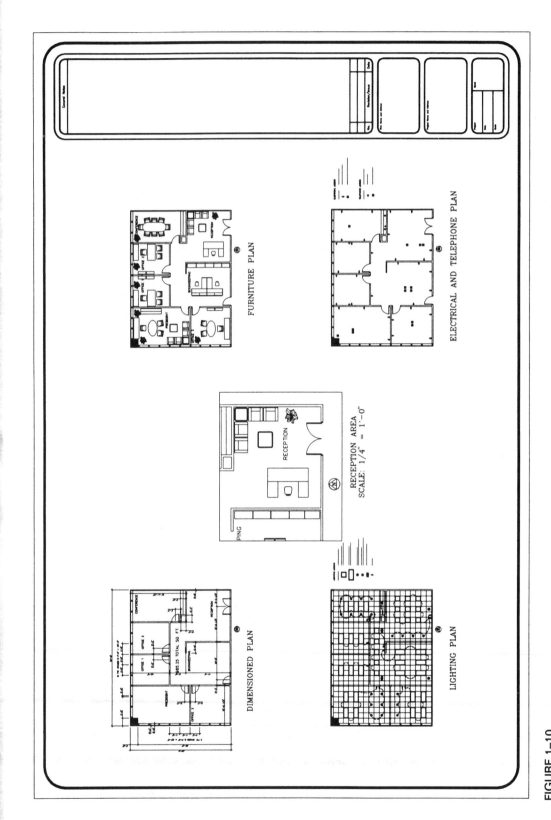

FIGURE 1–10
Tenant Space Project Presentation Drawing

8

FIGURE 1–11
3D Model of the Tenant Space
Reception Desk

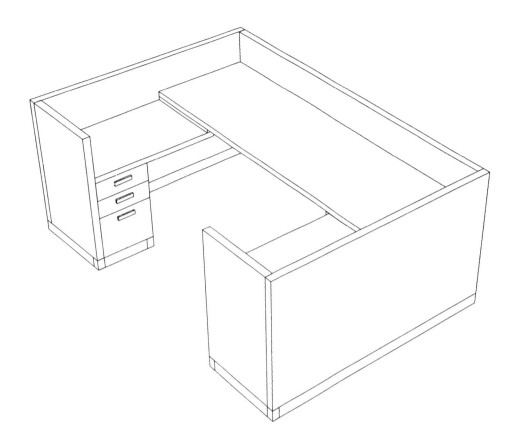

FIGURE 1–12
Solid Model of a Patio

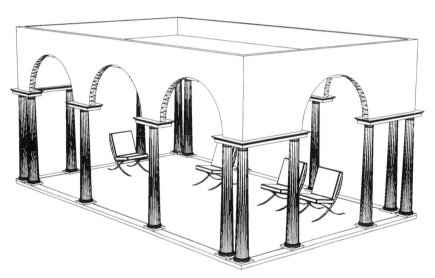

2 The Personal Computer and the AutoCAD Program

OBJECTIVES

When you have completed this chapter, you will be able to:

☐ Describe parts of the AutoCAD hardware system.
☐ Start the Windows 95 or Windows NT operating systems.
☐ Start AutoCAD for Windows.
☐ Describe the AutoCAD for Windows screen and begin using parts of the screen.
☐ Activate, hide, dock, float, reshape, and resize toolbars.

PARTS OF A PERSONAL COMPUTER SYSTEM

The parts of a typical personal computer system on which AutoCAD software can be used are the

Computer
Floppy disk drive
Compact disk drive
Hard disk drive
Display monitor
Keyboard
Mouse
Printer
Plotter

Computer

The computer should be of sufficient capacity to run AutoCAD Release 14 easily. The installation instructions recommend a minimum of 16 megabytes (MB) of RAM. It should also have a graphics card (a printed circuit board that allows a high-quality display of graphic data) and other features that will allow the display (the screen) to be easily read and quickly generated. In addition, AutoCAD requires a math-coprocessor chip. A slow response to commands or a poor display will defeat the advantages of this valuable drawing tool.

Floppy Disk Drive

At least one floppy disk drive is needed to move large blocks of information into and out of the computer. Floppy disks are inserted into a floppy disk drive. Similar to a record player, the disk drive spins the floppy disk on a spindle to read information from it or write information to it. The AutoCAD program is loaded into the computer from floppy disks, or diskettes, or from a compact disk. AutoCAD drawings can be stored on floppy disks. Floppy disk drives are identified by a one-letter name followed by a colon (for example, A:). If you have two floppy disk drives, they are commonly labeled drives A and B. Currently there are four types of floppy disk drives ($5\frac{1}{4}''$ drives are becoming obsolete).

1. The $5\frac{1}{4}''$ double-density drive uses a $5\frac{1}{4}''$ double-density floppy disk. This disk stores approximately 360K (360,000) bytes of information.

2. The $5\frac{1}{4}''$ high-density drive uses a $5\frac{1}{4}''$ high-density floppy disk. This disk stores approximatley 1.2MB (1,200,000 bytes) of information.

3. The $3\frac{1}{2}''$ double-density drive uses a $3\frac{1}{2}''$ floppy diskette. This diskette stores approximately 720K (720,000 bytes) of information.

4. The $3\frac{1}{2}''$ high-density disk drive uses a $3\frac{1}{2}''$ floppy diskette. This diskette stores approximatly 1.44MB (1,440,000 bytes) of information.

Compact Disk Drive

Compact disk drives are available in a variety of speeds. The faster they are, the higher the price. A relatively slow compact disk drive is sufficient to load AutoCAD software, but a faster speed drive is nice to have. Because much of the new software is available on compact disks and as a result is more convenient and faster to load, a compact disk drive is becoming a necessity.

Hard Disk Drive

A hard disk drive, also called a hard drive or hard disk, is usually permanently installed inside the computer. It can store much more information than the removable floppy disks and is used to store the AutoCAD program. AutoCAD drawings may also be stored on the hard disk drive. The hard disk drive is commonly called drive C (C:). A hard drive with adequate storage capacity for your situation is necessary. One to 6 gigabyte (GB) hard drives are commonly used.

Display Monitor

A display monitor is similar to a television screen. A color display monitor is a necessity for most drawings. The physical size of the screen is not as important as the resolution. The resolution of the display is stated in *pixels*, which is the number of dots arranged in rows and columns to make the visual display on the screen. The finer the resolution, the better. AutoCAD requires a display screen of reasonably high resolution. Types of display screens are CGA (color graphics adapter), EGA (enhanced graphics adapter), VGA (video graphics adapter), and Super VGA. CGA is coarse and is the least desirable for displaying AutoCAD, EGA is acceptable, VGA is better, and Super VGA is the highest resolution.

Keyboard

The keyboard has three parts:

Alphanumeric Keys

Located in the center of the keyboard, these are used to type the lettering and numbers that will appear on your drawings and occasionally to type commands. The number keys can also be used as a calculator with an AutoCAD command.

Function Keys

Keys labeled F1–F12, often located to the left or above the alphanumeric keys of many keyboards. These keys are used to perform special functions such as turning a grid on or off. These keys are used and their functions are explained in later chapters.

Numeric keys

Often located to the right of the alphanumeric keys. These keys can be used to type numbers that will appear on your drawings and can also be used as a calculator in combination with an AutoCAD command. The directional arrows, which can be toggled on or off, may be used to move the location of the pointer.

Mouse

A mouse is used to select commands from the AutoCAD menus that appear on the right edge or top of the AutoCAD screen display. The mouse allows the eyes of the operator to remain on the screen at all times. The mouse is also used to enter points of a drawing, such as where a line starts or where a circle is located. It is moved across a tabletop or pad, and its action is described on the display screen by the movement of crosshairs. The crosshairs are positioned to highlight a command or to locate a point. The pick button (usually the far-left button) on the mouse is pushed to select a command or enter a point on the drawing. The other buttons on a mouse can be assigned to perform different tasks. Most commonly one button is assigned <enter> (↵).

Printer

Laser printers are available that produce hard copies of excellent quality in black and white. Many of the newer color printers are relatively inexpensive and produce high-quality hard copies. The low-cost color printers are slow, however, so take the speed factor into account if you buy one.

Plotter

A plotter is essential for making high-quality, usable drawings (hard copies). One type of plotter commonly available uses pens similar to technical drawing pens for manual inking. Felt markers are also available for this type of plotter. Both types of pens can be used for multicolor drawings. A good plotter makes drawings with smooth curves, dense lines, and crisp connections. Plotters may have one pen or multiple pens. A plotter may accept only $8\frac{1}{2}'' \times 11''$ paper, or it may accept larger sizes and rolls of paper. Electrostatic plotters that use an electrical charge and toner to produce an image are also available as well as relativley low cost color ink jet plotters.

EXERCISE 2–1
Start Microsoft Windows, Start the AutoCAD
Program, Examine the AutoCAD Screen, and Exit AutoCAD

Exercise 2–1 will provide a step-by-step introduction to Microsoft Windows and the AutoCAD Program Release 14. To begin Exercise 2–1, turn on the computer.

Start Microsoft Windows

Start Microsoft Windows (Figure 2–1):
Windows may be activated in one of two ways:

1. You may have a menu that allows you to pick a picture or type a number or letter to activate Microsoft Windows.

2. Your computer may activate Microsoft Windows when it is turned on.

When Windows is started, the Windows opening screen known as the Desktop appears. Figure 2–1 shows a typical display of the Desktop with its icons (an icon is a picture). The taskbar appears at the bottom of the screen. It contains the **Start** button, which you can use to start the AutoCAD Program Release 14 as follows:

Start the AutoCAD Program

Start the AutoCAD Program (Figure 2–2):

Prompt	Response
The Desktop is displayed:	CLICK: **Start button**
The Start menu is displayed:	CLICK: **Programs**
A submenu of Programs is displayed:	CLICK: **AutoCAD R14**

FIGURE 2–1
Windows Desktop

FIGURE 2–2
Starting AutoCAD R14

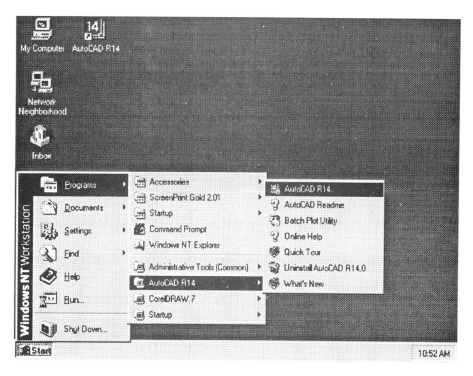

The AutoCAD R14 menu is displayed:

The AutoCAD screen appears with the Start Up dialog box:

CLICK: **AutoCAD R14**

CLICK: **Cancel Button** (on the Start Up dialog box)

Note: DOUBLE CLICK: means to place your cursor over the selection and press the left mouse button twice rapidly.

You may also double click the AutoCAD R14 icon shown in the upper left of the screen in Figure 2–1. This is a shortcut that Windows will create for you, to allow you to activate AutoCAD more quickly.

When AutoCAD R14 is started, the AutoCAD screen appears. It provides the display area for drawing and the commands used to create, modify, view, and plot drawings. The

Start Up dialog box, Figure 2–3, is displayed. For now, you clicked: **Cancel** to get rid of the Start Up dialog box. You can begin by naming the new drawing, or you may immediately begin drawing without naming the drawing. When you are ready to end the drawing session, the drawing must be saved using Save or SaveAs..., at which time the drawing must be named. AutoCAD communicates with you on various parts of the screen. You may have a slightly different appearing screen, depending on the preferences selected. A brief introduction to each part of the screen (Figure 2–4) follows.

FIGURE 2–3
Start Up Dialog Box

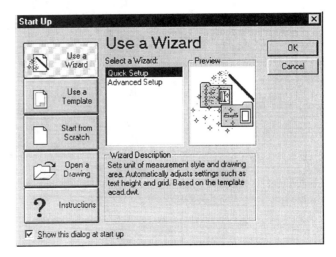

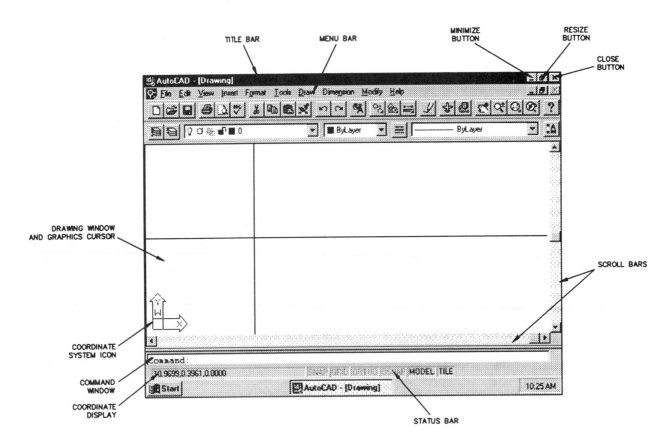

FIGURE 2–4
The AutoCAD Screen

Part I: Preparing to Draw with AutoCAD

The AutoCAD Screen

Title Bar

The title bar contains the name of the program, AutoCAD, and the name of the current drawing, in this case, [Drawing], because you have not named the drawing yet.

AutoCAD Program and Drawing Buttons

This button on the program window minimizes the AutoCAD program. The program remains active so you can return to it if you choose. To return to it, click the AutoCAD R14 button on the taskbar at the bottom of the screen. A drawing can also be minimized by clicking this button on the drawing window.

This button resizes the program or drawing window.

This button maximizes the size of the program or drawing window.

This button closes the AutoCAD program. It is grayed out on the drawing window, indicating that the drawing cannot be closed from this button.

Drawing Window and Graphics Cursor

The drawing window is where your drawing is displayed. The graphics cursor (or crosshairs) follow the movement of a mouse when points of a drawing are entered or a command is selected.

Command Window

The command window shown at the bottom of the screen (which may be moved and resized if you want) is where AutoCAD communicates with you once a command is activated. AutoCAD prompts you to enter specific information to further define a command and then responds with action on the screen or additional prompts. Always watch the command window to make sure you and AutoCAD are communicating.

Coordinate System Icon

The coordinate system icon in the lower left corner of the drawing window shows the orientation of the X, Y, and Z axes of the current coordinate system. When AutoCAD is started, you are in the world coordinate system (WCS) as indicated by the W in the coordinate system icon.

Coordinate Display

Using an X- and Y-axis coordinate system, the coordinate display numbers in the extreme lower left corner tell you where the cursor or crosshairs on the screen are located in relation to point 0,0 (the lower left corner).

Status Bar

The status bar at the bottom of the screen keeps you informed about your drawing by displaying the status of modes that affect your drawing: SNAP, GRID, ORTHO, OSNAP, MODEL, and TILE. These modes can be turned on and off by double clicking on the mode name with the pick button of your mouse. The time is also displayed.

Scroll Bars

The scroll bars on the bottom and right side of the screen area allow you to move the drawing display at the same magnification up and down, left and right. The scroll bars can be turned on and off using the Display tab of the Preferences... dialog box under Tools in the menu bar. The menu bar is described next.

Menu Bar

Practice using the menu bar (Figures 2–5 through 2–14):
You can open a menu item on the menu bar by holding the pointer on the menu name and clicking it; click the menu item again to close the menu, or use the Esc key to cancel any command activated. A pull-down menu will appear for each item on the menu bar when the item is clicked (Figures 2–5 through 2–13). Pull-down menus provide access to many

of the same commands that are included on the tool bars. The commands followed by an ellipsis (...) display a dialog box when clicked. Use the Esc key or click the Cancel button in the dialog box to cancel it. Those pull-down menu items with an arrow to the right have a cascading menu.

When you hold your mouse steady over each menu bar item, pull-down menu command, or cascading menu command, a text string at the bottom of the display screen (in the coordinate display and status bar area) gives a brief description of the commands. Many of the menu bar commands are used in the following chapters; however, the following brief description of the general content of the menu bar provides an introduction:

File (Figure 2–5) This menu bar item contains the commands needed to start a new drawing, open an existing one, save drawings, print a drawing, import and export data, manage files, and exit from AutoCAD. It also shows the most recently active drawings, which may be opened by clicking on them.

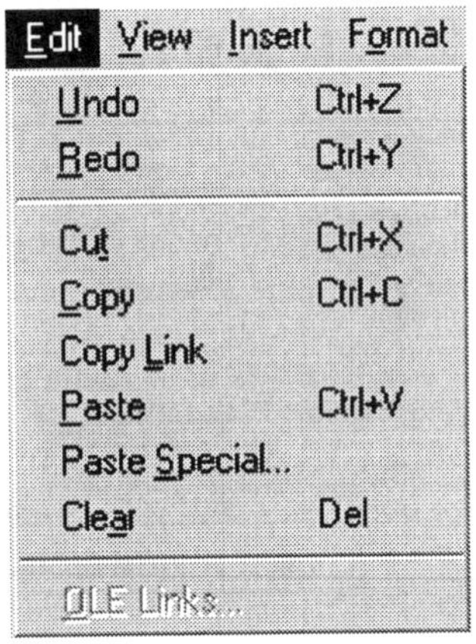

Edit (Figure 2–6) This item contains the Undo command (allows you to undo or reverse the most recent command) and the Redo command (will redo one undo). It also contains the commands related to the Windows Clipboard: Cut, Copy, Copy Link, Paste, and Paste Special.... Drawings or text from other applications (such as Word or Paintbrush) can be cut or copied onto the Windows Clipboard and then pasted from the Clipboard into an AutoCAD drawing. The reverse is also possible; AutoCAD drawings can be pasted into other applications. The OLE Links... command is a Windows feature that allows you to link or unlink an AutoCAD drawing and another application's object (document or drawing). When a drawing is copied and placed in a document in another program such as Paintbrush or Word and then linked, editing it updates the information in both the original drawing and the new document.

View (Figure 2–7) This menu contains commands that control the display of your drawing. The Redraw and Regen commands redraw the display screen to remove blips, and redraw any part of the drawing that is missing. The Zoom commands control the magnification of the drawing display, and Pan allows you to move the drawing up and down, left and right. There are some 3D commands on the pull-down menu and also commands for model space (where your drawing is created) and paper space (where a presentation is created). The Named Views... command provides a dialog box that allows you to name drawing views, save them, and restore them as needed. The Hide, Shade, and Render commands are used to render solid models, and the Toolbars... command allows you to display or hide toolbars.

Insert (Figure 2–8) This menu contains the commands that allow you to insert previously drawn objects into an AutoCAD drawing. These objects may be other AutoCAD drawings or pictures from other drawing programs.

Format (Figure 2–9) This menu bar item contains commands that help you set up your drawing environment and prepare to draw with AutoCAD. The Layer... command creates layers on which different parts of a drawing can be placed. Every drawing entity (such as an arc, line, or circle) will have a Color and Linetype. You will learn in later chapters to create a Text Style and a Dimension Style, so you can add text and dimensions to your drawing. Point Style... allows you to set the style and size for points that are drawn. Multiline Style... allows you to draw up to 16 lines at a time. The Units... command establishes the drawing units. For example, an inch is a drawing unit. Thickness allows you to give an object height. The Drawing Limits command sets the page size you draw on. The Rename... command allows you to rename layers, text styles, dimension styles, and more.

Tools (Figure 2–10) This menu has a spell checker and a display order command that allows you to place images on top of each other. Inquiry allows you to obtain information about the size and location of the entities and about the amount of time spent on the drawing when it was done and to place a date and time stamp on your drawing. Tools also has commands for running scripts (described in a later chapter) and adding external data. The next seven items are settings that you will use often in drawing. The Tools menu also has a command for customizing menus and toolbars, and activating

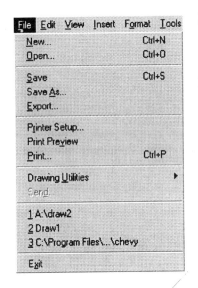

FIGURE 2–5
File Menu

FIGURE 2–6
Edit Menu

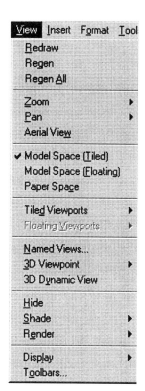

FIGURE 2–7
View Menu

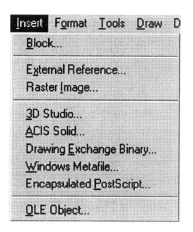

FIGURE 2–8
Insert Menu

FIGURE 2–9
Format Menu

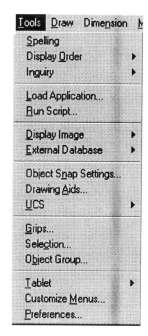

FIGURE 2–10
Tools Menu

FIGURE 2–11
Draw Menu

the Preferences... dialog box. This dialog box gives you several options for arranging and coloring your screen display and other configuration options.

Draw (Figure 2–11) The Draw menu has all the commands used to draw objects in AutoCAD.

Dimension (Figure 2–12) This menu contains the commands used to place dimensions on drawings. All these commands are described in detail in a later chapter.

Modify (Figure 2–13) The Modify commands are used to change the position, shape, or number of objects after they have been drawn. Commands to change text are also on this menu.

Help (Figure 2–14) This menu bar item has commands that teach you how to use the Help command. The AutoCAD Help Topics command provides information about how to use AutoCAD commands. It is a very helpful tool for any AutoCAD user. The four introductory items on this menu, Quick Tour, What's New, Learning Assistance, and Connect to Internet, are very worthwhile. Take the time to run those now to familiarze yourself with the basics of this program. Other commands in this menu item provide technical information about AutoCAD.

Top Level Toolbars

The AutoCAD screen shown in Figure 2–4 has two top level toolbars displayed: a docked Object Properties toolbar (Figure 2–15) and a docked Standard Toolbar (Figure 2–16). Both are visible by default. The Standard Toolbar contains tools that represent frequently used commands. The Object Properties toolbar contains the Layer & Linetype Properties dialog box, used to create layers and assign properties such as color and linetype to every drawing entity (line, arc, circle, and so on). It also contains the commands for setting color and linetype and for modifying drawing entities.

Activate the Standard Toolbar's tooltips (Figure 2–16):
As you hold the mouse pointer steady (do not click) on each tool of the Standard toolbar, tooltips will display the name of the command, as shown in Figure 2–16. A text string at the bottom of the display screen (in the coordinate display and status bar area) gives a brief description of the command.

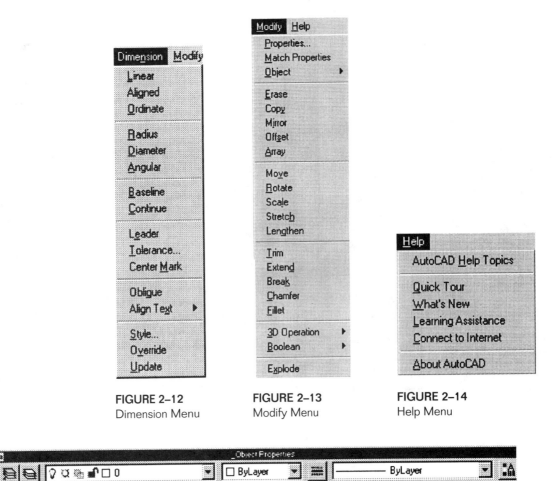

FIGURE 2-12
Dimension Menu

FIGURE 2-13
Modify Menu

FIGURE 2-14
Help Menu

FIGURE 2-15
Object Properties Toolbar

FIGURE 2-16
Standard Toolbar with Tooltip Displayed

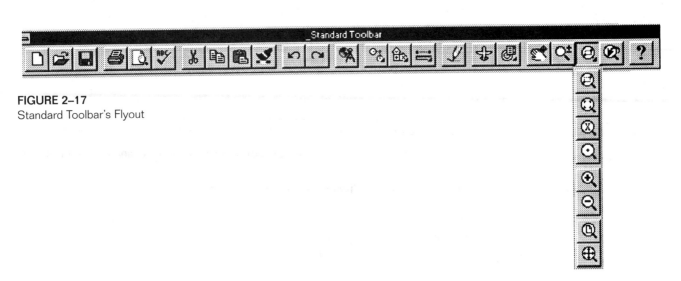

FIGURE 2-17
Standard Toolbar's Flyout

Part I: Preparing to Draw with AutoCAD

Activate the Standard Toolbar's flyouts (Figure 2–17):

Tools with a small black triangle have flyouts. Hold the pointer on the tool, press and hold the pick button, and the flyout will appear, as shown in Figure 2–17. When you position the pointer on a tool in the flyout and release the pick button, the command is activated; a dialog box will appear or a command sequence will begin. The most recently activated tool icon will replace the top icon that was previously visible in the standard toolbar; the location of the icon changes to reflect the most recently used command. Use the Esc key to cancel any command.

Locate the names of all the top level toolbars (Figure 2–18):

Prompt	Response
Command:	CLICK: **Toolbars...** (on the View menu)
The Toolbars dialog box (Figure 2–18) appears:	All the names of top level toolbars are displayed in the list.

Activate and close the Dimension toolbar:

To activate a toolbar, pick the check box to the left of the toolbar name, so that an X appears in it. After studying a toolbar, you can close it by clicking the bar in the upper left corner of the toolbar. You can also close a toolbar by picking the X in the Toolbars dialog box next to the toolbar name. Try this by opening and closing the Dimension toolbar.

Floating Toolbars

A floating toolbar floats or lies on any part of the AutoCAD screen. A floating toolbar can be moved to another part of the screen and can be reshaped and resized. Any of the top level toolbars can be displayed and will float on the screen as follows:

Display the Draw toolbar (Figure 2–19):

Prompt	Response
Command:	CLICK: **Toolbars...** (on the View menu)

FIGURE 2–18
Toolbars Dialog Box

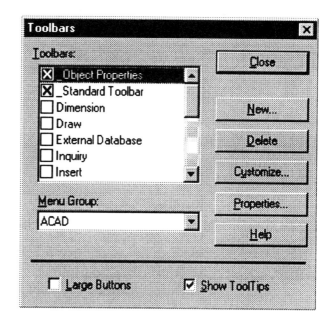

Prompt	Response
The Toolbars dialog box appears:	CLICK: **the box to the left of Draw** (Figure 2–19)
An X appears in the box. The Draw toolbar appears on the screen:	CLICK: **Close**

Display the Modify toolbar:

Use the same steps to display the Modify toolbar as you used to display the Draw toolbar.

To hide any toolbar you do not want visible, click on the bar in the upper left corner of the toolbar. Close the Toolbars dialog box by picking the X in the upper right corner, or pick close.

Reshape and move the Draw and Modify toolbars (Figure 2–20):

Change the shape of the toolbars to match those shown in Figure 2–20, by changing the width and height. Slowly move the pointer over the borders of each toolbar until you get the double-arrow pointer that allows you to resize it.

Move the Draw and Modify toolbars to the approximate position shown in Figure 2–21 by picking the title bar of each toolbar and dragging it to the new location.

FIGURE 2–19
Displaying the Draw Toolbar

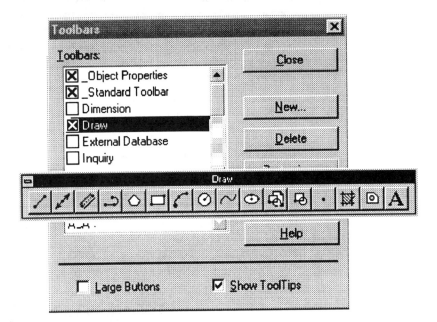

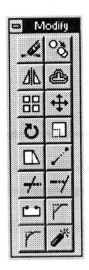

FIGURE 2–20
Reshaping Toolbars

Part I: Preparing to Draw with AutoCAD

FIGURE 2–21
Moving Toolbars

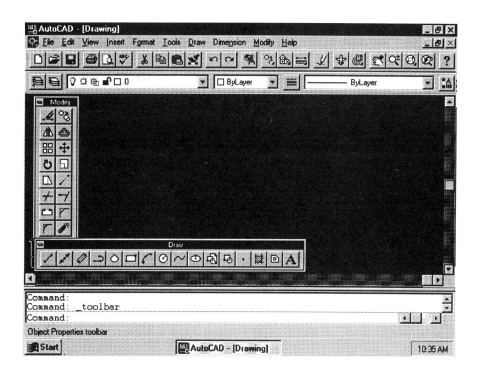

Change the size of the tool buttons (Figure 2–22):

Prompt	Response
Command:	CLICK: **Toolbars...** (from View on the menu bar)
The Toolbars dialog box appears (Figure 2–22):	CLICK: **Large Buttons** (the check box, to put a check in the box, turning it on)
A check appears in the Large Buttons check box:	CLICK: **Close** (to exit)
All the toolbars are larger:	**Use the same steps to change the tool bars back to the smaller size.**

Close all toolbars at once:

Prompt	Response
Command:	TYPE: **-TOOLBAR<enter>** (be sure to include the dash)
Toolbar name (or ALL):	TYPE: **ALL<enter>**
Show/Hide:	TYPE: **H<enter>**

Docked Toolbars

Display the Draw toolbar:

Prompt	Response
Command:	CLICK: **Toolbars...** (from View on the menu bar)
The Toolbars dialog box appears:	CLICK: **the box to the left of Draw**
An X appears in the box.	
The Draw toolbar appears on the screen:	CLICK: **Close**

FIGURE 2–22
Changing the Size of the Tool
Buttons

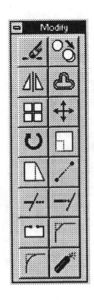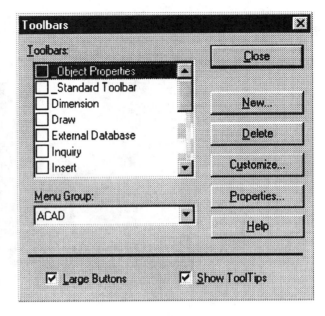

Dock the Draw toolbar:

A toolbar can be docked, which means it can be attached to any edge of the drawing window. Once docked, the toolbar does not lie on any part of the drawing area; it also cannot be reshaped. One way to dock a toolbar is to pick on the name of the toolbar and drag it to an edge. When you see an outline of the toolbar along an edge (showing you how the toolbar will look in the docking area), release the pick button on the mouse to dock the toolbar.

To undock the toolbar, pick in any part of the gray area (grab region) around the tools, and drag the toolbar away from the edge.

Pick on the name of the Draw toolbar and drag it to the left edge of the drawing area and dock it.

Toolbar Command

Use the Toolbar command to dock the Modify toolbar on the right side of the drawing area (Figure 2–23):

Prompt	Response
Command:	TYPE: **-TOOLBAR<enter>** (be sure to include the dash)
Toolbar name (or ALL):	TYPE: **Modify<enter>**
Show/Hide/Left/Right/Top/Bottom/Float: <Show>:	TYPE: **R<enter>**
Position <0,0>:	**<enter>**
The Modify toolbar is docked on the right side of the drawing area, Figure 2–23.	

The other options of the Toolbar command, when activated, allow you to dock a toolbar on the left, top, or bottom of the drawing area, float a docked toolbar, show a hidden toolbar, or hide a visible toolbar. You can use the ALL option to make all the toolbars visible or to hide all the toolbars.

Customizing Toolbars

You can customize toolbars using the Customize Toolbars dialog box by activating the Toolbars dialog box and clicking Customize... . Using this dialog box, you can add, delete, move, or copy existing tools, or create a new toolbar using existing or new tools.

FIGURE 2–23
Docking the Modify Toolbar

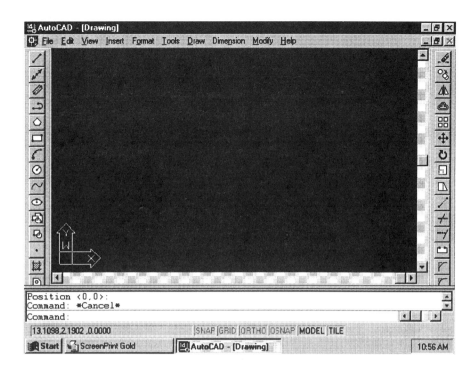

Using AutoCAD for Windows with Other Programs

All commands related to the Windows Clipboard such as Cut, Copy, Paste, and Insert Object, are available in AtuoCAD for Windows. Drawings or text from other applications (such as Word or Paintbrush) can be cut or copied onto the Windows Clipboard and then pasted from the Clipboard into an AutoCAD drawing. The reverse is also possible; Auto-CAD drawings can be pasted into other applications.

Exit AutoCAD

The Exit command takes you out of the AutoCAD program. If you have made changes to the drawing and have not saved those changes, AutoCAD will give you the message "Save changes to Drawing.dwg?". If you have named the drawing, the drawing name will replace the word "Drawing." This is a safety feature because the Exit command, by itself, does not update or save a drawing. For now, you will not name or save this exercise.

Exit AutoCAD (Figure 2–24):

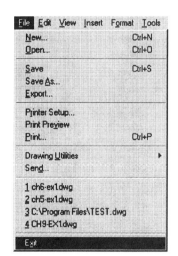

FIGURE 2–24
File Menu with Exit Clicked

Prompt	Response
Command:	**Exit**
The AutoCAD warning appears: Save changes to Drawing.dwg?	CLICK: **No**
	If you have not drawn anything or made any settings, the message will not appear.

REVIEW QUESTIONS

1. Which of the following is used to store the AutoCAD program?
   a. Plotter
   b. Printer
   c. Keyboard
   d. Hard drive
   e. Display monitor

2. What do you do to display the submenu of programs containing AutoCAD R14 in Windows?
   a. TYPE: OPEN<enter>
   b. Double click on the icon
   c. CLICK: the Start icon and then CLICK: Programs
   d. Hold the pointer on the icon and press <enter>
   e. TYPE: Enter<enter>
3. Picking the X in the upper right corner of the AutoCAD program window
   a. Closes the AutoCAD program
   b. Closes the Program Manager and displays the Exit Windows dialog box
   c. Enters the AutoCAD program
   d. Opens the AutoCAD screen
   e. Resizes the AutoCAD screen
4. To maximize the AutoCAD screen
   a. Pick the underscore in the upper right of the screen
   b. Pick the rectangle in the upper right of the screen
   c. Pick the X in the upper right of the screen
   d. Pick the icon to the left of File on the menu bar
   e. The AutoCAD screen cannot be maximized.
5. Which menu on the AutoCAD menu bar contains the command needed to start a new drawing?
   a. File
   b. Edit
   c. Tools
   d. Format
   e. Options
6. Which menu on the AutoCAD menu bar contains the commands related to Windows Clip-board?
   a. File
   b. Edit
   c. Tools
   d. Format
   e. Options
7. Which menu on the AutoCAD menu bar allows you to make and set layers, select drawing units, and set drawing limits?
   a. File
   b. Edit
   c. Tools
   d. Format
   e. Options
8. Which menu on the AutoCAD menu bar takes you to the Toolbar... command?
   a. File
   b. Edit
   c. Tools
   d. Format
   e. View
9. Which toolbar is usually on by default?
   a. Modify
   b. External Reference
   c. Standard Toolbar
   d. Draw
   e. Select Objects
10. Double clicking GRID in the status bar when it is grayed out does which of the following?
   a. Turns the grid off
   b. Displays the grid and turns snap on
   c. Displays the grid and turns snap off
   d. Displays the grid
   e. Has no effect on the display screen

Complete.

11. List the six modes displayed on the status bar.

   _____

12. If you have not named a new drawing, what name does AutoCAD assign to it?

   _____

13. Describe the purpose of the command window.

   _____

14. List the two top level toolbars that are on by default.

   _____

15. Describe how to open or activate a toolbar.

   _____

16. Describe how to close or hide a toolbar.

   _____

17. Describe how to undock a toolbar.

   _____

18. Describe how to resize a toolbar.

   _____

19. Describe the function of the scroll bars on the bottom and right side of the AutoCAD for Windows screen.

   _____

20. Describe how to activate a toolbar's tooltips and flyouts.

   Tooltips: _____

   Flyouts: _____

3 Preparing to Draw with AutoCAD

OBJECTIVES

When you have completed this chapter, you will be able to:
- □ Begin an AutoCAD drawing without using a wizard.
- □ Make settings for an AutoCAD drawing to include Units, Limits, Grid, and Snap.
- □ Create layers and assign color and linetype to each layer.
- □ Use function keys F2 (flip screen), F7 (grid), and F9 (snap) to control the display screen, grid, and snap as required.
- □ Use the commands Save, SaveAs... and Exit to save work and exit AutoCAD.
- □ Save a drawing as a template.

INTRODUCTION

When a project that is to be manually drafted is started, decisions are made about the number of drawings required, the appropriate sheet size, scale, and so on. Similar decisions are made when preparing to draw with AutoCAD. This chapter describes the settings that must be made before drawing can begin.

The following is a hands-on step-by-step procedure to make the setup for your first drawing exercise in Chapter 4. Each step is followed by an explanation of the command used. To begin, turn on the computer and start AutoCAD.

FOLLOWING THE EXERCISES IN THIS BOOK

Before you start the exercises in this book, it will help to have a description of how to follow them.

Drives

This book will assume that the hard drive of the computer is called drive C. It will also assume that there is a floppy disk drive labeled A (your drive may be labeled B).

Prompt and Response Columns

Throughout the exercises in this book, Prompt and Response columns provide step-by-step instructions for starting and completing a command. The Prompt column text repeats the AutoCAD prompt that appears in the command prompt area of the display screen. The text in the Response Column shows your response to the AutoCAD prompt and appears as follows:

1. All responses are shown in bold type.
2. **<enter>** is used to indicate the enter response. Either a button on the mouse or a key on the keyboard may be used. Some keyboards may have this key marked ⏎, Enter, or Return.

3. A response that is to be typed and entered from the keyboard is preceded by the word "TYPE:" and is followed by **<enter>** to indicate the enter response (for example, TYPE: **WALLS<enter>**).

4. If a response is to click a command or command option from a menu or a toolbar, that command is shown in the response column in bold type (for example, **Units**).

5. Most commands can be entered by typing from the keyboard. For example, that option is shown as (or TYPE: **DDUNITS<enter>**).

6. If the response is to click a button in a dialog box, that button description is shown in the response column in bold type (for example, CLICK: **OK**).

7. Function keys are the keys marked F1 through F10 on the keyboard (F11 and F12 are available on some keyboards). If the response is to use a function key, the key name will be preceded by the word "PRESS:" (for example, PRESS: **F7**).

8. Helpful notes, such as (F2 is the flip screen function key), are provided in parentheses.

Margin Illustrations

Illustrations of the AutoCAD menu bar with items highlighted and toolbars are shown in the book margins. They show you where to find a command. Helpful notes, tips, and warnings are also included in the margins.

EXERCISE 3–1
Beginning an AutoCAD Drawing Using "Start from Scratch": Setting Units, Limits, Grid, and Snap; Creating Layers; Saving Your Work and Exiting AutoCAD

Begin a New Drawing Using "Start from Scratch"

Begin a new drawing (Figure 3–1):

Prompt	Response
The Start Up dialog box appears (Figure 3–1): (If the Start Up dialog box does not appear, from the Tools menu choose Preferences.... On the Compatibility menu, make a check beside the "Show the Start Up dialog box" button.)	CLICK: **Start from Scratch** CLICK: **English** CLICK: **OK**

FIGURE 3–1
Start Up Dialog Box

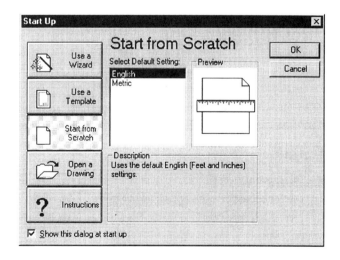

Start Up Dialog Box

When the AutoCAD program is started, the Start Up dialog box appears. It has three buttons that, when clicked, determine how you start a drawing, a button that allows you to open an existing drawing, and an instruction button.

Use a Wizard

When a new drawing is started by clicking the Use a Wizard button, AutoCAD leads you through making the drawing setup using tabbed dialog boxes. The two Wizard options are Quick Setup and Advanced Setup:

Quick Setup
The Quick Setup dialog box tabs include:

Step 1: Units
Step 2: Area (Drawing Limits)

Advanced Setup
The Advanced Setup dialog box tabs include:

Step 1: Units
Step 2: Angle
Step 3: Angle Measure
Step 4: Angle Direction
Step 5: Area (Drawing Limits)
Step 6: Title Block
Step 7: Layout

Use a Template

Any drawing can be saved as a template. You can create standard templates to suit your drawing needs or office standards. Templates save time because the drawings environment is already set. Those settings include:

Unit type and precision
Drawing limits
Snap, Grid, and Ortho settings
Layer organization
Title blocks, borders, and logos
Dimension and text styles
Linetypes

AutoCAD saves the template file in the template folder by default.

Start from Scratch

This button allows you to set up a drawing in English or metric using AutoCAD commands.

Open a Drawing

This button allows you to open an existing drawing.

Instructions

This button provides instructions about the buttons on the Start Up dialog box.

Turn off all the toolbars (so the screen will be larger):

Prompt	Response
Command:	TYPE: **-TOOLBAR\<enter>** (include the dash)
Toolbar name (or ALL):	TYPE: **ALL\<enter>**
Show/Hide:	TYPE: **H\<enter>**

Format Tools Draw
Layer...
Color...
Linetype...

Text Style...
Dimension Style...
Point Style...
Multiline Style...

Units...
Thickness
Drawing Limits

Rename...

Note: To cancel a command, PRESS: **Esc** (from the keyboard).

Note: The Precision: button has no bearing on how accurately AutoCAD draws. It controls the display of dimensions and other values displayed on the screen such as coordinates and defaults. No matter what the Precision: setting, AutoCAD draws with extreme accuracy.

Now that you have started a new drawing, select the units that will be used in making this drawing.

Units

Units refers to drawing units. For example, an inch is a drawing unit. In this book decimal units and architectural units, which provide feet and fractional inches, are used. The Precision: button in the Units Control dialog box allows you to set the smallest fraction to display when a unit value is shown on the screen. All other settings in the Units Control dialog box are for measuring angles, and there is no reason to change any of these settings at this time.

To set drawing Units... (Figure 3–2):

Prompt	Response
Command:	(Move the mouse across the top of the display screen on the menu bar.) **Units...** (or TYPE: **DDUNITS\<enter\>**)
The Units Control dialog box appears (Figure 3–2):	CLICK: **the circle to the left of Architectural so a dot appears in it** CLICK: 0'-0 1/16" (for Precision:) CLICK: **OK**

You can also set units by typing **UNITS\<enter\>** from the keyboard. When you do that, AutoCAD flips you to the text screen and allows you to select the same settings as shown in the Units Control dialog box. To exit from the text screen and return to the graphics screen, PRESS: **F2** (the function key). Flipping from the graphics screen to the text screen is often helpful to see what you have previously typed or what text is shown when a command is picked. PRESS: **F2** two times so you can see what it does for you.

Drawing Scale

A drawing scale factor does not need to be set. While using AutoCAD to make drawings for the exercises in this book you will automatically draw full scale, using real-world feet and inches. Full-scale drawings can be printed or plotted at any scale. Plotting and printing to scale is described in Chapter 8.

FIGURE 3–2
Units Control Dialog Box

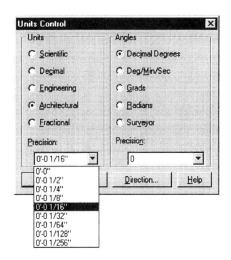

FIGURE 3–3
Drawing Limits

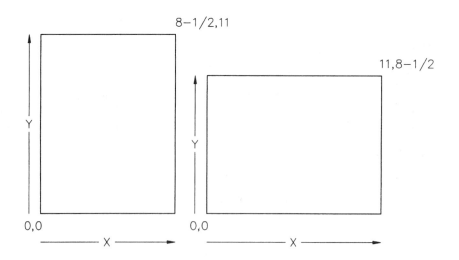

Drawing Limits

To set Drawing Limits:

Prompt	Response
Command:	**Drawing Limits** (or TYPE: **LIMITS** <enter>)
ON/OFF/<Lower left corner> <0'-0", 0'-0">:	<enter>
Upper right corner <1'-0", 0'-9">:	TYPE: **8-1/2,11 <enter>**

Think of drawing limits as the sheet size or sheet boundaries. Here 8-1/2,11 was set as the drawing limits. In AutoCAD that value is entered as 8-1/2,11 using a comma with no spaces to separate the X and Y axes. AutoCAD defaults to inches (or any other basic unit of measure), so the inch symbol is not required. The X axis is first (8-1/2) and measures drawing limits from left to right. The Y axis is second (11) and measures drawing limits from bottom to top. You will be drawing in a vertical $8\frac{1}{2}'' \times 11''$ area similar to a standard sheet of typing paper.

The lower left corner of the drawing boundaries is 0,0. The upper right corner is 8-1/2,11 (Figure 3–3). These are the limits for Chapter 4 Exercise 1. To turn the $8\frac{1}{2}'' \times 11''$ area horizontally, enter the limits as 11,8-1/2.

You can also respond to the Limits: prompt "ON/OFF/<Lower left corner>:" by typing ON or OFF. The ON mode, when activated, helps you avoid drawing outside the drawing limits. The OFF mode, when activated, allows you to draw outside the drawing limits.

If the drawing limits need to be changed, you may do so at any time by entering new limits to the "Upper right corner>:" prompt. Changing the drawing limits will automatically change the grid pattern to the new limits.

Grid and Snap

Set the Grid and Snap Spacing:

Prompt	Response
Command:	TYPE: **GRID<enter>**
Grid spacing (X) or ON/OFF/ Snap/Aspect <0'-0">:	TYPE: **1/4<enter>**
Command:	TYPE: **SNAP<enter>**
Snap spacing or ON/OFF/Aspect/ Rotate/Style <0'-0">:	TYPE: **1/8<enter>**

Grid

You have just set $\frac{1}{4}''$ as the grid spacing. The grid is the visible pattern of dots on the display screen. With a setting of $\frac{1}{4}''$, each grid dot is spaced $\frac{1}{4}''$ vertically and horizontally. The grid is not part of the drawing, but it helps in getting a sense of the size and relationship of the drawing elements. It is never plotted.

Function key F7 turns the grid on or off. The grid can also be turned on or off by selecting either option in response to the prompt "Grid spacing (X) or ON/OFF/Snap/Aspect:" or by double clicking GRID at the bottom of the screen.

Snap

You have set $\frac{1}{8}''$ as the snap spacing. Snap is an invisible pattern of dots on the display screen. As you move the mouse across the screen, the crosshairs will snap, or lock, to an invisible snap grid when SNAP is on. With a setting of $\frac{1}{8}''$, each snap point is spaced $\frac{1}{8}''$ horizontally and vertically.

Function key F9 turns the snap on or off. The snap can also be turned on or off by selecting either option in response to the prompt "Snap spacing or On/OFF/Aspect/Rotate/Style>:" or by double clicking SNAP at the bottom of the screen. Rotate and Style options are used in later chapters.

It is helpful to set the snap spacing the same as the grid spacing or as a fraction of the grid spacing so the crosshairs snap to every grid point or to every grid point and in between. The snap can be set to snap several times in between the grid points.

Some drawings or parts of drawings should never be drawn with snap off. Snap is a very important tool for quickly locating or aligning elements of your drawing. You may need to turn snap off and on while drawing, but remember that a drawing entity drawn on snap is easily moved, copied, or otherwise edited.

Zoom

To view the entire drawing area:

Prompt	Response
Command:	TYPE: **Z\<enter\>**
All/Center/Dynamic/Extents/Previous/Scale (X/XP)/Window/\<Realtime\>:	TYPE: **A\<enter\>**

The Zoom-All command lets you view the entire drawing area. Use it after setting up or entering an existing drawing so that you are familiar with the size and shape of your limits and grid. Otherwise, you may be viewing only a small part of the drawing limits and not realize it.

Drawing Aids Dialog Box and Components of All Dialog Boxes

You can also set snap and grid by using the Drawing Aids dialog box.

To locate the Drawing Aids dialog box, move the pointer across the top of the display screen and highlight "Tools" on the menu bar that appears. When you click: **TOOLS** a pull-down menu appears. Move your pointer to highlight Drawing Aids... and click: **Drawing Aids....** The Drawing Aids dialog box (Figure 3–4) now appears on your screen.

All dialog boxes have some basic components. The following is a description of the components that appear in the Drawing Aids dialog box (Figure 3–4) as well as in other dialog boxes you will use:

1. *Cursor:* Changes to an arrow.
2. *OK button:* Click this button to complete the command, leave the dialog box, and return to the drawing. If any changes have been made, they will remain as changes. Pressing **\<enter\>** has the same effect.

FIGURE 3–4
The Drawing Aids Dialog Box

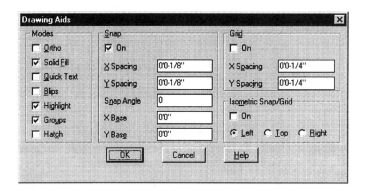

3. *Cancel button:* Click this button to cancel the command, leave the dialog box, and return to the drawing. If any changes have been made, they will be canceled and the original settings will return. Pressing the Esc key has the same effect.

4. *Input buttons:* An input button has two parts, its name and the area where changes can be made by typing new input. Click the second part of the input button, X Spacing, under Snap and experiment with the text cursor that is attached to the point of the arrow. As you move the mouse and pick a new spot, the text cursor moves also. The following editing keys can be used to edit the text in input buttons:

   Backspace key: Deletes characters to the left of the text cursor one at a time as it is pressed.
   Delete key: Deletes characters to the right of the text cursor one at a time as it is pressed.
   Left arrow: Moves the text cursor to the left without changing the existing text.
   Right arrow: Moves the text cursor to the right without changing the existing text.
   Character keys: After deleting existing settings, new settings can be typed from the keyboard.
   Snap X spacing input button: Enter the X spacing in this input button, and the Y spacing is automatically set to the same spacing.
   Grid X spacing input button: Enter the X spacing in this input button, and the Y spacing is automatically set to the same spacing.
   Snap angle, X base, and Y base input buttons: These buttons relate to the Rotate option and are discussed in later chapters.

5. *Check buttons:* A check button has two parts, its mode name and the area that can be clicked to toggle the check mark and mode on and off. A check mark in the box indicates the mode is on.

6. *Radio buttons:* A round button within a circle. A dark circle in the selection indicates that selection is picked.

While in the Drawing Aids dialog box, experiment with the different editing keys to become familiar with their functions. The dialog box is a handy tool to use in setting the snap and grid spacing, but if you are a fair typist, typing these commands from the keyboard is faster. After experimenting, be sure to return the grid spacing to $\frac{1}{4}$ and the snap to $\frac{1}{8}$ to have the correct settings for Exercise 4–1.

Layers

The layer concept in AutoCAD is like using transparent overlays with a manually drafted project. Different parts of the project can be placed on separate layers. The building shell may be on one layer, the interior walls on another, the electrical on a third layer, the furniture on a fourth layer, and so on. There is no limit to the number of layers you may use in a drawing. Each is perfectly aligned with all the others. Each layer may be viewed on the display screen separately, one layer may be viewed in combination with one or more of the other layers, or all layers may be viewed together. Each layer may also be plotted separately or in combination with other layers, or all layers may be plotted at the same time. The layer name may be from 1 to 31 characters in length.

Create layers using the Layer & Linetype Properties dialog box (Figures 3–5 and 3–6):

Prompt	Response
Command:	**Layer...**
The Layer & Linetype Properties dialog box appears (Figure 3–5):	CLICK: **New** (**three times**)
Layer1, Layer2, Layer3 appear in the Layer Name list (Figure 3–6):	CLICK: **Layer1** (as shown in Figure 3–6)

FIGURE 3–5
Layer & Linetype Properties
Dialog Box

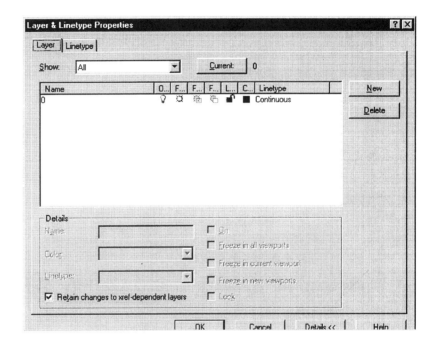

FIGURE 3–6
Select Layer1 to Assign a Color
to It

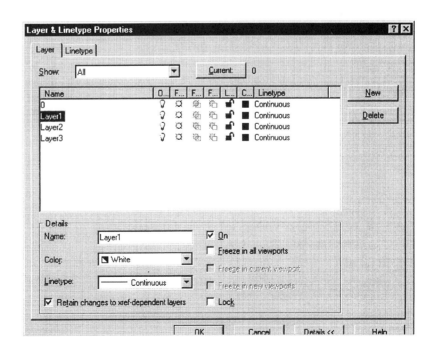

FIGURE 3–7
Select Color Dialog Box

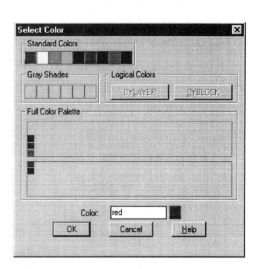

Assign colors to layers (Figure 3–7):

Prompt	Response
Layer1 is highlighted:	CLICK: **the box under C...,** **beside Layer1**
The Select Color dialog box appears (Figure 3–7):	CLICK: **the color Red**
	CLICK: **OK**
The Layer & Linetype Properties dialog box appears:	CLICK: **Layer2**
Layer2 is highlighted:	CLICK: **the box under C...,** **beside Layer2**
The Select Color dialog box appears:	CLICK: **the color Yellow**
	CLICK: **OK**
The Layer & Linetype Properties dialog box appears:	CLICK: **Layer3**
Layer3 is highlighted:	CLICK: **the box under C...,** **beside Layer3**
The Select Color dialog box appears:	CLICK: **the color Blue**
	CLICK: **OK**

Assign linetypes to layers (Figures 3–8, 3–9, and 3–10):

Prompt	Response
The Layer & Linetype Properties dialog box appears:	CLICK: **the word Continuous** **under Linetype, beside Layer2**
The Select Linetype dialog box appears (Figure 3–8):	CLICK: **Load...** (to load linetypes so they can be selected)
The Load or Reload Linetypes dialog box appears (Figure 3–9):	**Move the mouse to the center of the** **dialog box** and
	CLICK: **the right mouse button**
	CLICK: **Select All**
	CLICK: **OK**

FIGURE 3–8

Select Linetype Dialog Box

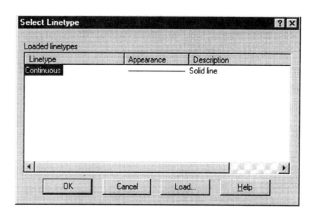

FIGURE 3–9

Load or Reload Linetypes
Dialog Box

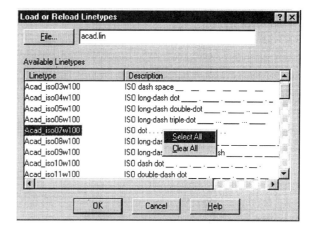

FIGURE 3–10

Select Linetype Dialog Box

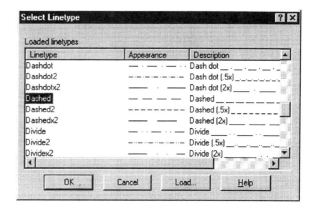

Individual linetypes can be loaded, or several can be loaded by holding down the Shift key as they are selected. The AutoCAD library of standard linetypes provides you with three different sizes of each standard linetype other than continuous. For example, the dashed line has the standard size called Dashed, a linetype half the standard size called Dashed2(.5x), and a linetype twice the standard size called Dashedx2(2x).

Prompt	Response
The Select Linetype dialog box appears (Figure 3–10):	CLICK: **Dashed** CLICK: **OK**

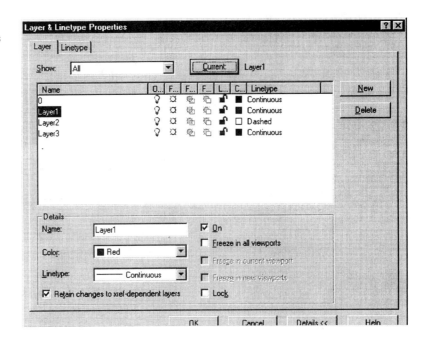

Make a layer current (Figure 3-11):

Prompt	Response
The Layer & Linetype Properties dialog box appears with layer names, colors, and linetypes assigned as shown in Figure 3–11:	CLICK: **Layer1** (to select it)
	CLICK: **Current**
	CLICK: **OK**

Anything drawn from this point until another layer is set current will be on Layer1.

Make the Object Properties toolbar visible (Figures 3–12 and 3–13):

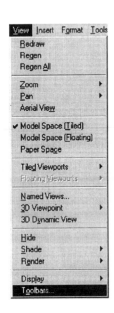

Prompt	Response
Command:	**Toolbars...**
The Toolbars dialog box appears (Figure 3–12):	CLICK: **the check box beside Object Properties** (so an X appears as shown in Figure 3–12)
	CLICK: **Close**
The Object Properties toolbar appears docked at the top of the screen with Layer1 current:	CLICK: **the down arrow** (as shown in Figure 3–13)

The layer icons on the Object Properties Toolbar, reading from left to right, are:

1. *On or Off:* These pertain to the visibility of layers. When a layer is turned OFF, it is still of the drawing, but any entity drawn on that layer is not visible on the screen and cannot be plotted. For instance, the building exterior walls layer, interior walls layer, and electrical layer are turned ON and all other layers turned OFF to view, edit, or plot an electrical plan. One or more layers can be turned OFF and ON as required.

2. *Frozen or Thawed:* These also pertain to the visibility of layers. The difference between ON/OFF and FREEZE/THAW is a matter of how quickly the drawing regen-

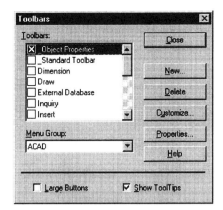

FIGURE 3–12
Toolbars Dialog Box

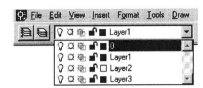

FIGURE 3–13
Show Layer Status on the Object
Properties Toolbar

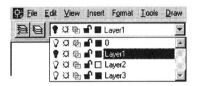

FIGURE 3–14
Turn Off Layer1

Note: With the Object Properties Toolbar displayed, CLICK: the highlighted icon (showing three sheets of paper) to activate the Layer and Linetype Properties dialog box.

erates on the display screen. If a layer is frozen, it is not visible, cannot be plotted, and AutoCAD spends no time regenerating it. A layer that is turned OFF is not visible and cannot be plotted, but AutoCAD does regenerate it.

3. *Frozen or Thawed in Selected Viewports:* This one is not available now because only one viewport is active. Freezing layers in separate viewports will be discussed in a later chapter.

4. *Locked or Unlocked:* When a layer is locked, it is visible, and you can draw on it. You cannot use any of the Edit commands to edit any of the drawing entities on the layer. You cannot accidentally change any entity that is already drawn.

To change the state of any layer pick the icon to select the alternate state. For example, Figure 3–14 shows that LAYER1 was turned off by picking the light bulb to turn it off. Experiment with changing the state of layers, then open the Layer and Linetype Properties dialog box to see the changed state reflected in it.

Experiment with all parts of the Layer and Linetype Properties dialog box. If you create some layers that you do not need, delete them by highlighting them and picking the Delete button. To change a layer name, color, or linetype, highlight the layer, and change it in the Details area of the dialog box. Return all layers to their original state before you exit. Pick any open spot on the screen to close the layer list.

Saving the Drawing and Exiting AutoCAD

Three commands, Save, SaveAs, and Exit (or Quit), and their uses must be understood to save your work in the desired drive and directory and to exit AutoCAD after you have saved your work.

Save

When the command Save is clicked and the drawing has been named, the drawing is saved automatically to the drive and directory in which you are working and a backup file is created with the same name but with the extension .bak. If the drawing has not been named, Save behaves like SaveAs.

SaveAs

SaveAs activates the Save Drawing As dialog box whether or not the drawing has been named and allows you to save your drawing to any drive or directory you choose.

Some additional features of the SaveAs command are as follows:

1. A drawing file can be saved and you may continue to work because with the SaveAs command the drawing editor is not exited.

2. If the default drive is used (the drive on which you are working), and the drawing has been opened from that drive, .dwg and .bak files are created.

3. If a different drive is specified (a floppy disk in the floppy drive), only a .dwg file is created.

4. To change the name of the drawing, you may save it under a new name by typing a new name in the File Name: button.

5. If the drawing was previously saved or if a drawing file already exists with the drawing file name you typed, AutoCAD gives you the message "This file already exists. Do you want to replace it?"

   When a drawing file is updated, the old .dwg file is replaced with the new drawing, so the answer to click is Yes. If an error has been made and you do not want to replace the file, click No.

6. A drawing may be saved to as many floppy disks or to as many directories on the hard disk as you wish. You should save your drawing in two different places as insurance against catastrophe.

Save the settings and layers for Exercise 4–1 on the hard drive (Figure 3–15):

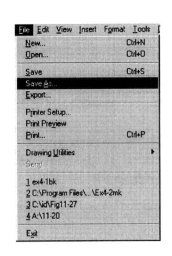

Prompt	Response
Command:	SaveAs...
The Save Drawing As dialog box appears with the File Name: Drawing highlighted:	TYPE: **CH4-EX1** (Because the File Name: Drawing was highlighted, you were able to type in that place. If you had used any other part of the dialog box first, you would have had to pick to the left of the File Name: Drawing, hold down the pick button, and drag the cursor across the name or double click the text to highlight it and then begin typing.) The drawing name may be from 1 to 255 characters. Auto-CAD adds the .dwg extension automatically.
The Save Drawing As dialog box appears as shown in Figure 3–15:	CLICK: **Save**

Be sure to make note of the drive and folder where the drawing is being saved so you can retrieve it easily when you need it.

FIGURE 3–15
Save CH4-EX1

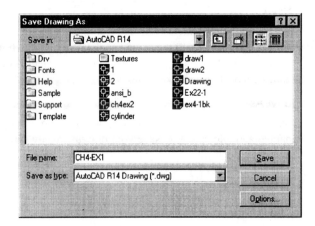

FIGURE 3–16

Save CH4-EX1 on the Disk in the $3\frac{1}{2}$ Floppy Drive [A:]

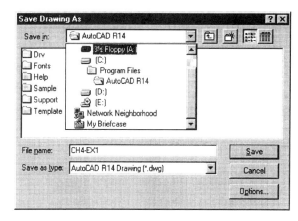

Save the same drawing to a floppy disk in the A: drive. (Substitute B: for A: if your computer is so labeled.) (Figure 3–16):

Insert a formatted diskette into the A drive.

Prompt	Response
Command:	**<enter>** (to repeat the previous command)
The Save Drawing As dialog box appears:	CLICK: **the down arrow in the Save in: button, highlight the $3\frac{1}{2}$ Floppy [A:]**
The Save Drawing As dialog box appears as shown in Figure 3–16:	CLICK: **$3\frac{1}{2}$ floppy [A:]**
	CLICK: **Save**

The light should brighten on the A drive, indicating that the drawing is being saved. Because the drawing was named when you saved it on the hard drive, you did not have to type the name again to save it with that name on the floppy disk. You could have chosen to give the drawing another name when you saved it on the floppy disk, in which case the new name would have to be typed in the File name: input button.

Save the drawing as a template to a floppy disk in the A drive (Figures 3–17 and 3–18):

Prompt	Response
Command:	**SaveAs...**
The Save Drawing As dialog box appears:	CLICK: **the down arrow in the Save as type: button and move the cursor to**

FIGURE 3–17

Save A:A-SIZE As a Template

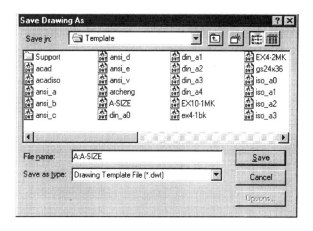

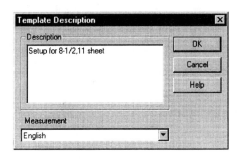

FIGURE 3–18
Template Description Dialog Box

Prompt	Response
	CLICK: **Drawing Template File[*.dwt]**
	TYPE: **A:A-SIZE** (in the File name: input area, so the Save Drawing As dialog box appears as shown in Figure 3–17)
	CLICK: **Save**
The Template Description dialog box appears (Figure 3–18):	TYPE: **Setup for 8-1/2,11 sheet** (as shown in Figure 3–18)
	CLICK: **OK**

Save Drawing As Dialog Box

The parts and functions of the Save Drawing As dialog box are as follows:

File name: Input Button

The drawing file name that will be saved appears here.

When you double click any folder an alphabetized list of all files of the type defined by the Save as type: button in the drive and directory specified in the Save In: button appears. If you want to use one of the names in this list, click it, and that name will replace the one in the File name: button. You will need to use the scroll bar if the list of files is longer than the area shown.

Save as type: Button

Clicking the down arrow reveals a list of file types under which the drawing may be saved. All have the extension .dwg except the Drawing Template File, which has the extension .dwt. Some of these file types can be used interchangeably, but others require that a specific file type be used. In this book you will use only the AutoCAD R14 Drawing file type for drawings.

Save in:

The drive and folder where the file will be saved is listed in the area. The list shown in Figure 3–19 indicates that the Template folder under the ACAD R14 folder is open. The list of files in this area shows the files with the .dwt extension that exist in this folder. If you double click the drive labeled C:, a list of other directories on the C drive appears.

Save Button

When clicked, this button executes the SaveAs... command. If you have already saved the drawing with the same name in the same folder, the warning shown in Figure 3-20 appears. Click Yes if you want to replace the drawing, No if you don't.

Cancel Button

When clicked, this button cancels the command or closes any open button on the dialog box. The Esc key has the same effect.

Note: The drawing C4-EX1 could have been saved as a template (.dwt) with the extension .dwt instead of .dwg. If you need to use the drawing in another version of AutoCAD, however, the file would have to be renamed to .dwg before the other version of AutoCAD would recognize the drawing as a valid file name.

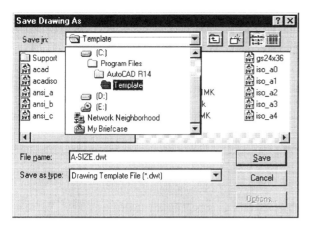

FIGURE 3–19
The Template Folder Is Open

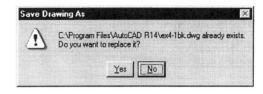

FIGURE 3–20
Save Drawing As Warning.

Exit (or Quit)

Note: The File menu **Exit** and the Command line: QUIT are the same command.

If you have not made any changes to the drawing since you last saved it, the Exit command takes you out of the AutoCAD program. If you have made changes to the drawing and have not saved these changes, AutoCAD will give you the message "Save changes to C:\Auto-CAD R14\CH4-EX1.dwg?" (or whatever the drawing name is). This is a safety feature because the Exit command, by itself, *does not update or save a drawing*. You have three options: Yes, save the changes; No, do not save changes; or Cancel the Exit command.

If you have just entered a drawing, have made a lot of mistakes, and just want to get rid of everything, respond with No to the Save changes question. If you opened an existing drawing and use the Exit command without making any changes, the stored .dwg file and .bak files are preserved unchanged.

While you are making a new drawing, AutoCAD is creating a .dwg (drawing) file of your drawing. There is no .bak (drawing file backup) file for a new drawing.

Each time an existing drawing file is opened for editing, the original drawing file (.dwg) becomes the drawing file backup (.bak). The new edited version of the drawing becomes the .dwg file. Thus there is a copy of the original drawing file (.bak) and a copy of the new edited version (.dwg).

Exit AutoCAD:

Prompt	Response
Command:	**Exit** (You may also TYPE: **QUIT<enter>** to exit.)

EXERCISES

EXERCISE 3–1. Complete Exercise 3–1 using the procedure described in this chapter.

REVIEW QUESTIONS

1. Which of the following is *not* on the list of units on the Unit Control dialog box?
   a. Scientific
   b. Metric
   c. Decimal
   d. Fractional
   e. Architectural

2. The Precision: button on the Units Control dialog box does which of the following?
   a. Determines how accurately AutoCAD draws
   b. Has a default value of 1/16″, which may not be changed
   c. Sets decimal places for fractional units
   d. Allows you to set the smallest fraction to display
   e. Sets decimal places for architectural units
3. The limits of a drawing may be set using a dialog box.
   a. True
   b. False
4. The default lower left corner of the drawing limits is 8-1/2,11.
   a. True
   b. False
5. The function key F7 described in this chapter does which of the following?
   a. Provides a check list of the layers created
   b. Turns snap ON or OFF
   c. Flips the screen from the text display to the graphics display
   d. Turns grid ON or OFF
   e. Turns ortho ON or OFF
6. Units, Limits, Grid, and Snap can all be found under the Format menu.
   a. True
   b. False
7. Which of the following function keys is used to turn snap ON or OFF?
   a. F1
   b. F2
   c. F7
   d. F8
   e. F9
8. How many layers may be set current at the same time?
   a. 1
   b. 2
   c. 3
   d. 16
   e. An unlimited number
9. When a layer is OFF, it will regenerate but is not visible.
   a. True
   b. False
10. AutoCAD provides how many sizes of each standard linetype (except continuous)?
    a. 1
    b. 2
    c. 3
    d. 4
    e. As many as you want

Complete.

11. Describe the effect of using the Esc key while in a command.

    _____

12. What is an invisible grid to which the crosshairs will lock called?

    _____

13. What is the maximum number of characters that may be used in a layer name?

    _____

14. How many layers may be used in a drawing?

    _____

15. What is the maximum number of characters that may be used in a drawing name?

    _____

16. Explain what .dwg and .dwt files are.

.dwg: _____

.dwt: _____

17. Before a linetype other than continuous may be selected or changed in the Layer Control dialog box, what must be done?

_____

18. List the toolbar on which the layer status is displayed.

_____

19. What does the Exit or Quit command do when used by itself?

_____

20. Describe how Save differs from SaveAs when the drawing has been named.

_____

TWO-DIMENSIONAL AUTOCAD

4 Drawing with AutoCAD: Basic Commands and Settings

OBJECTIVES

When you have completed this chapter, you will be able to:

☐ Correctly use the following commands and settings:

2D Solid	Ellipse	Move	Redo	Select
Arc	Erase	Oops	Redraw	Undo
Blipmode	Line	Ortho	Regen	Viewres
Circle	Ltscale	Pan	Scale	Zoom
Donut				

☐ Turn ORTHO mode on and off to control drawing as required.
☐ Turn the screen coordinate display off and on.
☐ Correctly use the following selection set options contained in many Modify commands:

All	Previous	Add	Window Polygon
Window	Crossing Window	Undo	Crossing Polygon
Last	Remove	Fence	

☐ Use the transparent Zoom and Pan commands while another command is in progress.

INTRODUCTION

Exercises 4–1 and 4–2 provide step-by-step instructions describing how to use many of the AutoCAD commands. Exercises 4–3, 4–4, and 4–5 provide drawings for you to practice the commands learned in Exercises 3–1, 3–2, 4–1, and 4–2.

Several options are available for each command, and you can access many commands from the toolbars or menu bar. Experiment with each new command to become familiar with it; you can then decide which options you prefer to use and how you like to access the commands. Upon completion of Chapter 4 and mastery of the commands included in the chapter, you will have a sound foundation upon which to continue learning AutoCAD and the remaining commands.

Following the Exercises in This Book

Prompt and Response columns continue to provide the steps required to start and complete each new command sequence. A new Response column item used in this and following chapters describes the location of points picked on the screen. Figures are provided throughout the chapters to show the location of the points. Points are indicated in bold type in the Response column by a **D** followed by a number (for example, **D1,D2**). Look at the figure provided to locate the point on the drawing, and pick a point in the same place on your screen drawing. Another feature added to this and following chapters is that sometimes the response is described generally in the Response column (for example, **Pick the middle of the windowed view**).

EXERCISE 4–1
Drawing Lines and Circles

In Chapter 3, the settings and layers were made for drawing CH4-EX1. In Exercise 4–1, that setup is used to complete your first drawing exercise. When you have completed Exercise 4–1, your drawing will look similar to the drawing in Figure 4–1.

To begin Exercise 4–1, turn on the computer and start AutoCAD. The Start Up dialog box is displayed.

Open an Existing Drawing on the Hard Drive

If your drawing CH4-EX1 is stored on a floppy disk, proceed with the following. If your drawing CH4-EX1 is stored on the hard disk, skip to the section "To open existing drawing CH4-EX1 on the hard drive, when it is stored on the hard disk."

FIGURE 4–1

Exercise 4–1: Drawing Lines and Circles

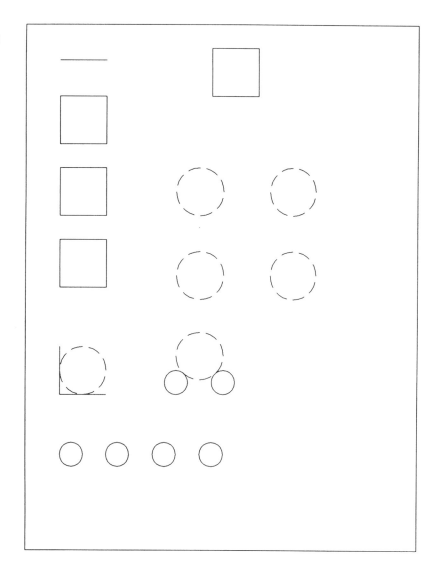

To open existing drawing CH4-EX1 when it is stored on a floppy disk that has no directories:

Prompt	Response
The Start Up dialog box is displayed:	**Insert the floppy disk in drive A.**
	CLICK: **Open a Drawing button**
	DOUBLE CLICK: **A:\CH4-EX1.dwg**
	-or-
	If A:\CH4-EX1.dwg is not listed in the Select a File: selection: DOUBLE CLICK: **More files...**
The Select File dialog box appears:	CLICK: $3\frac{1}{2}$ **Floppy[A:]**
	CLICK: **CH4-EX1**
	CLICK: **Open** (or DOUBLE CLICK: **CH4-EX1**)

Note: DOUBLE CLICK: means to place your cursor over the selection and press the left mouse button twice rapidly.

CH4-EX1 is opened.

Save the drawing to the hard drive:

Prompt	Response
Command:	**Save As...**
The Save Drawing As dialog box is displayed:	CLICK: **[C:]** (and the correct folder if needed)
	CLICK: **Save**

Now you are working on the hard drive. Do not work on a floppy disk. Always work on the hard drive.

To open existing drawing CH4-EX1 on the hard drive, when it is stored on the hard disk:

If your drawing is stored on the hard disk, CLICK: **Open a Drawing** and DOUBLE CLICK: **CH4-EX1** or CLICK: **CH4-EX1** to preview it, then CLICK: **OK**.

   If your drawing file is not listed, DOUBLE CLICK: **Move files...** to locate it.

Toolbars

The Object Properties toolbar and the Standard Toolbar are usually visible by default. Illustrations of the AutoCAD menu bar and toolbars of the commands needed to complete the exercises are shown in the book margins. If you plan to use any of the toolbars, be sure to select **Toolbars...** from the **View** menu in the menu bar, and activate the toolbar that contains the tools for the commands that will be used. The name of the toolbar used is included in the margin art.

ZOOM

The Zoom-All command lets you view the entire drawing area. Use it after setting up or entering a drawing so that you are familiar with the size and shape of your limits and grid. Otherwise, you may be working on a small part of the drawing and not realize it.

Use Zoom-All to view the entire drawing area:

Prompt	Response
Command:	**Zoom-All** (or TYPE: **Z<enter>**)
All/Center/Dynamic/Extents/Previous/ Scale(X/XP)/Window/<Realtime>:	TYPE: **A<enter>**

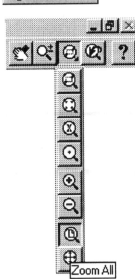

GRID

The grid is visible when it is on. Press the F7 function key to turn the grid off and on, or DOUBLE CLICK: **GRID** at the bottom of your screen. Turn the grid off and on to clean up any blips that appear on the screen while you are drawing.

On Your Own

Turn the grid on.

ORTHO

Note: When Ortho mode is on, drawing or editing of a drawing part is restricted to horizontal and vertical movements only. Turn Ortho ON and OFF to accommodate your drawing activity.

Press the F8 function key to turn Ortho on and off, or DOUBLE CLICK: **ORTHO** at the bottom of your screen. Ortho mode, when on, helps you to draw lines perfectly horizontally and vertically. It does not allow you to draw at an angle, so turn Ortho off and on as needed.

On Your Own

Turn Ortho on.

SNAP

Function key F9 turns Snap on and off, or you may DOUBLE CLICK: **SNAP** at the bottom of your screen. Snap helps you to draw accurately; it is desirable to draw with Snap on most of the time. If you need to turn Snap off to draw or edit a drawing entity, remember to turn it back on as soon as possible.

On Your Own

1. Turn Snap on.
2. Check the Layer Control; Layer1 should be current.

LINE and ERASE

Use Figure 4–1 as a guide when locating the line and squares drawn using the Line command.

Drawing Lines Using the Grid Marks

Lines can be drawn by snapping to the grid marks visible on the screen.

Draw a horizontal line 1″ long, using the grid marks (Figure 4–2):

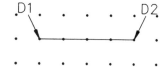

FIGURE 4–2
Draw a Horizontal Line 1″ Long,
Using Grid Marks

Prompt	Response
Command:	**Line** (or TYPE: **L<enter>**)
From point:	**D1** (click a point three grid spaces down ($\frac{3}{4}''$) and three grid spaces to the right of the upper left corner of the page)
To point:	**D2** (move four grid marks to the right)
To point:	**<enter>** (to complete the command)

Erase the line and bring it back again:

Prompt	Response
Command:	**Erase** (or TYPE: **E<enter>**)

Prompt	Response
Select objects:	**Position the small box that replaces the crosshairs any place on the line and click the line.**
Select objects: 1 found	
Select objects:	**<enter>** (the line disappears)
Command:	TYPE: **OOPS<enter>** (the line reappears)

Do not be afraid to draw with AutoCAD. If you make a mistake, you can easily erase it using the Erase command. When you are using the Erase command, a small box replaces the screen crosshairs. The small box is called the *object selection target*. You will learn more about the object selection target later in this exercise. The Oops feature will restore everything erased by the *last* erase command. Oops cannot be used to restore lines erased by a previous command.

Draw a 1″ square using the grid marks and undo the last two lines (Figure 4–3):

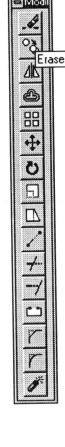

FIGURE 4–3
Draw a 1″ Square Using Grid Marks

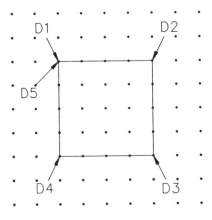

Prompt	Response
Command:	**Line**
LINE From point:	**D1** (click a point $\frac{3}{4}$″ directly below the left end of the line just drawn)
To point:	**D2**
To point:	**D3**
To point:	**D4**
To point:	**D5**
To point:	TYPE: **U<enter>**
To point:	TYPE: **U<enter>**
To point:	**<enter>** (to stop and return to the Command: prompt)

While in the line command if you decide you do not like the last line segment drawn, use the undo command to erase it and continue on with the "To point:" prompt. Clicking more than one undo will backtrack through the line segments in the reverse of the order in which they were drawn.

Complete the square (Figure 4–3):

Prompt	Response
Command:	**<enter>** (to return the Line command prompt)
From point:	**<enter>** (the line is attached)
To point:	**D4,D5**
To point:	**<enter>** (to stop)

The Line command has a very handy feature: If you respond to the prompt "To point:" by pressing the enter key or the space bar, the line will start at the end of the most recently drawn line.

Drawing Lines Using Absolute Coordinates

Note: Pressing the Esc key cancels the command selection process and returns AutoCAD to the "Command:" prompt. Use Esc if you get stuck in a command.

Remember, 0,0 is the lower left corner of the page. When you are using absolute coordinates to draw, the X-axis coordinate is entered first and identifies a location on the horizontal axis. The Y-axis coordinate is entered second and identifies a location on the vertical axis. The page size is 8-1/2,11. A little adding and subtracting to determine the absolute coordinates will locate the square on the page as follows.

Draw a 1″ square using absolute coordinates (Figure 4–4):

FIGURE 4–4
Draw a 1″ Square Using Absolute Coordinates

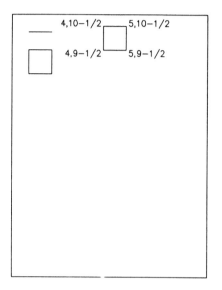

Prompt	Response
Command:	**Line** (move the crosshairs to the center of the screen)
From point:	TYPE: **4,10-1/2<enter>** (the line begins)
To point:	TYPE: **5,10-1/2<enter>**
To point:	TYPE: **5,9-1/2<enter>**
To point:	TYPE: **4,9-1/2<enter>**
To point:	TYPE: **C<enter>**

On Your Own

1. Function key F6 controls the screen coordinate display located in the lower left corner of the screen. Press the F6 function key to turn the coordinate display off and on. Turn the screen coordinate display on and move your pointer to each corner of the square. Watch how the screen coordinate display shows the X,Y coordinate position of each corner. Compare those coordinates with the coordinates you just typed and entered. They are the same.

2. Hold the crosshairs of the cursor (with snap on) on the lower left corner of the grid; the coordinate display reads 0′-0″,0′-0″. Move the cursor to the upper right corner of the grid; the coordinate display reads 0′-8-1/2″,0′-11″. This is a good way to check the limits of a drawing.

Drawing Lines Using Relative Coordinates

Relative coordinates are used after a point is entered. (Relative to what? Relative to the point just entered.) After a point has been clicked on the drawing, relative coordinates are entered by typing @, followed by the X,Y coordinates. For example, after a point is entered to start a line, typing and entering @ 1,0 will draw the line 1″ in the X direction, 0″ in the Y direction.

Draw a 1″ square using relative coordinates:

Prompt	Response
Command:	**Line**
From point:	**Click a point on the grid $\frac{1}{2}$″ below the lower left corner of the first square drawn.**
To point:	TYPE: **@1,0<enter>**
To point:	TYPE: **@0,−1<enter>**
To point:	TYPE: **@−1,0<enter>**
To point:	TYPE: **C<enter>**

A minus sign (−) is used for negative line location with relative coordinates. Negative is to the left for the X axis and down for the Y axis.

Drawing Lines Using Polar Coordinates

Absolute and relative coordinates are extremely useful in some situations. However, for many design applications (for example, drawing walls) polar coordinates or direct distance entry is used. Be sure you understand how to use all four types of coordinates.

Polar coordinates are also relative to the last point entered. They are typed starting with an @, followed by a distance and angle of direction. Figure 4–5 shows the polar coordinate angle directions. The angle of direction is always preceded by a < sign when polar coordinates are entered.

Draw a 1″ square using polar coordinates:

FIGURE 4–5
Polar Coordinate Angles

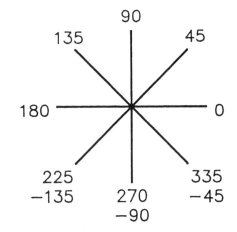

Prompt	Response
Command:	**<enter>** (to return the Line command prompt)
From point:	**Click a point on the grid $\frac{1}{2}$″ below the lower left corner of the last square drawn.**
To point:	TYPE: **@1<0<enter>**
To point:	TYPE: **@1<−90<enter>**
To point:	TYPE: **@1<180<enter>**
To point:	TYPE: **C<enter>**

On Your Own

1. Practice using the Erase command by erasing the entire last square you just drew. Then replace it using Direct Distance Entry as described next.

Part II: Two-Dimensional AutoCAD

Drawing Lines Using Direct Distance Entry

Direct Distance Entry is a quick, accurate, and easy way to draw horizontal and vertical lines (it can also be used to draw at an angle if you know which direction to move your mouse or with any other command that asks you to specify a point). With ORTHO ON move your mouse in the direction you want to draw, TYPE: **the distance**, and PRESS: **<enter>**.

Draw a 1″ square using direct distance entry:

Prompt	Response
Command:	**With ORTHO ON** **Line** (or TYPE: **L<enter>**)
LINE From point:	**Click a point on the grid in the same location as the beginning of the square you just erased.**
To point:	**Move your mouse to the right.** TYPE: **1<enter>**
To point:	**Move your mouse down.** TYPE: **1<enter>**
To point:	**Move your mouse to the left.** TYPE: **1<enter>**
To point:	TYPE: **C<enter>**

CIRCLE

In the following part of this exercise, four circles of the same size are drawn, using four different methods.

On Your Own

1. Look at Figure 4–1 to determine the approximate location of the four circles you will draw.
2. Set Layer2 current. Layer2 has a dashed linetype.

Center, Radius

Draw a circle with a $\frac{1}{2}″$ radius (Figure 4–6):

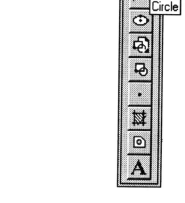

FIGURE 4–6
Draw the Same Size Circle Using Four Different Methods

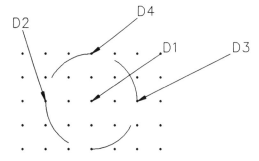

Prompt	Response
Command:	**Circle-Center, Radius**
3P/2P/TTR<Center point>:	**D1**
Diameter/<Radius>:	TYPE: **1/2<enter>** (the circle appears)

Center, Diameter

Refer to Figure 4–1 to determine the approximate location of the next circle.

Draw a circle with a 1″ diameter (Figure 4–6):

Prompt	Response
Command:	**<enter>** (to return Circle command prompt)
3P/2P/TTR<Center point>:	**D1**
Diameter/<Radius><0′-0 1/2″>:	TYPE: **D<enter>**
Diameter<0′-1″>:	TYPE: **<enter>** (the circle appears)

2 points

Draw a 1″ diameter circle by locating the two endpoints of its diameter (Figure 4–6):

Prompt	Response
Command:	**Circle-2 Points**
2p First point on diameter:	**D2** (on a grid mark)
Second point on diameter:	**D3** (move four grid spaces to the right)

3 points

Draw a 1″ diameter circle by clicking three points on its circumference (Figure 4–6):

Prompt	Response
Command:	**Circle-3 Points**
3p First point on diameter:	**D2**
Second point:	**D3** (move four grid spaces to the right)
Third point:	**D4** (the center of the top of the circle)

You have just learned four different methods of drawing the same size circle. You can watch the size of the circle change on the screen by moving the pointer, and you can select the desired size by clicking the point that indicates the size.

On Your Own

1. Experiment with different size circles and the different methods until you become comfortable with them.
2. Set Layer1 current.
3. Draw two 1″ lines that form a corner and two $\frac{1}{2}$″ diameter circles, 1″ on center as shown in Figure 4–7. Figure 4–1 will help you to determine the approximate location of the corner and two circles on your drawing.
4. Set Layer2 current again.

FIGURE 4–7
Draw Two 1″ Lines That Form a Corner and Two $\frac{1}{2}$″ Diameter Circles, 1″ on Center

TTR

The next option of the Circle command is Tan, Tan, Radius. This stands for tangent, tangent, and radius. A tangent touches a circle at a single point.

Draw a circle with a $\frac{1}{2}$″ radius tangent to two lines (Figure 4–8):

Prompt	Response
Command:	**Circle-Tangent, Tangent, Radius**
Enter Tangent spec:	**D1** (pick any place on the line)

Prompt	Response
Enter second Tangent spec:	**D2** (pick any place on the line)
Radius<default>:	TYPE: 1/2 **<enter>**

Draw a circle with a $\frac{1}{2}''$ radius tangent to two other circles (Figure 4–8):

FIGURE 4–8
Draw a Circle with a $\frac{1}{2}''$ Radius Tangent to Two Lines; Draw a Circle with a $\frac{1}{2}''$ Radius Tangent to Two Other Circles

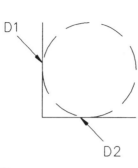
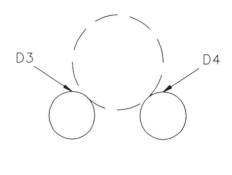

Prompt	Response
Command:	**<enter>** (to return Circle command prompt)
3P/2P/TTR/<Center point>:	TYPE: **TTR<enter>**
Enter Tangent spec:	**D3**
Enter second Tangent spec:	**D4**
Radius<0′-0 1/2″>:	TYPE: **<enter>**

On Your Own

1. Experiment with different size circles. The location of the tangent circle will change with different radius sizes. Also, the location of the tangent circle between the two circles will change, depending on the location of the first and second tangents specified.

2. Use the Tangent, Tangent, Tangent option to experiment with drawing circles that are tangent to three objects.

LTSCALE

AutoCAD provides a variety of linetypes that you may use. For example, the dashed linetype provided by AutoCAD consists of $\frac{1}{2}''$ line segments with $\frac{1}{4}''$ spaces in between. The given line segment length ($\frac{1}{2}''$) and spacing ($\frac{1}{4}''$) for the dashed linetype are drawn when the global linetype scale factor is set to 1 (the default).

To make the line segment length or spacing smaller, a linetype scale factor smaller than 1 but larger than 0 is entered to the Ltscale prompt. To make the line segment length and spacing larger, a linetype scale factor larger than 1 is entered. Look closely to see the circle's DASHED linetype scale change when the following is entered.

Use Ltscale to change the size of the DASHED linetype:

Prompt	Response
Command:	TYPE: **LTSCALE<enter>**
New scale factor <1.0000>:	TYPE: **1/2<enter>**
Regenerating drawing.	

ZOOM

The different Zoom commands (Realtime, Previous, Window, Dynamic, Scale, Center, In, Out, All, Extents) control how you view the drawing area on the display screen. While drawing the lines and circles for this chapter you have been able to view the entire $8\frac{1}{2}'' \times 11''$ drawing limits on the screen. The Zoom-All command was used earlier to assure that view.

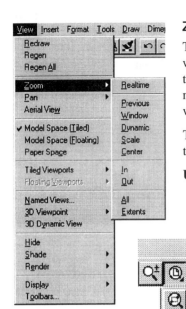

Zoom-Window

The Zoom-Window command allows you to pick two opposite corners of a rectangular window on the screen. The cursor changes to form a rubber band that shows the size of the window on the screen. The size of the window is controlled by the movement of the mouse. The part of the drawing inside the windowed area is magnified to fill the screen when the second corner of the window is clicked.

The following will use the Zoom-Window command to look more closely at the three tangent circles previously drawn.

Use Zoom-Window to look more closely at the three tangent circles (Figure 4–9):

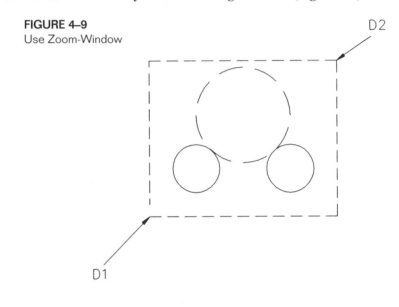

FIGURE 4–9
Use Zoom-Window

Prompt	Response
Command:	TYPE: **Z\<enter>**
All/Center/Dynamic/Extents/Previous/Scale (X/XP/Window/\<Realtime>):	**D1** (lower left corner of the window)
Other corner:	**D2** (upper right corner of the window)

The area that was windowed is now displayed to fill the screen.

When the magnification of the circles was enlarged with the Zoom-Window command, to save time AutoCAD did not regenerate the drawing. The part of the drawing that was windowed and magnified was *redrawn* only. That is why the circles are not smooth. Small line segments called vectors make up a circle. When the entire page is displayed, fewer line segments are used to make up the smaller circles. By zooming in and not regenerating, you are able to see the small number of vectors.

Use REGEN to regenerate the drawing:

Prompt	Response
Command:	TYPE: **REGEN\<enter>**

By typing and entering REGEN, you issued a regeneration of the drawing. AutoCAD regenerated the circles with the optimal number of line segments (making the circle smoother) for the larger magnification.

Zoom-All

Now that you have a windowed area of the drawing, how do you view the entire drawing again? Zoom-All will provide a view of the entire drawing area.

Part II: Two-Dimensional AutoCAD

Use Zoom-All to view the entire drawing:

Prompt	Response
Command:	**Zoom-All** (or TYPE: **Z<enter>**)
All/Center/Dynamic/Extents/Previous/Scale (X/XP)/Window/<Realtime>:	TYPE: **A<enter>**

Zoom-Previous

Zoom-Previous is a very convenient feature. AutoCAD remembers up to ten previous views. This is especially helpful and saves time if you are working on a complicated drawing.

Use Zoom-Previous to see the last view of the tangent circles again:

Prompt	Response
Command:	**<enter>**
All/Center/Dynamic/Extents/Previous/Scale (X/XP)/Window/<Realtime>:	TYPE: **P<enter>**

Zoom-Dynamic

Another Zoom command that saves time is Zoom-Dynamic.

Use Zoom-Dynamic to change the display (Figure 4–10):

Prompt	Response
Command:	**<enter>**
All/Center/Dynamic/Extents/Previous/Scale (X/XP)/Window/<Realtime>:	TYPE: **D<enter>**

You now see three areas on the screen (Figure 4–10):

1. The tangent circle area previously windowed.
2. The drawing limits or the drawing extents, whichever is larger.
3. The box with the X in it is the same size as the window that you just made when you windowed the circles. This window can be moved; it follows the movement of your mouse. Experiment by moving it around the screen.

The size of the window can also be changed. Change the size of the window by pressing the pick button on the mouse. The X inside changes to an arrow when you press the left button. When the arrow is in the window, the movement of the pointer changes the size of the window. Experiment with changing the size of the window. Press the left button on the mouse to return the X to the center of the window. With the X in the center of

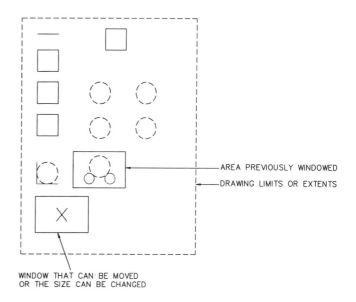

FIGURE 4–10
Use Zoom-Dynamic

AREA PREVIOUSLY WINDOWED
DRAWING LIMITS OR EXTENTS
WINDOW THAT CAN BE MOVED OR THE SIZE CAN BE CHANGED

the window, the size remains constant and you may move the window to the area of the drawing that you want to window or zoom in on next.

When you have decided which area of the drawing you want to view next and have the size of window needed, with an X in the center, place the window on the area to be enlarged. When you press the enter button on the mouse, the area inside the window will appear enlarged on the screen.

Zoom-Extents

Zoom-Extents always performs a regeneration of the drawing. The Zoom-Extents command allows you to view the extents of a drawing. To understand Zoom-Extents, you need to understand the difference between drawing limits and drawing extents. The limits of a drawing are the size of the sheet set with the LIMITS command. The extents of a drawing include whatever graphics are actually drawn on the page. If only one half of the page is full, the extents will be one half the page. Sometimes a drawing entity is drawn outside the limits; this too is considered the drawing extents. The Zoom-Extents command provides a view of all drawing entities on the page as large as possible to fill the screen. The Zoom-All command displays the entire drawing limits or extents, whichever is larger. The extents are larger than the limits when a drawing entity is drawn outside of the limits.

Use Zoom-Extents to view the extents of drawing CH4-EX1:

Prompt	Response
Command:	**Zoom-Extents**

The remaining Zoom commands are Scale, Center, Realtime, In and Out. A brief explanation of each follows.

Zoom-Scale

Zoom-Scale is stated as Scale(X/XP). The Scale feature allows you to increase or decrease the magnification of the objects on the screen when you are viewing the entire page or a windowed view. If, while viewing the entire page or limits of the drawing, you type and enter 2 to the Zoom prompt, the new displayed view will have a magnification twice as large as the full view. If you type and enter 1/4, the view will be decreased to one quarter of the full view. To view the entire drawing as displayed within the limits, enter 1 to the Zoom-Scale prompt, "Enter scale factor:".

While in a windowed view, with an object displayed, enter 2 followed by an X (2X) to the Zoom prompt, to increase the magnification of the windowed view by 2. A number followed by an X increases or decreases the object *currently* displayed. If while you are in the windowed area the number 2 is not followed by an X, the full view or entire drawing area (not the windowed area) will be magnified by 2 and displayed.

The "XP" in the Scale part of the Zoom command prompt refers to model space and paper space, which will be discussed in a later chapter.

Zoom-Center

When Zoom-Center is clicked, AutoCAD asks you for a center point of a window. After you have clicked the center point of the window on the drawing, the prompt asks for "Magnification or Height <current height>:". The current height (for example, 11″ on your current drawing) is shown in default brackets. If 2 is typed and entered, a view of 2″ of the current drawing is enlarged to fill the screen. A height larger than the current height (such as 15) decreases the magnification by changing the height of the displayed view to 15″ instead of 11″.

If 2X (an X following the number) is entered to the prompt, "Magnification or Height <current height>:", the current drawing display is magnified by 2.

Real-Time Zoom

The Real-Time Zoom command is located on the Standard Toolbar and on the menu bar View menu under Zoom. You may also TYPE: **RTZOOM <enter>** from the keyboard to activate this command. To zoom in or out, hold down the left mouse button and move the

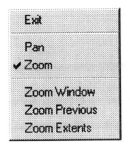

Note: PRESS:<enter> to the Zoom prompt to activate Real-Time Zoom.

mouse up or down to change the magnification of the drawing. PRESS: **the right mouse button** to get a shortened zoom and pan menu as shown in the margin. PRESS: **Esc** to exit from the command.

Zoom-In

Zoom In makes the objects in the drawing appear to be larger.

Zoom-Out

Zoom Out makes the objects in the drawing appear to be smaller.

PAN

Tip: The Zoom and Pan commands may also be activated by typing **Z** or **P** from the keyboard.

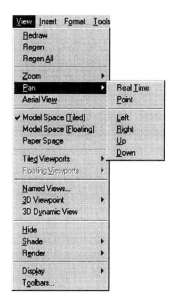

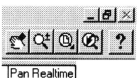

The Pan command allows you to maintain the current display magnification and see parts of the drawing that may be off the screen and not visible in the display. It allows you to move the entire drawing in any direction. Pan does not change the magnification of the view. It is not necessary to window an area to use the Pan command, but in the following exercise, a windowed view will be used.

On Your Own

Magnify any portion of the drawing using the Zoom-Window option.

Use Pan to move the drawing while in a windowed view:

Prompt	Response
Command:	**Pan-Point**
'pAN Displacement:	**Click the middle of the windowed view.**
Second point:	**Click a point two grid marks to the right of the first point.**

You can also enter the 'pan Displacement (the direction of the drawing movement) using relative coordinates. For instance, typing and entering -.5,0 or -1/2,0 to the first prompt "'Pan Displacement:" and pressing the enter key for the "Second point:" prompt will move the drawing $\frac{1''}{2}$ to the left.

Real-Time Pan

The Real-Time Pan command is located on the Standard Toolbar and on the menu bar View menu under Pan. You may also TYPE: **RTPAN<enter>** to activate this command. To move the view of your drawing at the same magnification, hold down the left button on your mouse and move the mouse in any direction to change the view of your drawing. PRESS: **the right mouse button** while in Real-Time Pan to get a shortened zoom and pan menu. PRESS: **Esc** to exit from the command.

Pan Scroll Bars

The scroll bars on the right side and bottom of the display may also be used to pan from one area of the drawing to another.

Transparent Commands

A transparent command is a command that can be used while another command is in progress. It is very handy to be able to change the display while a command such as Line is in progress. To use the Zoom commands transparently, after you have entered the Line command, TYPE: **'Z<enter>**. An apostrophe (') must precede the command name. The **'Z** prompt is ">>All/Center/Dynamic/Extents/Previous/Scale(X/XP)/Window/<Real-time>:". The >> preceding the command prompt indicates that the command is being used transparently.

You can also use Pan as a transparent command, while another command is in progress: TYPE: **'P<enter>**, or click it from the view menu in the menu bar.

All of the Zoom commands from the View menu in the Menu Bar may be used transparently; you can simply click them.

REDRAW

When you pick Redraw from the View Menu or TYPE: **R<enter>**, AutoCAD redraws and cleans up your drawing. Any marker blips (when a point is entered, AutoCAD generates small marker blips on the screen) on the screen disappear, and drawing entities affected by editing of other objects are redrawn. Pressing function key F7 twice turns the grid off and on and also redraws the screen.

REGEN

When you click Regen from the View menu, AutoCAD regenerates the entire drawing and redraws the current view. As you have already learned, other View commands do this, and it is seldom necessary to issue a regeneration with the Regen command.

VIEWRES

When you TYPE: **VIEWRES<enter>** AutoCAD prompts "Do you want fast zooms? <Y>". If you respond yes, AutoCAD maintains the virtual screen and performs redraws when possible. If the response is no, AutoCAD always regenerates the drawing when the view is changed. Viewres must be set to yes if you want to use transparent commands.

The next prompt from Viewres is "Enter circle zoom percent (1-20000) <100>:". Remember the line segments, or vectors (discussed earlier), that make up circles and arcs? The circle zoom percent affects the number of vectors that make up circles, arcs, and linetypes. The AutoCAD default of 100 tells AutoCAD to use its internal computation to set the number of vectors. If you enter a number less than 100, the circles and arcs may not look as smooth, but the drawing regenerates more quickly. If you enter a number higher than 100, the circles and arcs appear very smooth as you zoom in, but regeneration time increases. Viewres affects the display screen only; it does not affect how the circles, arcs, and linetypes plot.

BLIPMODE

When a point is entered on a drawing, AutoCAD generates small marker blips on the screen. Commands such as Redraw or Regen that redraw or regenerate the drawing erase the marker blips. When you TYPE: **BLIPMODE<enter>**, the Blipmode command has two responses: ON and OFF. When the Blipmode command is OFF, no marker blips are displayed. When the Blipmode command is ON, the marker blips appear. A Blips check button is also located in the Drawing Aids dialog box, when you click Drawing Aids... from the Tools menu.

MOVE and Editing Commands Selection Set

You may want to move some of the items on your page to improve the layout of the page. The Move command lets you do that.

On Your Own

1. Set Layer3 current.
2. Use Zoom-All to view the entire drawing.
3. Draw a row of four $\frac{1}{2}''$ diameter circles, 1" on center, as shown in Figure 4–11.
4. Pick Move from the Modify menu (or TYPE: **M<enter>**).

After you pick Move, the prompt in the prompt line asks you to "Select objects:". Also, a small box replaces the screen crosshairs. This box, called an object selection target, helps you to select the item or group of items to be moved by positioning the target box on the item. The item or group of items selected is called the *selection set*. Many of the Auto-CAD Modify commands provide the same prompt, the object selection target, and also the same options used to select the object or objects to be edited. The options are: All, Window, Window Polygon, Last, Previous, Crossing, Crossing Polygon, Fence, Remove, Add, and Undo. You can also select an item by clicking any point on it.

FIGURE 4–11
Draw a Row of Four $\frac{1}{2}''$ Diameter
Circles, $1''$ on Center

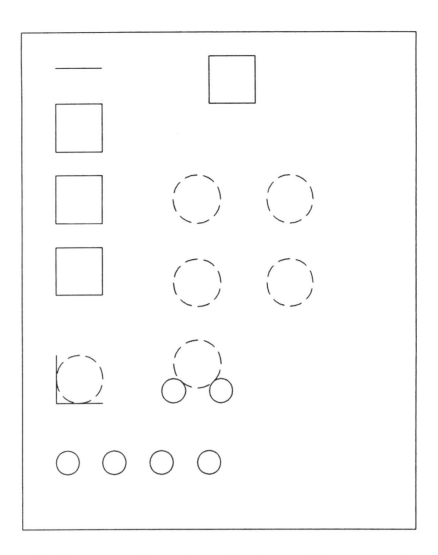

The Move command is used in the following part of this exercise to demonstrate the various options many of the Modify commands use to select objects. Notice that when the item is selected, AutoCAD confirms your selection by highlighting it.

Select a circle by clicking a point on the circle, and move it by clicking a point on the drawing (Figure 4–12):

FIGURE 4–12
Select a Circle by Clicking a Point
on the Circle, and Move It by
Clicking a Point on the Drawing

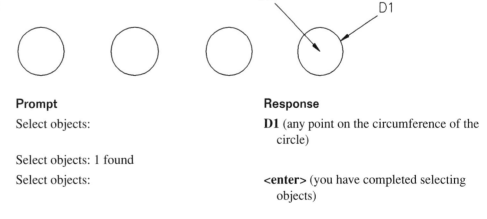

Prompt	Response
Select objects:	**D1** (any point on the circumference of the circle)
Select objects: 1 found	
Select objects:	**<enter>** (you have completed selecting objects)

Prompt	Response
Base point or displacement:	**D2** (the center of the circle—be sure SNAP is ON)
Second point of displacement:	**Click a point three grid marks ($\frac{3}{4}''$) to the right.**

Select a circle by clicking a point on the circle, and move it by entering relative coordinates (Figure 4–13):

FIGURE 4–13
Select a Circle by Clicking a Point on the Circle, and Move It by Entering Relative Coordinates

Note: Keep Snap ON while moving a drawing entity. Snap from one grid point (Base point or displacement) to another (Second point of displacement).

Prompt	Response
Command:	**<enter>** (to return Move command prompt)
Select objects:	**D1**
Select objects: 1 found	
Select objects:	**<enter>**
Base point or displacement:	**D2** (the center of the circle)
Second point of displacement:	TYPE: **@-3/4,0<enter>**

You can give the second point of displacement by clicking a point on the screen or by using absolute, relative, polar coordinates, or direct distance entry.

Select items to be edited by using a window, and then remove an item from the selection set (Figure 4–14):

FIGURE 4–14
Select Items to Be Edited by Using a Window, and Then Remove an Item from the Selection Set

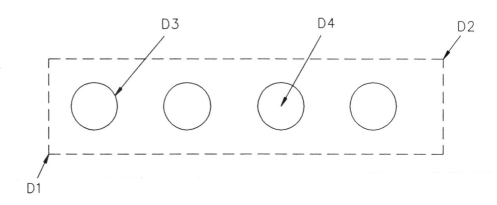

Prompt	Response
Command:	**<enter>**
Select objects:	**D1**
Other corner:	**D2**
4 found	
Select objects:	TYPE: **R<enter>**
Remove objects:	**D3**
Remove objects:	**<enter>**

Prompt	Response
Base point or displacement:	**D4** (the center of the circle)
Second point of displacement:	**Click a point two grid marks down the Y axis.**

Window (W), Crossing Window (C), Window Polygon (WP), and Crossing Polygon (CP)

The Window and Crossing (Window) responses allow you to pick two opposite corners of a rectangular window on the screen. The crosshairs of the pointer change to form a rubber band that shows the size of the window on the screen. The size of the window is controlled by the movement of the pointer. Window Polygon and Crossing Polygon allow you to make a polygon by clicking points that are used to select objects.

Tip: Typing W<enter> and C<enter> to activate window and crossing window is helpful when the drawing area is dense and clicking an empty area is difficult or impossible.

With the Window response, only the parts of the drawing that are *entirely contained within the window* are selected to be edited. If the window covers only a part of a drawing entity, that entity is not selected. You may also type and enter **W** to activate the Window response, or **WP** to activate Window Polygon.

When you use the Crossing Window command, any part of the drawing that is contained within or *crossed by the crossing window* is included in the selection set. With a crossing window, a drawing entity such as a line or circle does not have to be entirely contained within the window to be selected.

Picking an empty area on the drawing and moving your mouse to the right creates a window. Picking and moving to the left creates a crossing window.

On Your Own

1. Experiment with the difference between Window and Crossing Window. You may also type and enter **C** to activate the Crossing Window response, or **CP** to activate Crossing Polygon.

2. Return the circles to the approximate location as shown in Figure 4–11.

All (All)

Selects all objects on thawed layers.

Fence (F)

Fence allows you to click points that draw a line that selects any objects it crosses.

Remove (R) and Add (A)

The Remove response allows you to remove a drawing part from the selection set. If you are in the remove mode and decide to add another drawing part to the selection set, TYPE: **A<enter>** to return to the add mode.

Last (L) and Previous (P)

The Last response selects the most recent drawing entity created. The Previous response selects the most recent selection set. Both are handy if you want to use several editing commands on the same drawing entity or the same selection set. You may also type and enter **L** or **P** from the keyboard.

Undo (U)

While in an editing command, if you decide you do not want something in a selection set, you may use the Undo command to remove it and continue on with the "Select objects:" prompt. Picking more than one Undo backtracks through the selection sets in the reverse order in which they were selected. You may also type and enter **U** from the keyboard.

SELECT

The Select command allows you to preselect the items to be edited. Then you can use the "Previous" option in the Modify commands to refer to the selection set. TYPE: **SELECT<enter>** to the Command: prompt.

Save Your Drawing and Exit AutoCAD

When you have completed Exercise 4–1, save your drawing in at least two places and exit AutoCAD. Exercise 4–1 will be printed in Chapter 8.

EXERCISE 4–2
Drawing Arcs, Ellipses, and Solids

When you have completed Exercise 4–2, your drawing will look similar to the drawing in Figure 4–15. To begin Exercise 4–2, turn on the computer and start AutoCAD.

Begin Drawing CH4-EX2 on the Hard Drive

1. CLICK: **Use a Wizard**

2. CLICK: **Quick Setup**

   CLICK: **OK**

3. Set drawing Units: **Architectural**

   CLICK: **Next>>**

4. Set drawing Width: $8\frac{1}{2}''$ × Length: **11″**

   CLICK: **Done**

5. **Use SaveAs... to save the drawing on the hard drive with the name CH4-EX2.**

6. Set Grid: $\frac{1}{4}''$

7. Set Snap: $\frac{1}{8}''$

8. Create the following Layers:

Note: To change a layer name after using New to create layers: Click the layer name to highlight it, double click the name in the Name: input area, and type over the existing name. You can also name the layers by clicking New and then typing the layer names separated by commas. When you type the comma you move to the next layer.

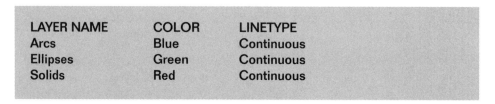

LAYER NAME	COLOR	LINETYPE
Arcs	Blue	Continuous
Ellipses	Green	Continuous
Solids	Red	Continuous

9. Be sure to use **Zoom-All** to view the entire drawing area.

UNDO

Understanding how to use the Undo command can be very helpful while drawing with AutoCAD.

When **U** is typed from the keyboard to the Command: prompt, and the enter key is pressed (or undo is selected) the most recent command operation is undone. Most of the time the operation that is undone is obvious, such as when a line that you have just drawn is undone. The most recent mode settings that are not obvious, such as snap, will be undone also. Typing **REDO** and pressing enter will redo only one undo.

When **U** is typed and entered from the keyboard, no prompt line appears. If **UNDO** is typed and entered, the prompt "Auto/Control/BEgin/End/Mark/Back/<Number>:" appears.

<Number>

The default is "number". You may enter a number for the number of operations to be undone. For instance, if 5 is entered to the prompt, five operations will be undone. If you decide you went too far, you can type and enter **REDO** or select Redo from the standard Toolbar, and all five operations will be restored.

Typing **U** from the keyboard and pressing the enter key is the same as entering the number 1 to the Undo prompt. In that instance, **Redo** will redo only one undo, no matter how many times you typed and entered **U**.

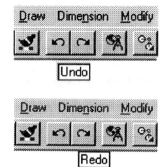

FIGURE 4–15
Exercise 4–2: Drawing Arcs,
Ellipses, and Solids

Mark and Back

The Undo subcommands Mark and Back can be very helpful if you want to practice or experiment while in a drawing. By using Mark and Back you can easily erase a practice session or experiment.

When Mark is selected in response to the Undo prompt, AutoCAD makes a special mark in the undo information; it is not a visible mark. Any drawing or editing that is done after Mark is selected can be easily undone when you click Back in response to the prompt. The Back subcommand will backtrack through the drawing one mark at a time and remove the mark when it's found. An example of the command sequence follows.

Use UNDO, Mark, and Back for a practice session:

Prompt	Response
Command:	TYPE: **UNDO<enter>**
Auto/Control/BEgin/End/Mark/Back/ <number>:	TYPE: **M<enter>**
Command:	**Draw several lines and circles.**
Command:	TYPE: **UNDO<enter>**
Auto/Control/BEgin/End/Mark/Back/ <number>:	TYPE: **B<enter>**

Everything drawn since Mark was picked is undone.

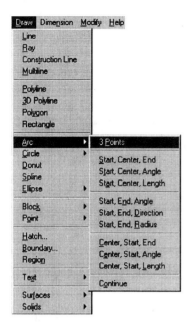

ARC

There are many methods from which to choose when you are drawing arcs. Whatever the situation, you can select a method to suit your needs. Experiment with the different methods described next and decide which ones you prefer to use. Use Figure 4–15 as a guide when locating the arcs on your drawing.

On Your Own

Set Layer Arcs current.

3-point

Using the 3-point method, you can draw an arc clockwise or counterclockwise by specifying the start point, second point, and end point of the arc.

Draw three arcs using the 3-point method (Figure 4–16):

Prompt	Response
Command:	**Arc-3 Points** (or TYPE: **A\<enter\>**)
Center/\<Start point\>:	**D1** (pick a point five grid marks down ($1\frac{1}{4}''$) and three grid marks to the right of the upper left corner of the page)
Center/End/\<Second point\>:	**D2**
End point:	**D3**
Command:	**\<enter\>**
Center/\<Start point\>:	**D4**
Center/End/\<Second point\>:	**D5**
End point:	**D6**
Command:	**\<enter\>**
Center/\<Start point\>:	**D7**
Center/End/\<Second point\>:	**D8**
End point:	**D9**

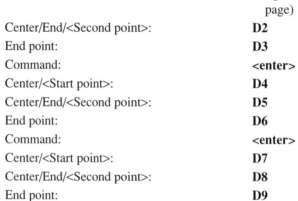

FIGURE 4–16
Draw Arcs Using the 3-Point Method

Start, Center, End

The Start, Center, End method allows an arc to be drawn only counterclockwise, by specifying the start, center, and end. You can draw the same arc using the Center, Start, End method, which also draws counterclockwise. Refer to Figure 4–17.

Draw two arcs using the Start, Center, End method:

Prompt	Response
Command:	**Arc-Start, Center, End**
Center/\<Start point\>:	**D1** (pick a point $1\frac{3}{4}''$ directly below the left end of the first arc drawn)

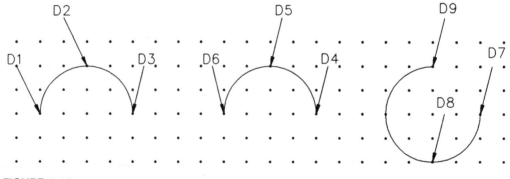

Part II: Two-Dimensional AutoCAD

FIGURE 4-17
Draw Arcs Using the Start, Center, End Method

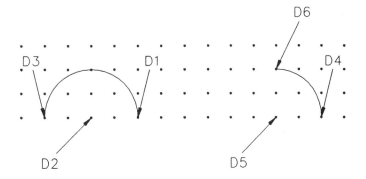

Prompt	Response
Center/End/<Second point>: c Center:	**D2**
Angle/Length of chord/<End point>:	**D3**
Command:	**Arc-Start, Center, End**
Center/<Start point>:	**D4**
Center/End/<Second point>: c Center:	**D5**
Angle/Length of chord/<End point>:	**D6**

Start, Center, Angle

In the Start, Center, Angle method, A is the included angle (the angle the arc will span). A positive angle will draw the arc counterclockwise; a negative angle will draw the arc clockwise. Refer to Figure 4–18.

FIGURE 4-18
Draw Arcs Using the Start, Center, Angle and Start, Center, Length Methods

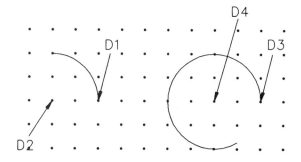

Draw an arc using the Start, Center, Angle method:

Prompt	Response
Command:	**Arc-Start, Center, Angle**
Center/<Start point>:	**D1** ($2\frac{1}{4}''$ to the right of the last arc drawn)
Center/End/<Second point>: c Center:	**D2**
Angle/Length of chord/<End point>: a Included angle:	TYPE: **90<enter>**

Start, Center, Length

In the Start, Center, Length method, L is the chord length. A *chord* is a straight line that connects an arc's start point and end point. A positive chord length can be entered to draw a minor arc (less than 180°), and a negative chord length can be entered to draw a major arc (more than 180°). Both are drawn counterclockwise. See Figure 4–18.

Draw an arc using the Start, Center, Length method:

Prompt	Response
Command:	**Arc-Start, Center, Length**
Center/<Start point>:	**D3**

Prompt	Response
Center/End/<Second point>: c Center	**D4**
_l Length of chord:	TYPE: **-1/2<enter>**

Start, End, Angle

With the Start, End, Angle method, after the start point and end point of the arc have been picked, a positive angle draws the arc counterclockwise; a negative angle keeps the same start and end points but draws the reverse arc or draws clockwise.

Start, End, Radius

In the Start, End, Radius method, Radius is the arc radius. When you use the method, a positive readius can be entered to draw a minor arc (less than 180°), and a negative radius can be entered to draw a major arc (more than 180°). Both are drawn counterclockwise.

Start, End, Direction

In this method, Direction is the specified direction that the arc takes, from the start point. The direction is specified in degrees. You can also specify the direction by pointing to a single point. Major, minor, counterclockwise, and clockwise arcs can be drawn with the Start, End, Direction method.

Continue

If Continue is picked at the first prompt of any of the arc methods that start with S, the new arc starts at the end point of the last arc or line drawn. Pressing the enter key has the same effect. The new arc's direction follows the direction of the last arc or line drawn.

ELLIPSE

Look at Figure 4–15 to determine the approximate location of the ellipses drawn with the Ellipse command.

On Your Own

Set Layer Ellipses current.

Axis,End

The minor axis of an ellipse is its smaller axis, and the major axis is the larger axis. Refer to Figure 4–19.

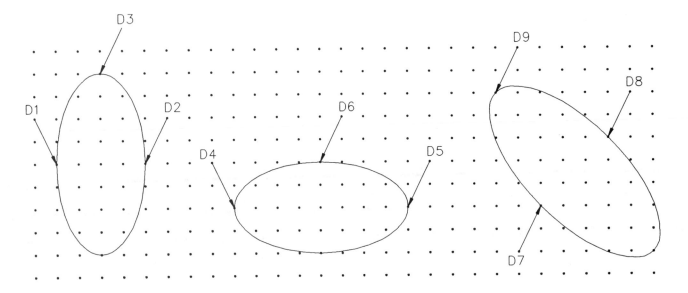

FIGURE 4–19
Draw an Ellipse by Entering Points for the Minor and Major Axes of the Ellipse, and Draw an Ellipse at an Angle

Part II: Two-Dimensional AutoCAD

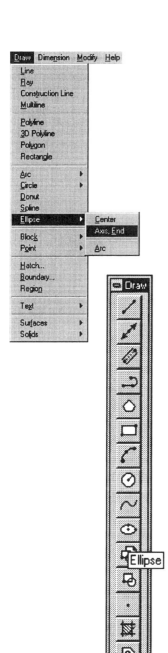

Draw an ellipse by entering points for the minor axis of the ellipse:

Prompt	Response
Command:	**Ellipse-Axis,End** (or TYPE: **EL<enter>**)
Arc/Center/<Axis endpoint 1>:	**D1**
Axis endpoint 2:	**D2**
<Other axis distance>/Rotation:	**D3**

Draw an ellipse by entering points for the major axis of the ellipse:

Prompt	Response
Command:	**Ellipse-Axis,End**
Arc/Center/<Axis endpoint 1>:	**D4**
Axis endpoint 2:	**D5**
<Other axis distance>/Rotation:	**D6**

Draw an ellipse at an angle by entering points for the minor axis of the ellipse:

Prompt	Response
Command:	**Ellipse-Axis,End**
Arc/Center/<Axis endpoint 1>:	**D7**
Axis endpoint 2:	**D8**
<Other axis distance>/Rotation:	**D9**

Rotation

The Rotation option specifies an actual rotation into the third dimension, around the major axis. To visualize this, hold a coin between two fingers and rotate it.

Draw two ellipses by entering points for the major axis and specifying the rotation angle around the major axis (Figure 4–20):

Prompt	Response
Command:	**Ellipse-Axis,End**
Arc/Center/<Axis endpoint 1>:	**D1**
Axis endpoint 2:	**D2**
<Other axis distance>/Rotation:	TYPE: **R<enter>** (rotation changes the minor axis to the major axis)
Rotation around major axis:	TYPE: **0<enter>** (a 0° ellipse is a circle)
Command:	**<enter>**
Arc/Center/<Axis endpoint 1>:	**D3**
Axis endpoint 2:	**D4**
<Other axis distance>/Rotation:	TYPE: **R<enter>**
Rotation around major axis:	TYPE: **60<enter>**

FIGURE 4–20
Draw Ellipses by Specifying the Rotation Angle

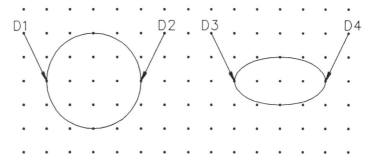

Center

You may also draw an ellipse by specifying the center point, the endpoint of one axis, and the length of the other axis. Type **C** and press enter to the prompt "Arc/Center/<Axis endpoint 1>:" to start with the center of the ellipse. Entering the center point first is similar to the first two methods described above, and either the minor or major axis may be constructed first. As with all methods of drawing an ellipse, you can specify the points either by clicking a point on the drawing or by typing and entering coordinates.

DONUT

Look at Figure 4–15 to determine the approximate location of the solid ring and solid circle drawn using the Donut command.

On Your Own

Set Layer Solids current.

Use the Donut command to draw a solid ring (Figure 4–21):

FIGURE 4–21
Use the Donut Command to Draw a Solid Ring and a Solid Circle

Prompt	Response
Command:	**Donut** (or TYPE: **DO<enter>**)
Inside diameter <default>:	TYPE: **1/2<enter>**
Outside diameter <default>:	TYPE: **1<enter>:**
Center of donut:	**Click a point on the drawing.**
Center of donut:	<enter>

Use the Donut command to draw a solid circle (Figure 4–21):

Prompt	Response
Command:	<enter>
Inside diameter <0'-0 1/2">:	TYPE: **0<enter>** (so there is no center hole)
Outside diameter <0'-1">:	<enter>
Center of donut:	**Click a point on the drawing.**
Center of donut:	<enter>

Donut can be used to draw solid dots of any size as well as solid rings with different inside and outside diameters.

2D SOLID

With the 2D Solid command you can draw angular solid shapes by entering them as three-sided (triangle) or four-sided (square and rectangle) sections. The trick with the 2D Solid command is entering the third point; to draw a square or a rectangle, you must pick the third point diagonally opposite the second point. If four points are picked in a clockwise or counterclockwise progression, a bow-tie shape is drawn.

In the following part of this exercise, first, the 2D Solid command will be used to draw a solid rectangle and a solid triangle at the bottom of the page. Second, the Scale command will be used to reduce the rectangle and enlarge the triangle.

FIGURE 4–22
Use the 2D Solid Command to
Draw a Solid Rectangle and a
Solid Triangle

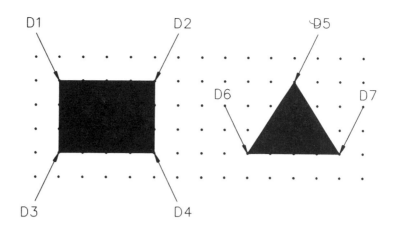

Use the 2D Solid command to draw a solid rectangle (Figure 4–22):

Prompt	Response
Command:	**2D Solid** (or TYPE: **SO<enter>**)
First point:	**D1**
Second point:	**D2**
Third point:	**D3** (notice that D3 is diagonally opposite D2)
Fourth point:	**D4**
Third point:	**<enter>**

Use the Solid command to draw a solid triangle (Figure 4–22):

Prompt	Response
Command:	**<enter>**
First point:	**D5**
Second point:	**D6**
Third point:	**D7**
Fourth point:	**<enter>**
Third point:	**<enter>**

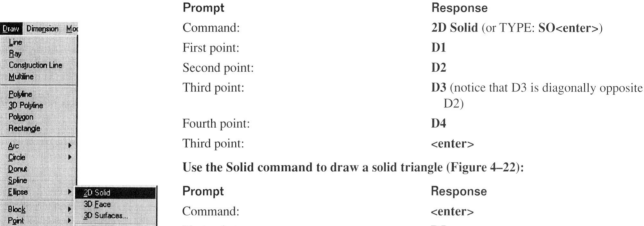

When the "Third point:" prompt appears a second time, you can continue with another section of the shape or press enter to complete a shape.

FILL ON and FILL OFF

The options FILL ON and FILL OFF affect both the Donut and the 2D Solid commands and any other "filled" areas.

On Your Own

1. TYPE: **FILL<enter>**, then TYPE: **OFF<enter>,** and then TYPE: **REGEN<enter>** to regenerate the drawing. All the shapes made with the Donut and 2D Solid commands will no longer be solid.

2. TYPE: **Fill<enter>,** then **ON<enter>** to make them solid again and regenerate the drawing.

FIGURE 4–23
Use the Scale Command to
Reduce the Solid Rectangle and
Enlarge the Solid Triangle

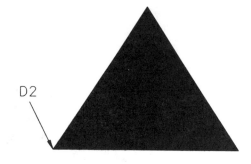

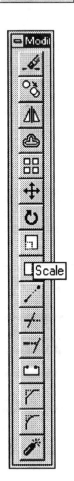

SCALE

The Scale command lets you reduce or enlarge either drawing entities or an entire drawing.

<Scale factor>

Use the Scale command to reduce the solid rectangle (Figure 4–23):

Prompt	Response
Command:	**Scale** (or TYPE: **SC<enter>**)
Select objects:	**Window the rectangle** (or click the outside edge of the solid).
Select objects:	**<enter>**
Base point:	**D1**
<Scale factor>/Reference:	TYPE: **.5<enter>**

The relative scale factor of .5 was used to reduce the rectangle. A relative scale factor of 2 would have enlarged the rectangle.

Reference

Use the Scale command to enlarge the solid triangle (Figure 4–23):

Prompt	Response
Command:	**<enter>**
Select objects:	**Window the triangle**
Select objects:	**<enter>**
Base point:	**D2**
<Scale factor>/Reference:	TYPE: **R<enter>**
Reference length <1>:	**<enter>** (to accept 1″ default)
New length:	TYPE: **2<enter>**

The Reference option allows you to type and enter a number for the Reference (current) length of a drawing entity. You can also enter the Reference (current) length by picking two points on the drawing to show AutoCAD the Reference (current) length. You can type and enter the New length by using a number, or you can enter it by picking two points on the drawing to show the New length.

The Reference option is especially useful when you have drawn a project full scale and want to reduce it to scale. To reduce a full-scale drawing to $\frac{1}{4}'' = 1'\text{-}0''$, the Reference length is 12 and the new length $\frac{1}{4}''$. The drawing can then be inserted into a border format. The Insert command is described later in this book.

Save Your Drawing and Exit AutoCAD

When you have completed Exercise 4–2, save your drawing in at least two places and exit AutoCAD. Exercise 4–2 will be printed in Chapter 8.

EXERCISE 4–3
Drawing Shapes I

Draw, full size, the shapes shown in Figure 4–24. Use the dimensions shown. Locate the shapes approximately as shown. To begin Exercise 4–3, turn on the computer and start AutoCAD. The Start Up dialog box is displayed.

Begin Drawing CH4-EX3 on the Hard Drive

1. CLICK: **Start from Scratch**
   CLICK: **OK**
2. **Use SaveAs... to save the drawing on the hard drive with the name CH4-EX3.**
3. Set drawing Units: **Architectural**
4. Set Drawing Limits: **8-1/2,11**
5. Set Grid: $\frac{1''}{4}$
6. Set Snap: $\frac{1''}{8}$
7. Create the following Layers:

LAYER NAME	COLOR	LINETYPE
Single	Blue	Continuous (for all single-line shapes)
Solid	Red	Continuous (for all solid shapes)

FIGURE 4–24
Exercise 4–3: Drawing Shapes I
(Scale: $\frac{1}{2}''$ = 1")

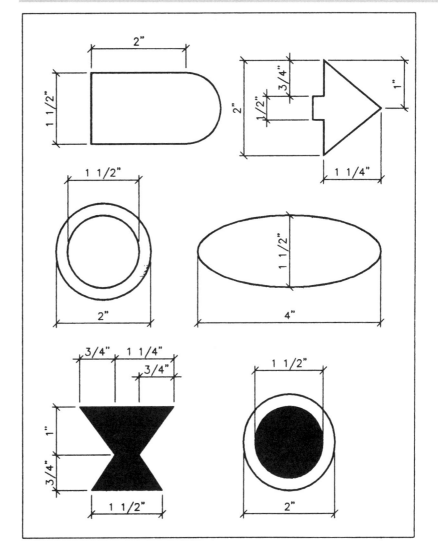

EXERCISE 4–4
Drawing a Pattern

Draw the pattern design shown in Figure 4–25. Use a $\frac{1}{2}'' = 1''$ architectural scale to measure the pattern design and draw it full scale. Your drawing will be twice the size shown in the figure. To begin Exercise 4–4, turn on the computer and start AutoCAD. The Start Up dialog box is displayed.

Begin Drawing CH4-EX4 on the Hard Drive

1. CLICK: **Start from Scratch**
   CLICK: **OK**
2. **Use SaveAs... to save the drawing on the hard drive with the name CH4-EX4.**
3. Set drawing Units: **Architectural**
4. Set Drawing Limits: **8-1/2,11**
5. Set Grid: $\frac{1}{4}''$
6. Set Snap: $\frac{1}{8}''$
7. Create the Layers on your own.

FIGURE 4–25
Exercise 4–4: Drawing a Pattern
(Scale: $\frac{1}{2}'' = 1''$)

EXERCISE 4–5
Drawing Shapes II

Draw the shapes shown in Figure 4–26. Use a $\frac{1}{2}'' = 1''$ architectural scale to measure the shapes and draw them full scale. Your drawing will be twice the size shown in the figure. To begin Exercise 4–5, turn on the computer and start AutoCAD. The Start Up dialog box is displayed.

Begin Drawing CH4-EX5 on the Hard Drive

1. CLICK: **Start from Scratch**
   CLICK: **OK**
2. **Use SaveAs... to save the drawing on the hard drive with the name CH4-EX5.**
3. Set drawing Units: **Architectural**
4. Set Drawing Limits: **8-1/2,11**
5. Set Grid: $\frac{1}{4}''$
6. Set Snap: $\frac{1}{8}''$
7. Create the Layers on your own.

FIGURE 4–26

Exercise 4–5: Drawing Shapes II
(Scale: $\frac{1}{2}'' = 1''$)

1. When an existing drawing is stored on a floppy disk, you should open the drawing and immediately save it on the hard disk.
   a. True
   b. False

2. To make the line segment length and spacing larger for a dashed linetype, enter a number higher than 1 to the Ltscale prompt, "New scale factor <1.0000>:".
   a. True
   b. False

3. Always use the Zoom-All command after setting up a new drawing.
   a. True
   b. False

4. Snap may be turned OFF and ON while you are drawing.
   a. True
   b. False

5. Typing and entering a response of 1/2 to the Circle prompt "Diameter/<Radius>:" will produce a circle of
   a. $\frac{1}{2}''$ radius
   b. $\frac{1}{2}''$ diameter
   c. 6" radius
   d. 6" diameter

6. To view the entire drawing area, which Zoom command should you use immediately after you have set up a new drawing?
   a. All
   b. Center
   c. Dynamic
   d. Extents
   e. Scale

7. Many of the Modify commands use the same variety of subcommands to select the object or objects to be edited. Which of the following commands is *not* used to select the objects to be edited?
   a. Window
   b. Remove
   c. Circle
   d. Crossing
   e. Add

8. The 3-point method of drawing arcs allows you to draw arcs clockwise or counterclockwise.
   a. True
   b. False

9. The Reference option of the Scale command allows you to pick two points on the drawing to show AutoCAD the current length of the drawing entity to be reduced or enlarged.
   a. True
   b. False

10. Pressing the Esc key cancels a command.
    a. True
    b. False

11. Name the key on the keyboard that when pressed brings back the last command used in response to the command prompt line.

    _____

12. Using relative coordinates to draw a 3" square, write the information you type and enter in response to the Line "To point:" prompt after the first point of the square has been clicked. Draw the square to the right and up.
    1. _____ 3. _____
    2. _____ 4. _____

13. Using absolute coordinates to draw a 3" square, write the information that you type and enter in response to the Line "To point:" prompt after the first point of the square has been clicked. The first point of the square is at coordinates 4,4. Draw the square to the right and up.
    1. _____ 3. _____
    2. _____ 4. _____

14. Using polar coordinates to draw a 3″ square, write the information that you type and enter in response to the Line "To point:" prompt after the first point of the square has been clicked. Draw the square to the right and up.

    1. _____ 3. _____
    2. _____ 4. _____

15. Write the names of the 10 Zoom commands that can be used transparently.

    _____ _____ _____ _____

    _____ _____ _____ _____

    _____ _____

16. Write the name of the function key that can be pressed twice to redraw the screen.

    _____

17. Write the name of the function key that when pressed helps to draw lines perfectly horizontally and vertically.

    _____

18. Describe what Direction means in the arc method Start, End, Direction.

    _____

19. Describe what Length means in the arc method Start, Center, Length.

    _____

20. What command can be typed and entered to the Command: prompt to make the appearance of circles and arcs smoother?

    _____

5 Drawing with AutoCAD: Conference and Lecture Rooms

OBJECTIVES

When you have completed this chapter, you will be able to:
☐ Correctly use the following pull-down commands and settings:

Break	Edit Polyline	Offset	Polyline
Cancel	Explode	Osnap	Rectangle
Chamfer	Fillet	Osnap-Tracking	Rotate
Copy	Help	Pickbox	Sketch
Distance	ID Point	Point	Trim
Divide	Measure	Polygon	

EXERCISE 5–1
Drawing a Rectangular Conference Room Including Furniture

A conference room, including walls and furnishings, is drawn in Exercise 5–1. When you have completed Exercise 5–1, your drawing will look similar to Figure 5–1. To prepare to draw Exercise 5–1, turn on the computer and start AutoCAD. The Start Up dialog box is displayed.

1. CLICK: **Use a Wizard**
2. CLICK: **Quick Setup**
   CLICK: **OK**
3. Set drawing Units: **Architectural**
   CLICK: **Next>>**
4. Set drawing Width: **25′** × Length: **35′**
   CLICK: **Done**
5. **Use SaveAs... to save the drawing on the hard drive with the name CH5–EX1.**
6. Set Grid: **12″**
7. Set Snap: **6″**
8. Create the following Layers:

LAYER NAME	COLOR	LINETYPE
Walls	White	Continuous
Furniture	Red	Continuous

9. Set Layer Walls current.
10. Use **Zoom-All** to view the limits of the drawing.

FIGURE 5–1

Exercise 5–1: Drawing a Rectangular Conference Room Including Furniture (Scale: $\frac{1''}{4} = 1'\text{-}0''$)

POLYLINE

We will begin by drawing the conference room walls using the Polyline command. Polylines are different from regular lines in that regardless of the number of segments that make up a polyline, AutoCAD treats a polyline drawn with one operation of the Polyline command as a single entity. This is especially helpful when you are drawing walls, because after you draw the outline of a single room or entire building, the entire polyline can be offset to show the thickness of the walls. Any of the various linetypes may be drawn with Polyline, but the CONTINUOUS linetype will be used to draw the walls of the conference room.

Use Polyline to draw the inside lines of the conference room walls (Figure 5–2):

Prompt	Response
Command:	**Polyline** (or TYPE: **PL<enter>**)
From point:	TYPE: **5',5'<enter>**
	Set ORTHO On (Press: **F8** or DOUBLE CLICK: **ORTHO**)
Current line-width is 0'-0" Arc/Close//Halfwidth/Length/Undo/Width/ <Endpoint of line>:	**Move your mouse to the right and** TYPE: **15'<enter>**
Arc/Close/ ... <Endpoint of line>:	**Move your mouse up** and TYPE: **20'<enter>**

FIGURE 5–2
Draw the Conference Room
Walls

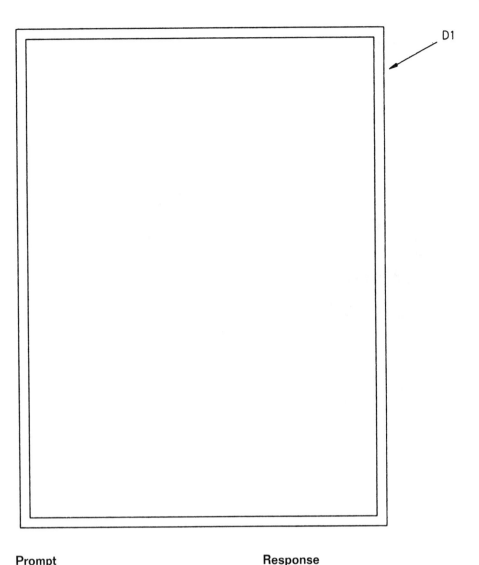

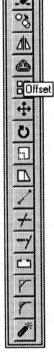

Prompt	Response
Arc/Close/ ... <Endpoint of line>:	**Move your mouse to the left and** TYPE: **15′<enter>**
Arc/Close/ ... <Endpoint of line>:	TYPE: **C<enter>**

<Endpoint of line>

<Endpoint of line>, the default option in the Polyline prompt, was used when you entered a direct distance while drawing the outline of the conference room. You could have also drawn the room outline by clicking points on the drawing for each line segment.

Undo

The Polyline Undo option is similar to the Line command: If you do not like the last polyline segment drawn, use the Undo option to erase it and continue with the <Endpoint of line>: prompt.

You can enter all the options in the Polyline prompt from the keyboard by typing (upper- or lowercase) the letters that are capitalized in each option. The remaining options in the Polyline prompt will be described later in this chapter.

OFFSET

Because the polyline is treated as a single entity, when you click one point on the polyline, you are able to offset the entire outline of the conference room at once. If the outline of the room had been drawn with the Line command, using Offset would offset each line segment individually, and the corners would not meet.

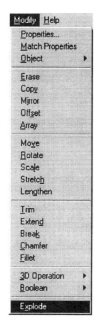

Use Offset to draw the outside line (showing depth) of the conference room walls (Figure 5–2):

Prompt	Response
Command:	**Offset** (or TYPE: **O<enter**)
Offset distance or Through <Through>:	TYPE: **5<enter>**
Select object to offset:	**Click any place on the polyline.**
Side to offset?	**D1** (outside of the rectangle)
Select object to offset:	**<enter>**

There are two options in the Offset prompt, offset distance and Through. To complete the conference room walls, 5″ was set as the offset distance. The following is an *example* of the Offset command prompt sequence for Through.

Through

Prompt	Response
Offset distance or Through <Through>:	**<enter>** (to accept the default)
Select object to offset:	**Click the drawing entity that you want to offset.**
Through point:	**Click the point on the drawing through which you want the entity offset.**

EXPLODE

Because the polyline is treated as a single entity, it must be "exploded" before individual line segments can be edited. The Explode command splits the solid polyline into separate line segments. After the polyline is exploded into separate line segments, you will be able to add the conference room door.

Use Explode to split the two polylines that make the conference room walls:

Prompt	Response
Command:	**Explode** (or TYPE: **X<enter>**)
Select objects:	**Click any place on the outside polyline**
Select objects:	**Click any place on the inside polyline <enter>**

After you use the Explode command, the walls do not look different, but each line segment is now a separate entity.

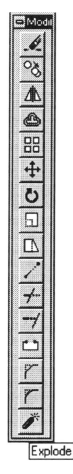

ID POINT

A very useful command, ID Point allows you to locate a point on a drawing and have the position of the point displayed in coordinates. AutoCAD remembers the coordinate location of the point. A Draw command, such as Line, can be initiated immediately after the ID Point command has located a point on the drawing. You can enter the start point of the Line command by using relative or polar coordinates to specify a distance from the established ID Point location.

On Your Own

Use Zoom-Window to magnify the corner of the conference room where the door will be located.

Use ID Point to locate a point on the drawing. Use Line to draw the right side of the door opening (Figure 5–3):

FIGURE 5–3

Draw the Door Opening and
Door; Draw a Credenza and Conference Table

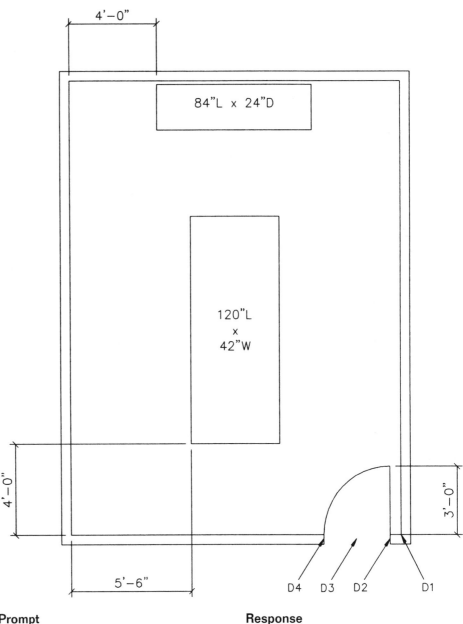

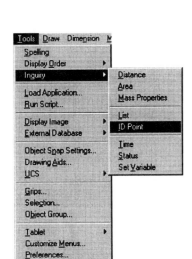

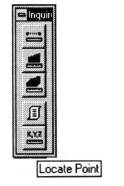

Locate Point

Prompt	Response
Command:	**ID Point** (or TYPE: ID<enter>)
Point:	**D1** (snap to the inside lower right corner of the conference room)
Point: X = 20′-0″ Y = 5′-0″ Z = 0′-0″	
Command:	TYPE: **L<enter>**
From point:	TYPE: **@6<180<enter>** (move your mouse so you can see where the line is attached)
To point:	TYPE @5<-90<enter>
To point:	**<enter>**

Offset the line 3′ to the left to form the door opening:

Prompt	Response
Command:	**Offset** (or TYPE: O<enter>)
Offset distance or Through <default>:	TYPE: **3′<enter>**
Select object to offset:	**D2** (the door opening line you just drew; turn SNAP off if needed)

80

Part II: Two-Dimensional AutoCAD

Prompt	Response
Side to offset?	**D3** (to the left)
Select object to offset:	**<enter>**

TRIM

Use Trim to trim the wall lines out of the door opening (Figure 5–3):

Prompt	Response
Command:	**Trim** (or TYPE: **TR<enter>**)
Select cutting edges: (Projmode=UCS, Edgemode=No extend)	
Select objects:	**D2**
Select objects: 1 found	
Select objects:	**D4**
Select objects: 1 found	
Select objects:	**<enter>**
<Select object to trim>/Project/Edge/Undo:	**Click the two horizontal wall lines between D2 and D4.**
	<enter> (if you turn SNAP off to pick the lines, be sure to turn it back on)

Watch the Trim prompts carefully. Not until all cutting edges have been selected and the enter key is pressed so that the prompt "<Select object to trim>Project/Edge/Undo:" appears, can you pick the objects to trim. When you have many lines to trim, use the Crossing or Fence option to select the cutting edges, then click the lines after you PRESS: **<enter>** to trim. If you are unable to trim an entity because it does not intersect a cutting edge, use the Erase command.

On Your Own

See Figure 5–3.

1. Use the Line command to draw a 3′ vertical door line. Snap (be sure SNAP is ON) to the upper right corner of the door opening to begin the door line. Draw the line using polar coordinates or direct distance entry.

2. Use the Arc-Start, Center, End method to draw the door swing arc, counterclockwise. Note that the start of the arc is the top of the door line, the center is the bottom of the door line, and the end is the upper left corner of the door opening.

3. Change the current layer to Furniture.

4. Use the Polyline command to draw a credenza (84″ long by 24″ deep) centered on the 15′ rear wall of the conference room, 2″ away from the wall. Locate an ID point by snapping to the inside upper left corner of the conference room. Start the Polyline @48,-2 (relative coordinates) away from the point. Finish drawing the credenza by using polar coordinates. Use your own personal preference to enter feet or inches. Remember, Auto-CAD defaults to inches in Architectural Units, so use the foot (′) symbol if you are using feet. Be sure to draw the credenza using one operation of polyline so it is one continuous polyline. Use the Close option for the last segment of the polyline.

5. Draw a conference table 120″ long by 42″ wide using the Line command. You can determine the location of the first point by using ID Point or by using grid and snap increments. Use direct distance entry to complete the table. Refer to Figure 5–3 for the location of the table in the room.

6. Use Zoom-Window to zoom in on the table.

CHAMFER

A chamfer is an angle (usually 45°) formed at a corner. The following will use the Chamfer command to make the beveled corners of the conference table and credenza.

Use Chamfer to bevel the corners of the table (Figure 5–4):

Prompt	Response
Command:	**Chamfer** (or TYPE: **CHA<enter>**)
Polyline/Distance/Angle/Trim/Method/ <Select first line>:	TYPE: **D<enter>**
Enter first chamfer distance <default>:	TYPE: **2<enter>**
Enter second chamfer distance <0'-2">:	**<enter>**
Command:	**<enter>**
Polyline/Distance/Angle/Trim/Method/ <Select first line>:	**D1**
Select second line:	**D2**
Command:	**<enter>**
Polyline/Distance/Angle/Trim/Method/ <Select first line>:	**D2**
Select second line:	**D3**

FIGURE 5–4
Bevel the Corners of the Table and Credenza; Draw a Rectangle Shape

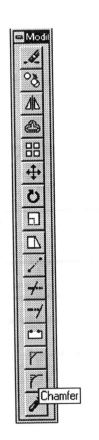

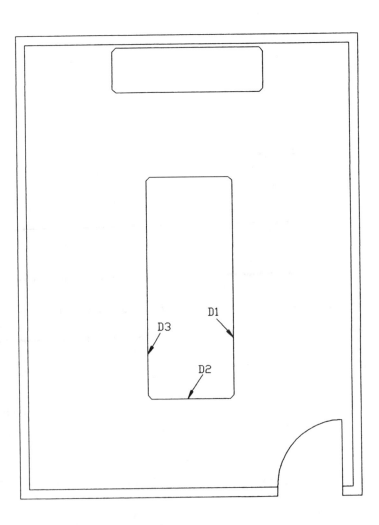

On Your Own

1. Chamfer the other corners of the table (Figure 5–4).

2. Use Zoom-Dynamic to zoom in on the credenza.

Polyline

Because the credenza was drawn using one operation of the Polyline command, it is treated as a single entity. The Chamfer command Polyline option chamfers all corners of a continuous polyline with one click.

Angle

This option of the Chamfer command allows you to specify an angle and a distance to create a chamfer.

Trim

This option of both the Chamfer and Fillet commands allows you to specify that the part of the original line removed by the chamfer or fillet remains as it was. To do this, TYPE: **T<enter>** at the Chamfer prompt and **N<enter>** at the Trim/No Trim <Trim>: prompt. Test this on a corner of the drawing so you know how it works. Be sure to return it to the Trim option.

Method

The Method option of the Chamfer command allows you to specify whether you want to use the Distance or the Angle method to specify how the chamfer is to be drawn. The default is the Distance method.

Use Chamfer to bevel the corners of the credenza (Figure 5–4):

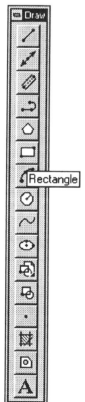

Prompt	Response
Command:	**Chamfer**
Polyline/Distance/Angle/Trim/Method/ <Select first line>:	TYPE: **D<enter>** (to verify the distances)
Enter first chamfer distance <0'-2">:	**<enter>** (to accept 2″ as previously set)
Enter second chamfer distance <0'-2">:	**<enter>**
Command:	**<enter>** (to return the Chamfer prompt)
Polyline/Distance/Angle/Trim/Method/ <Select first line>:	TYPE: **P<enter>**
Select 2D polyline:	**Click any place on the credenza line.**

All corners of the credenza are chamfered.

When setting the chamfer distance, you can set a different distance for the first and second chamfers. The first distance applies to the first line clicked, and the second distance applies to the second line clicked. You can also set the distance by clicking two points on the drawing.

You can set a chamfer distance of zero and use it to remove the chamfered corners from the table. Using a distance of zero will make 90° corners on the table. Then you can erase the old chamfer lines. This will change the table but not the credenza, because it does not work with a polyline. If you have two lines that do not meet to form an exact corner or that overlap, use the Chamfer command with 0 distance to form an exact corner. The Chamfer command will chamfer two lines that do not intersect. It automatically extends the two lines until they intersect, trims the two lines according to the distance entered, and connects the two trimmed ends with the chamfer line.

RECTANGLE

The Rectangle command allows you to draw a rectangle, chamfer or fillet the corners, and give width to the polyline that is created. It also allows you to give elevation and thickness to

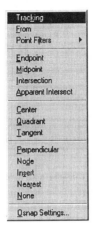

Tip: If you have a two-button mouse, hold down the shift key on your keyboard and press the right mouse button to activate the Osnap menu.

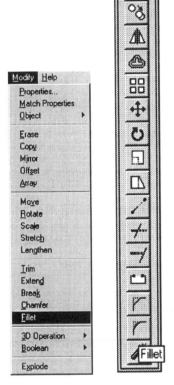

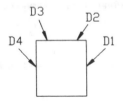

FIGURE 5–5
Use Fillet to Create the Chair Symbol

the polyline. Elevation and thickness are covered in chapters on three-dimensional drawing. To give you an idea of how the Rectangle command works, in the next part of this exercise, you will erase the table and redraw it with the Rectangle command and Osnap-Tracking.

OSNAP-TRACKING

Osnap-Tracking, which is similar to the ID Point command, allows you to specify points except that you can activate Tracking any time AutoCAD asks for a point. You can also specify as many points as you need until you arrive at the desired location, then you press ENTER to end the tracking mode.

Erase the table:

Prompt	Response
Command:	TYPE: **E\<enter>**
Select objects:	**Window the table\<enter>**

Draw the table using Rectangle and Osnap-Tracking (Figure 5–3):

Prompt	Response
Command:	**Rectangle** (or TYPE: **REC\<enter>**)
Chamfer/Elevation/Fillet/Thickness/Width/ \<First corner>:	TYPE: **C\<enter>**
First chamfer distance for rectangles <0'-0">:	TYPE: **2\<enter>**
Second chamfer distance for rectangles <0'-2">:	**\<enter>**
Chamfer/Elevation/Fillet/Thickness/Width/ \<First corner>:	CLICK: **the middle button on your mouse**
	CLICK: **Tracking** (or TYPE: **TRACK\<enter>**)
First tracking point:	**With SNAP on, CLICK: the lower left inside corner of the room.**
	Turn ORTHO Off (F8).
Next point (Press ENTER to end tracking):	TYPE: **@5'6,4'\<enter>**
Next point (Press ENTER to end tracking):	**\<enter>**
Other corner:	TYPE: **@42,120\<enter>**

On Your Own

See Figure 5–4.

1. Zoom in on a portion of the grid outside the conference room walls.

2. Draw a rectangle 26″ wide by 28″ deep using the Line command. Be sure to have SNAP on when you draw the rectangle. You will now edit this rectangle using the Fillet command to create the shape of a chair.

FILLET

The Fillet command is similar to Chamfer, except the Fillet command creates a round instead of an angle.

Use Fillet to edit the back of the rectangle to create the symbol of a chair (Figure 5–5):

Part II: Two-Dimensional AutoCAD

Prompt	Response
Command:	**Fillet** (or TYPE: **F<enter>**)
Polyline/Radius/Trim/<Select first object>:	TYPE: **R<enter>**
Enter fillet radius <0'-0">:	TYPE: **12<enter>**
Command:	**<enter>**
Polyline/Radius/Trim/<Select first object>:	TYPE: **T<enter>**
Trim/No trim<No trim>:	TYPE: **T<enter>**
Polyline/Radius/Trim/<Select first object>:	**D1**
Select second object:	**D2**
Command:	**<enter>**
Polyline/Radius/Trim/<Select first object>:	**D3**
Select second object:	**D4**

The Polyline option of Fillet automatically fillets an entire continuous polyline with one click. Remember to set the fillet radius first.

Fillet will also fillet two circles, two arcs, a line and a circle, a line and an arc, or a circle and an arc. When Fillet is used with arcs and circles, AutoCAD uses the select object points to determine the fillet endpoints.

COPY and OSNAP-Midpoint

The Copy command allows you to copy any part of a drawing either once or multiple times. Object Snap modes when combined with other commands help you to draw very accurately. As you become more familiar with the Object Snap modes, you will use them constantly to draw with extreme accuracy. The following introduces the Midpoint Osnap mode. The Osnap-Midpoint mode helps you to snap to the midpoint of a line or arc.

Use the Copy command, combined with Osnap-Midpoint, to copy three times the chair you have just drawn (Figure 5–6):

Prompt	Response
Command:	**Copy** (or TYPE: **CP<enter>**)
Select objects:	**Click the first corner of a window that will include the chair.**
Other corner:	**Click the other corner of the window to include the chair.**
Select objects:	**<enter>**
<Base point of displacement>/Multiple:	TYPE: **M<enter>**
Multiple Base point:	CLICK: **the middle mouse button**
	CLICK: **Midpoint** (or TYPE: **MID<enter>**)
Mid of	**D1**

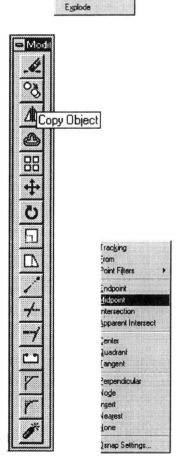

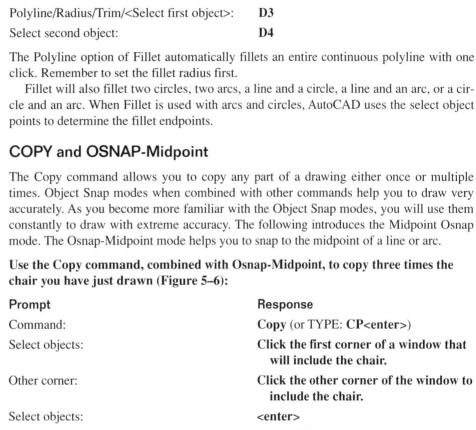

FIGURE 5–6
Copy the Chair Three Times; Use Rotate to Rotate the Chairs

Prompt	Response
Second point of displacement:	**D2,D3,D4** (be sure snap is on, and snap to a grid point)
Second point of displacement:	**<enter>**

By selecting the option Multiple in response to the Copy prompt, you were able to copy the chairs multiple times. If Multiple is not selected, you can copy the chair only once.

The Osnap-Midpoint mode helped you snap very accurately to the midpoint of the line; you used the midpoint of the line that defines the front of the chair as the base point. When using the Copy command, carefully choose the base point so that it helps you easily locate the copies.

ROTATE

The Rotate command rotates a selected drawing entity in the counterclockwise direction; 90° is to the left, and 270° (or -90°) is to the right. You select a base point of the entity to be rotated, and the entity rotates about that base point.

Use the Rotate command to rotate chairs 2 and 3 (Figure 5–6):

Prompt	Response
Command:	**Rotate** (or TYPE: **RO<enter>**)
Select objects:	**Start the window to include chair 2.**
Other corner:	**Complete the window to include chair 2.**
Select objects:	**<enter>**
Base point:	**Osnap-Midpoint**
Mid of	**D2**
<Rotation angle>/Reference:	TYPE: **90<enter>**
Command:	**<enter>**
Select objects:	**Window chair 3**
Select objects:	**<enter>**
Base point:	TYPE: **MID<enter>**
Base point: mid of	**D3**
<Rotation angle>/Reference:	TYPE: **180<enter>**

On Your Own
See Figure 5–7.
Rotate chair 4 using a 270° (or -90°) rotation angle.

Reference

The Reference option of the Rotate prompt is sometimes easier to use, especially if you do not know the rotation angle. It allows you to select the object to be rotated and click the base

Note: If part of the entity that is to be rotated lies on the specified base point, that part of the entity remains on the base point while the entity's orientation is changed.

FIGURE 5–7
Rotated Chairs

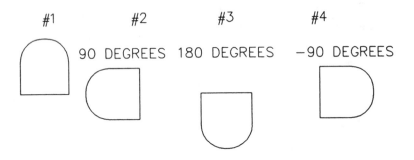

#1   #2   #3   #4

90 DEGREES   180 DEGREES   −90 DEGREES

Part II: Two-Dimensional AutoCAD

point. Type: **R<enter>** for Reference. Then you can enter the "Reference angle:" (current angle) of the object by typing it and pressing enter. If you don't know the current angle you can show AutoCAD the "Reference angle:" by picking the two endpoints of the line to be rotated. You can specify the "New angle:" by typing it and pressing enter. If you don't know the new angle, you can show AutoCAD the "New angle:" by picking a point on the drawing.

POINT

The Point command allows you to draw points on your drawing. Object Snap recognizes these points as nodes. The Osnap mode Node is used to snap to points.

There are many different types of points to choose from. The appearance of these points is determined by the pdmode (point definition mode) and pdsize (point definition size) options within the Point command.

Use the Point Style... command to set the appearance of points:

Prompt	Response
Command:	**Point Style...** (or TYPE: **DDPTYPE<enter>**)
The Point Style dialog box appears (Figure 5–8):	CLICK: **the X box**
	CLICK: **Set Size in Absolute Units**
	TYPE: **6 in the Point Size entry box**

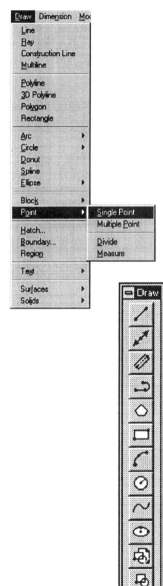

FIGURE 5–8
Point Style Dialog Box

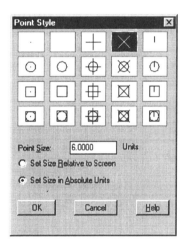

You have just set the points to appear as an X, and they will be 6″ high. The Point Style dialog box shows the different type of points available. The size of the point may be set in a size relative to the screen or in absolute units. Your Point Style dialog box should appear as shown in Figure 5–8.

Response
CLICK: **OK**

On Your Own

See Figure 5–9.

1. Use the Explode command on the table.

2. Use the Offset command to offset the two lines that define the long sides of the conference table. These lines will be used as construction lines to help locate the chairs. The chairs will be placed 6″ from the edge of the table, so set 6″ as the offset distance. Offset the lines on each side, outside the table as shown in Figure 5–9.

DIVIDE

The Divide command divides an entity into equal parts and places point markers along the entity at the dividing points. The pdmode has been set to 3 (an X point), so an X will appear as the point marker when you use Divide.

Use Divide to divide the offset lines into eight equal segments (Figure 5–9):

Prompt	Response
Command:	**Divide** (or TYPE: **DIV<enter>**)
Select object to divide:	**Click any place on one of the offset lines.**
<Number of segments>/Block:	TYPE: **8<enter>**

The X points divide the line into eight equal segments.

You can divide lines, circles, arcs, and polylines by selecting them. The Divide command also draws a specified Block at each mark between the equal segments. You will learn about blocks in Chapter 9.

On Your Own

See Figure 5–9. Continue with the Divide command and divide the other offset line into eight equal segments.

FIGURE 5–9

Offset the Two Lines Defining the Long Sides of the Conference Table; Divide the Lines Into Eight Equal Segments; Copy Chair 4

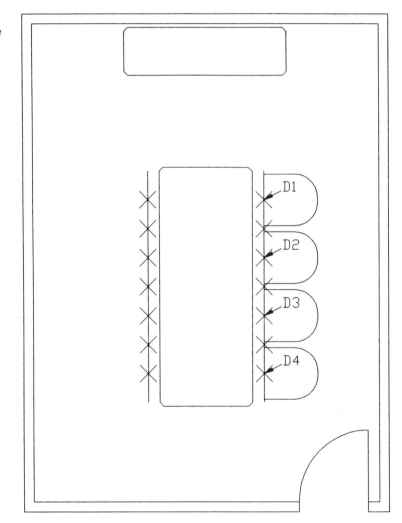

COPY, OSNAP-Midpoint, OSNAP-Node

Use the Copy command (combined with Osnap-Midpoint and Osnap-Node) to copy chair 4 four times on the right side of the conference table (Figure 5–9):

Prompt	Response
Command:	**Copy (or TYPE: CP\<enter\>)**
Select objects:	**Click below and to the left of chair 4.**
Other corner:	**Window chair 4**
Select objects:	**\<enter\>**
Base point or displacement\>/Multiple:	**TYPE: M\<enter\>**
Multiple Base point:	**Osnap-Midpoint**
_mid of	**Click any place on the straight line that forms the front of the chair symbol.**
Second point of displacement:	**TYPE: NOD\<enter\>**
of	**D1**
Second point of displacement:	**TYPE: NOD\<enter\>**
of	**D2**
Second point of displacement:	**TYPE: NOD\<enter\>**
of	**D3**
Second point of displacement:	**TYPE: NOD\<enter\>**
of	**D4**
Second point of displacement:	**\<enter\>**

By selecting the option Multiple in response to the Copy prompt, you were able to copy the chairs multiple times.

The points act as nodes (snapping exactly on the center of the X) for Object Snap purposes.

On Your Own

See Figure 5–10.

1. Continue with the Copy, Osnap-Midpoint, and Osnap-Node commands, and place four chairs on the left side of the table.

2. Use the Copy command to place a chair at each end of the conference table. Because you will be copying each chair only once, do not pick Multiple but go immediately to Osnap-Midpoint to specify the base point. Use the grid and snap to determine the "Second point of displacement:" for each chair.

3. TYPE: **PDMODE\<enter\>** at the Command: prompt. Set the Pdmode to 1, then regenerate the drawing. The X's will disappear. You have set the Pdmode to be invisible.

4. Erase the offset lines used to locate the chairs on each long side of the table. Use F7 to redraw when it looks like part of the chairs have been erased.

5. Erase the chairs you have drawn outside the conference room walls.

6. Exercise 5–1 is complete.

FIGURE 5–10
Complete Exercise 5–1

HELP

If you have forgotten the name of a command or the options that are available for a specific command, the Help command is available to refresh your memory. The Help command provides a list of the AutoCAD commands as well as information about specific commands.

Use HELP to obtain information about a specific command:

Prompt	Response
Command:	TYPE: **HELP<enter>**
The Help Topics: AutoCAD Help dialog box with tabs appears on the screen:	TYPE: **DONUT** (or type the name of any other command you have questions about)
	DOUBLE CLICK: **DONUT command**
The Topics Found dialog box is displayed:	CLICK: **Display button**
Information about the DONUT command is shown:	CLICK: **X** (upper right corner) to close when you are through

Don't forget that the Help command is available. You can also use the Help command while you are in the middle of another command. If you type 'help in response to any prompt that is not asking for a text string, information is supplied about the current command. The information is sometimes specific to the current prompt.

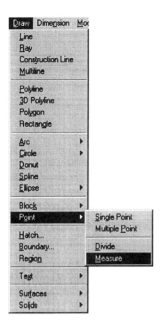

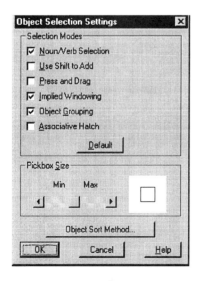

MEASURE

The Measure command is similar to the Divide command, except that with Measure you specify the distance. Divide calculates the interval to divide an entity into a specified number of equal segments. The Measure command places point markers at a specified distance along an entity.

The measurement and division of a circle start at the angle from the center that follows the current Snap rotation. The measurement and division of a closed polyline start at the first vertex drawn. The Measure command also draws a specified Block at each mark between the divided segments.

PICKBOX SIZE

The Pickbox Size slider bar on the Object Selection Settings dialog box under Selection... on the Tools menu can be used to change the size of the target box, the small box that replaces the screen crosshairs when the Modify commands are used.

On Your Own

1. Activate a Modify command to confirm visually the current size of the pickbox.

2. Cancel the command and complete the following to change the size of the pickbox.

Change the size of the pickbox:

Prompt	Response
Command:	TYPE: **PICKBOX<enter>**
New value for PICKBOX <default>:	TYPE: **a number larger or smaller than the default<enter>**

OSNAP

It is very important that you become familiar with and use Object Snap modes in combination with Draw, Edit, Modify, and other AutoCAD commands while you are drawing. When an existing drawing entity is not located on a snap point, it is impossible to connect a line or other drawing entity exactly to it. You may try, and you might think that the two points are connected, but a close examination (Zoom-Window) will reveal that they are not. Object Snap modes are used in combination with other commands to connect exactly to specific points of existing objects in a drawing. You need to use Object Snap modes constantly for complete accuracy while drawing.

An Osnap mode can be activated in four different ways: by picking from the Standard Toolbar, by picking from the Object Snap Toolbar, by pressing a button on your mouse, or by typing the first three letters of the mode from the keyboard.

When Osnap is activated, a target box is added to the screen crosshairs. This small box shows the area within which AutoCAD will search for Object Snap candidates. The size of the box is controlled by the Aperture command.

Osnap Modes That Snap to Specific Drawing Features

You have already used Osnap-Midpoint and Node. They are examples of Osnap modes that snap to specific drawing features. Midpoint snaps to the midpoint of a line or arc, and Node snaps to a point entity.

The following list describes other Osnap modes that snap to specific drawing features. AutoCAD Osnap modes treat each edge of a solid, and each polyline segment as a line. 3D faces and viewports (described in later chapters) are treated in the same manner. You will use many of these Osnap modes while completing the exercises in this book.

Endpoint Snaps to the endpoint of a line or arc. The end of the line or arc nearest the point picked is snapped to.

Midpoint Snaps to the midpoint of a line or arc.

Center Snaps to the center of an arc or circle.

Node Snaps to a point (POINT: command) entity.

Note: Press function key F9 to turn Snap off if the snap setting interferes with picking a drawing entity. Use an Osnap mode to select the entity accurately. When the task is complete, turn Snap back on.

Note: You can enter each Osnap mode while you are in a command by typing the first three letters of the mode and pressing the enter key.

Quadrant Snaps to the closest quadrant point of an arc or circle. These are the 0°, 90°, 180°, and 270° points on a circle or arc.

Intersection Snaps to the intersection of two lines, a line with an arc or circle, or two circles and/or arcs. You will use this often to snap to the intersection of two lines.

Insertion Snaps to the insertion point of text, attribute, or Block entities. (These entities are described in later chapters.)

Perpendicular Snaps to the point on a line, circle, or arc that forms a 90° angle from that object to the last point. For example, if you are drawing a line, click the first point of the line, then use Perpendicular to connect the line to another line, circle, or arc. The new line will be perpendicular to form a 90° angle with the first pick.

Tangent Snaps to the point on a circle or arc that when connected to the last point entered forms a line tangent to (touching at one point) the circle or arc.

Nearest Snaps to the point on a line, arc, or circle that is closest to the position of the crosshairs; also snaps to any point (POINT: command) entity that is visually closest to the crosshairs. You will use this when you want to be sure to connect to a line, arc, circle, or point, and cannot use another Osnap mode.

Apparent Intersection Snaps to what appears to be an intersection even though one object is above the other in 3D space.

For the Line command, you can also use the Tangent and Perpendicular modes when picking the first point of the line. This allows you to draw a line tangent to, or perpendicular to, an existing entity.

Snap to Quick You can use Snap to Quick in combination with one of the other Osnap modes when you are working with a very complicated drawing. Quick makes the Osnap search faster. You will not use Snap to Quick in the exercises in this book.

Running Osnap Modes

You can use individual Osnap modes while in another command (as you did with Midpoint and Node) by picking them directly from the Osnap menu (activated with the middle mouse button), or by typing them when AutoCAD prompts for a point. You can also set a running Osnap mode. A running Osnap mode is constantly in effect while you are drawing, until it is disabled. For example, if you have many intersections to which you are connecting lines, set the Intersection mode as a running mode. This saves time by eliminating your constant return to the Osnap command for each intersection pick.

You can set a running Osnap mode using Object Snap Settings... from the Tools menu. When the Osnap Settings dialog box appears, Figure 5–11, make sure the Running Osnap

FIGURE 5–11
Osnap Settings, Running Osnap

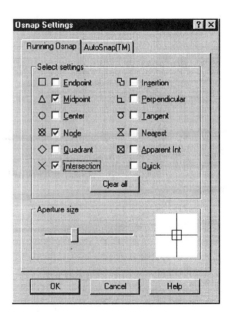

FIGURE 5–12
Osnap Settings, AutoSnap(TM)

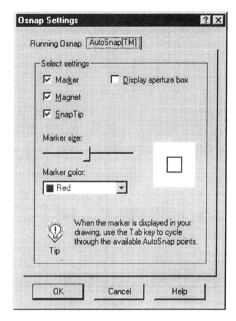

tab is active. Click a check mark beside the desired Osnap mode or modes. Be sure to disable the running Osnap mode when you are through using it, as it will interfere with your drawing. CLICK: **Clear all**, or click to clear the check marks to disable the running Osnap modes. Note the markers (small symbols) beside each Osnap mode. These can be activated by selecting the AutoSnap(TM) tab of this dialog box. When you click on the AutoSnap(TM) tab, the AutoSnap(TM) tab (Figure 5–12) appears.

The **Aperture size** slider bar specifies the size of the Osnap target box, the small box that can be added to the crosshairs when Osnap is activated. This can be activated by selecting the AutoSnap(TM) tab of this dialog box.

AutoSnap(TM)

A check mark beside **Display aperture box** will add a small box to the crosshairs when Osnap is activated. Its size is specified under the Running Osnap tab.

A check mark beside **Marker** will turn the Osnap marker on. It corresponds to the markers shown beside the Osnap modes shown under the Running Osnap tab. The marker size can be changed by using the slider bar under **Marker Size:.** The marker color can be changed by clicking the down arrow under **Marker color:.** When the marker is displayed in a drawing, the Tab key can be used to cycle through any specified running Osnap modes. The marker symbol will change as you Tab through the modes.

The **Magnet** locks the aperture box onto the snap point. The **Snap Tip** is like a Tool Tip and will appear on the screen when on.

Save Your Drawing

When you have completed Exercise 5–1, save your work in at least two places. Exercise 5–1 will be printed in Chapter 8.

EXERCISE 5–2
Drawing a Rectangular Lecture Room Including Furniture

A lecture room, including walls and furnishings, is drawn in Exercise 5–2. When you have completed Exercise 5–2, your drawing will look similar to Figure 5–13. To prepare to draw Exercise 5–2, turn on the computer and start AutoCAD. The Start Up dialog box is displayed.

1. CLICK: **Use a Wizard**

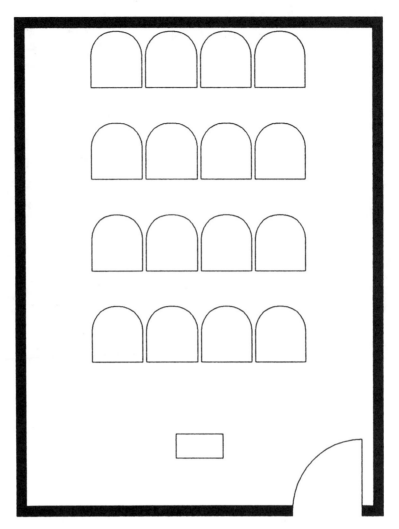

2. CLICK: **Quick Setup**
   CLICK: **OK**

3. Set drawing Units: **Architectural**
   CLICK: **Next>>**

4. Set drawing Width: **25′** × Length: **35′**
   CLICK: **Done**

5. **Use SaveAs... to save the drawing on the hard drive with the name CH5-EX2.**

6. Set Grid: **12″**

7. Set Snap: **6″**

8. Create the following Layers:

LAYER NAME	COLOR	LINETYPE
Walls	White	Continuous
Furniture	Red	Continuous

9. Set Layer Walls current.

10. Use **Zoom-All** to view the limits of the drawing.

POLYLINE

The Polyline prompt is "Arc/Close/Halfwidth/Length/Undo/Width/<Endpoint of line>:". In Exercise 5–1, a simple continuous polyline was used to draw the inside lines of the conference room walls. Then Offset was used to draw the outside line showing wall depth. The Width option of the Pline prompt allows you to specify a thickness for the polyline. The Width option is used to draw the lecture room walls in Exercise 5–2.

Width

The Width option allows you to draw wide polylines. In Exercise 5–2, a 5″ wide polyline is used to draw the walls of the lecture room. The *interior dimensions* of the lecture room are 15′ × 20′. The starting and ending points of a wide polyline are the *center* of the polyline's width. Because the starting and ending points of the wide polyline segments are the center of the line segment, 5″ is added to each line length to compensate for the $2\frac{1}{2}″$ wall thickness on each side of the center line.

When a wide polyline is exploded, the width information is lost and the polyline changes to a line segment.

Use Polyline Width to draw the walls of the lecture room (Figure 5–14):

Prompt	Response
Command:	**Polyline** (or TYPE: **PL<enter>**)
From point:	TYPE: **4′9-1/2,4′9-1/2<enter>**
Current line-width is 0′0″	

FIGURE 5–14

Use a Wide Polyline to Draw the Lecture Room Walls

Prompt	Response
Arc/Close/Halfwidth/Length/Undo/Width/ <Endpoint of line>:	TYPE: **W**<enter>
Starting width <0'0">:	TYPE: **5**<enter>
Ending width <0'-5">:	<enter>
Arc/Close/Halfwidth/Length/Undo/Width/ <Endpoint of line>:	**Turn ORTHO On** **Move your mouse to the right** and TYPE: **15'5**<enter>
Arc/Close/Halfwidth/Length/Undo/Width/ <Endpoint of line>:	**Move your mouse up** and TYPE: **20'5**<enter>
Arc/Close/Halfwidth/Length/Undo/Width/ <Endpoint of line>:	**Move your mouse to the left** and TYPE: **15'5**<enter>
Arc/Close/Halfwidth/Length/Undo/Width/ <Endpoint of line>:	TYPE: **C**

When you subtract $2\frac{1}{2}''$ (half the polyline width) from coordinates 5',5' to get your starting point of coordinates 4'9-1/2,4'9-1/2, the inside lower left corner of the lecture room is located on the grid mark at coordinates 5',5'. Turn coordinates (F6) on and snap to the lower left inside corner of the lecture room to verify this.

With 5" added to each measurement, the inside dimensions of the lecture room are 15' × 20'. If we had wanted the *outside* of the lecture room walls to measure 15' × 20', we would have *subtracted* 5" from each measurement.

Notice that you do not have to insert the inch symbol in the polar coordinates, because architectural units default to inches.

Close

It is always best to use the Close option when you are completing a wide polyline. The effect of using Close is different from clicking or entering a point to complete the polyline. With the Close option, a beveled corner will appear. A 90° corner will appear if the point is entered or clicked.

Halfwidth

The Halfwidth option in the polyline prompt is similar to the Width option, except that half the total width is specified.

Length

The Length option in the Polyline prompt allows you to draw a polyline segment at the same angle as the previously drawn polyline segment, by simply specifying the length of the new segment. It also allows you to return to straight line segments after you have drawn a polyline arc.

FILL ON, FILL OFF

The settings FILL ON and FILL OFF affect the appearance of the polyline. To have an outline of the polyline, TYPE: FILL<enter>, then OFF<enter> and regenerate the drawing. To have it appear solid again, TYPE: FILL<enter>, then TYPE: ON<enter> and regenerate the drawing.

On Your Own

1. TYPE: **FILL**<enter>, then TYPE: **OFF** and regenerate the drawing to create an open polyline.
2. Use Zoom-Window to magnify the corner of the lecture room where the door will be drawn.

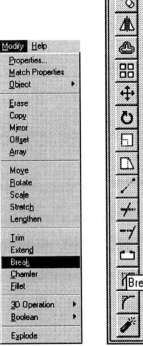
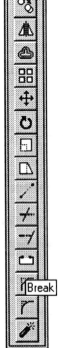

Part II: Two-Dimensional AutoCAD

FIGURE 5–15
Use Break to Create an Opening
for the Lecture Room Door

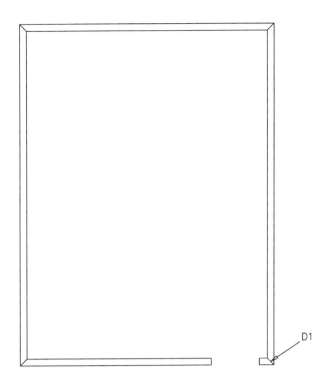

BREAK

The Break command can be used to erase a part of a drawing entity.

Use Break to create an opening for the lecture room door (Figure 5–15):

Prompt	Response
Command:	**Break** (or TYPE: **BR<enter>**)
Select object:	TYPE: **INT<enter>**
int of	**D1**
Enter second point (or F for first point):	TYPE: **F<enter>**
Enter first point:	**With ORTHO On, move your mouse to the left** and TYPE: **44-1/2<enter>**
Enter second point:	**Move your mouse to the right and** TYPE: **36<enter>**

When a closed polyline is broken, the break goes counterclockwise from the first to the second point.

First

When selecting an entity to break, you may use the point entered in the selection process as the first break point, or you may TYPE: **F<enter>** to be able to select the first break point.

@

Sometimes you need only to break an entity and not erase a section of it. In that case, use @ as the second break point. The line will be broken twice on the same point; no segments will be erased from the line.

On Your Own

With snap on, use the Line command to draw a 5′ × 5′ square in the approximate location shown in Figure 5–16, and proceed with the following to see how Edit Polyline will join lines to form a single polyline.

FIGURE 5–16
Edit Polyline Join Option

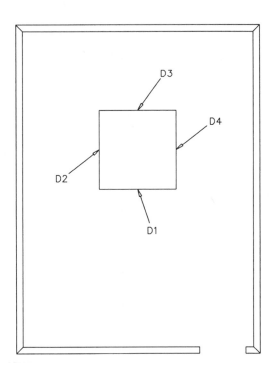

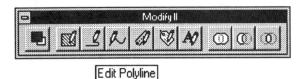

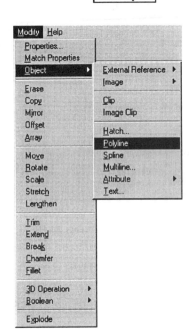

Edit Polyline

Edit Polyline is a special edit command that is used only to edit polylines. The prompt is "Close/Join/Width/Edit vertex/Fit/Spline/Decurve/Ltypegen/Undo/ eXit<X>:".

The following will describe how to use the Join and Width options available in the Edit Polyline prompt. All options can be used on either a simple polyline or a wide polyline.

Join

The Join option joins any line, arc, or other polyline to an existing polyline if it meets that existing polyline's endpoints. The Join option also joins lines or arcs together and changes them into a single polyline. You will do this in the following part of this exercise.

Use Edit Polyline Join to join four separate lines (drawn with the Line command) to form a single polyline (Figure 5–16):

Prompt	Response
Command:	**Edit Polyline** (or TYPE: **PE<enter>**)
Select polyline:	**D1**
Object selected is not a polyline	
Do you want to turn it into one? <Y>	**<enter>**
Close/Join/Width/Edit vertex/Fit/Spline/ Decurve/Ltype gen/Undo/eXit<X>:	TYPE: **J<enter>**
Select objects:	**D2,D3,D4**
Select objects:	**<enter>**
3 segments added to polyline	
Open/Join/Width/Edit vertex/Fit/Spline/ Decurve/Ltypegen/Undo/eXit<X>:	**<enter>**

On Your Own

To verify that all segments of the line have been joined to form a single polyline, use the Erase command and pick a point on the new polyline. If all segments are highlighted, it is a polyline, and you can enter Esc to cancel the Erase command.

Width

The width option allows you to change the width of an existing polyline.

98

Use Edit Polyline Width to change the width of the polyline that makes the **5′ × 5′ square:**

Prompt	Response
Command:	**Edit Polyline**
Select polyline:	**Click a point on the polyline that forms the 5′ × 5′ square**
Open/Join/Width/Edit vertex/Fit/Spline/ Decurve/Ltypegen/Undo/eXit<X>:	TYPE: **W<enter>**
Enter new width for all segments:	TYPE: **5<enter>**
Open/Join/Width/Edit vertex/Fit/Spline/ Decurve/Ltypegen/Undo/eXit<X>:	**<enter>**

On Your Own

See Figure 5–17.

1. Use the Erase command to erase the 5′ × 5′ square that you have drawn in the middle of the lecture room walls.

2. Use the Line command to draw a 3′ vertical door line. Use Osnap-Endpoint to snap to the end (center of the polyline's width) of the wide polyline.

FIGURE 5–17
Draw the Chairs for the Lecture Room

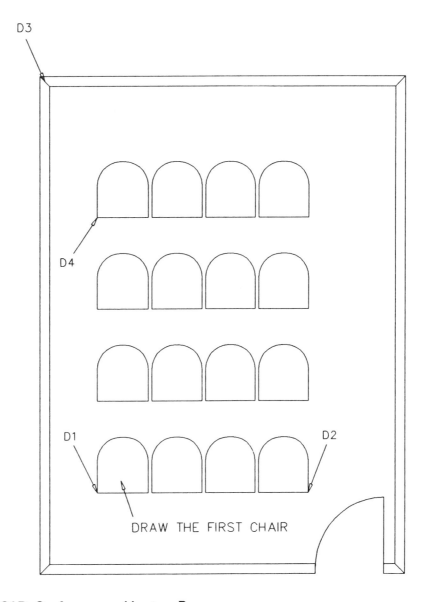

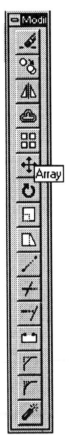

3. Use the Arc-Start, Center, End method to draw the counterclockwise door swing arc. Use Osnap-Endpoint for all connections.

4. Set the current layer to Furniture. To draw the first chair in the group of chairs, zoom in on a portion of the grid inside the lecture room walls in the lower left area.

5. Use the Line command to draw a rectangle 26″ wide by 28″ deep. This chair shape will be used to draw the entire group of 16 chairs and will be moved to the correct position later. For now, just be sure it is located in the general area shown in Figure 5–17.

6. Edit the rectangle, using the Fillet command, 12″ Radius to form the shape of the chair.

7. Zoom-Extents after you finish drawing the chair.

ARRAY

Array allows you to make multiple copies of an object in a rectangular or polar (circular) array. The rectangular option is used to draw all the chairs in the lecture room; the polar option is described in Exercise 5–3.

Use the Array command to make a rectangular pattern of 16 chairs (Figure 5–17):

Prompt	Response
Command:	**Array (or TYPE: AR<enter>)**
Select objects:	PICK: **any point to locate the first corner of a window to include the entire chair**
Other corner:	**Window the chair just drawn.**
Select objects:	**<enter>**
Rectangular or Polar array (R/P):	TYPE: **R<enter>**
Number of rows (- - -) <1>:	TYPE: **4<enter>**
Number of columns(!!!) <1>:	TYPE: **4<enter>**
Unit cell or distance between rows (- - -):	TYPE: **46<enter>** (chair depth of 28″ + 18″)
Distance between columns (!!!):	TYPE: **28<enter>** (chair width of 26″ + 2″)

Rectangular

The Rectangular option of Array allows you to make multiple copies of an object in a rectangular array. The array is made up of horizontal rows and vertical columns. The direction and spacing of the rows and columns are determined by the distance you specify between each. In the previous example we used the chair as the cornerstone element in the lower left corner of the array. Positive numbers were entered for the distance between the rows and columns, and the array was generated up and to the right. When a positive number is entered for the rows, they proceed up; when a negative number is entered, they proceed down. When a positive number is entered for the columns, they proceed to the right; when a negative number is entered, they proceed to the left. Spacing and direction of rows and columns may also be specified by picking two points on a diagonal.

DISTANCE

The Distance command can be used to determine measurements. We know the interior width of the room is 15′. To center the array of chairs accurately in the lecture room, we need to measure the width of the array. The depth appears to be fine for the room size.

Use Distance to measure a specified distance (Figure 5–17):

Hint: In the Array command, include the original cornerstone item in the number of rows and columns.

Note: To rotate a rectangular array, set the snap rotation to the desired angle and then create the array.

Part II: Two-Dimensional AutoCAD

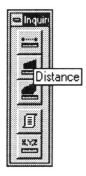

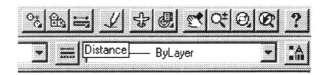

Prompt	Response
Command:	**Distance** (or TYPE: **DIST\<enter>**)
First point:	TYPE: **INT\<enter>**
int of	**D1**
Second point:	TYPE: **INT\<enter>**
int of	**D2**
Distance = 9'-2"	

The room width, 180", minus the array width, 110", is 70". You can leave 35"-wide aisles on each side of the array.

Position the Chair Array

To locate the chair array precisely, use a combination of commands—ID, Point, and Move—as well as some Osnap modes. The array will be located 2" away from the back wall of the lecture room and will have 35"-wide aisles on each side. Be sure to set pdmode and pdsize so that you will be able to see a point on your drawing.

To locate the chair array (Figure 5–17):

Prompt	Response
Command:	TYPE: **ID\<enter>**
ID Point:	TYPE: **INT\<enter>**
int of	**D3**
Command:	TYPE: **PO\<enter>**
Point:	TYPE: **@37-1/2,-32-1/2\<enter>**

The aisle width, 35", plus half the width of the polyline, $2\frac{1}{2}''$, is $37\frac{1}{2}''$ on the X axis. The chair depth, 28", plus half the width of the polyline, $2\frac{1}{2}''$, plus the distance away from the wall, 2", is $32\frac{1}{2}''$ on the Y axis.

Prompt	Response
Command:	**Move** (or TYPE: **M\<enter>**)
Select objects:	CLICK: **any point to locate the first corner of a window to include the entire array**
Other corner:	**Window the entire array.**
Select objects:	**\<enter>**
Base point of displacement:	TYPE: **INT\<enter>**
int of	**D4**
Second point of displacement:	TYPE: **NODE**
node of	**Click the point.**

On Your Own

See Figure 5–18.

1. Draw the lectern centered on the chair array, as shown.

2. Set pdmode so that the point is no longer visible.

FIGURE 5–18
Complete Exercise 5–2

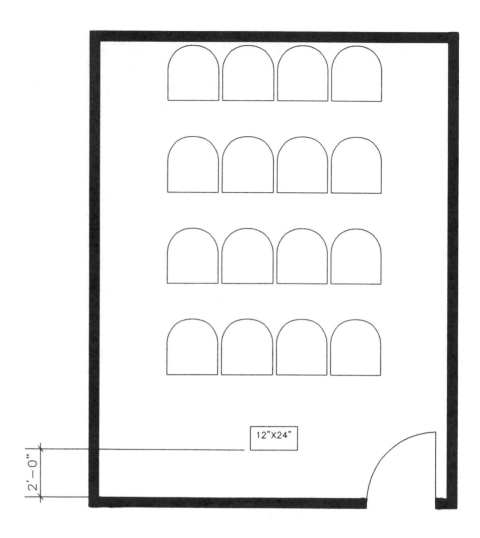

12"X24"

2'–0"

3. TYPE: **FILL<enter>**, then TYPE: **ON<enter>** and regenerate the drawing to have the walls appear solid again.

4. Exercise 5–2 is complete.

Save Your Drawing

When you have completed Exercise 5–2, save your work in at least two places. Exercise 5–2 will be printed in Chapter 8.

EXERCISE 5–3
Drawing a Curved Conference Room Including Furniture

A conference room, including walls and furnishings, is drawn in Exercise 5–3. When you have completed Exercise 5–3, your drawing will look similar to Figure 5–19. To prepare to draw Exercise 5–3, turn on the computer and start AutoCAD. The Start Up dialog box is displayed.

1. CLICK: **Use a Wizard**

2. CLICK: **Quick Setup**
   CLICK: **OK**

FIGURE 5–19

Exercise 5–3: Drawing a Curved Conference Room Including Furniture (Scale: $\frac{1''}{4}$ = 1'-0")

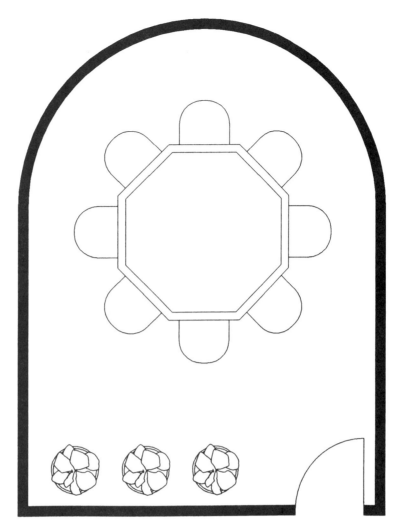

3. Set drawing Units: **Architectural**

 CLICK: **Next>>**

4. Set drawing Width: **25'** × Length: **35'**

 CLICK: **Done**

5. **Use SaveAs... to save the drawing on the hard drive with the name CH5-EX3.**

6. Set Grid: **12"**

7. Set Snap: **6"**

8. Create the following Layers:

LAYER NAME	COLOR	LINETYPE
Walls	White	Continuous
Furniture	Red	Continuous

9. Set Layer Walls current.

10. Use **Zoom-All** to view the limits of the drawing.

Hint: Use the Coordinate Display at the
bottom of your screen to determine the
absolute coordinates of a point.

POLYLINE

The last option we discuss in the Polyline prompt is Arc. The Polyline Arc command is
similar to the Arc command in the Draw menu.

Draw the walls of the conference room, using a wide polyline and wide polyarc (Figure 5–20):

Prompt	Response
Command:	**Polyline** (or TYPE: **PL<enter>**)
From point:	TYPE: **4′9-1/2,4′9-1/2<enter>**
Current line-width is 0′0″	
Arc/Close/Halfwidth/Length/Undo/Width/ <Endpoint of line>:	TYPE: **W**
Starting width <0′0″>:	TYPE: **5<enter>**
Ending width <0′-5″>:	**<enter>**
Arc/Close/Halfwidth/Length/Undo/Width/ <Endpoint of line>:	TYPE: **@15′5<0<enter>**
Arc/Close/Halfwidth/Length/Undo/Width/ <Endpoint of line>:	TYPE: **@12′9<90<enter>**

FIGURE 5–20
Draw Exercise 5–3

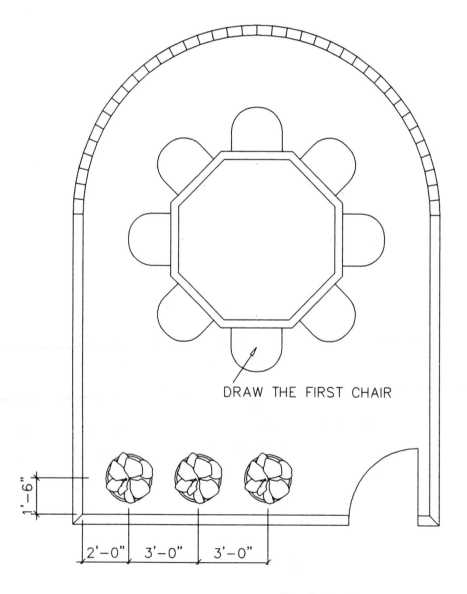

DRAW THE FIRST CHAIR

1′–6″

2′–0″   3′–0″   3′–0″

Prompt	Response
Arc/Close/Halfwidth/Length/Undo/Width/ <Endpoint of line>:	TYPE: **A<enter>**
<Endpoint of arc>:	TYPE: **@15'5<180<enter>**
Angle/CEnter/CLose/Direction/Halfwidth/ Line/Radius/Second pt/Undo/ /Width/ <Endpoint of arc>:	TYPE: **L<enter>**
Arc/Close/Halfwidth/Length/Undo/Width/ <Endpoint of line>:	TYPE: **C<enter>**

Arc, <Endpoint of arc>

The Arc, <Endpoint of arc> option allows you to pick or specify the end point of the arc, as you did in the preceding exercise.

Arc, Line

The Arc, Line option returns you to the straight line polyline mode and the Polyline prompts.

Arc, Angle

If you select Angle from the prompt, you can specify the included angle. A positive angle draws the arc counterclockwise; a negative angle draws the arc clockwise.

Arc, CEnter

The Arc, CEnter option draws an arc segment tangent to the previous polyline segment unless otherwise specified. This option allows you to specify a center point other than the one AutoCAD automatically calculates.

Arc, Direction

The Arc, Direction option allows you to specify a direction other than the one AutoCAD automatically sets (the direction equal to the previous segment's ending direction).

Radius

The Radius option allows you to specify the radius of the arc.

CLose

The CLose option closes the polyline to be with an arc segment rather than a straight line segment.

Second pt

The Second pt option allows you to specify a second and third point of the polyarc.

Halfwidth, Undo, Width

The Halfwidth, Undo, and Width options here are similar to the same options in the straight polyline prompt.

On Your Own

See Figure 5–20.

1. TYPE: **FILL<enter>**, then TYPE: **OFF<enter>** and regenerate the drawing to create an open polyline.

2. Use the Break command to create a 3' door opening, 6" in from the lower inside right corner of the room. Be sure to allow 2-1/2" for the polyline width on the left side of the center line.

3. Use the Line command to draw a 3' vertical door line. Use Osnap-Endpoint to snap to the end (center of the polyline's width) of the polyline.

4. Use the Arc-Start, Center, End method to draw the counterclockwise door swing arc. Use Osnap-Endpoint for all connections.

5. Set the current layer to Furniture.

POLYGON

The Polygon command draws a polygon with 3 to 1024 sides. After the number of sides is specified, the Polygon prompt is "Edge/<Center of polygon>:". When the center of the polygon (default option) is specified, the polygon can then be inscribed in a circle or circumscribed about a circle. When the polygon is inscribed in a circle, all the vertices lie on the circle, and the edges of the polygon are inside the circle. When the polygon is circumscribed about a circle, the midpoint of each edge of the polygon lies on the circle, and the vertices are outside the circle. A polygon, which is actually a closed polyline, must be exploded before it can be edited. Edit Polyline can be used to edit a polygon.

Use the Polygon command to draw the conference table (Figure 5–20):

Prompt	Response
Command:	**Polygon** (or TYPE: **POL<enter>**)
Number of sides:	TYPE: **8<enter>**
Edge/<Center of polygon>:	TYPE: **12′6,16′6<enter>**
Inscribed in circle/Circumscribed about circle (I/C):<I>:	TYPE: **I<enter>** (or just **<enter>** if I is the default
Radius of a circle:	TYPE: **48<enter>**

The method of specifying the radius controls the orientation of the polygon. When the radius is specified with a number, as above, the bottom edge of the polygon is drawn at the current snap angle—horizontal in the polygon just drawn. When the radius of an inscribed polygon is specified with a point, a vertex of the polygon is placed at the point location. When the radius of a circumscribed polygon is specified with a point, an edge midpoint is placed at the point's location.

Edge

When the Edge option of the prompt is selected, AutoCAD prompts for "First endpoint of edge:" and "Second endpoint of edge:". The two points entered to the prompts specify one edge of a polygon that is drawn counterclockwise.

On Your Own

See Figure 5–20.

1. To draw the first chair of the eight chairs that are placed around the conference table, zoom in on a portion of the grid inside the conference room walls.

2. Use the Line command to draw a rectangle 26″ wide by 28″ deep using polar coordinates or direct distance entry.

3. Edit one of the 26″ wide sides of the rectangle, using the Fillet command, 12″ Radius to form the back of the chair.

4. Locate an ID point on the Midpoint of the bottom edge of the polygon. In relation to the ID point, draw a point (node) 6″ inside the midpoint of the bottom edge of the polygon. Use the Move command, Osnap-Midpoint (to the front of the chair), and Osnap-Node to locate the front of chair 6 inside the midpoint of the bottom edge of the conference table polygon.

5. Use the Trim and Erase commands to erase the part of the chair that is under the conference table.

6. Use the Offset command to offset the outside edge of the conference table 4″ to the inside, to form the 4″ band.

7. Zoom-Extents after you have finished Step 6.

ARRAY

Use the Array command to make a polar (circular) pattern of eight chairs (Figure 5–20):

Prompt	Response
Command:	**Array** (or TYPE: **AR\<enter\>**)
Select objects:	CLICK: **the first corner for a window to select the chair just drawn**
Other corner:	**Window the chair just drawn.**
Select objects:	**\<enter\>**

Prompt	Response
Rectangular or Polar array (R/P):	TYPE: **P\<enter\>**
Base/\<Specify center point of array\>:	CLICK: **the center point of the polygon** (or TYPE: **12′6,16′6\<enter\>**)
Number of items:	TYPE: **8\<enter\>** (include the original chair)
Angle to fill (+=ccw, −=cw) \<360\>:	**\<enter\>**
Rotate objects as they are copied? \<Y\>	**\<enter\>**

Polar

The Polar option of Array allows you to make multiple copies of an object in a circular array. The 360° "Angle to fill" can be specified to form a full circular array. An angle less than 360° can be specified to form a partial circular array. As shown in the "Angle to fill" prompt, when a positive angle is specified, the array is rotated counterclockwise (+=ccw). When a negative angle is specified, the array is rotated clockwise (−=cw).

AutoCAD constructs the array by determining the distance from the array's center point to a point on the entity selected. If more than one object is selected, the reference point is on the last item in the selection set. When multiple items are arrayed and are not rotated as they are copied, the resulting array depends on the reference point used.

If one of the two array parameters used above—the number of items in the array or the angle to fill—is not specified, AutoCAD will prompt for a third parameter—"Angle between items:". Any two of the three array parameters must be specified to complete an array.

SKETCH

The Sketch command (TYPE: **SKETCH\<enter\>**) allows you to draw freehand using a pointing device, such as a mouse. When you enter **P** in response to the prompt "Pen eXit Quit Record Erase Connect.", an imaginary sketching pen is raised and lowered. When the pen is lowered and the pointer is moved, the sketch lines follow the mouse's movements.

Freehand drawing, especially with very fine accuracy, generates a large number of lines and consumes a lot of disk space. It is used for signatures and other irregular items. It should not be used when another AutoCAD command is sufficient.

On Your Own

See Figure 5–20.

1. Use Zoom-Window to zoom in on the area of the conference room where the plants and planters are located.

2. Use the Circle command, 12″ Radius, to draw the outside shape of one planter.

3. Use the Offset command, offset distance 1″, offset to the inside of the planter, to form a thickness to the planter.

4. Use the Polyline command, 0 width, to draw multisegmented shapes (to show a plant) in the planter.

5. Use Trim to trim any lines you need to remove. Window the entire planter to select the cutting edges, and then select the lines to trim.

6. Use the Copy command to draw the next two planters.

7. Set FILL ON and regenerate the drawing to have the walls appear solid again.

8. Exercise 5–3 is complete.

Save Your Drawing

When you have completed Exercise 5–3, save your work in at least two places. Exercise 5–3 will be printed in Chapter 8.

EXERCISE 5–4
Drawing a Rectangular Conference Room Including Furniture

A rectangular conference room including furniture (Figure 5–21) is drawn in Exercise 5–4. To prepare to draw Exercise 5–4, turn on the computer and start AutoCAD. The Start Up dialog box is displayed.

1. CLICK: **Use a Wizard**

2. CLICK: **Quick Setup**

   CLICK: **OK**

3. Set drawing Units: **Architectural**

   CLICK: **Next>>**

FIGURE 5–21

Exercise 5–4: Drawing a Rectangular Conference Room Including Furniture (Scale: $\frac{1''}{4} = 1'$-$0''$)

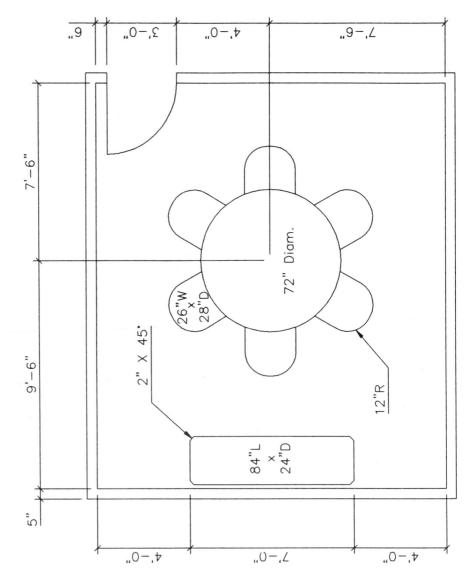

Part II: Two-Dimensional AutoCAD

4. Set drawing Width: **27′** × Length: **22′**

   CLICK: **Done**

5. **Use SaveAs... to save the drawing on the hard drive with the name CH5-EX4.**

6. Set Grid: **12″**

7. Set Snap: **6″**

8. Create the following Layers:

LAYER NAME	COLOR	LINETYPE
Walls	Blue	Continuous
Furniture	Red	Continuous

9. Use the measurements shown in Figure 5–21 to draw the conference room full scale.

10. You can plot Exercise 5–4 after completing Chapter 8.

11. Save the drawing in at least two places.

EXERCISE 5–5
Drawing a Rectangular Lecture Room Including Furniture

A lecture room including furniture (Figure 5–22) is drawn in Exercise 5–5. To prepare to draw Exercise 5–5, turn on the computer and start AutoCAD. The Start Up dialog box is displayed.

1. CLICK: **Use a Wizard**

2. CLICK: **Quick Setup**

   CLICK: **OK**

3. Set drawing Units: **Architectural**

   CLICK: **Next>>**

4. Set drawing Width: **25′** × Length: **27′**

   CLICK: **Done**

5. **Use SaveAs... to save the drawing on the hard drive with the name CH5-EX5.**

6. Set Grid: **12″**

7. Set Snap: **6″**

8. Create the following Layers:

LAYER NAME	COLOR	LINETYPE
Walls	White	Continuous
Furniture	Magenta	Continuous

9. Use the measurements shown in Figure 5–22 to draw the lecture room full scale.

10. You can plot Exercise 5–5 after completing Chapter 8.

11. Save the drawing in at least two places.

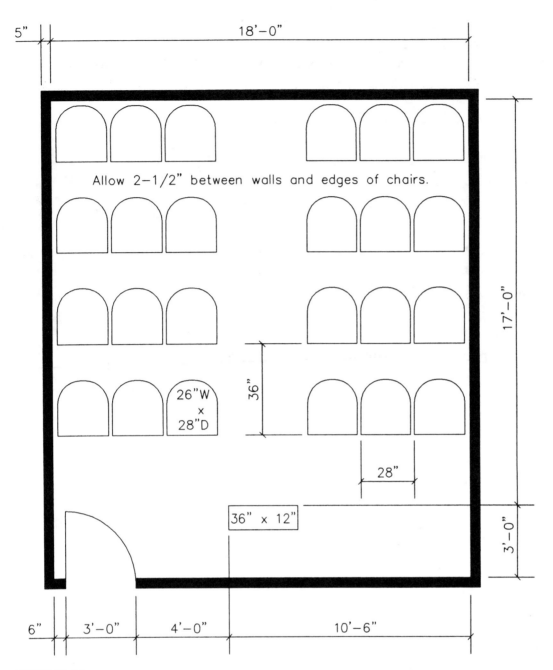

FIGURE 5–22
Exercise 5–5: Drawing a Rectangular Lecture Room Including Furniture (Scale: $\frac{1}{4}'' = 1'\text{-}0''$)

REVIEW QUESTIONS

1. When the outline of the walls of a room is drawn with a polyline, which of the following commands can be used to draw most quickly the second line that shows the depth of the walls?
   a. Line
   b. Polyline
   c. Offset
   d. Copy
   e. Array
2. Which of the following commands is used to split a solid polyline into separate line segments?
   a. ID Point
   b. Offset

c. Array

d. Trim

e. Explode

3. Which of the following commands is used to identify, on a drawing, a point that AutoCAD uses as the origin for a single DRAW command?

a. ID Point

b. Inquiry

c. First point

d. Aperture

e. Distance

4. The Chamfer command will chamfer two lines that do not intersect.

a. True

b. False

5. Which of the following commands can be used to draw a rounded corner?

a. Chamfer

b. Fillet

c. Offset

d. Trim

e. Edit Polyline

6. Which of the following Osnap modifiers is used to snap to a point entity?

a. Perpendicular

b. Endpoint

c. Node

d. Midpoint

e. Intersection

7. Which of the following rotation angles is the same as -90°?

a. 90

b. 180

c. 270

d. 300

e. 330

8. Which of the following settings controls the appearance of the markers used in the Divide command?

a. Aperture

b. Pdmode

c. Osnap

d. Pickbox

e. ID

9. Which of the following settings is used to change the size of the target box that appears when Modify commands are used?

a. Aperture

b. Pdmode

c. Osnap

d. Pickbox

e. ID

10. Which of the following commands can be used to join lines or arcs together and make them a single polyline?

a. Explode

b. Edit Polyline

c. Polyline

d. Close

e. Edit vertex

11. Describe the difference between a square drawn with the Line command and a square drawn with the Polyline command.

_____

_____

_____

_____

12. Describe what the Trim prompt "Select cutting edge(s)... Select objects:" means.

_____

_____

13. Describe how to chamfer the corners of a rectangle using only the Rectangle command.

_____

14. Which Polyline-arc option allows you to draw an arc in a direction other than the one Auto-CAD automatically sets?

_____

15. Which command is used to determine the exact distance from one point to another?

_____

16. Describe the difference between a polygon that has been inscribed in a circle and one that has been circumscribed about a circle.

Inscribed in a circle: _____

_____

Circumscribed about a circle: _____

_____

17. When creating a counterclockwise polar array of six chairs arranged in a half circle, which "Angle to fill" would you use to form the partial array?

_____

18. What is the disadvantage of using the Sketch command?

_____

19. Which Polyline Arc option allows you to draw a straight line polyline after a Polyline arc has been drawn?

_____

20. Describe the use of Osnap-Tracking.

_____

Part II: Two-Dimensional AutoCAD

6 Using Raster Images in AutoCAD Drawings

OBJECTIVES

When you have completed this chapter, you will be able to:

- ☐ Define the terms vector and raster images.
- ☐ List file types for raster images.
- ☐ Insert raster images into AutoCAD drawings.
- ☐ Select raster images for editing.
- ☐ Use grips to stretch, move, scale, copy, rotate, and mirror raster images.
- ☐ Clip raster images.
- ☐ Change the order of images lying on top of each other.
- ☐ Adjust the brightness and contrast of raster images.
- ☐ Turn image boundaries ON and OFF.
- ☐ Delete and Detach raster images.

INTRODUCTION

Release 14 of AutoCAD allows raster images to be easily imported into and exported from AutoCAD drawings. A raster image is one made up of dots similar to the photographs you find printed in newspapers and magazines. A vector image is one made up of lines and solids. Most AutoCAD drawings are made up entirely of vector images.

Being able to use raster images easily in AutoCAD drawings means that you can now bring many different types of images into your drawing. For example, you can use files from CorelDraw, Paintbrush, Powerpoint and many other popular graphics programs. You can also take photographs with a digital camera and import them into your drawing. AutoCAD uses the following four raster file types:

BMP (Bitmap)
TGA (TrueVision Targa)
PCX (Paintbrush)
TIFF (Tagged Image File Format)

Many of the same commands you use with vector images can be used with raster images. How these commands are used, however, varies a little. The following exercise will give you some experience in using raster images.

EXERCISE 6–1
Inserting and Modifying Raster Images

The drawing template A-size, created in Chapter 3, will be used for this exercise. You will use that template to create a new drawing and then insert some raster images that are in the AutoCAD R14 program. After the images are inserted some standard commands will be used to modify the images and create the pictures for an advertisement for a travel agency. Your final drawing will look similar to Figure 6–1.

FIGURE 6-1

Exercise 6–1: Inserting and Modifying Raster Images (This material has been reprinted with permission from and under the copyright of Autodesk, Inc.)

In Chapter 7 you will place text on the ad to complete it.

To prepare to draw Exercise 6–1, turn on the computer and start AutoCAD. The Start Up dialog box is displayed (Figure 6–2).

1. CLICK: **Use a Template**
2. **Insert the floppy disk that has A-SIZE.dwt stored on it in drive A.**
3. CLICK: **$3\frac{1}{2}$ Floppy [A:]**
4. CLICK: **A-SIZE.dwt**, Figure 6–2
5. CLICK: **Open**
6. **Use SaveAs... to save the drawing on the hard drive with the name CH6-EX1.**
7. Use Zoom-All to view the limits of the drawing.

Inserting Raster Images into AutoCAD Drawings

Find the sample raster files that are in AutoCAD R14 and insert the one named jblake (Figures 6–3 and 6–4):

Prompt	Response
Command:	CLICK: **Raster Image...**
The Image dialog box appears:	CLICK: **Attach...**
The Attach Image File dialog box appears:	DOUBLE CLICK: **the Sample Folder** (as shown in Figure 6–3) to open it
	CLICK: **jblake** (as shown in Figure 6–4)
	CLICK: **Open**

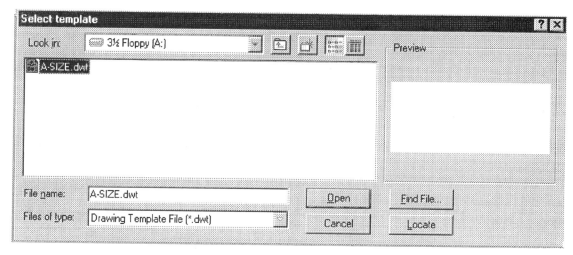

FIGURE 6–2
Select Template Dialog Box

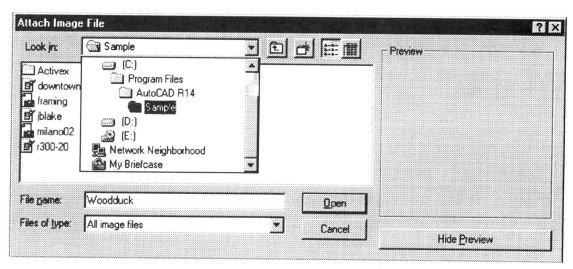

FIGURE 6–3
Double Click the Sample Folder to Open It

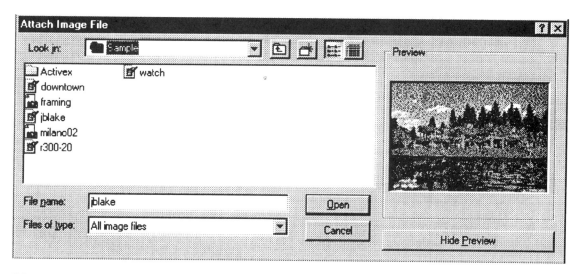

FIGURE 6–4
Attach jblake to Your Drawing

Chapter 6: Using Raster Images in AutoCAD Drawings

FIGURE 6–5
Insert the Watch Image

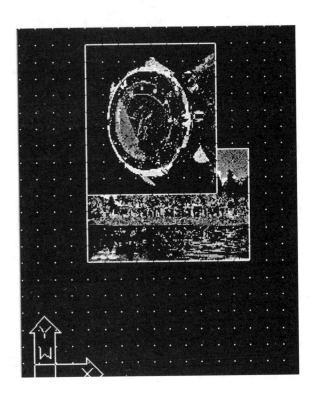

Prompt	Response
The Attach Image dialog box appears:	CLICK: **OK**
Insertion point <0,0>:	TYPE: **2,4<enter>** (This locates the lower left corner of the picture 2″ to the right and 4″ up from the lower left corner of the drawing.)
Base image size: Width: 1.00, Height: 0.67 <Unitless> Scale factor <1>:	TYPE: **5<enter>** (This enlarges the picture to five times its original size.)

The jblake image is inserted into the drawing.

On Your Own (Figure 6–5)

1. Locate the file named **watch** in the same folder as the first image. You will have to CLICK: **Browse...** in the Attach Image dialog box.

2. Look at Figure 6–5, and insert the watch image with an Insertion point: **2,6** and a Scale factor: **4**.

The watch picture is too big, so you will have to scale it down. Now would be a good time to do that.

Modifying Raster Images

Before you can do anything to an image you have to select it. Raster images have to be selected by using a window or by clicking any point on the image frame. After selecting the object, you may then move, stretch, scale, copy, mirror, or rotate it using grips or one of the standard commands.

Next you will select the watch raster image, then use grips to scale and move it.

Select the watch raster image (Figures 6–6 and 6–7):

Prompt	Response
Command:	CLICK: **any point on the frame of the watch image, shown as D1** (Figure 6–6)

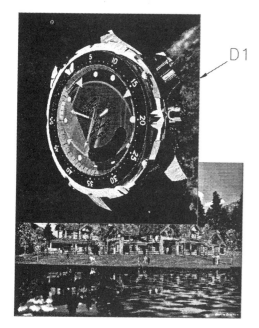

FIGURE 6–6
Select the Watch Image

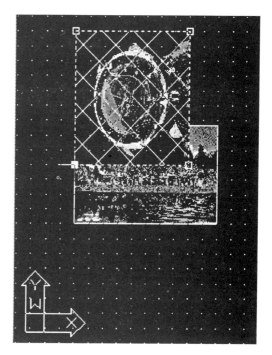

FIGURE 6–7
Click the Grip on the Lower Left Corner

Prompt	Response
Small blue boxes (grips) appear at each corner of the image:	**Center the pickbox on the lower left grip.**
	CLICK: **the lower left grip** (Figure 6–7)
The lower left grip changes to a solid color.	

Scale the watch image to 1/4 its size:

Prompt	Response
<Stretch to point>/Base point/Copy/ Undo/eXit:	**PRESS: <enter> until the prompt reads as shown in the following Prompt column.**
<Scale factor>/Base point/Copy/Undo/ Reference/eXit:	TYPE:**1/4<enter>**
The watch image is reduced to a smaller size.	

The watch image is in the wrong place. The following steps will use grips to move it up.

Move the watch image up $\frac{3''}{4}$ using grips (Figure 6–8):

Prompt	Response
The small blue squares should still be displayed at the corners of the image. If they are not, CLICK: the image so that they are:	**Center the pickbox on the lower left grip.** CLICK: **the grip on the lower left corner** (Figure 6–8)
The lower left grip changes to a solid color.	
<Stretch to point>/Base point/Copy/ Undo/eXit:	PRESS: **<enter>**
<Move to point>/Base point/Copy/Undo/eXit:	TYPE: **@3/4<90<enter>**

FIGURE 6–8
Click the Grip on the Lower Left Corner

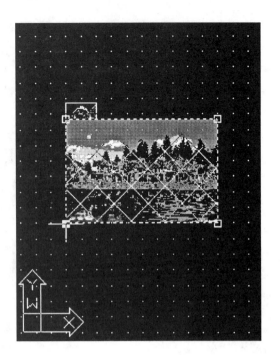

FIGURE 6–9
Click the Lower Left Grip

Prompt	Response
The image moves up $\frac{3}{4}''$:	PRESS: **Esc** twice (to cancel grips)

Next, you will make a copy of the jblake image, enlarge it, and then clip a small area from the enlarged image to make the third picture in the ad.

Select the jblake raster image (Figure 6–9):

Prompt	Response
Command:	CLICK: **any point on the frame of the jblake image**
Small blue boxes (grips) appear at each corner of the image:	CLICK: **the lower left grip** (Figure 6–9)
The lower left grip changes to a solid color.	

Copy and scale the jblake image to two times its present size:

Prompt	Response
<Stretch to point>/Base point/Copy/Undo/ eXit:	PRESS: **<enter> until the prompt reads as shown in the following Prompt column.**
<Scale factor>/Base point/Copy/Undo/ Reference/eXit:	TYPE: **C<enter>**
<Scale factor>/Base point/Copy/Undo/ Reference/eXit:	TYPE: **2<enter>** (Scale factor)
<Scale factor>/Base point/Copy/Undo/ Reference/eXit:	TYPE: **X<enter>** (to exit)

On Your Own (Figure 6–10)

1. Activate the Reference toolbar by Picking Toolbars... .

2. Check the box to the left of Reference and Close the Toolbars dialog box (Figure 6–10).

FIGURE 6–10
View the Reference Toolbar

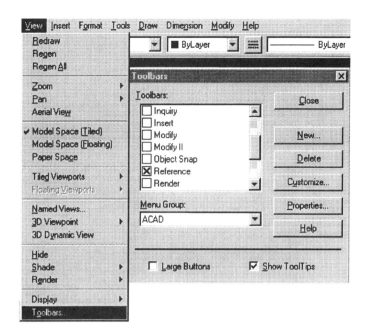

Clip an area from the enlarged jblake image (Figure 6–11):

Prompt	Response
Command:	CLICK: **Image Clip**
Select image to clip:	CLICK: **any point on the boundary of the enlarged jblake image**
On/OFF/Delete/<New boundary>:	**<enter>**
Polygonal/<Rectangular>:	**<enter>**
First point:	CLICK: **D1** (Figure 6–11; D1 and D2 are approximate points.)
Other corner:	CLICK: **D2**

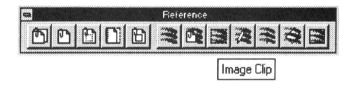

Image Clip

FIGURE 6–11
Clip the Enlarged Image

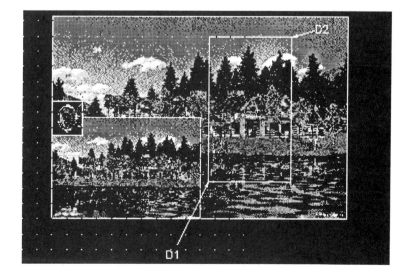

FIGURE 6–12
Move the Clipped Image to Overlap the Original jblake Image

On Your Own (Figure 6–12)

1. Use grips to move the clipped image to the approximate location shown in Figure 6–12. Click the image to select it, and then click the lower left grip.

2. PRESS: **<enter>** to toggle to the Move grips mode. Move your mouse and click a new point to locate the lower left corner of the image, to the approximate location shown in Figure 6–12.

3. Press Esc twice to cancel grips.

4. Notice that Figure 6–12 shows the clipped image behind the original image. Your drawing may show the clipped image in front. In any case, complete the next step so you will know how to arrange images in overlapping order.

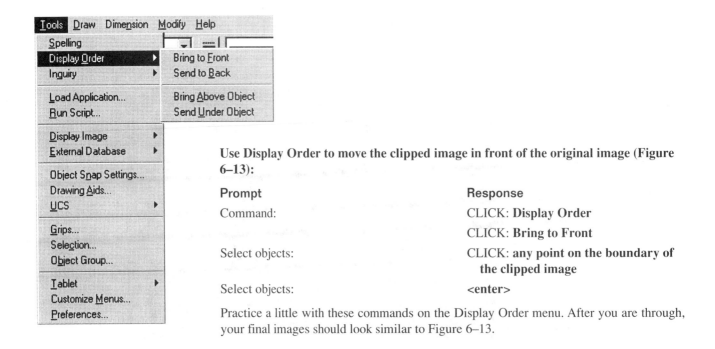

Use Display Order to move the clipped image in front of the original image (Figure 6–13):

Prompt	Response
Command:	CLICK: **Display Order**
	CLICK: **Bring to Front**
Select objects:	CLICK: **any point on the boundary of the clipped image**
Select objects:	**<enter>**

Practice a little with these commands on the Display Order menu. After you are through, your final images should look similar to Figure 6–13.

Part II: Two-Dimensional AutoCAD

FIGURE 6–13
Bring the Clipped Image to the
Front

Using a Standard Vector Command with a Raster Image

One part of the message of the advertisement is that time is to be ignored when you are on vacation. To display that part of the message you will draw a wide polyline (a vector image) across the watch image in the following part of this exercise.

Draw a wide polyline across the watch image (Figure 6–14):

Prompt	Response
Command:	TYPE: **PL\<enter>**
From point:	CLICK: **D1**

FIGURE 6–14
Draw a Wide Polyline across the
Watch Image

Prompt	Response
Arc/Close/Halfwidth/Length/Undo/Width/ <Endpoint of line>:	TYPE: **W\<enter\>**
Starting width <0-0">:	TYPE: **1/4\<enter\>**
Ending width <0'-0 1/4">:	TYPE: **1/8\<enter\>**
Arc/Close/Halfwidth/Length/Undo/Width/ <Endpoint of line>:	CLICK: **D2**
Arc/Close/Halfwidth/Length/Undo/Width/ <Endpoint of line>:	**\<enter\>**

Adjusting the Brightness and Contrast of a Raster Image

Adjust the brightness and contrast of the original jblake image (Figure 6–15):

FIGURE 6–15
Adjust Brightness and Contrast

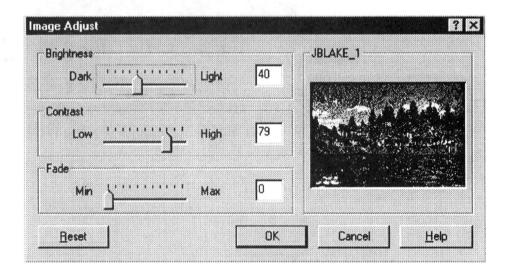

Prompt	Response
Command:	CLICK: **Image Adjust**
Select image to adjust:	CLICK: **any point on the boundary of the original jblake image**
The Image Adjust dialog box appears:	**Move the slider for brightness to 40 and the contrast to 79 as shown in Figure 6–15.**
	CLICK: **OK**

Turning Raster Image Frames On and Off

Turn image frames off:

Prompt	Response
Command:	CLICK: **Image Frame**
ON/OFF <ON>:	TYPE: **OFF\<enter\>**

You cannot select an image with the frame turned off. If you need to select an image later, you will have to turn the image frame ON again using the Image Frame command.

Deleting and Detaching Images

When you want to delete one or more images, select them and press the Delete key on your keyboard. You should not delete any of the images you presently have unless you have made a mistake and have more images than are shown in Figure 6–13.

Deleting the images does not Detach the image from your drawing. To detach the image, activate the Image command, select the image file name in the Image dialog box and CLICK: **Detach**. When the image is detached, it is removed from the drawing database and all those images are erased from the drawing.

Save Your Drawing and Exit AutoCAD

When you have completed Exercise 6–1, save your drawing in at least two places. Exercise 6–1 will be printed in Chapter 8.

REVIEW QUESTIONS

1. A raster image is made up of dots.
    a. True
    b. False
2. Which of the following is not a raster file type?
    a. BMP
    b. DWG
    c. PCX
    d. TIFF
    e. TGA
3. Which of the following folders contains the raster images used in this chapter?
    a. Sample
    b. R14
    c. Support
    d. Template
    e. Fonts
4. To select a raster image
    a. Pick any point inside the frame.
    b. Pick any point outside the frame.
    c. Use a dialog box to select it.
    d. Pick any point on the frame.
    e. Type the name of the image.
5. When a raster image is selected
    a. It changes color.
    b. Small blue squares called grips appear on each corner.
    c. Vertical white lines appear on the image.
    d. Horizontal white lines appear on the image.
    e. A round dot appears in the center of the image.
6. When a Scale factor of 1/4 is used with the grips Scale mode
    a. The selected image is reduced to $\frac{1}{4}$ its original size.
    b. The selected image is reduced to $\frac{1}{2}$ its original size.
    c. The selected image is reduced to $\frac{1}{25}$ its original size.
    d. The selected image is enlarged to 4 times its original size.
    e. The selected image is enlarged to 25 times its original size.

7. To activate the move grip mode, select the image, pick a grip, and press <enter>
   a. Once
   b. Twice
   c. Three times
   d. Four times
   e. Do not press <enter> at all.
8. An image can be copied and enlarged at the same time.
   a. True
   b. False
9. When you select Image Clip you have a choice of two types of boundaries to specify. They are
   a. Circular/<Rectangular>
   b. Rectangular/<Elliptical>
   c. Polygonal/<Rectangular>
   d. Circular/<Polygonal>
   e. Elliptical/<Circular>
10. The Display Order command is used to
    a. Show which image was inserted first
    b. Move an image from the bottom of a stack of images to the top
    c. Arrange images in alphabetical order
    d. Arrange images in rows
    e. Arrange images in columns
11. List the command that is used to insert a raster image.

    _____

12. List the command that is used to clip a raster image.

    _____

13. List the command that is used to turn off the frame around raster images.

    _____

14. Write the name of the small blue squares that appear at the corners of a raster image when it is selected.

    _____

15. List the command that will allow you to save a drawing on more than one disk.

    _____

16. What two letters do you type to activate the Polyline command?

    _____

17. Describe how to delete a raster image from the screen.

    _____

18. Describe how to Detach a raster image from your drawing.

    _____

7

Adding Text to the Drawing

OBJECTIVES

When you have completed this chapter, you will be able to:

☐ Define the terms *style* and *font* and describe the function of each.
☐ Use different fonts on the same drawing.
☐ Place text on several different parts of the drawing with a single command.
☐ Use the modifiers Center, Align, Fit, Middle, Right, Top, and Style.
☐ Use the Text Style... setting to create condensed, expanded, rotated, backward, inclined, and upside-down text.
☐ Use the Text Style... setting to change any style on the drawing to a different font.
☐ Use standard codes to draw special characters such as the degree symbol, the diameter symbol, the plus and minus symbol, and underscored and overscored text.
☐ Use Mtext (multiline text) to create paragraph text.
  Spell check your drawing.

EXERCISE 7–1
Placing Text on Drawings

To make complete drawings with AutoCAD, you need to know how text is added to the drawings. The following AutoCAD commands, used to place lettering on drawings, are examined in Exercise 7–1.

Text Style... Used to control the appearance of text.
Single Line Text (Dtext) Used to draw text that is not in paragraph form.
Multiline Text (Mtext) Used to draw text that is in paragraph form.

When you have completed Exercise 7–1, your drawing will look similar to the drawing in Figure 7–1. To begin Exercise 7–1, turn on the computer and start AutoCAD. The Start Up dialog box is displayed.

1. CLICK: **Open a Drawing**
2. Open existing drawing **CH6–EX1**.
3. **Use SaveAs... to save the drawing on the hard drive with the name CH7–EX1.**
4. Set Layer1 current.
5. Use Zoom-All to view the limits of the drawing.

Making Settings for Text Style...

It is very important to understand the difference between the terms *Style Name* and *Font Name* with regard to text:

Style Name: This is a general category that can be assigned any name you choose. The style name is used to separate fonts. You may use the same name for the style as is used for the font, or you may use a different name, single number, or letter for the style name.

FIGURE 7–1
Exercise 7–1: Placing Text on
Drawings (This material has been
reprinted with permission from
and under the copyright of
Autodesk, Inc.)

Font Name: This is the name of a particular alphabet that you select to assign to a style name. A font has to be in the AutoCAD program before it can be selected and assigned to a style name.

You may have only one font per style, but you can have many styles with the same font. For example,

Style Name	Font Name
SIMPLEX	SIMPLEX
CLIENT NAME	ITALIC
NOTES	SIMPLEX
ITALIC	ITALIC
BANNER	MONOTEXT
COMPANY NAME	ROMAND
ROMAND	ROMAND

In the following procedure, the Text Style... setting is used.

Make the setting for the STANDARD style (Figure 7–2):

Prompt	Response
Command:	**Text Style...** (or TYPE: **STYLE<enter>**)
The Text Style dialog box appears:	CLICK: **TechnicLite** (in the Font Name: list)
	CLICK: **Apply**

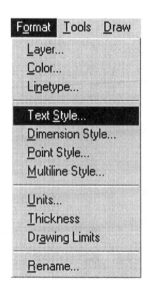

Any text typed while the STANDARD style is active will now contain the TechnicLite font. Notice the preview area in the lower right corner that shows you what the font looks like. Notice also that the vertical setting is grayed out, indicating that this font cannot be drawn running up and down.

The other settings should be left as they are. If you leave the text height set at 0, you will be able to draw different heights of the same style and you will be able to change the height of text if you need to. Leave the text height set to 0 in all cases. The Width Factor allows you to stretch letters so they are wider by making the width factor greater than 1, narrower by making the width factor less than 1. The Oblique Angle slants the letters to the right if the angle is positive and to the left if the angle is negative.

FIGURE 7–2
Select the TechnicLite Font for
the Standard Style

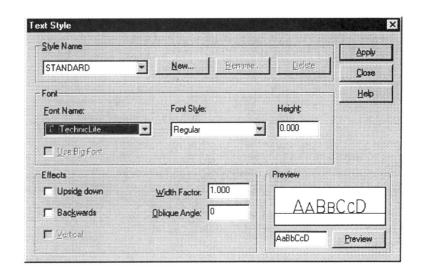

Make the settings for a new style that will be used on the drawing (Figures 7–3 and 7–4):

Prompt	Response
The Text Style dialog box:	CLICK: **New...**
The New Text Style dialog box appears with a Style Name that AutoCAD assigns, style1:	TYPE: **HEADING** (to name the style, Figure 7–3)
	CLICK: **OK**
The Text Style dialog box appears:	CLICK: **Futura Lt BT** (in the Font Name: list, Figure 7–4)
	CLICK: **Apply**

You now have two styles that have been defined on your drawing, STANDARD and HEADING.

FIGURE 7–3
Name the New Style, HEADING

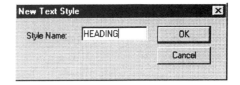

FIGURE 7–4
Select the Futura LtBt Font for
the HEADING Style

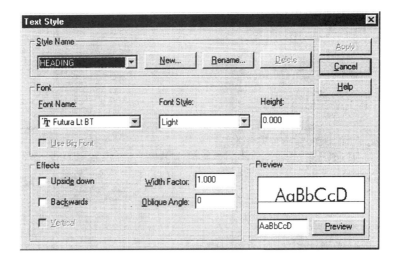

FIGURE 7–5
Make Settings for the VERTICAL
Style

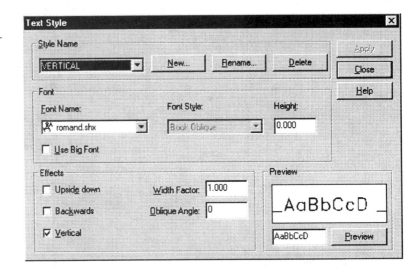

FIGURE 7–6
Check the Style Name List

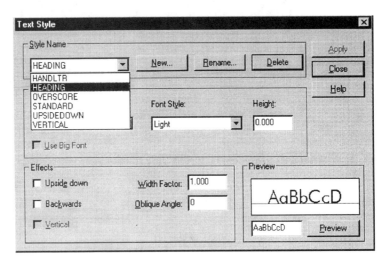

On Your Own (Figures 7–5 and 7–6)

1. Make the settings for the following styles:

Style Name	Font Style	Other Settings
HANDLTR	CityBlueprint	None
OVERSCORE	AvantGarde Bk BT	None
UPSIDEDOWN	AvantGarde Bk BT	Place checks in the Effects box labeled Upside down and the box labeled Backwards.
VERTICAL	romand.shx	Place a check in the Effects box labeled Vertical, Figure 7–5.

2. Click the down arrow in the Style Name list to determine if your list matches the one shown in Figure 7–6.

3. Click the HEADING style name to make it current.

4. Close the dialog box.

Using the Single Line Text Command to Draw Text

The Single Line Text command (also known as Dtext) is used to draw text that is not in paragraph form. Although the name of the command might lead you to believe that only a single line can be drawn, such is not the case. To draw one line under another just PRESS: <enter>, and the next line will be ready to be drawn with the same settings as the first line. To demonstrate this, draw several of the lines of text on your current drawing.

If you are not happy with the location of the text, use the Move command to relocate it.

Draw the heading at the top of the drawing using single line text (Figures 7–7 and 7–8):

Prompt	Response
Command:	CLICK: **Single Line Text** or TYPE: **DT<enter>**
Justify/Style/<Start point>:	TYPE: **C<enter>** to center the heading about a point
Center point:	CLICK: **a point in the approximate location shown in Figure 7–7**
Height <default>:	TYPE: **1/4<enter>**
Rotation angle <0>:	<enter>
Text:	TYPE: **CANCEL TIME AND PLAN THE<enter>** (The text will be centered when you press <enter> the second time after the next line.)
Text:	TYPE: **PERFECT SUMMER VACATION<enter>**
Text:	<enter>

Your drawing looks like Figure 7–8.

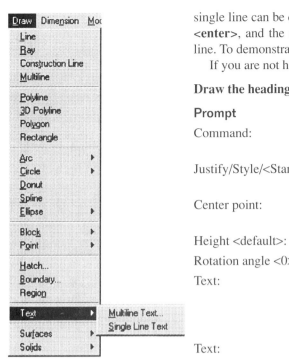

FIGURE 7–7
Click a Center Point for the Heading Text

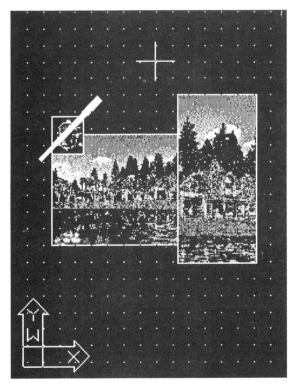

FIGURE 7–8
The Completed Heading

Make a different style current:

Prompt	Response
Command:	CLICK: **Single Line Text** or TYPE: **DT\<enter\>**
Justify/Style/\<Start point\>:	TYPE: **S\<enter\>** (to change to a different style that is defined)
Style name (or ?) \<HEADING\>:	TYPE: **HANDLTR\<enter\>**

Draw the two labels (THIS and NOT THIS) using single line text with the HAN-DLTR style (Figure 7–9):

Prompt	Response
Justify/Style/\<Start point\>:	TYPE: **C\<enter\>** to center the heading about a point
Center point:	CLICK: **a center point for the NOT THIS text,** Figure 7–9. Remember that the point is the center of the bottom of the line of text.
Height \<default\>:	TYPE: **3/16\<enter\>**
Rotation angle \<0\>:	**\<enter\>**
Text:	TYPE: **NOT\<enter\>**
Text:	TYPE: **THIS\<enter\>**
Text:	**\<enter\>**
Command:	**\<enter\>** (to return to the Dtext prompt)
DTEXT Justify/Style/\<Start point\>:	TYPE: **C\<enter\>** to center the heading about a point
Center point:	CLICK: **a center point for the THIS text,** Figure 7–9. Remember that the point is the center of the bottom of the line of text.
Height \<0′-0 3/16″\>:	TYPE: **1/2\<enter\>**
Rotation angle \<0\>:	**\<enter\>**
Text:	TYPE: **THIS\<enter\>**
Text:	**\<enter\>**

FIGURE 7–9
Draw Two Labels Using the HAN-DLTR Style

CANCEL TIME AND PLAN THE
PERFECT SUMMER VACATION

FIGURE 7–10
Click a Start Point for Vertical
Text

Draw the vertical text (In Your State) using the VERTICAL style and single line text (Figure 7–10):

Prompt	Response
Command:	**<enter>** (to repeat the last command. If you have used any other command, TYPE: **DT<enter>**.)
Justify/Style/<Start point>:	TYPE: **S<enter>** (to change to a different style that is defined)
Style name (or ?) <HANDLTR>:	TYPE: **VERTICAL<enter>**
Justify/Style/<Start point>:	CLICK: **a point for the vertical text** (Figure 7–10). This point is the left side of the bottom of the first character in the line of text. The default for line text is left justified.
Height <default>:	TYPE: **1/4<enter>**
Rotation angle <270>:	**<enter>**
Text:	TYPE: **In Your State<enter>**
Text:	**<enter>**

Draw the label (SIGN UP NOW) using the Fit option of single line text with the STANDARD style (Figure 7–11):

Prompt	Response
Command:	**<enter>** (to repeat the last command. If you have used any other command, TYPE: **DT<enter>**.)
Justify/Style/<Start point>:	TYPE: **S<enter>** (to change to a different style that is defined)
Style name (or ?) <VERTICAL>:	TYPE: **STANDARD<enter>**

FIGURE 7–11
Use the Fit Option to Draw Condensed Text

Prompt	Response
Justify/Style/<Start point>:	TYPE: **F<enter>** to specify the Fit option
First text line point:	CLICK: **D1** (in the approximate location shown in Figure 7–11)
Second text line point:	CLICK: **D2** (approximately $1\frac{1}{2}''$ to the right)
Height <default>:	TYPE: **1/2<enter>**
Text:	TYPE: **SIGN UP NOW<enter>**
Text:	**<enter>**

When you activate the Single Line Text command, the prompt is "Justify/Style/<Start point>:". The Style option allows you to select a different style (that has already been defined) for the text you are about to draw. If you TYPE: **J<enter>**, the prompt then becomes "Align/Fit/Center/Middle/Right/TL/TC/TR/ML/MC/MR/BL/BC/BR:".

Align

Align draws the text between two points that you click. It does not condense or expand the font but instead adjusts the letter height so that the text fits between the two points.

Fit

Fit draws the text between two clicked points like the align option, but instead of changing the letter height, Fit condenses or expands the font to fit between the points.

Center

Center draws the text so that the bottom of the line of lettering is centered on the clicked point. Centering is not displayed until the second return is pressed. You may also choose the top or the middle of the line of lettering by typing TC or MC at the justify prompt.

Middle

Middle draws the text so that the middle of the line of lettering is centered around a clicked point. This is very useful when a single line of text must be centered in an area such as a box. Middle is not displayed until the second return is pressed. The top or bottom of the line may also be selected by typing MC or MB at the justify prompt.

45%%D

45°

FIGURE 7–12
Degree Symbol Code

%%C.500

⌀.500

FIGURE 7–13
Diameter Symbol Code

Right

Right draws the text so that each line of text is right justified (ends at the same right margin). Right justification is not displayed until the second return is pressed. The top or center of the line may also be selected by typing TR or MR at the justify prompt.

TL/TC/TR/ML/MC/MR/BL/BC/BR

These are alignment options, Top Left, Top Center, Top Right, Middle Left, Middle Center, Middle Right, Bottom Left, Bottom Center, Bottom Right. They are used with horizontal text.

Using Standard Codes to Draw Special Characters

Figures 7–12 through 7–16 show the use of codes to obtain several commonly used symbols, such as the degree symbol, the diameter symbol, the plus-minus symbol, and underscored and overscored text. The top line of Figure 7–12 shows the code that must be inserted to obtain the degree symbol following the number 45. The top line is displayed until the <enter> is pressed to obtain the degree symbol shown on the bottom line. Two percent symbols followed by the letter D produce the degree symbol.

Figure 7–13 illustrates that two percent symbols followed by the letter C produce the diameter symbol. Any text following the symbol must be typed immediately following the code.

Figure 7–14 shows the code for the plus-minus symbol.

Figure 7–15 shows the code for underscore: two percent symbols followed by the letter U. Notice that the first line contains only one code. The second line contains two codes: one to start the underline and one to stop it.

Figure 7–16 shows the code for overscored text. The same code sequence for starting and stopping the overscore applies.

%%UUNDERSCORE

UNDERSCORE

%%OOVERSCORE

OVERSCORE

%%P.005

±.005

FIGURE 7–14
Plus–Minus Symbol Code

%%UUNDERSCORE%%U LETTERS

UNDERSCORE LETTERS

FIGURE 7–15
Underscore Code

%%OOVERSCORE%%O LETTERS

OVERSCORE LETTERS

FIGURE 7–16
Overscore Code

Draw the three lines containing special codes for the degree and plus-minus symbols with the OVERSCORE style (Figure 7–17):

Prompt	Response
Command:	**<enter>** (to repeat the last command. If you have used any other command, TYPE: **DT<enter>**.)
Justify/Style/<Start point>:	TYPE: **S<enter>** (to change to a different style that is defined)
Style name (or ?) <STANDARD>:	TYPE: **OVERSCORE<enter>**
Justify/Style/<Start point>:	TYPE: **C<enter>** to center the heading about a point

	CLICK: **a center point** (for the three lines in the approximate location shown in Figure 7–17. Remember that the point is the center of the bottom of the line of text.)
Center point:	
Height <default>:	TYPE: **3/16<enter>**
Rotation angle <0>:	**<enter>**
Text:	TYPE: **In<enter>**
Text:	TYPE: **50%%D to 75%%D %%P5%%D <enter>**
Text:	TYPE: **Weather<enter>**
Text:	**<enter>**

Draw the overscored line FUN with the OVERSCORE style (Figure 7–18):

Prompt	Response
Command:	**<enter>** (to repeat the last command. If you have used any other command, TYPE: **DT<enter>**.)
Justify/Style/<Start point>:	TYPE: **C<enter>** to center the heading about a point

FIGURE 7–17
Click the Center Point for the
Three Lines of Text

FIGURE 7–18
Click the Center Point for FUN
Overscored Text

Part II: Two-Dimensional AutoCAD

Center point:	CLICK: **a center point** (for the FUN line in the approximate location shown in Figure 7–18)
Height <default>:	TYPE: **3/16<enter>**
Rotation angle <0>:	**<enter>**
Text:	TYPE: **%%OFUN<enter>**
Text:	**<enter>**

On Your Own

1. Make the Style Name UPSIDEDOWN current.
2. Use Single Line Text to draw the word FUN ($\frac{3}{16}$ height) upsidedown and backward with an overscore in the approximate location shown in Figure 7–19.
3. Change the current style to STANDARD.

Use Single Line Text to draw your name in the lower right corner so it ends at a point 1″ from the right and 1″ from the bottom:

Prompt	Response
Command:	CLICK: **Single Line Text** or TYPE: **DT<enter>**
Justify/Style/<Start point>:	TYPE: **R<enter>** to specify right justification
End point:	TYPE: **7-1/2,1<enter>** to locate the end of your name $7\frac{1}{2}″$ in the X direction and 1″ in the Y direction
Height <default>:	TYPE: **3/16<enter>**
Rotation angle <0>:	**<enter>**
Text:	TYPE: **YOUR NAME<enter>** (The text will be right justified when you press <enter> the second time.)
Text:	**<enter>**

FIGURE 7–19
Specify the Size for the Paragraph

Using the Multiline Text Command to Draw Text Paragraphs

The Multiline Text command (also known as Mtext) is used to draw text in paragraph form. The command activates the Multiline Text Editor, which has many of the same features that other Windows Text Editors have. You can select a defined style, change the text height, boldface and italicize some fonts, select a justification style, specify the width of the line, rotate a paragraph, search for a word and replace it with another, undo, import text, and select symbols for use on your drawing. In this exercise you will create a paragraph using the STANDARD text style.

FIGURE 7–20
The Multiline Text Editor

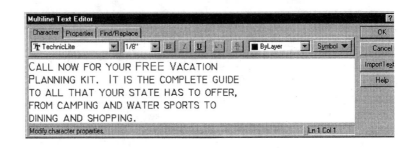

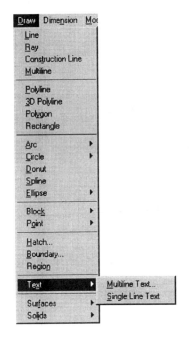

Use Multiline Text to draw a paragraph (Figures 7–19 and 7–20):

Prompt	Response
Command:	**Multiline Text** (or TYPE: **MT<enter>**)
Specify first corner:	CLICK: **D1** (Figure 7–19) $\frac{3}{4}''$ below the lower left corner of the picture)
Specify opposite corner or [Height/Justify/ Rotation/Style/Width]:	TYPE: **@3-1/4,5/8<enter>** (to make the paragraph $3\frac{1}{4}''$ wide and $\frac{5}{8}''$ high)
The Multiline Text Editor appears:	**Change the text height to 1/8** and TYPE: **the paragraph shown in Figure 7–20.** (You will have to press <enter> after the first sentence.)
	CLICK: **OK**

If you have trouble getting the Multiline Text to change text height, cancel the command and TYPE: **DT** to activate Single Line Text and change the default text height to 1/8. The Multiline Text height will then be set at 1/8, and you can proceed with typing the paragraph. Be sure you do not cancel the Single Line Text command before you have changed the default text height.

Changing Text Properties

There will be occasions when you will need to change the text font, height, or content. AutoCAD has several commands that can be used to do these tasks:

Text Style... Use this command to change the font of text that already exists on your drawing.

CHANGE Use this command to change the endpoint of a line, the radius of a circle, and for Single Line Text. When used for Single Line Text, you can change the text properties, the insertion point, the text style, the text height, the text rotation angle, or the text content.

DDEDIT(Edit Text) Use this command if you want to change the text contents only for Single Line Text. This command gives you the Multiline Text Editor when you select multiline text and allows you to change all its properties.

DDMODIFY(Properties) Use this command to change any of the text's characteristics: properties, origin, style, height, rotation angle, the text content, or any of several other properties.

Use the Text Style... command to change the font of text typed with the STANDARD name from TechnicLite to scriptc.shx (Figure 7–21):

Prompt	Response
Command:	**Text Style...** (or TYPE: **ST<enter>**)
The Text Style dialog box appears:	CLICK: **scriptc.shx** (from the Font Name: list, Figure 7–21)
	CLICK: **Apply**
	CLICK: **Close**

FIGURE 7–21
Select the scriptc.shx Font for the
STANDARD Style

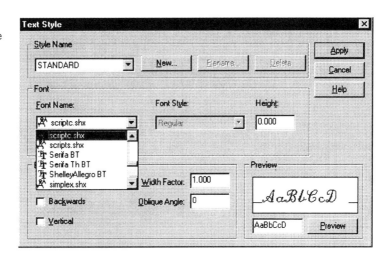

Notice that everything you typed with the STANDARD style name is now changed to the scriptc font.

Use the CHANGE command to change the height of the word $\overline{\text{FUN}}$ and remove the overscore:

Prompt	Response
Command:	TYPE: **CHANGE<enter>**
Select objects:	CLICK: **the word $\overline{\text{FUN}}$**
Select objects:	**<enter>**
Properties/<Change point>:	**<enter>**
Enter text insertion point:	**<enter>**
New style or press ENTER for no change:	**<enter>**
New height <0'-0 3/16">:	TYPE:**1/4<enter>**
New rotation angle <0>:	**<enter>**
New text <%%OFUN>:	TYPE: **FUN<enter>**

Use the DDEDIT (Edit Text) command to change SIGN UP NOW to SIGN UP SOON (Figure 7–22):

Prompt	Response
Command:	**Modify-Object Text...** or TYPE: **DDEDIT<enter>**
<Select an annotation object>/Undo:	CLICK: **SIGN UP NOW**

Edit Text

FIGURE 7–22
Change Text Using the Edit Text
Dialog Box

FIGURE 7–23
Change Text to LAYER2

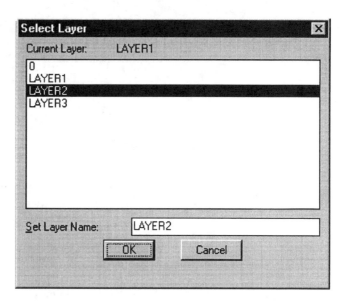

Prompt	Response
The Edit Text dialog box appears:	CLICK: **to the right of NOW, backspace over NOW** and TYPE: **SOON**
	CLICK: **OK**

Use the DDMODIFY (Properties) command to change the vertical line of text from LAYER1 to LAYER2 (Figure 7–23):

Prompt	Response
Command:	**Properties...** or TYPE: **DDMODIFY<enter>**
Select objects:	CLICK: **the vertical line of text (In Your State)<enter>**
The Modify Text dialog box appears:	CLICK: **Layer...**
The Select Layer dialog box appears:	CLICK: **LAYER2**
	CLICK: **OK**
The Modify Text dialog box appears:	CLICK: **OK**

In Your State is now changed to LAYER2.

On Your Own

Use the Undo command to undo the changes you made to the text (TYPE: **U<enter>** and continue to press <enter> until you remove all changes, or CLICK: **Undo** from the Standard Toolbar).

Checking the Spelling

AutoCAD has a spell checker that allows you to accurately check the spelling on your drawing. If the word is correctly spelled but is not in the current dictionary, you can select Ignore All to ignore all instances of that word on the drawing. You can also add the word to the current dictionary. You can change the spelling of a single use of a word or all instances of the word on the drawing by picking Change All. AutoCAD also allows you to change dictionaries.

On Your Own

Purposely misspell the word CANCEL. Use Edit Text... to change CANCEL TIME AND PLAN THE to CNACEL TIME AND PLAN THE.

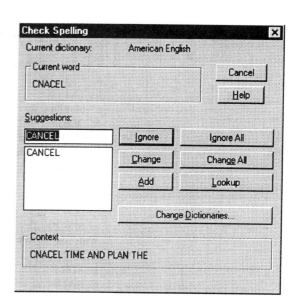

FIGURE 7–24
Change CNACEL to CANCEL

Use the Spelling command to check the spelling on your drawing (Figures 7–24 and 7–25):

Prompt	Response
Command:	**Spelling** (or TYPE: **SP<enter>**)

Prompt	Response
Select objects:	TYPE: **ALL<enter>** to select all the text on your drawing
Select objects:	**<enter>**
The Check Spelling dialog box appears (Figure 7–24):	CLICK: the word **CANCEL** if it is not already highlighted in the suggestions box
	CLICK: **Change**
The AutoCAD Message appears:	CLICK: **OK** (Figure 7–25)

Save Your Drawing and Exit AutoCAD

When you have completed Exercise 7–1, save your drawing in at least two places. Exercise 7–1 will be printed in Chapter 8.

FIGURE 7–25
CLICK: OK to Complete the Spell Check

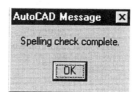

1. The command used in this chapter to place line text on drawings is
   a. Single Line Text (Dtext)
   b. TXT
   c. Multiline Text (Mtext)
   d. DDedit
   e. MS-DOS Text Editor

2. The command used in this chapter to place paragraph text on drawings is
   a. Single Line Text (Dtext)
   b. TXT
   c. Multiline Text (Mtext)
   d. DDedit
   e. MS-DOS Text Editor

3. Which of the following could be used as a Style name?
   a. SIMPLEX
   b. TITLE
   c. NAMES
   d. A
   e. All the above could be used as a Style name.

4. Which of the following is a font name?
   a. SIMPLEX
   b. TITLE
   c. NAMES
   d. A
   e. All the above are font names.

5. You can change from one text style to another from within the Single Line Text command.
   a. True
   b. False

6. When you set the text style, which of the following text height settings will allow you to draw different heights of the same text style?
   a. 1/4
   b. 0' - 0"
   c. 1
   d. 1000
   e. -

7. Which of the following Single Line Text options draws text between two clicked points and adjusts the text height so that it fits between the two points?
   a. Fit
   b. Align
   c. Justify
   d. Middle
   e. Style

8. Which of the following Single Line Text options draws text between two clicked points and condenses or expands the text to fit between the two points but does not change the text height?
   a. Fit
   b. Align
   c. Justify
   d. Middle
   e. Style

9. The justification letters MR stand for
   a. Middle, Right-justified
   b. Margin, Right-justified
   c. Midpoint, Left-justified
   d. Bottom, Right-justified
   e. Margin Release

10. Which of the following modifiers should be selected if you want the bottom of the line of text to end $\frac{1}{2}''$ above and $\frac{1}{2}''$ to the left of the lower right corner of the drawing limits?
   a. TL
   b. BR
   c. BL
   d. TR
   e. MR

11. List three commands that can be used to edit text.

   _____   _____   _____

12. List the command that allows you to change only the text contents.

   _____

13. List the command that allows you to change text height, contents, properties, justification, style, and origin.

   _____

14. List the command used to create a paragraph of text.

   _____

15. List the command that will spell check any line or paragraph of text you select.

   _____

16. Describe the difference between text style name and font name.

   _____

   _____

17. List the setting for Style height that must be used for AutoCAD to prompt you for height when Dtext is used.

   _____

18. Write the description for the abbreviations TL, ML, BR.

   _____

   _____

19. Describe how to quickly change all the text on a drawing done in the STANDARD style, TXT font, to the SIMPLEX font.

   _____

   _____

20. List the standard codes for the following.

   a. Degree symbol: _____

   b. Plus-minus symbol: _____

   c. Diameter symbol: _____

   d. Underscore: _____

   e. Overscore: _____

8 Printing and Plotting

OBJECTIVES

When you have completed this chapter, you will be able to:

☐ Print drawings on paint-jet or laser printers to scale or to fit on standard sheets.
☐ Plot drawings at various scales using pen or laser plotters with two or more different-size pens on standard sheets.

INTRODUCTION

In Release 14, a single Print/Plot Configuration dialog box is used for obtaining hard copies of your work. This chapter describes the parts of the Print/Plot Configuration dialog box. Exercise 8–1 describes responses for using a printer to print Exercise 7–1. Exercise 8–2 describes responses for using a plotter to plot Exercise 5–1.

The system variable command dialog (CMDDIA) controls whether the Print/Plot Configuration dialog box is turned on. TYPE: **CMDDIA<enter>** to make sure CMDDIA is set to 1 (ON) so the dialog box shows up.

EXERCISE 8–1
Print/Plot Responses for Exercise 7–1

The following is a hands-on, step-by-step exercise to make a printer plot of Exercise 7–1. To begin, turn on the computer and start AutoCAD. The Start Up dialog box is displayed.

Open drawing CH7–EX1:

Prompt	Response
The Start Up dialog box is displayed:	**Insert the floppy disk containing drawing CH7-EX1 in drive A.**
	CLICK: **Open a Drawing button**
	DOUBLE CLICK: **A:\CH7-EX1.dwg**

Exercise CH7-EX1 is opened.

Save the drawing to the hard drive:

Prompt	Response
Command:	SaveAs...
The Save Drawing As dialog box is displayed:	CLICK: **[C:]** (and the correct folder if needed)
	CLICK: **Save**

Now you are working on the hard drive. Do not work on a floppy disk.

FIGURE 8–1
Print/Plot Configuration Dialog
Box

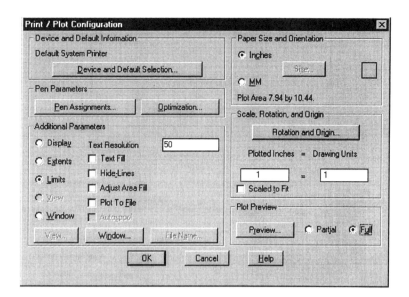

On Your Own

1. CLICK: **Print...** from the File Menu or from the Standard Toolbar, or TYPE:
   PLOT\<enter> to access the Print/Plot Configuration dialog box, Figure 8–1.

2. Follow the step-by-step information to make a printer plot of drawing CH7-EX1.

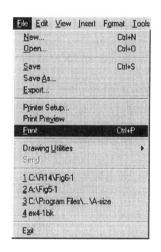

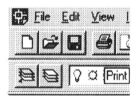

Device and Default Information

The text line in the Device and Default Information area shows the current plot device.
When the Device and Default Selection... button is clicked, a Device and Default Selection
dialog box appears, Figure 8–2. It has a list box that shows all the plot devices that are con-
figured to your computer. The device in the list box that is highlighted is the current plot
device. You can select the printing or plotting device that you want to use. Each time you
select a different device, the settings of the parameters change to the default for that device.

In the Configuration File Area of the Device and Default Selection dialog box you can
save and retrieve plot parameter settings. The Device Specific Configuration buttons
allow you to view additional configuration requirements or to change them.

STEP 1. Select the printer device that you will use.

If the text line does not show the correct printer, use the Device and Default Selection
dialog box to select the printer that you will use to print your drawing. If the correct

FIGURE 8–2
Device and Default Selection
Dialog Box

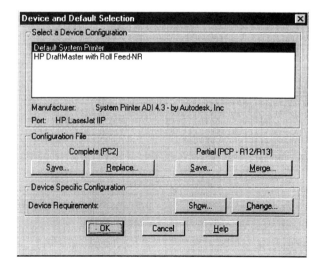

printer is not shown in the Device and Default Selection list, cancel the plot and configure AutoCAD for the correct printer. TYPE: **CONFIG<enter>**, then click the Printer tab to configure the printer or plotter.

Pen Parameters

Pens will be used and described in Exercise 8–2, when Exercise 5–1 is plotted on a plotter. You can change the width of lines on a printer by clicking the color in the Pen Assignments dialog box and changing the width in the Width: text box.

Additional Parameters: Specify the Part of the Drawing That Is to Be Plotted

A dialog box radio button is a button that is part of a group that are mutually exclusive—only one button in the group can be picked. The five radio buttons in the Additional Parameters area—Display, Extents, Limits, View, and Window—specify the part of the drawing that is to be printed, and only one can be selected at a time. When the button is selected, a black dot appears inside the button.

STEP 2. Specify the part of the drawing that is to be plotted.
Click the Limits radio button to select limits as the part of the drawing that is to be printed.

Display

This option plots the part of a drawing that is displayed on the screen at the time the plot is made.

Extents

This option plots the drawing extents. The drawing extents are whatever graphics are actually drawn, including any graphics that lie outside the limits of the drawing area.

Limits

You have chosen Limits as the part of the drawing to be plotted. This option plots the part of the drawing that lies within the drawing limits. The limits for drawing CH7-EX1 are 8-1/2,11.

View

This selection plots any view that has been named and saved as a result of using the View command. No view was named and saved for drawing CH7-EX1. If you have saved a view, pick the View... button (below the Window radio button) to use the View Name dialog box to select the named view.

Window

This selection allows you to pick two corners of a window and plot only the part of the drawing that is within the window. When the Window... button is clicked, it displays a Window Selection dialog box (Figure 8–3). Selecting the Pick< button on the Window Selection dialog box clears the dialog boxes so you can view your drawing and use your mouse to click the two corners of a window. AutoCAD then returns to the Print/Plot Configuration dialog box.

Additional Parameters: Text Resolution

Text Resolution sets the resolution, in dots per inch, of TrueType fonts (file extension .ttf) while plotting. To see examples of each TrueType font, open truetype.dwg drawing. Higher values increase resolution and decrease plotting speed. When TrueType fonts are used, print first using the default number, and then adjust the resolution as needed.

STEP 3. Setting Text Resolution.
TrueType fonts were not used, so do not change text resolution.

Additional Parameters: Check Buttons

There are five check buttons in the Additional Parameters area—Text Fill, Hide Lines, Adjust Area Fill, Plot to File, and Autospool. When the button is selected, a check appears inside the button. A check mark in the button indicates the mode is on.

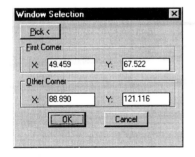

FIGURE 8–3
Window Selection Dialog Box

Text Fill

If the Text Fill button is checked, TrueType fonts will fill in when they are printed.

STEP 4. Setting Text Fill.

TrueType fonts were not used, so do not check the Text Fill Mode button.

Hide Lines

The Hide Lines check button refers to 3D objects only. When you use the Hide command, AutoCAD hides any surface of a drawing on the display screen that is behind another surface in 3D space. If you are working in 3D and want to do the same on your plot, you must turn this mode on so a check appears in it.

STEP 5. Setting Hide Lines.

Drawing CH7-EX1 is not 3D, so do not check the Hide Lines button.

Adjust Area Fill

The Adjust Area Fill check button is used in conjunction with the pen width. For example, if you check the button, all filled areas, such as solids, arrowheads, donuts, and wide polylines, will be drawn $\frac{1}{2}$ pen width smaller all around (with a .010 wide pen, that is .005). For most plotting applications this is not appropriate.

STEP 6. Setting Adjust Area Fill.

Do not check the Adjust Area Fill button.

Plot to File

STEP 7. Setting Plot to File.

If you do not check the Plot to File button, AutoCAD plots directly from your computer. If there is a cable leading from your computer to the printer or plotter, do not check the Plot to File button.

If you do check the Plot to File button, a file is created with the extension .PLT. Pick the File Name... button (just above the Cancel button) to see the Create Plot File dialog box (Figure 8–4) with the plot file name. The plot file may be copied onto a floppy disk or created on the floppy disk (add the drive information in front of the file name in the File Name: edit box) and carried to a plot station, where the plot is performed with a plotting software package. The plot station is often faster and more convenient and requires less expensive equipment than a computer dedicated to plotting .DWG drawing files. The plot file may also be created on the hard drive and sent via a network to the plot station.

Autospool

Sends a plot file to an assigned device for printing in the background while you continue working.

Paper Size and Orientation

The radio buttons Inches and MM allow you to select either inches or millimeters for specifying the paper size.

FIGURE 8–4
Create Plot File Dialog Box

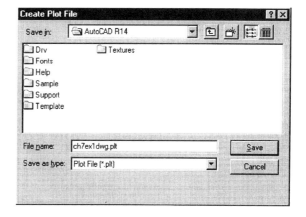

FIGURE 8–5
Paper Size Dialog Box

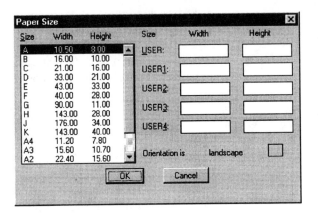

The text line below the MM button lists the current paper size selected. When the Size... button is picked, the Paper Size dialog box (Figure 8–5) appears. It lists the paper sizes the printer or plotter can accommodate; the current size is highlighted. An A or B displayed beside the size indicates a standard American National Standards Institute (ANSI) size area. You can enter a USER plotting size by entering the Width and Height in the USER: input boxes. The size then appears in the list box labeled USER.

If your printer naturally accepts an $8\frac{1}{2}'' \times 11''$ sheet of paper in the vertical position, that is a portrait orientation (not landscape); enter the paper size as 8.5 Width and 11 Height. If the size is entered as 11 Width and 8.5 Height, the printer cuts off the drawing graphics at $8\frac{1}{2}''$ on the 11'' height. You may specify a plotting size that is smaller than the actual paper size and then trim the paper.

STEP 8. Setting paper size and orientation.
Select the Inches radio button and enter 8.5'' Width $\times$ 11'' Height as the paper size, if your printer will accommodate more than one size. If your printer accepts only one size paper, click the Inches radio button and the paper size will be grayed out.

Scale, Rotation, and Origin: Determine the Plot Rotation

When the Rotation and Origin... button of the Print/Plot Configuration dialog box is clicked, the Plot Rotation and Origin dialog box (Figure 8–6) appears. AutoCAD allows you to rotate the drawing to change its orientation within the specified paper size.

Drawing CH7-EX1 does not need to be rotated because it has the same orientation as the 8.5'' $\times$ 11'' paper size entered in step 7. If drawing CH7-EX1 had limits of 11,8.5 it would be rotated 90°, to fit within the 8.5'' $\times$ 11'' paper size.

STEP 9. Set the plot rotation.
Set the plot rotation to 0.

Scale, Rotation, and Origin: Determine the Plot Origin

For a printer, the plot origin (0,0) is normally located in the upper left corner of the printer paper. A plot origin of 0,0 is a good place to start when you are making a print. If the drawing is not plotted in the desired location, changing the X Origin by $\frac{1}{2}''$ (for example, from 0.00 to 0.50) moves the print $\frac{1}{2}''$ to the right. Changing the Y Origin from 0.00 to 0.50 moves the plot $\frac{1}{2}''$ down from the upper left corner of the paper.

To verify the location of 0,0 and how the printer moves the origin of the plot, plot a simple drawing such as a border only. First, plot the drawing with a plot origin of 0,0. Second, change only the X Origin by $\frac{1}{2}''$ and replot. Third, change only the Y Origin by $\frac{1}{2}''$ and replot again. Keep careful notes as you vary the plot origin, and make a chart to be posted on the printer for future plots.

STEP 10. Set the plot origin.
Set the X and Y Origins to 0.

FIGURE 8–6
Plot Rotation and Origin Dialog
Box

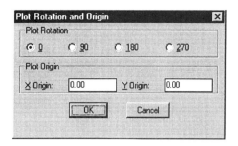

Scale, Rotation, and Origin: Specify the Plotting Scale

You can specify a plot drawing scale by entering the scale in the Plotted Inches = Drawing Units input buttons. Some basic calculations can help you determine the correct scale so that the drawing will fit within the specified paper size. To be able to measure a plotted drawing accurately using a scale, you must enter a specific plotting scale, such as the following:

1=1	(full size)	one plotted inch = 1 drawing unit
.5=1'	($\frac{1}{2}''$=1')	$\frac{1}{2}$ plotted inch = 1 foot on the drawing
.25=1'	($\frac{1}{4}''$=1')	$\frac{1}{4}$ plotted inch = 1 foot on the drawing
.125=1'	($\frac{1}{8}''$=1')	$\frac{1}{8}$ plotted inch = 1 foot on the drawing
.5=1	(half size)	$\frac{1}{2}$ plotted inch = 1 drawing inch
.75=1	($\frac{3}{4}$ size)	$\frac{3}{4}$ plotted inch = 1 drawing inch
1=4	($\frac{1}{4}$ size)	one plotted inch = 4 drawing inches
2=1	(twice size)	two plotted inches = 1 drawing inch

You can enter fractions in Architectural units, but AutoCAD shows the fraction in decimal units (Example: 1/2 = 12 defaults to .5 =1').

You may respond by checking the Scaled to Fit check box instead of entering a specific scale. When you check this box, AutoCAD scales the drawing as large as possible to fit the specified paper size.

STEP 11. Set the plotting scale.
TYPE: **1** Plotted Inches = **1** Drawing Units for plotting your drawing CH7-EX1.

Plot Preview

When you pick the Partial radio button and the Preview... button, the Preview Effective Plotting Area dialog box (Figure 8–7) appears. This allows you to preview the plot and, if any warnings appear, change the plotting parameters. A Partial preview shows only an outline of the effective plotting area of the drawing, while the Full preview shows the entire drawing.

FIGURE 8–7
Preview Effective Plotting
Area Dialog Box

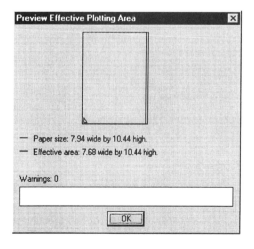

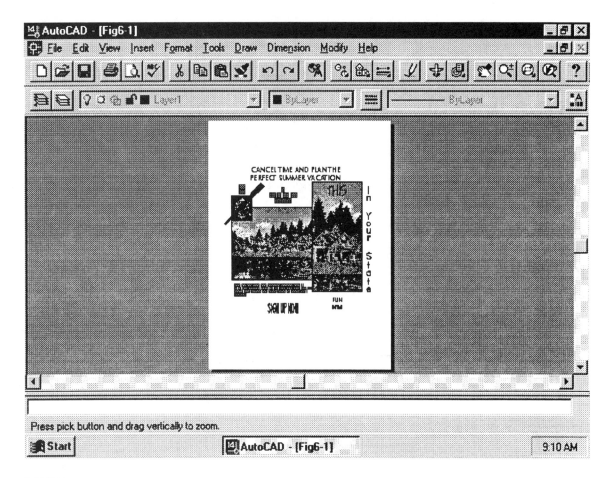

FIGURE 8–8
Full Plot Preview CH7-EX1

The effective plotting area, measured from the plot origin, is the actual size of the graphics to be plotted on the paper. If the maximum size for the printer is exceeded, Auto-CAD prompts in the Warnings area, "Plotting area truncated to maximum." If this warning appears, or if the effective plotting area appears too small, cancel the plot and recheck the drawing limits, or extents, and any layers that are off, and see how they relate to the plot parameters. Review the plot parameters that include the plot origin, paper size, plot rotation, and scale, and change them accordingly to get a successful plot.

STEP 12. Preview your plot.
Pick the Full preview radio button and preview your plot for CH7-EX1. It should look similar to Figure 8–8. If there is something wrong with the plot, press the spacebar to end the preview and make the necessary adjustments. If the preview looks OK, press the spacebar or <enter> to end the preview.

STEP 13. Complete the plot.
CLICK: **OK** on the Print/Plot Configuration dialog box. The printer plot proceeds from this point. Remove the completed plot from the printer and exit AutoCAD if you are finished with this session. If you have created a .PLT file, take your floppy disk to the plot station or send your plot via a network.

EXERCISE 8–2
Print/Plot Responses for Exercise 5–1

The following is a hands-on, step-by-step exercise to make a plotter plot of Exercise 5–1. To begin, turn on the computer and start AutoCAD. The Start Up dialog box is displayed.

Part II: Two-Dimensional AutoCAD

Open drawing CH5-EX1:

Prompt	Response
The Start Up dialog box is displayed:	**Insert the floppy disk containing the drawing, CH5-EX1, in drive A.**
	CLICK: **Open a Drawing button**
	DOUBLE CLICK: **A:\CH5-EX1.dwg**

Exercise CH5-EX1 is opened.

Save the drawing to the hard drive:

Prompt	Response
Command:	**SaveAs...**
The Save Drawing As dialog box is displayed:	CLICK: **[C:]** (and the correct folder if needed)
	CLICK: **Save**

Now you are working on the hard drive. Do not work on a floppy disk.

On Your Own

1. CLICK: **Print...** from the File menu or from the Standard Toolbar, or TYPE: **PLOT<enter>** to access the Print/Plot Configuration dialog box.
2. Follow the step-by-step information to make a plotter plot of drawing CH5-EX1.

Device and Default Information

STEP 1. Select the plotter device that you will use.
If the text line does not show the plotter device, use the Device and Default Selection dialog box to select the plotter that you will use to plot your drawing CH5-EX1.

Pen Parameters: Pen Assignments

When the Pen Assignments... button is picked, if your plotter supports multiple pens, a Pen Assignments dialog box (Figure 8–9) appears. Let's examine the meaning of the items in the dialog box, and then select pens for plotting drawing CH5-EX1.

Entity Color

The list box lists as many colors as your system supports. Each drawing entity has a color associated with it (such as the color associated with a layer). The Color portion of the chart cannot be changed. Each entity color may be plotted with a different pen number, plotter linetype, pen speed, and pen width, and those parameters can be changed.

FIGURE 8–9
Pen Assignments
Dialog Box

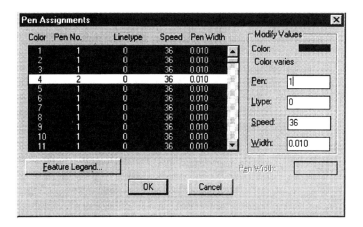

Pen No.

This is the number of the slot on the plotter's pen carousel. A pen of any color or width may be inserted into the slot. Any pen number may be used for any entity color. To change Pen No.s hold down the Ctrl key and click the lines you want to change, then click the Pen: edit box and change the Pen No., PRESS: <enter>. The following examples further describe how a pen is selected to draw an entity color.

Example 1

Place a thin black pen into the number 1 slot of the plotter's pen carousel. Change the pen numbers on the chart to read as follows:

Color	Pen No.
1 (red)	1
2 (yellow)	1
3 (green)	1
4 (cyan)	1
5 (blue)	1
6 (magenta)	1
7 (white)	1

RESULT: All the red, yellow, green, cyan, blue, magenta, and white lines on the drawing are plotted as thin black lines.

Example 2

Place a thin black pen in slot number 1 of the plotter's pen carousel and a thick black pen in slot number 2. Change the pen numbers on the pen chart to read:

Color	Pen No.
1 (red)	1
2 (yellow)	2
3 (green)	1
4 (cyan)	1
5 (blue)	1
6 (magenta)	1
7 (white)	1

RESULT: The yellow lines of your drawing are plotted with a thick black pen. All red, green, cyan, blue, magenta, and white lines are drawn with a thin black pen.

Linetype

Although most users do not change linetypes during plotting, this option allows you to do that. The plotter linetypes are listed 0 through 6 when you pick the Feature Legend... button. Do not combine entity linetypes (such as those associated with a layer) and plotter linetypes. Use a plotter linetype only if the entity linetype is CONTINUOUS. If the entity linetype is any linetype *other* than CONTINUOUS, use the plotter's continuous linetype, number 0.

Speed

Note: If you have a laser plotter, some of the information such as placing pens in a carousel does not apply.

Pen speed varies with the pen used and the paper or film on which the drawing is plotted. AutoCAD normally starts with the fastest pen speed. You will need to test the speed for your situation, and if the pen skips or moves too quickly, you can slow the pen speed.

Pen Width

The pen width setting is not a concern when you are plotting on a pen plotter. When you are plotting on a laser printer or plotter pen, widths can be varied based on the color of the lines on your drawing. A pen width of .003 will give you very thin lines. A pen width of .03 will give you much thicker lines. Vary pen widths between .003 and .03 for a variety of line widths to provide interest in your drawings. Be sure to convert a metric mea-

     Part II: Two-Dimensional AutoCAD

surement on any pen to an inches measurement before setting the pen width when you are using the inch unit.

Modify Values

Pick and highlight the item or items you want to change from the list box. Use the edit boxes in the Modify Values area to change the values of the pen number, linetype, pen speed, or pen width.

STEP 2. Select the pens for your drawing.
For drawing CH5-EX1, the following Layers were used:

LAYER NAME	COLOR	LINETYPE
Walls	White	Continuous
Furniture	Red	Continuous

Determine the pens you have available and select two slots in the plotter's carousel (Examples: 1 and 2). Insert two different colors or widths of pens in the two slots. Set the two different pen numbers for Color 1—red (Example: Pen No. 1) and Color 7—white (Example: Pen No. 2). Keep Linetype set at 0, continuous line for both colors.

Pen Parameters: Optimization

When this button is clicked, the Optimizing Pen Motion dialog box appears (Figure 8–10). The check boxes show different levels of optimizing pen motion (minimizing wasted pen motion) and reducing plotting time.

STEP 3. Setting pen optimization.
Do not change any of the Optimizing Pen Motion check boxes.

FIGURE 8–10
Optimizing Pen Motion Dialog Box

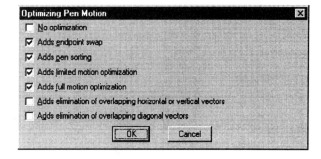

Additional Parameters

STEP 4. Specify the part of the drawing that is to be plotted.
Click the Limits radio button to select limits as the part of the drawing that is to be printed.

STEP 5. Setting Text Resolution.
TrueType fonts were not used, so do not change text resolution.

STEP 6. Setting Text Fill.
TrueType fonts were not used, so do not check the Text Fill button.

STEP 7. Setting Hide Lines.
Drawing CH5-EX1 is not 3D, so do not check the Hide Lines button.

STEP 8. Setting Adjust Area Fill.
Do not check the Adjust Area Fill button.

STEP 9. Setting Plot to File.
If you have a plot station, check the Plot to File check button.

Paper Size and Orientation

STEP 10. Setting paper size and orientation.

Select the Inches radio button and click the Size... button. Click the A size, 10.50 Width, 8.00 Height paper size in the Paper Size dialog box.

The list box in the Paper Size dialog box lists the paper sizes the plotter can accommodate and highlights the current selection. When these sizes match the ANSI standard size paper, the size is shown as A, B, C, D, or E. The MAX size is the maximum size the plotter can plot. When a plotting size is entered that is different from the MAX or standard ANSI plotting sizes for your plotter, it will appear in the list box labeled USER:.

The ANSI standard sheet sizes for paper are as follows:

Size	Width	Height
A	11	8.5
B	17	11
C	22	17
D	34	22
E	44	34

The sheet sizes listed in the list box may reflect the standard ANSI sheet sizes reduced by ¼″ to ½″. This is because the rollers that grip the plotter paper use this space and reduce the plotting size accordingly.

Many users specify a plotting size that is larger than the actual plotting size the drawing requires. That allows a drawing with an effective plotting area that is touching the boundaries of the smaller paper size to be plotted without interference from the rollers that grip the plotter paper. The paper is then trimmed to the smaller standard sheet size.

If you are using a standard Architectural paper size, you must enter that size in the USER: edit boxes. Standard Architectural sheet sizes are as follows:

Size	Width	Height
A	12	9
B	18	12
C	24	18
D	36	24
E	48	36

A new plotting size is usually entered using the landscape paper orientation. If your plotter allows you to insert the paper in the plotter in only the vertical orientation, test the 0,0 location to verify that the plotter automatically changes the X-Y direction and the 0,0 location accordingly.

Scale, Rotation, and Origin: Determine the Plot Rotation

STEP 11. Set the plot rotation.

Set the plot rotation to 90.

Scale, Rotation, and Origin: Determine the Plot Origin

For a plotter plot, the plot origin (0,0) is normally located in the lower left corner of the paper, assuming a horizontal paper orientation (for example, 11,8 1/2). Changing the X Origin by 1″ moves the plot 1″ to the right. Changing the Y Origin by 1″ moves the plot 1″ up from the home position. Changing the X Origin to −1″ moves the plot 1″ to the left. Changing the Y Origin to −1″ moves the plot 1″ down.

STEP 12. Set the plot origin.

Set the X and Y Origins to 0.

Scale, Rotation, and Origin: Specify the Plotting Scale

STEP 13. Set the plotting scale.

TYPE: **.25** Plotted Inches = **1′** (be sure to include the foot mark after the 1) Drawing Units for plotting your drawing CH5-EX1.

Plot Preview

STEP 14. Preview your plot.

Pick the Full preview radio button and preview your plot for CH5-EX1. It should look similar to Figure 8–11. If there is something wrong with the plot, PRESS: **<enter>** to end the preview and make the necessary adjustments. If the preview looks OK, PRESS: **<enter>** to end the preview.

STEP 15. Complete the plot.

CLICK: **OK** on the Print/Plot Configuration dialog box. The plotter plot proceeds from this point. If you have not created a plot file, remove the completed plot from the plotter and exit AutoCAD if you are finished with this session. If you have created a .PLT file, take your floppy disk to the plot station or send your plot via a network.

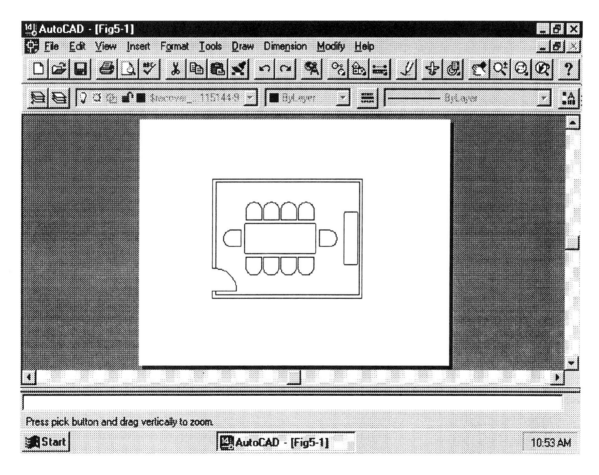

FIGURE 8–11
Full Plot Preview CH5-EX1

REVIEW QUESTIONS

1. A printer plot may not be performed while the drawing is active (displayed on the screen).
   a. True
   b. False

2. Which of the following pull-down menus contains the Print... command?
   a. File
   b. Data
   c. Options
   d. Tools
   e. Service

3. Which of the following will produce a plot of the screen display only?
   a. Display
   b. Extents
   c. Limits
   d. View
   e. Window

4. Which of the following will produce a plot of the entire drawing, even if part of it is outside the limits?
   a. Display
   b. Extents
   c. Limits
   d. View
   e. Window

5. A plot file has which of the following extensions?
   a. .BAK
   b. .DWG
   c. .PLT
   d. .CFK
   e. .PWD

6. A plot that shows only half of what should have been plotted could probably be corrected by doing which of the following?
   a. Moving the origin .5
   b. Selecting View instead of Extents
   c. Rotating the plot 90°
   d. Writing the plot to a file
   e. Selecting a smaller page size

7. The question "remove hidden lines?" on the plot routine refers to which of the following?
   a. 3D objects
   b. Isometric drawings
   c. Hidden linetypes
   d. 2D objects
   e. Slide files

8. A drawing that is to be plotted so that it fits on a particular size sheet without regard to the scale requires which scale response?
   a. 1 = 1
   b. Full
   c. 1 = 2
   d. Scaled to Fit
   e. MAX

9. A drawing that is to be plotted at a scale of $\frac{1''}{4} = 1'$ should use which scale response?
   a. Full
   b. FIT
   c. 48 = 1
   d. .25 = 1'
   e. $\frac{1}{4} = 1$

10. For a plotter plot, the plot origin (0,0) is normally located in the
    a. Upper right corner of the paper
    b. Lower left corner of the paper
    c. Lower right corner of the paper
    d. Upper left corner of the paper

11. If a pen plotter has a thick pen in slot 2 and a thin pen in slot 1, which pen numbers should be selected for each of the drawing lines shown? Write 1 or 2 in the Pen No. blank.

Color	Width	Pen No.
Red	Thick	_____
Blue	Thin	_____
Yellow	Thick	_____
Cyan	Thin	_____

12. If red lines on the drawing should be plotted red, blue lines plotted blue, and white lines plotted black, which pens should be placed in the plotter slots? Fill in red, blue, or black in the correct plotter pen slots.

Color	Pen No.	Plotter Slot
Red	1	1 _____
Blue	2	2 _____
White	3	3 _____

13. Which radio button must be selected to make sure you plot the entire drawing even if part of it is outside the drawing limits?

_____

14. Give the plotting scale needed to plot a drawing twice the size it was drawn.

Plotted Inches = **Drawing Units**

_____ _____

15. Give the plotting scale needed to plot a drawing at $\frac{1}{2}$ size.

Plotted Inches = **Drawing Units**

_____ _____

16. Give the plotting scale needed to plot a drawing at a scale of $\frac{1}{8}'' = 1'$.

Plotted Inches = **Drawing Units**

_____ _____

17. Describe the major function of the Device and Default Selection button.

_____

_____

18. Describe how "Pen width" and "Adjust Area Fill" are related.

_____

_____

_____

_____

19. List the five radio buttons that specify the part of the drawing that is to be printed or plotted.

1. _____

2. _____

3. _____

4. _____

5. _____

20. List the size name, width, and height of standard architectural sheet sizes.

1. _____

2. _____

3. _____

4. _____

5. _____

9 Drawing the Floor Plan: Walls, Doors, and Windows

OBJECTIVES

When you have completed this chapter, you will be able to:

☐ Correctly use the following commands and settings:

Base	Edit Multiline	List	Named Views
Block-Make...	Extend	MINSERT	Properties...
Change	Insert-Block...	Multiline	Status
Color	Linetype	Multiline Style...	Wblock

THE TENANT SPACE PROJECT

The Polyline or Multiline commands can be used to draw walls quickly. Polyline was described and used in Chapter 5. With Polyline, solid walls are drawn. With Multiline, walls with up to 16 lines are drawn. Exercise 9–1 contains step-by-step instructions for using Multiline to draw the exterior and interior walls of a tenant space that is located in the northwest corner of a building. The exercise also contains step-by-step instructions for inserting windows and doors into the plan.

Chapters 10 through 13 provide step-by-step instructions to complete the tenant space project started in Chapter 9. Each chapter will use the building plan drawn in Chapter 9 to complete a part of the project as described next.

Chapter 10: The tenant space is dimensioned and the square feet calculated.

Chapter 11: Elevations, sections, and details are drawn.

Chapter 12: Furniture is drawn, attributes are assigned (furniture specifications), and the furniture is added to the plan.

Chapter 13: The reflected ceiling plan and power plan are drawn.

EXERCISE 9–1
Tenant Space Floor Plan

When you have completed Exercise 9–1, the tenant space floor plan, your drawing will look similar to Figure 9–1. To prepare to draw Exercise 9–1, turn on the computer and start AutoCAD. The Start Up dialog box is displayed.

1. CLICK: **Use a Wizard**

2. CLICK: **Quick Setup**

   CLICK **OK**

3. Set drawing Units: **Architectural**

   CLICK: **Next>>**

4. Set drawing Width: **75′** x Length: **65′**

   CLICK: **Done**

5. **Use SaveAs... to save the drawing on the hard drive with the name CH9-EX1.**

6. Set Grid: **12″**

7. Set SNAP: **6″**

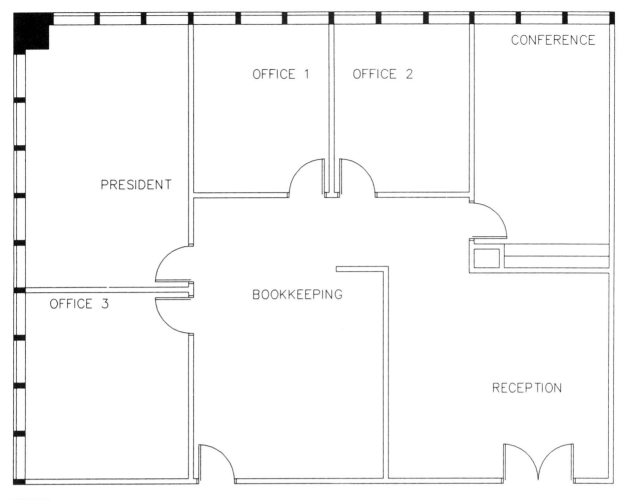

FIGURE 9–1
Exercise 9–1: Tenant Space Floor Plan (Scale: $\frac{1}{8}'' = 1'\text{-}0''$)

8. Create the following Layers:

LAYER NAME	COLOR	LINETYPE
A-area	White	Continuous
A-clng	Green	Continuous
A-door	Yellow	Continuous
A-flor-iden	White	Continuous
A-flor-wdwk	White	Continuous
A-furn	Magenta	Continuous
A-glaz	White	Continuous
A-pflr-dims	Cyan	Continuous
A-wall-ext	Blue	Continuous
A-wall-int	Red	Continuous
E-comm	Green	Continuous
E-lite	White	Continuous
E-powr	White	Continuous

The layers listed include those that will be used in Chapters 10, 12, and 13. The layer names are based on the guidelines provided by the document *CAD LAYER GUIDELINES Recommended Designations for Architecture, Engineering, and Facility Management Computer-Aided Design*, prepared by the Task Force on CAD Layer Guidelines.

9. Set Layer A-wall-ext current.

10. Use **Zoom-All** to view the limits of the drawing.

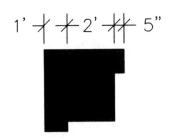

FIGURE 9-2
Use the 2D Solid Command to
Draw the Corner Column and Two
Mullions

2D SOLID

The 2D Solid command was described in Chapter 4. The following part of Exercise 9–1 used the 2D Solid command to draw the window mullions and the 3'-square corner column located in the northwest corner of the tenant space.

Use 2D Solid to draw the 3'-square corner column (Figure 9–2):

Prompt	Response
Command:	**2D Solid** (or TYPE: **SO<enter>**)
First point:	TYPE: **17',51'<enter>**
Second point:	TYPE: **@3'<0<enter>**
Third point:	TYPE: **@-3',-3'<enter>**
Fourth point:	TYPE: **@3'<0<enter>**
Third point:	**<enter>**

On Your Own

Zoom in close around the column, and use the 2D Solid command to draw the two separate mullions (5″ × 12″) that are on the east and south sides of the column just drawn, as shown in Figure 9–2.

ARRAY

The Array command was described in Chapter 5. The following part of Exercise 9–1 uses the Array command to draw the window mullions on the north and west exterior walls.

Use Array to finish drawing the mullions on the north exterior wall (Figure 9–3):

Prompt	Response
Command:	**Array** (or TYPE: **AR<enter>**)
Select objects:	**Click the mullion located on the east side of the column.**
Select objects: 1 found	
Select objects:	**<enter>**
Rectangular or Polar array (R/P):	TYPE: **R<enter>**
Number of rows (---) <default>:	TYPE: **1<enter>**
Number of columns (I I I) <default>:	TYPE: **13<enter>**
Distance between columns (I I I):	TYPE: **4'<enter>**

On Your Own

1. Use the Array command to draw the remaining mullions on the west exterior wall, as shown in Figure 9–3. Specify 10 rows, 1 column, and −4' distance between rows.

2. Next, you will draw the walls using Multiline after you set Multiline Style.... It is helpful if the column and mullions are not solid. Set FILL OFF and regenerate the drawing so that the columns and mullions are not solid.

3. Zoom-Extents to see the entire drawing.

MULTILINE STYLE...

With the column and mullions now completed, you are ready to use Multiline to draw the walls. The Multiline Style... dialog box allows you to make the settings necessary to draw up to 16 lines at the same time with the Multiline command. You can specify color and linetype for any of the 16 lines as well as the background color and endcaps for each multiline. You must add the name of the multiline style to the list of current styles before you can draw with it.

Next, you will use Multiline Style... to make the settings for the north exterior wall of the tenant space. You will have one line at 0, one at 9″, and one at 12″ (the 3″ glass line is offset 3″ from the outside line of the 12″ wall).

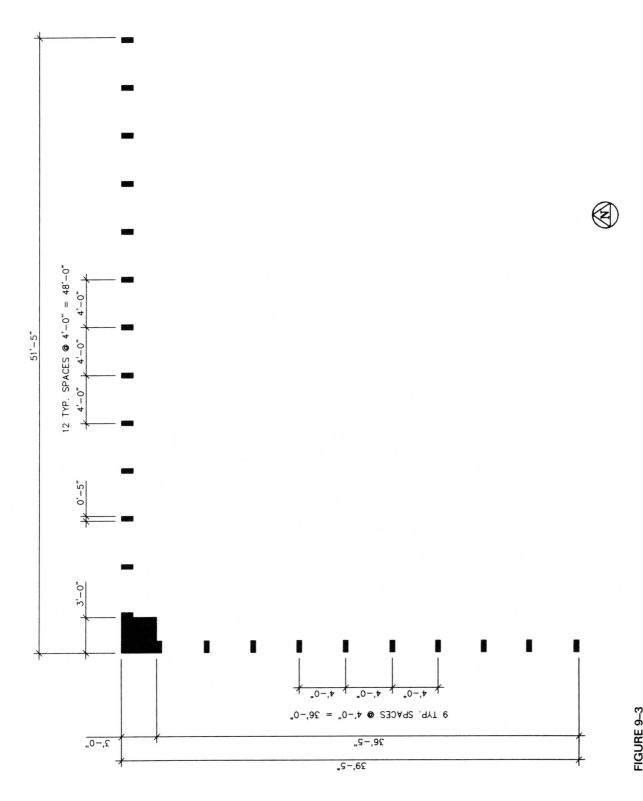

FIGURE 9–3
Use the Array Command to Finish Drawing the Mullions (Scale: 1/8″ = 1′-0″)

159

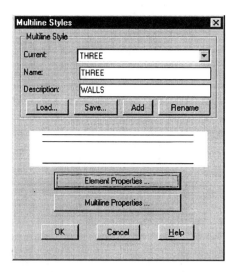

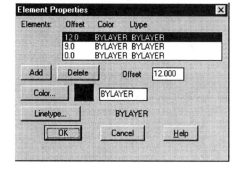

FIGURE 9–4
Multiline Style Named THREE

FIGURE 9–5
Element Properties with Offsets of 0, 9, and 12″

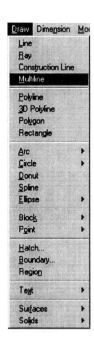

Use Multiline Style... to set a three-line wall that is 12″ thick with a 3″ glass line (Figures 9–4 and 9–5):

Prompt	Response
Command:	**Multiline Style...** (or TYPE: **MLSTYLE<enter>**)
The Multiline Styles dialog box appears (Figure 9–4):	Highlight: **STANDARD** in the Name: button and TYPE: **THREE** as shown in Figure 9–4
	CLICK: the **Description: input button** and TYPE: **WALLS**
	CLICK: **Add** to make the style current
	CLICK: **Element Properties...**
The Element Properties dialog box appears:	HIGHLIGHT: **0.500** in the Offset input button and TYPE: **9**
	CLICK: **Add**
	HIGHLIGHT: **0.000** in the Offset input button and TYPE: **12**
	CLICK: **Add**
	Do you have a scroll bar in the Elements list box that indicates more lines? If so, scroll down to look. If you have a -0.5 offset, CLICK: **−.05** in the list and CLICK: **Delete** to delete an unnecessary offset

You should now have a 12.0, a 9.0, and 0.0 in the Element Properties list as shown in Figure 9–5 and nothing else—no scroll bar to the right indicating more lines. You could now assign colors and linetypes to the lines. If you do not assign colors or linetypes, the lines will assume the color and linetype of the layer on which the multilines are drawn. Leave colors and linetypes assigned by layer so you can look at the drawing and see which layers they are on.

Part II: Two-Dimensional AutoCAD

Prompt	Response
	CLICK: **OK**
The Multiline Styles dialog box appears:	CLICK: **OK**

MULTILINE

The Multiline prompt is "Justification/Scale/Style/<From point>:". The Multiline command uses the current Multiline Style to draw up to 16 lines with or without endcaps at the same time.

Style

You can set any style current that has been defined with the Multiline Style... command if it is not already current (TYPE: **ST<enter>** then TYPE: **the style name<enter>** and begin drawing).

Justification

This option allows you to select Top, Zero, or Bottom lines to begin drawing multilines. The default is Top. In this case Zero and Bottom are the same because there are no negative offsets. If you have a positive 3 offset, a 0, and a negative 3 offset, your three lines will be drawn from the middle line with justification set to 0.

Scale

This option allows you to set the scale at which lines will be drawn. If your multiline style has a 10 offset, a 6 offset, and a 0, and you set the scale at .5, the lines will be drawn 5 and 3″ apart. The same style with a scale of 2 draws lines 20 and 12″ apart.

FIGURE 9–6
Use Multiline to Draw Exterior Walls with the Multiline Styles THREE, THREE-WEST, and TWO (Scale: $\frac{1}{8}″ = 1'\text{-}0″$)

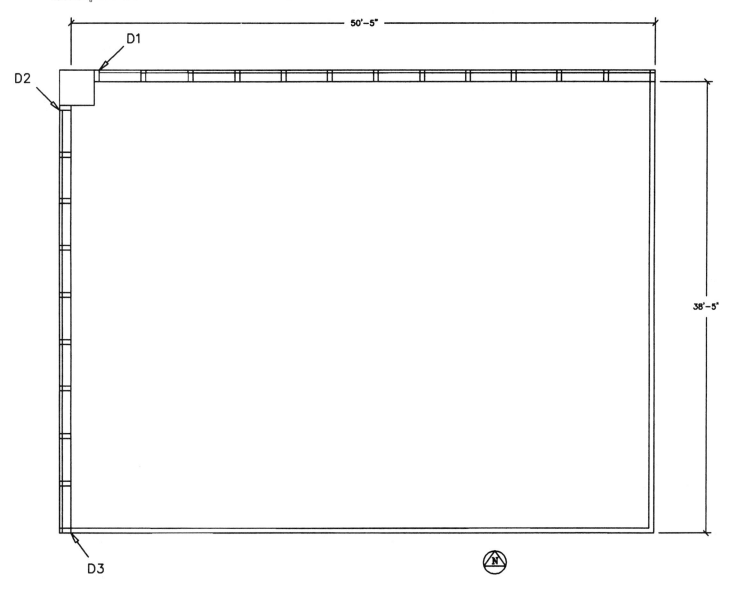

Use Multiline to draw the north exterior wall of the tenant space (Figure 9–6):

Prompt	Response
Command:	**Multiline** (or TYPE: **ML\<enter>**)
Justification/Scale/STyle/\<From point>:	TYPE: **INT\<enter>**
INT of	**D1**
\<To point>:	**Turn ORTHO ON. Move your mouse to the right** and TYPE: **48'\<enter>**
Undo/\<To point>:	**\<enter>**

On Your Own (Figures 9–6, 9–7, and 9–8)

1. Set a new multiline style with the name THREE-WEST; Description, Walls, and off-sets of 0, 3, and 12 (Figure 9–7).

2. Use Multiline with a justification of bottom to draw the west wall of the tenant space with the THREE-WEST multiline style. Use Osnap-Intersection and CLICK: **D2** (Figure 9–6) to start the multiline and make the line 36' long (subtract 2'5" from the dimension on the right side of Figure 9–6 to account for the 3'-square corner column and the 5" mullion).

3. Set a new multiline style with the name TWO; Description, INTERIOR WALLS, and offsets of 0 and 5 (Figure 9–8).

4. Use Multiline with a justification of bottom to draw the south and east walls of the tenant space. Use Osnap-Intersection and CLICK: **D3** (Figure 9–6) and make the line to the right 50'5" and the line up 38'5".

5. Next, draw the interior walls. Remember to use transparent Zoom commands to move to different parts of the drawing while in the Multiline command. TYPE: **'Z** from the keyboard and press enter. An apostrophe (') must precede the **Z** or use the Zoom commands from the new menu in the menu bar.

Use Multiline with the Multiline Style TWO to draw 5"-wide horizontal and vertical interior walls inside the tenant space. Keep layer A-WALL=EXT current. The layer on which the interior walls are drawn will be changed to A-WALL-INT in this exercise with the Properties... command (Figure 9–9):

Prompt	Response
Command:	**Multiline** (or TYPE: **ML\<enter>**)
Justification/Scale/STyle/\<From point>:	**Osnap-Intersection**

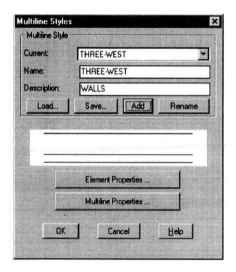

FIGURE 9–7
Set a New Multiline Style Named
THREE-WEST

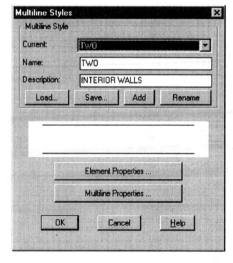

FIGURE 9–8
Set a New Multiline Style Named TWO

Part II: Two-Dimensional AutoCAD

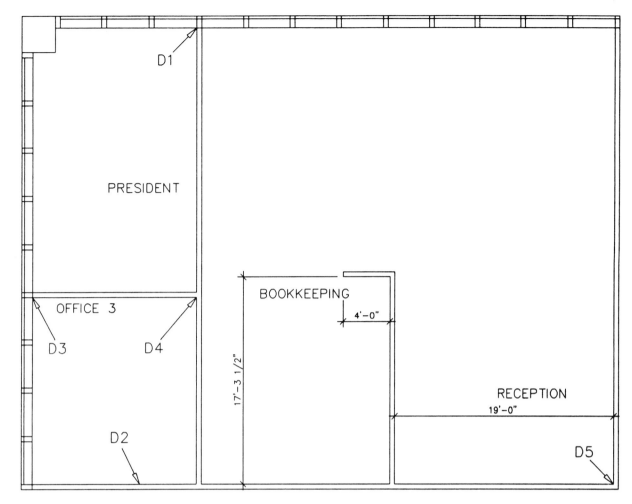

FIGURE 9–9
Use Multiline to Draw Interior Walls (Scale: $\frac{1}{8}''$ = 1'-0")

Prompt	Response
of	CLICK: **D1** (Figure 9–9)
<To point>:	**Osnap-Perpendicular**
To	**D2**
Undo/<To point>:	**<enter>**
Command:	**<enter>**
Justification/Scale/STyle/<From point>:	**Osnap-Intersection**
of	**D3**
<To point>:	**Osnap-Perpendicular**
To	**D4**
<To point>:	**<enter>**(the intersections will be edited later)

Set a new multiline style that uses the settings of the TWO style but adds an end cap at the end of the line. Then use Multiline and Osnap-From to draw the wall that separates the reception and bookkeeping areas (Figures 9–9 and 9–10):

Prompt	Response
Command:	**Multiline Style...**
The Multiline Styles dialog box appears:	DOUBLE CLICK: **Name: TWO** and TYPE: **TWO-CAP-END**

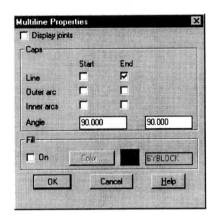

FIGURE 9–10
Multiline with End Cap

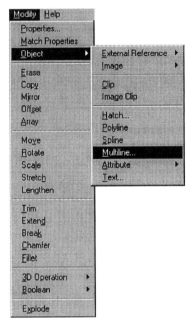

	CLICK: **Add**
	CLICK: **Multiline Properties**
The Multiline Properties dialog box appears:	In the caps area CLICK: **End** on the Line row so a check appears in it as shown in Figure 9–10.
	CLICK: **OK**
The Multiline Styles dialog box appears:	CLICK: **OK**
Command:	TYPE: **ML<enter>**
Justification/Scale/STyle/<From point>:	**Osnap-From**
Base point:	**Osnap-Endpoint**
Endp of	**D5**
<Offset>:	TYPE: **@19′5<180**
<To point>:	**Turn ORTHO ON. Move your mouse up** and TYPE: **17′3-1/2<enter>**
Undo/<To point>:	**Move your mouse to the left** and TYPE: **4′<enter>**
Close/Undo/<To point>:	**<enter>**

Tip: Use Zoom-Window, Zoom-Dynamic, and Zoom-Previous often to zoom in on parts of the drawing you are working on; drawing is easier, and you will be more accurate.

EDIT MULTLINE

The Edit Multiline command allows you to change the intersections of multilines in a variety of ways as shown in Figure 9–9. Just CLICK: the change you want, CLICK: **OK**, and then CLICK: the two multilines whose intersection you want to change.

Use Edit Multiline to trim the intersections of the multilines forming the interior walls to an Open Tee (Figures 9–11 and 9–12).

Prompt	Response
Command:	**Edit Multiline** (or TYPE: **MLEDIT<enter>**)
The Multiline Edit Tools dialog box appears:	CLICK: **Open Tee**
	CLICK: **OK**

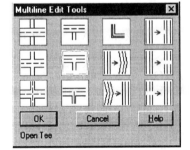

FIGURE 9–11
Edit Multiline Open Tee

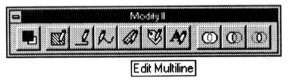

Edit Multiline

Part II: Two-Dimensional AutoCAD

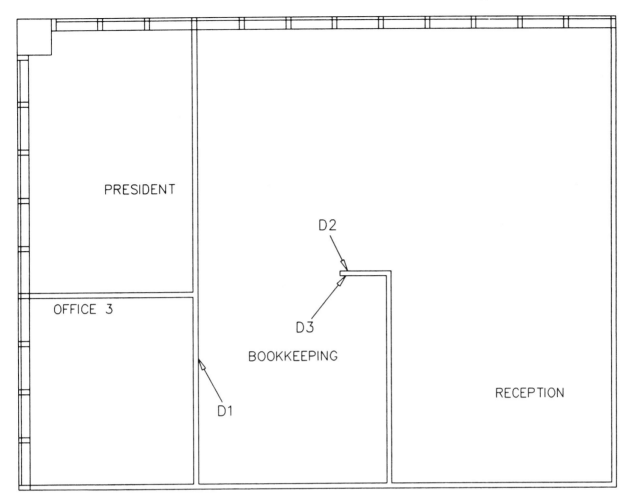

FIGURE 9–12
Practice Using the Extend Command (Scale: $\frac{1''}{8}$ = 1′-0″)

Select first mline:	CLICK: **the vertical wall separating the reception and bookkeeping areas**
Select second mline:	CLICK: **the south horizontal exterior wall**
Select first mline (or Undo):	CLICK: **the interior vertical wall of office 3**
Select second mline:	CLICK: **the south horizontal exterior wall**
Select first mline (or Undo):	CLICK: **the interior horizontal wall of the president's office**
Select second mline:	CLICK: **the interior vertical wall of the president's office**
Select first mline (or Undo):	**<enter>**

EXTEND

The Extend command allows you to lengthen an existing line or arc segment to meet a specified boundary edge. You will find it very useful when drawing walls. In the following part of this exercise, a boundary edge will be selected, and the horizontal wall of the bookkeeping area will be extended. The Undo option will then be used to erase it.

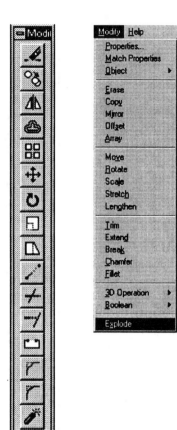

Practice using the Extend command, and then undo the practice session. You must first Explode the Multilines using the Explode command to make the separate lines. (Figure 9–12):

Prompt	Response
Command:	**Explode** (or TYPE: **X\<enter>**)
Select objects:	**D1**
Select objects:	**D2**
Select objects:	**\<enter>**
Command:	**Extend** (or TYPE: **EX\<enter>**)
Select boundary edge(s)...	
Select objects:	**D1**
Select objects: 1 found	
Select objects:	**\<enter>**
\<Select object to extend>/Project/Edge/Undo:	**D2**
\<Select object to extend>/Project/Edge/Undo:	**D3**
\<Select object to extend>/Project/Edge/Undo:	**\<enter>**

The points D2 and D3 were picked close to the left end of the line segment because the selected line (or arc) is extended from the end closest to the point picked. If the boundary edge does not intersect the entity to be extended, the prompt "Entity does not intersect an edge" appears.

On Your Own

After examining how precisely the lines are extended to meet the selected boundary edge, use the Undo command to erase the practice session.

CHANGE

The Change command can be used to change six properties—Color, Elevation, Layer, Linetype, Linetype scale, and Thickness—of an entity. You are familiar with the Color, Layer, and Linetype properties. The Elevation and Thickness properties, used in drawing basic three-dimensional models, is discussed in Chapter 17.

On Your Own

Before using the Change command, explode the outside wall line of the exterior north and west walls of the tenant space.

Use the Change command to change the layer property of the glass line from the A-wall layer to the A-glaz layer:

Prompt	Response
Command:	TYPE: **CHANGE\<enter>**
Select objects:	**Click any points on both glass lines (the middle line on the north and west walls).**
Select objects: 1 found	
Select objects: 1 found	
Select objects:	**\<enter>**
Properties/\<Change point>:	TYPE: **P\<enter>**
Change what property (Color/Elev/LAyer/LType/ltScale/Thickness)?	TYPE: **LA\<enter>**
New layer \<A-WALL-EXT>:	TYPE: **A-GLAZ\<enter>**
Change what property (Color/Elev/LAyer/LType/ltScale/Thickness)?	**\<enter>**

Part II: Two-Dimensional AutoCAD

The prompts for changing the Color and Linetype properties of any entity are the same as for changing the Layer property. To keep your drawing simple, do not mix multiple colors and linetypes within one layer. It is best to create a new layer with the desired linetypes and colors and change the layer property of the entity.

Change <Change point>

In Chapter 7, we examined the <Change point> option of the change command with regard to text. This option can also be used to move an endpoint of a line to a new location or to change the radius of a circle.

If a line is picked when the "Select objects:" prompt appears, the endpoint closest to the point picked is moved to the new point picked when the "Properties/<Change point>:" prompt appears. If a circle is picked when the "Select objects:" prompt appears, the radius of the circle is changed to pass through the new point picked when the "Properties/<Change point>:" prompt appears.

PROPERTIES...

The Properties... command allows you to change the properties of existing objects. Auto-CAD displays a different dialog box depending on the object selected. There are dialog boxes for lines, polylines, arcs, circles text, 3D objects, dimensions, and many others.

Use the Properties... command to change the layer of the interior walls from the A-wall-ext layer to the A-wall-int layer.

Prompt	Response
Command:	**Properties...**
Select objects:	**Use a crossing window to select all the interior walls.**
Select objects:	**<enter>**
The Change Properties dialog box appears:	CLICK: **Layer...**
The Select Layer dialog box appears:	CLICK: **A-wall-int**
	CLICK: **OK**
The Change Properties dialog box appears:	CLICK: **OK**

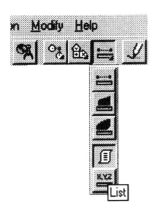

LIST

After you have changed the property of an entity and would like to confirm the change, or if you need additional information about an entity, using the List command is very helpful. The List command provides a screen display of the data stored for an entity.

Use the List command to examine the data stored for one line of an interior wall:

Prompt	Response
Command:	**List** (or TYPE: **LIST<enter>**)
Select objects:	**Click only one line of an interior wall.** **<enter>**

Depending on the type of entity selected, the List command displays data information for the entity. For the line selected, this data information includes the Layer on which the line is drawn, the length of the line, and its position relative to the current UCS. If several entities are selected, the list can become very long. Use Esc to cancel the listing and return to the Command: prompt when the listing is longer than needed.

STATUS

The Status command reports the current values of many of the defaults, modes, and extents used by AutoCAD.

Use the Status command to examine the Status Report for your drawing:

Prompt	Response
Command:	TYPE: **STATUS<enter>**
The Status Report appears,	
—Press RETURN for more—	**<enter>**
Command:	PRESS: **F2** (flip screen)

COLOR

Set color bylayer

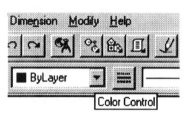

We have discussed and used the entity property of Color as determined by the color assigned to a Layer. This is controlling the entity color "bylayer". The entity is drawn with a layer current and inherits the color assigned to the layer. The Color command sets the color for drawing entities. The Color command prompt (TYPE: **color<enter>**) is "New/object/color <default>:". When BYLAYER is typed and entered, the entities subsequently drawn inherit the color of the layer on which they are drawn.

Set color individually

The color property of entities can also be set individually. When a color, such as red, is selected from the Object Properties toolbar, or typed and entered to the "New object color <default>:" prompt, the entities subsequently drawn inherit the color property red. The entities will be red regardless of the layer that is current when they are drawn.

To keep your drawing simple, do not mix the two methods of setting color. When a new color is needed, create a layer and assign the new color to that layer.

Set color byblock

Tip: If everything you draw is one color regardless of the layer it is drawn on, check the color setting, and set it to bylayer.

When you have completed drawing the interior walls of the tenant space, you will draw the doors and insert them into the walls. The Wblock command will be used to make blocks of the two different types of doors used in the tenant space. Blocks can be stored on a floppy disk or hard disk and recalled and inserted into a drawing. Thus you can create a library of often used parts, such as doors, windows, and furniture, using the Wblock command.

Most library parts that are blocks need to be drawn on the 0 Layer, which is the same as setting the color property to by ByBlock. The reason for this is explained in the following examples.

Example 1

A door (library part) is drawn on a Layer named DOOR that is assigned the color property red, and a Wblock is made of the door. The door block is inserted into a new project. Because the block was originally drawn on a layer named DOOR (color red) the layer name is dragged into the new drawing layer listing, and the door will be red, regardless of the layer current in the new drawing.

Example 2

A door (library part) is drawn on the 0 Layer. A Wblock is made of the door. The door Wblock is inserted into a new project. Because the block was originally drawn on the 0 Layer, the door is generated on the drawing's current layer and inherits all properties of that layer.

Before any drawing entity that will be used as a block is drawn, you need to decide how it will be used in future drawings; that will determine the color property that it is assigned.

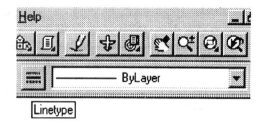

Part II: Two-Dimensional AutoCAD

LINETYPE

When the Linetype command is typed and entered or selected from the Object Properties toolbar, the Linetype tab of the Layer & Linetype Properties dialog box appears. Similar to the Color command, the linetype property can be set to bylayer, individually, or byblock. Most library parts that are blocks should be drawn on the 0 Layer, which is the same as setting the linetype to byblock. When inserted as a block, they will inherit the linetype of the current layer.

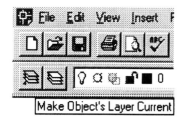

MAKE OBJECT'S LAYER CURRENT

This is another command that is very useful on the Object Properties toolbar. When you activate this command and pick any object, the layer that object is on becomes current.

On Your Own

1. Set Layer A-wall-int current. Use Multiline with the correct Multiline Style current to finish drawing the interior walls of the tenant space. Use the dimensions shown in Figure 9–13. Remember that you can use the Modify commands (Extend, Trim, Edit Multiline, and so on) to fix the Multiline.

2. Set FILL ON and regenerate the drawing.

3. Set 0 as the current layer. Use the dimensions shown in Figure 9–14 to draw the two door types—single door and double door—that will be defined as blocks and inserted

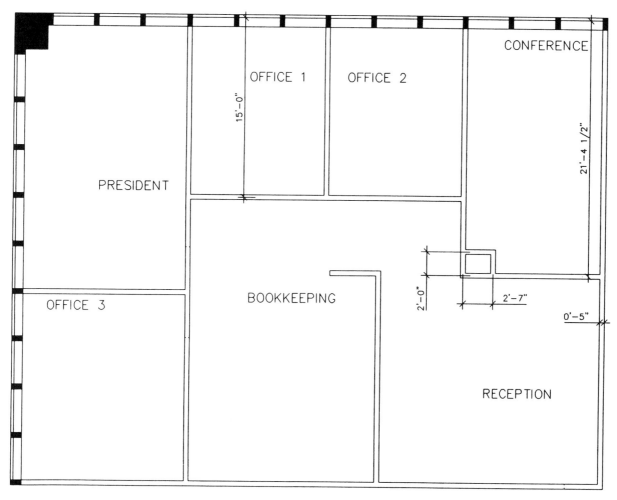

FIGURE 9–13
Use Multiline to Finish Drawing the Interior Walls (Scale: $\frac{1}{8}'' = 1'\text{-}0''$)

FIGURE 9–14
Two Door Types That Will Be Defined As Blocks and Inserted into the Tenant Space

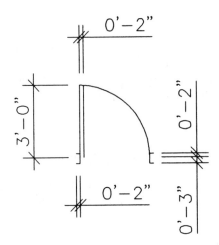

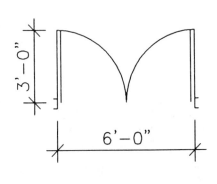

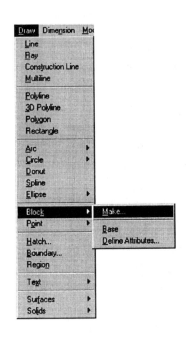

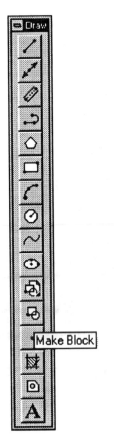

into the tenant space. Pick any open space on your drawing and draw each door full size. In the following part of this exercise the Block and Wblock commands are used to define the doors as blocks.

BLOCK-MAKE...

The Block-Make... command allows you to define any part of a current drawing as a block. Copies of the block can be inserted only into that drawing. Copies of a block defined with the Block-Make... command cannot be used in any other drawing.

Use the Block-Make... command to define the single door drawing as a block named DOOR stored in the current drawing (Figures 9–15 and 9–16):

Prompt	Response
Command:	**Block-Make...** (or TYPE: **B<enter>**)
The Block Definition dialog box appears:	TYPE: **DOOR** in the Block name: box
	CLICK: **the Retain Objects check box to put a check in the box**
	CLICK: **Select Point<**
Insertion base point:	**Osnap-Endpoint**
Endp of:	**D1** (Figure 9-15)
The Block Definition dialog box appears:	CLICK: **Select Objects<**
	CLICK: **a point to locate the first corner of a selection window**
Other corner:	**Window only the single-door drawing.**
Select objects:	**<enter>**
The Block Definition dialog box appears:	CLICK: **OK**
The single door is now defined as a block within your drawing.	

If the Retain Objects check box is not selected, AutoCAD deletes the selected object (the door) from the drawing after it has been included in the block.

A Block name can be 1 to 31 characters long. It may include only letters, numbers, and three special characters—$ (dollar sign), - (hyphen), and _ (underscore).

The Insert command is used later in this exercise to insert copies of the DOOR block into your drawing. The "insertion base point:" is the point on the inserted block to which the crosshairs attach. It allows you to position copies of the block exactly into the drawing. It is also the point around which the block can be rotated when it is inserted.

170

Part II: Two-Dimensional AutoCAD

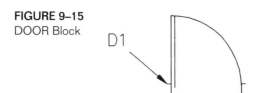

FIGURE 9–15
DOOR Block

D1

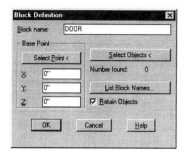

FIGURE 9–16
The Block Definition Dialog Box

Use the Block-Make... command to view a listing of the block just created:

Prompt	Response
Command:	**Block-Make...** (or TYPE: **B<enter>**)
The Block Definition dialog box appears:	CLICK: **List Block Names...**
The Block Names in This Drawing dialog box appears:	CLICK: **OK**
The Block Definition Dialog box appears:	CLICK: **Cancel**

OOPS

If the Retain Objects check box is not selected, the drawing part (for example, the door) that is windowed disappears after you define it as a block using the Block command. When you want to bring the part back to your drawing, use the Oops command to make the part appear again. Typing and entering the Oops command brings the part back to the drawing and keeps it defined as a block within your drawing. Using the Undo command to bring the block back makes the part appear again, but it will also undo the definition of the block within the drawing.

As described earlier, blocks defined with the Block command can be inserted only into the drawing in which they are defined. When you want to build a library of parts defined as blocks that can be inserted into any drawing, use the Wblock command, described next.

WBLOCK

The Wblock command allows you to define any part of a drawing or an entire drawing as a block. Blocks created with the Wblock command can be stored on a floppy disk or on the hard disk. Copies of the blocks can then be inserted into any drawing. These Wblocks become drawing files with a .DWG extension, just like any other AutoCAD drawing.

Use Wblock to save the double-door drawing as a block on a floppy disk in drive A (Figure 9–17)

Prompt	Response
Command:	TYPE: **WBLOCK<enter>**
The Create Drawing File dialog box appears:	TYPE: **A:DOORD** in the File name: box
	CLICK: **Save**
Block name:	PRESS: **<enter>**
Insertion base point:	**Endpoint**
of	**D1**
Select objects:	**Window the entire double-door drawing.**
Select objects:	**<enter>**

The double-door drawing disappears and is saved as a block on drive A.

The double-door drawing is now saved as a drawing file with a .DWG file extension on the floppy disk in drive A. Copies of the DOORD drawing can be recalled and inserted into any other drawing. It is obvious that building a library of parts that can be inserted into any drawing saves time.

The Wblock prompt "Block name:" appears to help define a block that is stored in the current drawing (and was defined using the Block-Make... command) as a block that is

FIGURE 9–17
DOORD Block

D1

defined using the Wblock command. There are four possible responses to the "Block name:" prompt. The responses and results are as follows:

1. TYPE: **The existing block name that is stored in the current drawing and was created with the Block-Make... command.** You can create a Wblock (with a new name) by copying an existing Block. The named block is saved as a drawing file on the disk you choose and is stored under the new name entered in the Create Drawing File dialog box.

2. TYPE: =. You can create a Wblock (with the same name) by copying an existing Block. Use this when the existing block name that is stored in the current drawing and was created with the Block-Make... command is the same as the name entered in the Create Drawing File dialog box.

3. TYPE: *. This response saves the entire drawing on the disk you choose. Named views, user coordinate systems, and unreferenced blocks, layers, linetypes, and text styles are not saved.

4. **blank** (or <enter>). As used in the preceding exercise, this allows you to name and select any part of the drawing to be saved to the disk you choose.

Undo

The drawing part that is windowed disappears after you define it as a block using the Wblock command. When you want to bring the part back to your drawing, use the Undo command. Using the Undo command to bring back a block defined with the Wblock command keeps the Wblock drawing file on the disk; you cannot do this for a block defined with the Block-Make... command.

BASE

Not only parts of a drawing but also an entire drawing can be defined as a block. When you plan to define an entire drawing as a block, you can use the Base command to identify the insertion base point of the drawing. The Base command prompt is "Base point <0'-0", 0'-0", 0'-0">:". Pick, or type and enter, a new base point to define the insertion base point of the drawing.

On Your Own

1. Use the Wblock command to write the DOOR block stored in your current drawing to the disk in drive A. Use A:DOOR as the Wblock File name, and = for the Block name.

2. In the following part of this exercise, the doors will be inserted into the tenant space. Before the doors are inserted, openings for all doors must be added to the drawing. Each single door is 3'4" wide, including the 2" frame, so each opening for a single door is 3'4" wide. As shown in Figure 9–18, the dimension from the corner of each room to the outside edge of the singe door frame is $3\frac{1}{2}"$. The dimensions shown in Figure 9–18 for the door to office 1 apply to all single-door openings.

Use the dimensions shown in Figure 9–18 to draw the openings for the five single doors (layer A-wall-int) and for the double entry door (layer A-wall-ext). A helpful hint: Use Osnap-Tracking or ID with the Line command to draw the first door opening line, and Offset for the second door opening line. Then use Trim to complete the opening.

INSERT-BLOCK...

The Insert-Block... command allows you to insert the defined blocks into your drawing. It may be used to insert a block defined with the Block-Make command or the Wblock command.

The Insert mode found in the Osnap menu allows you to snap to the insertion point of Text or a Block entity.

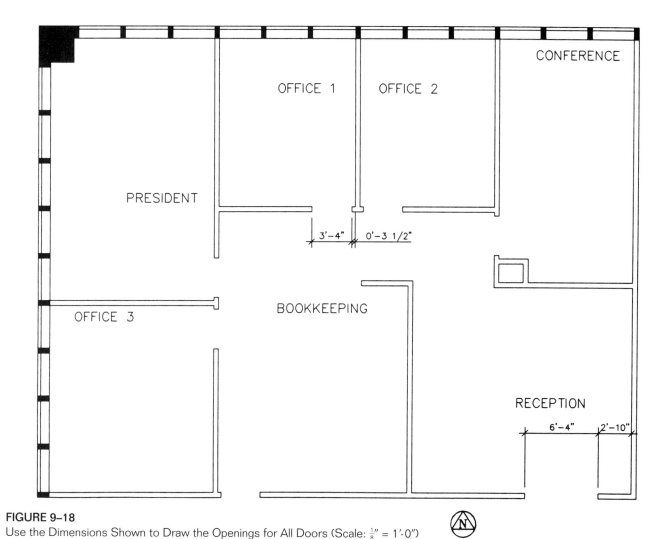

FIGURE 9–18
Use the Dimensions Shown to Draw the Openings for All Doors (Scale: $\frac{1}{8}'' = 1'\text{-}0''$)

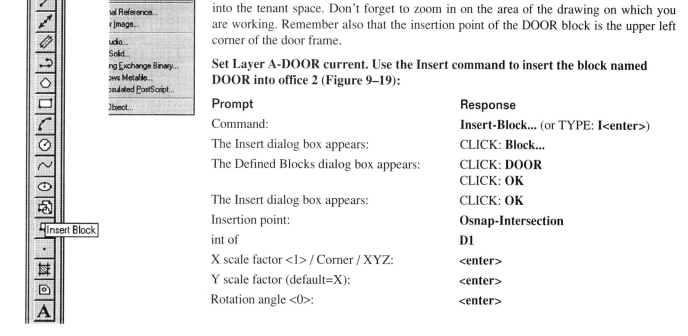

The following part of the exercise uses the Insert command to insert the DOOR block into the tenant space. Don't forget to zoom in on the area of the drawing on which you are working. Remember also that the insertion point of the DOOR block is the upper left corner of the door frame.

Set Layer A-DOOR current. Use the Insert command to insert the block named DOOR into office 2 (Figure 9–19):

Prompt	Response
Command:	**Insert-Block...** (or TYPE: **I<enter>**)
The Insert dialog box appears:	CLICK: **Block...**
The Defined Blocks dialog box appears:	CLICK: **DOOR**
	CLICK: **OK**
The Insert dialog box appears:	CLICK: **OK**
Insertion point:	**Osnap-Intersection**
int of	**D1**
X scale factor <1> / Corner / XYZ:	**<enter>**
Y scale factor (default=X):	**<enter>**
Rotation angle <0>:	**<enter>**

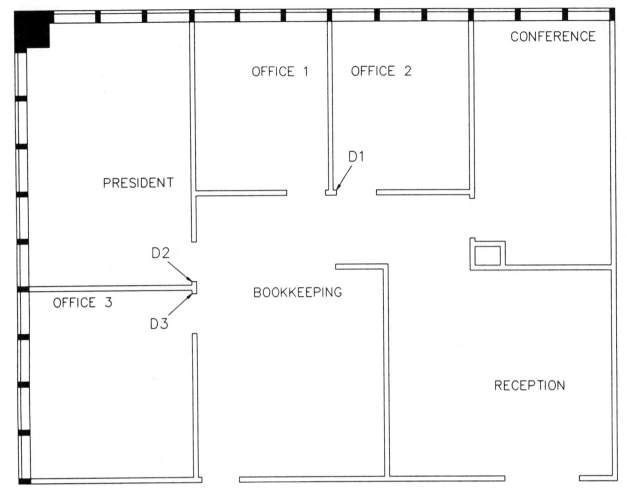

FIGURE 9-19
Use the Insert-Block... Command to Insert the Block Named DOOR (Scale: $\frac{1}{8}'' = 1'\text{-}0''$)

Use the Insert-Block... command to insert the block named DOOR into the president's office (Figure 9–19):

Prompt	Response
Command:	**Insert-Block...** (or TYPE: **I\<enter\>**)
The Insert dialog box appears with DOOR in the Block... box:	CLICK: **OK**
Insertion point:	**Osnap-Intersection**
int of	**D2**
X scale factor \<1\> / Corner / XYZ:	**\<enter\>**
Y scale factor (default=X):	**\<enter\>**
Rotation angle \<0\>:	TYPE: **90\<enter\>**

Because the doors were drawn on the 0 Layer, when inserted as blocks on the A-door Layer, they assumed the properties of the A-door Layer and are yellow.

When a copy of a block is inserted into the drawing, it is inserted as a single entity. The openings for the doors were prepared before the blocks were inserted, because the Trim command will not work to trim the walls out using a block as the cutting edge. Before the Trim command can be used, or a copy of a block can be edited, the block must be exploded with the Explode command. When a block is exploded, it returns to separate entities; it also changes color because it returns to the 0 Layer.

Part II: Two-Dimensional AutoCAD

If you want a block to be inserted retaining its separate entities, check the Explode box on the Insert dialog box.

Insertion Point

The "Insertion point:" of the incoming block is the point where the "insertion base point" specified when the door was defined as a block will be placed. In the preceding exercises, the Osnap mode Intersection was used to position copies of the block exactly into the drawing. You can also use the ID command when inserting a block. Use the ID command to identify a point on the drawing, and then initiate the Insert-Block... command after the point has been located. You can then enter the "Insertion point:" of the block by using relative or polar coordinates to specify a distance from the established point location.

X Scale Factor, Y Scale Factor

The X and Y scale factors provide a lot of flexibility in how the copy of the block will appear when it is inserted. The default X and Y scale factor is 1. A scale factor of 1 inserts the block as it was originally drawn.

New scale factors can be typed and entered in response to the prompts. AutoCAD multiplies all X and Y dimensions of the block by the X and Y scale factors entered. By default, the Y scale factor equals the X scale, but a different Y scale factor can be entered separately. This is especially helpful when you are inserting a window block into a wall with windows of varying lengths. The block can be inserted, the X scale factor can be increased or decreased by the desired amount, and the Y scale factor can remain stable by being entered as 1.

Negative X or Y scale factors can be entered to insert mirror images of the block. When the X scale factor is negative, the Y scale factor remains positive. When the Y scale factor is negative, the X scale factor remains positive. Either a negative X or Y scale factor will work in the following example, but negative X will be used.

Note: The Measure command draws a specified Block at each mark between divided segments. The Divide command also draws a specified Block at each mark between equal segments.

Use the Insert-Block... command, a negative X scale factor, and rotate the angle of the block using Ortho to insert the block named DOOR into office 3 (Figure 9–19):

Prompt	Response
Command:	**Insert-Block...**
The Insert dialog box with DOOR in the Block... box:	CLICK: **OK**
Insertion point:	**Osnap-Intersection**
int of	**D3**
X scale factor <1> / Corner / XYZ:	TYPE: **−1<enter>**
Y scale factor (default=X):	TYPE: **1<enter>**
Rotation angle <0>:	**Turn Ortho on and drag the door into position before picking the point on the drawing.**

Corner

If a block has equal X and Y dimensions or will exactly fit into a 1 × 1 box, you can use the Corner option to increase or decrease the scale factor. The first corner of the box is picked in response to the "X scale factor <1>:" prompt, and then AutoCAD prompts for the Corner point. The second point picked is the upper right corner of the box. With this method it is difficult to make sure that the X and Y scale factors are identical; therefore it is recommended that you use the normal specification method instead of the Corner method.

XYZ

The Insert XYZ option is used for inserting three-dimensional blocks. It allows you to specify a different scale for any of the three coordinates if you choose to do so.

On Your Own

See Figure 9–20.

1. Use the Insert-Block... command to complete the insertion of all doors in the tenant space.

2. Set Layer A-flor-wdwk current. Draw two lines to show the cabinets in the conference room. The upper cabinets are 12″ deep.

3. Set Layer A-flor-iden current. Create a Text Style with the Simplex Font. Use Dtext, height 9″, to type the identifying name in each room. Use the approximate locations as shown in Figure 9–20; the names can be moved as needed when furniture is inserted into the drawing.

Inserting Entire Drawings as Blocks

The Insert-Block... command can be used to insert into the current drawing any drawing that has not been defined as a block and to define it as a block within that drawing. Simply use the Insert-Block... command to insert the drawing. AutoCAD first copies the inserted drawing into the current drawing as a Block definition and then continues with the Insert command as usual, drawing a copy of the newly defined block. If a drive or directory name is used in front of the drawing name, it does not become part of the block name.

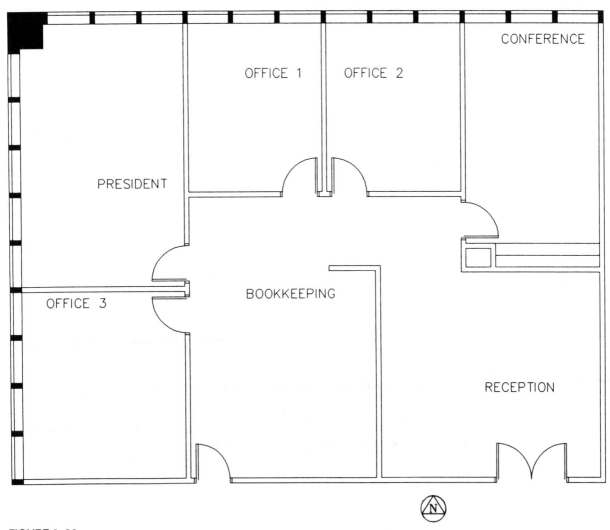

FIGURE 9–20
Exercise 9–1: Tenant Space Floor Plan (Scale: $\frac{1}{8}″$ = 1′-0″)

Part II: Two-Dimensional AutoCAD

If you want to define an existing drawing as a block within the current drawing but do not need a copy of the drawing at that time, press the Esc key at the "Insertion point:" prompt.

Redefining an Inserted Block Using the Block Command

The appearance of any block, defined as a block within a drawing, and all copies of the block within the drawing may be changed easily. As an example, we use the DOOR block that is defined as a block within the tenant space drawing. The following steps describe how to change the appearance of a block and all copies of the block that have already been inserted within a drawing. If you use this example to change the appearance of the DOOR block, be sure to return it to the original appearance.

1. Insert a copy of the DOOR block in an open space in the tenant space drawing.
2. Explode the DOOR block and edit it so that it is different from the original DOOR block.
3. Use the Block-Make... command as follows to redefine the block.

Prompt	Response
Command:	**Block-Make...**
The Block Definition dialog box appears:	TYPE: **DOOR** in the Block name: box
	CLICK: **Select Point<**
Insertion base point:	**Pick the insertion base point**.
The Block Definition dialog box appears:	CLICK: **Select Objects<**
Select objects:	**Window the single door.**
Select objects:	**<enter>**
The Block Definition dialog box appears:	CLICK: **OK**
The AutoCAD Warning "A Block with this name already exists in the drawing. Do you want to redefine it?" appears:	CLICK: **Redefine** (or TYPE: **R**)

The DOOR block is redefined, and all copies of the DOOR block that are in the drawing are redrawn with the new definition of the DOOR block.

Advantages of Using Blocks

1. A library of drawing parts allows you to draw an often-used part once instead of many times.
2. Blocks can be combined with customized menus to create a complete applications environment around AutoCAD that provides the building and furnishings parts that are used daily. Customized menus are discussed in Chapter 16.
3. Once a block is defined and inserted into the drawing, you can update all references to that block by redefining the block.
4. Because AutoCAD treats a block as a single entity, less disk space is used for each insertion of a block. For example, the door contains an arc and approximately 10 lines. If each door were drawn separately, the arcs and lines would take up a lot of disk space. When inserted as a block, the arcs and lines are treated as one definition. The more complicated a block, the greater is the disk space saved. A block that is inserted as exploded is inserted as separate entities and does not save disk space.

MINSERT

The MINSERT (Multiple Insert) command (TYPE: **MINSERT<enter>**) allows you to insert multiple copies of a block in a rectangular array pattern. Only a single entity reference is created with the MINSERT command, and the standard scaling and rotation option prompts are supplied. There is no way to edit a Minsert because it cannot be exploded.

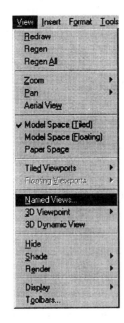

NAMED VIEWS

Many of the drawings that architects and space planners work with are large. The Named Views command is useful when you are working with a complex drawing. It allows you to window a portion of the drawing and save it as a named view that can be recalled to the screen with the Named Views-Restore command. For example, you may View Window each room in the tenant space and assign a View Name; then you can recall each room for editing by using the Named Views-Restore command.

Use Zoom-All to view the entire tenant space drawing. Use the Named Views command to create, name, and restore a view of the president's office:

Prompt	Response
Command:	**Named Views** (or TYPE: **V<enter>**)
The View Control dialog box appears:	CLICK: **New...**
The Define New View dialog box appears:	TYPE: **PRESIDENT** in the New Name: box
	CLICK: **Define Window**
	CLICK: **Window<**
First corner:	**Window only the president's office.**
Other corner	
The Define New View dialog box appears:	CLICK: **Save View**
The View Control dialog box appears:	CLICK: **PRESIDENT**
	CLICK: **OK**
Command:	**<enter>**
The View Control dialog box appears:	CLICK: **PRESIDENT**
	CLICK: **Restore**
	CLICK: **OK**

The View named PRESIDENT appears on the screen.

A View name can be 1 to 31 characters long. It may include only letters, numbers, and three special characters—$ (dollar sign), - (hyphen), and _ (underscore).

When you first enter the Drawing Editor, you can recall a named View by using the Named View... command. You can also print or plot a portion of a drawing by supplying the View name.

Delete

Delete removes one or more views from the list of saved Views. CLICK: the view name, then CLICK: Delete.

On Your Own

Use the Named Views... command to create and name a view of each room in the tenant space.

SAVE

When you have completed Exercise 9–1, save your work in at least two places.

PLOT

Printer Plot or Plotter Plot Exercise 9–1 to scale.

EXERCISE 9–2
Office I Floor Plan

1. Draw the office I floor plan as shown in Figure 9–21. Use an Architectural scale of $\frac{1}{8}''$ = 1'-0'' to measure the office floor plan, and draw it full scale. Use Multiline or Polyline to draw the walls.

2. Printer Plot or Plotter Plot the drawing to scale.

EXERCISE 9–3
Office II Floor Plan

1. Draw the office II floor plan as shown in Figure 9–22. Use an Architectural scale of $\frac{1}{8}''$ = 1'-0'' to measure the office floor plan, and draw it full scale. Use Multiline or Polyline to draw the walls.

2. Printer Plot or Plotter Plot the drawing to scale.

EXERCISE 9–4
House Floor Plan

1. Draw the lower and upper levels of the house floor plan as shown in Figure 9–23. Use an Architectural scale of $\frac{1}{8}''$ = 1'-0'' to measure the house floor plan, and draw it full scale. Use Multiline or Polyline to draw the walls.

2. Printer Plot or Plotter Plot the drawing to scale.

EXERCISE 9–5
Country Club Floor Plan

1. Draw the country club floor plan as shown in Figure 9–24 (pages 184–85). Use an Architectural scale of $\frac{1}{8}''$ = 1'-0'' to measure the country club floor plan, and draw it full scale. Use Multiline or Polyline to draw the walls.

2. Printer Plot or Plotter Plot the drawing to scale.

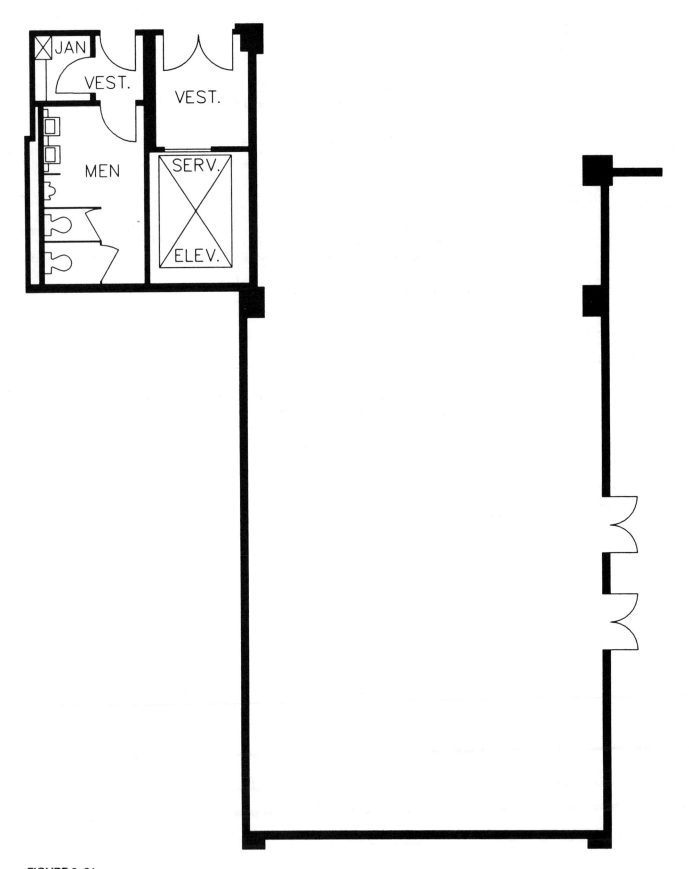

FIGURE 9–21
Exercise 9–2: Office I Floor Plan (Scale: $\frac{1''}{8}$ = 1'-0") (Courtesy of Business Interiors Design Department, Irving, Texas, and GTE Directories.)

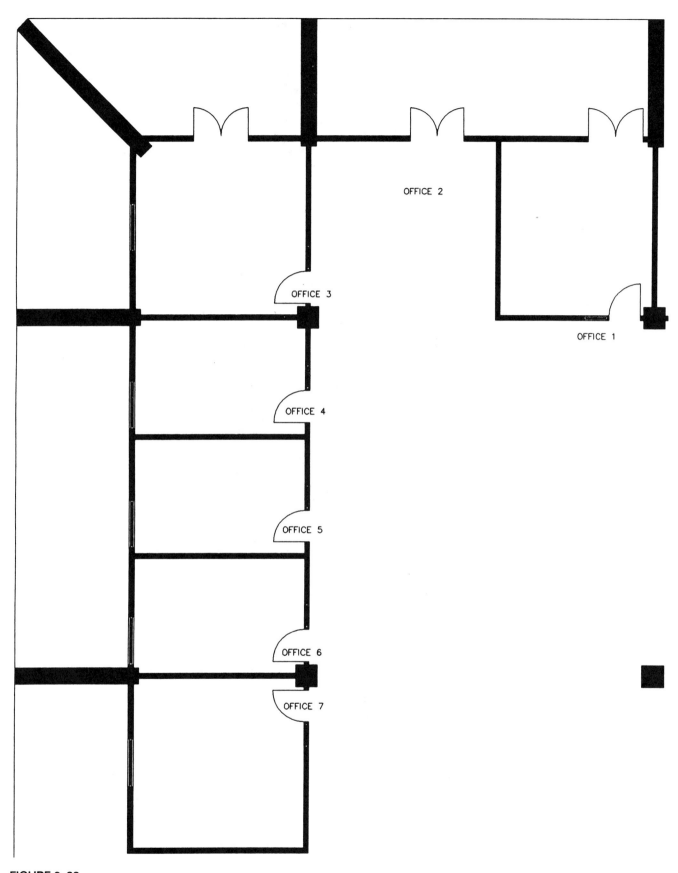

FIGURE 9–22
Exercise 9–3: Office II Floor Plan (Scale: $\frac{1}{8}'' = 1'\text{-}0''$) (Courtesy of Business Interiors Design Department, Irving, Texas, and GTE Directories.)

Chapter 9: Drawing the Floor Plan: Walls, Doors, and Windows

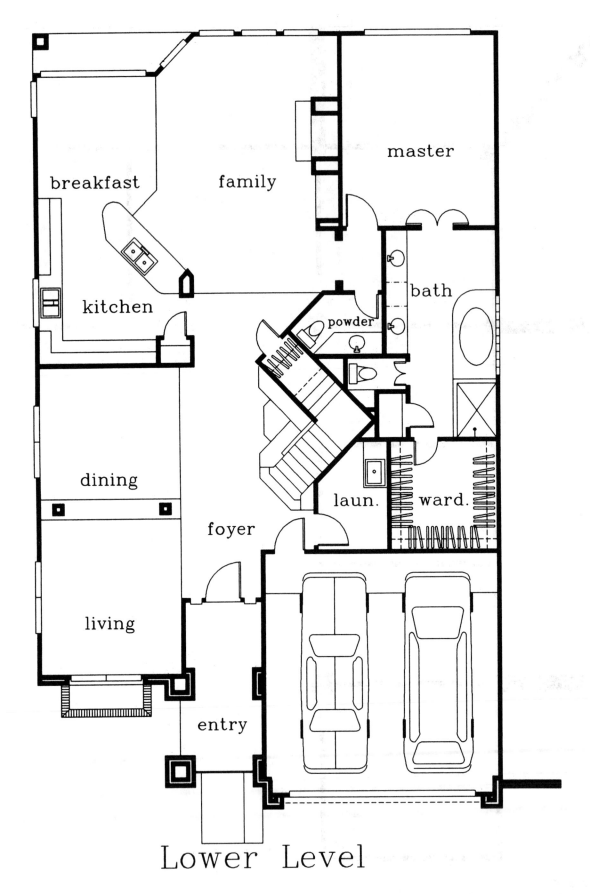

breakfast

family

master

kitchen

bath

powder

dining

laun.

ward.

foyer

living

entry

Lower Level

FIGURE 9–23
Exercise 9–4: House Floor Plan (Scale: $\frac{1}{8}'' = 1'\text{-}0''$) (Courtesy of John Brooks, AIA, Dallas, Texas.)

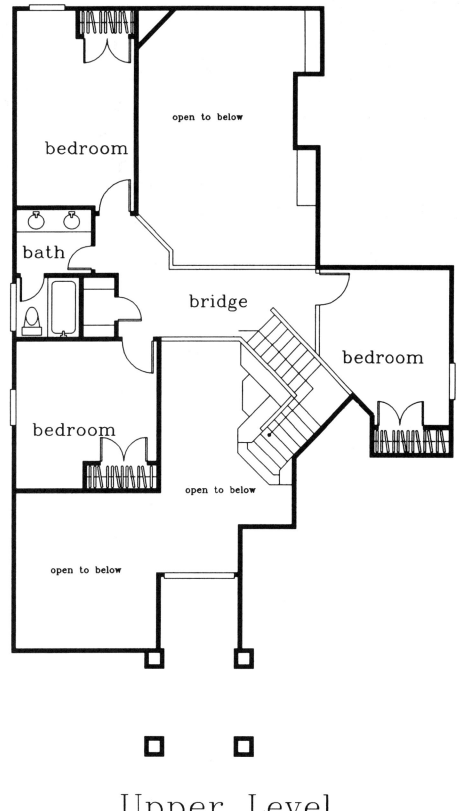

bedroom

open to below

bath

bridge

bedroom

bedroom

open to below

open to below

Upper Level

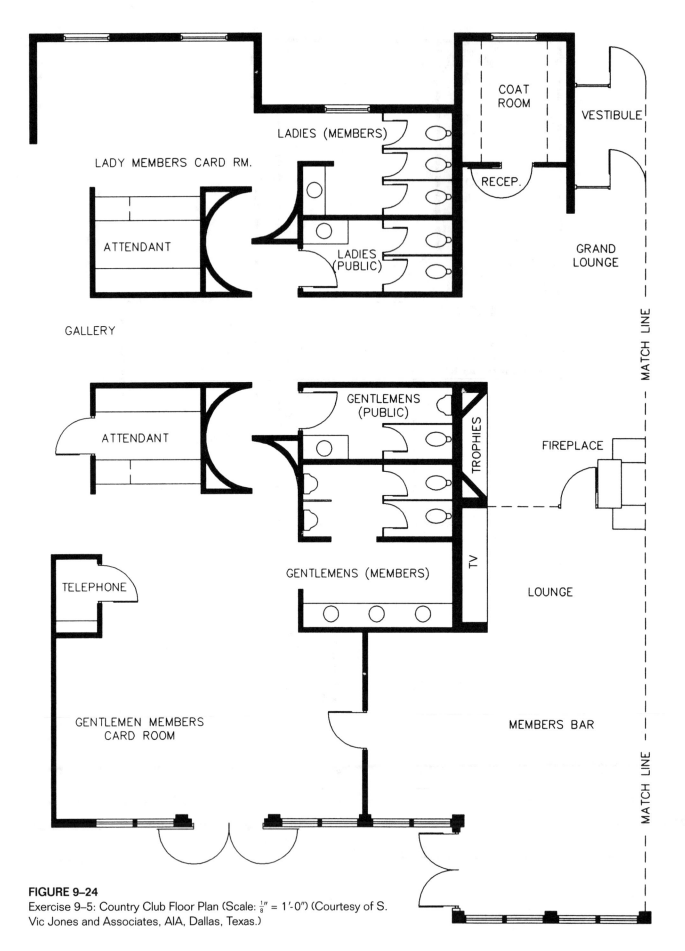

FIGURE 9–24

Exercise 9–5: Country Club Floor Plan (Scale: $\frac{1}{8}'' = 1'\text{-}0''$) (Courtesy of S. Vic Jones and Associates, AIA, Dallas, Texas.)

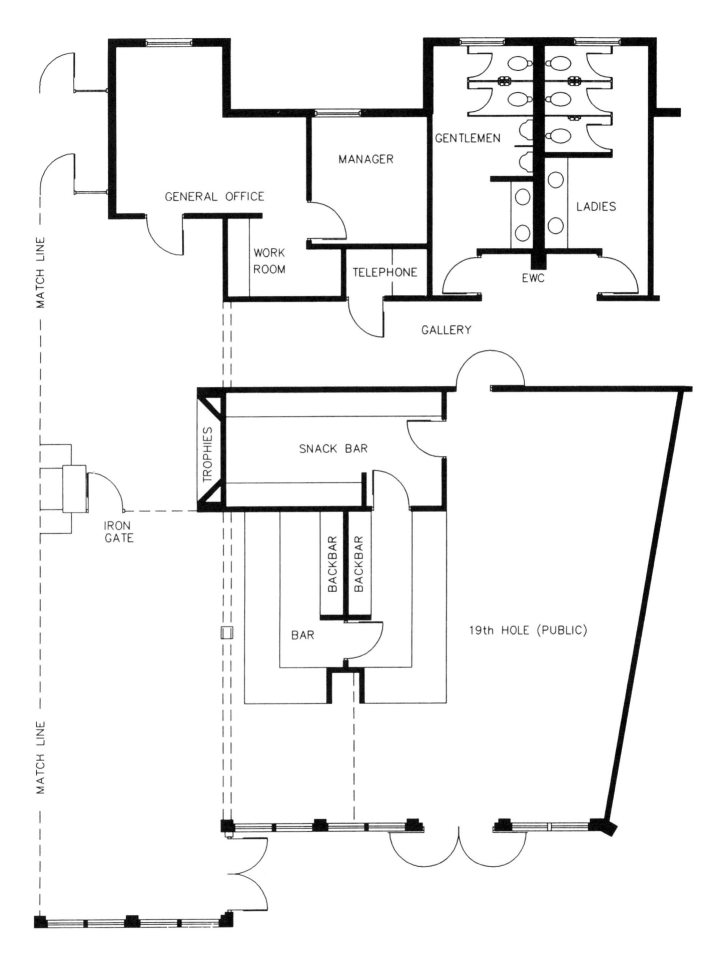

MATCH LINE

GENERAL OFFICE

MANAGER

GENTLEMEN

LADIES

WORK ROOM

TELEPHONE

EWC

GALLERY

TROPHIES

SNACK BAR

IRON GATE

BACKBAR

BACKBAR

BAR

19th HOLE (PUBLIC)

MATCH LINE

REVIEW QUESTIONS

1. What is the maximum number of lines you can draw at the same time with Multiline?
   a. 2   d. 12
   b. 4   e. 16
   c. 8

2. Which of the following Multiline justification options can be used to draw a three-line wall using the middle line?
   a. Top   d. Left
   b. Right   e. Zero
   c. Bottom

3. When you are setting a new Multiline Style what must you pick in the Multiline Style dialog box to set the new style current?
   a. Add   d. Load...
   b. Save...   e. Current
   c. New

4. Which of the following may *not* be changed with the Change command?
   a. Color   d. Circle Radius
   b. Layer   e. Polyline Width
   c. Text Position

5. Which of the following may *not* be changed with the Properties... command?
   a. Color   d. Thickness
   b. Layer   e. Drawing Name
   c. Linetype

6. Which of the following commands tells you the layer a line is on and its length?
   a. Status
   b. Dist
   c. Area
   d. List
   e. Utility

7. On which layer should most blocks be constructed?
   a. 0 Layer
   b. Any layer with a color other than white
   c. Blocks Layer
   d. BL Layer
   e. Any layer other than the 0 Layer

8. If a block is inserted with a check in the Explode block, which of the following is true?
   a. The block must be exploded before it can be edited.
   b. Each element of the block is a separate object.
   c. The block assumes the color of the current layer.
   d. A Wblock is created with the same name.
   e. AutoCAD will not accept the block name.

9. The Wblock command does which of the following?
   a. Creates a block that can be used on the current drawing only
   b. Creates a drawing file on any disk
   c. Creates a drawing file on the hard disk only
   d. Creates blocks of parts of the current drawing only
   e. Uses only named blocks on the current drawing

10. Which scale factor can be used to create a mirror image of a block with the use of the Insert-Block... command?
    a. Negative X, Positive Y
    b. Positive X, Positive Y
    c. Negative X, Negative Y
    d. Mirrored images cannot be created with the Insert-Block... command.

11. List the command you must use to set a new multiline style.

    _____

12. List five properties that can be changed with the Change command.

    1. _____

    2. _____

3. _____

4. _____

5. _____

13. List five items that can be changed with the Properties... command.

    1. _____

    2. _____

    3. _____

    4. _____

    5. _____

14. Describe how to use the Block-Make.. . command to redefine, on the current drawing, seven insertions of the block DOOR using an updated drawing file named DOOR.

_____

_____

15. Describe the basic difference between Block-Make... and Wblock.

_____

_____

_____

16. List the command that allows you to save and restore a view.

_____

17. Describe what happens when a block is created using the Block-Make… command, and the Retain objects check box is not selected.

_____

_____

18. Describe how several entities drawn on a single layer may each be a different color.

_____

_____

19. List four advantages of using blocks.

    1. _____

_____

    2. _____

_____

    3. _____

_____

    4. _____

_____

20. Compare the characteristics of the Minsert command with those of the Insert command.

_____

_____

_____

_____

10 Dimensioning and Area Calculations

OBJECTIVES

When you have completed this chapter, you will be able to:

☐ Understand the function of each dimensioning variable.
☐ Set dimensioning variables.
☐ Save and restore dimensioning styles.
☐ Correctly use the following commands and settings:

Aligned	Cal	Leader	Override
Align Text	Center Mark	Linear	Radius
Angular	Continue	Newtext	Style. . .
Area	Diameter	Oblique	Update
Baseline	Dimension Edit	Ordinate	

SIX BASIC TYPES OF DIMENSIONS

Dimensioning with AutoCAD can be fun and easy when the many options under the Dimension menu are thoroughly understood. Before dimensioning the tenant space floor plan completed in Chapter 9, we will describe some of those options.

Six basic types of dimensions can be automatically created using AutoCAD. They are linear, aligned, ordinate, radius, diameter, and angular. They are listed in the Dimension menu, and are shown on the Dimension toolbar. Each dimension type can be activated by selecting one of the following:

Linear   For dimensioning horizontal, vertical, and angled lines.
Aligned   For showing the length of features that are drawn at an angle.
Ordinate   To display the *x* or *y* coordinate of a feature.
Radius   To create radius dimensioning for arcs and circles.
Diameter   To create diameter dimensioning for arcs and circles.
Angular   For dimensioning angles.

Additionally, leaders and center marks can be drawn by selecting Leader or Center Mark.

The appearance of these six basic types of dimensions, leaders, and center marks when they are drawn and plotted is controlled by settings called dimensioning variables.

DIMENSIONING VARIABLES

A list of dimensioning variables and a brief description of each variable appears when STATUS is typed from the Dim: prompt. Figure 10–1 shows the list of dimensioning variables and the default setting for each, as they appear when STATUS is typed from the Dim: prompt and Architectural units have been set.

Some variables do not apply to the standard dimensioning techniques that architects use for drawings and will be less important to you than others. Once the variables are set

FIGURE 10–1
Dimensioning Variables

DIMALT	Off	Alternate units selected
DIMALTD	2	Alternate unit decimal places
DIMALTF	25.4000	Alternate unit scale factor
DIMALTTD	2	Alternate tolerance decimal places
DIMALTTZ	0	Alternate tolerance zero suppression
DIMALTU	2	Alternate units
DIMALTZ	0	Alternate unit zero suppression
DIMAPOST		Prefix and suffix for alternate text
DIMASO	On	Crate associative dimensions
DIMASZ	3/16″	Arrow size
DIMAUNIT	0	Angular unit format
DIMBLK		Arrow block name
DIMBLK1		First arrow block name
DIMBLK2		Second arrow block name
DIMCEN	1/16″	Center mark size
DIMCLRD	BYBLOCK	Dimension line and leader color
DIMCLRE	BYBLOCK	Extension line color
DIMCLRT	BYBLOCK	Dimension text color
DIMDEC	4	Decimal places
DIMDLE	0″	Dimension line extension
DIMDLI	3/8″	Dimension line spacing
DIMEXE	3/16″	Extension above dimension line
DIMEXO	1/16″	Extension line origin offset
DIMFIT	3	Fit text
DIMGAP	1/16″	Gap from dimension line to text
DIMJUST	0	Justification of text on dimension line
DIMLFAC	1.0000	Linear unit scale factor
DIMLIM	Off	Generate dimension limits
DIMPOST		Prefix and suffix for dimension text
DIMRND	0″	Rounding value
DIMSAH	Off	Separate arrow blocks
DIMSCALE	66.6667	Overall scale factor
DIMSD1	Off	Suppress the first dimension line
DIMSD2	Off	Suppress the second dimension line
DIMSE1	Off	Suppress the first extension line
DIMSE2	Off	Suppress the second extension line
DIMSHO	On	Update dimensions while dragging
DIMSOXD	Off	Suppress outside dimension lines
DIMSTYLE	STANDARD	Current dimension style (read-only)
DIMTAD	0	Place text above the dimension line
DIMTDEC	4	Tolerance decimal places
DIMTFAC	1.0000	Tolerance text height scaling factor
DIMTIH	On	Text inside extensions is horizontal
DIMTIX	Off	Place text inside extensions
DIMTM	0″	Minus tolerance
DIMTOFL	Off	Force line inside extension lines
DIMTOH	On	Text outside horizontal
DIMTOL	Off	Tolerance dimensioning
DIMTOLJ	1	Tolerance vertical justification
DIMTP	0″	Plus tolerance
DIMTSZ	0″	Tick size
DIMTVP	0.0000	Text vertical position
DIMTXSTY	STANDARD	Text style
DIMTXT	3/16″	Text height
DIMTZIN	0	Tolerance zero suppression
DIMUNIT	6	Unit format
DIMUPT	Off	User positioned text
DIMZIN	0	Zero suppression

you may make a template (or a prototype drawing) containing all the settings (Layers, Units, Limits, etc.) for a particular type of drawing. Notice that the variable names begin to make sense when you know what they are. For example: DIMSCALE is dimensioning scale, DIMTXT is dimensioning text, and DIMSTYLE is dimensioning style. The following describes the function of each dimensioning variable.

Dimensioning Variables That Govern Sizes, Distances, and Offsets

Before dimensioning a drawing, you must establish standards for how each element of the dimension will appear. For example, you may decide that the dimension text size will be $\frac{1}{8}''$ high and that tick marks (instead of arrows) will be used at the ends of the dimension lines. The following describes the dimensioning variables that govern the sizes, distances, and offsets of the dimensioning elements and provides an example of each element.

DIMTXT—text size

Tip: If the current Text Style height setting is other than 0, the DIMTXT setting has no effect on the height of dimensioning text. Be sure to set Text Style height to 0.

FIGURE 10–2
Dimension Text and Tick Marks

In Chapter 7, how to set a new Text Style and font was described. The dimension text uses the same font that is current in the Text Style setting. When the current Text Style setting does not have a fixed text height, the value of the DIMTXT variable specifies the height of the dimension text. Figure 10–2 shows dimension text.

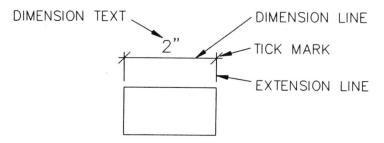

DIMTSZ—tick size

Tick marks are small, 45° lines drawn at the point where the dimension line meets the extension line. The value of the DIMTSZ variable specifies the size of the tick drawn at the ends of dimension lines for linear, radius, and diameter dimensioning. The value entered specifies half the tick size. For a $\frac{1}{8}''$ tick, enter a DIMTSZ value of 1/16″. When the DIMTSZ value is zero and DIMASZ (arrow size) is a positive value, arrows are drawn instead of ticks. Figure 10–2 shows ticks drawn at the ends of linear dimension lines.

DIMEXO—extension line offset

Extension lines extend from the object being measured to the dimension line. The value of the DIMEXO variable specifies how far the extension line is offset from the points picked on the object that is to be dimensioned. For example, you may snap precisely on the corners of a building, but the extension lines will be offset from the corners by the distance specified for the DIMEXO value. Figure 10–3 shows the extension line offset.

DIMEXE—extension line extension

The value of the DIMEXE variable specifies how far the extension line extends above the dimension line. Figure 10–3 shows the extension line extension.

DIMDLE—dimension line extension

The value of the DIMDLE variable specifies how far the dimension line extends past the extension line when ticks are specified instead of arrows. Figure 10–3 shows the dimension line extension.

FIGURE 10–3
Extension Line Offset, Extension Line Extension, and Dimension Line Extension

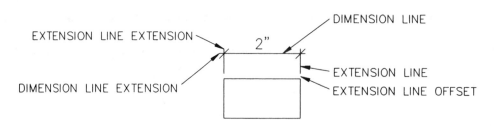

Part II: Two-Dimensional AutoCAD

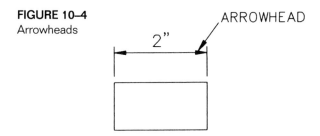

FIGURE 10–4
Arrowheads

DIMASZ—arrow size

Arrowheads may be drawn instead of ticks at the ends of dimension lines. The value of the DIMASZ variable specifies the length of the arrowheads drawn. When DIMTSZ (tick size) is set to a value other than zero, the DIMASZ variable has no effect for linear, aligned, radius, and diameter dimensioning, and ticks are drawn. Figure 10–4 shows arrowheads drawn at the ends of linear dimension lines.

A leader is used to show dimension text or other notes on a drawing. The value of DIMASZ also specifies the length of the arrowhead drawn at the end of a leader when the leader command is used. When DIMASZ is zero, no arrowhead is attached to the leader. When the value of DIMASZ is other than zero, it specifies the size of the arrowhead at the end of the leader. If the value of DIMASZ is a positive number and an arrowhead is not drawn on the leader, increase the leader length to allow for the arrow. Figure 10–5 shows an arrowhead drawn at the end of a leader.

The value of DIMASZ also specifies the length of arrowheads drawn in angular dimensioning. Figure 10–5 shows arrowheads drawn at the end of an angular dimension line arc.

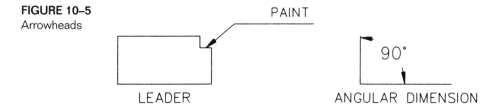

FIGURE 10–5
Arrowheads

DIMDLI—dimension line spacing

After the first segment of a line is dimensioned with a linear dimension, the Continue command automatically continues the next linear dimension. The next linear dimension uses the second extension line of the previous linear dimension as its first extension line. Typically, the dimension lines continue along on the same horizontal line. Sometimes, when the space is small and to avoid drawing over the previous dimension, the continued dimension line is offset. The DIMDLI variable setting determines the size of the offset. Figure 10–6 shows typical linear dimensioning with the Continue command and an offset linear dimension with the Continue command.

After the first segment of a line is dimensioned with a linear dimension, the Baseline command automatically continues the next linear dimension from the baseline (first

FIGURE 10–6
Typical Linear Dimensioning with the Continue Command, and an Offset Linear Dimension with the Continue Command

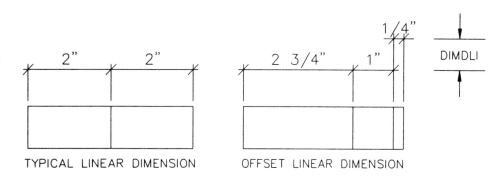

FIGURE 10–7
Linear Dimensioning with the
Baseline Command

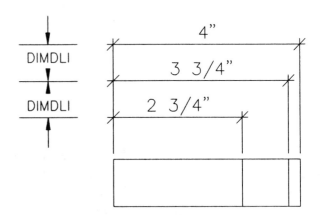

extension line) of the first linear dimension. The new dimension line is offset to avoid drawing on top of the previous dimension. The DIMDLI variable controls the size of the offset. Figure 10–7 shows a linear dimension with the Baseline command.

DIMCEN—center mark size

A center mark is the "+" that marks the center of a circle or arc. A center line includes the "+" and adds lines that intersect the circumference of the circle or arc. The value of DIMCEN controls the drawing of circle and arc center marks and center lines by the Diameter, Radius, and Center Mark commands.

The Diameter and Radius commands provide both the center mark (or center line) and dimensions. The Center Mark command is used to draw only a center mark (or center line) and does not provide dimensions.

When the value of DIMCEN is zero, center marks and center lines are not drawn. When the value of DIMCEN is greater than zero, it specifies the size of the center mark. The value of DIMCEN specifies the size of one arm of the "+". For example, if the value of DIMCEN is 1/8", the center mark is $\frac{1}{4}''$ wide and high overall. When the value of DIMCEN is less than zero (negative), center lines are drawn rather than center marks. The negative value specifies the size of one arm of the mark portion of the center line and how far outside the circumference of the circle the center line extends. For Radius and Diameter dimensioning, center marks or center lines are drawn only when the dimension line is placed outside the circle or arc. Figure 10–8 shows a center mark and a center line. The center mark (on the left) is a positive DIMCEN value. The center line (on the right) is a negative DIMCEN value.

FIGURE 10–8
Center Mark and Center Line

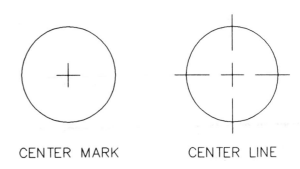

CENTER MARK   CENTER LINE

DIMGAP—gap from dimension line to text

Dimension text may be placed above a solid dimension line or along the dimension line when the dimension line is broken. The DIMGAP variable specifies the gap or distance AutoCAD maintains on each side of the dimension text when the dimension line is broken. Figure 10–9 shows the gap from the dimension line to the dimension text.

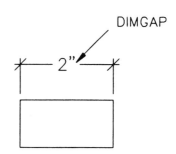

FIGURE 10–9
Gap from Dimension Line to Text

DIMGAP

Dimensioning Variable for Overall Scale Factor

DIMSCALE—overall scale factor

The preceding section described the dimensioning variables that govern the sizes, distances, and offsets of dimensioning elements. It is important to understand how the value that is entered for a variable that governs a size, distance, or offset of a dimensioning element relates to your drawing as it appears on the screen and when the drawing is plotted.

When a building that is drawn full scale is displayed on the screen, the dimensioning elements will be drawn in a larger scale and will thus measure larger than when plotted at a scale of $\frac{1}{8}'' = 12''$. DIMSCALE is the variable that controls the overall scale factor, or how the dimensioning parts appear on the screen display while you are drawing full scale and how they appear when plotted. For example, if you decide that the dimensioning text (DIMTXT) will be $\frac{1}{8}''$ high when a drawing is plotted, enter 1/8" for the DIMTXT value. If you plan to plot the drawing at $\frac{1}{2}'' = 12''$, set DIMSCALE to 24. While you are drawing full scale, the text height will be $\frac{1}{8}'' \times 24''$, or 3" high, on the screen. When the drawing is plotted at $\frac{1}{2}'' = 12''$, the entire drawing including the dimensioning is reduced by a scale factor of 24 ($\frac{1}{2} = 12$, 1 = 24).

The DIMSCALE for a drawing that is plotted at $\frac{1}{4}'' = 12''$ is 48 ($\frac{1}{4} = 12$, 1 = 48), and for a plotting ratio of $\frac{1}{8}'' = 12''$ the DIMSCALE is 96 ($\frac{1}{8} = 12$, 1 = 96).

Dimensioning Variable for Length Factor

DIMLFAC—linear unit scale factor

The DIMLFAC setting is the length factor by which all measured linear distances are multiplied before AutoCAD completes the dimension text on the drawing. The default, 1, is for drawing full scale, where one drawing unit equals one dimensioning unit. When you are drawing at a scale of $\frac{1}{2}'' = 1''$ or $6'' = 12''$, the DIMLFAC is set to 2 and all measured distances are multiplied by 2. When you are drawing at a scale of $\frac{1}{4}'' = 12''$, the DIMLFAC value is 48 and all measured distances are multiplied by 48. Because you will be drawing at full scale only, use the DIMLFAC default setting of 1.

Dimensioning Variables That Affect Location, Orientation, and Appearance of Dimension Text and Dimension Lines

DIMDEC—decimal places

This variable sets the number of decimal places to the right of the decimal point for the dimension value.

DIMTXSTY—text style

Specifies the text style of the dimension. The text style chosen must be defined in the current drawing.

DIMUNIT—unit format

Sets Units for primary dimensions as follows:

1. Scientific
2. Decimal

3. Engineering

4. Architectural (stacked)

5. Fractional (stacked)

6. Architectural

7. Fractional

8. Windows Desktop (decimal format using Control Panel settings for decimal separator and number grouping symbols)

DIMTAD—place text above the dimension line

The DIMTAD setting controls the vertical placement of dimension text that is drawn inside or outside the extension lines (text is placed outside the extension lines when there is not enough room for it inside the extension lines).

0   Centers the dimension text between the extension lines. When DIMTAD is off, DIMTVP controls the vertical placement of text. Figure 10–10 shows linear dimension lines and text that is inside the extension lines, with DIMTAD on (1) and off (0).

1   When DIMTAD is on, the dimension text is placed above the dimension line. The dimension line is not broken and is a single, solid line. DIMTIH and DIMTOH (described next) must be off for DIMTAD to work for vertical dimensions that are inside or outside the extension lines.

2   Places the dimension text on the side of the dimension line farthest away from the defining points.

3   Places the dimension text to conform to a Japanese Industrial Standards (JIS) representation.

DIMTVP—text vertical position

When DIMTAD is off, AutoCAD uses the DIMTVP value to determine the vertical placement of text above or below a solid dimension line or along a split dimension line. A value of .6 to −.6 splits the dimension line to accommodate the dimension text. A value of 1 places the text above a single, solid dimension line. A value of −1 places the text below a single, solid dimension line. Figure 10–10 shows dimension lines with different DIMTVP settings.

FIGURE 10–10
DIMTAD and DIMTVP Settings

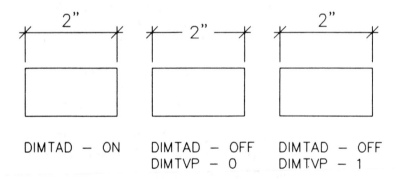

DIMTIH—text inside extension is horizontal

The DIMTIH setting controls the orientation of dimension text that fits between the extension lines. When DIMTIH is on, the text is always oriented horizontally. When DIMTAD is on and DIMTIH is on, the vertical dimension lines are split to accommodate the horizontal text. When DIMTIH is off, the text is aligned with the dimension line. Figure 10–11 shows linear dimension text with DIMTIH on and off.

DIMTOH—text outside horizontal

The DIMTOH setting affects dimension text that is drawn outside the extension lines. When DIMTOH is on, the text is always oriented horizontally. When DIMTOH is off, the text is aligned with the dimension line. Figure 10–12 shows dimension text that is outside the extension lines, with DIMTOH on and off.

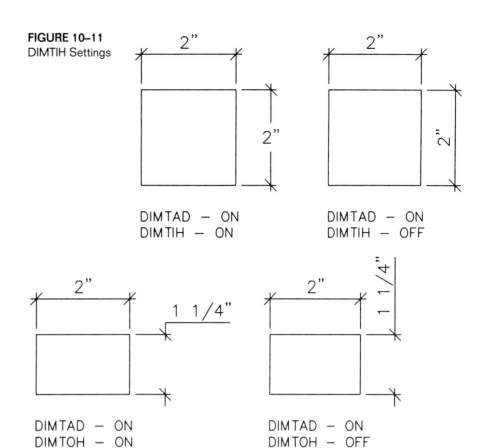

FIGURE 10–11
DIMTIH Settings

2"

2"

2"

2"

DIMTAD — ON
DIMTIH — ON

DIMTAD — ON
DIMTIH — OFF

FIGURE 10–12
DIMTOH Settings

2"

1 1/4"

2"

1 1/4"

DIMTAD — ON
DIMTOH — ON

DIMTAD — ON
DIMTOH — OFF

DIMTIX—place text inside extensions

AutoCAD automatically places the dimension text inside the extension lines when there is sufficient room and outside the extension lines when there is not. When DIMTIX is on, the dimension text is forced between the extension lines. This happens even if AutoCAD would have automatically placed it outside because of the limited room. When DIMTIX is off, the text location for linear, aligned, and angular dimensions varies depending on the type of dimension. If DIMTIX is off when you are drawing radius and diameter dimensions, the dimension text is forced outside the circle or arc. Figure 10–13 shows linear and diameter dimensions with DIMTIX on and off.

FIGURE 10–13
DIMTIX Settings

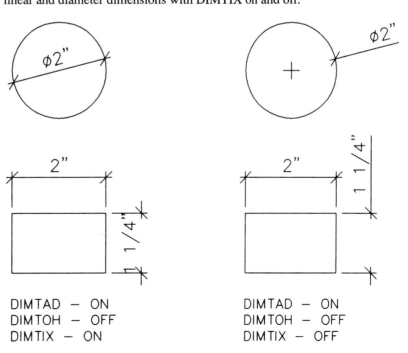

ø2"

ø2"

2"

1 1/4"

2"

1 1/4"

DIMTAD — ON
DIMTOH — OFF
DIMTIX — ON

DIMTAD — ON
DIMTOH — OFF
DIMTIX — OFF

FIGURE 10–14
DIMTIX and DIMSOXD Settings

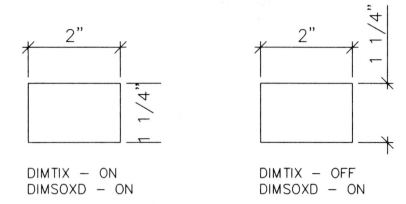

DIMTIX — ON
DIMSOXD — ON

DIMTIX — OFF
DIMSOXD — ON

DIMSOXD—suppress outside dimension lines

AutoCAD automatically draws dimension lines and text outside the extension lines when there is not sufficient room inside the extension lines for the text. DIMSOXD is effective only when DIMTIX is on. When DIMTIX and DIMSOXD are both on, the text is forced inside the extension lines and the dimension line is not drawn. Figure 10–14 shows linear dimensions with DIMTIX and DIMSOXD on. It also shows the same linear dimensions with DIMTIX off and DIMSOXD on.

DIMTOFL—force dimension line inside extension lines

When there is not sufficient room for the text and dimension lines between the extension lines, AutoCAD automatically places them outside the extension lines. When DIMTOFL is on, the dimension line is drawn between the extension lines, even when the text is drawn outside the extension lines. If DIMTOFL is on and DIMTIX is off when radius and diameter dimensions are drawn, the dimension line is drawn inside the circle or arc and the leader and text are drawn outside of the circle or arc. Figure 10–15 shows linear and diameter dimensions with DIMTOFL off and on.

DIMFIT—fit text

This variable controls the placement of text and arrowheads inside or outside extension lines based on the available space between extension lines as follows:

FIGURE 10–15
DIMTOFL Settings

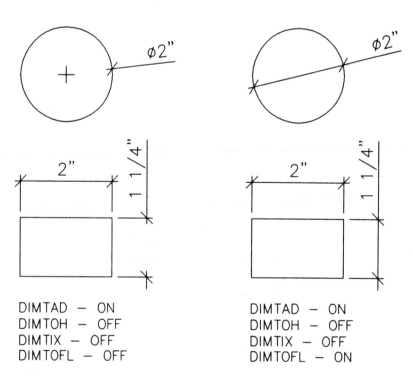

DIMTAD — ON
DIMTOH — OFF
DIMTIX — OFF
DIMTOFL — OFF

DIMTAD — ON
DIMTOH — OFF
DIMTIX — OFF
DIMTOFL — ON

Part II: Two-Dimensional AutoCAD

0	Places text and arrowheads between the extension lines if space is available. Otherwise places both text and arrowheads outside extension lines.
1	If space is available, places text and arrowheads between the extension lines. When enough space is available for text, places text between the extension lines and arrowheads outside them. When not enough space is available for text, places both text and arrowheads outside extension lines.
2	If space is available, places text and arrowheads between the extension lines. When space is available for the text only, AutoCAD places the text between the extension lines and the arrowheads outside. When space is available for the arrowheads only, AutoCAD places them between the extension lines and the text outside. When no space is available for either text or arrowheads, AutoCAD places them both outside the extension lines.
3	Creates leader lines when there is not enough space for text between extension lines. The dimensioning variable DIMJUST controls whether the text is drawn to the right or to the left of the leader.

DIMJUST—justification of text on dimension line

This variable controls the horizontal position of the text in the dimension as follows:

0	Positions the text above the dimension line and centers it between the extension lines.
1	Positions the text above the dimension line and next to the first extension line.
2	Positions the text above the dimension line and next to the second extension line.
3	Positions the text above the dimension line and rotates it so that it is centered above the first extension line
4	Positions the text above the dimension line and rotates it so that it is centered above the second extension line.

DIMUPT—user-positioned text

When this variable is on, it allows you to click the point where you wish the dimension line and the text to appear. If you want the text to appear nearer one end of the dimension line, select a single point that will place the dimension line where you want it and will place the text on the same point. The setting is 0 for off and 1 for on.

DIMSD1—suppress the first dimension line

When the DIMSD1 value is set to on, the dimension line nearest the first extension line origin is not drawn.

DIMSD2—suppress the second dimension line

When the DIMSD2 value is set to on, the dimension line nearest the second extension line origin is not drawn.

DIMSE1—suppress the first extension line

Setting the DIMSE1 value to on suppresses the drawing of the first extension line. Sometimes while you are drawing dimensions, it is convenient to be able to turn off the first extension line. When you are using Continue dimensioning, suppressing the first extension line prevents the overlapping of extension lines with each continuing dimension. When the first extension is suppressed, you have to draw it in (or turn DIMSE1 off and UPDATE the first dimension) to complete the first dimension segment drawn.

DIMSE2—suppress the second extension line

Setting the DIMSE2 value to on suppresses the drawing of the second extension line.

DIMZIN—zero suppression

The value of DIMZIN controls how the feet and inches of the dimensions appear. Figure 10–16 shows how DIMZIN affects feet and inches, using Architectural and Decimal units.

FIGURE 10–16
DIMZIN Values

DIMZIN Value	Meaning	Examples			
0	Suppress zero feet and inches	$\frac{1}{4}''$	$3''$	$2'$	$1'\text{-}0\frac{1}{2}''$
1	Include zero feet and inches	$0'\text{-}0\frac{1}{4}''$	$0'\text{-}3''$	$2'\text{-}0''$	$1'\text{-}0\frac{1}{2}''$
2	Include zero feet; suppress zero inches	$0'\text{-}0\frac{1}{4}''$	$0'\text{-}3''$	$2'$	$1'\text{-}0\frac{1}{2}''$
3	Suppress zero feet; include zero inches	$\frac{1}{4}''$	$3''$	$2'\text{-}0$	$1'\text{-}0\frac{1}{2}''$
4	Suppress leading zeros in decimal dimensions	.500	.50	.0010	
8	Suppress trailing zeros in decimal dimensions	0.5	1.5	.001	
12	Suppress leading and trailing zeros in decimal dimensions	.5	1.5	.001	

DIMPOST—prefix and suffix for dimension text

The DIMPOST variable defines a prefix, a suffix, or both for a dimension measurement. It is used when the Decimal unit of measurement is selected. For example, a DIMPOST setting of "<>mm" would produce a measurement of "10.50mm" for a measurement of 10.50 units. Use <> to indicate placement of the text. For example, to display mm 10.50, enter mm <>.

DIMAUNIT—angular unit format

This variable sets the angle format for angular dimensions as follows:

0 Decimal degrees
1 Degrees/minutes/seconds
2 Gradians
3 Radians
4 Surveyor's units

Dimensioning Variables for Setting Color

DIMCLRD—dimension line and leader color

The DIMCLRD setting controls the color of dimension lines, arrowheads, and leaders. When DIMCLRD is set to BYBLOCK the dimension lines and arrowheads take on the color of the current layer. You can also set DIMCLRD by entering a color number or name. For example, setting DIMCLRD to 1 will produce red dimension lines, arrowheads, and leaders. They will be red regardless of the layer that is current when they are drawn. This can be useful when you want different elements of the dimension to have varying line weights. When plotting, you should coordinate the dimension part colors to pens of varying widths.

DIMCLRE—extension line color

Similar to DIMCLRD, the DIMCLRE setting controls the color of the extension line.

DIMCLRT—dimension text color

Similar to DIMCLRD, the DIMCLRT setting controls the color of the dimension text.

Dimensioning Variables for Adding Dimension Tolerances, Generating Dimension Limits, and Rounding Dimensions

DIMTDEC—tolerance decimal places

Sets the number of decimal places in the tolerance value for a dimension.

DIMTOL—tolerance dimensioning

When DIMTOL is on, dimension tolerances that are specified by the values of DIMTP (Plus Tolerance) and DIMTM (Minus Tolerance) are added to the dimension text. Setting

FIGURE 10–17
Dimensioning with DIMTOL On

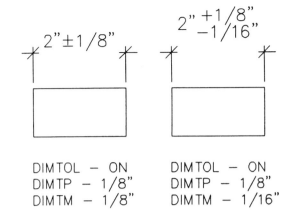

DIMTOL – ON   DIMTOL – ON
DIMTP – 1/8"   DIMTP – 1/8"
DIMTM – 1/8"   DIMTM – 1/16"

DIMTOL on forces DIMLIN (Generate Dimension Limits) off. When the plus tolerance and minus tolerance values are the same, AutoCAD draws a ± symbol followed by the tolerance value. When the plus and minus tolerances differ, the plus tolerance is drawn above the minus. Examples of dimensioning with dimension tolerances are shown in Figure 10–17.

DIMTOLJ—tolerance vertical justification

Controls the vertical placement of tolerance values relative to the dimension text as follows.

0   Top
1   Middle
2   Bottom

DIMTZIN—tolerance zero suppression

Suppresses zeros in tolerance values to the right of the value as follows:

0   Zeros are not suppressed (are shown; Example: .0500)
1   Zeros are suppressed (are not shown; Example: .05)

DIMLIM—generate dimension limits

When DIMLIM is on, dimension limits that are specified by the values of DIMTP and DIMTM are added to the dimension text. Setting DIMLIM on forces DIMTOL off. Examples of dimensioning with dimension limits are shown in Figure 10–18.

DIMTP—plus tolerance

The DIMTP setting specifies the plus tolerance used when DIMTOL is on and the upper dimension limits when DIMLIM is on.

FIGURE 10–18
Dimensioning with DIMLIM On

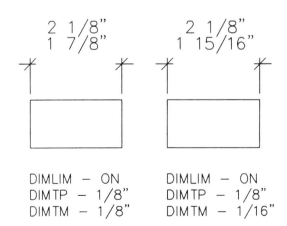

DIMLIM – ON   DIMLIM – ON
DIMTP – 1/8"   DIMTP – 1/8"
DIMTM – 1/8"   DIMTM – 1/16"

DIMTM—minus tolerance

The DIMTM setting specifies the minus tolerance used when DIMTOL is on and the lower dimension limits when DIMLIM is on.

DIMTFAC—tolerance text height scaling factor

Similar to DIMSCALE, DIMTFAC is the scale factor applied to the text height (DIMTXT) of the tolerance values specified in DIMTP and DIMTM. For example, if DIMTFAC is .5 and DIMTXT is 1/8″, the plus and minus tolerances are drawn with text $\frac{1}{16}$″ high.

DIMRND—rounding value

The value of DIMRND is used for rounding dimension distances. It does not apply to angular dimensions. For example, a rounding value of 1/2″ would result in rounding of all distances to the nearest $\frac{1}{2}$″ unit; $2\frac{3}{4}$″ would become 3″.

Dimensioning Variables for Alternate Units of Measurement

DIMALT—alternate units selected

When DIMALT is on, dimensions for two different systems of measurement, such as inches and metric, will be drawn. For example, when DIMALT is on and DIMALTF is set at 25.4, the dimension text appears as 2″ [50.80mm].

DIMALTD—alternate unit decimal places

The DIMALTD setting determines the number of places to the right of the decimal the alternate text will display. In the preceding alternate unit example, the DIMALTD setting is 2.

DIMALTF—alternate unit scale factor

The value of DIMALTF is the number by which the basic dimension is multiplied to obtain the value of the alternate unit. The default for DIMALFT is 25.4, the number of millimeters per inch. When DIMALT is on and DIMALTF is 25.4, the inch unit of measurement is multiplied by 25.4 to determine the alternate unit of measurement.

DIMALTTD—alternate tolerance decimal places

DIMALTTD sets the number of decimal places for the tolerance values of an alternate units dimension.

DIMALTTZ—alternate tolerance zero suppression

DIMALTTZ suppresses zeros in alternate tolerance values to the right of the decimal point as follows:

0   Zeros are not suppressed (are shown; example: 0.500)
1   Zeros are suppressed (are not shown; example: 0.5)

DIMALTU—alternate units

This variable sets units for alternate dimension as follows:

1. Scientific
2. Decimal
3. Engineering
4. Architectural

DIMALTZ—alternate unit zero suppression

DIMALTZ suppresses zeros in alternate dimension values to the right of the decimal point as follows:

0   Zeros are not suppressed (are shown; example: 2.00)

1   Zeros are suppressed (are not shown; example: 2)

DIMAPOST—prefix and suffix for alternate text

The DIMAPOST value is the prefix or suffix applied to the alternate unit of measurement. For example, when using metric, you enter the value of DIMAPOST as "mm", as shown in the DIMALT alternate unit example.

Dimensioning Variables for Designing Your Own Arrow Block

DIMBLK—arrow block

Tip: If you have defined a DIMBLK other than the standard arrowhead or tick and want to return to the standard form, respond with a period (.) to the DIMBLK name. Until you do this, the defined DIMBLK is in effect.

If you do not want an arrow or tick mark to be used at the ends of dimension lines, you may design your own mark. Use the Block command to make a block of the mark, and AutoCAD inserts your mark instead of arrows or ticks.

At the DIMBLK prompt, enter the name of the block to be drawn at the ends of the dimension line. The DIMASZ variable is used to determine the size of arrow blocks identified by the DIMBLK variable.

DIMSAH—separate arrow blocks, DIMBLK1—separate arrow block 1, DIMBLK2—separate arrow block 2

You may use different blocks for the marks at the two ends of the dimension line. When DIMSAH is on, the DIMBLK1 and DIMBLK2 variables specify different user-defined arrow blocks to be drawn at the two ends of the dimension line. DIMBLK1 names the block used for the mark drawn at one end of the dimension line, and DIMBLK2 names the block used for the mark drawn at the other end of the dimension line.

Dimensioning Variables for Associative Dimensions

DIMASO—create associative dimensions

The DIMASO setting is an important and very useful setting. You will find examples of the uses of DIMASO later in this chapter. When DIMASO is on, each dimension that is drawn is created as a block. That means that the extension lines, dimension lines, ticks or arrows, text, and all other parts of the dimension are entered as a single unit. When DIMASO is on, the dimensions drawn are called associative dimensions. When DIMASO is off, the extension lines, dimension lines, and all other parts of the dimension are drawn as separate entities.

DIMSHO—update dimensions while dragging

When DIMSHO is on, if a dimensioned object and its dimension are edited with the Stretch command, the dimension text is recomputed dynamically as the dimension entity is dragged. When DIMSHO is off, the original text is dragged.

Dimension Variable for Naming a Dimension Style

DIMSTYLE—current dimension style (read-only)

While dimensioning the same drawing, you may want some of the dimensions to have different variable settings from the rest of the dimensions. For example, you may want a different text height for some dimensions. You can do this easily by changing the DIMTXT setting and continuing to dimension. The dimensioning variables settings control the appearance of subsequent dimensions. Those dimensions that have already been drawn do not change when a variable is changed.

If you want to use two or more distinct styles of dimensioning in the same drawing, each style (and the variable settings for that style) may be saved separately and recalled when needed. The DIMSTYLE variable tells the name of the current dimension style.

EXERCISE 10–1
Dimensioning the Tenant Space Floor Plan Using Linear Dimensions

Exercise 10–1 provides instructions for setting the dimensioning variables for the tenant space floor plan drawn in Exercise 9–1, saving the dimensioning variables, and dimensioning the exterior and interior of the tenant space floor plan using linear dimensions. When you have completed Exercise 10–1, your drawing will look similar to Figure 10–19. To begin, turn on the computer and start AutoCAD. The Start Up dialog box is displayed.

Begin drawing CH10-EX1 on the hard drive by opening existing drawing CH9-EX1 from a floppy disk in drive A and saving it as CH10-EX1 on the hard drive.

Prompt	Response
The Start Up dialog box is displayed:	**Insert the floppy disk that has CH9-EX1 stored on it in drive A**
	CLICK: **Open a Drawing button**
	DOUBLE CLICK: **A:\CH9-EX1.dwg**
	-or-
	If A:\CH9-EX1.dwg is not listed in the Select a File: selection, DOUBLE CLICK: **More files...**
The Select File dialog box appears:	CLICK: **3½ Floppy [A:]**
	CLICK: **CH4-EX1**
	CLICK: **Open** (or DOUBLE CLICK: **CH4-EX1**)
CH9-EX1 is opened.	

Save the drawing to the hard drive.

Prompt	Response
Command:	**SaveAs...**
The Save Drawing As... dialog box is displayed:	TYPE: **CH10-EX1** (replace CH9-EX1 in the File Name: input box)
	CLICK: **[C:]** (and the correct folder if needed)
	CLICK: **Save**

You are now working on the hard drive with a drawing named CH10-EX1. Do not work on a floppy disk. Always work on the hard drive.

Setting the Dimensioning Variables

There are three different ways the dimensioning variables can be set. The following describes how to set dimensioning variables.

STATUS

Use STATUS to view the current status of all the dimensioning variables and change the setting for DIMASZ:

Prompt	Response
Command:	TYPE: **DIM<enter>**
Dim:	TYPE: **STATUS<enter>**
(The first page of dimension variable appears on the screen.)	
Press ENTER to continue:	**<enter>**

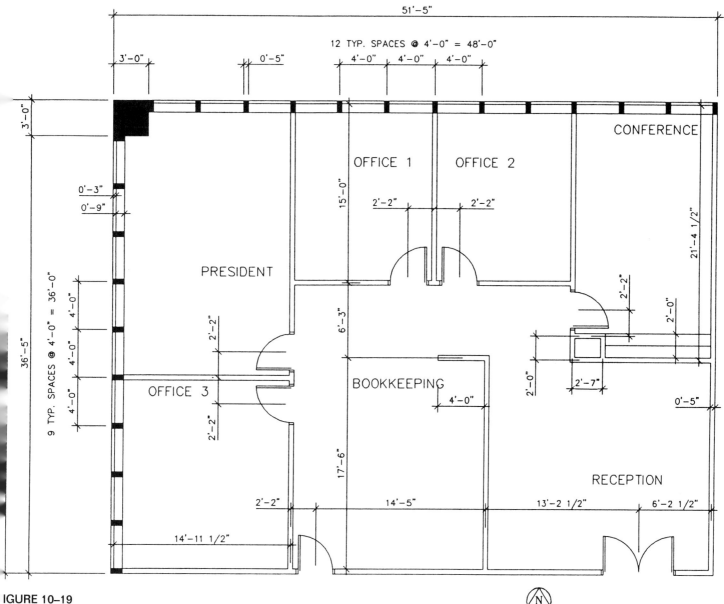

IGURE 10–19

xercise 10–1: Dimensioning the Tenant Space Floor Plan Using Linear Dimensions

Scale: $\frac{1}{8}'' = 1'$-$0''$)

Prompt	Response
(The second page of dimension variables appears on the screen.)	
Press ENTER to continue:	**\<enter\>**
(The remaining dimension variables list appears on the screen.)	
Dim:	TYPE: **ASZ\<enter\>**
Dim: asz	
Current value \<default\> New value:	TYPE: **1/16\<enter\>**
Dim:	PRESS: **F2**

Dimension Styles dialog box

The Dimension Styles dialog box (Figure 10–20) allows you to change dimension variables using dialog boxes. When **Geometry...** is clicked, the Geometry dialog box appears, Figure 10–21. When **Format...** is clicked, the Format dialog box appears, Figure 10–22. When **Annotation...** is clicked, the Annotation dialog box appears, Figure 10–23.

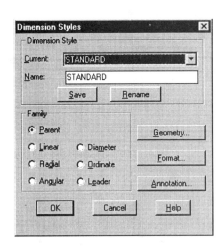

FIGURE 10–20
Dimension Styles Dialog Box

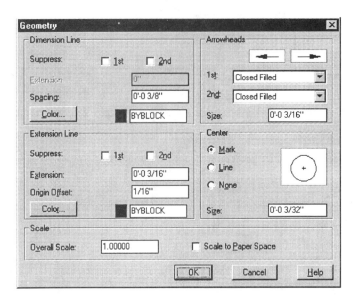

FIGURE 10–21
Geometry Dialog Box

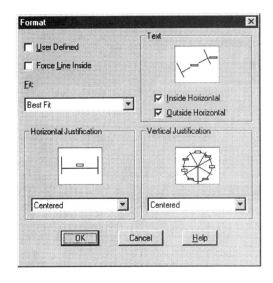

FIGURE 10–22
Format Dialog Box

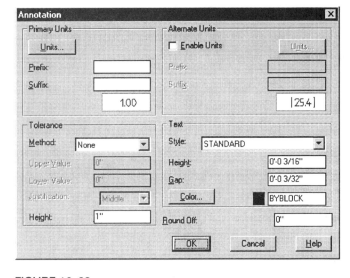

FIGURE 10–23
Annotation Dialog Box

The Family area of the Dimension Styles dialog box allows you to specify different settings for different members of the dimension family—Linear, Radial, Angular, Diameter, Ordinate, and Leader. When there are no differences in the settings for the different dimensioning family members, click the Parent radio box.

Use Dimension Styles dialog box to view the current setting for DIMUNIT, and change the setting for DIMUNIT (Figures 10–20, 10–21, 10–22, 10–23 and 10–24):

Prompt	Response
Dim:	**Dimension-Style...** (or TYPE: **DDIM<enter>**)
The Dimension Styles dialog box appears (Figure 10–20):	CLICK: **Annotation...**
The Annotation dialog box appears (Figure 10–23):	CLICK: **Units...** (in Primary Units area)

FIGURE 10–24
Primary Units Dialog Box

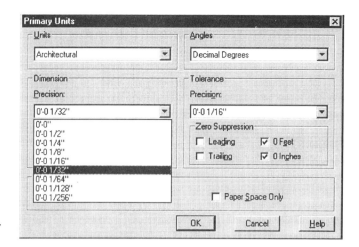

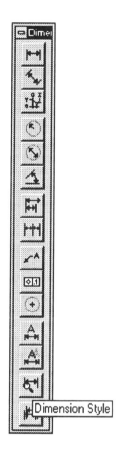

The Primary Units dialog box appears
    (Figure 10–24):

CLICK: **Architectural** (in Units area)

CLICK: **0′-0 1/32″** (in Dimension
    Precision area)

CLICK: **OK**

The Annotation dialog box appears:

CLICK: **OK**

The Dimension Styles dialog box appears:

CLICK: **OK**

Command: Prompt

From the Command: prompt, type DIMDLE to view the current setting for DIMDLE and change the current setting for DIMDLE

Prompt	Response
Command:	TYPE: **DIMDLE <enter>**
New value for DIMDLE <default>:	TYPE: **1/16<enter>**

On Your Own

Use any of the three ways described above to set the dimensioning variables for CH10-EX1. Many of the variables already have the correct setting. If you plan to plot or print CH10-EX1 at a scale of $\frac{1}{8}″$ = 12″, using an $8\frac{1}{2}″ \times 11″$ plotting size, set the variables as shown in Figure 10–25. Be sure 1/32 is set as the smallest fraction to display when setting drawing Units, so the 1/32 dimensioning variable will display that fraction. If you plan to plot CH10-EX1 at a scale of $\frac{1}{4}″$ = 12″, using an 18″ × 24″ plotting size, set the variables as shown in Figure 10–26.

Saving and Then Restoring Saved Dimension Styles

The dimensioning variable settings can be saved under a dimension style name. Any dimensions drawn while the style is current will be associated with the style. This can be done using the Dimension Styles dialog box.

After you define a dimension style by setting the variables, enter a name in the Dimension Styles dialog box Name: input box and choose Save. To rename a style, make the style current in the Current: input box, and enter the new name in the Name: input box and then choose Rename. To make a copy of the current style, enter the new name in the Name: input box and then choose Save.

On Your Own

1. Save all your variable settings to the dimension style name STYLE1.

2. Set Layer A-pflr-dims current.

3. Use Zoom-All to view the entire drawing.

Note: Be sure to select 32 as the denominator of the smallest fraction to display when setting drawing Units, so that the dimensioning variable settings may display the same fraction if they are set in the 32nds.

Note: Start a drawing, set the dimensioning variables, and save the drawing as a template for future dimensioning projects.

FIGURE 10–25

Exercise 10–1: Dimensioning
Variables (Plotting Scale: $\frac{1}{8}''$ =
1'-0"; Plotting Size: $8\frac{1}{2}'' \times 11''$)

DIMALT	Off	Alternate units selected
DIMALTD	2	Alternate unit decimal places
DIMALTF	25.40000	Alternate unit scale factor
DIMALTTD	2	Alternate tolerance decimal places
DIMALTTZ	0	Alternate tolerance zero suppression
DIMALTU	2	Alternate units
DIMALTZ	0	Alternate unit zero suppression
DIMAPOST		Prefix and suffix for alternate text
DIMASO	On	Crate associative dimensions
DIMASZ	1/16"	Arrow size
DIMAUNIT	0	Angular unit format
DIMBLK		Arrow block name
DIMBLK1		First arrow block name
DIMBLK2		Second arrow block name
DIMCEN	1/32"	Center mark size
DIMCLRD	BYBLOCK	Dimension line and leader color
DIMCLRE	BYBLOCK	Extension line color
DIMCLRT	BYBLOCK	Dimension text color
DIMDEC	0	Decimal places
DIMDLE	1/16"	Dimension line extension
DIMDLI	3/8"	Dimension line spacing
DIMEXE	1/16"	Extension above dimension line
DIMEXO	1/16"	Extension line origin offset
DIMFIT	3	Fit text
DIMGAP	1/32"	Gap from dimension line to text
DIMJUST	0	Justification of text on dimension
line		
DIMLFAC	1.00000	Linear unit scale factor
DIMLIM	Off	Generate dimension limits
DIMPOST		Prefix and suffix for dimension text
DIMRND	0"	Rounding value
DIMSAH	Off	Separate arrow blocks
DIMSCALE	96.00000	Overall scale factor
DIMSD1	Off	Suppress the first dimension line
DIMSD2	Off	Suppress the second dimension line
DIMSE1	Off	Suppress the first extension line
DIMSE2	Off	Suppress the second extension line
DIMSHO	On	Update dimensions while dragging
DIMSOXD	Off	Suppress outside dimension lines
DIMSTYLE	STYLE1	Current dimension style (read-only)
DIMTAD	1	Place text above the dimension line
DIMTDEC	4	Tolerance decimal places
DIMTFAC	1.00000	Tolerance text height scaling factor
DIMTIH	Off	Text inside extensions is horizontal
DIMTIX	Off	Place text inside extensions
DIMTM	0"	Minus tolerance
DIMTOFL	On	Force line inside extension lines
DIMTOH	Off	Text outside horizontal
DIMTOL	Off	Tolerance dimensioning
DIMTOLJ	1	Tolerance vertical justification
DIMTP	0"	Plus tolerance
DIMTSZ	1/32"	Tick size
DIMTVP	0.00000	Text vertical position
DIMTXSTY	STANDARD	Text style
DIMTXT	1/16"	Text height
DIMTZIN	0	Tolerance zero suppression
DIMUNIT	6	Unit format
DIMUPT	Off	User positioned text
DIMZIN	1	Zero suppression

FIGURE 10–26

Exercise 10–1: Dimensioning
Variables (Plotting Scale: $\frac{1}{4}''$ =
1'-0"; Plotting Size: $8\frac{1}{2}'' \times 11''$)

DIMALT	Off	Alternate units selected
DIMALTD	2	Alternate unit decimal places
DIMALTF	25.4000	Alternate unit scale factor
DIMALTTD	2	Alternate tolerance decimal places
DIMALTTZ	0	Alternate tolerance zero suppression
DIMALTU	2	Alternate units
DIMALTZ	0	Alternate unit zero suppression
DIMAPOST		Prefix and suffix for alternate text
DIMASO	On	Crate associative dimensions
DIMASZ	1/16"	Arrow size
DIMAUNIT	0	Angular unit format
DIMBLK		Arrow block name
DIMBLK1		First arrow block name
DIMBLK2		Second arrow block name
DIMCEN	1/32"	Center mark size
DIMCLRD	BYBLOCK	Dimension line and leader color
DIMCLRE	BYBLOCK	Extension line color
DIMCLRT	BYBLOCK	Dimension text color
DIMDEC	0	Decimal places
DIMDLE	1/16"	Dimension line extension
DIMDLI	3/8"	Dimension line spacing
DIMEXE	1/16"	Extension above dimension line
DIMEXO	1/16"	Extension line origin offset
DIMFIT	3	Fit text
DIMGAP	1/32"	Gap from dimension line to text
DIMJUST	0	Justification of text on dimension line
DIMLFAC	1.00000	Linear unit scale factor
DIMLIM	Off	Generate dimension limits
DIMPOST		Prefix and suffix for dimension text
DIMRND	0"	Rounding value
DIMSAH	Off	Separate arrow blocks
DIMSCALE	48.00000	Overall scale factor
DIMSD1	Off	Suppress the first dimension line
DIMSD2	Off	Suppress the second dimension line
DIMSE1	Off	Suppress the first extension line
DIMSE2	Off	Suppress the second extension line
DIMSHO	On	Update dimensions while dragging
DIMSOXD	Off	Suppress outside dimension lines
DIMSTYLE	STYLE1	Current dimension style (read-only)
DIMTAD	1	Place text above the dimension line
DIMTDEC	4	Tolerance decimal places
DIMTFAC	1.00000	Tolerance text height scaling factor
DIMTIH	Off	Text inside extensions is horizontal
DIMTIX	Off	Place text inside extensions
DIMTM	0"	Minus tolerance
DIMTOFL	On	Force line inside extension lines
DIMTOH	Off	Text outside horizontal
DIMTOL	Off	Tolerance dimensioning
DIMTOLJ	1	Tolerance vertical justification
DIMTP	0"	Plus tolerance
DIMTSZ	1/32"	Tick size
DIMTVP	0.00000	Text vertical position
DIMTXSTY	STANDARD	Text style
DIMTXT	1/16"	Text height
DIMTZIN	0	Tolerance zero suppression
DIMUNIT	6	Unit format
DIMUPT	Off	User positioned text
DIMZIN	1	Zero suppression

Linear and Continue Dimensioning

Using Linear, dimension the column and one mullion on the north exterior wall of the tenant space floor plan (Figure 10–27):

Prompt	Response
Command:	**Linear**
First extension line origin or press ENTER to select:	**D1** (on snap)
Second extension line origin:	**View, Zoom-Window** (from the menu bar)
>>First corner:	**Window the northwest corner of the president's office.**
>>Other corner:	
Second extension line origin:	**D2**
Dimension line location (Mtext/Text/Angle/Horizontal/Vertical/Rotated):	**D3** (on snap, three grid marks up, with 12″ grid)
Command:	**<enter>**
First extension line origin or press ENTER to select:	TYPE: **INT<enter>**
of	**D4**
Second extension line origin:	TYPE: **INT<enter>**
of	**D5** (may want to turn snap off)
Dimension line location (Mtext/Text/Angle/Horizontal/Vertical/Rotated):	**D6** (on snap, three grid marks up)

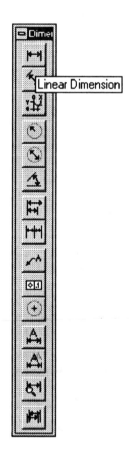

FIGURE 10–27
Linear Dimensioning

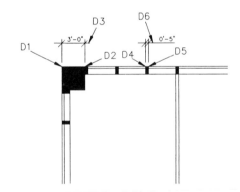

In the Linear command, after the second extension line origin is selected, the prompt reads:

Prompt

Dimension line location
(Mtext/Text/Angle/Horizontal/Vertical/Rotated):

Before you pick a dimension line location, you may type the first letter of any of the options in the parentheses and press enter to activate it. These options are as follows:

Mtext

To activate the multiline text command for dimensions requiring more than one line of text.

Text

To replace the default text with a single line of text. To suppress the text entirely, press the space bar.

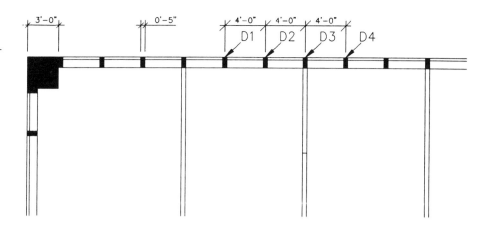

FIGURE 10–28
Linear Dimensioning with the Continue Command to draw Horizontal Dimensions

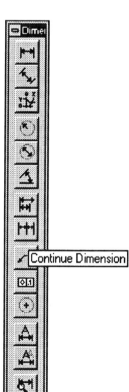

Angle

To rotate the text of the dimension to a specific angle.

Horizontal

To specify that you want a horizontal dimension; this is normally not necessary.

Vertical

To specify that you want a vertical dimension; this is normally not necessary.

Rotated

To specify that you want to rotate the entire dimension.

Using Linear and Continue, dimension horizontally (center to center) the distance between four mullions on the north exterior wall of the tenant space (Figure 10–28). (Before continuing, Zoom in or Pan over to the four mullions to be dimensioned.)

Prompt	Response
Command:	**Linear**
First extension line origin or press ENTER to select:	TYPE: **MID<enter>**
of	**D1**
Second extension line origin:	TYPE: **MID<enter>**
of	**D2**
Dimension line location (Mtext/Text/Angle/Horizontal/Vertical/Rotated):	**Click a point on snap, three grid marks up, to align with previous dimensions.**
Command:	**Continue**
Specify a second extension line origin or (Undo/<Select>):	TYPE: **MID <enter>**
of	**D3**
Specify a second extension line origin or (Undo/<Select>):	TYPE: **MID<enter>**
of	**D4**
Specify a second extension origin or (Undo/<Select>):	**<enter>**
Select continued dimension:	**<enter>**

Using Linear and Continue, dimension vertically (center to center) the distance between four mullions on the west exterior wall of the tenant space (Figure 10–29). (Before continuing, Zoom in on the four mullions to be dimensioned.)

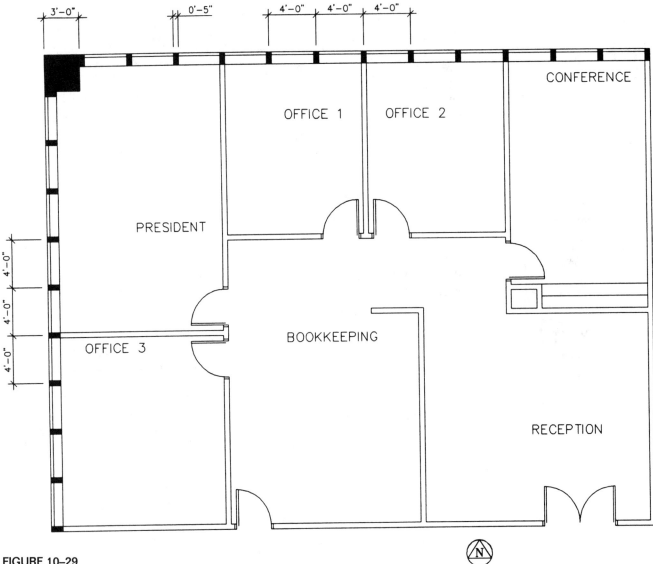

FIGURE 10–29
Linear Dimensioning with the Continue Command to Draw Vertical Dimensions
(Scale: $\frac{1''}{8}$ = 1'-0")

	Prompt	Response
	Command:	**Linear**
	First extension line origin or press ENTER to select:	TYPE: **MID<enter>**
	of	**Click the first mullion.** (Dimension south to north.)
	Second extension line origin:	TYPE: **MID<enter>**
Note: You may change the dimension string at the prompt "Dimension line location", by typing **T<enter>**, then typing new dimensions from the keyboard and pressing the enter key.	of	**Pick the second mullion.**
	Dimension line location (Mtext/Text/Angle/Horizontal/Vertical/ Rotated):	**Pick a point on snap, three grid marks to the left, similar to previous dimension line locations.**
Tip: Use Osnap commands often to select extension line origins.	Dim:	**Continue**
	Specify a second extension line origin or (Undo/<Select>):	TYPE: **MID<enter>**
Note: You can use the default dimension text, supply your own text, or suppress the text entirely.	of	**Pick the third mullion.**
	Specify a second extension line origin or (Undo/<Select>):	TYPE: **MID<enter>**

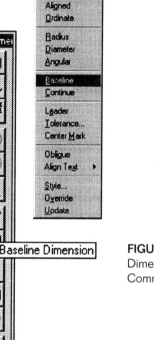

Aligned Dimension

Baseline Dimension

mid of

Specify a second extension line origin or
(Undo/<Select>):

Select continued dimension:

Pick the fourth mullion.

<enter>

<enter>

Aligned Dimensioning

When Aligned is used, you can select the first and second extension line origin points of a line that is at an angle, and the dimension line will run parallel to the origin points. Figure 10–30 shows an example of aligned dimensioning.

Baseline Dimensioning

With Linear dimensioning, after the first segment of a line is dimensioned, picking the Baseline Command in the Dimension menu automatically continues the next linear dimension from the baseline (first extension line) of the first linear dimension. The new

ALIGNED

FIGURE 10–30
Dimensioning with the Aligned
Command

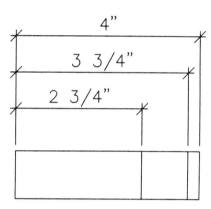

FIGURE 10–31
Linear Dimensioning with the Baseline
Command

dimension line is offset to avoid drawing on top of the previous dimension. The DIMDLI variable controls the size of the offset. Figure 10–31 shows linear dimensioning with the Baseline command.

Tip: Use the transparent Zoom and Pan commands while in the DIM: mode. You will find them very helpful.

Caution: When erasing construction lines, avoid selecting definition points; otherwise the dimension associated with that point will be erased.

On Your Own

See Figure 10–32.

1. Use Dtext, centered, to add the text "12 TYP. SPACES @4'-0" = 48'-0'" to the plan. Place it two grid marks (on a 12" grid) above the dimension line of the mullions dimension. Set the text height to 6".

2. Use Linear to dimension the overall north exterior wall of the tenant space. You may snap to the tick (intersection) of a previous dimension.

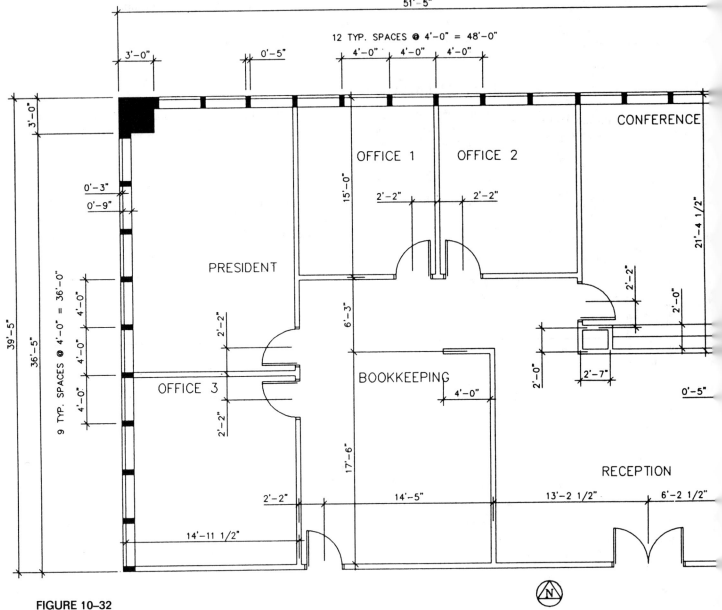

FIGURE 10-32
Complete Exercise 10-1 (Scale: $\frac{1}{8}'' = 1'-0''$)

Note: When stacking dimension lines, locate the first dimension line farther from the object being dimensioned than subsequent dimension lines are from each other. For example, locate the first dimension line three grid marks from the object and the second dimension line two grid marks from the first dimension line.

3. Use Dtext, centered, to add the text "9 TYP. SPACES @ 4'-0" = 36'-0" " to the plan. Place it two grid marks (on a 12" grid) above the dimension line of the mullions dimension. Set the text height to 6".

4. Use Linear to dimension from the southwest corner of the tenant space to the southern corner of the column. Use Continue to continue the dimension to the outside northwest corner of the building.

5. Use Linear to dimension the overall west exterior wall of the tenant space.

6. Complete the dimensioning using the Linear dimension commands. Use the Line command and appropriate Osnap modifiers to draw a temporary line across any doorways, or walls that are dimensioned to the center. Using Osnap-Midpoint, pick the lines to locate the extension line origin of the dimensions.

   When you are dimensioning from left to right, any outside dimension line and text will be placed to the right. Dimensioning from right to left draws any outside dimension line and text to the left.

7. Erase the temporary lines drawn in the doorways and walls. Be careful not to pick a def-point (small points on the drawing used to create associative dimensions); otherwise an entire dimension will be erased. Zoom in closely when you are erasing to avoid defpoints.

SAVE

When you have completed Exercise 10–1, save your work in at least two places.

PLOT

Printer Plot or Plotter Plot Exercise 10–1, at a scale to correspond with the specified DIMSCALE setting.

EXERCISE 10–2
Associative Dimension Commands and Grips

Exercise 10–2 describes the dimensioning commands that can be used only when DIMASO and Grips are on. When you have completed Exercise 10–2, your drawing will look similar to Figure 10–33. To begin, turn on the computer and start AutoCAD. The Start Up dialog box is displayed.

FIGURE 10–33
Exercise 10–2: Associative Dimension Commands (Scale: $\frac{1}{8}'' = 1'-0''$)

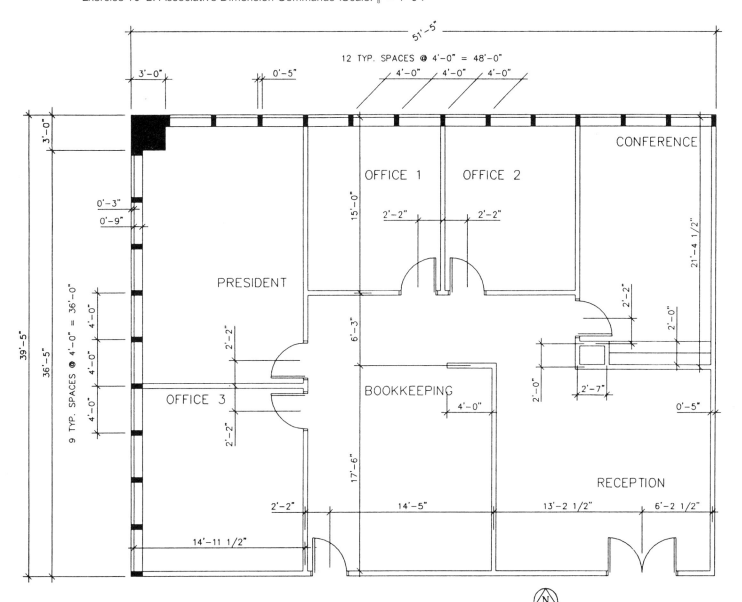

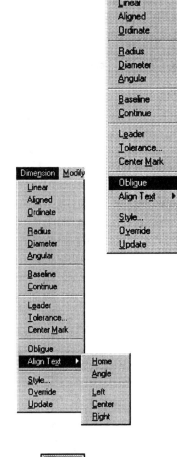

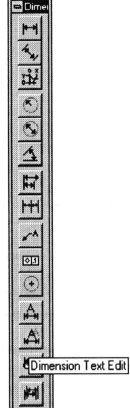

On Your Own

Open drawing CH10-EX1 from a floppy in drive A and save it as CH10-EX2 to the hard drive.

Associative Dimension Commands

When the DIMASO variable is on, each dimension that is drawn is created as a block. That means that the extension lines, dimension lines, ticks or arrows, text, and all other parts of the dimensions are entered as a single unit. When DIMASO is on, the dimensions drawn are called associative dimensions. When DIMASO is off, the extension lines, dimension lines and all other parts of the dimension are drawn as separate entities.

Six dimension commands—Oblique, Align Text, Dimension Edit, Override, Update, and Newtext—can be used only with associative dimensions (if DIMASO was on while you drew the dimensions). The following describes those commands.

Oblique

Create an oblique angle for the extension lines of the four mullions on the north exterior wall of the tenant space (Figure 10–34).

Prompt	Response
Command:	**Oblique** (or TYPE: **OB\<enter\>** from the DIM: prompt)
Select objects:	**Pick the extension lines of the mullion dimensions until they are all highlighted.**
Select objects:	**\<enter\>**
Enter obliquing angle (press ENTER for none):	TYPE: **45\<enter\>**

The extension lines of the mullion dimensions appear as shown in Figure 10–34.

Align Text-Angle

Rotate the text for the overall dimension on the north exterior wall of the tenant space. (Before continuing, Zoom in on the dimension text, "51′-5″".) (Figure 10–35)

Prompt	Response
Dim:	**Align Text-Angle**
Select dimension:	**Pick the dimension text, "51′-5″".**
Enter text angle:	TYPE: **30\<enter\>**

The text is rotated as shown in Figure 10–35.

Align Text-Home-Left-Center-Right

Change the placement of the text for the overall dimension on the west exterior wall of the tenant space to flush right, and return it to the center position:

Prompt	Response
Command:	**Align Text-Right**
Select dimension:	**Pick the dimension text, 39′-5″.**
Command:	**Align Text-Center**
Select objects:	**Pick the same dimension\<enter\>**

The Left option left justifies the text along the dimension line. The Angle option allows you either to type a new text angle (and press enter) or to pick two points to show AutoCAD new text angle. The Home option returns the dimension text to its home position.

Dimension Edit

When Dimension Edit is clicked from the Tool Bar or **DIMED** is typed at the Command: prompt, the Dimension Edit prompt is "Dimension Edit (Home/New/Rotate/Oblique) \<Home\>:" To activate any one of the options type the first letter:

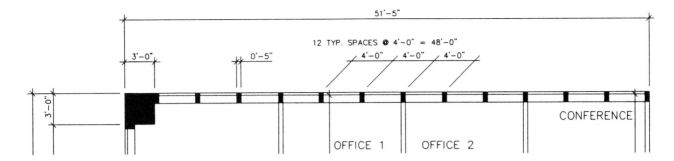

FIGURE 10–34
Using the Oblique Command

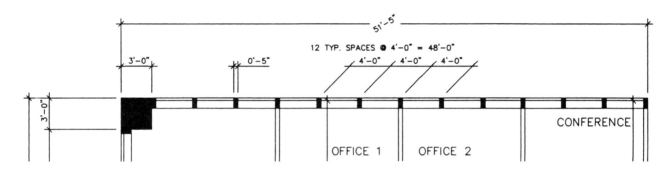

FIGURE 10–35
Using the Trotate Command

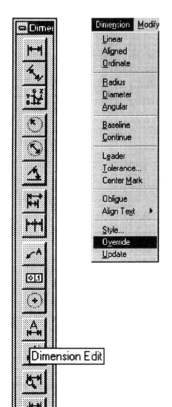

Home   Returns the dimension to its default (original) location in the dimension line.

New   Activates the Multiline Text Editor and allows you to change the existing text. The two brackets you see in the dialog box contain the original text and must be deleted if you want to replace it. Use the Backspace or Delete keys on your keyboard to do that. Then type the new text, click OK, and click the dimension whose text you want to change.

Rotate   Allows you to rotate existing text to a specified angle.

Oblique   Allows you to make an existing dimension into an oblique one.

Override

The Override command is helpful when you are in the middle of dimensioning a project or have completed dimensioning a project and decide that one or more of the dimension variables in a named style needs to be changed. The Override command can be used to change one or more dimension variables for selected dimensions but does not affect the current dimension style.

Use Override to change the DIMTXT variable of STYLE1 from 1/16″ to 1/8″:

Prompt	Response
Dim:	**Override** (or TYPE: **OV<enter>**)
Dimension variable to override (or Clear to remove overrides):	TYPE: **DIMTXT<enter>**
Current value <1/16″> New value:	TYPE: **1/8<enter>**
Dimension variable to override:	**<enter>**
Select objects:	**Pick any dimension entity on the drawing.**
Select objects:	**<enter>**
Dim:	TYPE: **DIMTXT <enter>**
New value for DIMTXT <0′-0 1/16″>:	**<enter>**

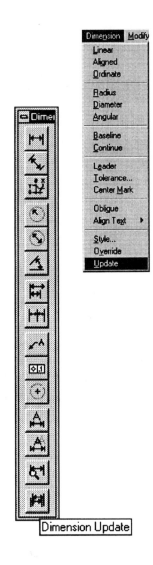

Dimension Update

The DIMTXT of 1/16″ setting has not changed.

Update

Update differs from Override in that it updates dimensions using the current settings of the dimension style. For example, if you decide a dimension variable needs to be changed in a dimension style—change the variable. You may click the Save button in the Dimension Styles dialog box to save the changed variable to the dimension style. If you do not save the changed variable, AutoCAD prompts you with an ALERT dialog box, "Save changes to current style?" when you change dimension styles. Use Update to include the new variable settings in all or part of the dimensions within the drawing.

Use Update to change the 1/8″ DIMTXT back to 1/16″:
Because the Override command did not change DIMTXT within the STYLE1 settings, it is still set at 1/16″.

Prompt	Response
Command:	**Update** (or TYPE: **UP<enter>** from the DIM: prompt)
Select objects:	**Click the dimension entity on the drawing changed with Override.**
Select objects:	**<enter>**

NEWTEXT

When NEWTEXT is typed from the DIM: prompt, AutoCAD prompts, "Dimension text <default>:" A new text string can then be typed and entered. The next prompt, "Select objects:", allows you to select one or more dimension entities that are to be changed to the new text string.

DEFPOINTS Layer

When associative dimensions are created, a special layer named Defpoints is also created. Definition points for associative dimensions are drawn on the Defpoints layer. They are small points on the drawing that are not plotted but are used to create the associative dimension. When an associative dimension is updated or edited, the definition points are redefined.

Modify Commands

In addition to the above commands used to edit associative dimensions, the following Modify commands can be used to edit *the dimensioned object and the accompanying associative dimension*. When editing a dimensioned object, be sure to include the accompanying associative dimension in the selection set.

Array   Scale
Extend   Stretch
Mirror   Trim
Rotate

Modify-Object-Text

Modify-Object-Text from the menu bar works when DIMASO is on or off. It activates the Multiline Text Editor and allows you to change the existing text.

GRIPS

Grips are particularly useful in modifying the placement of dimension text and the location of extension and dimension lines. To use grips to modify a dimension:

Note: Changing the DIMDLE variable and using Update does not change the dimension line increment for continuation of your drawing, because AutoCAD does not remember which dimensions were drawn using Baseline or Continue.

Prompt	Response
Command:	CLICK: **the 14′-11 1/2″ dimension in OFFICE 3**
Five squares appear on the dimension; one at the end of each extension line, one at the center of each tick, and one in the center of the dimension text:	CLICK: **the grip in the center of the dimension text**
The grip changes color (becomes HOT): <Stretch to point>/Base point/Copy/ Undo/eXit:	**With snap on, move your mouse up and** CLICK: **a point two grid marks up.**
The dimension is stretched up two grid marks:	CLICK: **the same grip to make it hot, move your mouse to the right, and** CLICK: **a point two grid marks to the right.**
The dimension text moves two grid marks to the right:	CLICK: **the grip at the origin of the first extension line to make it hot, and move your mouse up two grid marks**
The origin of the first extension line moves up two grid marks:	CLICK: **the grip in the center of the dimension text to make it hot, and press the space bar one time**
The prompt changes to <Move to point>/ Base point/Copy/Undo/eXit:	**Move your cursor two grid marks down and** CLICK: **a point.**
The entire dimension moves down two grid marks:	PRESS: **Esc twice**
The grips disappear:	TYPE: **U<enter>, and continue pressing <enter> until the dimension is returned to its original state.**

Using grips, you can toggle through STRETCH, MOVE, ROTATE, SCALE, and MIR-ROR. A more complete description of grips is given in a later chapter.

SAVE

When you have completed Exercise 10–2, save your work in at least two places.

PLOT

Printer Plot or Plotter Plot Exercise 10–2 at a scale to correspond with the specified DIM-SCALE setting.

EXERCISE 10–3
Angular, Diameter, Radius, and Ordinate Dimensioning

Exercise 10–3 describes four types of dimensioning: Angular, Diameter, Radius, and Ordinate dimensioning. It also describes drawing center marks and leaders. When you have completed Exercise 10–3, your drawing will look similar to Figure 10–36. To begin, turn on the computer and start AutoCAD. The Start Up dialog box is displayed.

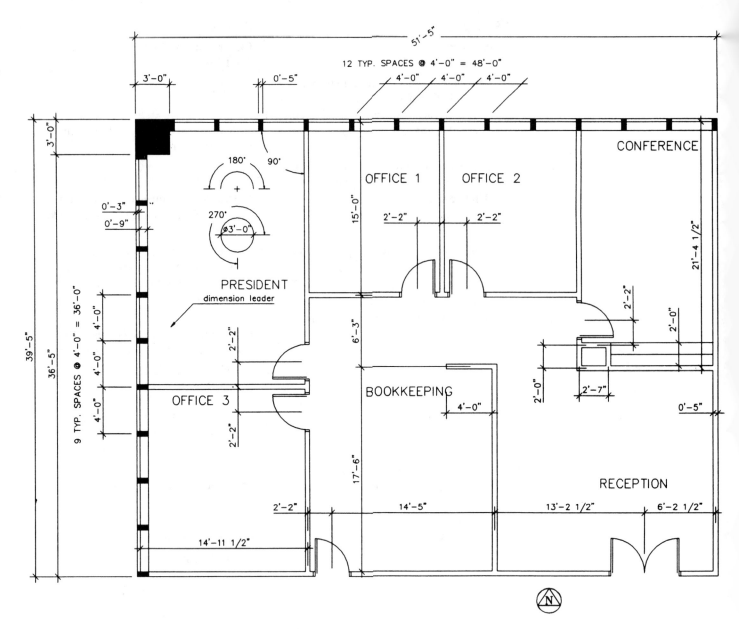

FIGURE 10–36
Exercise 10–3: Angular, Diameter, Radius, and Ordinate Dimensioning

On Your Own

1. Open drawing CH10-EX2 from a floppy disk in drive A and save it as CH10-EX3 to the hard drive.

2. The following part of Exercise 10–3 describes angular and radial dimensioning. To practice with both these dimension types, draw an arc (1'-6" radius) and a circle (1'-6" radius) in the president's office, as shown in Figure 10–37, on the current A-pflr-dims layer.

3. Change the following dimensioning variables:
   DIMTAD—to 0
   DIMTIH—to on

Angular Dimensioning

With the current layer A-pflr-dims, use the Angular command to dimension the angle of an arc (Figure 10–38):

Prompt	Response
Command:	**Angular**
Select arc, circle, line, or press ENTER:	**Click any point on the arc just drawn.**
Dimension arc line location (Mtext/Text/ Angle):	**Click a point on snap, one grid mark (12″) above the arc.**

Use the Angular command to dimension the angle of two points of a circle (Figure 10–38):

Prompt	Response
Command:	**Angular**
Select arc, circle, line, or press ENTER:	**D1** (snap on)
Second angle endpoint:	**D2** (snap on)

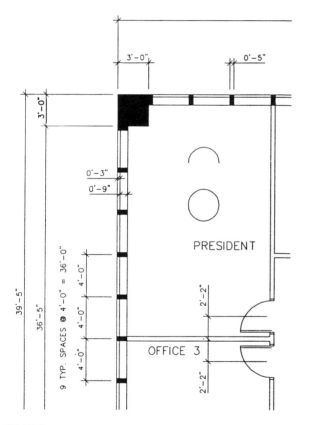

FIGURE 10–37
Draw an Arc and a Circle

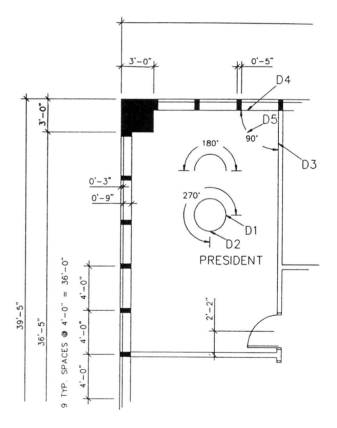

FIGURE 10–38
Using the Angular Command

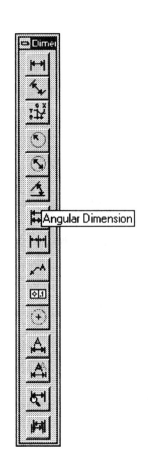

Prompt	Response
Dimension arc line location (Mtext/Text/ Angle):	**Click a point on snap, one grid mark above the circle.**

Use the angular command to dimension the angle of two lines (Figure 10–38):

Prompt	Response
Command:	**Angular**
Select arc, circle, line, or press ENTER:	**D3**
Second line:	**D4**
Dimension arc line location (Mtext/Text/ Angle):	**D5**

When dimensioning angles, AutoCAD uses three defining points—the angle vertex and two angle end points (the dimension extension lines location). When the arc is dimensioned, the center of the arc is the vertex and each end point of the arc locates the angle end points. When a circle is dimensioned, the center of the circle is the vertex, the first point selected is the first angle end point, and the second point selected is the second angle end point. When two lines are selected, the intersection of the two lines is the angle vertex, and either an arc spans the angle between the two lines or AutoCAD provides extension lines for the arc to span. When ENTER is pressed, AutoCAD prompts allow you to pick the angle vertex, the first angle end point, and the second angle end point.

Center Mark

Draw a center mark in an arc (Figure 10–39):

FIGURE 10–39
Using the Center Mark, Diameter, Radius, and Leader Commands

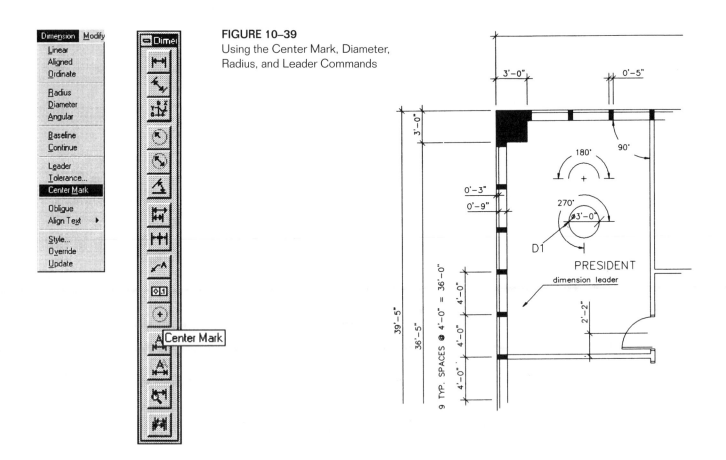

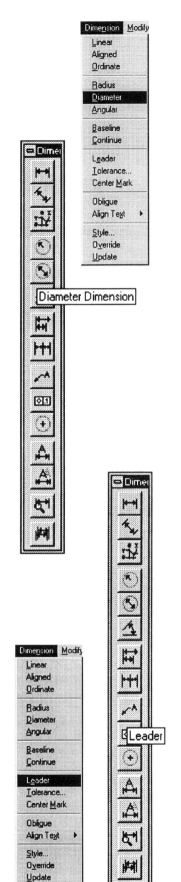

Prompt	Response
Command:	**Center Mark**
Select arc or circle:	**Click any place on the arc.**

A center mark is not associative and cannot be updated.

On Your Own

Change the following dimensioning variables:

DIMTAD—to 1
DIMFIT—to 0

Diameter

Dimension the diameter of a circle (Figure 10–39):

Prompt	Response
Command:	**Diameter**
Select arc or circle:	**D1**
Dimension text = 3′-0″	
Dimension line location (Mtext/Text/Angle):	**D1** (again)

Radius

The radius command is similar to the diameter command except that a radius line is drawn.

Leader

The Leader command draws a leader. It can be used to show dimensions or to place notes on a drawing.

Practice drawing a Leader (Figure 10–39):

Prompt	Response
Command:	**Leader**
From point:	**Pick a point in the president's office.**
To point:	**Pick another point at an angle, two grid marks up.**
To point (Format/Annotation/Undo) <Annotation>:	**<enter>**
Annotation (or press ENTER for options):	TYPE: **dimension leader<enter>**
Mtext:	**<enter>**

Ordinate Dimensioning

Ordinate dimensioning is a method of dimensioning that relates to an identified corner of a part that is the starting point, or point 0,0. The starting point of 0,0 is often called a *datum*. All dimensions are measured from the datum, as shown in Figure 10–40. This type of dimensioning, used for measuring mechanical or sheet-metal parts, is seldom used

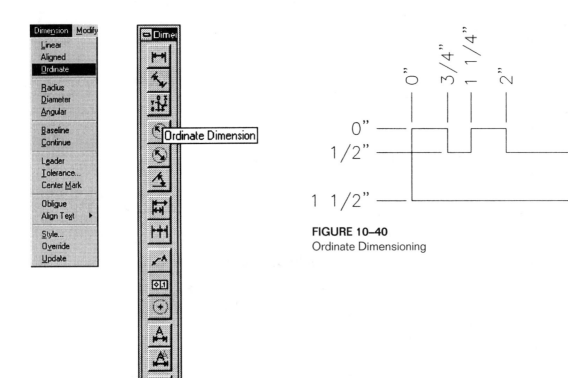

FIGURE 10–40
Ordinate Dimensioning

by architects and space planners. It is similar to baseline dimensioning but does not draw the dimension line.

SAVE

When you have completed Exercise 10–3, save your work in at least two places.

PLOT

Printer Plot or Plotter Plot Exercise 10–3 at a scale to correspond with the DIMSCALE setting.

EXERCISE 10–4
Tenant Space Total Square Feet

Exercise 10–4 provides step-by-step instructions for using the Area command to compute the total square feet of the tenant space floor plan. It also provides instructions for using the Cal (calculator) command. When you have completed Exercise 10–4, your drawing will look similar to Figure 10–41. To begin, turn on the computer and start AutoCAD. The Start Up dialog box is displayed.

On Your Own

Open drawing CH10-EX1 from a floppy disk in drive A and save it as CH10-EX4 to the hard drive.

AREA

To compute the total square feet of any space, the exact area that is to be included must be identified. In the tenant space, the face of the exterior building glass on the north and

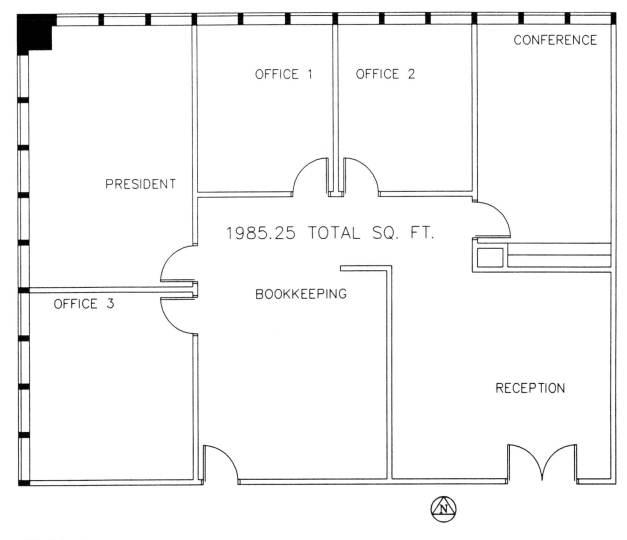

FIGURE 10–41

Exercise 10–4: Tenant Space Total Square Feet (Scale: $\frac{1}{8}'' = 1'\text{-}0''$)

west walls is used as the building's exterior measuring points, and the center of the south and east walls will be used as the interior measuring points.

On Your Own

Completing the following steps will help you to use the Area command (Figure 10–42):

1. Freeze layers A-pflr-dims and Defpoints, and set layer A-area current.

2. TYPE: **FILL\<enter>** then **OFF\<enter>** so that the column and mullions are not solid. Regenerate the drawing.

3. To be able to select the defining points of the exact area, as described above, use the Line command to draw separate lines in each corner of the tenant space to which you can snap using Osnap-Intersection-Midpoint. Each corner with the added lines is shown in Figure 10–42.

Compute the total square feet of the tenant space (Figure 10–42):

Prompt	Response
Command:	**Area** (or TYPE: **AREA\<enter>**)
\<First point>/Object/Add/Subtract:	TYPE: **INT\<enter>**
int of	**Zoom a window around the northwest corner.**

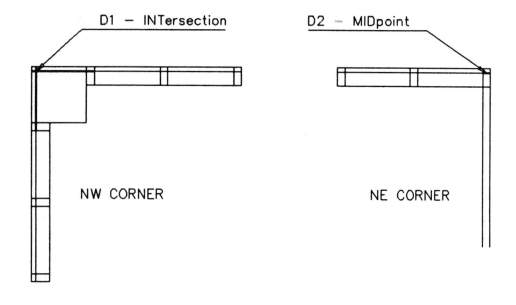

FIGURE 10–42
Defining Points of the Exact Area Included in the
Total Square Feet of the Tenant Space

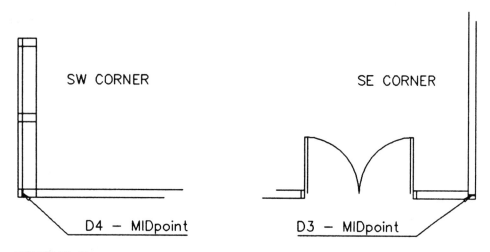

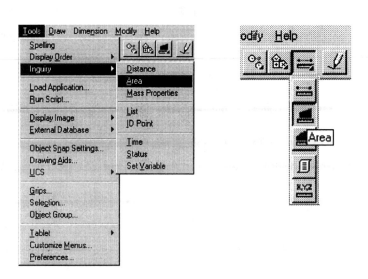

Prompt	Response
Resuming AREA command.	
of	**D1**
Next point:	**Use Zoom-Dynamic to window the northeast corner.**
Resuming AREA command.	
Next point:	**TYPE: MID\<enter\>**
of	**D2**
Next point:	**Use Zoom-Dynamic to window the southeast corner.**
Resuming AREA command.	
Next point:	**TYPE: MID\<enter\>**
of	**D3**
Next point:	**Use Zoom-Dynamic to window the southwest corner.**
Resuming AREA command.	
Next point:	**TYPE: MID\<enter\>**
of	**D4**
Next point:	**\<enter\>**
Area = 285876.25 square in. (1985.2517 square ft.), Perimeter = 179'-10"	
Command:	**Use the Dtext command (12" high) to write the number of total square feet of the drawing.**

Add   When Add is picked, the Area command is placed in an add mode. Add must be picked before the first space (of all the spaces to be added together) is specified. When the first space is specified, the area information is displayed. When the second space is specified, its individual area information is displayed along with the total area information of the two spaces together. Each subsequent space specified is displayed as an individual area total and is added to the running total.

Subtract   When Subtract is picked, each subsequent space specified is displayed as an individual area total and is subtracted from the running total.

Object   Object allows you to compute the area of a selected circle ellipse, polygon, solid, or polyline. For a circle, the area and circumference are displayed. When a wide, closed polyline is picked, the area defined by the center line of the polyline is displayed (the polyline width is ignored). Object is the fastest way to find the area of a closed polyline.

On Your Own

When you have completed practicing with the Area command, turn FILL ON.

CAL

AutoCAD provides a handy calculator function that is similar to many handheld calculators. The following uses the add and divide features of the calculator. You may want to try other features on your own.

Use CAL to add three figures:

+ = add
− = subtract
× = multiply
/ = divide

Prompt	Response
Command:	TYPE: **CAL<enter>**
>>Expression:	TYPE: **2′6″ + 6′2″ + 4′1″<enter>**
153.0	**<enter>**(Because the value is in inches it should be divided by 12 to arrive at feet.)
>>Expression	TYPE: **153/12<enter>**
12.75 (or 12′-9″)	

SAVE

When you have completed Exercise 10–4, save your work in at least two places.

PLOT

Printer Plot or Plotter Plot Exercise 10–4 to scale.

EXERCISE 10–5
Office I Dimensioned Plan

1. Set dimensioning variables for the office I floor plan completed in Exercise 9–2.
2. Create a new layer for dimensions, and dimension the interior of the office I floor plan.
3. Printer Plot or Plotter Plot the drawing to scale.

EXERCISE 10–6
Office II Dimensioned Plan

1. Set dimensioning variables for the office II floor plan completed in Exercise 9–3.
2. Create a new layer for dimensions, and dimension the interior of the office II floor plan.
3. Printer Plot or Plotter Plot the drawing to scale.

EXERCISE 10–7
House Dimensioned Plan

1. Set dimensioning variables for the house floor plan completed in Exercise 9–4.
2. Create a new layer for dimensions, and dimension the interior of the house floor plan.
3. Printer Plot or Plotter Plot the drawing to scale.

EXERCISE 10–8
Country Club Dimensioned Plan

1. Set dimensioning variables for the country club floor plan completed in Exercise 9–5.
2. Create a new layer for dimensions, and dimension the interior of the country club floor plan.
3. Printer Plot or Plotter Plot the drawing to scale.

REVIEW QUESTIONS

1. A complete list of current dimensioning variables and settings is displayed when which of the following is typed from the Dim: prompt?
   a. LINEAR
   b. DIM VARS
   c. STATUS
   d. DIMSTYLE
   e. UPDATE

2. Which of the following dimensioning variables controls the height of text used in the dimension?
   a. DIMSTYLE
   b. DIMTSZ
   c. DIMASZ
   d. DIMTXT
   e. DIMTIX
3. Which of the following dimensioning variables controls the length of the arrowhead used in the dimension?
   a. DIMSTYLE
   b. DIMTSZ
   c. DIMASZ
   d. DIMTXT
   e. DIMTIX
4. If a full-size drawing is to be plotted at a plotting ratio of $\frac{1}{8}'' = 12''$, the DIMSCALE value should be set to
   a. 1
   b. 12
   c. 24
   d. 48
   e. 96
5. For DIMTAD to place dimensions above vertical dimension lines, which of the following must be off?
   a. DIMLIM
   b. DIMTAD
   c. DIMTOL
   d. DIMTP
   e. DIMTIH
6. Which of the following dimensioning variables forces the dimensioning text between the extension lines?
   a. DIMTOFL
   b. DIMTIX
   c. DIMSOXD
   d. DIMTIH
   e. DIMTOH
7. Which of the following commands can be used only on associative dimensions?
   a. Linear
   b. Diameter
   c. Ordinate
   d. Oblique
   e. Angular
8. Which of the following commands can be used to change the dimension text string for an associative dimension?
   a. Update
   b. Change
   c. Trotate
   d. Modify-Object-Text
   e. Hometext
9. A DEFPOINTS layer is created when a dimension is drawn with which of the following dimensioning variables set to on?
   a. DIMSTYLE
   b. DIMTOH
   c. DIMTAD
   d. DIMASO
   e. DIMTIH
10. To find the area of a closed polyline most quickly, which of the Area options should be used?
    a. Object
    b. Poly
    c. Add
    d. Subtract
    e. First point

11. List the three categories of dimensioning variables described in the Dimension Styles dialog box.

1. _____

2. _____

3. _____

12. Describe the use of the dimensioning variable DIMDEC.

_____

_____

_____

_____

13. Describe the use of the dimensioning variable DIMUNIT.

_____

_____

14. Which settings must be made for dimensioning variable values to be displayed in 32nds of an inch?

_____

_____

15. Describe the use of the Continue command for linear dimensioning.

_____

_____

16. Write the name of the dimensioning variable that is used when you design your own arrow block.

_____

17. Describe how to save and name a set of dimensioning variables for a drawing.

_____

_____

_____

_____

18. Describe how the Update command differs from the Override command.

_____

_____

_____

_____

19. Describe the use of the Update command.

_____

_____

_____

_____

20. Describe the use of Grips to move dimensioning text.

_____

_____

_____

_____

11 Drawing Elevations, Wall Sections, and Details

OBJECTIVES

When you have completed this chapter, you will be able to:

☐ Correctly use the following commands and settings:

Edit Hatch	Rename...
Filters	Stretch
Hatch...	UCS
Mirror	UCS Icon
Named UCS... (DDUCS)	

INTRODUCTION

The AutoCAD program makes it possible to produce clear, accurate, and impressive drawings of elevations, sections, and details. Many of the commands you have already learned are used in this chapter, along with some new commands, to draw an elevation (Exercise 11–1), a section (Exercise 11–2), and a detail (Exercise 11–3) of parts of the tenant space project.

EXERCISE 11–1
Tenant Space: Elevation of Conference Room Cabinets

In Exercise 11–1, an elevation of the south wall of the tenant space conference room is drawn. The south wall of the tenant space conference room has built-in cabinets that include a refrigerator and a sink. When you have completed Exercise 11–1, your drawing will look similar to Figure 11–1. To begin, turn on the computer and start AutoCAD. The Start Up dialog box is displayed.

1. CLICK: **Use a Wizard**
2. CLICK: **Quick Setup**
   CLICK: **OK**
3. Set drawing Units: **Architectural**
   CLICK: **Next>>**
4. Set drawing Width: **25′** × Length: **24′**
   CLICK: **Done**
5. **Use SaveAs... to save the drawing on the hard drive with the name CH11-EX1.**
6. Set Grid: **12″**

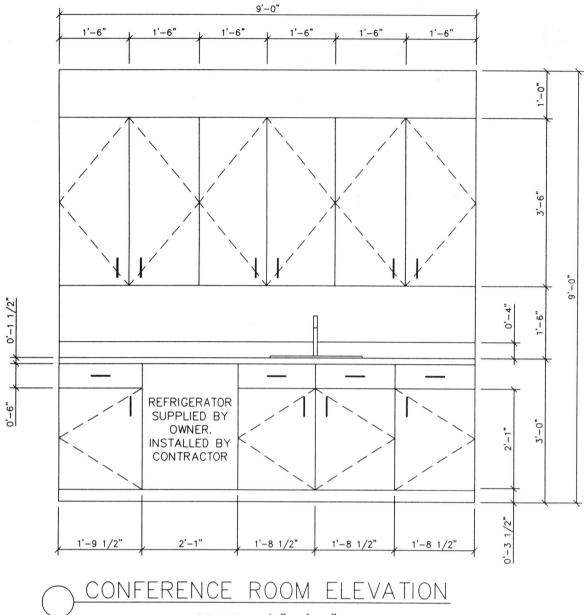

CONFERENCE ROOM ELEVATION

SCALE: 1/2"=1'-0"

FIGURE 11–1
Exercise 11–1: Tenant Space, Elevation of Conference Room Cabinets (Scale: $\frac{1}{2}''$ = 1'-0'')

7. Set Snap: **6"**

8. Create the following Layers:

LAYER NAME	COLOR	LINETYPE
A-elev	Red	Continuous
A-elev-hid	Green	Hidden
A-elev-text	White	Continuous
A-elev-dim	Blue	Continuous

9. Set Layer A-elev current.

FIGURE 11–2
The Typical UCS Icon, and
the UCS Icon as It Appears
in Paper Space

UCS

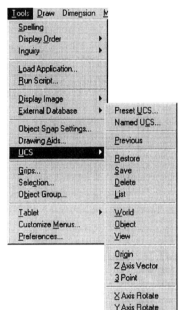

While you were drawing with AutoCAD in previous chapters, the UCS (User Coordinate System) icon was located in the lower left corner of your drawings. A coordinate system is simply the X, Y, and Z coordinates used in your drawings. For two-dimensional drawings, only the X and Y coordinates are meaningful. The Z coordinate is used for a three-dimensional model.

Notice that the UCS Icon (Figure 11–2) has a W on it. The W stands for World Coordinate System. This is the AutoCAD fixed coordinate system, which is common to all AutoCAD drawings.

The UCS command is used to set up a new User Coordinate System or to modify the existing one. When UCS is typed from the Command: prompt, the prompt is "Origin/ZAxis/3point/OBject/View/X/Y/Z/Prev/Restore/Sav/Del/?/<World>:".

The Z coordinate is described and used extensively in the chapters that cover three-dimensional modeling. The UCS command options that apply to two dimensions are listed next.

Origin

Used to define a new UCS at a different origin (0,0) point.

OBject

Allows you to define a new UCS by pointing to a drawing object such as an arc, point, circle, or line.

Save

Allows you to name and save a newly created UCS so that you can use it again.

Restore

Allows you to recall a UCS, using the name you gave it when you saved it.

Previous

Makes the previous UCS current.

Delete

Allows you to delete one or more saved UCSs.

World

This is the AutoCAD fixed coordinate system, which is common to all AutoCAD drawings. In most cases you will want to return to the World Coordinate System before plotting any drawing.

?

Lists the names of the saved User Coordinate Systems.

Use the UCS command to change the origin of the current UCS:

Prompt	Response
Command:	TYPE: **UCS<enter>**
Origin/ZAxis/3point/OBject/View/X/Y/Z/ Prev/Restore/Save/Del/?/<World>:	TYPE: **O<enter>** (to select origin) (or CLICK: **UCS-Origin**)
Origin point <0,0,0>:	TYPE: **8′, 12′<enter>**

The origin for the current user coordinate system is now 8′ in the X direction and 12′ in the Y direction. Notice that the UCS Icon did not move from where 0,0 was originally located. The UCS Icon command, described next, is used to control the orientation and visibility of the UCS Icon.

UCS Icon

The UCS Icon command is used to control the visibility and orientation of the UCS Icon (Figure 11–2). The UCS Icon appears as arrows (most often located in the lower left corner of an AutoCAD drawing) that show the orientation of the X-, Y-, and Z-axes of the current UCS. It appears as a triangle in paper space (paper space is discussed in Chapter 15). The UCS Icon command prompt is "ON/OFF/All/Noorigin/ORigin<ON>:". The UCS Icon command options are listed next.

ON

Allows you to turn on the UCS Icon if it is not visible.

OFF

Allows you to turn off the UCS Icon when it gets in the way. This has nothing to do with the UCS location—only the visibility of the UCS Icon.

All

Allows you to apply changes to the UCS Icon in all active viewports. (The Viewports command, which allows you to create multiple viewports, is described in Chapter 15.)

ORigin

Forces the UCS Icon to be displayed at the origin of the current UCS. For example, when USC Icon-Origin is clicked, the new UCS that you just created will appear in its correct position. If the origin of the UCS is off the screen, the icon is still displayed in the lower left corner of the screen.

Noorigin

When Noorigin is current, the UCS Icon is displayed at the lower left corner of the screen.

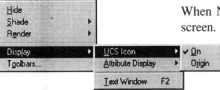

Use the UCS Icon command to force the UCS Icon to be displayed at the origin of the new, current UCS:

Prompt	Response
Command:	TYPE: **UCSICON<enter>**
ON/OFF/All/Noorigin/ORigin<ON>:	TYPE: **OR<enter>** (or CLICK: **UCS Icon-Origin**)

The UCS Icon now moves to the 8′, 12′ coordinate location. You can now begin to draw the cabinets using the new UCS location.

Using absolute coordinates, draw the lines forming the first upper cabinet door. Start the drawing at the 0,0, location of the new UCS (Figure 11–3):

Prompt	Response
Command:	**Line** (or TYPE: **L<enter>**)
From point:	TYPE: **0,0<enter>**
To point:	TYPE: **18,0<enter>**
To point:	TYPE: **18,3′6<enter>**
To point:	TYPE: **0,3′6<enter>**
To point:	TYPE: **C<enter>**

FIGURE 11–3
Draw the Lines Forming the First
Upper Cabinet Door

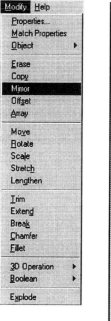

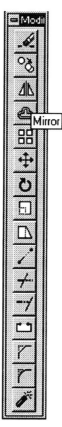

Use Polyline to draw the door hardware using absolute coordinates (Figure 11–3):

Prompt	Response
Command:	**Polyline** (or TYPE: **PL<enter>**)
From Point:	TYPE: **15,2<enter>**
Arc/Close/Halfwidth/Length/Undo/Width/ <Endpoint of line>:	TYPE: **W<enter>**
Starting width <0'-0">:	TYPE: **1/4<enter>**
Ending width <0'-0 1/4">:	**<enter>**
Arc/Close/Halfwidth/Length/Undo/Width/ <Endpoint of line>:	TYPE: **15,7<enter>**
Arc/Close/Halfwidth/Length/Undo/Width/ <Endpoint of line>:	**<enter>**

On Your Own

Set Layer A-elev-hid current.

Draw the dashed lines of the door using absolute coordinates (Figure 11–3):

Prompt	Response
Command:	**Line** (or TYPE: **L<enter>**)
From point:	TYPE: **18,3'6<enter>**
To point:	TYPE: **0,21<enter>**
To point:	TYPE: **18,0<enter>**
To point:	TYPE: **<enter>**

On Your Own

If needed, change the linetype scale of the Hidden linetype to make it appear as dashes, change the linetype to Hidden2, or both. A large linetype scale such as 24 is needed.

MIRROR

The Mirror command allows you to mirror about an axis any entity or group of entities. The axis can be at any angle.

Note: If you want to mirror a part of a drawing containing text but do not want the text to be a mirror image, change the MIRRTEXT system variable setting to 0. This allows you to mirror the part and leave the text "right reading." When MIRRTEXT is set to 1 (the default), text is given a mirror image. To change this setting TYPE: **MIRRTEXT<enter>**, then TYPE: **0<enter>**.

Draw the second cabinet door, using the Mirror command to copy part of the cabinet door just drawn. The top and bottom lines of the cabinet door are not mirrored (Figure 11–4):

FIGURE 11–4
Use the Mirror Command to Copy
Part of the Cabinet Door

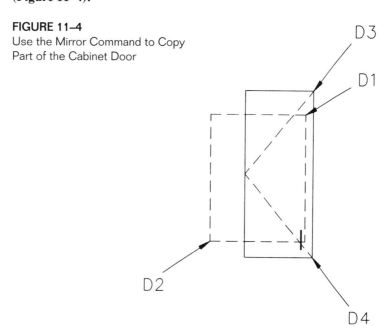

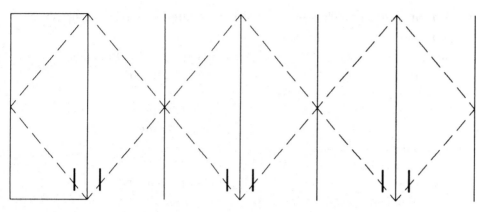

FIGURE 11–5
Use the Mirror Command to Draw the Inside of the Cabinet Doors and the Right Vertical
Edge of the Next Two Sets of Doors

Prompt	Response
Command:	**Mirror** (or TYPE: **MI\<enter>**)
Select objects:	**D1** (with SNAP On)
Other corner:	**D2**
Select objects:	**\<enter>**
First point of mirror line:	**D3** (with ORTHO and SNAP on)
Second point:	**D4**
Delete old objects? \<N>	**\<enter>**

On Your Own

Use the Mirror command to draw the inside and the right vertical cabinet edge of the next
two sets of doors. When this step is completed, your drawing will look like Figure 11–5.

You will extend the lines forming the top and bottom of the first cabinet later so that you
do not have 12 small lines instead of 2 long lines. Having extra line segments increases the
size of your drawing file and creates a drawing that is sometimes difficult to change.

Use the Mirror command to draw the first lower cabinet door (Figure 11–6):

Prompt	Response
Command:	**Mirror** (or TYPE: **MI\<enter>**)
Select objects:	**D2**
Other corner:	**D1**
Select objects:	**\<enter>**
First point of mirror line:	**D3** (with ORTHO and SNAP on; the lower cabinets will be moved to the accurate location later)
Second point:	**D4**
Delete old objects? \<N>	**\<enter>**

Note: A crossing window is clicked right to left.

The lower cabinet door is now too high and too narrow. The Stretch command can be
used to shrink the cabinet to the correct height and stretch it to the correct width.

STRETCH

The Stretch command can be used to stretch entities to make them longer or shorter. It can
also be used to move entities that have other lines attached to them without removing the
attached lines (described later in this exercise). Stretch requires you to use a crossing window
to select objects. As with many other Modify commands, you may select objects initially,
then remove or add objects to the selection set before you perform the stretch function.

Part II: Two-Dimensional AutoCAD

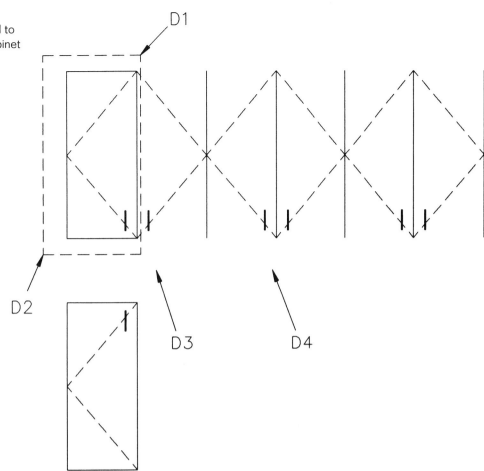

FIGURE 11–6
Use the Mirror Command to Draw the First Lower Cabinet Door

D1

D2

D3

D4

Use the Stretch command to change the height of the first lower cabinet door just drawn (Figure 11–7):

Prompt	Response
Command:	**Stretch** (or TYPE: **S\<enter\>**)
Select objects to stretch by crossing-window or crossing-polygon...	
Select objects:	**D1**
Other corner:	**D2**
Select objects:	**\<enter\>**
Base point or displacement:	**D3** (any point)
Second point of displacement:	TYPE: **@8-1/2<270\<enter\>** (the upper door height, 3'6", minus the lower door height, 2'1", divided by 2; take half off the top of the door and half off the bottom)
Command:	**Stretch** (or PRESS: **\<enter\>**)
Select objects to stretch by crossing-window or crossing-polygon...	
Select objects:	**D4**
Other corner:	**D5**
Select objects:	**\<enter\>**
Base point or displacement:	**D3** (any point)
Second point of displacement:	TYPE: **@8-1/2<90\<enter\>**

FIGURE 11–7
Use the Stretch Command to
Change the Height of the First
Lower Cabinet Door

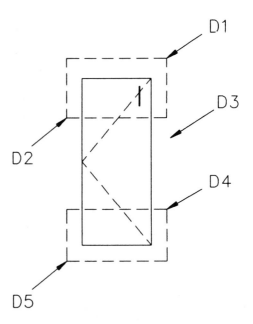

The lower cabinet door should now be 17″ shorter than the upper cabinet door from which it was mirrored (3′6″ minus 17″ equals 2′1″, the cabinet door height). Now let's use Stretch to make the door the correct width.

Use the Stretch command to change the width of the cabinet door (Figure 11–8):

Prompt	Response
Command:	**Stretch**
Select objects to stretch by crossing-window or crossing-polygon...	
Select objects:	**D1**
Other corner:	**D2**
Select objects:	**<enter>**
Base point or displacement:	**D3** (any point)
Second point of displacement:	TYPE: **@3-1/2<0<enter>** (the upper door width, 1′6″, plus $3\frac{1}{2}''$, equals the lower door width, $1'9\frac{1}{2}''$)

FIGURE 11–8
Use the Stretch Command to
Change the Width of the
Cabinet Door

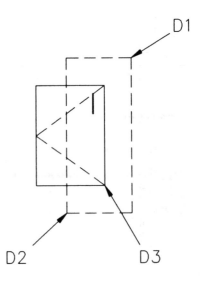

Complete the Following Steps to Finish Drawing the Elevation of the South Wall of the Tenant Space Conference Room

Step 1. Save the current UCS used to draw the upper cabinets:

Prompt	Response
Command:	TYPE: **UCS<enter>**
Origin/ZAxis/3point/OBject/View/X/Y/Z/ Prev/Restore/Save/Del?<World>:	TYPE: **S<enter>** (or CLICK: **UCS-Save**)
?/Desired UCS name:	TYPE: **UPPER<enter>**

Step 2. Create a new UCS origin for drawing the lower cabinets by moving the existing UCS origin -4'6" in the Y direction:

Prompt	Response
Command:	**<enter>**
Origin/ZAxis/3point/OBject/View/X/Y/Z/ Prev/Restore/Save/Del?<World>:	TYPE: **O<enter>**
Origin point <0,0,0>:	TYPE: **0,-4'6<enter>**

Step 3. Move the lower cabinet door to a point $3\frac{1}{2}''$ (the base height) above the origin of the current UCS (Figure 11–9):

Prompt	Response
Command:	**Move** (or TYPE: **M<enter>**)
Select objects:	**D1**
Other corner:	**D2**
Select objects:	**<enter>**
Base point or displacement:	**Osnap-Intersection**
of	**D3**
Second point of displacement:	TYPE: **0,3-1/2<enter>**

On Your Own

Step 4. Copy part of the lower cabinet $3'10\frac{1}{2}''$ in the 0 direction, as shown in Figure 11–10.

Step 5. Stretch the right side of the copied door 1" in the 180 direction, making it 1" narrower.

FIGURE 11–9
Move the Lower Cabinet Door to a Point $3\frac{1}{2}''$ above the Origin of the Current UCS

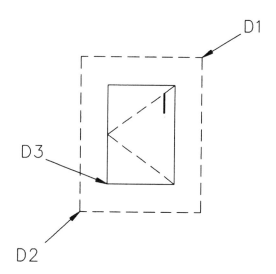

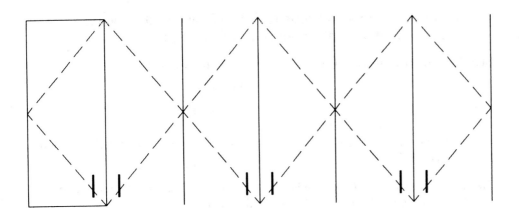

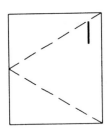
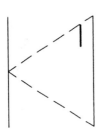

FIGURE 11–10
Copy Part of the Lower Cabinet 3'-10½" in the 0 Direction

Step 6. Use Mirror and Copy to draw the remaining doors, as shown in Figure 11–11.

Step 7. Use Extend to extend the top and bottom lines of both the upper and lower cabinets to the right edges of the cabinets, as shown in Figure 11–12.

Step 8. Use Offset to draw the bottom line of the base, the top and bottom (top of the drawers line) lines of the countertop, and the backsplash line (Figure 11–13).

Step 9. Use Erase and Extend to connect the sides of the upper and lower cabinets and the base (Figure 11–13).

Step 10. Set A-elev Layer current, and use Extend, Polyline, and Copy to draw the lower cabinet drawers and their 5" × 1/4" handles. Use Trim to trim the line out of the area where the refrigerator is located (Figure 11–13).

Step 11. Draw the sink in the approximate location shown in Figure 11–14 (the Stretch command will be used later to move the sink to the correct location):

Prompt	Response
Command:	**Line** (or TYPE: L<enter>)
From point:	**D1** (with SNAP on)
To point:	TYPE: @1/2<90<enter>
To point:	TYPE: @25<0<enter>
To point:	TYPE: @1/2<270<enter>
To point:	<enter>

Part II: Two-Dimensional AutoCAD

FIGURE 11–11
Use Mirror and Copy to Draw the
Remaining Doors

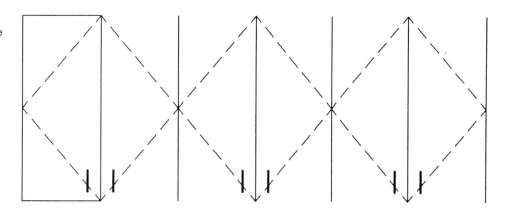

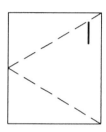
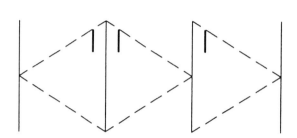

Prompt	Response
Command:	**<enter>**
From point:	**Osnap-Midpoint**
of	**D2** (turn SNAP off)
To point:	TYPE: **@10<90<enter>**
To point:	**<enter>**
Command:	**Offset (or TYPE: O<enter>)**
Offset distance or Through <default>:	TYPE: **1/2<enter>**
Select object to offset:	**D3**
Side to offset?	**D4**
Select object to offset:	**D3**
Side to offset?	**D5**
Select object to offset:	**<enter>**
Command:	**Line**
From point:	**Osnap-Endpoint**
of	**D6**
To point:	**Osnap-Endpoint**
of	**D7**
To point:	**<enter>**
Command:	**Offset**
Offset distance or Through <0'-1/2">:	TYPE: **3<enter>**

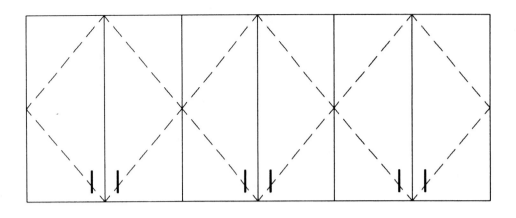

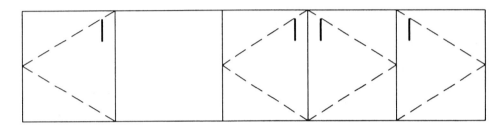

FIGURE 11–12
Use Extend to Extend the Top and Bottom Lines of Both the Upper and Lower Cabinets

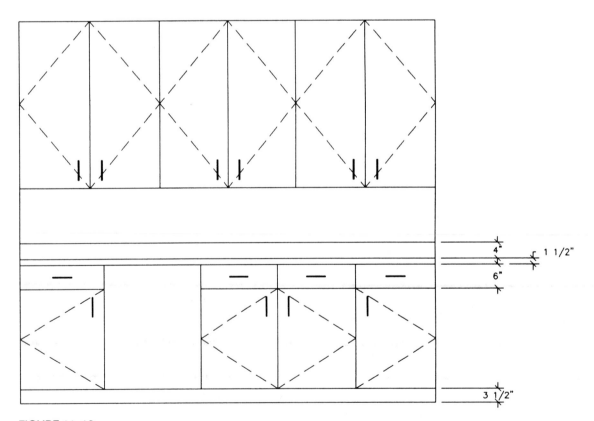

FIGURE 11–13
Finish Drawing the Cabinets As Shown

FIGURE 11–14
Draw the Sink in the Approximate
Location Shown

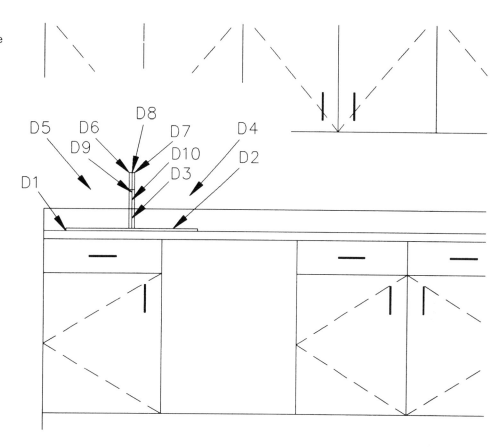

Prompt	Response
Select object to offset:	**D8**
Side to offset?	**D4**
Select object to offset:	**<enter>**
Command:	**Erase** (or TYPE: **E<enter>**)
Select objects:	**D9** (the center vertical line)
Select objects:	**<enter>**

On Your Own

Step 12. Trim out the line of the backsplash where it crosses the faucet.

Step 13. Set SNAP to 1″.

Step 14. **You can use the Stretch command to move entities that have other lines attached to them without removing the attached lines. Use Stretch to move the sink to its correct location (Figure 11–15):**

Prompt	Response
Command:	**Stretch** (or TYPE: **S<enter>**)
Select objects to stretch by crossing-window or crossing-polygon...	
Select objects:	**D2**
Other corner:	**D1**
Select objects:	**<enter>**
Base point or displacement:	**Osnap-Midpoint**

FIGURE 11–15
Use Stretch to Move the Sink to
Its Correct Location

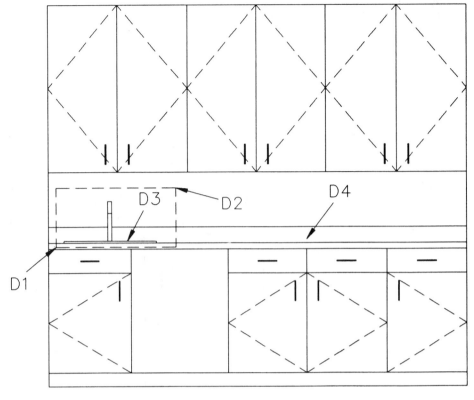

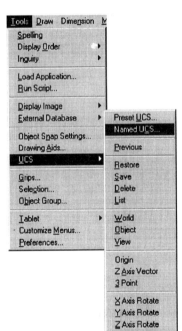

Prompt	Response
of	**D3**
New point:	**D4** (with ORTHO and SNAP ON, pick a point directly above where the two doors meet)

On Your Own

Step 15. Use Offset and Extend to draw the ceiling line above the cabinets (Figure 11–16).

Step 16. Set the A-elev-text Layer current, and use Simplex lettering to place the note on the refrigerator and to write the name of the elevation.

Step 17. Use the UCS command to save the current UCS, and name it LOWER. Set the UCS to World.

Step 18. Set the A-elev-dim Layer current, set the dimensioning variables, and add the dimensions as shown in Figure 11–16. You may want to change the GRID and SNAP settings to do the dimensioning.

NAMED UCS...

The Named UCS... (or TYPE: **DDUCS**) command displays a UCS Control dialog box (Figure 11–17). This dialog box can be used in a manner similar to the UCS command.

RENAME...

The Rename command provides the Rename dialog box, which allows you to rename an existing UCS, as well as many other objects such as Layers, Blocks, Text and Dimension Styles, Views, Linetypes, and Viewport configurations.

SAVE

When you have completed Exercise 11–1, save your work in at least two places.

Part II: Two-Dimensional AutoCAD

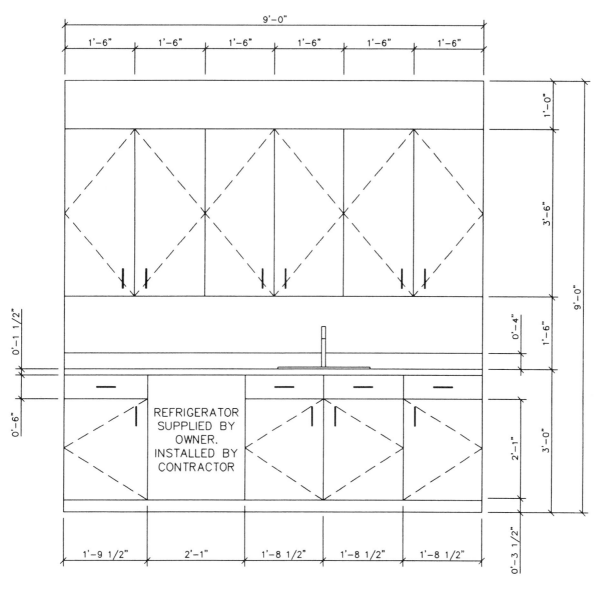

CONFERENCE ROOM ELEVATION

SCALE: 1/2"=1'-0"

FIGURE 11–16
Complete the Elevation Drawing (Scale: $\frac{1}{2}'' = 1'\text{-}0''$)

FIGURE 11–17
UCS Control Dialog Box

Chapter 11: Drawing Elevations, Wall Sections, and Details

243

PLOT

Printer Plot or Plotter Plot Exercise 11–1 to scale.

EXERCISE 11–2
Tenant Space: Section of Conference Room Cabinets with Crosshatching

In Exercise 11–2, a sectional view of the south wall of the tenant space conference room is drawn. The sectional view of the south wall of the conference room (Figure 11–18) shows many construction details that elevation and plan views cannot. Sectional views are imaginary cuts through an area. Crosshatched lines are used to show where the imaginary saw used to make these imaginary cuts, touches the cut objects. This crosshatching is done in AutoCAD by drawing hatch patterns. Exercise 11–2 will describe the Hatch command, used to draw hatch patterns.

When you have completed Exercise 11–2, your drawing will look similar to Figure 11–18. To begin, turn on the computer and start AutoCAD. The Start Up dialog box is displayed.

On Your Own

1. Begin drawing CH11-EX2 on the hard drive by opening existing drawing CH11-EX1 from a floppy disk in drive A and saving it to the hard drive with the CH11-EX2. You can use all the settings created for Exercise 11–1.

2. Reset Drawing Limits, Grid, and Snap as needed.

3. Create the following Layers by renaming the existing layers and changing the Hidden linetype to Continuous:

LAYER NAME	COLOR	LINETYPE
A-sect	Red	Continuous
A-sect-patt	Green	Continuous
A-sect-text	White	Continuous
A-sect-dim	Blue	Continuous

4. Set Layer A-sect current.

5. Use Erase to eliminate the entire drawing or most of the drawing that appears on the screen. After looking closely at Figure 11–18, you may want to keep some of the conference room elevation drawing parts.

6. The cabinet section must be drawn before you use the Hatch command to draw the crosshatching. Draw the sectional view of the south wall of the tenant space conference room full size, as show in Figure 11–19. Include the text and the dimensions. Use Layer A-sect to draw the view, Layer A-sect-text for the text and leaders, and Layer A-sect-dim for the dimensions. Hatch patterns as shown in Figure 11–18 will be drawn on Layer A-sect-patt.

7. When the cabinet section is complete with text and dimensions, freeze layers A-sect-text and A-sect-dim so that they do not interfere with drawing the hatch patterns.

Preparing to Use the Hatch Command
with the Select Objects< Boundary Option

The most important aspect of using the Hatch command when you use "Select Objects" to create the boundary is to have the boundary of the area to be hatched defined clearly on the drawing. If the boundary of the hatching area is not clearly defined, the hatch pattern will not appear as you want it to. For example, some of the hatch pattern may go outside the boundary area, or the boundary area may not be completely filled with the hatch pattern.

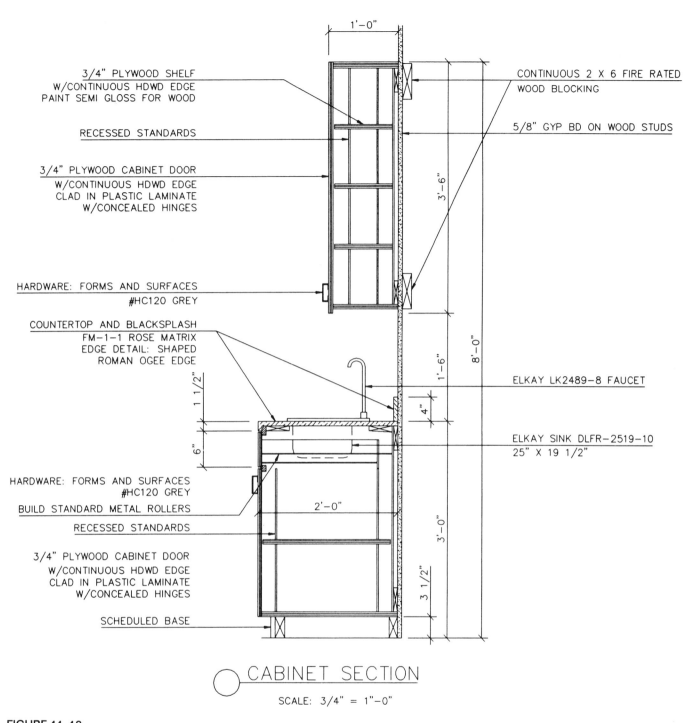

3/4" PLYWOOD SHELF
W/CONTINUOUS HDWD EDGE
PAINT SEMI GLOSS FOR WOOD

RECESSED STANDARDS

3/4" PLYWOOD CABINET DOOR
W/CONTINUOUS HDWD EDGE
CLAD IN PLASTIC LAMINATE
W/CONCEALED HINGES

HARDWARE: FORMS AND SURFACES
#HC120 GREY

COUNTERTOP AND BLACKSPLASH
FM-1-1 ROSE MATRIX
EDGE DETAIL: SHAPED
ROMAN OGEE EDGE

HARDWARE: FORMS AND SURFACES
#HC120 GREY

BUILD STANDARD METAL ROLLERS

RECESSED STANDARDS

3/4" PLYWOOD CABINET DOOR
W/CONTINUOUS HDWD EDGE
CLAD IN PLASTIC LAMINATE
W/CONCEALED HINGES

SCHEDULED BASE

CONTINUOUS 2 X 6 FIRE RATED
WOOD BLOCKING

5/8" GYP BD ON WOOD STUDS

ELKAY LK2489-8 FAUCET

ELKAY SINK DLFR-2519-10
25" X 19 1/2"

1'-0"
3'-6"
8'-0"
1'-6"
4"
1 1/2"
6"
2'-0"
3'-0"
3 1/2"

CABINET SECTION
SCALE: 3/4" = 1"-0"

FIGURE 11–18
Exercise 11–2: Tenant Space, Section of Conference Room Cabinets with Crosshatching (Scale: $\frac{3''}{4}$ = 1'-0")

Before you use the Hatch command in this manner, all areas to which hatching will be added must be prepared so that none of their boundary lines extend beyond the area to be hatched. When the views on which you will draw hatching have already been drawn, it is often necessary to use the Break command to break the boundary lines into line segments that clearly define the hatch boundaries. The Break command is used to break any of the lines that define the area to be hatched so that those lines do not extend beyond the boundary of the hatching area.

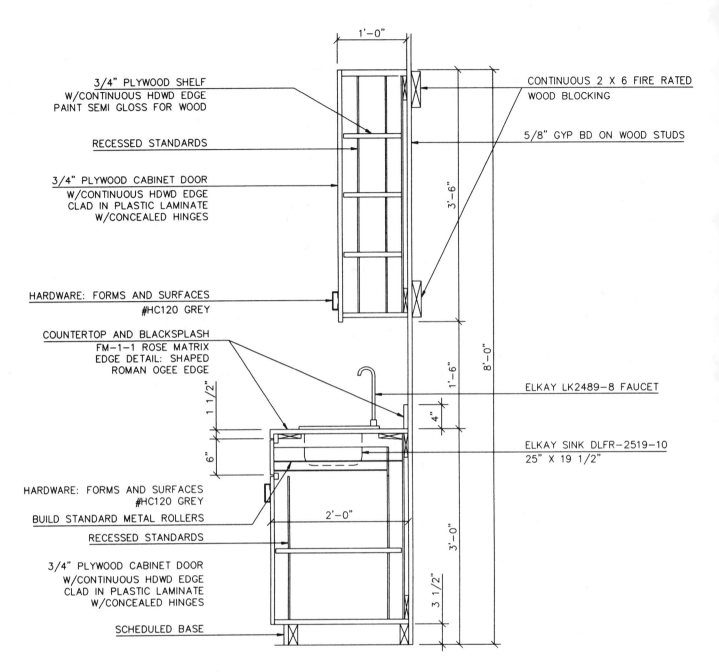

FIGURE 11–19

Exercise 11–2: Tenant Space, Section of Conference Room Cabinets Before Crosshatching (Scale: $\frac{3''}{4}$ = 1'-0")

Use the Break command to help clearly define the right side of the horizontal plywood top of the upper cabinets (Figure 11–20):

Prompt	Response
Command:	**Break** (or TYPE: **BR<enter>**)
Select object:	**D1** (to select the vertical line)
Enter second point (or F for first point):	TYPE: **F<enter>**
Enter first point:	**D2** (use Osnap-Intersection)
Enter second point:	TYPE: **@<enter>** (places the second point exactly at the same place as the first point, and no gap is broken out of the line)

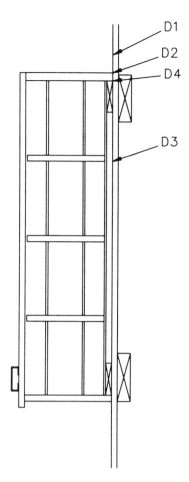

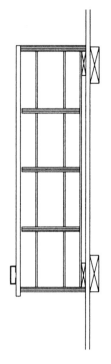

FIGURE 11–20
Use the Break Command to
Clearly Define the Right Side of the
Horizontal Top Area of the Upper
Cabinets

FIGURE 11–21
Upper Cabinets with
Hatch Patterns Drawn

Prompt	Response
Command:	**<enter>**
Break Select object:	**D3** (to select the vertical line)
Enter second point (or F for first point):	TYPE: **F<enter>**
Enter first point:	**D4** (use Osnap-Intersection)
Enter second point:	TYPE: **@<enter>**

You have just used the Break command with the @ option to break the vertical line so that it is a separate line segment that clearly defines the right side of the plywood top area.

The Break command can also be used to erase or break a gap out of an entity. To break a gap out of an entity, simply click the first and second points of the desired gap at the command prompts. As shown in the prompt, "Enter second point (or F for first point):", the point used to "Select object:" can be used as the first point of the break.

On Your Own

Before using the Hatch command to hatch the plywood top, the three plywood shelves, and the plywood bottom of the upper cabinet as shown in Figure 11–21, you need to define clearly the boundaries of those areas.

1. Use the Break command to break the vertical line at the intersection of the top and bottom of the left side of the plywood top boundary.

Note: Although the "Pick Points" method of creating hatch boundaries is often much easier, you must know how to use "Select Objects" as well. There are instances when "Pick Points" just does not work.

2. When the boundary of the plywood top is clearly defined, the top, bottom, right, and left lines of the top are separate line segments that do not extend beyond the boundary of the plywood top. To check the boundary, use the Erase command to pick and highlight each line segment. When each line is highlighted, you can see clearly if it needs to be broken. Use the Esc key to cancel the Erase command so that the lines are not actually erased. Use the Break command on the top horizontal line of the plywood top, if needed.

3. Use the Break command to prepare the three plywood shelves and the plywood bottom of the upper cabinet boundaries for hatching.

4. The Hatch command will also not work properly if the two lines of an intersection do not meet, that is, if there is any small gap. If you need to check the intersections of the left side of the plywood shelves to make sure they intersect properly, do this before continuing with the Hatch command as follows.

HATCH... Boundary Hatch Dialog Box

When the Hatch command is activated (TYPE: **H<enter>**), the Boundary Hatch dialog box appears, Figure 11–22. As shown in the Pattern Type Area, the Pattern Types can be as follows:

Tip: You may prefer to draw lines on a new layer over the ones existing to form the enclosed boundary area instead of breaking, as described in this procedure. These additional lines may be erased easily with a window after you turn off all layers except the one to be erased. This is sometimes faster and allows the line that was to be broken to remain intact.

Predefined   Makes the Pattern... button available.

User-defined   Defines a pattern of lines using the current linetype.

Custom   Specifies a pattern from the ACAD.pat file or any other PAT file.

To view the Predefined Hatch pattern options, pick the Pattern... button. The Hatch pattern palette appears, Figure 11–23. Other parts of the Boundary Hatch dialog box are as follows:

Pattern Properties Area

ISO Pen Width   If you select one of the 14 ISO (International Organization of Standardization) patterns at the bottom of the list of Hatch Patterns, this option scales the pattern based on the selected pen width. Each of these pattern names begins with ISO.

Pattern   Specifies a predefined pattern name.

Custom Pattern   This button shows a custom pattern name. This option is available when Custom is selected in the Pattern Type area.

Warning: Those of you who are still working on your floppy disk are even more likely to lose some of your work with Hatch. Hatching often creates a huge drawing file. Be aware of how large that file is, and be sure it will fit comfortably on your floppy disk when you Save it.

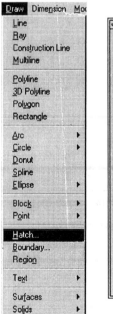

FIGURE 11–22
Boundary Hatch Dialog Box

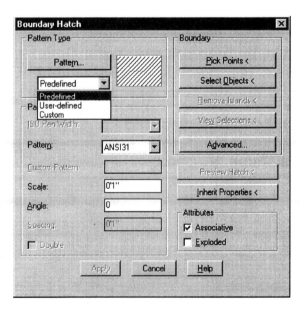

FIGURE 11–23
Hatch Pattern Palette

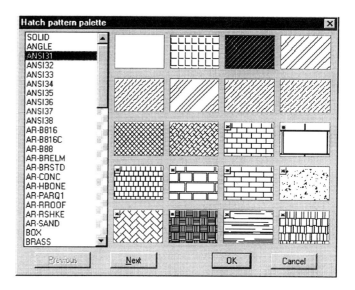

Scale   This allows you to enlarge or shrink the hatch pattern to fit the drawing. It is not available if you have selected User-defined in the Pattern Type.

Angle   Allows you to specify an angle for the hatch pattern relative to the X axis of the current UCS.

Spacing   Allows you to specify the space between lines on a user-defined hatch pattern.

Double   When you pick this button so that a ✓ appears in it, the area is hatched with a second set of lines at 90° to the first hatch pattern. This is called a double hatch.

Boundary Area

Pick Points<   Allows you to pick points inside a boundary to specify the area to be hatched.

Select Objects<   Allows you to select the outside edges of the boundary to specify the area to be hatched.

Remove Island<   Allows you to remove from the boundary set objects defined as islands by the Pick Points< option. You cannot remove the outer boundary.

View Selections<   Displays the currently defined boundary set. This option is not available when no selection or boundary has been made.

Advanced...   Displays the Advanced Options dialog box, Figure 11–24.

Preview Hatch<   Allows you to preview the hatch pattern before you apply it to the drawing.

Inherit Properties<   Allows you to pick an existing hatch pattern to specify the properties of that pattern. The pattern picked must be associative (attached to and defined by its boundary).

Attributes Area

Associative   When a ✓ appears in this button, the hatch pattern stretches when the area that has been hatched is stretched.

Exploded   When this button is clicked so that a ✓ appears in it, the hatch pattern is applied as individual line segments instead of a single entity. If you think you may have a hatch pattern that extends outside the hatch boundary, you should bring in the pattern exploded and then use the Trim command to correct the overlap.

Advanced Options Dialog Box

When the Advanced... button of the Boundary Hatch dialog box is clicked, the Advanced Options dialog box, Figure 11–24, appears.

FIGURE 11–24
Advanced Options Dialog Box;
Boundary Style Options: Normal,
Outer, and Ignore

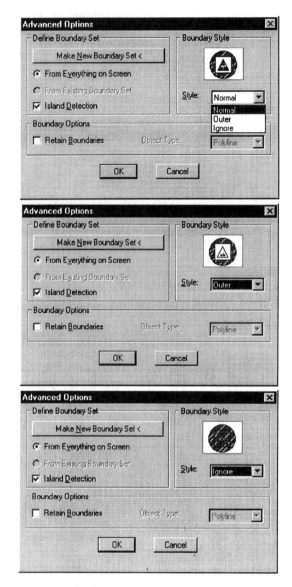

Define Boundary Set Area

Make New Boundary Set<   When this button is clicked, all dialog boxes close to allow object selection.

From Everything on Screen   When this radio button is clicked, a boundary set is created from everything that is visible on the screen.

From Existing Boundary Set   When this radio button is clicked, the current boundary set is selected. If you have just entered the Boundary Hatch dialog box, this option is not available because there is no current boundary set.

Island Detection   Specifies whether objects within the outermost boundary are used as boundary objects. These internal objects are known as *islands*.

Boundary Style Area

The following boundary style options are show in Figure 11–24:

Normal   When Style: is set to Normal (and a selection set is composed of areas inside other areas), alternating areas are hatched as shown in the Boundary Style area.

Outer   When Style: is set to Outer (and a selection set is composed of areas inside other areas), only the outer area is hatched as shown in the Boundary Style area.

Ignore   When Style: is set to Ignore (and a selection set is composed of areas inside other areas), all areas are hatched as shown in the Boundary Style area.

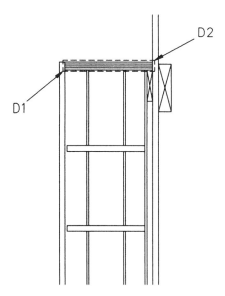

FIGURE 11–25
Use the Hatch Command with the Select Objects< Boundary Option to Draw a Uniform Horizontal-Line Hatch Pattern on the Plywood Top of the Upper Cabinets

Boundary Options

Retain Boundaries   Specifies whether the boundary objects will remain in your drawing after hatching is completed.

Object Type   Controls the type of the new boundary object. When the boundary is created, AutoCAD uses a region or polyline. For now, this box should read Polyline.

On Your Own

Set Layer A-sect-patt current.

Use the Hatch command with the Select Objects< Boundary option to draw a Uniform horizontal-line hatch pattern on the plywood top of the upper cabinets (Figure 11–25).

Prompt	Response
Command:	**Hatch** (or TYPE: **H<enter>**)
The Boundary Hatch dialog box appears:	CLICK: **User-defined** in the Pattern Type area
	Angle: **0**
	Spacing: **1/4″**
	CLICK: **Select objects<**
Select objects:	CLICK: **D1**
Other corner:	CLICK: **D2**
Select objects:	**<enter>**
The Boundary Hatch dialog box appears:	CLICK: **Preview Hatch<**
A preview of your hatching appears:	CLICK: **Continue**
The Boundary Hatch dialog box appears:	CLICK: **Apply** (if the correct hatch pattern was previewed; if not, CLICK: **Cancel** and fix the problem)

The plywood top of the upper cabinet is now hatched.

On Your Own

Use the same hatching procedure to draw a hatch pattern on the three plywood shelves and the plywood bottom of the upper cabinet, as shown in Figure 11–26.

When you use Pick Points< Boundary option to create a boundary for the hatch pattern, AutoCAD allows you to pick any point inside the area, and the boundary is automat-

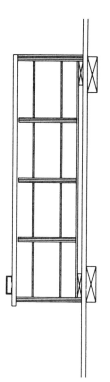

FIGURE 11–26
Draw a Hatch Pattern on the Three Plywood Shelves and the Plywood Bottom of the Upper Cabinet

Tip: When selecting objects using a Window, TYPE: **W<enter>** to use the crosshairs.

Tip: Turn off or freeze the text and dimension layers if they interfere with hatching.

Note: Be sure to zoom out so the entire boundary of the area to be hatched is visible or it will not hatch.

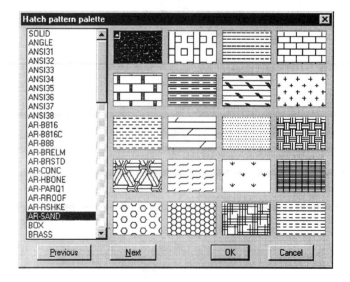

FIGURE 11–27
Use the Hatch Command with the Pick Points< Boundary Option to Draw a Uniform Vertical-Line Hatch Pattern on the Upper Cabinet Door

Tip: You may have to draw a line across the top of the 5/8″ gypsum board to create the hatch pattern.

ically created. You do not have to prepare the boundary of the area as you did with the Select Objects< Boundary option.

Use the Hatch command with the Pick Points< Boundary option to draw a uniform vertical-line hatch pattern on the upper cabinet door (Figure 11–27):

Prompt	Response
Command:	**Hatch** (or TYPE: **H<enter>**)
The Boundary Hatch dialog box appears:	CLICK: **User-defined** in the Pattern Type area
	Angle: **90**
	Spacing: **1/4**
	CLICK: **Pick Points<**
Select internal point:	CLICK: **D1** (inside the door symbol)
Select internal point:	**<enter>**
The Boundary Hatch dialog box appears:	CLICK: **Preview Hatch<**
A preview of your hatching appears:	CLICK: **Continue**
The Boundary Hatch dialog box appears:	CLICK: **Apply** (if the correct hatch pattern was previewed; if not, CLICK: **Cancel** and fix the problem)

Use the Hatch command with the Pick Points< Boundary option to draw the AR-SAND hatch pattern on the $\frac{5}{8}''$ gypsum board (Figures 11–28, 11–29, and 11–30):

Prompt	Response
Command:	**Hatch**
The Boundary Hatch dialog box appears:	CLICK: **Predefined**
	CLICK: **Pattern...**
The Hatch pattern palette appears:	CLICK: **AR-SAND** (Figure 11–28)
	CLICK: **OK**
The Boundary Hatch dialog box appears (Figure 11–29):	TYPE: **3/8″** (in Scale: box)
	CLICK: **Pick Points<**

FIGURE 11–28

252

Part II: Two-Dimensional AutoCAD

FIGURE 11–29

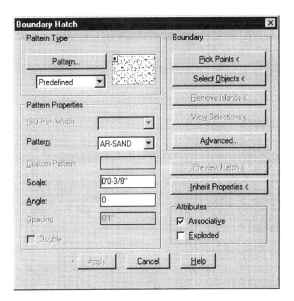

FIGURE 11–31

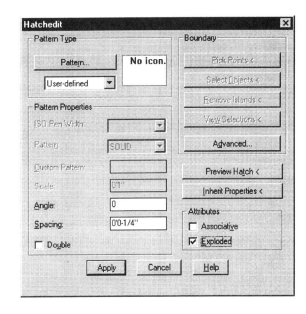

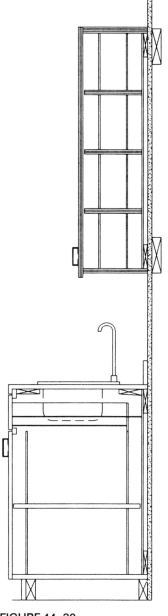

FIGURE 11–30
Use the Hatch Command to Draw the AR-SAND Hatch Pattern on the $\frac{5}{8}''$ Gypsum Board

Note: AutoCAD ensures proper alignment of hatch patterns in adjacent areas by generating all lines of every hatch pattern from the same reference point (usually 0,0). Use the Snap, Rotate command, Base point to change the reference point of a hatch pattern to vary the alignment.

Select internal point:	CLICK: **any point inside the lines defining the 5/8 gypsum board boundary**
Select internal point:	**<enter>**
The Boundary Hatch dialog box appears:	**Apply**

The 5/8″ gypsum board is now hatched.

Editing Hatch Patterns

If you have prepared a complex drawing to be hatched, and the hatch preview shows one or two lines extending outside the hatch area, click the Exploded box in the Boundary Hatch dialog box before you click Apply. The hatch pattern will then be inserted as individual lines that can be trimmed or otherwise edited.

If you already have a hatch pattern on the drawing that has one or two lines extending outside the hatch area, select Modify-Object-Hatch..., Edit Hatch (or TYPE: **HE<enter>**), click on the hatch pattern, and check the Exploded box in the resulting Hatch edit dialog

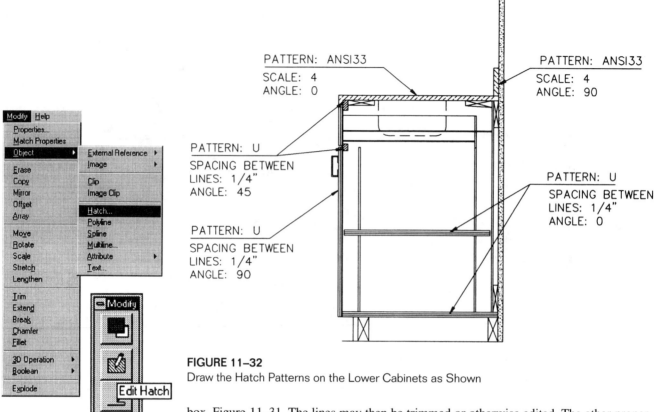

Modify Help
Properties...
Match Properties
Object ▶
Erase
Copy
Mirror
Offset
Array
Move
Rotate
Scale
Stretch
Lengthen
Trim
Extend
Break
Chamfer
Fillet
3D Operation ▶
Boolean ▶
Explode

External Reference ▶
Image ▶
Clip
Image Clip
Hatch...
Polyline
Spline
Multiline...
Attribute ▶
Text...

Edit Hatch

PATTERN: ANSI33
SCALE: 4
ANGLE: 0

PATTERN: ANSI33
SCALE: 4
ANGLE: 90

PATTERN: U
SPACING BETWEEN
LINES: 1/4"
ANGLE: 45

PATTERN: U
SPACING BETWEEN
LINES: 1/4"
ANGLE: 0

PATTERN: U
SPACING BETWEEN
LINES: 1/4"
ANGLE: 90

FIGURE 11–32
Draw the Hatch Patterns on the Lower Cabinets as Shown

box, Figure 11–31. The lines may then be trimmed or otherwise edited. The other properties of the hatch pattern may also be edited using the Hatch edit dialog box.

On Your Own

1. Using the patterns described in Figure 11–32, draw hatch patterns by using the Pick Points< Option on the lower cabinets.
2. Thaw layers A-sect-text and A-sect-dim.

SAVE

When you have completed Exercise 11-2, save your work in at least two places.

PLOT

Printer Plot or Plotter Plot Exercise 11–2 to scale.

EXERCISE 11–3
Detail of Door Jamb with Crosshatching

In Exercise 11–3, a detail of a door jamb is drawn. When you have completed Exercise 11–3, your drawing will look similar to Figure 11–33. To begin, turn on the computer and start AutoCAD.

On Your Own

1. Begin drawing CH11-EX3 on the hard drive by opening existing drawing CH11-EX1 from a floppy disk in drive A and saving it to the hard drive with the name CH11-EX3. You can use most of the settings you created for Exercise 11–1.
2. Reset Drawing Limits, Grid, and Snap as needed.

FIGURE 11–33

Exercise 11–3: Detail of a Door Jamb with Crosshatching (Scale: 3″ = 1′-0″)

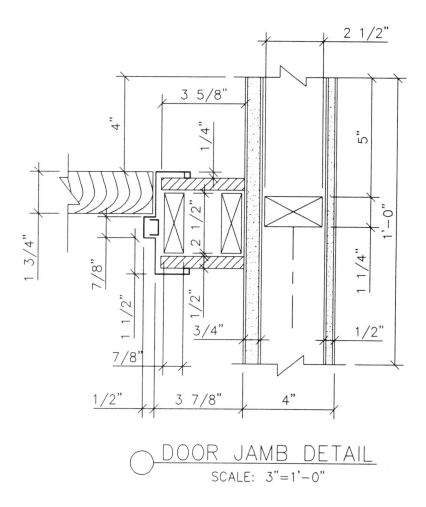

DOOR JAMB DETAIL
SCALE: 3"=1'-0"

3. Create the following Layers by renaming the existing Layers and changing the Hidden linetype to Continuous.

LAYER NAME	COLOR	LINETYPE
A-detl	Red	Continuous
A-detl-patt	Green	Continuous
A-detl-text	White	Continuous
A-detl-dim	Blue	Continuous

4. Set Layer A-detl current.

5. Use Erase to eliminate the entire drawing that appears on the screen.

6. Using the dimensions shown in Figure 11–33, draw all the door jamb components. Drawing some of the components separately and copying or moving them into place will be helpful. Measure any dimensions not shown with a scale of 3″ = 1′-0″.

7. Set Layer A-detl-patt current, and draw the hatch patterns as described in Figure 11–34. Use a Spline and array it to draw the curved wood grain pattern.

8. Set Layer A-detl-dim current, and draw the dimensions as shown in Figure 11–33.

9. Set Layer A-detl-text current, and add the name of the detail as shown in Figure 11–33.

10. Save the drawing in two places, and Printer Plot or Plotter Plot the drawing to scale.

FIGURE 11–34
Exercise 11–3: Hatch Patterns

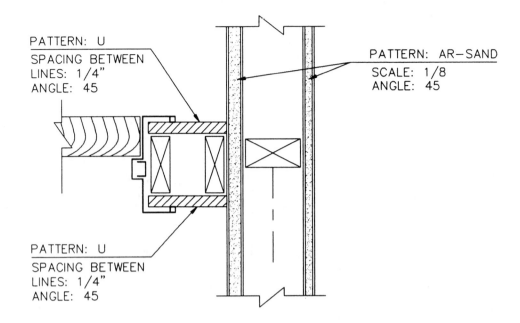

PATTERN: U
SPACING BETWEEN
LINES: 1/4"
ANGLE: 45

PATTERN: AR–SAND
SCALE: 1/8
ANGLE: 45

PATTERN: U
SPACING BETWEEN
LINES: 1/4"
ANGLE: 45

EXERCISE 11–4
Using Filters to Draw an Orthographic Drawing of a Conference Table

In Exercise 11–4, the AutoCAD feature called FILTERS is used. Using FILTERS is especially helpful when you are making orthographic drawings showing the top, front, and right views of an object.

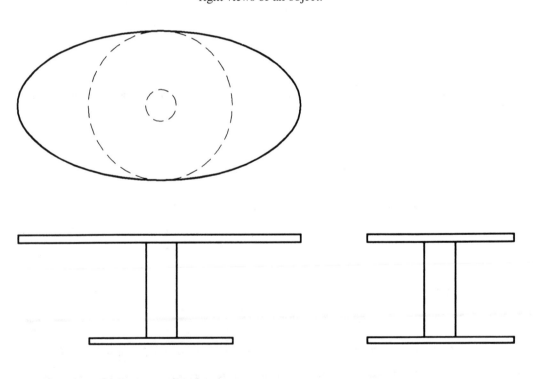

CONFERENCE TABLE
SCALE: 1/2"=1'-0"

FIGURE 11–35
Exercise 11–4: Using FILTERS to Draw an Orthographic Drawing of a Conference Table
(Scale: $\frac{1}{2}'' = 1'-0''$)

In Exercise 11–4, an orthographic drawing of a conference table, showing the top, front, and right sides, is drawn using FILTERS. When you have completed Exercise 11–4, your drawing will look similar to Figure 11–35. To begin, turn on the computer and start AutoCAD. The Start Up dialog box is displayed.

1. CLICK: **Use a Wizard**
2. CLICK: **Quick Setup**

   CLICK: **OK**
3. Set drawing units: **Architectural**

   CLICK: **Next>>**
4. Set drawing width: **12′** × Length: **9′**

   CLICK: **Done**
5. **Use SaveAs... to save the drawing on the hard drive with the name CH11-EX4.**
6. Set Grid **2″**
7. Set Snap **1″**
8. Create the following Layers:

LAYER NAME	COLOR	LINETYPE
A-furn-s	Red	Continuous
A-furn-h	Green	Hidden
A-furn-text	White	Continuous

9. Set Layer A-furn-h current.
10. Set Ltscale **12**

FILTERS

In many instances you will find filters to be a valuable tool for locating points. Filters relate to the X, Y, and Z coordinates of a point. They allow you to avoid drawing unnecessary construction lines and to save considerable time when used effectively. An X filter, for example, says to AutoCAD, "I am pointing to the X location for the point now; then I will point to the Y location." (You will find it helpful to ignore the Z component for now. The Z component is used for drawing 3D models.)

You may filter one or two of the X, Y, and Z components of any point in any command that requires the location of a point. Some of these commands are as follows:

Line	Copy
Polyline	Move
Ellipse	Polygon
Circle	

Draw the base and column of the table (HIDDEN Line), as shown in the top view (Figure 11–36):

Prompt	Response
Command:	**Circle-Center, Diameter**
circle 3P/2P/TTR/<Center point):	TYPE: **4′,6′<enter>**
Diameter/<Radius>: d Diameter:	TYPE: **3′1-1/2<enter>**
Command:	**<enter>**
circle 3P/2P/TTR<Center point>:	**Osnap-Center**
of	**D1**
Diameter/<Radius><default>:	TYPE: **4<enter>**

FIGURE 11–36
Draw the Base, Column, and Top
of the Table

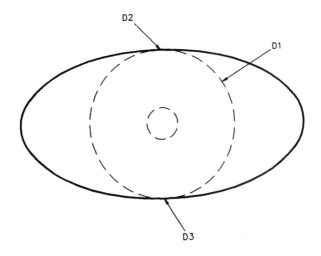

On Your Own

Set Layer A-furn-s current.

Draw the elliptical top of the table (Continuous Line), as shown in the top view (Figure 11–36):

Prompt	Response
Command:	**Ellipse-Axis, End**
Arc/Center/<Axis endpoint 1>:	**Osnap-Quadrant**
of	**D2**
Axis endpoint 2:	**Osnap-Quadrant**
of	**D3**
<Other axis distance>/Rotation:	TYPE: **36-3/4<enter>**

Use FILTERS to draw the front view of the top of this odd-size elliptical table (Figure 11–37):

Prompt	Response
Command:	**Line**
From point:	TYPE: **.X<enter>**
of	**Osnap-Quadrant**
of	**D1**
(need YZ):	**D2** (with SNAP on, pick a point in the approximate location shown in Figure 11–37)

FIGURE 11–37
Draw the Front View of the Top
of the Table

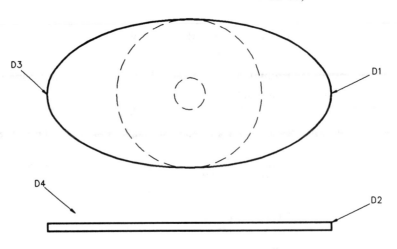

Part II: Two-Dimensional AutoCAD

To point:	TYPE: **.X<enter>**
of	**Osnap-Quadrant**
of	**D3**
(need YZ):	**D4** (with Ortho on, pick any point to identify the Y component of the point; Ortho says that the Y component of the new point is the same as the Y component of the previous point)
To point:	TYPE: **@2<270<enter>**
To point:	TYPE: **.X<enter>**
of	**Osnap-Endpoint**
of	**D2**
(need YZ)	**D2** (with Ortho on, pick any point)
To point:	TYPE: **C<enter>**

Use FILTERS to draw the column of the front view of the table (Figure 11–38):

Prompt	Response
Command:	**Line**
From point:	TYPE: **.X<enter>**
of	**Osnap-Quadrant**
of	**D1**
(need YZ)	**Osnap-Nearest**
to	**D2** (any point on this line to identify the Y component of the point)
To point:	TYPE: **@24<270<enter>**
To point:	**<enter>**
Command:	**Offset** (or TYPE: **O<enter>**)
Offset distance or Through <Through>:	TYPE: **8<enter>**
Select object to offset:	**D3**
Side to offset?	**D4**
Select object to offset:	**<enter>**

Use FILTERS to draw the front view of the base of the table (Figure 11–38):

Prompt	Response
Command:	**Line**
From point:	TYPE: **.Y<enter>**
of	**Osnap-Endpoint**
of	**D5**
(need XZ)	**Osnap-Quadrant**
of	**D6**
To point:	TYPE: **.X<enter>**
of	**Osnap-Quadrant**
of	**D7**
(need YZ)	**D8** (with Ortho on, any point will do)
To point:	TYPE: **@1-1/2<270<enter>**
To point:	TYPE: **.X<enter>**
of	**Osnap-Endpoint**

FIGURE 11–38
Draw the Front View of the Column and Base of the Table

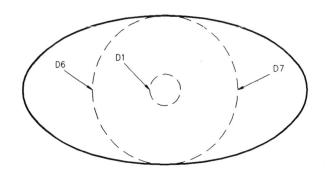

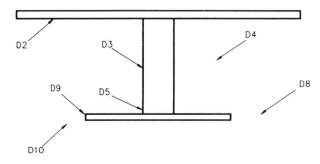

of	**D9**
(need YZ):	**D10** (with Ortho on, any point)
To point:	TYPE: **C\<enter>**

On Your Own

1. Use filters to draw the right side view of the table with the Line command. Be sure to get depth dimensions from the top view.

FIGURE 11–39
Draw the Right Side View of the Table

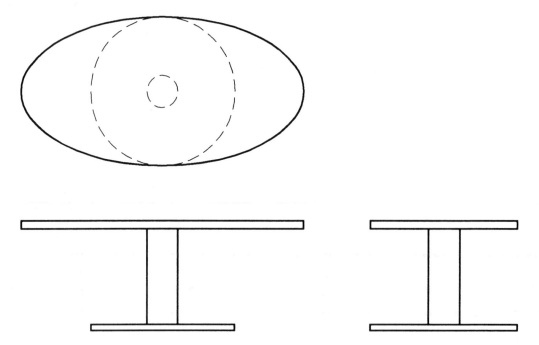

CONFERENCE TABLE
SCALE: 1/2"=1'–0"

260

Part II: Two-Dimensional AutoCAD

2. Set Layer A-furn-text current, and add the name of the drawing as shown in Figure 11–39.

3. Save the drawing in two places, and Printer Plot or Plotter Plot the drawing to scale.

EXERCISE 11–5
Different Hatch Styles

1. Draw the figure (without hatching) shown in Figure 11–40. Use an Architectural scale of $\frac{1}{2}'' = 1''$ to measure the figure, and draw it full scale. Copy it two times, leaving $1''$ between figures.

2. Shade each figure with a different Hatch Style as shown: Normal, Outermost, and Ignore. Use the same hatch pattern: User-defined, 1/8 spacing, 45 angle.

3. Save the drawing in two places, and Printer Plot or Plotter Plot the drawing to scale.

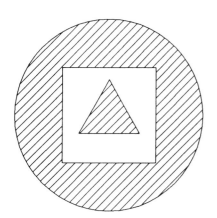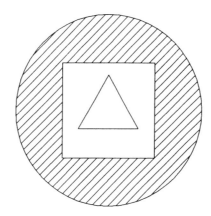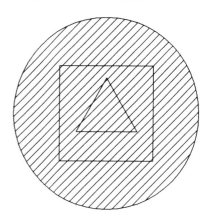

FIGURE 11–40
Practice Exercise 11–5: Different Hatch Styles (Scale: $\frac{1}{2}'' = 1''$)

REVIEW QUESTIONS

1. Which of the following patterns produces evenly spaced dots?
   a. U
   b. DOTS
   c. ANSI34
   d. DOLMIT
   e. LINE

2. Which of the following angles produces the User-defined pattern shown in Figure 11–41?
   a. 45
   b. 90
   c. 0
   d. 135
   e. 105

FIGURE 11–41

3. Which of the following angles produces the User-defined pattern shown in Figure 11–42?
   a. 45
   b. 90
   c. 0
   d. 135
   e. 105

FIGURE 11–42

4. Which of the following commands can be used to correct a hatch pattern that extends outside a hatch boundary, after it has been exploded?
   a. Array
   b. Copy
   c. Move
   d. Trim
   e. Break

FIGURE 11–43

5. Which of the following describes the User-defined pattern shown in Figure 11–43?
   a. X pat
   b. 45, 145
   c. Double
   d. Double section
   e. Line-two

6. Which of the following in the Spacing: input area in the Boundary Hatch dialog box produces Hatch lines $\frac{1}{4}''$ apart (User-defined pattern)?
   a. 1/4
   b. 1
   c. 1-4
   d. 4
   e. Depends on the size of the drawing.

7. After a Hatch command that spaced lines $\frac{1}{8}''$ apart has been performed, what is the default setting in the Spacing: input area for the next hatch pattern?
   a. 0
   b. 1/4
   c. 1/8
   d. 1
   e. Depends on the size of the drawing.

8. Which setting allows an image to be Mirrored without mirroring the text?
   a. MIRRTEXT = 1
   b. MIRRTEXT = 0
   c. MIRRTXT = 1
   d. MIRRTXT = 0
   e. DTEXT-STYLE = 0

9. The Stretch command is best used for
   a. Stretching an object in one direction
   b. Shrinking an object in one direction
   c. Moving an object along attached lines
   d. All the above
   e. None of the above

10. Which Hatch option allows you to hatch only the outermost boundary of multiple areas within a selection window?
    a. Pattern
    b. Scale
    c. Style
    d. Angle
    e. Spacing

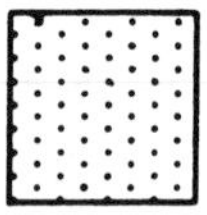

FIGURE 11–44

11. What is the correct name of the pattern in Figure 11–44?

   _____

12. How can the predefined Hatch pattern options (Hatch pattern palette) be called up on the screen?

   _____

   _____

   _____

FIGURE 11–45

13. Correctly label the User-defined pattern shown in Figure 11–45. Show angle and spacing at full scale.

   Angle _____   Spacing _____

Part II: Two-Dimensional AutoCAD

FIGURE 11–46

14. Correctly label the Predefined pattern shown in Figure 11–46. Show pattern and angle.

   Pattern _____   Angle _____

15. How can a hatch pattern line that extends outside a hatch boundary be corrected?

   _____

   _____

   _____

   _____

   _____

16. What is the name of the UCS Icon command option that forces the UCS Icon to be displayed at the 0,0 point of the current UCS?

   _____

17. How can all the lines of an unexploded 35-line hatch pattern be erased?

   _____

18. List the command that allows you to change a hatch pattern from Associative to Exploded.

   _____

19. Describe a practical use for the UCS command for two-dimensional drawing.

   _____

   _____

   _____

   _____

20. List the prompts and responses for getting the UCS Icon to move to the UCS origin after the UCS has been moved.

   Prompt   **Response**

   Command: _____

   _____   _____

12 Drawing and Adding Specifications to Furnishings

OBJECTIVES

When you have completed this chapter, you will be able to:

☐ Correctly use the following commands and settings:

ATTDIA systems variable
ATTEXT (Attribute Extraction)
ATTREDEF (Attribute Redefinition)
Attribute Definition (ATTDEF)
Attribute Display (ATTDISP)
DDATTEXT (Dynamic Dialog Attribute Extraction)
Define Attributes... (DDATTDEF)
Edit Text (DDEDIT)
External Reference (XREF)
Modify Attribute Global (ATTEDIT)
Modify Attribute Single (DDATTE)
XBIND (External Bind)

INTRODUCTION

This chapter describes the AutoCAD commands that allow specifications to be added to furnishings and how the specifications are extracted from the drawing. These commands are especially important because they reduce the amount of time it takes to add furniture to the plan, and total large amounts of like furniture pieces (with specifications) from the plan. There are many software programs available that can be used with AutoCAD to save even more time. These programs provide furniture symbols already drawn and programs that extract specification information in a form that suits your individual needs. Although you may ultimately combine one of these programs with the AutoCAD program, learning the commands included in this chapter will help you to understand how they interact with AutoCAD.

EXERCISE 12–1
Tenant Space Furniture Plan with Furniture Specifications

When you have completed Exercise 12–1, your drawing will look similar to Figure 12–1. To draw Exercise 12–1 turn on the computer and start AutoCAD. The Start Up dialog box is displayed.

1. Begin drawing CH12-EX1 on the hard drive by opening existing drawing CH10-EX1 from a floppy disk in drive A and saving it as CH12-EX1 on the hard drive.

2. Set Layer 0 current.

3. Freeze Layers: A-pflr, Defpoints, and A-area.

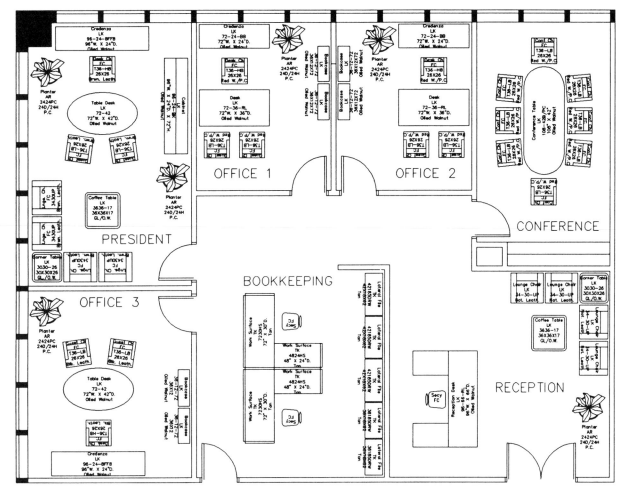

FIGURE 12-1

Exercise 12–1: Tenant Space Furniture Plan with Furniture Specifications (Scale: $\frac{1}{8}'' = 1\text{-}'0''$)

4. Use Zoom-All to view the limits of the drawing.

On Your Own

The furniture symbols must be drawn in plan view before you use the ATTDEF (Attribute Definition) or Define Attributes... (DDATTDEF-Dynamic Dialog Attribute Definition) commands to add specifications. Draw the tenant space reception furniture symbols as show in Figure 12–2. Use a $\frac{1}{4}'' = 1'\text{-}0''$ architectural scale to measure the symbols, and draw each piece full scale on your drawing. Pick any open space on your drawing to draw the furniture. Draw each symbol on the 0 Layer. Blocks will be made of each symbol after you use the ATTDEF and Define Attributes... commands, so it does not matter where the furniture is drawn on the plan. Use short, straight sections of a polyline to draw the plant inside the planter.

ATTDEF and Define Attributes... (DDATTDEF-Dynamic Dialog Attribute Definition)

The ATTDEF (Attribute Definition) command allows you to add attributes (furniture specifications) to the furniture symbols drawn in plan view. Define Attributes... (DDATTDEF-Dynamic Dialog Attribute Definition) allows you to do the same thing using a dialog box. In this exercise you will use both commands. After the attributes are added, a block is made of the symbol. When the block is inserted into a drawing, the

TENANT SPACE — RECEPTION

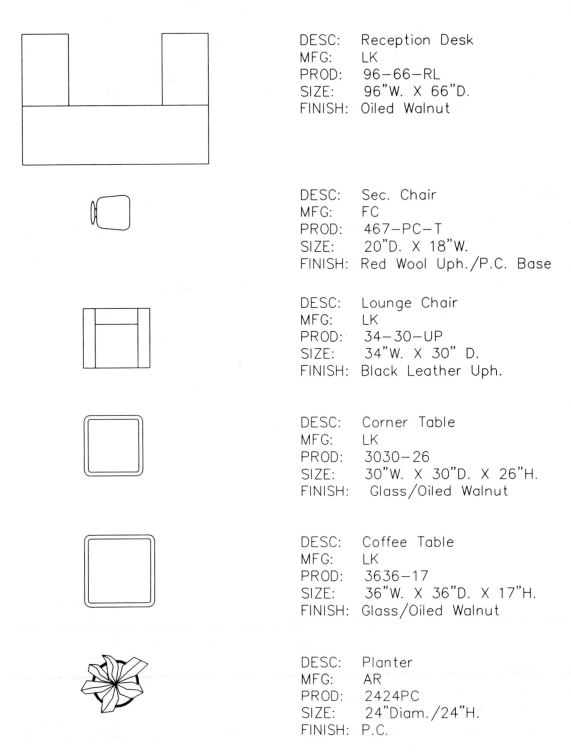

DESC: Reception Desk
MFG: LK
PROD: 96–66–RL
SIZE: 96"W. X 66"D.
FINISH: Oiled Walnut

DESC: Sec. Chair
MFG: FC
PROD: 467–PC–T
SIZE: 20"D. X 18"W.
FINISH: Red Wool Uph./P.C. Base

DESC: Lounge Chair
MFG: LK
PROD: 34–30–UP
SIZE: 34"W. X 30" D.
FINISH: Black Leather Uph.

DESC: Corner Table
MFG: LK
PROD: 3030–26
SIZE: 30"W. X 30"D. X 26"H.
FINISH: Glass/Oiled Walnut

DESC: Coffee Table
MFG: LK
PROD: 3636–17
SIZE: 36"W. X 36"D. X 17"H.
FINISH: Glass/Oiled Walnut

DESC: Planter
MFG: AR
PROD: 2424PC
SIZE: 24"Diam./24"H.
FINISH: P.C.

FIGURE 12–2
Reception Furniture Symbols and Specifications (Scale: $\frac{1}{4}'' = 1\text{-}0''$)

specifications appear on the drawing if they have been defined as visible (attributes can be visible or invisible). You can then extract the attribute information from the drawing using the ATTEXT command or DDATTEXT using the Attribute Extraction dialog box.

As shown in Figure 12–2, each piece of furniture in the reception area has five attributes. An attribute is made up of two parts, the tag and the value. The tag is used to help define the attribute but does not appear on the inserted drawing. It does appear on the drawing while attributes are being defined and before it is made into a block. The tags on the reception area furnishings are DESC., MFG., PROD., SIZE, and FINISH. The tag is used when the attribute information is extracted from the drawing. The ATTEXT command lists each occurrence of an attribute in the drawing. The attribute tag may contain any characters, but no spaces, and it is automatically converted to uppercase.

The value is the actual specification, such as Reception Desk, LK, 96-66-RL, 96″W. × 66″D., and Oiled Walnut. The attribute value may contain any characters, and it may also have spaces. The value appears on the drawing after it is inserted as a block. It appears exactly as it was entered.

There are five optional modes for the value of ATTDEF; these are set at the beginning of the attribute definition:

Invisible   This value is not displayed on the screen when the block is inserted. You may want to use the Invisible mode for pricing, or you may want to make some attributes invisible so that the drawing does not become cluttered.

Constant   This value is fixed and cannot be changed. For example, if the same chair is used throughout a project but the fabric varies, then the furniture manufacturer value of the chair will be constant but the finish value will not be constant. A Constant value cannot be edited.

Verify   This mode allows the value to be variable and allows you to check (verify) the value you have entered. Changes in the value may be entered as needed when the block is inserted. A second set of prompts appears while you are inserting the block. These prompts allow you to verify that the value you entered is correct.

Preset   This mode allows the value to be variable, but the changes are not requested as the block is inserted. It is similar to Constant in that fewer prompts appear. But unlike a Constant value, the Preset value can be changed with ATTEDIT, DDATTE, DDEDIT, and Properties... commands.

Variable   If none of the above modes is selected, the value is Variable. The Variable mode allows the value to be changed and prompts you once when the block is inserted to type any value other than the default value.

On Your Own

1. Keep the 0 Layer current.

2. Zoom in on the reception desk.

Use ATTDEF to define the attributes of the reception desk. Make all the attributes of the reception desk Constant (Figure 12–3):

Prompt	Response
Command:	TYPE: **ATTDEF<enter>**
Attribute modes—Invisible:N	

FIGURE 12–3
Use ATTDEF to Define the Attributes of the Reception Desk

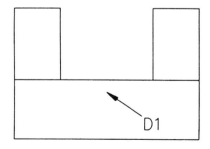

Prompt	Response

Constant:N Verify:N Preset:N
Enter (ICVP) to change, or press ENTER
   when done:
	TYPE: **C\<enter\>** (to set the mode to
	   Constant)

Attribute modes—Invisible:N
ConstantY: Verify:N Preset:N
Enter (ICVP) to change, or press ENTER
   when done:
(NOTE: The "N" after Constant has
   changed to "Y".)
	\<enter\>

Attribute tag:	TYPE: **DESC\<enter\>**
Attribute value:	TYPE: **Reception Desk\<enter\>**
Justify/Style/\<Start point\>:	TYPE: **C\<enter\>**
Center point:	**D1**
Height \<default\>:	TYPE: **3\<enter\>**
Rotation angle \<0\>:	**\<enter\>**
Command: (The first attribute is complete; the Attribute tag appears on the drawing.)	**\<enter\>**
Attribute modes—Invisible:N Constant:Y Verify:N Preset:N Enter (ICVP) to change, or press ENTER when done:	**\<enter\>** (to keep the Constant mode)
Attribute tag:	TYPE: **MFG\<enter\>**
Attribute value:	TYPE: **LK\<enter\>**

Justify/Style/\<Start point\>:	**\<enter\>** (AutoCAD automatically aligns
	   each new definition below the previous
	   attribute definition)

Command: (The second attribute is complete.)	**\<enter\>** (to return the ATTDEF prompt)
Attribute modes—Invisible:N Constant:Y Verify:N Preset:N Enter (ICVP) to change, or press ENTER when done:	**\<enter\>**
Attribute tag:	TYPE: **PROD\<enter\>**
Attribute value:	TYPE: **96-66-RL\<enter\>**
Justify/Style/\<Start point\>:	**\<enter\>**
Command: (The third attribute is complete.)	**\<enter\>**
Attribute modes—Invisible:N Constant:Y Verify:N Preset:N Enter (ICVP) to change, or press ENTER when done:	**\<enter\>**
Attribute tag:	TYPE: **SIZE\<enter\>**
Attribute value:	TYPE: **96"W X 66"D\<enter\>**
Justify/Style/\<Start point\>:	**\<enter\>**
Command: (The fourth attribute is complete.)	**\<enter\>**

Part II: Two-Dimensional AutoCAD

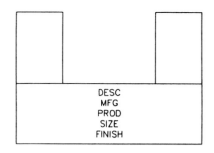

FIGURE 12–4
Reception Desk with Attribute Tags

Prompt	Response
Attribute modes—Invisible:N Constant:Y Verify:N Preset:N Enter (ICVP) to change, or press ENTER when done:	**<enter>**
Attribute tag:	TYPE: **FINISH<enter>**
Attribute value:	TYPE: **Oiled Walnut<enter>**
Justify/Style/<Start point>:	**<enter>**
Command: (The fifth attribute is complete.)	

When you have completed defining the five attributes, your drawing of the reception desk will look similar to the desk in Figure 12–4.

In the next part of this exercise, you will see how the ATTDEF prompts for a Constant attribute differ from an attribute defined with the Verify mode.

Note: If you are not happy with the location of the Attribute Tags, use the Move command to relocate them before using the Block command.

On Your Own

1. Keep the 0 Layer current.
2. Zoom in on the corner table.

Use ATTDEF to define the attributes of the corner table. Make the DESC. and MFG. attributes of the corner table Constant, and use the Verify mode for the PROD., SIZE, and FINISH attributes (Figure 12–5):

FIGURE 12–5
Use ATTDEF to Define the Attributes of the Corner Table

Prompt	Response
Command:	TYPE: **ATTDEF<enter>**
Attribute modes—Invisible:N Constant:Y Verify:N Preset:N Enter (ICVP) to change, or press ENTER when done: (*Note:* The "Y" indicates Constant is still the current mode.)	**<enter>**
Attribute tag:	TYPE: **DESC<enter>**
Attribute value:	TYPE: **Corner Table<enter>**
Justify/Style/<Start point>:	TYPE: **C<enter>**
Center point:	**D1**
Height <0'-3">:	**<enter>**
Rotation angle <0>:	**<enter>**
Command:	**<enter>**

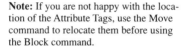

Prompt	Response
(The first attribute is complete; the Attribute tag appears on the drawing.)	
Attribute modes—Invisible:N Constant:Y Verify:N Preset:N Enter (ICVP) to change, or press ENTER when done:	**<enter>** (to keep the Constant mode)
Attribute tag:	TYPE: **MFG<enter>**
Attribute value:	TYPE: **LK<enter>**
Justify/Style/<Start point>:	**<enter>**
Command:	**<enter>**
(The second attribute is complete.)	
Attribute modes—Invisible:N Constant:Y Verify:N Preset:N Enter (ICVP) to change, or press ENTER when done:	TYPE: **C<enter>** (to cancel the Constant mode)
Attribute modes—Invisible:N Constant:N Verify:N Preset:N Enter (ICVP) to change, or press ENTER when done:	TYPE: **V<enter>** (to set the Verify mode)
Attribute modes—Invisible:N Constant:N Verify:Y Preset:N Enter (ICVP) to change, or press ENTER when done:	**<enter>**
Attribute tag:	TYPE: **PROD<enter>**
Attribute prompt:	TYPE: **Enter product number<enter>**
Default attribute value:	TYPE: **3030-26<enter>**
Justify/Style/<Start point>:	**<enter>**
Command:	**<enter>**
(The third attribute is complete.)	
Attribute modes—Invisible:N Constant:N Verify:Y Preset:N Enter (ICVP) to change, or press ENTER when done:	**<enter>**
Attribute tag:	TYPE: **SIZE<enter>**
Attribute prompt:	TYPE: **Enter product size<enter>**
Default attribute value:	TYPE: **30″W X 30″D X 26″H<enter>**
Justify/Style/<Start point>:	**<enter>**
Command:	**<enter>**
(The fourth attribute is complete.)	
Attribute modes—Invisible:N Constant:N Verify:Y Preset:N Enter (ICVP) to change, or press ENTER when done:	**<enter>**
Attribute tag:	TYPE: **FINISH<enter>**
Attribute prompt:	TYPE: **Enter product finish<enter>**
Default attribute value:	TYPE: **Glass/Oiled Walnut<enter>**

Note: The Constant mode must be canceled for the Verify and Preset modes to function. The Constant mode overrides the other two.

Note: The "Attribute prompt:" line may say whatever you want it to say.

Prompt	Response
Justify/Style/<Start point>:	<enter>
Command:	
(The fifth attribute is complete.)	

When the attribute mode is set to Verify, two additional ATTDEF prompts appear—"Attribute prompt:" and "Default attribute value:". The attribute prompt information that is typed and entered will appear when the block of the corner table is inserted into the drawing; it will appear and prompt you to enter the product finish, size, and number. The default attribute value appears if a different value is not typed and entered. These ATTDEF prompts do not appear while you are defining Constant attributes, because a Constant attribute value cannot vary.

In the following part of this exercise, you will use DDATTDEF and notice that the prompts for the Variable and Preset modes are the same as for the Verify mode. If none of the modes—Constant, Verify, or Preset—is set, the mode is Variable. You will also use the Invisible mode to define attributes.

On Your Own

1. Keep the 0 Layer current.

2. Zoom in on the secretarial chair.

3. If you need to, rotate your secretarial chair to appear oriented like the chair in Figure 12–6.

FIGURE 12–6
Use DDATTDEF to Define the Attributes of the Secretarial Chair

Use Define Attributes... (DDATTDEF-Dynamic Dialog Attribute Definition) to define the attributes of the secretarial chair. Make the DESC. and MFG. attributes of the secretarial chair variable. Use the Preset and Invisible modes for the PROD., SIZE, and FINISH attributes (Figures 12–6, 12–7, 12–8, 12–9, 12–10, and 12–11):

Prompt	Response
Command:	**Define Attributes...**
	or TYPE: **DDATTDEF<enter>**
The Attribute Definition dialog box appears:	**Clear all the checks in the Mode area.**
	(The attribute will now be variable.)
	TYPE: **DESC** in the Tag: box

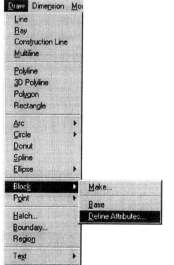

FIGURE 12–7
Defining the First Attribute for the Secretarial Chair

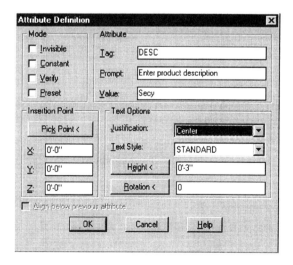

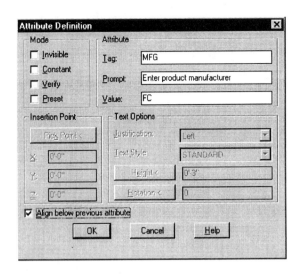

FIGURE 12–8
Defining the Second Attribute for the Secretarial Chair

Prompt	**Response**
	TYPE: **Enter product description** in the Prompt: Box
	TYPE: **Secy** in the Value: box
	CLICK: **The down arrow** in the Justification: box and CLICK: **Center**

All other parts of the dialog box should be as shown in Figure 12–7.

Prompt	**Response**
	CLICK: **Pick Point<**
Start point:	**D1** (Figure 12–6)
The Attribute Definition dialog box reappears:	CLICK: **OK**
The first attribute is complete; the Attribute Tag appears on the drawing.	
Command:	**<enter>**
The Attribute Definition dialog box appears:	**Complete the dialog box as shown in Figure 12–8. Notice that the Align below previous attribute button is checked, so that the Insertion Point and Text Options areas are grayed out.**
	CLICK: **OK**
The second attribute is complete; the Attribute Tag appears on the drawing aligned below the first attribute.	
Command:	**<enter>**
The Attribute Definition dialog box appears:	**Complete the dialog box as shown in Figure 12–9. Notice that the Align below previous attribute button is checked again and that the Preset and Invisible modes are checked.**
	CLICK: **OK**

FIGURE 12–9
Defining the Third Attribute for
the Secretarial Chair

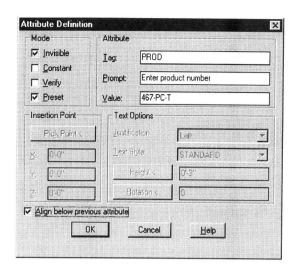

FIGURE 12–10
Defining the Fourth Attribute for
the Secretarial Chair

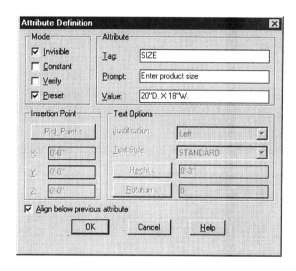

Prompt	Response
The third attribute is complete; the Attribute Tag appears on the drawing aligned below the second attribute.	
Command:	**<enter>**
The Attribute Definition dialog box appears:	**Complete the dialog box as shown in Figure 12–10. Notice that the Align below previous attribute button is checked again and that the Preset and Invisible modes are checked.**
	CLICK: **OK**
The fourth attribute is complete; the Attribute Tag appears on the drawing aligned below the third attribute.	
Command:	**<enter>**
The Attribute Definition dialog box appears:	**Complete the dialog box as shown in Figure 12–11. Notice that the Align below previous attribute button is checked again and that the Preset and Invisible modes are checked.**

FIGURE 12–11
Defining the Fifth Attribute for the Secretarial Chair

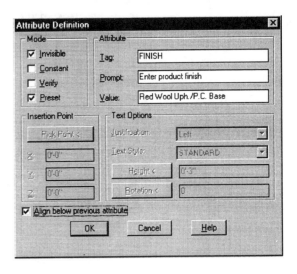

Prompt	Response
	CLICK: **OK**

The fifth attribute is complete; the Attribute Tag appears on the drawing aligned below the fourth attribute.

Edit Text (DDEDIT)

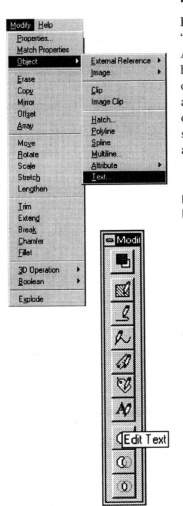

Did you make a mistake while responding to the "Attribute tag", "Attribute prompt", or "Default attribute value" prompts? The Edit Text command allows you to use an Edit Attribute Definition Dialog Box (Figure 12–12) to correct any typing mistakes you may have made while defining the attributes. The Edit Text prompt is "<Select an annotation object>/Undo:". When a tag is picked, the Edit Attribute Definition dialog box appears and allows you to change the attribute tag, prompt, or default value for a Variable, Verify, or Preset attribute. The tag and the default (actually the Value) can be changed for a Constant attribute; adding a prompt for an attribute defined as Constant does not change the attribute mode, and the prompt does not appear.

The Edit Text command can be used only before the symbol is made into a block.

FIGURE 12–12
Edit Attribute Definition Dialog Box

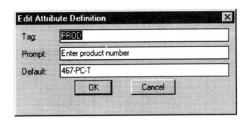

On Your Own

1. Use Wblock to save the reception desk as a Wblock (a drawing) on a floppy disk in drive A. Name the Wblock RDSK. Use the insertion base point as shown in Figure 12–13. Have the desk oriented as shown in Figure 12–13.

2. Use Wblock to save the corner table as a Wblock (a drawing) on a floppy disk in drive A. Name the Wblock CRTBL. Use the insertion base point as shown in Figure 12–13. If the table was drawn on snap, you can use the snap point of the two sides of the table as if they met at a 90° angle.

3. Use Wblock to save the secretarial chair as a Wblock on a floppy disk in drive A. Name the block SECY. Pick the center of the chair as the insertion base point.

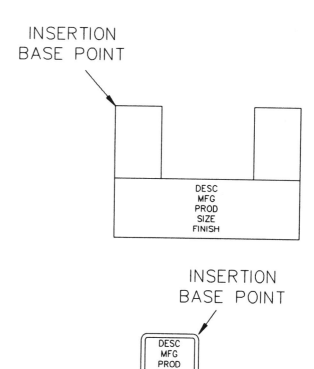

FIGURE 12–13
Save the Reception Desk and the Corner Table as a Wblock (a Drawing) on a Floppy Disk

INSERTION BASE POINT

DESC
MFG
PROD
SIZE
FINISH

INSERTION BASE POINT

DESC
MFG
PROD
SIZE
FINISH

Inserting a Block with Attributes—Using the Command: Prompt Line

The Insert command is used to insert the blocks with attributes into the tenant space floor plan. Let's insert the reception desk into the drawing. Remember, all five attribute values were defined as Constant. They will appear on the drawing as you entered them.

On Your Own

Set the A-furn Layer current.

Use the Insert command to insert the RDSK block stored on a floppy disk in drive A into the tenant space floor plan. Use the ID command to help position the block (Figure 12–14):

Prompt	Response
Command:	TYPE: **ID<enter>**
Point:	**Osnap-Intersection**
of	**D1**
ID Point: Int of	
X = 49'-0″ Y = 12'-0″ Z = 0'-0″	
Command:	TYPE: **INSERT<enter>**
Block name (or ?):	TYPE: **A:RDSK<enter>**
Insertion point:	TYPE: **@24,30<enter>**
X scale factor <1> / Corner / XYZ:	**<enter>**
Y scale factor (default=X):	**<enter>**
Rotation angle <0>:	TYPE: **90<enter>** (the RDSK block is inserted; the Values appear on the block)

Let's insert the corner table into the drawing. Remember, the Description and Manufacturer attribute values of the corner table were defined with the Constant mode. The Prod-

FIGURE 12–14
Use the Insert Command to
Insert the RDSK Block into the
Tenant Space Floor Plan

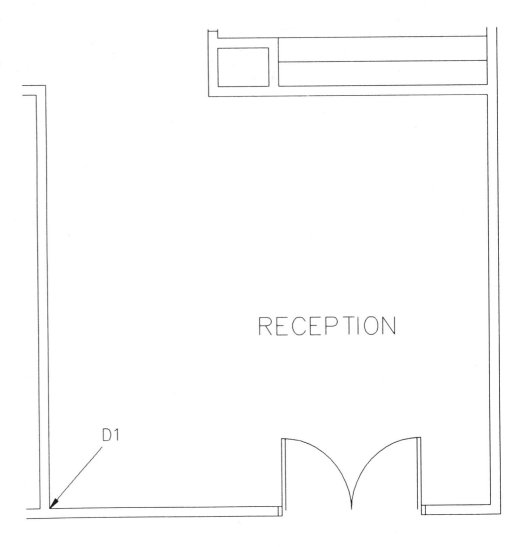

RECEPTION

D1

uct, Size, and Finish attribute values were defined with the Verify mode. The prompts entered during the ATTDEF command for the values defined with Verify will appear while you insert the CRTBL block. Those prompts allow you to change the attribute value or accept the Default attribute value that was also entered during the ATTDEF command.

Keep the A-furn Layer current. Use the Insert command to insert the CRTBL block stored on a floppy disk in drive A into the tenant space floor plan. Use the ID command to help position the block (Figure 12–15):

Prompt	Response
Command:	TYPE: **ID<enter>**
Point:	**Osnap-Intersection**
Int of	**D1**
ID Point: INT of	
X = 68'-0″ Y = 29'-2″ Z = 0'-0″	
Command:	TYPE: **INSERT<enter>**
Block name (or ?) <RDSK>:	TYPE: **A:CRTBL<enter>**
Insertion point:	TYPE: **@-2,-2<enter>**
X scale factor <1> / Corner / XYZ:	**<enter>**
Y scale factor (default=X):	**<enter>**

FIGURE 12-15
Use the Insert Command to
Insert the CRTBL Block into the
Tenant Space Floor Plan

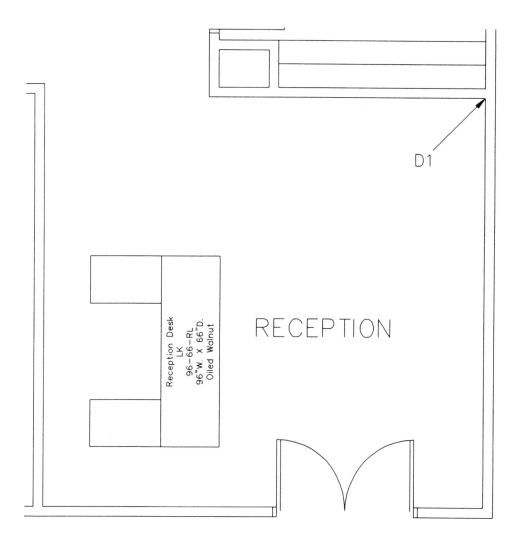

RECEPTION

D1

Reception Desk
LK
96-66-RL
96"W. X 66"D.
Oiled Walnut

Note: If the Enter Attributes dialog box appears, escape from the command, and turn the dialog box off. TYPE: ATTDIA <enter> and 0<enter> for the new value.

Rotation angle <0>:	**<enter>**
Enter attribute values	
Enter product finish <Glass/Oiled Walnut>:	**<enter>** (to accept the default)
Enter product size <30″W × 30″D × 26″H>:	**<enter>**
Enter product number <3030-26>:	**<enter>**
Verify attribute values	
Enter product finish <Glass/Oiled Walnut>:	**<enter>**
Enter product size <30″W × 30″D × 26″H>:	**<enter>**
Enter product number <3030-26>:	**<enter>**

Some of the values that appeared on the corner table are too long; they go outside the table symbol. We will fix this later in the exercise with the ATTEDIT command.

When you insert a block with attributes defined using the Verify mode, you may type and enter a new value or accept the default value at the first prompt. A second prompt appears, allowing you to verify that the attribute values you entered by accepting the default or typing from the keyboard are correct.

Tip: If you are not happy with a Block location after insertion, use the Move command to relocate it.

FIGURE 12–16
Enter Attributes Dialog Box

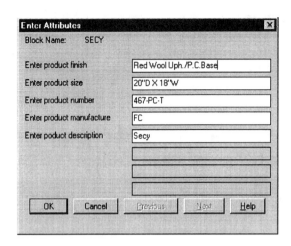

Inserting a Block with Attributes—Using an Enter Attributes Dialog Box

An Enter Attributes dialog box (Figure 12–16) can be used to insert blocks with attributes. The dialog box allows you to change or accept the default values of the attributes you defined using the Variable, Verify, or Preset modes. Its appearance is controlled by the ATTDIA system variable.

Set the ATTDIA system variable to 1 to make the dialog box appear while you insert blocks with attributes:

Prompt	Response
Command:	TYPE: **ATTDIA<enter>**
New value for ATTDIA <0>:	TYPE: **1<enter>**

Let's insert the secretarial chair into the drawing. Remember, the DESC and MFG attributes were defined as Variable, and PROD, SIZE, and FINISH attributes were defined as Preset and Invisible.

Keep the A-furn Layer current. Use the Insert command to insert the SECY block stored on a floppy disk in drive A into the tenant space reception area.

Prompt	Response
Command:	**Insert** (or TYPE: **I<enter>**)
The Insert dialog box appears:	CLICK: **File...**
The Select Drawing File dialog box appears:	In the File name: box TYPE: **A: SECY** (or CLICK: **the down arrow in the Look in: box**, CLICK: **$3\frac{1}{2}$ Floppy [A:]** and CLICK: on the **SECY** drawing file)
	CLICK: **Open**
The Insert dialog box appears with SECY in the Block... box.	CLICK: **OK**
Insertion point:	**The block is dragged in with the crosshairs on the insertion point of the chair. Click a point behind the reception desk close to the location of the center of the chair.**
X scale factor <1> / Corner / XYZ:	**<enter>**
Y scale factor (default = X):	**<enter>**

Tip: Change your SNAP setting if it helps your accuracy when inserting a Block.

Part II: Two-Dimensional AutoCAD

Prompt	Response
Rotation angle <0>:	<enter>
(The Enter Attributes dialog box appears.)	CLICK: **OK**

The last three attributes, because they were defined using the Invisible mode, are not visible on the inserted chair.

Using the dialog box, you may change the values for attributes defined using the Verify, Preset, or Variable modes. Prompts do not appear in the Command: prompt area for the values defined with the Preset mode, but with a dialog box, the Preset mode values can be changed as they are inserted.

Attribute Display (ATTDISP)

The Attribute Display (ATTDISP) command allows you to turn ON the Invisible attributes of the secretarial chair. The prompt is "ATTDISP Normal/ON/OFF<Default>:".

ON

Pick ON to make the Invisible attributes appear. Try this, and you will be able to see the Invisible attributes of the secretarial chair.

OFF

Pick OFF to make all the attributes on the drawing Invisible. Try this, and you will see that all the attributes are not visible.

Normal

Pick Normal to make visible attributes defined as Visible and to make invisible attributes defined as Invisible. Set Normal as the default.

Modify-Attribute-Single (DDATTE-Dynamic Dialog Attribute Edit)

The Modify-Attribute-Single (Dynamic Dialog Attribute Edit) command uses the Edit Attributes dialog box (Figure 12–17) to edit Variable, Verify, and Preset Attributes values of an inserted block. Attributes defined with the Constant mode cannot be edited.

Some of the values on the corner table are too long. Let's use the Modify-Attribute-Single command to make them shorter.

Use the Modify-Attribute-Single command to edit the values (created with the Verify mode) on the inserted corner table:

Prompt	Response
Command:	**Modify-Attribute-Single**
	(or TYPE: **ATE<enter>**)

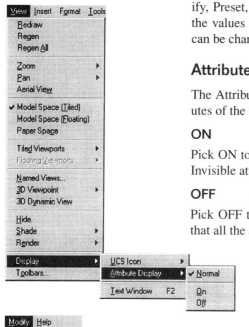

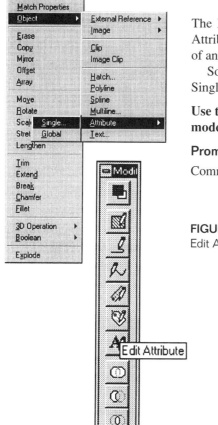

Note: The Preset ATTDEF mode is used to eliminate prompts and save time but still allows you to edit the attributes after insertion.

FIGURE 12–17
Edit Attributes Dialog Box

Prompt	Response
Select block:	**Pick any place on the corner table.**
(The Edit Attributes dialog box appears.)	**Use the dialog box to insert the following two new values:**
	Enter product finish: GL/O.W.
	Enter product size..: 30X30X26.
	CLICK: **OK**

The values that appear on the corner table now fit within the table symbol.

On Your Own

1. Set the 0 Layer current. Use the Define Attributes... command to add to the lounge chair, coffee table, and planter the attributes shown in Figure 12–2. Make each attribute Variable and Visible. Set the text height at 3″. Refer to the inserted blocks in Figure 12–18 for the value text (may be abbreviated to fit) and location.

2. Use Wblock to save the lounge chair, coffee table, and planter as blocks on a floppy disk in drive A. Name the blocks LGCH, CFTBL, and PLANT. Look at the location of each inserted block in Figure 12–18, and select a point for the insertion base point of each block.

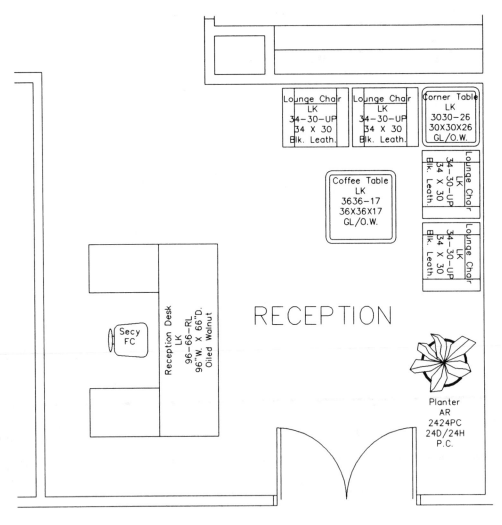

FIGURE 12–18
Tenant Space Reception Area (Scale: $\frac{1}{4}$″ = 1′-0″)

Tip: To save time while using the ATTDEF command, press the enter key at the "Attribute prompt:" prompt line. The Attribute prompt will then automatically be the same as the tag.

3. Set the A-furn Layer current. Use the Insert command to complete the insertion of all furniture in the tenant space reception area. Changing the SNAP setting to 2″ may help with insertion of the blocks. Remember, once a block is inserted, it can be moved to a new location.

Modify-Attribute-Global (ATTEDIT-Attribute Edit)

The Modify-Attribute-Global (Attribute Edit) command allows you to edit inserted attribute values, independent of their block reference. It allows you to edit one at a time the text string, text string position, text height, text angle, text style, layer, or color of inserted attribute values. It also provides prompts that allow you globally to edit the value text strings of many attributes all at once. Constant values cannot be edited.

On Your Own

Zoom in on the coffee table. We will begin by using Modify-Attribute-Global to edit attribute values one at a time.

Use the Modify-Attribute-Global command to edit the text height of the description value, "Coffee Table", and the manufacturer value, "LK":

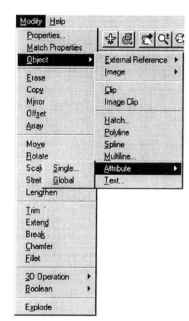

Prompt	Response
Command:	**Modify-Attribute-Global** (or TYPE: **ATTEDIT<enter>**)
Edit attributes one at a time? <Y>	**<enter>**
Block name specification <*>:	**<enter>**
Attribute tag specification <*>:	**<enter>**
Attribute value specification <*>:	**<enter>**
Select Attributes:	**Pick the text strings "Coffee Table" and "LK"**
Select Attributes:	**<enter>**
2 attributes selected. Value/Position/Height/Angle/Style/Layer/ Color/Next <N>: ("Coffee Table" is highlighted and an X appears at the beginning of the text string.)	TYPE: **H<enter>**
New height <0′-3″>:	TYPE: **4<enter>**
Value/Position/Height/Angle/Style/Layer/ Color/Next <N>:	**Next** (or PRESS:**<enter>**)
Value/Position/Height/Angle/Style/Layer/ Color/Next <N>: ("LK" is highlighted)	TYPE: **H<enter>**
New height <0′-3″>:	TYPE: **4<enter>**
Value/Position/Height/Angle/Style/Layer/ Color/Next <N>:	**<enter>**

The Modify-Attribute-Global prompts allow you to narrow the value selection by entering a specific block name, tag specification, and value specification. In the preceding exercise, we accepted the default "*" to include all of the blocks.

Only visible attributes can be edited when you respond with "Yes" to the prompt "Edit attributes one at a time?". If you respond with "No" to the prompt, visible and invisible attribute value text strings can be edited.

Let's use the Modify-Attribute-Global command to edit all at once a value on the four lounge chairs.

On Your Own

Zoom in on the four lounge chairs.

Use the Modify-Attribute-Global command to edit the text string of the finish value on all the chairs at once:

Prompt	Response
Command:	**Modify-Attribute-Global** (or TYPE: **ATTEDIT<enter>**)
Edit attributes one at a time? <Y>	TYPE: **N<enter>**
Edit only attributes visible on screen? <Y>	**<enter>**
Block name specification <*>:	TYPE: **LGCH<enter>**
Attribute tag specification <*>:	TYPE: **FINISH<enter>**
Attribute value specification <*>:	TYPE: **Blk. Leath.<enter>**
Select Attributes:	**Window all four chairs and the coffee table<enter>**
4 attributes selected.	
String to change:	TYPE: **Blk. Leath.<enter>**
New string:	TYPE: **Brwn. Leath.<enter>**

When you use this option of the Modify-Attribute-Global command, the wild-card character "*" is interpreted literally by AutoCAD, so it cannot be used. Type and enter the block name, tag, and value exactly. You may also enter "No" in response to the prompt "Edit only attributes visible on screen?", and invisible attribute values may also be changed.

On Your Own

Use the Modify-Attribute-Global command to change the text height of the coffee table description value, "Coffee Table", and the manufacturer value, "LK", back to 3″.

ATTREDEF

Any drawing defined as a block with the Wblock command and inserted into a drawing then becomes available for use as a block in the current drawing. Once inserted, these blocks are similar to blocks defined with the Block command.

The ATTREDEF command allows you to redefine a block within the drawing and updates all previous insertions of the block in your drawing. In the following part of this exercise, the LGCH block will be redefined. Before redefining the block, you must complete a new definition of the block attributes.

On Your Own

1. Select "?" from the Block prompt, and view the list of blocks available within the drawing.
2. Set 0 Layer current.
3. Insert a copy of the LGCH block in an open space in the tenant space drawing.
4. Explode the LGCH block and erase the tags.
5. Use the ATTDEF command to create the following new attributes. Make all the attributes variable.

Tag	Value
DESC	Lnge. Ch.
MFG	FC
PROD	34-30-UP
UPH	Nat. Leath.

FIGURE 12–19
Redefined LGCH Block

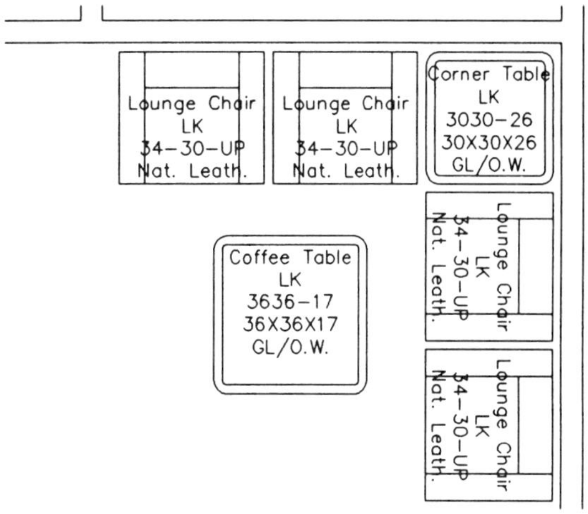

Use ATTREDEF to redefine the LGCH block:

Prompt	Response
Command:	TYPE: **ATTREDEF<enter>**
Name of Block you wish to redefine:	TYPE: **LGCH<enter>**
Select objects for new Block…	
Select objects:	**Window the newly drawn lounge chair.**
Other corner: 11 found	
Select objects:	**<enter>**
Insertion base point of new Block:	**Select the same insertion base point you previously selected**

The drawing is regenerated and all previous insertions of the LGCH block are redefined (Figure 12–19). The values on the block may not have changed exactly as you thought they would. When ATTREDEF is used to redefine a block:

1. New attributes to existing block references are given their default values.

2. Old attributes to existing block references retain their old values.

3. Old attributes not included in the new block definition are deleted from the existing block references.

The shape of the block can also be changed with ATTREDEF. If the lounge chair needed to be smaller, it could have been redrawn before you redefined the block.

On Your Own

Future insertions of the block will use the redefined variable attribute tags and values. To see how future insertions of the block appear:

1. Use the Insert command to insert a copy of the redefined LGCH block in an open space in the tenant space drawing.

2. Erase the block after comparing the differences between the existing redefined blocks and the newly inserted redefined block.

Redefining an Inserted Block with Attributes Using the BLOCK Command

As described in Chapter 9, you can redefine a block using the Block command. When a block that has attributes assigned is redefined using the Block command, previous insertions of the block are affected as follows:

1. Old constant attributes are lost, replaced by new constant attributes, if any.

Tip: Be consistent with the position of the "Insertion base point" location of the furniture symbol blocks. For example, always pick up the upper right or upper left corner. This helps you to remember the "Insertion base point" location when inserting the furniture symbols. It is especially necessary to be consistent when using ATTREDEF, so the newly redefined block is oriented correctly.

DESC: Conference Table
MFG: LK
PROD: 108-42B/PC
SIZE: 108" X 42"
FINISH: Oiled Walnut

DESC: Conference Chair
MFG: FC
PROD: T36-LB
SIZE: 26"W. X 26"D.
FINISH: Red Wool Uph./P.C. Base

FIGURE 12–20
Conference Room Furniture Symbols and Specifications (Scale: $\frac{1}{4}$" = 1'-0")

Tip: If the furniture symbols are inserted on the wrong layer, use the Properties... command to change the symbols to the correct layer.

2. Variable attributes remain unchanged, even if the new block definition does not include those attributes.

3. New variable attributes are not added.

Future insertions of the block will use the new attributes. The previous insertions of the block must be erased and inserted again to use the new attributes.

On Your Own

1. Set the 0 Layer current. Draw the remaining furniture symbols as shown in Figures 12–20 through 12–24 for the tenant space. Be sure to note furniture pieces that are repeated, and draw them only once. For example, the planter and secretarial chair symbols have already been drawn, attributes have been added, and a block has been made.

2. Use the ATTDEF command to add the attributes shown in Figures 12–20 through 12–24 to the furniture symbols. Make all attributes Variable. Make all the attributes Visible, except the attributes of the bookkeeping systems panels, which need to be Invisible. Set the Text height at 3". Refer to the inserted blocks in Figure 12–25 for the value text (may be abbreviated to fit) and location.

3. Use Wblock to save the new furniture symbols as blocks on a floppy disk in drive A. Create a name for each new block. Look at the location of each inserted block in Figure 12–25, and select a point for the insertion base point of each block.

4. Set the A-furn Layer current, and use the Insert command to complete the insertion of all furniture symbols in the tenant space reception plan.

ATTEXT and DDATTEXT

The ATTEXT (Attribute Extraction) command allows you to extract attribute information from a drawing using the command line. The DDATTEXT command extracts attribute information using a dialog box. Both are typed and entered from the Command: line. To use the ATTEXT command, you must create a template file. A template file specifies which attributes are to be extracted, what information is to be included for each Block having those attributes, and how that information is to appear for CDF and SDF formats. You create the template file using a database program, text editor, or word processor. The *AutoCAD User's Guide*, Chapter 11, describes how to create a template file.

The ATTEXT prompt is "CDF, SDF, or DXF Attribute extract (or Objects)?<C>:". The Objects option allows you to pick selected objects for attribute extraction. The CDF, SDF, and DXF options specify attribute extraction formats. CDF is a comma-delimited format, and SDF has fixed-width fields. DXF is similar to the AutoCAD Drawing Interchange File format. All are described in the *AutoCAD User's Guide*.

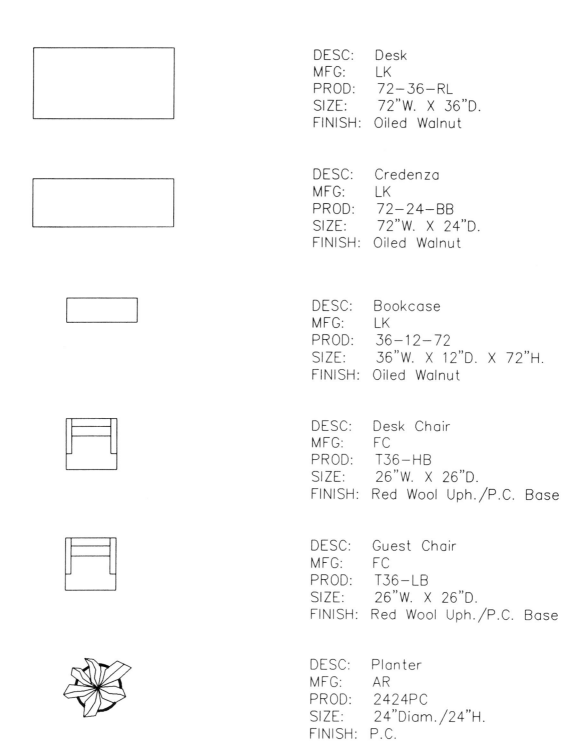

DESC: Desk
MFG: LK
PROD: 72—36—RL
SIZE: 72"W. X 36"D.
FINISH: Oiled Walnut

DESC: Credenza
MFG: LK
PROD: 72—24—BB
SIZE: 72"W. X 24"D.
FINISH: Oiled Walnut

DESC: Bookcase
MFG: LK
PROD: 36—12—72
SIZE: 36"W. X 12"D. X 72"H.
FINISH: Oiled Walnut

DESC: Desk Chair
MFG: FC
PROD: T36—HB
SIZE: 26"W. X 26"D.
FINISH: Red Wool Uph./P.C. Base

DESC: Guest Chair
MFG: FC
PROD: T36—LB
SIZE: 26"W. X 26"D.
FINISH: Red Wool Uph./P.C. Base

DESC: Planter
MFG: AR
PROD: 2424PC
SIZE: 24"Diam./24"H.
FINISH: P.C.

FIGURE 12–21
Office 1 and Office 2 Furniture Symbols and Specifications (Scale: $\frac{1}{4}'' = 1'\text{-}0''$)

TENANT SPACE — OFFICE 3

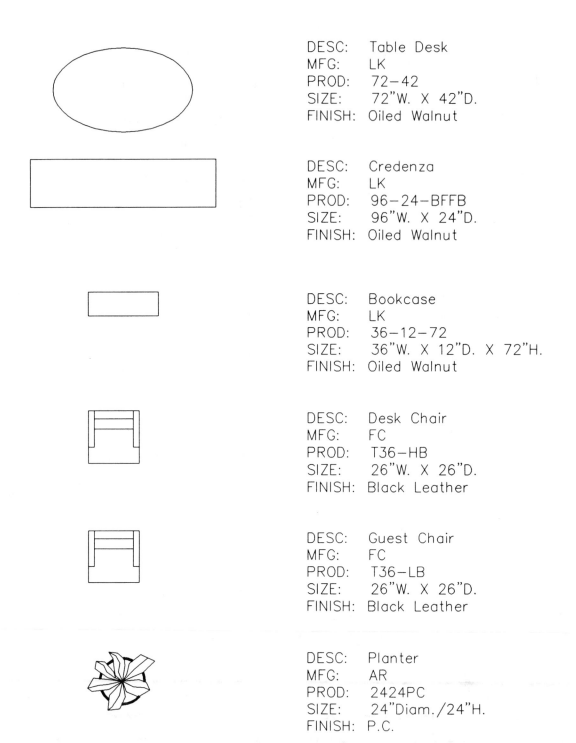

DESC: Table Desk
MFG: LK
PROD: 72—42
SIZE: 72"W. X 42"D.
FINISH: Oiled Walnut

DESC: Credenza
MFG: LK
PROD: 96—24—BFFB
SIZE: 96"W. X 24"D.
FINISH: Oiled Walnut

DESC: Bookcase
MFG: LK
PROD: 36—12—72
SIZE: 36"W. X 12"D. X 72"H.
FINISH: Oiled Walnut

DESC: Desk Chair
MFG: FC
PROD: T36—HB
SIZE: 26"W. X 26"D.
FINISH: Black Leather

DESC: Guest Chair
MFG: FC
PROD: T36—LB
SIZE: 26"W. X 26"D.
FINISH: Black Leather

DESC: Planter
MFG: AR
PROD: 2424PC
SIZE: 24"Diam./24"H.
FINISH: P.C.

FIGURE 12–22
Office 3 Furniture Symbols and Specifications (Scale: $\frac{1}{4}$" = 1'-0")

TENANT SPACE — BOOKKEEPING

DESC: Panel
MFG: TK
PROD: T4812TS
SIZE: 48" X 2" X 62"H.
FINISH: Rose Fabric

DESC: Panel
MFG: TK
PROD: T3612TS
SIZE: 36" X 2" X 62"H.
FINISH: Rose Fabric

DESC: Panel
MFG: TK
PROD: T3012TS
SIZE: 30" X 2" X 62"H.
FINISH: Rose Fabric

DESC: Panel
MFG: TK
PROD: T2412TS
SIZE: 24" X 2" X 62"H.
FINISH: Rose Fabric

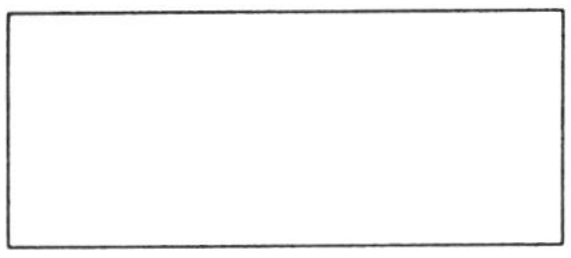

DESC: Work Surface
MFG: TK
PROD: 7230HS
SIZE: 72" X 30"D.
FINISH: Tan

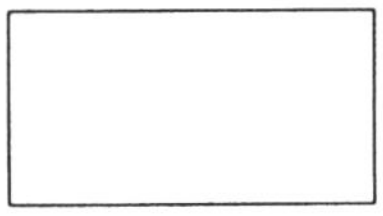

DESC: Work Surface
MFG: TK
PROD: 4824HS
SIZE: 48" X 24"D.
FINISH: Tan

FIGURE 12–23
Bookkeeping Furniture Symbols and Specifications (Scale: $\frac{1}{4}'' = 1'-0''$)

TENANT SPACE — BOOKKEEPING (CONT.)

DESC: Lateral File
MFG: TK
PROD: 42185DRW
SIZE: 42" X 18" X 62"H.
FINISH: Tan

DESC: Lateral File
MFG: TK
PROD: 36185DRW
SIZE: 36" X 18" X 62"H.
FINISH: Tan

DESC: Sec. Chair
MFG: FC
PROD: 467—PC—T
SIZE: 20"D. X 18"W.
FINISH: Red Wool Uph./P.C. Base

FIGURE 12–23 *continued*

After you specify CDF, SDF, or DXF you are prompted to enter the template filename and the extract filename. Then the extract file is created. The extract file does not total like furniture pieces; for example, if five like chairs are on the plan, the extract file will contain five references to the chair. Once the extract file has been created, it can be processed by a database program to create lists that total like pieces and other similar totals.

Furniture Symbol and Specification Software Programs

Creating a library of all the furniture symbols you may need while completing a furniture plan can be very time consuming. Many programs are available on the market today that have the furniture symbols already drawn. Most of the major furniture manufacturers' furniture symbols and catalog specifications are available in programs that work easily with AutoCAD. Some already have the specifications or attributes assigned and allow you to enter variables. Programs are also available that extract attribute information from a drawing and provide a list of information that can be tailored to include such data as item totals, specifications, total costs, and total selling price.

TENANT SPACE − PRESIDENT

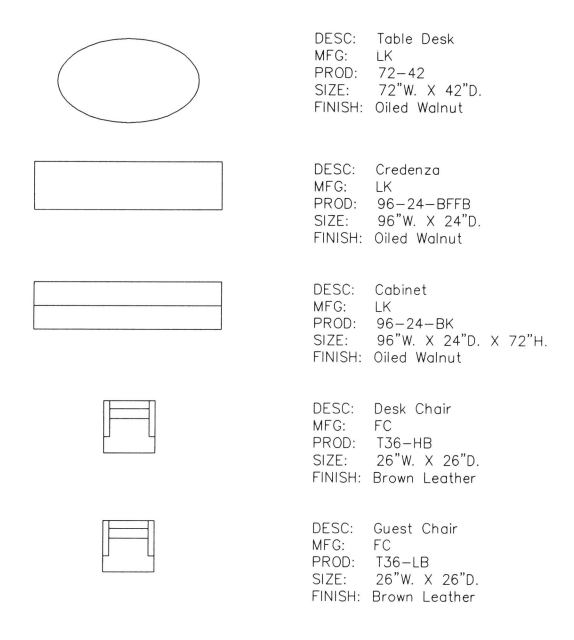

DESC: Table Desk
MFG: LK
PROD: 72−42
SIZE: 72"W. X 42"D.
FINISH: Oiled Walnut

DESC: Credenza
MFG: LK
PROD: 96−24−BFFB
SIZE: 96"W. X 24"D.
FINISH: Oiled Walnut

DESC: Cabinet
MFG: LK
PROD: 96−24−BK
SIZE: 96"W. X 24"D. X 72"H.
FINISH: Oiled Walnut

DESC: Desk Chair
MFG: FC
PROD: T36−HB
SIZE: 26"W. X 26"D.
FINISH: Brown Leather

DESC: Guest Chair
MFG: FC
PROD: T36−LB
SIZE: 26"W. X 26"D.
FINISH: Brown Leather

DESC: Planter
MFG: AR
PROD: 2424PC
SIZE: 24"Diam./24"H.
FINISH: P.C.

FIGURE 12–24
President's Furniture Symbols and Specifications (Scale: $\frac{1}{4}'' = 1'\text{-}0''$)

TENANT SPACE — PRESIDENT (CONT.)

DESC: Corner Table
MFG: LK
PROD: 3030—26
SIZE: 30"W. X 30"D. X 26"H.
FINISH: Glass/Oiled Walnut

DESC: Coffee Table
MFG: LK
PROD: 3636—17
SIZE: 36"W. X 36"D. X 17"H.
FINISH: Glass/Oiled Walnut

DESC: Lounge Chair
MFG: FC
PROD: 3430UP
FINISH: Brown Leather

FIGURE 12–24 *continued*

External Reference (XREF)

The External Reference command allows you to attach an external reference (drawing) to a primary drawing. For each drawing, the data is stored in its own separate file. Any changes made to the external reference drawing are reflected in the primary drawing each time the primary drawing is loaded into the Drawing Editor.

There are three distinct advantages to using External References:

1. The primary drawing always contains the most recent version of the External Reference.

2. There are no conflicts in layer names and other similar features (called named objects), such as linetypes, text styles, and block definitions. AutoCAD automatically precedes the external reference layer name or other object name with the drawing name of the XREF and a slash (/). For example, if the primary drawing and the external reference (named CHAIR) have a layer named Symbol, then the current drawing layer retains the name Symbol, and the external reference layer in the current drawing becomes Chair/symbol.

3. Drawing files are often much smaller.

External references are used, for example, when you are drawing a large furniture plan containing several different levels of office types, such as assistant, associate, manager, vice president, and president. Each office typical (furniture configuration used in the office) is attached to the current drawing as an external reference. When changes are made to the external reference drawing of the manager's office (as a result of furniture substitution, for example), the change is reflected in each instance of a manager's office in the primary large furniture plan when it is loaded into the Drawing Editor.

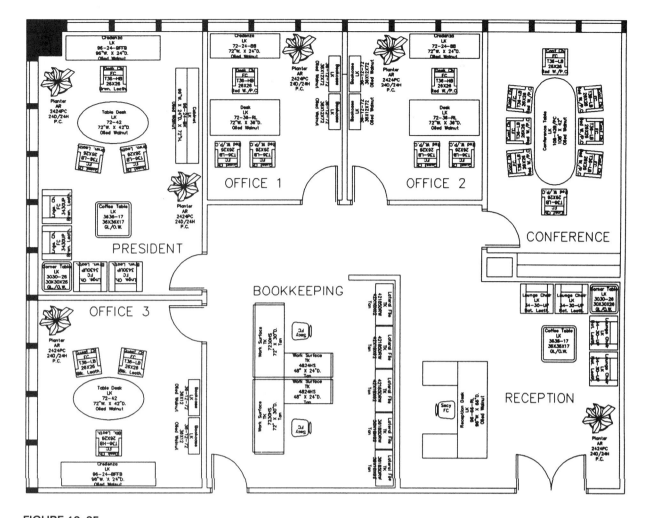

FIGURE 12–25

Exercise 12–1: Tenant Space Furniture Plan with Furniture Specifications (Scale: $\frac{1}{8}'' = 1'\text{-}0''$)

When the External Reference command is activated, the External Reference dialog box appears. After you attach a drawing to your current drawing, the following options are available in the External Reference dialog box:

Attach

The Attach option allows you to attach as an external reference any drawing to the current drawing. There is no limit to the number of external references that you can attach to your drawing.

Detach

The Detach option lets you remove unneeded external references from your drawing.

Reload

The Reload option allows you to update the current drawing with an external reference that has been changed since you began the current drawing. You do not have to exit from the current drawing to update it with an external reference that you or someone else changed while in the current drawing.

Unload

Temporarily clears the external reference from the current drawing until the drawing is reloaded.

Bind...

The insert option in the Bind dialog box creates a block of the external reference in the current drawing and erases any reference to it as an external reference. The Bind option binds the selected Xref to the drawing and renames layers in a manner similar to the attached Xref.

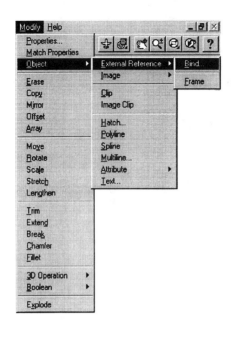
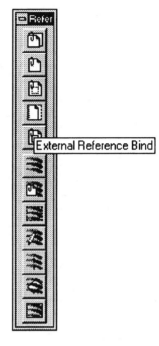

Features of External References

1. An External Reference cannot be exploded.
2. An External Reference can be changed into a block with the Bind-Insert option and then exploded. The advantage of using the External Reference is then lost. The Bind option would be used if you wanted to send a client a disk containing only the current drawing without including External References on the same disk.
3. External References can be nested. That means that a current drawing containing External References can itself be used as an External Reference on another current drawing. There is no limit to the number of drawings you can nest like this.

XBIND

The XBIND (External Bind) command allows you to bind a selected subset of an External Reference's dependent symbols to the current drawing. For example, if you did not want to create a block of the entire External Reference but wanted permanently to add only a dimension style of the external reference to the drawing, you could use XBIND.

SAVE

When you have completed Exercise 12–1, save your work in at least two places.

PLOT

Printer Plot or Plotter Plot Exercise 12–1 to scale.

EXERCISE 12–2
Office I Furniture Plan

1. Start a new drawing named CH12-EX2 by copying the Office I floor plan drawn in Exercise 9–2 or by copying the Office I floor plan dimensioned in Exercise 10–5.
2. Create a new layer for furniture, and draw the furniture as shown in Figure 12–26 for the Office I furniture plan. Use a $\frac{1''}{8} = 1'\text{-}0''$ architectural scale to measure the furniture, and draw it full scale.
3. Save the drawing in two places, and Printer Plot or Plotter Plot the drawing to scale.

Part II: Two-Dimensional AutoCAD

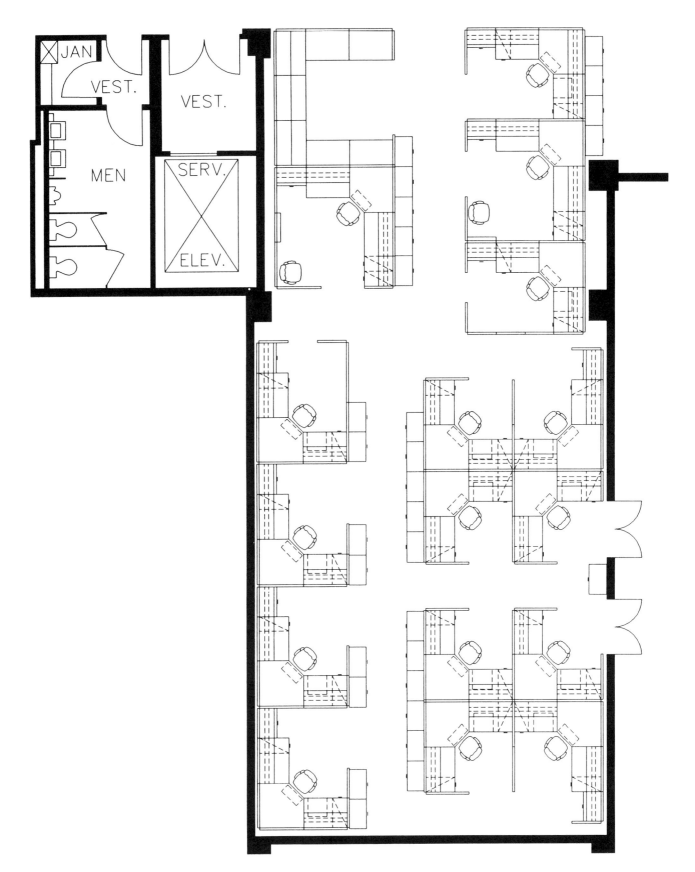

FIGURE 12–26
Exercise 12–2: Office I Furniture Plan (Scale: $\frac{1}{8}'' = 1'\text{-}0''$)
(Courtesy of Business Interiors Design Department, Irving, Texas, and GTE Directories.)

Chapter 12: Drawing and Adding Specifications to Furnishings

EXERCISE 12-3
Office II Furniture Plan

1. Start a new drawing named CH12-EX3 by copying the Office II floor plan drawn in Exercise 9–3 or by copying the Office II floor plan dimensioned in Exercise 10–6.

2. Create a new layer for furniture, and draw the furniture as shown in Figure 12–27 for the Office II furniture plan. Use a $\frac{1}{8}'' = 1'-0''$ architectural scale to measure the furniture, and draw it full scale.

3. Save the drawing in two places, and Printer Plot or Plotter Plot the drawing to scale.

EXERCISE 12-4
House Furniture Plan

1. Start a new drawing named CH12-EX4 by copying the house floor plan drawn in Exercise 9–4 or by copying the house floor plan dimensioned in Exercise 10–7.

2. Create a new layer for furniture, and draw the furniture as shown in Figure 12–28, Lower and Upper Levels, for the house furniture plan. Use a $\frac{1}{8}'' = 1'-0''$ architectural scale to measure the furniture, and draw it full scale.

3. Save the drawing in two places, and Printer Plot or Plotter Plot the drawing to scale.

EXERCISE 12-5
Country Club Furniture Plan

1. Start a new drawing named CH12-EX5 by copying the country club floor plan drawn in Exercise 9–5 or by copying the country club floor plan dimensioned in Exercise 10–8.

2. Create a new layer for furniture, and draw the furniture as shown in Figure 12–29 for the country club furniture plan. Use a $\frac{1}{8}'' = 1'-0''$ architectural scale to measure the furniture, and draw it full scale.

3. Save the drawing in two places, and Printer Plot or Plotter Plot the drawing to scale.

REVIEW QUESTIONS

1. Which of the following modes must be selected to create a variable attribute that gives you two chances to type the correct value?
   a. Invisible
   b. Constant
   c. Verify
   d. Preset
   e. Do not select any of these

2. The prompt "Attribute modes–Invisible:Y Constant:Y Verify:N Preset:N" indicates which of the following?
   a. Verify mode is active.
   b. Preset mode is active.
   c. Invisible and Constant modes are active.
   d. Verify and Preset modes are active.
   e. Invisible mode only is active.

3. To change the prompt in Question 2 to "Attribute modes—Invisible:N Constant:N Verify:N Preset:N", you must:
   a. TYPE: IC, then N
   b. TYPE: I, then CI, then N
   c. TYPE: I, then C
   d. TYPE: IC, then OFF
   e. TYPE: IC, then Y

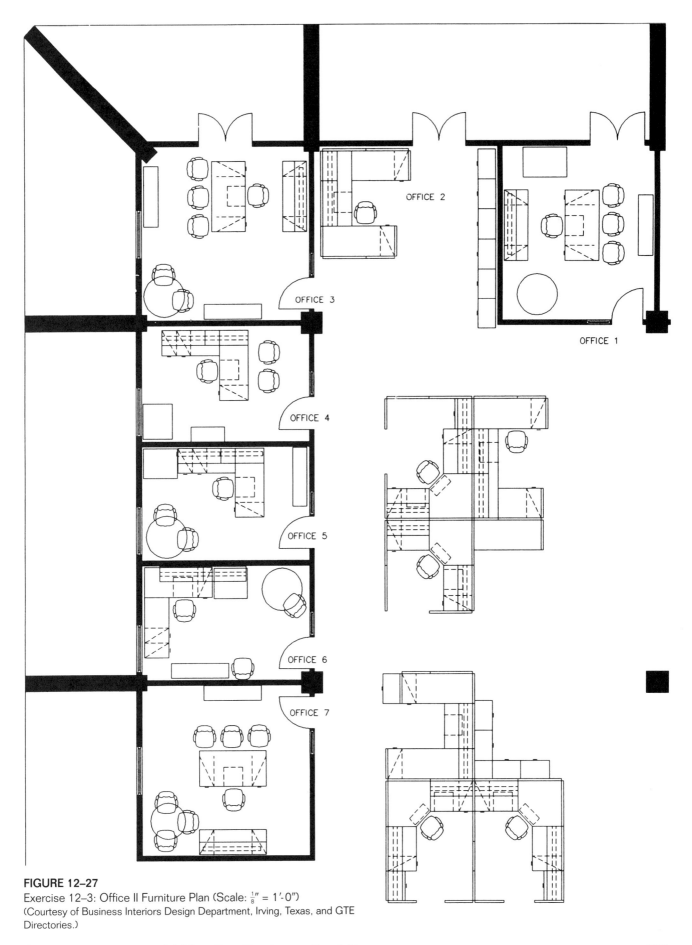

FIGURE 12–27
Exercise 12–3: Office II Furniture Plan (Scale: $\frac{1}{8}'' = 1'\text{-}0''$)
(Courtesy of Business Interiors Design Department, Irving, Texas, and GTE Directories.)

Chapter 12: Drawing and Adding Specifications to Furnishings

295

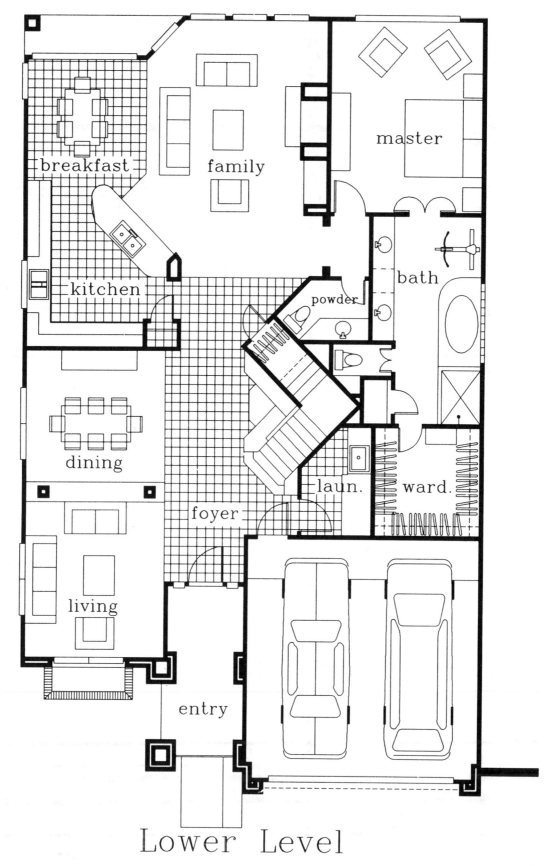

master

breakfast

family

kitchen

bath

powder

dining

laun.

ward.

foyer

living

entry

Lower Level

FIGURE 12–28
Exercise 12–4: House Furniture Plan (Scale: $\frac{1}{8}'' = 1'\text{-}0''$)
(Courtesy of John Brooks, AIA, Dallas, Texas.)

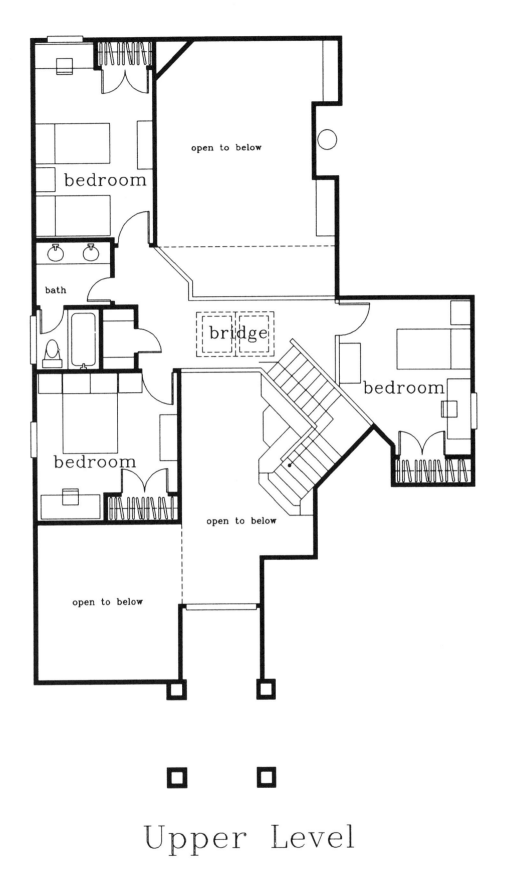

open to below

bedroom

bath

bridge

bedroom

bedroom

open to below

open to below

Upper Level

FIGURE 12–28 *continued*

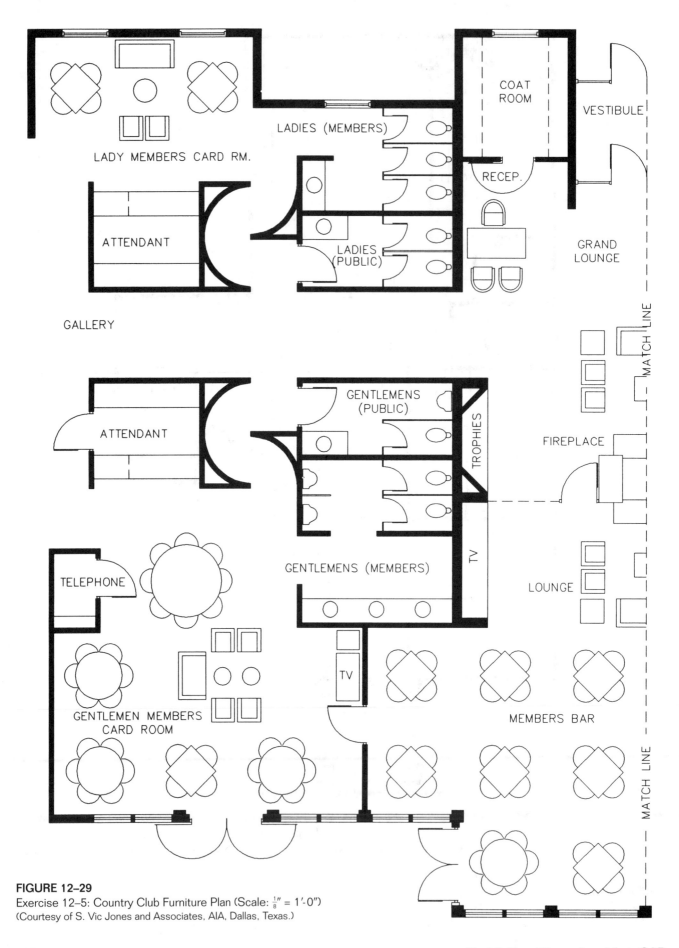

COAT ROOM

VESTIBULE

LADIES (MEMBERS)

LADY MEMBERS CARD RM.

RECEP.

GRAND LOUNGE

ATTENDANT

LADIES (PUBLIC)

GALLERY

MATCH LINE

GENTLEMENS (PUBLIC)

TROPHIES

FIREPLACE

ATTENDANT

TV

TELEPHONE

GENTLEMENS (MEMBERS)

LOUNGE

TV

GENTLEMEN MEMBERS CARD ROOM

MEMBERS BAR

MATCH LINE

FIGURE 12–29
Exercise 12–5: Country Club Furniture Plan (Scale: $\frac{1}{8}'' = 1'\text{-}0''$)
(Courtesy of S. Vic Jones and Associates, AIA, Dallas, Texas.)

Part II: Two-Dimensional AutoCAD

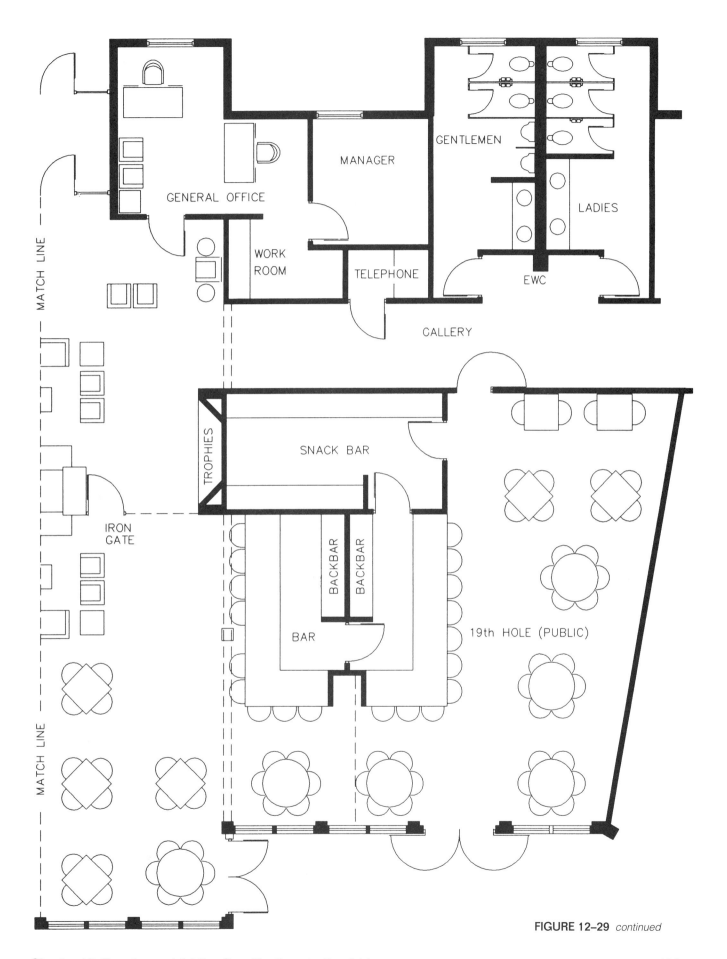

GENTLEMEN

MANAGER

GENERAL OFFICE

LADIES

MATCH LINE

WORK ROOM

TELEPHONE

EWC

CALLERY

TROPHIES

SNACK BAR

IRON GATE

BACKBAR

BACKBAR

19th HOLE (PUBLIC)

BAR

MATCH LINE

FIGURE 12–29 *continued*

Chapter 12: Drawing and Adding Specifications to Furnishings

4. In which of the following may spaces *not* be used?
   a. Value
   b. Default Value
   c. Prompt
   d. Tag
   e. Spaces may be used in all the above.
5. AutoCAD automatically places an attribute definition below one that was defined with the previous ATTDEF command:
   a. True
   b. False
6. Which of the following part of an attribute appears on the inserted furniture symbol when the attribute mode is *not* Invisible?
   a. Tag
   b. Prompt
   c. Value
   d. Mode
   e. Block name
7. If you insert a block with attributes into a drawing and no attribute prompts occur, which of the following is true?
   a. All attributes are Constant.
   b. All attributes are Variable.
   c. All attributes are Verify.
   d. All attributes are Invisible.
   e. The block has not been inserted on the correct layer.
8. To use the Enter Attributes dialog box to change or accept default values of attributes, which of the following system variables must be set to 1?
   a. ATTREQ
   b. ATTDIA
   c. ATTMODE
   d. ANGDIR
   e. AUPREC
9. Which of the following commands can be used to make invisible all the visible attributes on the drawing?
   a. DDATTE
   b. ATTEXT
   c. ATTDEF
   d. ATTEDIT
   e. ATTDISP
10. Which of the following commands can be used to edit Variable, Verify, Preset, and Constant attribute values of an inserted block using a dialog box?
    a. ATTEXT
    b. ATTDEF
    c. ATTEDIT
    d. ATTDISP
    e. Constant attributes cannot be edited
11. The command used to edit attribute values without a dialog box is:

    _____

12. After you have selected several attribute values for editing using ATTEDIT, how do you know which attribute you are currently editing?

    _____

13. What command will change all the attribute values "Black" to "Brown" on all occurrences of the Tag "COLOR" at the same time, independent of the block reference?

    _____

14. The command that allows you to redefine a block within a drawing and update all previous insertions of the block in your drawing is:

    _____

15. When a block that has attributes assigned is redefined with the Block command, what happens to existing Variable attributes on the drawing?

_____

16. The command that uses a dialog box to extract attributes from a drawing is:

_____

17. Describe how an external reference drawing differs from a block drawing.

_____

_____

18. Which External Reference option allows you to make an external reference a Block on the present drawing?

_____

19. Describe the main purpose of using blocks with attributes.

_____

_____

20. List three advantages of using external references.

_____

_____

13 Drawing the Reflected Ceiling Plan and Power Plan

OBJECTIVES

When you have completed this chapter, you will be able to:

☐ Draw a lighting legend.
☐ Draw a reflected ceiling plan.
☐ Draw an electrical and telephone legend.
☐ Draw a power plan.

INTRODUCTION

Previously learned commands are used to draw the tenant space reflected ceiling plan in Exercise 13–1, Part 1, and power plan in Exercise 13–1, Part 2. Helpful guidelines for drawing Exercise 13–1, Parts 1 and 2, are provided.

EXERCISE 13–1, PART 1
Tenant Space Lighting Legend and Reflected Ceiling Plan

In Exercise 13–1, Part 1, two separate drawings are drawn—a lighting legend and a reflected ceiling plan for the tenant space. The lighting legend is drawn first and then inserted into the tenant space reflected ceiling plan. When you have completed Exercise 13–1, Part 1, your reflected ceiling plan drawing will look similar to Figure 13–1.

Tenant Space Lighting Legend Drawing

1. Begin the lighting legend drawing on the hard drive.

2. Create a Layer named E-lite-txt, color Green.

3. Draw the lighting legend as shown in Figure 13–2, full scale. Draw the lighting symbols on the 0 Layer, and the text on the E-lite-txt Layer. Typically, the lighting symbols and related circuitry have heavier line weights than the floor plan. You may accomplish this using either of two methods:

☐ Plot the lighting symbols and circuitry with a thicker pen.
☐ Draw the lighting symbols and circuitry with a thicker line (polyline or donut).

4. Wblock the lighting legend drawing to a floppy disk in drive A.

Tenant Space Reflected Ceiling Plan

1. Begin drawing CH13-EX1 on the hard drive by opening existing drawing CH12-EX1 from a floppy disk in drive A and saving it as CH13-EX1 on the hard drive.

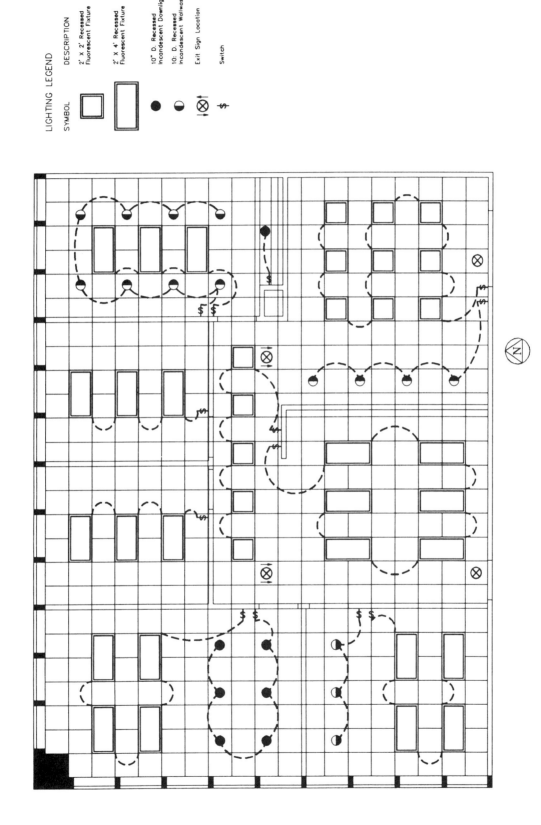

LIGHTING LEGEND

SYMBOL	DESCRIPTION
□	2' x 2' Recessed Fluorescent Fixture
▭	2' x 4' Recessed Fluorescent Fixture
●	10" D. Recessed Incandescent Downlight
◐	10: D. Recessed Incandescent Wallwasher
⊗	Exit Sign Location
$	Switch

FIGURE 13–1

Exercise 13–1, Part 1: Tenant Space Reflected Ceiling Plan (Scale: $\frac{1''}{8} = 1'\text{-}0''$)

FIGURE 13–2

Tenant Space Lighting Legend (Scale: $\frac{1}{4}'' = 1'\text{-}0''$)

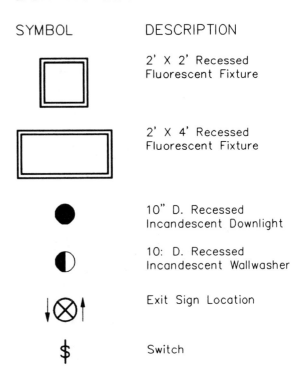

LIGHTING LEGEND

SYMBOL	DESCRIPTION
	2' X 2' Recessed Fluorescent Fixture
	2' X 4' Recessed Fluorescent Fixture
	10" D. Recessed Incandescent Downlight
	10: D. Recessed Incandescent Wallwasher
	Exit Sign Location
	Switch

2. Freeze the following Layers that have entities drawn that are not needed to draw the reflected ceiling plan:

A-area
A-door
A-flor-iden
A-furn
A-pflr-dims

3. Create a layer named E-lite-d, color red, and make it current. Draw lines across the door openings as shown in Figure 13–1 (A-door Layer is Frozen) on layer E-lite-d.

If you plan to plot the exterior and interior walls with pens of different thicknesses, you may create two separate layers to draw these lines: one for the interior walls (red) and one for the exterior walls (blue). A running Osnap-Intersection mode will help to draw the lines quickly. Be sure to cancel the Osnap mode when you are finished.

4. Set Layer A-clng current and draw the 2' × 2' ceiling grid: Draw half of a 2' × 2' ceiling tile symbol, as shown in Figure 13–3, in the lower left corner of the tenant space floor plan. Use the Array command to complete the ceiling grid, making it rectangular with 19 rows and 25 columns and having 2' distance between rows and columns.

Erase the extra ceiling line out of the larger corner column. You may erase or leave the ceiling grid lines that are drawn on top of the south and west interior wall lines of the tenant space floor plan.

5. Set Layer E-lite current and Insert-Block... the lighting legend drawing, full scale, into the location shown on the tenant space reflected ceiling plan in Figure 13–1. Check the Explode box in the Insert dialog box so that each symbol is inserted as a separate entity.

FIGURE 13–3

Draw Half of the 2' × 2' Ceiling Grid in the Lower Left Corner of the Tenant Space Floor Plan

6. Prepare the ceiling grid for insertion of the 2′ × 4′ recessed fixture symbols by using the Erase command to erase the ceiling grid lines that will cross the centers of the symbols.

Use the Copy (Multiple) command and an Osnap modifier to copy the lighting symbols from the legend and place them on the plan, as shown in Figure 13–1. You may also snap to a grid point when possible.

The wallwasher, 2′ × 4′ fixture, and switch symbols appear on the reflected ceiling plan in several different orientations. Copy each symbol and Rotate the individual symbols into the various positions, then use Copy (Multiple) to draw the additional like symbols in the correct locations on the plan.

7. Create an E-lite-w Layer, color white, with a DASHEDX2 linetype, and set it current. Use the Arc command to draw the symbol for the circuitry.

8. The lighting symbols and circuitry are both on layers with the color property white. If you plan to plot the lighting symbols and circuitry with a thicker pen, change the A-flor-wdwk and A-glaz Layers (also both white) to a different color.

9. When you have completed Exercise 13–1, Part 1, save your work in at least two places.

10. Printer Plot or Plotter Plot Exercise 13–1, Part 1, to scale.

EXERCISE 13–1, PART 2
Tenant Space Power Plan

In Exercise 13–1, Part 2, three separate drawings are drawn—an electrical legend, a telephone legend, and a power plan for the tenant space project. The electrical and telephone legends are drawn first and then inserted into the tenant space power plan. When you have completed Exercise 13–1, Part 2, your tenant space power plan drawing will look similar to Figure 13–4.

Tenant Space Electrical Legend Drawing

1. Begin the drawing of the electrical legend on the hard drive.

2. Create a Layer named E-power-txt, color Green.

3. Draw the electrical legend as shown in Figure 13–5, full scale. Draw the electrical symbols on the 0 Layer, and the text on the E-power-txt Layer. You may decide to draw the symbols with a heavier line weight than shown or to plot them with a thicker pen.

4. Wblock the electrical legend drawing to a floppy disk in drive A.

Tenant Space Telephone Legend Drawing

1. Begin the drawing of the telephone legend on the hard drive.

2. Draw the telephone legend as shown in Figure 13–6, full scale, on the 0 Layer (both text and symbols).

3. Wblock the telephone legend drawing to a floppy disk in drive A.

Tenant Space Power Plan

1. Open drawing CH13-EX1 and save it on the hard drive.

2. Freeze all layers that are not required to draw the power plan.

3. Set Layer E-powr current and Insert-Block... the electrical legend drawing full scale in the location shown on the tenant space power plan in Figure 13–4. Check the Explode box in the Insert dialog box to separate the symbols into individual entities.

4. Use the Copy (Multiple) command and an Osnap modifier to copy the electrical symbols from the legend and place them on the plan as shown in Figure 13–4. You may also snap to a grid point when possible.

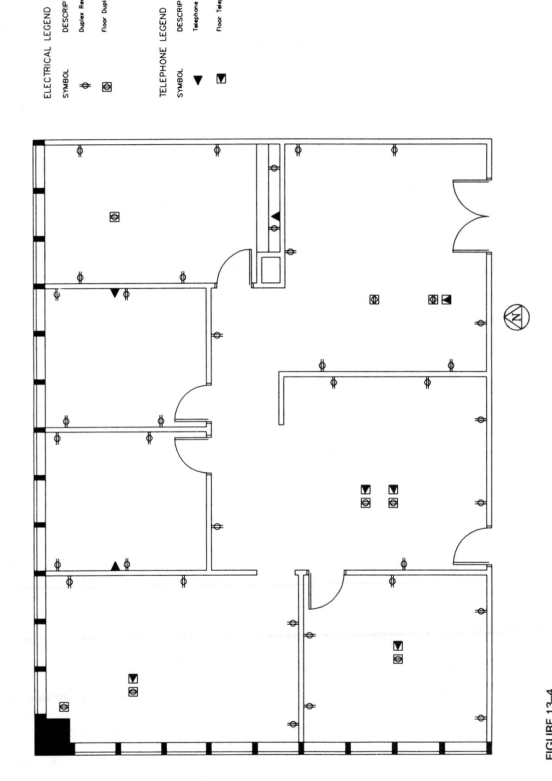

ELECTRICAL LEGEND

SYMBOL   DESCRIPTION

⊕   Duplex Receptacle

⊟   Floor Duplex Receptacle

TELEPHONE LEGEND

SYMBOL   DESCRIPTION

▼   Telephone

▼   Floor Telephone

FIGURE 13–4

Exercise 13–1, Part 2: Tenant Space Power Plan (Scale: $\frac{1''}{8} = 1'\text{-}0''$)

ELECTRICAL LEGEND

SYMBOL   DESCRIPTION

Duplex Receptacle

Floor Duplex Receptacle

TELEPHONE LEGEND

SYMBOL   DESCRIPTION

Telephone

Floor Telephone

The duplex receptacle symbol appears on the plan in several different orientations. Copy the symbol, and use Rotate to obtain the rotated positions as shown on the plan. Use the Copy command to draw like rotated symbols in the correct locations on the plan.

It is helpful to draw a line connecting the two endpoints of the two lines in the duplex receptacle. Use the Midpoint of this line to locate the duplex receptacle along the walls. Do not include this line in the selection set of the Copy command. Use Osnap-Center to help locate the floor receptacle symbol.

5. Set Layer E-comm current and Insert the telephone legend drawing full scale in the location shown on the tenant space power plan in Figure 13–4.

6. Copy the telephone symbols from the legend, and place them on the plan as shown in Figure 13–4.

7. The power symbols are on a layer with the color property white. If you plan to plot the power symbols with a thicker pen, change the A-flor-wdwk and A-glaz Layers (also both white) to a different color.

8. When you have completed Exercise 13–1, Part 2, save your work in at least two places.

9. Printer Plot or Plotter Plot Exercise 13–1, Part 2, to scale.

EXERCISE 13–2
Office I Reflected Ceiling Plan and Power Plan

In Exercise 13–2, a reflected ceiling plan and power plan are drawn for Office I.

1. Begin drawing CH13-EX2 on the hard drive by opening existing drawing CH12-EX2 from a floppy disk in drive A and saving it as CH13-EX2 on the hard drive.

2. Freeze the layers that are not needed to draw the reflected ceiling plan.

3. Insert-Block... on the correct layer the lighting legend drawn in Exercise 13–1, Part 1, into drawing CH13-EX2. Check the Explode box in the Insert dialog box so that each symbol is inserted as a separate entity. Modify the inserted legend for Office I as shown in Figure 13–7.

LICHTING LEGEND

SYMBOL   DESCRIPTION

2' X 4' Recessed
Fluorescent Fixture

                    Switch

ELECTRICAL LEGEND

SYMBOL   DESCRIPTION

                    Duplex Receptacle

TELEPHONE LEGEND

SYMBOL   DESCRIPTION

                    Telephone

4. Complete the Office I reflected ceiling plan as shown in Figure 13–8.

5. Freeze the layers that are not needed to draw the power plan.

6. Insert-Block... on the correct layers the electrical and telephone legends drawn in Exercise 13–1, Part 2. Modify the inserted legends for Office I as shown in Figure 13–7.

7. Complete the Office I power plan as shown in Figure 13–9.

8. When you have completed Exercise 13–2, save your work in at least two places.

9. Printer Plot or Plotter Plot the drawings to scale.

EXERCISE 13–3
Office II Reflected Ceiling Plan and Power Plan

In Exercise 13–3, a reflected ceiling plan and power plan are drawn for Office II.

1. Begin drawing CH13-EX3 on the hard drive by opening existing drawing CH12-EX3 from a floppy disk in drive A and saving it as CH13-EX3 on the hard drive.

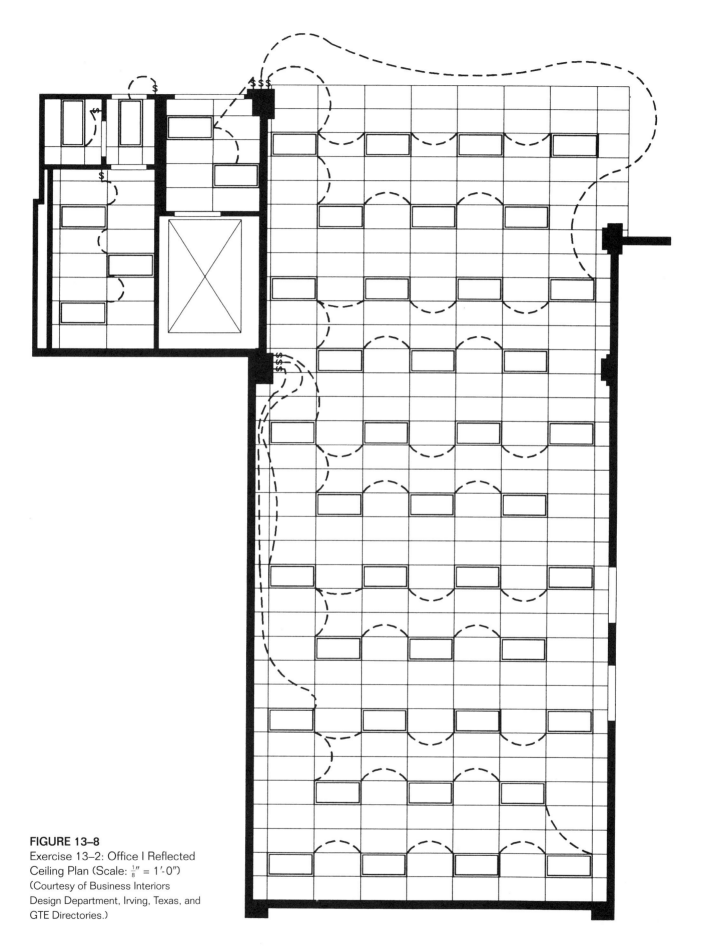

FIGURE 13–8
Exercise 13–2: Office I Reflected
Ceiling Plan (Scale: $\frac{1}{8}'' = 1'\text{-}0''$)
(Courtesy of Business Interiors
Design Department, Irving, Texas, and
GTE Directories.)

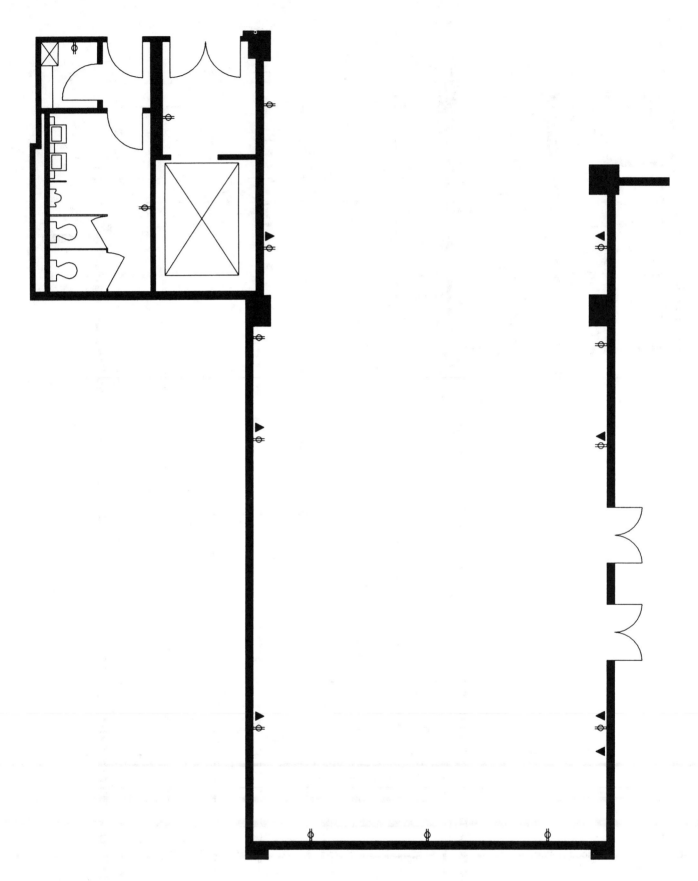

FIGURE 13–9

Exercise 13–2: Office I Power Plan (Scale: $\frac{1}{8}'' = 1'\text{-}0''$)

(Courtesy of Business Interiors Design Department, Irving, Texas, and GTE Directories.)

Part II: Two-Dimensional AutoCAD

2. Freeze the layers that are not needed to draw the reflected ceiling plan.

3. Insert-Block... on the correct layer the lighting legend drawn in Exercise 13–1, Part 1, into drawing CH13-EX3. Check the Explode box in the Insert dialog box so that each symbol is inserted as a separate entity. Modify the inserted legend for Office II as shown in Figure 13–10.

4. Complete the Office II reflected ceiling plan as shown in Figure 13–11.

5. Freeze the layers that are not needed to draw the power plan.

6. Insert-Block... on the correct layers the electrical and telephone legends drawn in Exercise 13–1, Part 2.

7. Complete the Office II power plan as shown in Figure 13–12.

8. When you have completed Exercise 13–3, save your work in at least two places.

9. Printer Plot or Plotter Plot the drawing to scale.

FIGURE 13–10
Office II Lighting, Electrical, and Telephone Legends
(Scale: $\frac{1}{4}'' = 1'\text{-}0''$)

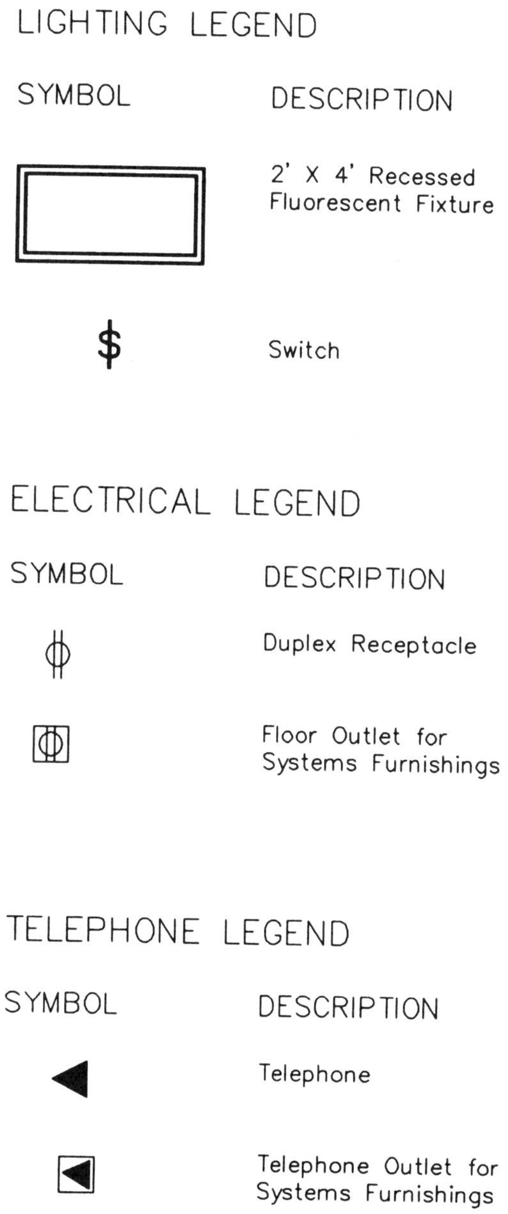

LIGHTING LEGEND

SYMBOL   DESCRIPTION

2' X 4' Recessed
Fluorescent Fixture

Switch

ELECTRICAL LEGEND

SYMBOL   DESCRIPTION

Duplex Receptacle

Floor Outlet for
Systems Furnishings

TELEPHONE LEGEND

SYMBOL   DESCRIPTION

Telephone

Telephone Outlet for
Systems Furnishings

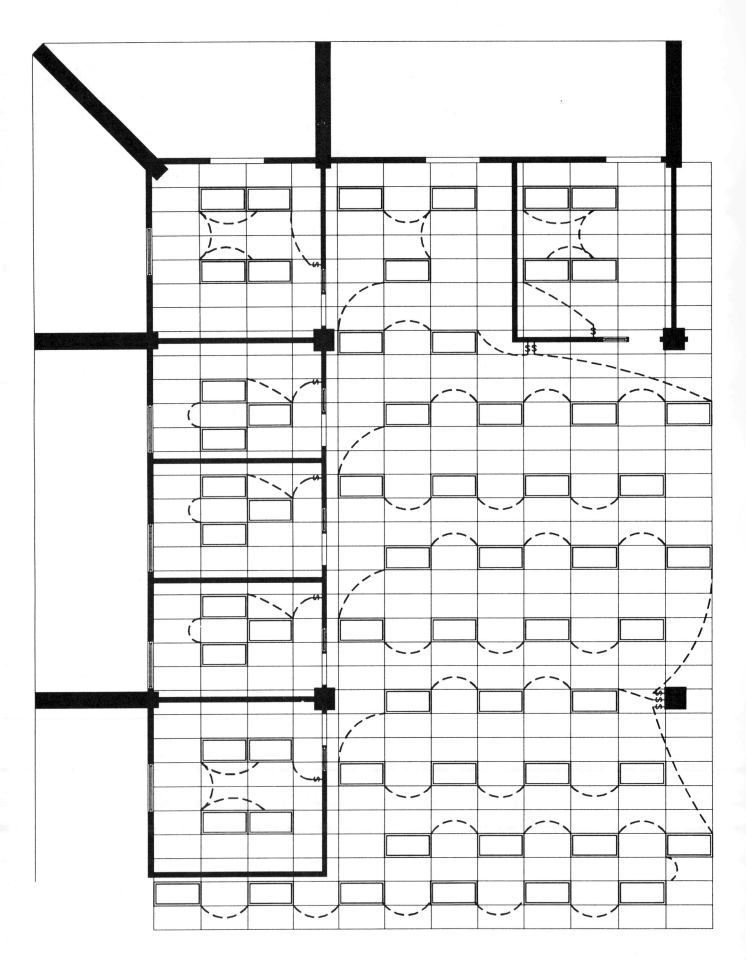

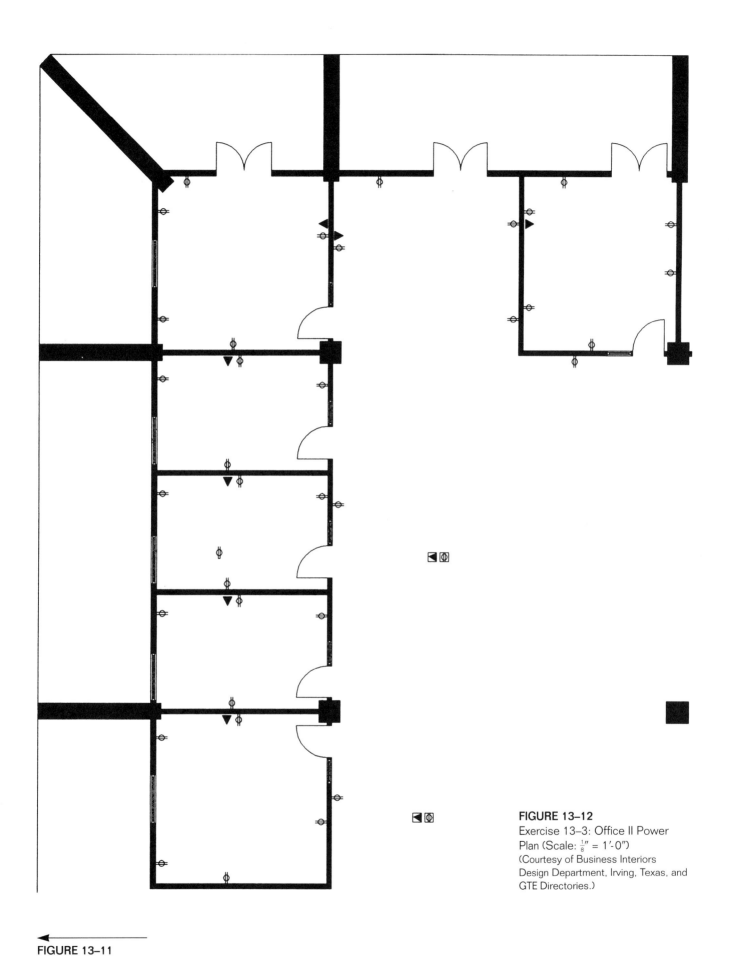

FIGURE 13–12
Exercise 13–3: Office II Power
Plan (Scale: $\frac{1}{8}'' = 1'\text{-}0''$)
(Courtesy of Business Interiors
Design Department, Irving, Texas, and
GTE Directories.)

FIGURE 13–11
Exercise 13–3: Office II Reflected Ceiling Plan (Scale: $\frac{1}{8}'' = 1'\text{-}0''$)
(Courtesy of Business Interiors Design Department, Irving, Texas, and GTE Directories.)

EXERCISE 13–4
House Lighting and Outlet Plan

In Exercise 13–4, a lighting and outlet plan is drawn for the house.

1. Begin drawing CH13-EX4 on the hard drive by opening existing drawing CH12-EX4 from a floppy disk in drive A and saving it as CH13-EX4 on the hard drive.

2. Freeze the layers that are not needed to draw the lighting and outlet plan.

3. Insert-Block... on the correct layers the lighting, electrical, and telephone legends drawn in Exercise 13–1, Parts 1 and 2, into drawing CH13-EX4. Check the Explode box in the Insert dialog box so that each symbol is inserted as a separate entity. Modify the inserted legends as shown in Figure 13–13.

4. Complete the lighting and outlet plan for the house as shown in Figure 13–14.

5. When you have completed Exercise 13–4, save your work in at least two places.

6. Printer Plot or Plotter Plot the drawing to scale.

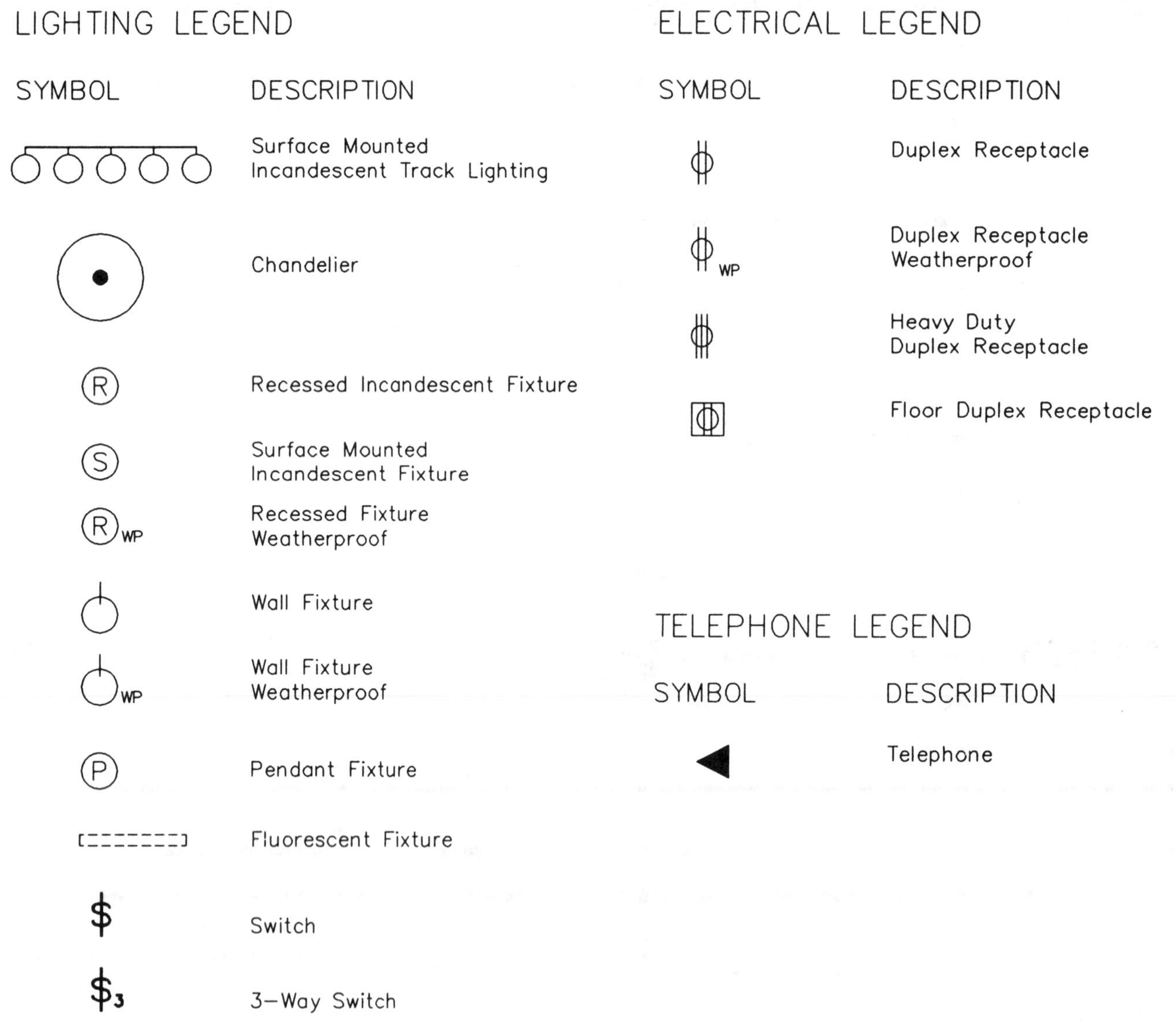

LIGHTING LEGEND

SYMBOL	DESCRIPTION
	Surface Mounted Incandescent Track Lighting
	Chandelier
(R)	Recessed Incandescent Fixture
(S)	Surface Mounted Incandescent Fixture
(R)wp	Recessed Fixture Weatherproof
	Wall Fixture
wp	Wall Fixture Weatherproof
(P)	Pendant Fixture
[=======]	Fluorescent Fixture
$	Switch
$3	3−Way Switch

ELECTRICAL LEGEND

SYMBOL	DESCRIPTION
	Duplex Receptacle
wp	Duplex Receptacle Weatherproof
	Heavy Duty Duplex Receptacle
	Floor Duplex Receptacle

TELEPHONE LEGEND

SYMBOL	DESCRIPTION
◄	Telephone

FIGURE 13–13
House Lighting, Electrical, and Telephone Legends (Scale: $\frac{1}{4}'' = 1'\text{-}0''$)

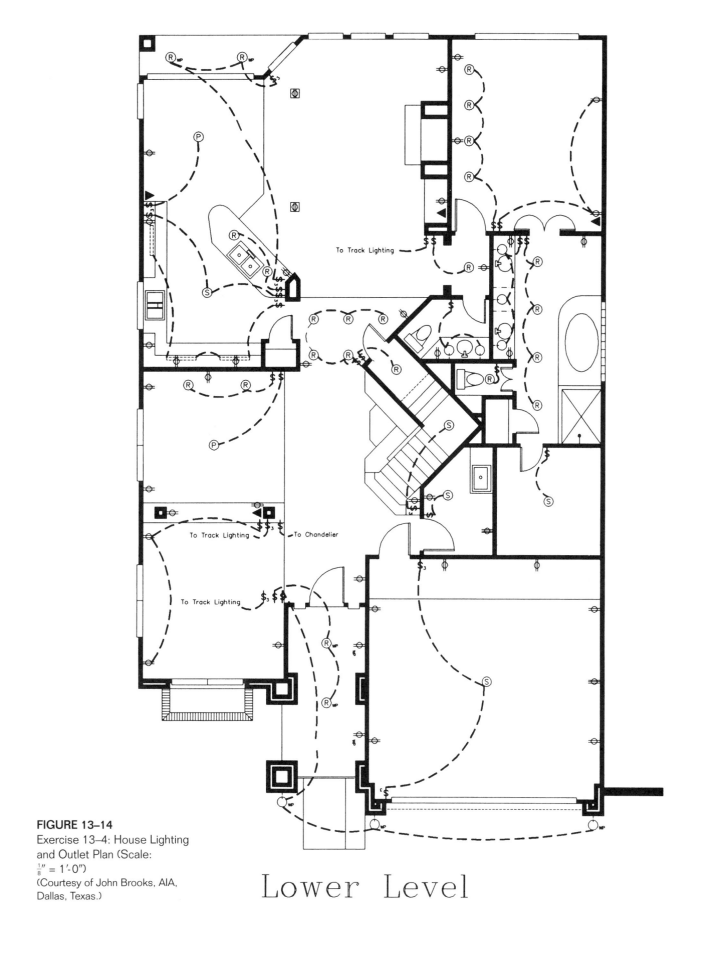

FIGURE 13–14
Exercise 13–4: House Lighting
and Outlet Plan (Scale:
$\frac{1}{8}'' = 1'\text{-}0''$)
(Courtesy of John Brooks, AIA,
Dallas, Texas.)

Lower Level

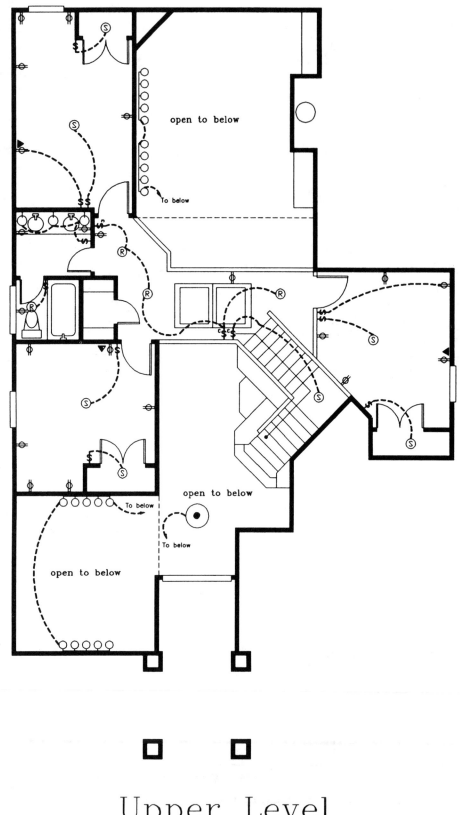

Upper Level

FIGURE 13–14 *continued*

316   Part II: Two-Dimensional AutoCAD

EXERCISE 13–5
Country Club Reflected Ceiling Plan and Power Plan

In Exercise 13–5, a reflected ceiling plan and power plan are drawn for the country club.

1. Begin drawing CH13-EX5 on the hard drive by opening existing drawing CH12-EX5 from a floppy disk in drive A and saving it as CH13-EX5 on the hard drive.
2. Freeze the layers that are not needed to draw the ceiling plan.
3. Insert-Block... on the correct layer the lighting legend drawn in Exercise 13–1, Part 1, into drawing CH13-EX5. Check the Explode box in the Insert dialog box so that each symbol is inserted as a separate entity. Modify the inserted legend for the country club as shown in Figure 13–15.
4. Complete the country club reflected ceiling plan as shown in Figure 13–16.
5. Freeze the layers that are not needed to draw the power plan.
6. Insert-Block... on the correct layers the electrical and telephone legends drawn in Exercise 13–1, Part 2. Modify the inserted legends for the country club as shown in Figure 13–15.
7. Complete the country club power plan as shown in Figure 13–17.
8. When you have completed Exercise 13–5, save your work in at least two places.
9. Printer Plot or Plotter Plot the drawings to scale.

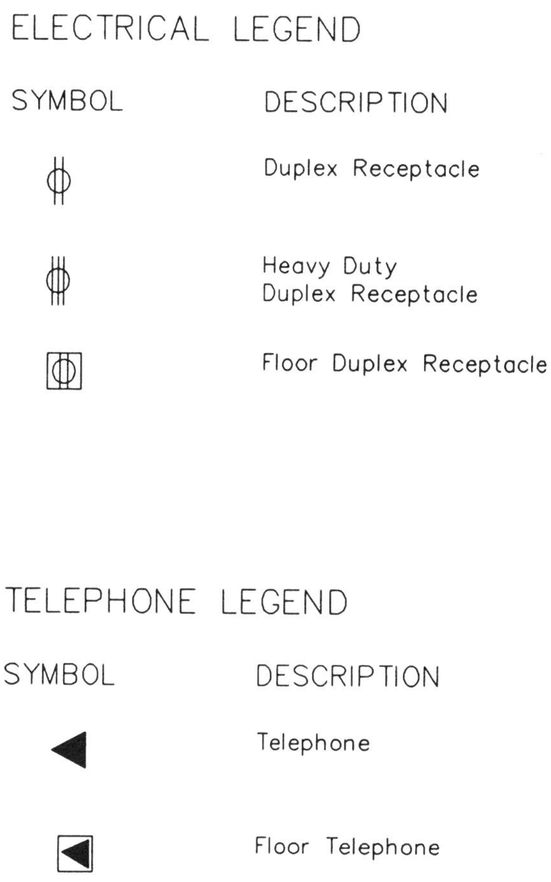

FIGURE 13–15
Country Club Lighting, Electrical, and Telephone Legends (Scale: $\frac{1}{4}'' = 1'\text{-}0''$)

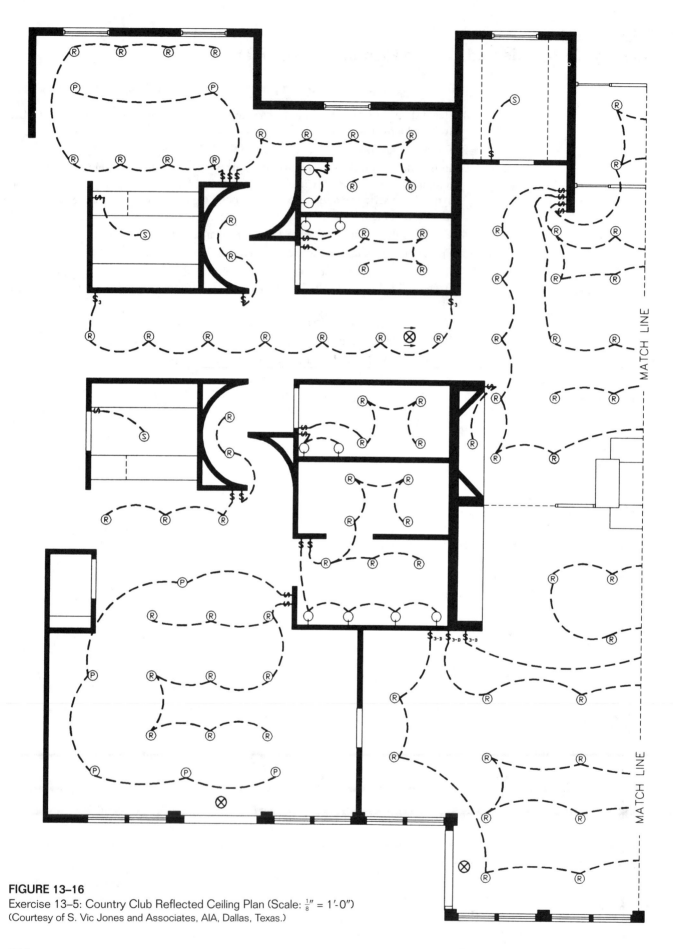

FIGURE 13–16

Exercise 13–5: Country Club Reflected Ceiling Plan (Scale: $\frac{1}{8}'' = 1'\text{-}0''$)

(Courtesy of S. Vic Jones and Associates, AIA, Dallas, Texas.)

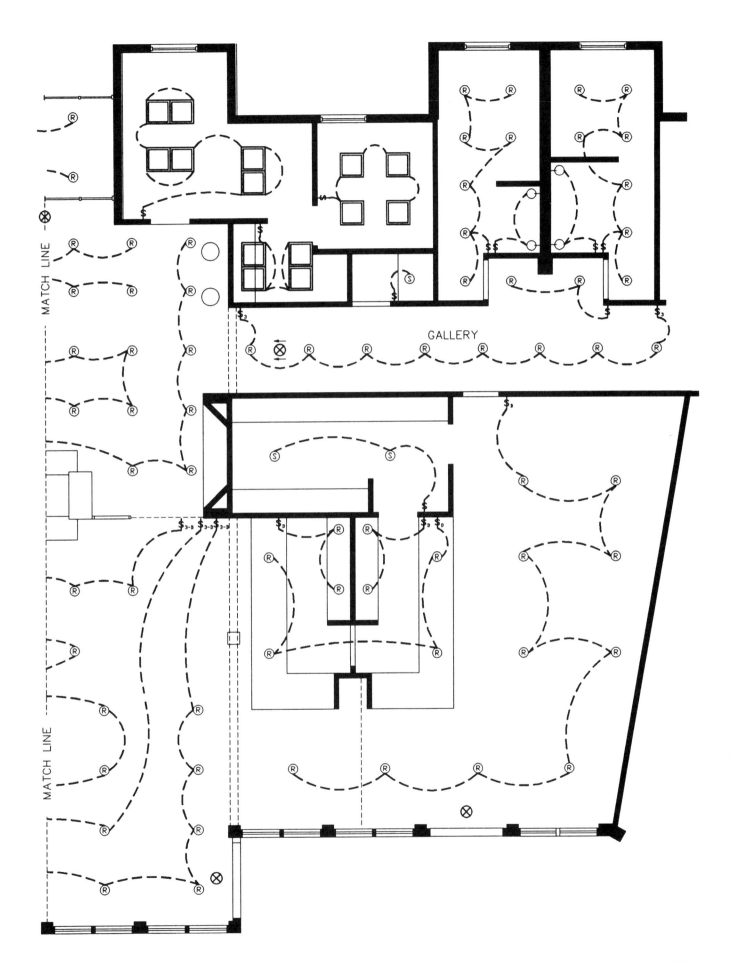

Chapter 13: Drawing the Reflected Ceiling Plan and Power Plan

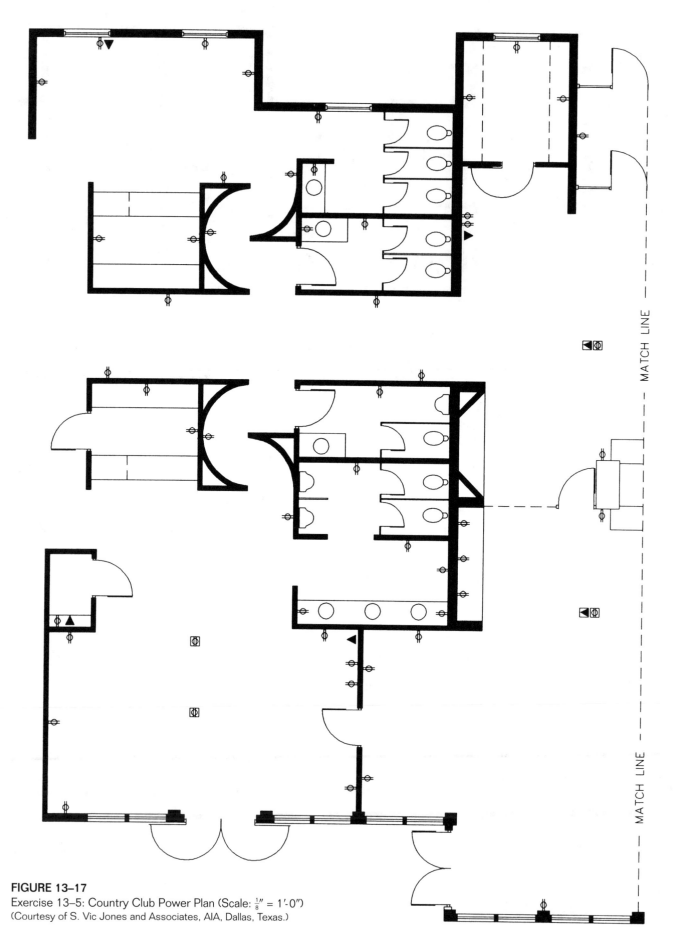

MATCH LINE

MATCH LINE

FIGURE 13–17
Exercise 13–5: Country Club Power Plan (Scale: $\frac{1''}{8} = 1'\text{-}0''$)
(Courtesy of S. Vic Jones and Associates, AIA, Dallas, Texas.)

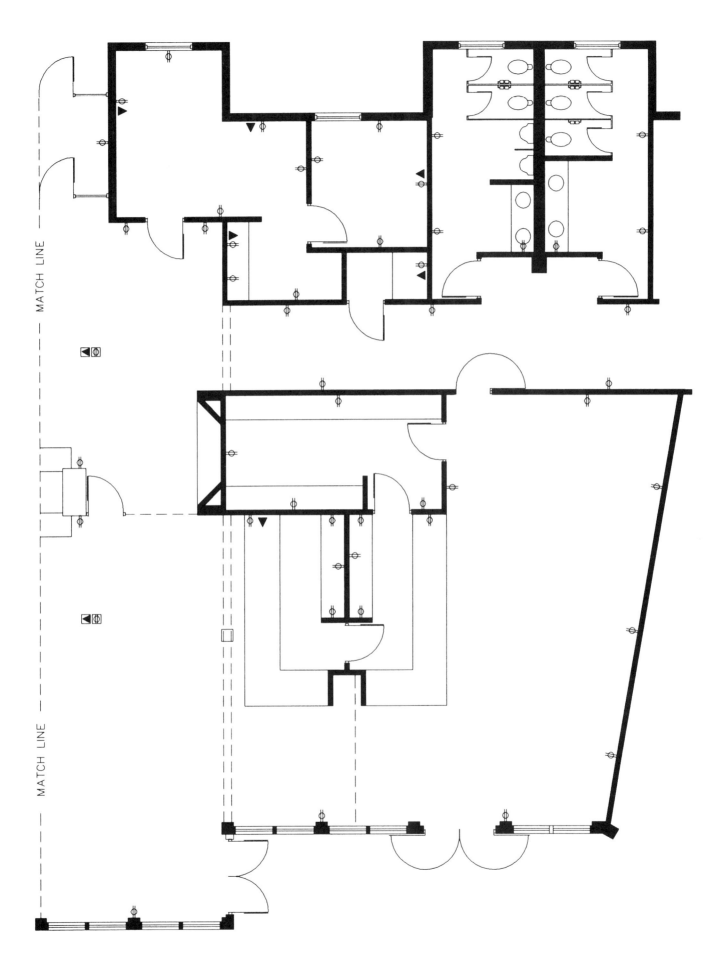

Chapter 13: Drawing the Reflected Ceiling Plan and Power Plan   321

REVIEW QUESTIONS

1. List two methods that you can use to have the lighting symbols and related circuitry have heavier line weights that the floor plan when plotted.

   _____

   _____

   _____

   _____

2. Write the drawing name you used when you Wblocked the lighting legend to a floppy disk. Include the floppy drive destination in the name.

   _____

3. How do you use an existing drawing to create a new drawing?

   _____

4. List the steps needed to set a running Osnap-Intersection mode.

   _____

5. Describe what checking the Explode box in the Insert dialog box does when a drawing is inserted into another drawing, using the Insert-Block... command.

   _____

   _____

6. Why do you freeze layers instead of turning them off?

   _____

   _____

7. List the prompts and responses used to create an array of the ceiling grid.

Prompt	**Response**
Command:	_____
_____	_____
_____	_____
_____	_____
_____	_____
_____	_____
_____	_____

8. List the setting that controls the sizes of linetypes as they appear on the screen.

   _____

9. If a Wblock is created on a layer that has the color property green, what color does it assume when it is inserted on a layer with the color property red?

   _____

10. How do you insert a block so that all its lines are separate objects?

   _____

14 Drawing a Plat

OBJECTIVES

When you have completed this chapter, you will be able to:

☐ Draw an open traverse.
☐ Draw a closed traverse.
☐ Draw a plat.
☐ Draw a plat and add a building outline.

INTRODUCTION

Drawing Types

The most common types of drawing used in land drafting are shown in Figure 14–1. These are easily produced using AutoCAD. In this chapter an open traverse, a closed traverse, a plat, and a plat with a building added are drawn.

Surveying Basics

All maps and associated drawings begin with a survey. A survey is a process used to measure land. The basic elements of this measuring process are distance, direction, and elevation.

Distance

Distance along a line is measured in feet and decimal parts of a foot (252.5′) or feet and inches (252′6″). Many AutoCAD drafters or engineers find it convenient to work full scale and use the plotting ratio to reduce a map to a standard plot size.

Direction

Note: There are 60 seconds in an angular minute; 60 minutes in a degree. The symbol ° indicates degrees, the symbol ′ indicates minutes, and the symbol ″ indicates seconds.

The direction of a surveying line is most often shown as a bearing. Bearings are measurements of angles. They measure from 0 to 90°, taken from a north or south line, and point either east or west (e.g., N49°15′0″E). AutoCAD allows you to specify a bearing in these same terms using surveyor's units.

Elevation

The elevation or height of a point is measured from sea level. This measurement is often taken from any known point, and further elevation readings are measured from there. AutoCAD provides an elevation setting or Z-axis measurement to provide the elevation measurement.

The three elements of distance, direction, and elevation are used to collect data for the six survey types. The procedure of surveying is not included in this book. The six survey types are as follows.

Survey Types

Land or boundary survey The plat is one of the most commonly used boundary surveys. It is used to describe any tract when it is not necessary to show elevation (often called *relief*). Any property you own should have a plat describing its boundaries.

323

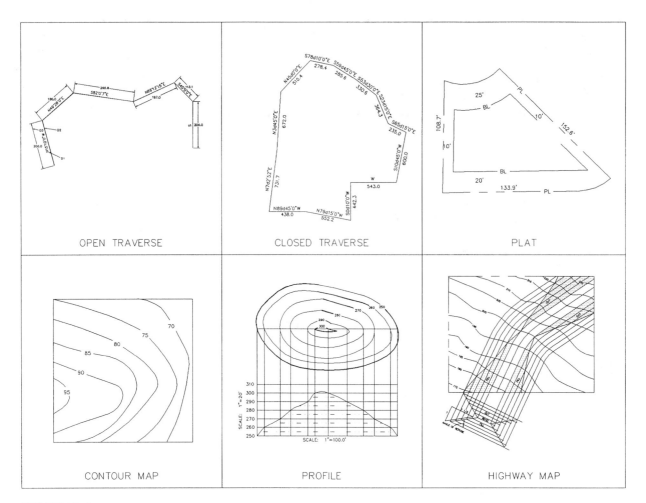

FIGURE 14–1
Drawing Types

Topographic survey This survey is used to produce maps that show the elevations (artificial or natural) and features of the land. These are contour maps.

Geodetic survey This is a survey covering large areas, often entire countries. These areas are so large that the curvature of the earth is a factor in measurement.

Photo survey This survey consists of a series of aerial photographs that are combined to produce a complete photogrammetric map.

Route survey This survey is used to describe highways, pipelines, or power lines. It consists of straight lines and angles originating from an identified point. No elevations are shown on a route survey.

Construction survey This survey is used in the construction of buildings and highways where the elevation of points are needed. It is often used to show where earth must be removed (cut) or added (fill).

Now that you have an idea of how data are gathered, let's use AutoCAD to produce traverses (a series of straight lines showing distance and direction) that are used to create site plans and highway maps.

EXERCISE 14–1
Drawing an Open Traverse

When you have completed Exercise 14–1, your drawing will look similar to the drawing in Figure 14–2. To begin Exercise 14–1, turn on the computer and start AutoCAD.

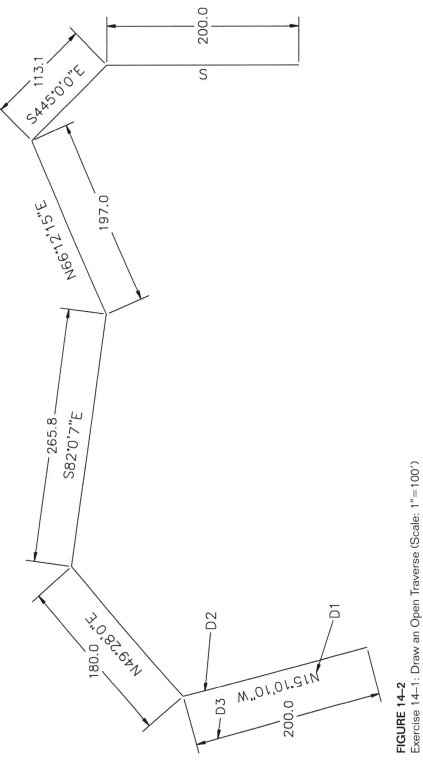

FIGURE 14–2
Exercise 14–1: Draw an Open Traverse (Scale: 1″=100′)

Begin Drawing CH14-EX1 on the Hard Drive

1. CLICK: **Use a Wizard**
2. CLICK: **Quick Setup**
   CLICK: **OK**

Note: Either decimal or engineering can be selected. Decimal allows units to be entered without respect to feet or inches. The unit can be inches, millimeters, feet, miles, or any other unit of measure. Engineering sets inches as the default and allows feet and inches to be entered.

3. Set drawing Units: **Decimal**
   CLICK: **Next>>**
4. Set drawing Width: **800** × Length **500**
   CLICK: **Done**
5. **Use Save As... to save the drawing on the hard drive with the name CH14-EX1**
6. Set Grid: **40**
7. Set Snap: **20**
8. Create the following Layers:

LAYER NAME	COLOR	LINETYPE
Bearing	Magenta	Continuous
Text	Green	Continuous

9. Set Bearing as the current layer.
10. Create a text style with a simplex font.
11. **Zoom-All** to view the entire drawing area.

Set Surveyor's units:

Prompt	Response
Command:	TYPE: **UNITS<enter>**
Enter Choice, 1 to 5<2>	**<enter>** (to accept Decimal)
Number of digits to right of decimal point (0 to 8)<4>	TYPE: **1<enter>**
Enter Choice, 1 to 5<1>	TYPE: **5** (to select Surveyor's units) **<enter> <enter> <enter>** (to accept defaults) **F2** (to flip to graphics display)

Draw the open traverse (Figure 14–2)

Prompt	Response
Command:	**Polyline** (or TYPE: **PL<enter>**)
From point:	TYPE: **133,47<enter>**
Arc/Close/Halfwidth/Length/Undo/Width/ <Endpoint of line>	TYPE: **@200<N15D10′W<enter>**
Arc/Close/Halfwidth/Length/Undo/Width/ <Endpoint of line>	TYPE: **@180<N49D28′E<enter>**
Arc/Close/Halfwidth/Length/Undo/Width/ <Endpoint of line>	TYPE: **@265.8<S82D0′7″E<enter>**
Arc/Close/Halfwidth/Length/Undo/Width/ <Endpoint of line>	TYPE: **@197<N66D12′15″E<enter>**
Arc/Close/Halfwidth/Length/Undo/Width/ <Endpoint of line>	TYPE: **@113.1<S45DE<enter>**
Arc/Close/Halfwidth/Length/Undo/Width/ <Endpoint of line>	TYPE: **@200<S<enter>**

Arc/Close/Halfwidth/Length/Undo/Width/
    <Endpoint of line>   **<enter>**

The traverse of Figure 14–2 is now complete. Add identifying text and dimensions using the following procedures:

On Your Own

Set Text as the current layer.

Note: The rotation angle for the text is the same as the bearing angle.

Place text on the first bearing using the following procedure (Figure 14–2):

Prompt	Response
Command:	**Single Line Text** (or TYPE: **DT<enter>**)
Justify/Style/<Start point>:	**D1** (the starting point for the label)
Height <default>:	TYPE: **10<enter>**
Rotation angle <E>:	TYPE: **N15D10′W<enter>** (or click on the endpoints of the line)

Note: %%D is the code for the degree symbol.

Text:	TYPE: **N15%%D10′10″W<enter>**
Text:	**<enter>**

On Your Own

1. Use a similar procedure to place text on all other bearings.
2. Set DIMSALE=50.
3. Set DIMDEC to 1.

Place dimensions on the first bearing using the following procedure (Figure 14–2):

Prompt	Response
Command:	**Aligned** (from the Dimensioning menu)
First extension line origin or press ENTER to select:	**<enter>**
Select object to dimension:	**D2**
Dimension line location <Mtext/Text/Angle>:	**D3**

On Your Own

Use a similar procedure to place dimensions on all other bearings.

Save

When you have completed Exercise 14–1, save your work in at least two places.

Plot

Printer Plot or Plotter Plot Exercise 14–1 on an $8\frac{1}{2}″ \times 11″$ sheet at a scale of 1 plotted unit = 100 drawing units (Scale: $1″ = 100′$ on the plotted drawing).

EXERCISE 14–2
Drawing a Closed Traverse

The closed traverse of Figure 14–3 is drawn in a manner similar to the one used to draw the open traverse of Figure 14–2. The last bearing, however, may be drawn with the **C,** or **Close,** modifier of the line command. An inquiry using the Distance command will provide a positive check to determine how accurately you have drawn the traverse.

When you have completed Exercise 14–2, your drawing will look similar to the drawing in Figure 14–3. To begin Exercise 14–2, turn on the computer and start AutoCAD.

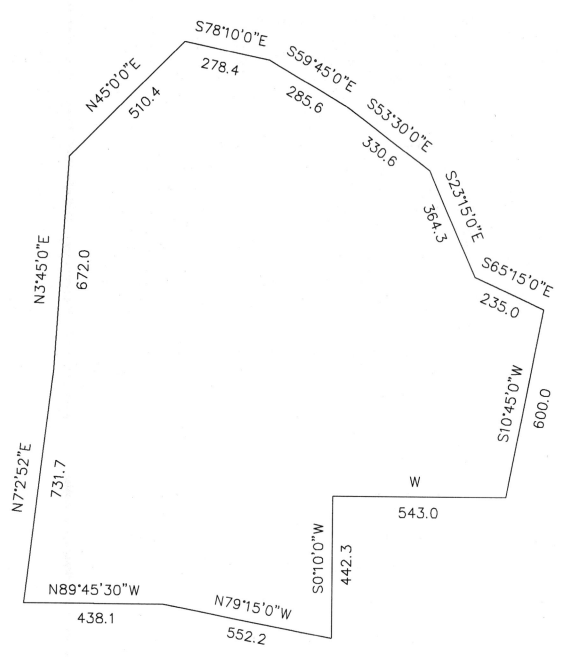

FIGURE 14–3

Exercise 14–3: Drawing a Closed Traverse (Scale: 1″=300′)

Begin Drawing CH14-EX2 on the Hard Drive

1. CLICK: **Use a Wizard**

2. CLICK: **Quick Setup**

   CLICK: **OK**

3. Set drawing Units: **Decimal**

   CLICK: **Next>>**

4. Set drawing Width: **2400** × Length **2500**

   CLICK: **Done**

5. **Use Save As… to save the drawing on the hard drive with the name CH14-EX2**

6. Set Grid: **100**

7. Set Snap: **25**

8. Create the following Layers:

LAYER NAME	COLOR	LINETYPE
Bearing	Magenta	Continuous
Text	Green	Continuous

9. Set Bearing as the current layer.

10. Create a text style with a simplex font.

11. **Zoom-All** to view the entire drawing area.

Set Surveyor's units:

Prompt	Response
Command:	TYPE: **UNITS<enter>**
Enter Choice, 1 to 5<2>	**<enter>** (to accept Decimal)
Number of digits to right of decimal point (0 to 8)<4>	TYPE: **1<enter>**
Enter Choice, 1 to 5<1>	TYPE: **5** (to select Surveyor's units)

Draw the traverse (Figure 14–3):

Prompt	Response
Command:	**Line** (or TYPE: **L<enter>**)
From point:	TYPE: **400,400 <enter>**
To point:	TYPE: **@731.7<N7D2′52″E<enter>**
To point:	TYPE: **@672<N3D45′E<enter>**
To point:	TYPE: **@510.4<N45DE<enter>**
To point:	TYPE: **@278.4<S78D10′E<enter>**
	Continue drawing bearings around the traverse, as shown in Figure 14–3, until you come to the last bearing, N89D45′30″W. For this bearing:
To point:	TYPE: **C<enter>**

Use List to see how well you drew the traverse:

Prompt	Response
Command:	**List** (or TYPE: **LIST<enter>**)
Select objects:	CLICK: **on the last bearing (the one drawn with the C response)**
Select objects:	**<enter>**
	A description of the bearing appears. It should show an angle in the X-Y plane of N89D45′30″W and a length of 438.1.
Command:	**F2** (to return to the graphics screen)

Note: The Area command allows you to pick points to describe an enclosed area by digitizing points immediately after the first Area prompt. It also allows you to add or subtract areas from other areas. This is a good command with which to experiment a little.

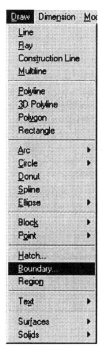

On Your Own (Figure 14–3)

1. Set the current layer to Text.

2. Place 30″ text describing the bearing direction and length on the drawing as you did in Figure 14–2. Do not use arrowheads and dimension lines.

Use Area to find the area and perimeter of the closed traverse:

Prompt	Response
Command:	**Boundary**
The Boundary Creation dialog box appears:	CLICK: **Pick Points<**
Select internal point:	CLICK: **on any point inside the closed traverse**
Select internal point:	**<enter>**
BOUNDARY created 1 polyline Command:	**Area** (or TYPE: **AREA<enter>**)
<First point>/Object/Add/Subtract:	TYPE: **O<enter>**
Select objects:	CLICK: **on any point on the closed traverse**

Area=2064012.7, Perimeter=5983.6

Note: CLICK: F2 (or the down arrow) to return to the graphics screen.

Save

When you have completed Exercise 14–2, save your work in at least two places.

Plot

Printer Plot or Plotter Plot Exercise 14–2 on an $8\frac{1}{2}'' \times 11''$ sheet at a scale of 1 plotted unit = 300 drawing units (Scale: $1'' = 300'$ on the plotted drawing).

EXERCISE 14–3
Drawing a Plat

The plat of Figure 14–4 has many of the same elements as the closed traverse. It also has curve data and building line offsets that must be accurately drawn. When you have completed Exercise 14–3, your drawing will look similar to the drawing in Figure 14–5. All the data shown in Figure 14–4 are needed to draw Figure 14–5. To begin Exercise 14–3, turn on the computer and start AutoCAD.

Begin Drawing CH14-EX3 on the Hard Drive

1. CLICK: **Use a Wizard**
2. CLICK: **Quick Setup**
   CLICK: **OK**
3. Set Drawing Units: **Decimal**
   CLICK: **Next>>**
4. Set drawing Width: **200** × Length **160**
   CLICK: **Done**
5. **Use Save As… to save the drawing on the hard drive with the name CH14-EX2**
6. Set Grid: **10**
7. Set Snap: **2**
8. Create the following Layers:

LAYER NAME	COLOR	LINETYPE
Bl	Magenta	Dashedx2
Pl	Green	Phantom2
Text	Cyan	Continuous

CURVE DATA

CURVE	CHORD BEARING	CHORD LENGTH	CURVE RADIUS
C70	S68°44'46"W	33.4'	50'
C74	N77°50'57"E	55.4'	50'

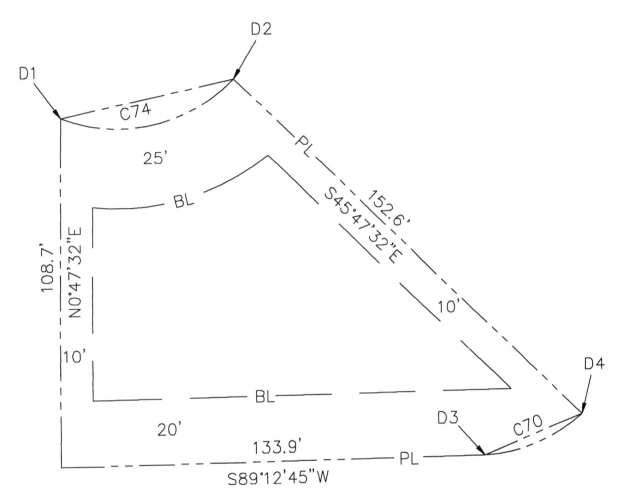

FIGURE 14–4
Information Needed to Draw the Plat (Scale: 1"=30')

9. Set Pl as the current layer
10. Create a text style with a simplex font.
11. **Zoom-All** to view the entire drawing area.

Set Surveyor's units:

Prompt	Response
Command:	TYPE: **UNITS<enter>**
Enter Choice, 1 to 5<2>	**<enter>** (to accept Decimal)
Number of digits to right of decimal point (0 to 8)<4>	TYPE: **1<enter>**
Enter Choice, 1 to 5<1>	TYPE: **5** (to select Surveyor's units) **<enter> <enter> <enter>** (to accept defaults) **F2** (to flip to graphics display)

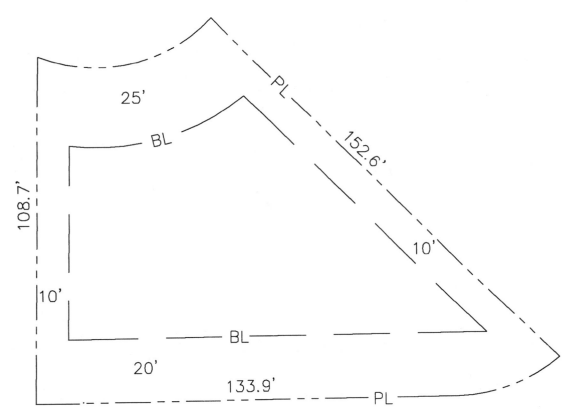

FIGURE 14–5
Exercise 14–3: Drawing a Plat (Scale: 1″=30′)

Use the following procedure to draw a plat (Figure 14–5):

Prompt	Response
Command:	**Line (or TYPE: L<enter>)**
From point:	TYPE: **20,10<enter>**
To point:	TYPE: **@108.7<N0D47′32″E<enter>**
To point:	TYPE: **@55.4<N77D50′57″E<enter>**
	(This is the bearing for curve C74.)

Notice that the bearing for the curve C74 was taken from the curve data chart shown on Figure 14–4. Curve data are an essential part of the information you need for this type of drawing.

Prompt	Response
To point:	TYPE: **@152.6<S45D47′32″E<enter>**
To point:	TYPE: **@33.4<S68D44′47″W<enter>**
To point:	TYPE: **C<enter>**

Use the Arc command to draw curves C70 and C74 (Figure 14–4):

Prompt	Response
Command:	**Arc-Start, End, Radius**
Center/<start point>:	**D1** (Use Osnap-Endpoint.)
End point:	**D2** (Use Osnap-Endpoint.)
Radius:	TYPE: **50<enter>**
Command:	**Arc-Start, End, Radius**
Center/<start point>:	**D3** (Use Osnap-Endpoint.)

| End point: | **D4** (Use Osnap-Endpoint.) |
| Radius: | TYPE: **50<enter>** |

On Your Own (Figure 14–5)

1. Erase the two chords of C70 and C74.

2. Use Offset to form the building line.

3. Use zero-radius Fillet to clean up the corners of the building line.

4. Use Properties... to change the building line layer to Bl.

5. Set the current layer to Text, and place the required text in the locations shown on Figure 14–5 using Single Line Text 3.5 units high. When you enter the Single Line Text rotation angle for the bearing S10°45′0″W, enter N10D45′0″E to get the correct angle. Do the same for similar Single Line Text entries.

6. Break lines where they cross Text, as shown in Figure 14–5.

Save

When you have completed Exercise 14–3, save your work in at least two places.

Plot

Printer Plot or Plotter Plot Exercise 14–3 on an $8\frac{1}{2}'' \times 11''$ sheet at a scale of 1 plotted unit = 30 drawing units (Scale: $1'' = 30'$ on the plotted drawing).

EXERCISE 14–4
Drawing a Plat and Adding the Structure

When you have completed Exercise 14–4, your drawing will look similar to the drawing in Figure 14–8. To begin Exercise 14–4, turn on the computer and start AutoCAD.

Begin Drawing CH14-EX4 on the Hard Drive

1. CLICK: **Use a Wizard**

2. CLICK: **Quick Setup**
   CLICK: **OK**

3. Set drawing Units: **Architectural**
   CLICK: **Next>>**

4. Set drawing Width: **125′** × Length **160′**
   CLICK: **Done**

5. **Use Save As... to save the drawing on the hard drive with the name CH14-EX4**

6. Set Grid: **4′**

7. Set Snap: **1′**

8. Create the following Layers:

LAYER NAME	COLOR	LINETYPE
Pl	Red	Dashdot
Building	Green	Continuous
Bl	Yellow	Dashed
Labels	Blue	Continuous

9. Set Pl as the current layer.

10. Set Ltscale=240. The drawing will be plotted at a scale of $1'' = 20'$ (or $1'' = 240''$).

11. Create a text style with a simplex font (try CIBT or COBT for a different architectural font).

12. Zoom-All to view the entire drawing area.

Set Surveyor's units:

Prompt	Response
Command:	TYPE: **UNITS<enter>**
Enter Choice, 1 to 5<4>	**<enter>** (to accept Architectural)
Denominator of smallest fraction to display... <16>	**<enter>** (to accept 16)
Enter Choice, 1 to 5<1>	TYPE: **5** (to select Surveyor's units) **<enter> <enter> <enter>** (to accept defaults) **F2** (to flip to graphics display)

Use the bearings on the site plan to draw the property lines of lot 11 (Figure 14–6):

Prompt	Response
Command:	**Line** (or TYPE: **L<enter>**)
From point:	TYPE: **15′,20′<enter>** (This point will locate the drawing in the center of the limits.)
To point:	TYPE: **@120′<N0D47′32″W<enter>**
To point:	TYPE: **@95′<N89D12′32″E<enter>**
To point:	TYPE: **@120′<S0D47′32″E<enter>**
To point:	TYPE: **C<enter>**

On Your Own (Figures 14–7, 14–8, 14–9)

1. Draw the building lines (Figure 14–7). On the north and south sides of this lot, the building lines are taken from the site plan. They are the lines labeled BL. On the east and west sides of the lot, many building codes require a 10′ distance from the building to the property line. Use Offset and Trim to make the building lines; then use Properties... to change them to layer BL.

FIGURE 14–6
Site Plan

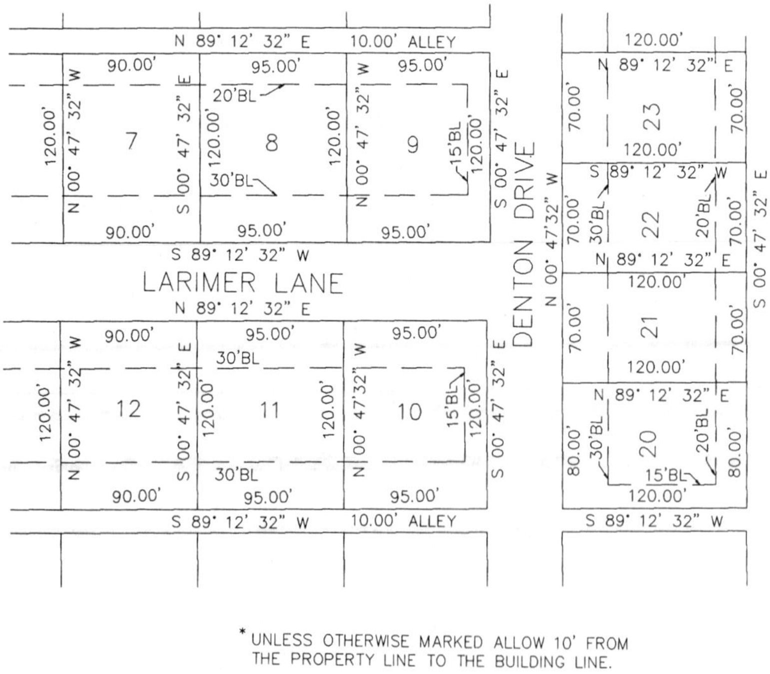

* UNLESS OTHERWISE MARKED ALLOW 10′ FROM THE PROPERTY LINE TO THE BUILDING LINE.

Part II: Two-Dimensional AutoCAD

FIGURE 14–7
Drawing the Property and Building Lines (Scale: 1″=20′)

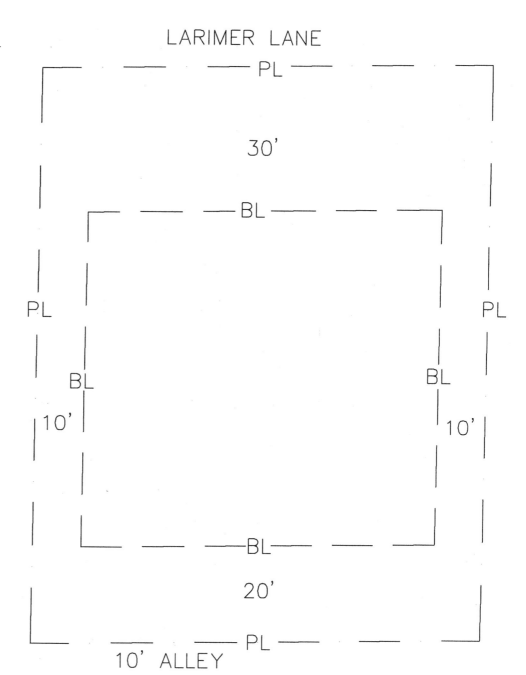

LARIMER LANE

2. Draw the house outline inside the building lines (Figure 14–8). Locate the house shown in Figure 14–9 inside the building lines. Use only the outside dimensions of the building and hatch the house as shown in Figure 14–8.

3. Add the driveway and walks.

4. Add labels as indicated, using Dtext 3′ high.

Save

When you have completed Exercise 14–4, save your work in at least two places.

Plot

Printer Plot or Plotter Plot Exercise 14–4 on an $8\frac{1}{2}'' \times 11''$ sheet at a scale of $1'' = 20'$.

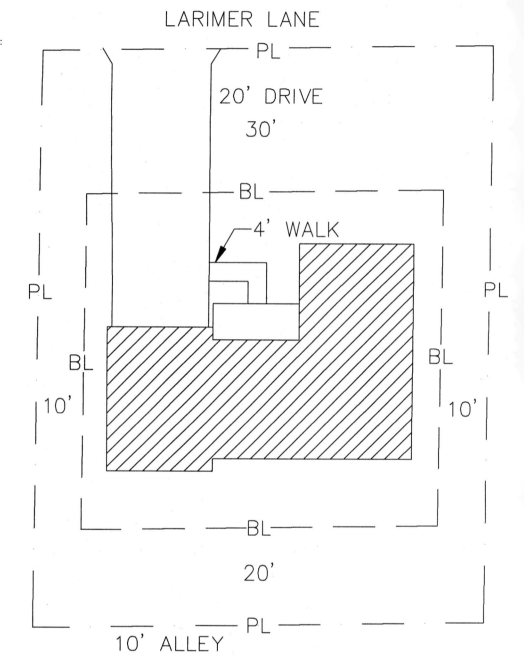

FIGURE 14–8
Exercise 14–4: Drawing a Plat
and Adding the Structure (Scale:
1"=20')

LARIMER LANE

PL

20' DRIVE

30'

BL

4' WALK

PL

PL

BL

BL

10'

10'

BL

20'

PL

10' ALLEY

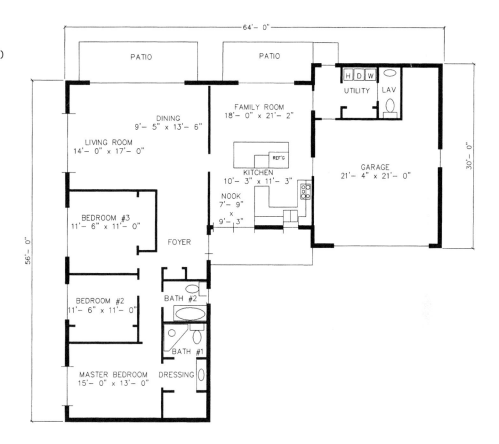

FIGURE 14–9
Drawing the House Outline inside the Building Lines (Scale: $\frac{1}{8}''=1'0''$)

REVIEW QUESTIONS

1. The selection of decimal units allows drawings to made
   a. In feet
   b. In inches only
   c. In millimeters only
   d. In any metric measurement
   e. In any unit of measure
2. The selection of Surveyor's units permits lines to be drawn as bearings.
   a. True
   b. False
3. Which of the following is a correct response to the Line command prompt "To point:" when Surveyor's units have been selected?
   a. @100<N30D<enter>
   b. @100<N30D0'0"<enter>
   c. @100<N30%%D0'0"E<enter>
   d. @100<N30D0'ME<enter>
   e. @100<ND30"0'0E
4. Which of the following surveys does not require elevation measurements?
   a. Topographic
   b. Photo
   c. Plat
   d. Route
   e. Construction
5. Which of the following variables was set to 50 to allow dimensions to be added to the open traverse in Figure 14–2?
   a. Ltscale
   b. Plot Ratio
   c. Dimscale
   d. Dim
   e. Dimvar

Chapter 14: Drawing a Plat

6. Which of the following is called a plat?
   a. Land survey
   b. Topographic survey
   c. Geodetic survey
   d. Photo survey
   e. Route survey
7. Which of the following commands is used to discover the length and direction of a bearing?
   a. Dist
   b. Inquiry
   c. List
   d. Type
   e. Status
8. A crossing window may be created (when Erase is selected from the pull-down menu) by
   a. Clicking on a spot that contains no entities and dragging downward to the left
   b. Clicking on a spot that contains no entities and dragging upward to the right
   c. Clicking on a spot that contains an entity and dragging upward to the right.
   d. Clicking on a spot that contains no entities and dragging downward to the right
   e. None of the above
9. There is no response to a Single Line Text prompt that will allow text to be placed at the same angle as the bearing.
   a. True
   b. False
10. The linetype of Figure 14–5 that was used to draw the building line is
    a. DASHED
    b. HIDDEN
    c. CONTINUOUS
    d. DASHEDX2
    e. PHANTOM
11. List the six survey types.

    _____   _____

    _____   _____

    _____   _____

12. List the setting that allows linetypes such as DASHED to be displayed correctly on a large drawing.

    _____

13. List the three basic surveying measuring elements.

    _____   _____   _____

14. List the text code for the degree symbol.

    _____

15. List the command used to change the closed traverse from separate line segments into a single closed polyline.

    _____

PART **III** SPECIAL TOPICS

15 Isometric Drawing

OBJECTIVES

When you have completed this chapter, you will be able to:

☐ Make isometric drawings to scale from two-dimensional drawings.
☐ Correctly use the following commands and settings:

ELLIPSE-Isocircle   SNAP-Style Iso

☐ Use the Ctrl-E or F5 keys to change from one isoplane to another.

INTRODUCTION

Isometric drawing is commonly used to show how objects appear in three dimensions. This drawing method is a two-dimensional one (you are drawing on a flat sheet of paper) that is used to give the appearance of three dimensions. It is not a 3D modeling form such as those that are covered in later chapters. In 3D modeling you actually create three-dimensional objects that can be viewed from any angle and can be placed into a perspective mode.

You can make isometric drawings quickly and easily using AutoCAD software. Once the proper Grid and Snap settings are made, the drawing itself proceeds with little difficulty. The three isometric axes are 30° right, 30° left, and vertical.

EXERCISE 15–1
Fundamentals of Isometric Drawing

Seven isometric shapes are drawn in this exercise to acquaint you with the fundamentals of making isometric drawings using AutoCAD. We will begin with a simple isometric box (Figure 15–1, shape 1) so that you can become familiar with drawing lines on an isometric axis. All seven of these shapes are drawn on the same sheet and plotted on one $8\frac{1}{2}'' \times 11''$ sheet. When you have completed Exercise 15–1, your drawing will look similar to Figure 15–1. To begin Exercise 15–1, turn on the computer and start AutoCAD.

1. CLICK: **Use a Wizard**
2. CLICK: **Quick Setup**
   CLICK: **OK**
3. Set drawing Units: **Architectural**
   CLICK: **Next>>**
4. Set drawing Width: **11′** × Length: **8′6″**
   CLICK: **Done**

339

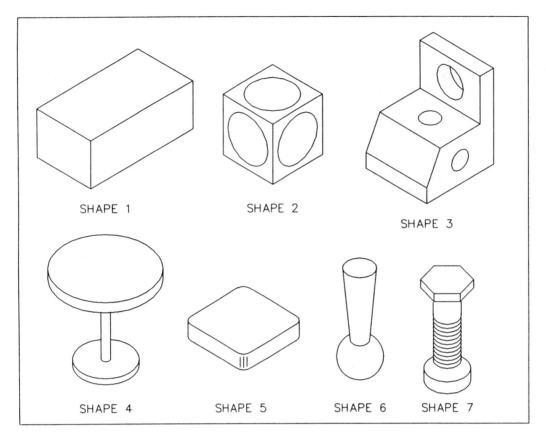

FIGURE 15–1
Exercise 15–1: Fundamentals of Isometric Drawing (Scale: $\frac{1}{2}'' = 1'\text{-}0''$)

5. Use SaveAs... to save the drawing on the hard drive with the name CH15-EX1.

6. Set Snap as follows.

Set Snap for an isometric grid:

Prompt	Response
Command:	TYPE: **SNAP<enter>**
Snap spacing or ON/OFF/Aspect/Rotate/ Style <0'-6"):	TYPE: **S<enter>**
Standard/Isometric <S>:	TYPE: **I<enter>**
Vertical spacing <0'-6">:	TYPE: **1<enter>** (if 1" is not the default)

When you want to exit the isometric grid, TYPE: **SNAP<enter>** and then TYPE: **S<enter>**, then TYPE: **S<enter>** again to select the standard grid. Keep the isometric grid for this exercise.

7. Set Grid: **3"**

8. Create the following Layers:

LAYER NAME	COLOR	LINETYPE
A-furn-iso-r	Red	Continuous
A-furn-iso-g	Green	Continuous

9. Set Layer A-furn-iso-g current.

FIGURE 15–2
Drawing Aids Dialog Box

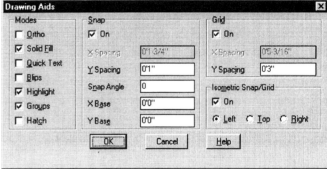

Drawing Aids Dialog Box

You may also use the Drawing Aids dialog box from the Tools menu on the pull-down menu bar (Figure 15–2) to make the settings.

When the isometric snap (and the grid) is set, and the Drawing Aids dialog box is entered, the 1″ Snap and 3″ Grid settings will appear as shown in Figure 15–2.

Shape 1: Drawing the Isometric Rectangle

Drawing shape 1 (Figure 15–3) helps you become familiar with drawing lines using isometric polar coordinates.

FIGURE 15–3
Shape 1: Drawing the Isometric
Rectangle (Scale: $\frac{3}{4}'' = 1'\text{-}0''$)

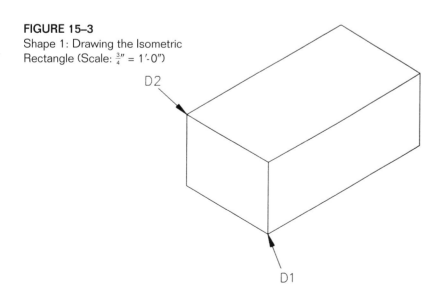

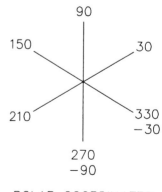

POLAR COORDINATES
FOR ISOMETRIC DRAWING

Draw the right face of an isometric rectangular box measuring 12″ × 16″ × 30″ using isometric polar coordinates:

Prompt	Response
Command:	**Line** (or TYPE: **L<enter>**)
LINE From point:	**D1** (Figure 15–3) (absolute coordinates 1′7-1/16″,4′11″)
To point:	TYPE: **@30<30<enter>**
To point:	TYPE: **@12<90<enter>**
To point:	TYPE: **@30<210<enter>**
To point:	TYPE: **C<enter>**

Draw the left face of the isometric rectangular box:

Prompt	Response
Command:	**<enter>**
From point:	**D1**
To point:	TYPE: **@16<150<enter>**
To point:	TYPE: **@12<90<enter>**
To point:	TYPE: **@16<330<enter>**
To point:	**<enter>**

Draw the top of the isometric rectangular box:

Prompt	Response
Command:	**<enter>**
From point:	**D2**
To point:	TYPE: **@30<30<enter>**
To point:	TYPE: **@16<-30<enter>**
To point:	**<enter>**

When using polar coordinates to draw lines in isometric, you can ignore Isoplanes. Isoplanes are isometric faces—Top, Right, and Left. Pressing two keys, Ctrl and E, at the same time toggles your drawing to the correct Isoplane—Top, Right, or Left. The function key F5 can also be used to toggle to the correct Isoplane.

Shape 2: Drawing Isometric Ellipses

Shape 2 (Figure 15–4) has a circle in each of the isometric planes of a cube. When drawn in isometric, circles appear as ellipses. You must use the isoplanes when drawing isometric circles using the Ellipse command. The following part of the exercise starts by drawing a 15″ isometric cube.

Draw the right face of a 15″ isometric cube using isometric polar coordinates:

Prompt	Response
Command:	**Line** (or TYPE: **L<enter>**)
From point:	**D1** (absolute coordinates 5′5-13/16,5′)
To point:	TYPE: **@15<30<enter>**
To point:	TYPE: **@15<90<enter>**
To point:	TYPE: **@15<210<enter>**
To point:	TYPE: **C<enter>**

FIGURE 15–4
Shape 2: Drawing Isometric
Ellipses (Scale: $\frac{3}{4}'' = 1'\text{-}0''$)

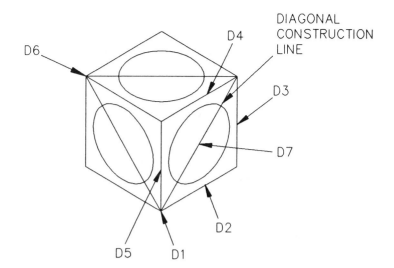

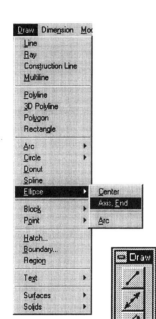

Use the Mirror command to draw the left face of the isometric cube:

Prompt	Response
Command:	**Mirror** (or TYPE: **MI<enter>**)
Select objects:	**D2,D3,D4<enter>**
First point of mirror line:	**D1** (be sure Ortho is on)
Second point:	**D5** (PRESS: **F5** to be sure you are in either the right or left isoplane.)
Delete old objects? <N>	**<enter>**

Complete the top face of the isometric cube:

Prompt	Response
Command:	**Line** (or TYPE: **L<enter>**)
From point:	**D6**
To point:	TYPE: **@15<30<enter>**
To point:	TYPE: **@15<-30<enter>**
To point:	**<enter>**

On Your Own

1. Draw construction lines, as shown in Figure 15–4, across diagonally opposite corners in each of the visible surfaces. Be sure to turn Ortho off. The construction lines will be used to locate accurately the centers of the ellipses.

Draw an isometric ellipse (6″ radius) that represents a circle in the right isoplane:

Prompt	Response
Command:	**Ellipse** (or TYPE: **EL<enter>**)
Arc/Center/Isocircle/<Axis endpoint 1>:	TYPE: **I<enter>**
Center of circle:	**Osnap-Midpoint**
mid of	**D7**
<Circle radius>/Diameter:	PRESS: **the F5 function key until the command line reads <Isoplane Right>, then** TYPE: **6<enter>**

When you type and enter **D** in response to the prompt "<Circle radius>/Diameter:", you can enter the diameter of the circle. The default is radius.

On Your Own

1. Follow a similar procedure to draw ellipses in the left and top isoplanes. Be sure to specify Isocircle after you have selected the Ellipse command, and be sure you are in the correct isoplane before you draw the ellipse. Use F5 to toggle to the correct isoplane.

2. Erase the construction lines.

When you have completed this part of the exercise, you have the essentials of isometric drawing. Now apply these essentials to a more complex shape.

Shape 3: Drawing Angles in Isometric and Drawing Ellipses to Show the Thickness of a Material

Shape 3 (Figure 15–5) has an angle and also a hole that shows the thickness of the material that makes up the shape. This part of the isometric exercise describes how to draw an angle and how to draw two ellipses to show the thickness of the material. Begin by drawing the front face of the shape.

Begin to draw the front face of shape 3:

Prompt	Response
Command:	**Line** (or TYPE: **L<enter>**)
From point:	**D1** (Figure 15–5) (Pick a point in the approximate location shown in Figure 15–1.)
To point:	TYPE: **@1'8<30<enter>**
To point:	TYPE: **@2'<90<enter>**
To point:	TYPE: **@4<210<enter>**
To point:	TYPE: **@1'<-90<enter>**
To point:	TYPE: **@1'<210<enter>**
To point:	**<enter>**

Because you do not know the angle for the next line, you must locate the other end of it and connect the two endpoints. This is a common practice in isometric drawing. Any time an angle is encountered in isometric, locate the two endpoints of the angle and connect those points to draw a line that is not one of the isometric axes.

Locate the two endpoints of the angle, and draw the line that is at an angle to complete the front face of shape 3:

Prompt	Response
Command:	**Line** (or TYPE: **L<enter>**)
From point:	**D1**
To point:	TYPE: **@4<90<enter>**
To point:	**Osnap-Endpoint**
of	**D2**
To point:	**<enter>**

Use the Copy command to draw the identical back plane:

Prompt	Response
Command:	**Copy** (or TYPE: **CP<enter>**)
Select Objects:	**D3,D4,D5,D6,D7<enter>**
<Base point or displacement>/Multiple:	**D1**
Second point of displacement:	TYPE: **@1'6<150<enter>**

FIGURE 15–5
Shape 3: Drawing Angles in Isometric and Drawing Ellipses to
Show the Thickness of the Mate-
rial (Scale: $\frac{3}{4}'' = 1'\text{-}0''$)

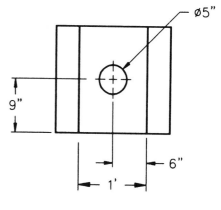

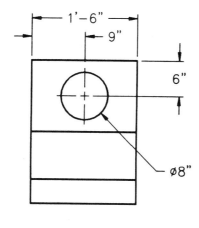

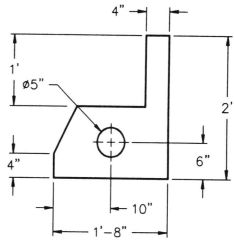

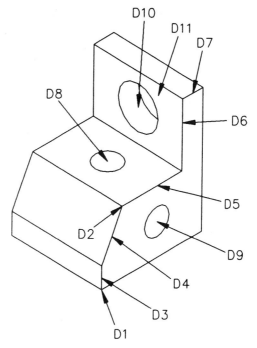

On Your Own

Draw lines connecting the front and back surfaces.

Draw an isometric ellipse (5″ diameter) that represents a circle in the top isoplane:

Prompt	Response
Command:	**Ellipse (or TYPE: EL<enter>)** **(Toggle to the top isoplane using F5.)**
Arc/Center/Isocircle/<Axis endpoint 1>:	TYPE: **I<enter>**
Center of circle:	**D8** (Count the 3″ grid marks (1″ snap) to locate the center of the plane, or draw construction lines from the midpoints of two parallel sides.)
<Circle radius>/Diameter:	TYPE: **D<enter>**
Circle diameter:	TYPE: **5<enter>**

On Your Own

1. Toggle to the right isoplane, and draw a 5″-diameter ellipse in the right isometric plane using D9 as its center.

2. Two ellipses are required in the left isoplane, on the part of the shape that sits on top. One is needed on the front surface and part of one is needed on the back surface to describe the thickness of the material. To do this:

   ☐ Toggle to the left isoplane, and draw an 8″-diameter ellipse in the left isometric plane using D10 as its center.

   ☐ Draw a line from D10 (the center of the first ellipse) to D11 (the center of the second ellipse that is yet to be drawn). Draw this line using **@4<30** (4″ is the depth) as the polar coordinates for the second point of the line.

   ☐ Draw the second 8″-diameter ellipse in the left isoplane using D11 as its center (the endpoint of the 4″ line).

   ☐ Use the Trim and Erase commands to trim and erase the back part of the second ellipse and center line.

Tip: You can also skip drawing this 9″ center line and simply copy the ellipse using @4<30 as the second point of displacement.

Shape 4: Drawing a Shape That Has a Series of Ellipses Located on the Same Center Line

Shape 4 (Figure 15–6), similar to a round table, will help you become familiar with drawing a shape that has a series of ellipses located on the same center line. Five ellipses must be drawn. The centers of two of them, the extreme top and bottom ellipses, can be located by using Endpoints of the center line. Centers for the other three can be located by using construction lines or the ID command. Construction lines are used for this exercise so that you can see where the centers are.

The following part of the exercise begins by drawing a center line through the entire height of the object.

Begin to draw a shape containing several ellipses of different sizes located on the same center line by drawing the center line:

Prompt	Response
Command:	**Line (or TYPE: L<enter>)**
From point:	**D1**
To point:	TYPE: **@24<90<enter>**
To point:	**<enter>**

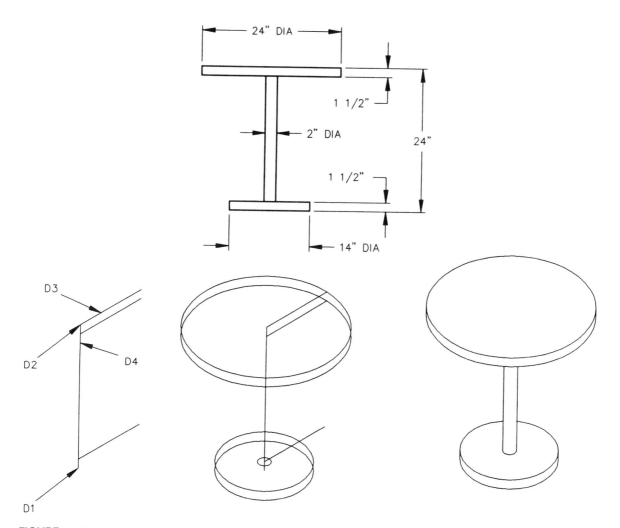

FIGURE 15–6
Shape 4: Drawing a Shape That Has a Series of Ellipses Located on the Same Center Line (Scale: $\frac{3}{4}'' = 1'\text{-}0''$)

Draw construction lines used to locate the centers of three ellipses:

Prompt	Response
Command:	**Line** (or TYPE: **L<enter>**)
From point:	**D2**
To point:	TYPE: **@12<30<enter>**
To point:	**<enter>**
Command:	**Copy** (or TYPE: **CP<enter>**)
Select objects:	**D3**
Select objects:	**<enter>**
<Base point or displacement>/Multiple:	TYPE: **M<enter>**
Base point:	**Osnap-Endpoint**
of	**D4**
Second point of displacement:	TYPE: **@1-1/2<270<enter>**
Second point of displacement:	TYPE: **@22-1/2<270<enter>**
Second point of displacement:	**<enter>**

On Your Own

To draw the five ellipses:

1. Toggle to the top isoplane and use Endpoint to locate the center of the uppermost ellipse on the endpoint of the vertical line. Draw it with a diameter of 24″.

2. Draw a second 24″-diameter ellipse using as its center the Intersection of the construction line that is located $1\frac{1}{2}$″ from the top end of the vertical line, or copy the 24″ ellipse $1\frac{1}{2}$″ down.

3. Draw two isometric ellipses with their centers located at the Intersection of the construction line located $1\frac{1}{2}$″ from the bottom of the vertical line. One ellipse is 2″ in diameter; the other is 14″ in diameter.

4. Draw the 14″-diameter ellipse again using the bottom Endpoint of the vertical line as its center, or copy the 14″ ellipse $1\frac{1}{2}$″ down.

On Your Own

See Figure 15–7.

Note: Although Osnap-Nearest can be used to end an isometric line on another line, the position is not exact. A more exact method is to draw the line beyond where it should end and trim it to the correct length.

1. To draw the 2″ column, toggle to the right or left isoplane (the top isoplane does not allow you to draw vertical lines using a pointing device if Ortho is on). Turn Ortho (F8) on. Draw a vertical line from the Quadrant of one side of the 2″-diameter ellipse to just above the first 24″-diameter ellipse. Draw a similar line to form the other side of the column.

2. With Ortho (F8) on and toggled to the right or left isoplane, draw vertical lines from the Quadrants of the ellipse segments to connect ellipses as shown in Figure 15–7.

3. Use Trim and Erase to remove unneeded lines. The drawing is complete.

FIGURE 15–7
Shape 4: Drawing Tangents to the Ellipses (Scale: $\frac{3}{4}$″ = 1′-0″)

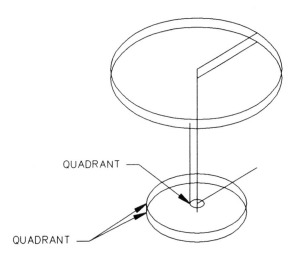

QUADRANT

QUADRANT

Shape 5: Isometric Detail with Rounded Corners

The fifth drawing (Figure 15–8) in this exercise is a shape that has rounded corners. Rounded corners are common in many items. In two-dimensional drawing, the Fillet command allows you to obtain the rounded corners quickly and easily. This is not so in isometric. Drawing shape 5 will help you to become familiar with how rounded corners must be constructed with isometric ellipses.

Turn on Ortho and Snap, and toggle to the top isoplane. Draw an 18″ × 18″ square shape in the top isoplane.

Prompt	Response
Command:	**Line** (or TYPE: **L<enter>**)
LINE From point:	**D1** (on a grid mark)
To point:	TYPE: **@18<30<enter>**

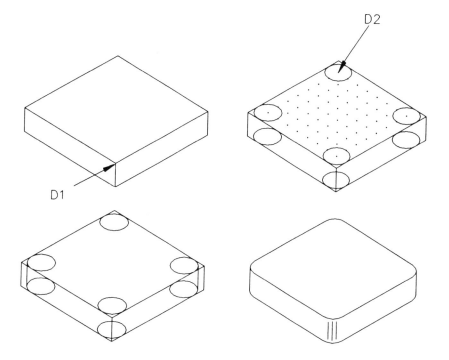

Prompt	Response
To point:	TYPE: **@18<150<enter>**
To point:	TYPE: **@18<210<enter>**
To point:	TYPE: **C<enter>**

On Your Own

1. Copy the front two edges of the square to form the bottom of the shape. Copy using **@4<270** (4″ is the depth) as the polar coordinates for the second point of displacement.

2. Draw lines connecting the top and bottom edges. (These lines are for reference only. You may skip this step if you choose.)

Draw a 2″ radius ellipse in the top isoplane:

Prompt	Response
Command:	**Ellipse** (or TYPE: **EL<enter>**) (Toggle to the top isoplane.)
Arc/Center/Isocircle/<Axis endpoint 1>:	TYPE: **I<enter>**
Center of circle:	**D2** (Count 2″ from the corner to locate the center of the ellipse.)
<Circle radius>/Diameter:	TYPE: **2<enter>**

On Your Own

To complete shape 5:

1. Copy the ellipse just drawn to the other four top corners, locating them in a similar manner.

2. Copy the front three ellipses 4″ in the 270 direction to form corners in the bottom plane.

3. Draw lines connecting the two outside ellipses using Osnap-Quadrant.

4. Use the Trim and Erase commands to remove the extra lines.

5. Add highlights on the front corner to complete the drawing.

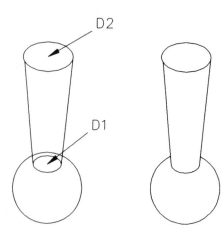

FIGURE 15–9
Shape 6: Isometric Detail—A
Rounded Shape Intersecting a
Sphere (Scale: $\frac{3}{4}$″ = 1′-0″)

D2

D1

Shape 6: Isometric Detail—A Rounded Shape Intersecting a Sphere

While drawing in isometric, you may encounter a cylinder intersecting a sphere (Figure 15–9). The cylinder in Figure 15–9 is also tapered.

Draw the sphere:

Prompt	Response
Command:	**Circle-Center, Radius** (or TYPE: **C<enter>**)
3P/2P/TTR/<Center point>:	**Click the center of the circle on a grid mark, in the approximate location shown in Figure 15–1.**
Diameter/<Radius>:	TYPE: **6<enter>**

Draw the bottom ellipse of the tapered cylinder:

Prompt	Response
Command:	**Ellipse** (or TYPE: **EL<enter>**) (Toggle to the top isoplane.)
Arc/Center/Isocircle/<Axis endpoint 1>:	TYPE: **I<enter>**
Center of circle:	**D1** (2″ down from the top of the center of the circle)
<Circle radius>/Diameter:	TYPE: **2<enter>**

Draw the top ellipse of the tapered cylinder:

Prompt	Response
Command:	**<enter>**
Arc/Center/Isocircle/<Axis endpoint 1>:	TYPE: **I<enter>**
Center of circle:	**D2** (Click a point 18″ above the center of the first ellipse.)
<Circle radius>/Diameter:	TYPE: **3.5<enter>**

On Your Own

1. Complete the shape by drawing lines connecting the top and bottom ellipses using Osnap-Quadrant.

2. Trim the circle and the bottom ellipse to complete the shape. Although the true shape of the intersection between the cylindrical shape and the sphere is a compound curve, it is often simplified in isometric as you have done here. The compound curve is difficult to construct and looks no better than the simplified version.

Shape 7: Isometric Detail—A Polygon and a Threaded Shape

The final shape in this exercise combines several features (Figure 15–10).

Draw the hexagonal head of a threaded spacer (Figure 15–10A):

Prompt	Response
Command:	**Polygon (or TYPE: POL<enter>)**
Number of sides <4>:	TYPE: **6<enter>**
Edge/<Center of polygon>:	**Click a point on a grid mark, in the approximate location shown in Figure 15–1.**
Inscribed in circle/Circumscribed about circle (I/C) <I>:	TYPE: **C<enter>**
Radius of circle:	TYPE: **6<enter>**

Now you have a hexagon that cannot be used in isometric drawing. To use it, you must block the hexagon and then insert it with different X and Y values. **Be sure to toggle to the top isoplane when you insert the hexagonal block.**

Block and insert the hexagon (Figure 15–10B):

Prompt	Response
Command:	**Block (or TYPE: B<enter>)**
The Block Definition dialog box appears:	TYPE: **HEX** in the Block name: box.
	Make sure Retain Objects is not selected.
	CLICK: **Select Point<**
Insertion base point:	CLICK: **the center of the hexagon**
The Block Definition dialog box appears:	CLICK: **Select Objects<**
Select objects:	CLICK: **any point on the hexagon**
Select objects:	**<enter>**
The Block Definition dialog box appears:	CLICK: **OK**
Command:	**Insert-Block... (or TYPE: I<enter>)**
The Insert dialog box appears:	CLICK: **Block...**
The Defined Blocks dialog box appears:	CLICK: **HEX**
	CLICK: **OK**

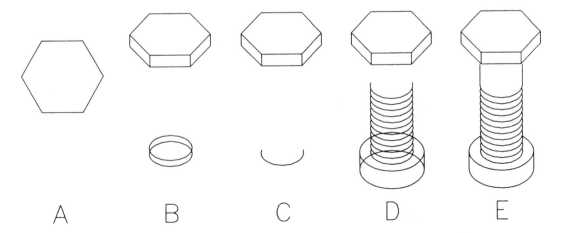

A   B   C   D   E

FIGURE 15–10
Shape 7: Isometric Detail—A Polygon and a Threaded Shape (Scale: $\frac{3}{4}'' = 1'\text{-}0''$)

Prompt	Response
The Insert dialog box appears:	CLICK: **OK**
Insertion point:	**Pick the location of the isometric hexagon as shown in Figure 15–1.**
X scale factor <1> / Corner / XYZ:	**<enter>**
Y scale factor (default=X):	TYPE: **.58<enter>** (This is a very close approximation to the isometric Y scale factor.)
Rotation angle <0>:	**<enter>**

On Your Own

Complete drawing shape 7, and add text to your drawing as follows:

1. Draw 2″ vertical lines from each of the visible corners of the hexagon in the 270 direction (Figure 15–10B).

2. Using Osnap-Endpoint, draw lines to form the bottom of the hexagon (Figure 15–10B).

3. At a center point 20″ below the center of the isometric hexagon, draw an isometric ellipse with a 3″ radius in the top isoplane. Copy the ellipse 1″ in the 90 direction (Figure 15–10B).

4. Trim the back of the bottom ellipse using the top ellipse as the cutting edge. Erase the top ellipse (Figure 15–10C).

5. Array the trimmed ellipse using 12 rows, 1 column, and a space between rows of +1″ (Figure 15–10D).

6. Draw a 10″-diameter isometric ellipse using the center of the bottom thread ellipse. Copy the ellipse 3″ in the 270 direction (Figure 15–10D).

7. Draw lines connecting the Quadrants of the two 10″ ellipses (Figure 15–10D).

8. Draw lines from the top thread to just below the lower surface of the hexagon (Figure 15–10E).

9. Trim and Erase as needed to complete the drawing (Figure 15–10E).

10. Set Layer A-FURN-ISO-R current, and use Single Line Text, 2″H, Simplex font to identify shapes 1 through 7 as shown in Figure 15–1.

SAVE

When you have completed Exercise 15–1, save your work in at least two places.

PLOT

Plot or Print the drawing on an $8\frac{1}{2}″ \times 11″$ sheet of paper. Use a plotting scale of $1″ = 1′\text{-}0″$.

EXERCISE 15–2
Tenant Space Reception Desk in Isometric

The tenant space solid wood reception desk is drawn in isometric in Exercise 15–2. When you have completed Exercise 15–2, your drawing will look similar to Figure 15–11. To begin Exercise 15–2, turn on the computer and start AutoCAD.

1. CLICK: **Use a Wizard**

2. CLICK: **Quick Setup**

   CLICK: **OK**

3. Set drawing Units: **Architectural**

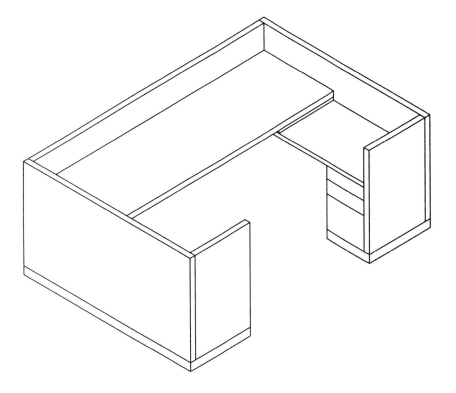

CLICK: **Next>>**

4. Set drawing Width: **15'** × Length: **15'**

   CLICK: **Done**

5. **Use SaveAs... to save the drawing on the hard drive with the name CH15-EX2.**

6. Set Snap: **Style-Isometric-1"**

7. Set Grid: **4"**

8. Create the following Layer:

LAYER NAME	COLOR	LINETYPE
A-furn-iso-g	Green	Continuous

9. Set Layer A-furn-iso-g current.

10. **Zoom-All**

This exercise is a series of straight lines, all of which are on the isometric axes. It is suggested that you follow the step-by-step procedure described next so that you get some ideas about what you can and cannot do when using the isometric drawing method. To draw an isometric view of the reception desk (Figure 15–11) use the dimensions shown in Figure 15–13.

Set Snap and Ortho on. Draw the top edge of the panels (Figure 15–12):

Prompt	Response
Command:	**Line** (or TYPE: **L<enter>**)
From point:	**D1** (Figure 15–12) (absolute coordinates 8'1,7'4)
To point:	TYPE: **@24<210<enter>**
To point:	TYPE: **@66<150<enter>**
To point:	TYPE: **@96<30<enter>**

FIGURE 15–12
Drawing the Top Edge of the
Panels

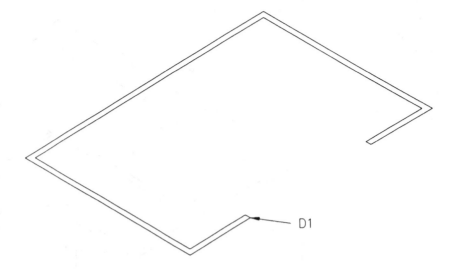

D1

Tip: Remember that direct distance
entry can be used to draw lines if you
choose.

Prompt	Response
To point:	TYPE: **@66<-30<enter>**
To point:	TYPE: **@24<210<enter>**
To point:	TYPE: **@2<150<enter>**
To point:	TYPE: **@22<30<enter>**
To point:	TYPE: **@62<150<enter>**
To point:	TYPE: **@92<210<enter>**
To point:	TYPE: **@62<330<enter>**
To point:	TYPE: **@22<30<enter>**
To point:	TYPE: **C<enter>**

Use the Extend command to extend the inside lines of the panels to form the separate panels (Figure 15–14):

Prompt	Response
Command:	**Extend** (or TYPE: **EX<enter>**)
Select boundary edges: (Projmode = UCS, Edgemode = No extend)	
Select objects:	**D1**
Other corner:	**D2**
Select objects:	**<enter>**
<Select object to extend>/Project/Edge/Undo:	**D3,D4,D5,D6<enter>**

Copy the top edges of the panels to form the lower kickplate surfaces (Figure 15–15):

Tip: You can also use direct distance
to specify distances when you copy.

Prompt	Response
Command:	**Copy** (or TYPE: **CP<enter>**)
Select objects:	**D1,D2,D3,D4**
Select objects:	**<enter>**
<Base point or displacement>/Multiple:	TYPE: **M<enter>**
Base point:	**D1** (any point is OK)
Second point of displacement:	TYPE: **@35<270<enter>**
Second point of displacement:	TYPE: **@38<270<enter>**
Second point of displacement:	**<enter>**

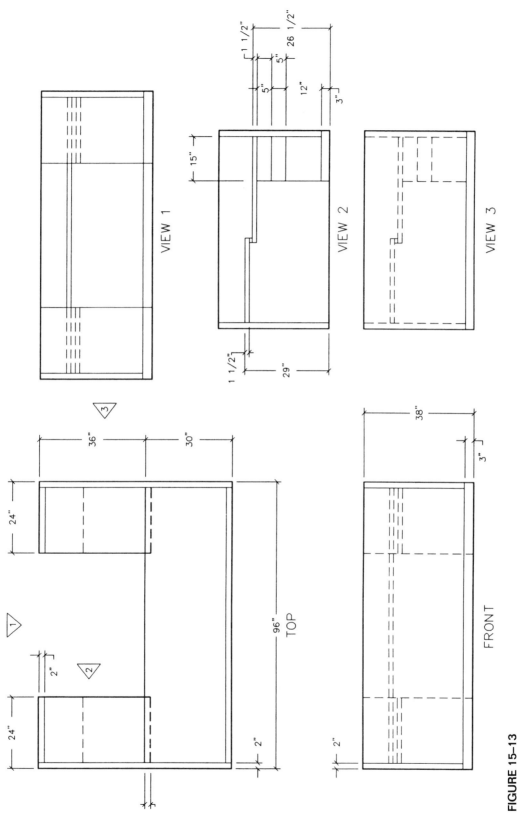

FIGURE 15–13
Dimensions of the Tenant Space Reception Desk (Scale: $\frac{3''}{8} = 1'\text{-}0''$)

VIEW 1

VIEW 2

VIEW 3

TOP

FRONT

355

FIGURE 15–14
Extending Lines to Form the
Separate Panels

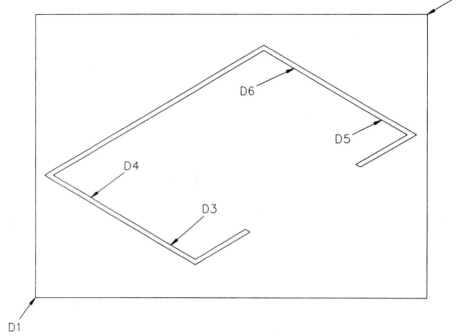

Use the Copy command to draw the edge of the main work surface against the inside of the panel (Figure 15–15):

Prompt	Response
Command:	**Copy** (or TYPE: **CP\<enter\>**)
Select objects:	**D5**
Select objects:	**\<enter\>**
\<Base point or displacement\>/Multiple:	**D5** (any point is OK)
Second point of displacement:	TYPE: **@9\<270\<enter\>**

FIGURE 15–15
Copy the Top Edges to Form the
Lower Kickplate Surfaces and the
Edge of the Main Work Surface

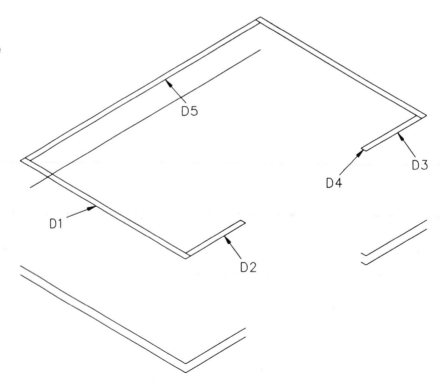

On Your Own

See Figure 15–16.

Set a running Osnap mode of Endpoint and draw vertical lines connecting top and bottom outside lines and the inside corner above the work surface. Turn the running Osnap mode off when you have completed this part of the exercise. Next you will draw the work surface.

Draw the work surfaces (Figure 15–16):

Prompt	Response
Command:	**Line** (or TYPE: **L<enter>**)
From point:	**Osnap-Endpoint, D1**
To point:	TYPE: **@28<330<enter>**
To point:	**D2** (With Ortho on and the top isoplane active, pick any point beyond the inside of the left partition; you can Trim these later.)
To point:	**<enter>**
Command:	**<enter>**
From point:	**Osnap-Endpoint, D3**
To point:	TYPE: **@1-1/2<270<enter>**
To point:	**D4** (Pick another point outside the left partition.)
To point:	**<enter>**
Command:	**<enter>**
From point:	**Osnap-Endpoint, D5**
To point:	TYPE: **@1<270<enter>**
To point:	TYPE: **@22<210<enter>**
To point:	TYPE: **@1<90<enter>**

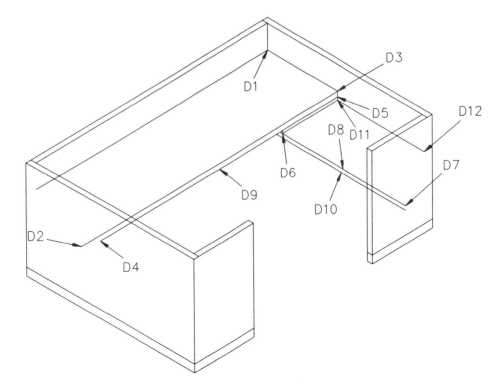

FIGURE 15–16
Drawing the Vertical Lines Connecting Top and Bottom Edges; Drawing the Work Surfaces

Prompt	Response
To point:	<enter>
Command:	<enter>
From point:	Osnap-Endpoint, D6
To point:	D7 (Pick a point outside the right rear panel.)
To point:	<enter>
Command:	<enter>
From point:	Osnap-Endpoint, D11
To point:	D12 (Pick a point outside the right rear panel.) <enter>
Command:	Copy (or TYPE: CP<enter>)
Select objects:	D8
Select objects:	<enter>
<Base point or displacement>/Multiple:	D8
Second point of displacement:	TYPE: @1-1/2<270<enter>
Command:	Extend (or TYPE: EX<enter>)
Select boundary edges: (Projmode = UCS, Edgemode = No extend)	
Select objects:	D9<enter>
<Select object to extend>/Project/Edge/Undo:	D8, D10<enter>

Trim lines that extend outside the panels (Figure 15–17):

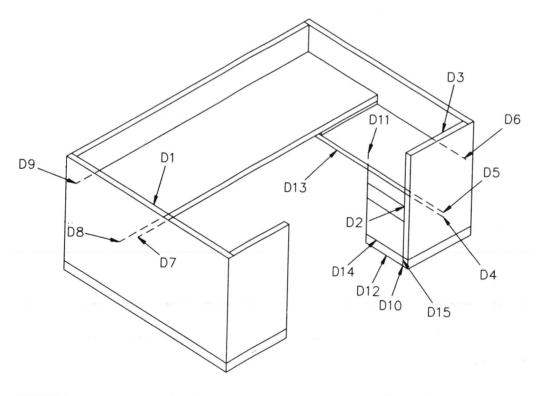

FIGURE 15–17
Trimming Lines and Drawing the Drawer Pedestal

Prompt	Response
Command:	**Trim** (or TYPE: **TR<enter>**)
Select cutting edges: (Projmode = UCS, Edgemode = No extend)	
Select objects:	**D1,D2,D3<enter>**
<Select object to trim>/Project/Edge/Undo:	**D4,D5,D6,D7,D8,D9<enter>**

Draw the drawer pedestal:

Prompt	Response
Command:	**Line** (or TYPE: **L<enter>**)
LINE From point:	**Osnap-Endpoint, D10**
To point:	TYPE: **@15<150<enter>**
To point:	**D11** (With Ortho on and the left isoplane active, pick a point above the bottom edge of the desktop.)
To point:	**<enter>**
Command:	**Copy** (or TYPE: **CP<enter>**
Select objects:	**D12** (Figure 15–17)
Select objects:	**<enter>**
<Base point or displacement>/Multiple:	TYPE: **M<enter>**
Base point:	**D12**
Second point of displacement:	TYPE: **@3<90<enter>**
Second point of displacement:	TYPE: **@15<90<enter>**
Second point of displacement:	TYPE: **@20<90<enter>**
Second point of displacement:	**<enter>**

Trim the extra lines:

Prompt	Response
Command:	**Trim** (or TYPE: **TR<enter>**)
Select cutting edges: (Projmode = UCS, Edgemode = No extend)	
Select objects:	**D13,D14<enter>**
<Select object to trim>/Project/Edge/Undo:	**D15,D11<enter>**

Dimensioning in Isometric

You can resolve the problem of placing dimensions on an isometric drawing by buying a third-party software dimensioning package designed specifically for isometric. Other methods, such as using the aligned option in dimensioning and using an inclined font with the style setting, solve only part of the problem. Arrowheads must be constructed and individually inserted for each isoplane. If you spend a little time blocking the arrowheads and customizing your menu, you can speed up the process significantly.

SAVE

When you have completed Exercise 15–2, save your work in at least two places.

PLOT

Plot or Print the drawing on an $8\frac{1}{2}'' \times 11''$ sheet of paper. Use a plotting ratio of $\frac{1}{2}'' = 1'\text{-}0''$).

EXERCISE 15–3
Tenant Space Reception Seating Area in Isometric

1. Make an isometric drawing, full size, of the chairs, coffee table, and corner table to show the entire reception room seating area. Use the dimensions shown in Figure 15–18.
2. Plot or Print the drawing to scale on an $8\frac{1}{2}'' \times 11''$ sheet of paper.

EXERCISE 15–4
Tenant Space Conference Chair in Isometric

1. Make an isometric drawing, full size, of the conference room chair. Use the dimensions shown in Figure 15–19.
2. Plot or Print the drawing to scale on an $8\frac{1}{2}'' \times 11''$ sheet of paper.

FIGURE 15–18

Exercise 15–3: Tenant Space Reception Seating Dimensions (Scale: $\frac{3''}{8} = 1'\text{-}0''$)

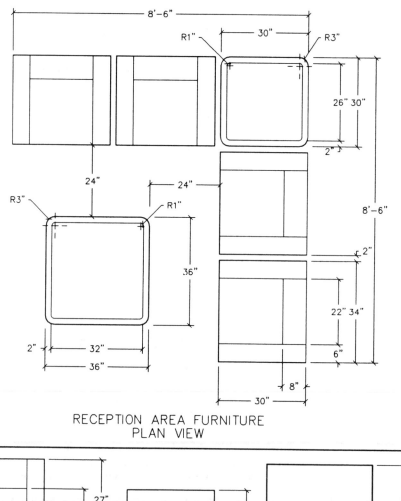

RECEPTION AREA FURNITURE
PLAN VIEW

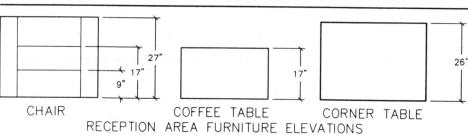

CHAIR   COFFEE TABLE   CORNER TABLE

RECEPTION AREA FURNITURE ELEVATIONS

FIGURE 15–19
Exercise 15–4: Tenant Space
Conference Chair Dimensions
(Scale: $\frac{3}{8}$" = 1'-0")

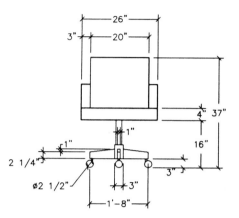

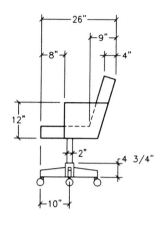

EXERCISE 15–5
Conference Room Walls and Furniture in Isometric

1. Make an isometric drawing, full size, of the conference room shown in Figure 15–20. Draw a view from the direction shown by the arrow in Figure 15–20(A).

   The following figures provide the information needed to complete Exercise 5:

   □ Figure 15–19: Tenant space conference chair dimensions.
   □ Figure 15–20(A): Plan view of the conference room.
   □ Figure 15–20(B): Elevation of the north wall of the conference room.
   □ Figure 15–20(C): Elevation of the east wall of the conference room.
   □ Figure 15–20(D): Plan and elevation views of the conference table.

   Show the chairs 6″ under the conference table. Two chairs on each side of the table are rotated at a 10° angle. You will have to draw a rectangular box (parallel to the walls) touching the outside points of the plan view of the rotated chairs. Project lines from points on the plan view to the rectangular box, and measure points of intersection with the box to get accurate measurements on the left and right isometric axes.

2. Plot or Print the drawing to scale on an $8\frac{1}{2}″ \times 11″$ sheet of paper.

REVIEW QUESTIONS

1. From which of the following selections on the Tools menu on the menu bar are the isometric snap and grid obtained?
   a. Layer Control...
   b. Drawing Aids...
   c. Set SysVars
   d. Grid On/Off
   e. UCS Control...
2. From which of the Snap options is the isometric Snap obtained?
   a. ON
   b. OFF
   c. Aspect
   d. Rotate
   e. Style

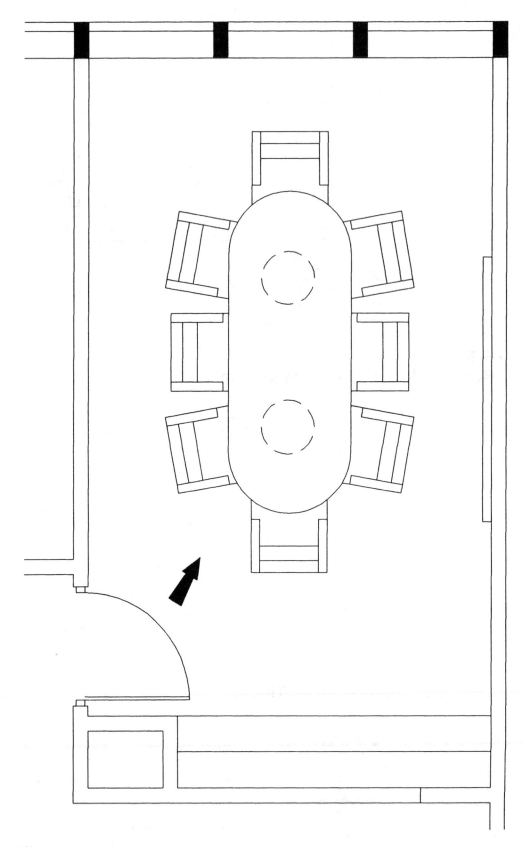

FIGURE 15–20 (A)
Exercise 15–5: Plan View of the Conference Room (Scale: $\frac{3}{8}'' = 1'\text{-}0''$)

FIGURE 15–20 (B)

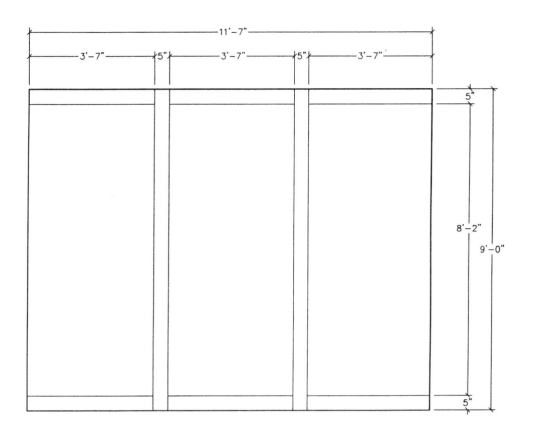

Exercise 15–5: Elevation of the
North Wall of the Conference
Room (Scale: $\frac{3''}{8}$ = 1'-0")

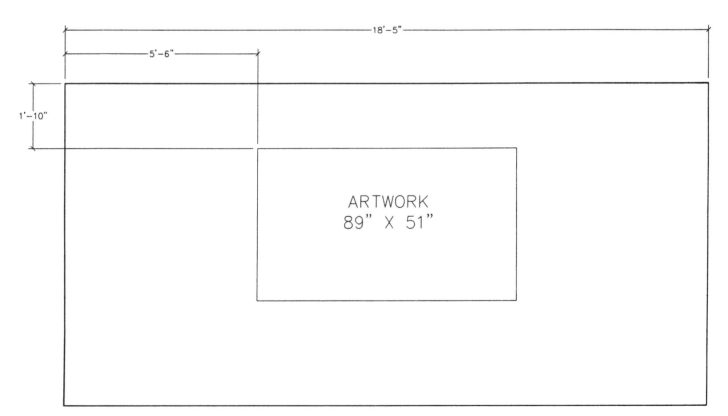

FIGURE 15–20 (C)
Exercise 15–5: Elevation of the East Wall of the Conference Room (Scale: $\frac{3''}{8}$ = 1'-0")

FIGURE 15–20 (D)

Exercise 15–5: Plan and Elevation
Views of the Conference Table
(Scale: $\frac{3}{8}'' = 1'\text{-}0''$)

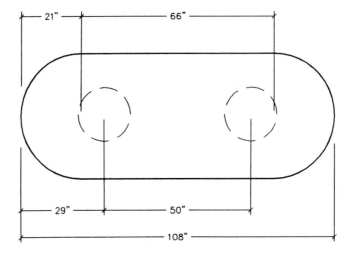

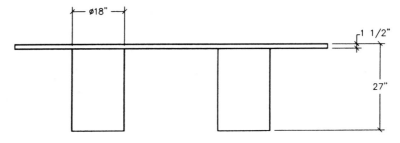

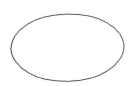

FIGURE 15–21

FIGURE 15–22

FIGURE 15–23

3. Which of the following is not one of the normal isometric axes?
   a. 30
   b. 60
   c. 90
   d. 210
   e. 330

4. From which of the Ellipse prompts is the isometric ellipse obtained?
   a. <Axis endpoint 1>
   b. Center
   c. Isocircle
   d. Axis endpoint 2
   e. Rotation

5. Which isoplane is used to draw the ellipse shown in Figure 15–21?
   a. Top
   b. Left
   c. Right

6. Which isoplane is used to draw the ellipse shown in Figure 15–22?
   a. Top
   b. Left
   c. Right

7. Which isoplane is used to draw the ellipse shown in Figure 15–23?
   a. Top
   b. Left
   c. Right

8. Which key(s) toggle from one isoplane to another?
   a. Ctrl-C
   b. F9
   c. F7
   d. F5
   e. Alt-F1

Part III: Special Topics

9. Which of the following is the same as –30°?
   a. 60°
   b. 150°
   c. 180°
   d. 210°
   e. 330°
10. Which of the following isoplanes will not allow vertical lines to be drawn with a mouse when ORTHO is on?
    a. Top
    b. Left
    c. Right
11. Which function key is used to turn the isometric grid ON and OFF?

   _____

12. Write the correct syntax (letters and numbers) to draw a line 5.25″ at a 30° angle upward to the right.

   _____

13. Write the correct sequence of keystrokes, using polar coordinates, to draw the right side of the isometric rectangle shown in Figure 15–24, after the first point (lower left corner) has been picked. Draw to the right and up.

   1. _____   3. _____
   2. _____   4. _____

FIGURE 15–24

14. In Exercise 15–2, why were lines drawn beyond where they should stop and then trimmed to the correct length?

   _____

   _____

15. Which command used in this chapter has a feature labeled "Multiple"?

   _____

16. List the six angles used for polar coordinates in drawing on isometric axes.

   _____

17. Describe how to draw an angled line that is not on one of the isometric axes.

   _____

   _____

18. Describe how to draw a cylindrical object in isometric that has several ellipses of different sizes located on the same center line.

   _____

   _____

19. Describe two problems that must be solved to place dimensions on an isometric drawing.

   _____

   _____

20. Describe the difference between isometric drawing and 3D modeling.

   _____

   _____

16 Presentation Capabilities

OBJECTIVES

When you have completed this chapter, you will be able to:

☐ Correctly use the following commands and settings:

EDIT	Regen
Floating Viewports (MVIEW)	RegenAll
Model Space [Floating]	RESUME
Model Space [Tiled]	SCRIPT
MSLIDE	SLDSHOW
MVSETUP	Tiled Viewports (VPORTS)
Paper Space	Tilemode
Redraw	VPLAYER
RedrawAll	VSLIDE

MODEL SPACE AND PAPER SPACE

This chapter presents the details of how to use model space and paper space and how to plot multiple viewports. It also describes how to write a script file and prepare a slide presentation of your work. Let's begin with the concepts of model space and paper space.

Model Space

Model space is the 2D environment (and also 3D, as you will discover in Chapters 18 and 19) in which you have been working to this point. While in model space you can use the Tiled Viewports (VPORTS) command to divide the display screen into multiple viewports, as shown in Figure 16–1. Model space is limited in that although several viewports may be visible on the display screen, only one viewport can be active on the display screen at a time and only one viewport can be plotted. Model space is where your 2D or 3D model (drawing) is created and modified. When you start a new drawing, you are in model space.

Paper Space

Paper space is similar to a piece of illustration board used to paste up a presentation. The MVIEW command, which operates only when Tilemode is off (0), is used to create and control viewport display; the display screen may be divided into multiple viewports. Each viewport can be treated as a single sheet of paper (on the illustration board) and may be copied, stretched, erased, moved, or scaled, as shown in Figure 16–2. The drawing within the viewport cannot be edited while it is in paper space. However, you may draw something over the viewport; for example, you may add dimensions or labels to a drawing. You may even overlap a viewport over one or more of the other viewports. You can also place the viewports into a single architectural format sheet, and you can plot all the viewports at the same time.

FIGURE 16–1
Viewports Created in Model
Space

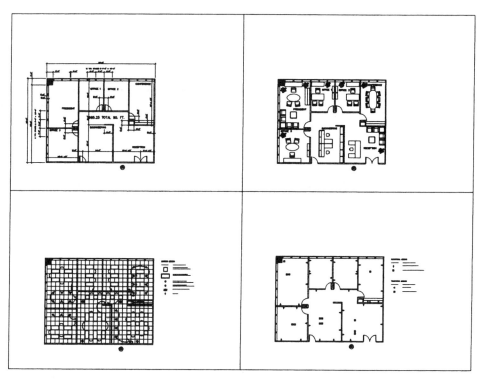

EXERCISE 16–1
Creating a Printed Presentation of the Tenant Space Project by Combining Multiple Plans on One Sheet of Paper

When you have completed Exercise 16–1, your drawing will look similar to Figure 16–3. To begin Exercise 16–1, turn on the computer and start AutoCAD.

1. Open existing drawing CH13-EX1 from a floppy disk in drive A and save it as CH16-EX1 to the hard drive.
2. Use **Zoom-All** to view the limits of the drawing.

TILED VIEWPORTS (VPORTS)

Begin by dividing the screen into four viewports. Remember that while it is in model space the model (drawing) is the same in each viewport. If you edit the model in any one viewport, you are doing it in all viewports. You may, however, freeze different layers in each viewport—which you will do later in this exercise—and you may zoom in or out in a viewport without affecting other viewport magnification.

Divide the screen into four viewports:

Prompt	Response
Command:	TYPE: **VPORTS<enter>**
Save/Restore/Delete/Join/SIngle/?/2/<3>/4:	TYPE: **4<enter>** (or CLICK: **Tiled Viewports: 4 viewports**)

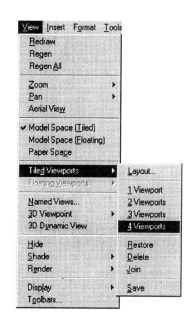

The screen is now divided into four viewports. The active viewport, outlined with a solid line, displays the lines of the cursor when the cursor is moved into it. Inactive viewports display an arrow when the cursor is moved into those areas. To make a different viewport active, position the arrow in the desired viewport and press the Click button on your mouse. The options of the viewports command are:

Save

Allows you to name a set of viewports and save it for future use. Restore recalls the saved viewports. Any number of sets of viewports may be named, saved, and recalled.

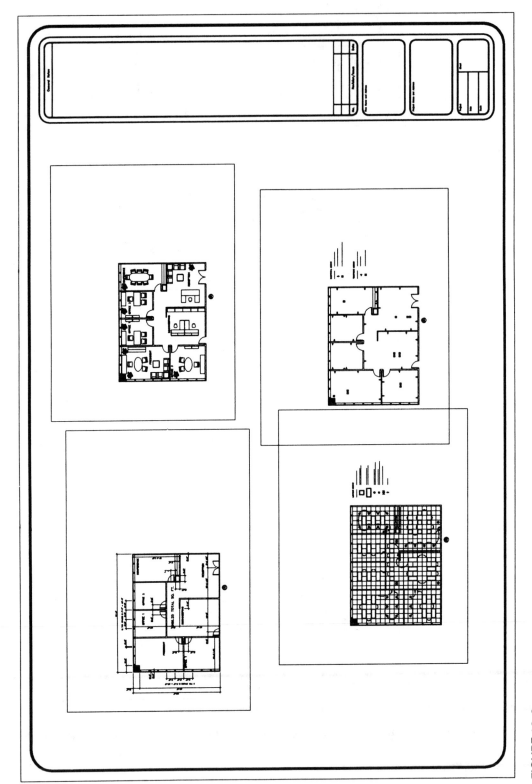

FIGURE 16–2
Viewports Modified in Paper Space

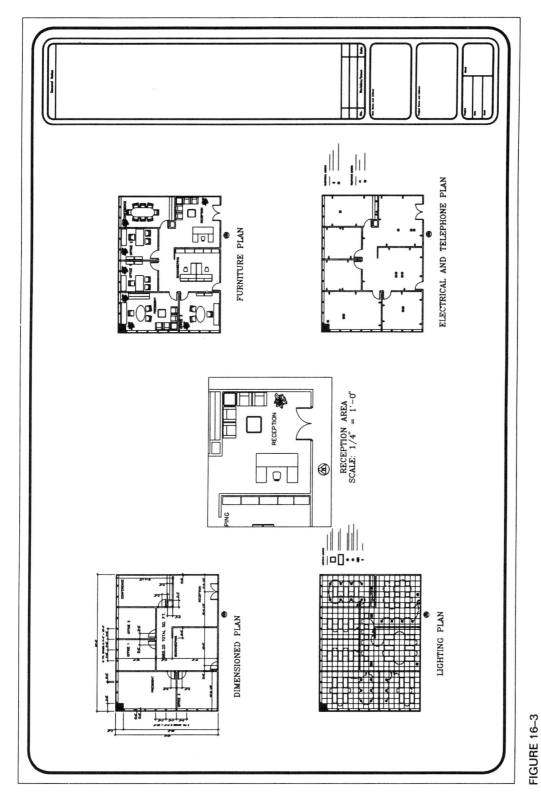

FIGURE 16–3

Exercise 15–1: Creating a Printed Presentation of the Tenant Space by Combining Multiple Plans on One Sheet of Paper

Restore

Restores a saved set of viewports. AutoCAD prompts you for the name of the saved viewport.

Delete

Deletes a named viewport set. AutoCAD prompts you for the name of the saved viewport set to be deleted.

Join

Joins two viewports into a larger one. The resulting view is the dominant viewport. AutoCAD prompts for the following when Join is picked:

Prompt	Response
Select dominant viewport <current>:	**<enter>** (to accept the current active viewport, or Click the one you want)
Select viewport to join:	**Click the other viewport.**

Single

Returns the display to a single viewport. The resulting view is the current active viewport before single was selected.

?

Lists the identification numbers and the screen positions of the current arrangement of viewports and all previously saved viewports by name if you accept the default <*> when AutoCAD prompts you for the viewport configuration to list.

2,3,4

Divides the current viewport into two, three, or four viewports with the same view, snap, grid, and layer settings. Selections 2 and 3 also allow you to select a vertical or horizontal arrangement. Selection 3 allows for two smaller viewports to the left or right of one larger one. You can divide the screen into as many as 64 viewports depending on your display.

On Your Own

See Figure 16–4. Experiment with the viewports so that you may get an idea of how viewports can be useful in drawing as well as in presentation:

1. Click the upper left viewport to make it active, and zoom a window around the lower right corner of the building in the upper left viewport.

2. Click the upper right viewport to make it active, and zoom a window around the upper left corner of the building in the upper right viewport.

3. Draw a line from the lower right corner of the building to the upper left corner. Click the upper left viewport to make it active, start the Line command in the upper left viewport, and then click the upper right viewport to make it active, ending the line in the upper right viewport. (Be sure Ortho is off.)

When you begin a command in any viewport you must first click the viewport to make it active, so ending the line in the upper right viewport requires two picks: one to make the viewport active and one to complete the Line command. Experiment with this a little, and then use Undo or Zoom-All in each viewport to return all displays to their original magnification. Use Redraw in the View menu to refresh the display in all viewports at the same time.

FIGURE 16–4
Start a Command in One Viewport and End It in Another

Part III: Special Topics

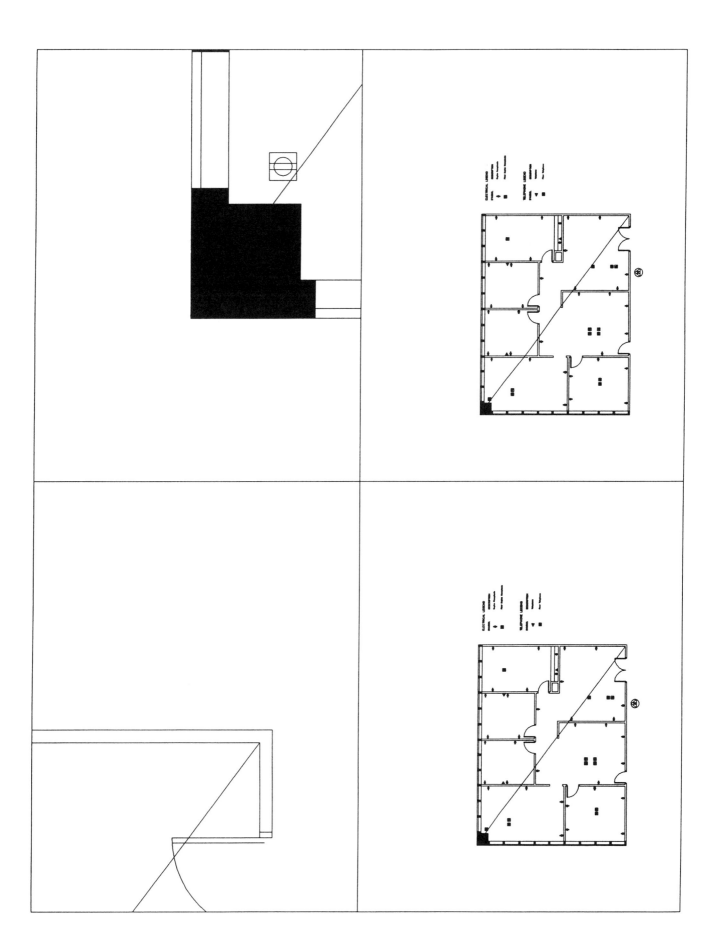

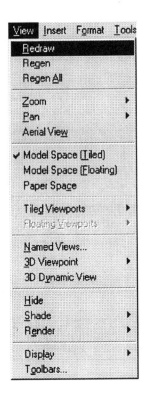

REDRAW, REDRAWALL, REGEN, and REGENALL

The Redraw and Regen commands redraw or regenerate the drawing in the current viewport only. The RedrawAll and RegenAll commands redraw or regenerate the drawing in all viewports at the same time. When you TYPE: **R<enter>**, you activate Redraw. When you CLICK: **Redraw** on the View menu you activate RedrawAll.

TILEMODE

Two types of viewports, tiled and nontiled, are available to you in AutoCAD.

Tiled Viewport Characteristics   Tiled viewports are those that exist in model space. They have the following characteristics:

- ☐ They fill the graphics screen, lie side-by-side like ceramic tile, and cannot be moved.
- ☐ They are fixed and cannot overlap.
- ☐ They can be deleted only by changing the viewport configuration.
- ☐ Only one tiled viewport can be active at a time.
- ☐ Only the active viewport can be plotted.
- ☐ Nothing drawn in a tiled viewport can be edited in a nontiled viewport.
- ☐ A ✓ appears beside Model Space [Tiled] in the View menu on the menu bar.

Nontiled Viewport Characteristics   Nontiled viewports are those that exist in paper space or model space. They have the following characteristics:

- ☐ They may or may not fill the graphics screen.
- ☐ They can overlap.
- ☐ They can be moved, copied, scaled, stretched, or erased while they are in paper space.
- ☐ They can have different layers frozen in any viewport.
- ☐ All nontiled viewports can be plotted at the same time when they are in paper space.
- ☐ Nothing drawn in paper space (a nontiled viewport) can be edited in model space.
- ☐ A ✓ appears beside Model Space [Floating] when in model space.

Tilemode Settings   Settings for Tilemode are 1 (on) and 0 (off). The Tilemode setting determines whether the viewports displayed are tiled (1—on) or nontiled (0—off). DOUBLE CLICK: **TILE** at the bottom of your screen to turn Tilemode on or off. Gray is off.

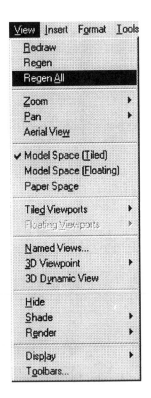

- ☐ You can work in model space with Tilemode set either to 1 (on) or 0 (off).
- ☐ When Tilemode is 0 (off) the VPORTS command is disabled. The MVIEW command (described next) must be used to create and manipulate viewports when Tilemode is 0 (off).
- ☐ Tilemode must be 0 (off) for you to work in paper space.
- ☐ The default for Tilemode is 1 (on).

MODEL SPACE [FLOATING] AND FLOATING VIEWPORTS (MVIEW)

The first time you select Model Space [Floating] from the View menu in the menu bar, AutoCAD automatically sets Tilemode to 0 (off), regenerates the drawing, and switches you to paper space in a nontiled viewport, and the Command: line displays the MVIEW prompts. Anytime you pick Model Space [Floating] again, in the same drawing, it switches you from paper space to model space.

The Floating Viewports command on the View menu in the menu bar displays most of the MVIEW options. The Floating Viewports (MVIEW) command operates only when Tilemode is set to 0 (off) and is used to create and control viewport display in model space and paper space. When you TYPE: **MV<enter>**, the Tilemode setting must first be set to 0 (off). The Floating Viewports (MVIEW) options are:

SNAP |GRID |ORTHO |OSNAP |**PAPER** |TILE

Part III: Special Topics

OFF

Think of each viewport as a single sheet of paper (on the illustration board). The viewport may be copied, stretched, erased, moved, or scaled. The drawing within the viewport cannot be edited while it is in paper space. The OFF option turns off the views inside the viewport and saves regeneration time while you are editing the viewports. When the viewports are located so that you are pleased with the format, you can turn the views back on.

ON

Turns on the model space view (drawing inside the viewport).

Hideplot

Used to hide surfaces covered by other surfaces in a 3D model. This option is used in Chapter 18.

Fit

Creates a single viewport to fill current paper space limits. Other viewports can be erased before or after the Fit option is used.

2,3,4

Creates two, three, or four viewports in a specified area or to fit the current paper space limits.

Restore

Restores saved model space viewports (saved with the Tiled Viewports (VPORTS) command) into paper space.

<First point>

Creates a new viewport defined by picking two corners or by typing the X and Y coordinates of lower left and upper right corners.

Save the current viewport configuration in model space and restore it in paper space:

Prompt	Response
Command:	TYPE: **VPORTS<enter>**
Save/Restore/Delete/Join/SIngle/?/2/<3>/4:	TYPE: **S<enter>** (or CLICK: **Tiled Viewports - Save**)
?/Name for new viewport configuration:	TYPE: **VP1<enter>** (or any other 31-character name consisting of letters, digits, and the characters $, -, and __)
Command:	**View-Model Space [Floating]** (from the menu bar)
ON/OFF/Hideplot/Fit/2/3/4/Restore/ <First point>:	TYPE: **R<enter>**
?/Name of window configuration to insert <*ACTIVE>:	TYPE: **VP1<enter>**
Fit/<First Point>:	TYPE: **0,0<enter>**
Second point:	TYPE: **24,18<enter>** (the 24″ × 18″ size will fit into a 36″ × 24″ sheet when it is plotted)
Command:	**Zoom-All**

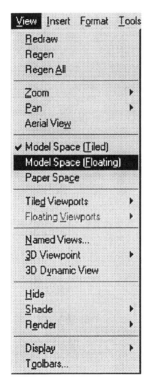

Note: If you get a single model space viewport when you click Model Space [Floating], TYPE: **PS<enter>** to go to paper space, erase the paper space viewport by clicking the outside edge when erase asks you to select objects, then TYPE: **MV<enter>** to get the mview prompt.

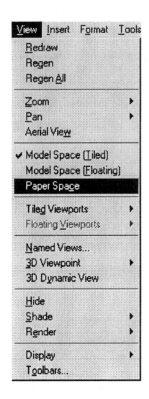

Note: The UCS Icon appears as a triangle in paper space.

Prompt	Response
Command:	**Paper Space** (or TYPE: **PS<enter>** or DOUBLE CLICK: **MODEL** at the bottom of your screen if you are not already in Paper Space)

The Model Space [Floating] command switches you from paper space to model space. You may work in model space with Tilemode either on or off.

To use the Model Space [Floating] command, you must set Tilemode to 0 (off). Since you are presently in paper space, you know that Tilemode is 0 because paper space cannot be active unless Tilemode is 0. To return to model space, simply select Model Space [Floating] (or TYPE: **MS<enter>** or CLICK: **PAPER** at the bottom of your screen).

Return to model space with Tilemode: set to 0:

Prompt	Response
Command:	**Model Space [Floating]** (or TYPE: **MS<enter>**) (or CLICK: **PAPER** on the status bar)

On Your Own

In the next part of this exercise, the VPLAYER command is used to freeze different layers in each viewport, to create a unique drawing in each viewport.

1. Before continuing with the VPLAYER command, thaw all frozen layers. When all layers are thawed, they will all be visible in each viewport.

2. Set Attribute Display (TYPE: **ATTDISP<enter>**, then TYPE: **OFF<enter>**) to off so that the attributes will not appear on the furniture symbols.

VPLAYER

The VPLAYER command allows you to freeze different layers in any viewport. It works in either paper space or model space. To use the VPLAYER command, you must set TILEMODE to 0 (off).

In model space, you can use the Layer and Linetype Properties dialog box to freeze layers in individual viewports by clicking the Freeze/Thaw in current viewport button beside the layer name. When you click the Freeze/Thaw in new viewports button, that layer is frozen for all new viewports created. Both of these buttons should be picked to freeze layers for newly created viewports.

The VPLAYER command options are:

?

Lists layers frozen in selected paper space viewports.

Freeze

Prompts you to list the names of layers you want to freeze, then prompts you for the viewports in which you want to freeze the layers. The viewport options are:
All—All viewports, while in model space or paper space.
Select—Switches to paper space (when you are in model space) and allows you to pick viewports for layer freeze.
Current—Selects the current viewport while in model space for layer freeze.

Thaw

Prompts you as before to name the layers you want to thaw, then prompts you for the viewports in which you want to thaw the layers.

Reset

After you use the Freeze or Thaw option to change a layer's visibility, you can use the Reset option to restore the default visibility setting for a layer in a selected viewport.

Newfrz

Creates new layers that are frozen in all viewports. If you then want to thaw a layer in a single viewport, use the Thaw option.

Vpvisdfl

If a layer is frozen in some viewports and thawed in others, you can use the Vpvisdfl option to set the default visibility per viewport for any layer. This default setting then determines the layer's visibility in any new viewport created with the MVIEW command.

Use the VPLAYER command to freeze layers in the upper left viewport:

Prompt	Response
Command:	**Click the upper left viewport to make it active.**
Command:	TYPE: **VPLAYER<enter>**
?/Freeze/Thaw/Reset/Newfrz/Vpvisdfl:	TYPE: **F<enter>**
Layer(s) to Freeze:	TYPE: **A-AREA,A-FURN,A-CLNG, E-LITE,E-LITE-D,E-LITE-W, E-POWR,E-COMM<enter>**
All/Select/<Current>:	**<enter>** (the current viewport)
?/Freeze/Thaw/Reset/Newfrz/Vpvisdfl:	**<enter>**

On Your Own

1. Click the upper right viewport to make it active. Use the Layer and Linetype Properties dialog box to freeze layers in the active (current) viewport. Click "Freeze/Thaw in current viewport" in the column as shown in Figure 16–5. CLICK: **OK**.

2. Click the lower left viewport to make it active. Use the Layer and Linetype Properties dialog box to freeze layers in the active (current) viewport. Click "Freeze/Thaw in current viewport" in the column as shown in Figure 16–6. CLICK: **OK**.

3. Click the lower right viewport to make it active. Use the Layer and Linetype Properties dialog box to freeze layers in the active (current) viewport. Click "Freeze/Thaw in current viewport" in the column as shown in Figure 16–7. CLICK: **OK**.

There will be occasions when you will want to select or deselect all Layers at the same time. To do that, position the cursor in an open area in the dialog box and press the right mouse button. Then click Select All or Clear All.

FIGURE 16–5
Frozen Layers in the Upper Right
Viewport

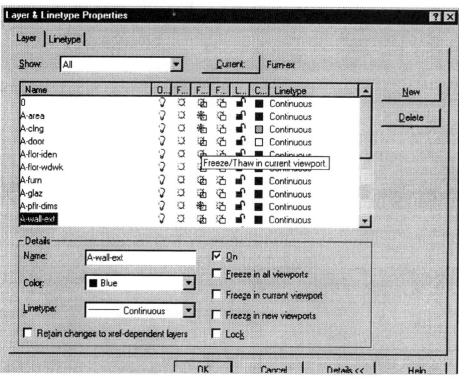

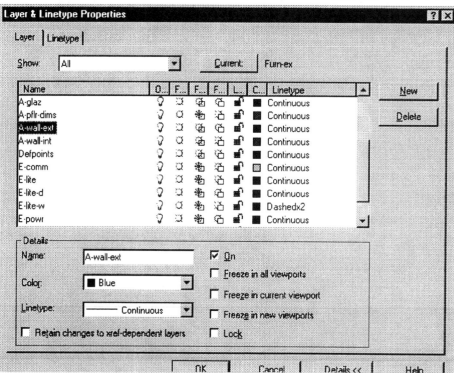

FIGURE 16–6
Frozen Layers in the Lower Left
Viewport

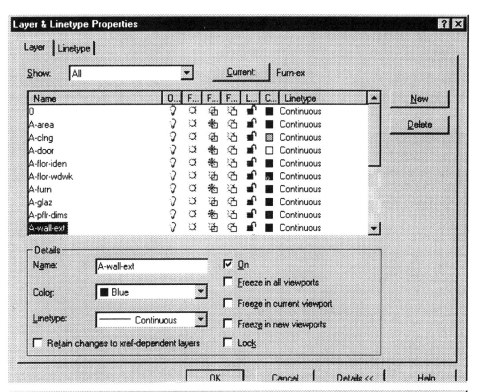

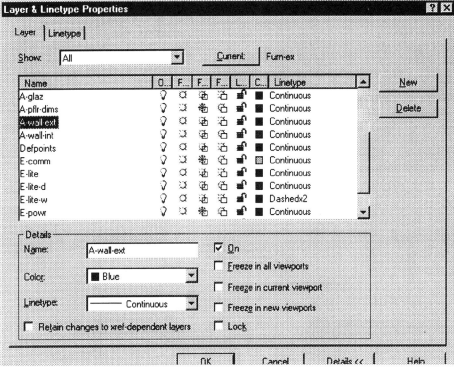

FIGURE 16–7
Frozen Layers in the Lower Right
Viewport

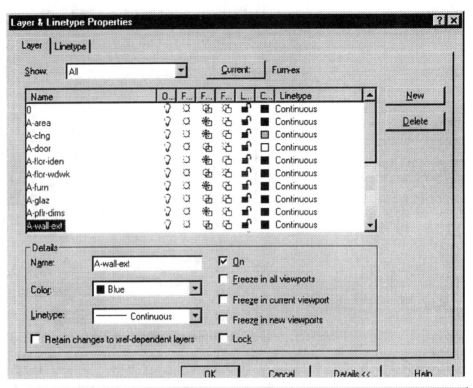

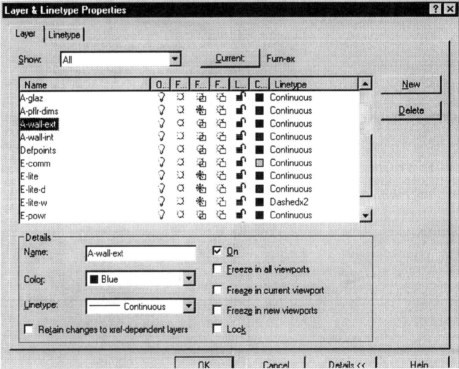

PAPER SPACE

The Paper Space command switches you from model space to paper space. Tilemode must be 0 (off) for Paper Space to work. Tilemode is still set to 0. You have been working in model space with Tilemode set to 0.

Use the Paper Space command to return to paper space:

Prompt	Response
Command:	**Paper Space** (or TYPE: **PS\<enter\>**)
	(or DOUBLE CLICK: **MODEL** at the bottom of your screen)

MVSETUP

Now that you have a paper space display (24″ × 18″) containing four views with different layers frozen, let's use the MVSETUP command to place these views into an architectural format that is 36″ × 24″.

Use MVSETUP to place the paper space views into an architectural format:

Prompt	Response
Command:	TYPE: **MVSETUP\<enter\>**
Align/Create/Scale viewports/Options/ Title block/Undo:	TYPE: **T\<enter\>**
Delete objects/Origin/Undo/ \<Insert title block\>:	**\<enter\>**
Available title block options:	
0: None	
1: ISO A4 Size(mm)	
2: ISO A3 Size(mm)	
3: ISO A2 Size(mm)	
4: ISO A1 Size(mm)	
5: ISO A0 Size(mm)	
6: ANSI-V Size(in)	
7: ANSI-A Size(in)	
8: ANSI-B Size(in)	
9: ANSI-C Size(in)	
10: ANSI-D Size(in)	
11: ANSI-E Size(in)	
12: Arch/Engineering (24 x 36in)	
13: Generic D size Sheet (24 x 36in)	
Add/Delete/Redisplay\<Number of entry to load\>:	TYPE: **12\<enter\>**
Align/Create/Scale viewports/Options/ Title block/Undo:	**\<enter\>**

On Your Own

1. You now have a 36″ × 24″ architectural format with the four viewports in it. Use the Move command to move the viewports so that they are centered in the space approximately as shown in Figure 16–8. You will have to pick the outside edge of any viewport to move it, or select all four viewports by using a crossing window.

2. Use the Model Space [Floating] command to return to model space. In the next part of this exercise the Zoom XP command is used to scale each viewport to a standard size of 1/8″ = 1′-0″.

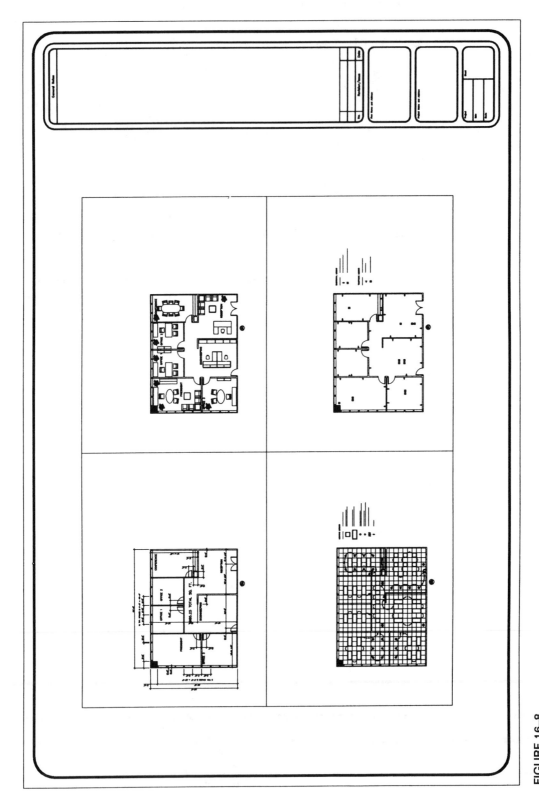

FIGURE 16-8
Position the Paper Space Viewports in the Architectural Format

380

Use the Zoom command to scale each viewport to a standard scale size:

Prompt	Response
Command:	**Pick the upper left viewport to make it active.**
Command:	TYPE: **Z<enter>**
All/Center/Dynamic/Extents/Previous/ Window/Scale(X/XP)/<Realtime>:	TYPE: **1/96XP<enter>**

While working in model space with Tilemode set to 0, you can use the XP option of the Zoom command to scale the current model space view relative to paper space. The 1/96XP entered previously gives you a scale of $\frac{1''}{8} = 1'$-$0''$ ($8 \times 12 = 96$) on your viewport.

On Your Own

1. Use the Zoom XP command to establish a scale of $\frac{1''}{8} = 1'$-$0''$ on the other three model space viewports. Use Pan to center images in each viewport.

2. Use the Paper Space command to return to paper space.

3. Use the MVIEW command to turn off the model space views (drawings inside the viewports), as shown in Figure 16–9. Turning the viewports off decreases regeneration time and allows you to work faster on complex drawings. Pick the outside edge of the viewport to turn the views off.

4. Use the Move command to move all viewports to the approximate locations as shown in Figure 16–9.

5. Use the Mview command to turn on the model space views.

Because the viewports have been moved, it is likely that your model space views are not lined up vertically and horizontally. The Mvsetup command can be used to align the views (drawings) within each viewport.

Use the Mvsetup command to align viewports in model space (Figure 16–10):

Prompt	Response
Command:	TYPE: **MVSETUP<enter>**
Align/Create/Scale viewports/Options/ Title block/Undo:	TYPE: **A<enter>**
Angled/Horizontal/Vertical alignment/ Rotate view/Undo:	TYPE: **H<enter>** (AutoCAD changes to model space)
Basepoint:	**Click the lower right viewport to make it active.**
	Osnap-Intersection
of	**D1**
Other point:	**Click the lower left viewport to make it active.**
	Osnap-Intersection
of	**D2**
Angled/Horizontal/Vertical alignment/ Rotate view/Undo?	TYPE: **V<enter>**
Basepoint:	**Osnap-Intersection**
of	**Click the upper right viewport to make it active.**
	D3
Other point:	**Click the lower right viewport to make it active.**

FIGURE 16-9
Turn Off the Model Space Views and Move the Viewports

382

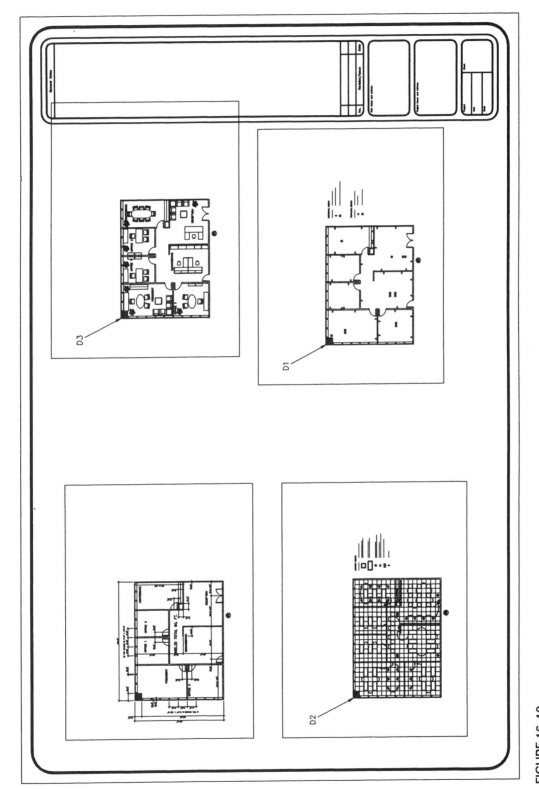

FIGURE 16–10
Use MVSETUP to Align the Views within Each Viewport

383

Prompt	Response
	Osnap-Intersection
of	**D1**

On Your Own

Align, horizontally and vertically, any remaining model space views that need to be aligned.

A brief description of the MVSETUP options follows:

Tilemode Set to 1 (On)

When Tilemode is on, MVSETUP acts just like SETUP in earlier versions of AutoCAD. You set Units, Scale, and Paper Size using prompts for each setting.

Tilemode Set to 0 (Off)

When Tilemode is off, MVSETUP has the following options:

Align This option lets you Pan the view so that it aligns with a basepoint in another viewport. You may align viewports horizontally and vertically; you may align them at a specified distance and angle from a basepoint in another viewport; and you may rotate the view in a viewport about a basepoint. This option also has an undo feature.

Create This option allows you to delete existing viewports. It also allows you to create one or more standard-size viewports. If more than one is created, this option allows you to specify the distance between viewports. It also allows you to create an array of viewports. This option also has an undo feature.

Scale viewports This option allows you to set the scale of the drawing displayed in the viewports; it is similar to the Zoom XP feature.

Options This option allows you to specify a layer for the title block, reset paper space limits, change different units, or attach an Xref as the title block.

Title block This option allows you to delete objects from paper space and to select the origin point for this sheet. It then prompts you to select one of 13 standard formats. This option also has an undo feature.

Undo This is an undo option for the major routine.

Adding Details and Annotating Paper Space Viewports

Add another viewport (Figure 16–11):

Prompt	Response
Command:	TYPE: **MV<enter>**
ON/OFF/Hideplot/Fit/2/3/4/Restore/ <First point>:	TYPE: **1',9<enter>**
Other corner:	TYPE: **1'7,1'3<enter>**
Switching to model space.	

You are now in model space and have a viewport containing a view of the active model space viewport. All the layers are turned on. Later in the exercise, the borders of the viewports will be frozen.

Use the Zoom command to scale the view:

Prompt	Response
Command:	TYPE: **Z<enter>**
All/Center/Dynamic/Extents/Previous/ Window/Scale(X/XP)/<Realtime>:	TYPE: **1/48XP<enter>** (this value represents a scale of $\frac{1}{4}'' = 1'\text{-}0''$)

On Your Own

1. Use the Layer and Linetype Properties dialog box to freeze layers in the newly added, current viewport. Freeze the same layers as you did for the upper right viewport.

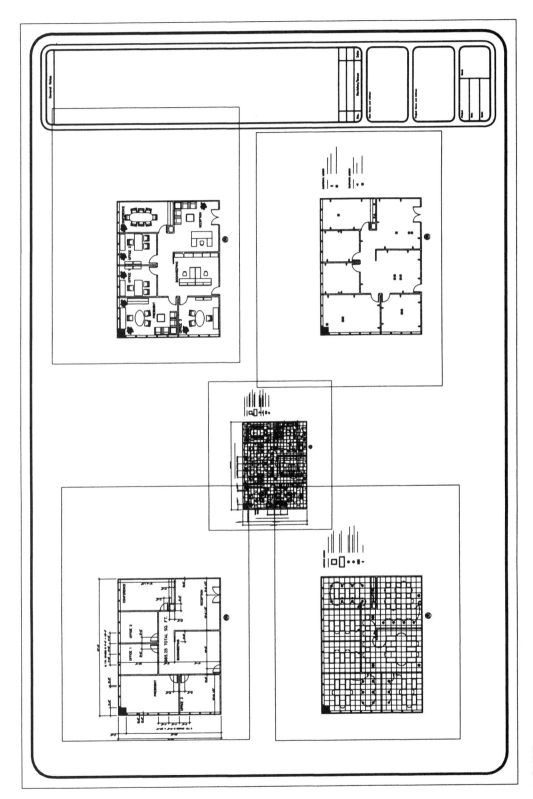

FIGURE 16–11
Use Mview to Create Another Viewport

2. Use Zoom-Dynamic to obtain a view of the reception area of the tenant space.

3. If needed, use the Move command to locate the views so that they are located approximately as shown in Figure 16–12. Align them as needed.

4. Use the VPLAYER command to create a new frozen layer named VPORT. While in paper space use the Properties... command to change the outside edges of the four large viewports to the VPORT layer. Do not select the outside edge of the viewport that has the detail of the reception area in it. Use the Layer and Linetype Properties dialog box to turn the VPORT Layer off. The outside edges of the viewports will no longer be visible.

5. Label the views using Dtext (single line text) with the STYLE name Label, FONT—COMPLEX. Height—1/4, as shown in Figure 16–12. Use the Zoom-Window command to zoom in on the viewports so that the text is visible.

6. Fill in the title block information as appropriate using the Dtext (single line text) command.

SAVE

When you have completed Exercise 16–1, save your work in at least two places.

PLOT

Plot Exercise 16–1 at a plotting ratio of 1 = 1. You will be plotting a 36″ × 24″ sheet.

EXERCISE 16–2
Creating a Slide Show of the Tenant Space Project Drawings

Another means of creating a presentation is with the use of slides. A slide is made of a drawing while it is active on the display screen; it is a file containing a "snapshot" (a raster image) of the display on the screen. A script file is used to display the slides in the correct order and with an appropriate amount of delay between slides.

Use the following steps to create a slide show:

Step 1. Select and organize the drawings to be included in the slide show:

Decide which drawings you wish to include in your slide show. Make a storyboard consisting of quick sketches of the drawings in the order in which you want them to appear. Identify each drawing by the name under which you have it stored. You may include as many drawings as you want (for this exercise use a minimum of 10).

Step 2. Use MSLIDE to make slides of each drawing:

Using AutoCAD, bring each drawing to be included in the slide show from the floppy disk to the hard drive, one at a time. Zoom a window around a drawing so that it fills the screen. Inserting drawings into a blank area may be the fastest means of accomplishing this. Insert, make the slide, then Undo to get rid of the drawing.

You may also use the Layer and Linetype Properties dialog box to control the display of different layers to create different drawings and make slides of each drawing. The view of the drawing as displayed on the screen is what your slide will look like.

Make slides of each displayed drawing by using the following procedure:

Prompt	Response
Command:	TYPE: **MSLIDE<enter>**
The Create Slide File dialog box appears:	TYPE: **A:SLIDE1** in the File name: input area (use an empty floppy disk so that all your slides and the script file will fit on it; label each slide with a different consecutive number)
	CLICK: **Save**

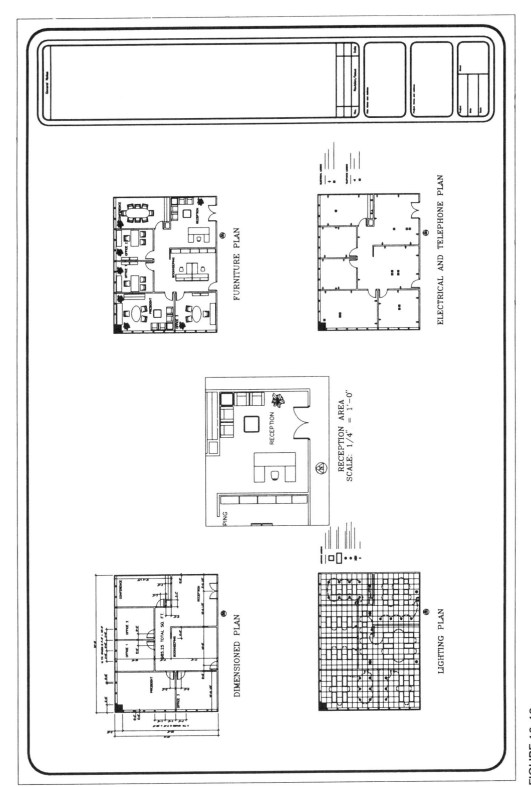

FURNITURE PLAN

ELECTRICAL AND TELEPHONE PLAN

RECEPTION AREA
SCALE: 1/4" = 1'-0"

DIMENSIONED PLAN

LIGHTING PLAN

FIGURE 16–12
Complete Exercise 16–1

Continue this procedure for each drawing until all slides are made. Number each slide with a different consecutive number. Be sure to save the slides on the floppy disk in drive A by including A: as the destination.

Step 3. Use VSLIDE to view any slide that you have created:

When the VSLIDE command is used, the slide recalled replaces the current drawing on the display screen. View any slide that you have created by using the following procedure:

Prompt	Response
Command:	TYPE: **VSLIDE<enter>**
The Select Slide File dialog box appears:	CLICK: **SLIDE1** (on the $3\frac{1}{2}$ Floppy [A:] drive)
	CLICK: **Open** (to view Slide1)

Step 4. Make a script file for your slide show:

AutoCAD provides the Script command, which allows other commands to be read and executed from a script file. The following procedure describes how to use the Edit command to make a script file for 10 slides while you are in the drawing editor. Read through the description first, and if you have more than 10 slides, you will be able to add to the script file.

Prompt	Response
Command:	TYPE: **EDIT<enter>**
File to edit:	TYPE: **A:SLDSHOW.SCR<enter>** (SLDSHOW is the name of your script file—it can be any standard 8 characters—the SCR extension identifies this as a script file to AutoCAD)
The MS-DOS Editor appears:	Type the following exactly as described:
	TYPE: **VSLIDE A:SLIDE1<enter>** (VSLIDE is the VSLIDE command that tells AutoCAD to display a slide; A:SLIDE1 tells AutoCAD where the slide is located and its name)
	TYPE: **VSLIDE *A:SLIDE2<enter>** (tells AutoCAD to load the next file— * means load—A:SLIDE2 is the name of the slide located on a floppy disk in drive A)
	TYPE: **DELAY 2500<enter>** (tells AutoCAD to delay 2500 milliseconds before proceeding to the next line)
	TYPE: **VSLIDE<enter>** (tells AutoCAD to display the slide that was loaded with line 2—Slide 2)
	TYPE: **VSLIDE *A:SLIDE3<enter>**
	TYPE: **DELAY 2500<enter>**
	TYPE: **VSLIDE**
	TYPE: **VSLIDE *A:SLIDE4<enter>**
	TYPE: **DELAY 2500<enter>**
	TYPE: **VSLIDE<enter>**
	TYPE: **VSLIDE *A:SLIDE5<enter>**
	TYPE: **DELAY 2500<enter>**

Note: Leave one space only between the following:
VSLIDE and **A:**
VSLIDE and ***A:**
DELAY and **2500**

Note: Press <enter> only once at the end of each line, otherwise your script file will not work.

Prompt	Response
	TYPE: **VSLIDE\<enter>**
	TYPE: **VSLIDE *A:SLIDE6\<enter>**
	TYPE: **DELAY 2500\<enter>**
	TYPE: **VSLIDE\<enter>**
	TYPE: **VSLIDE *A:SLIDE7\<enter>**
	TYPE: **DELAY 2500\<enter>**
	TYPE: **VSLIDE\<enter>**
	TYPE: **VSLIDE *A:SLIDE8\<enter>**
	TYPE: **DELAY 2500\<enter>**
	TYPE: **VSLIDE\<enter>**
	TYPE: **VSLIDE *A:SLIDE9\<enter>**
	TYPE: **DELAY 2500\<enter>**
	TYPE: **VSLIDE\<enter>**
	TYPE: **VSLIDE *A:SLIDE10\<enter>**
	TYPE: **DELAY 2500\<enter>**
	TYPE: **VSLIDE\<enter>**
	TYPE: **RSCRIPT\<enter>** (tells AutoCAD to rerun the script file)

You must now check each line of your file to be sure it contains no errors:

Check each line of your script file to be sure there are no extra spaces or returns.

Save your script file:

Prompt	Response
	CLICK: **File-Save**
	CLICK: **File-Exit**

You now have a floppy disk containing your script file named Sldshow.Scr and 10 (or more) slides named SLIDE1.sld through SLIDE10.sld.

Step 5. Test your slide show and script file:

Prompt	Response
Command:	TYPE: **SCRIPT\<enter>**
(The Select Script File dialog box appears.)	CLICK: **Sldshow.scr** (on the $3\frac{1}{2}$ Floppy [A:])
	CLICK: **Open**

If all is well, your slide show will run uninterrupted until you decide to stop it. To stop the slide show at any point, press Esc. To start it again, TYPE: **RESUME\<enter>**.

If the file does not run, make sure the script file and your slide files are on the floppy disk and your script file is correct. Also make sure you have typed the script file name correctly. If the delay period is not what you want, you may edit your script file and make the delay longer or shorter as you wish.

To edit your script file:

Prompt	Response
Command:	TYPE: **EDIT\<enter>**
File to edit:	TYPE: **A:SLDSHOW.SCR\<enter>**
The MS-DOS Editor appears with the script file displayed:	**Edit the file as needed.**

EXERCISE 16–3
Create a Presentation

Use the procedures described in Exercise 16–1 to prepare a 36″ × 24″ sheet containing the architectural format and similar plans of one of the other projects you have completed. All viewports should be at a standard scale ($\frac{1''}{8} = 1'\text{-}0''$ or $\frac{1''}{4} = 1'\text{-}0''$). Your final sheet should contain five paper space viewports and should appear similar to Figure 16–12.

EXERCISE 16–4
Create a Presentation

Use the procedures described in Exercise 16–1 to prepare a 36″ × 24″ sheet containing the architectural format and similar plans of still another of the projects you have completed. All viewports should be at a standard scale ($\frac{1''}{8} = 1'\text{-}0''$ or $\frac{1''}{4} = 1'\text{-}0''$). Show two details of different spaces at a scale of $\frac{1''}{4} = 1'\text{-}0''$. Your final sheet should contain six paper space viewports and should appear similar to Figure 16–12.

EXERCISE 16–5
Create a Slide Show

Prepare a slide show containing 20 slides of your work plus a title slide. The title slide should contain the following:

Your Name
Title of the Class
Course and Section Number
Instructor's Name
Date

Make your title slide as fancy or as simple as you like. Make a drawing of the title slide, and then use MSLIDE to create the slide.

REVIEW QUESTIONS

1. Which of the following is a characteristic of paper space?
   a. Viewports are tiled.
   b. Tilemode is set to 1.
   c. Viewports can overlap.
   d. Models are created.
   e. The VPORTS command will work.
2. How many model space viewports can be created on any one drawing?
   a. 2
   b. 4
   c. 16
   d. 64
   e. Unlimited
3. Which of the following letters must you type to save a viewport configuration?
   a. S
   b. R
   c. D
   d. J
   e. N

4. Which of the following VPORTS options allows for both vertical and horizontal arrangements?
   a. Single
   b. J
   c. 3
   d. 4
   e. S
5. A command can be started in one viewport and completed in a different viewport.
   a. True
   b. False
6. Which of the following is a characteristic of a nontiled viewport?
   a. Fills the graphics screen and touches all other viewports
   b. Is fixed and cannot overlap
   c. Can be erased or moved
   d. Only one of these viewports may be plotted at one time.
   e. Only one viewport may be active at one time.
7. Model Space may be active with Tilemode set at either 0 or 1.
   a. True
   b. False
8. Which of the following MVIEW options creates several viewports at the same time?
   a. ON
   b. OFF
   c. Fit
   d. 2,3,4
   e. <First point>
9. Which of the following will produce a model space view within a viewport that is at a scale of $\frac{1}{4}'' = 1'\text{-}0''$ in relation to paper space?
   a. Zoom-1/4XP
   b. Zoom-1/48XP
   c. Zoom-1/4"=1'XP
   d. Zoom-1/4=12XP
   e. Zoom-1/4-12XP
10. Which of the following can be used to align viewports accurately in model space?
    a. MVIEW
    b. VPORTS
    c. Move
    d. MVSETUP
    e. Align
11. Which option of the MVSETUP command is used to obtain an architectural format 24″ × 36″?

    _____

12. List the command and its option that will insert a set of saved model space viewports into paper space.

    _____

13. List the prompts and responses needed to freeze layers A-AREA and A-FURN in one of four paper space viewports (Tilemode is off). The viewport is active.

    Prompt   **Response**
    Command: TYPE: _____
    _____   TYPE: _____
    _____   TYPE: _____

    _____   _____

14. List the command used to switch from model space to paper space when Tilemode is off.

    _____

15. List five characteristics of tiled viewports that are different from nontiled viewports.

_____

_____

_____

_____

_____

16. List the prompts and responses needed to create a slide named SLD1 on a floppy disk in drive A.

Prompt	**Response**
Command:	TYPE: _____
_____	TYPE: _____
_____	CLICK: _____

17. Write the command used to view a slide.

_____

18. Write the command used in this chapter to create a script file.

_____

19. Describe what each line of the following script file does.

VSLIDE A:DRAW1 _____

VSLIDE *A:DRAW2_____

DELAY 1500 _____

VSLIDE _____

20. To run the script file described in this chapter, what files must be contained on the floppy disk in drive A?

_____

_____

17 Customizing Toolbars and Menus

OBJECTIVES

After completing this chapter, you will be able to

- ☐ Make new toolbars.
- ☐ Add tools to a toolbar.
- ☐ Delete tools from a toolbar.
- ☐ Move tools from one toolbar to another toolbar.
- ☐ Copy tools from one toolbar to another toolbar.
- ☐ Delete toolbars.
- ☐ Position toolbars.
- ☐ Display toolbars.
- ☐ Hide toolbars.
- ☐ Create and edit tools.
- ☐ Make a new menu bar.
- ☐ Make a new .mnu (menu) file.
- ☐ Copy the acad.mnu file under another name.
- ☐ Add macros to a menu.
- ☐ Delete commands from a menu.
- ☐ Move commands from one position to another.
- ☐ Copy commands from one menu to another.
- ☐ Delete menus.
- ☐ Position menus on the menu bar.
- ☐ Load menus.
- ☐ Unload menus.

EXERCISE 17–1
Customizing Toolbars

AutoCAD allows you to create custom toolbars that allow you to be more productive by arranging tools so they can be found easily and quickly. When you make a new toolbar it has no tools. You have to drag tools onto the new toolbar from the Customize Toolbars dialog box. In Exercise 17–1 you will start a new toolbar and load it with tools you use frequently. Your final toolbar will look similar to the one shown in Figure 17–1. Turn on the computer and start AutoCAD. The Start Up dialog box is displayed.

1. CLICK: **Use a Wizard**
2. CLICK: **Quick Setup**
   CLICK: **OK**
3. Set drawing Units: **Architectural**
   CLICK: **Done**
4. **Use SaveAs… to save the drawing on the hard drive with the name CH17-EX1.**

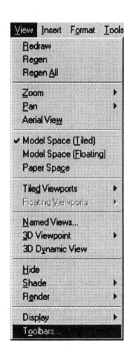

Making a New Toolbar

Make a new toolbar (Figures 17–2 and 17–3):

Prompt	Response
Command:	**Toolbars...** (or CLICK: **any tool with the RETURN button of your pointing device**)
The Toolbars dialog box appears:	CLICK: **New...**
The New Toolbar dialog box (Figure 17–2) appears:	TYPE: (**your initials**)**TOOLS** in the Toolbar Name: text box
	CLICK: **OK**

Your new toolbar (Figure 17–3) is displayed. (If the toolbar is not visible, it is hidden behind other toolbars. Either move the other toolbars or turn them off.)

On Your Own (Figure 17–4)

Move your new toolbar to the left side of the screen (Figure 17–4) so it will be to the left of the Toolbars dialog box. Position your cursor over the toolbar title area, hold down the click button on your mouse, and release the click button when the toolbar is where you want it to be.

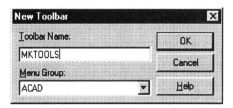

FIGURE 17–2
New Toolbar Dialog Box with Your New Name

FIGURE 17–3
Your New Toolbar

FIGURE 17–1
Your New Toolbar

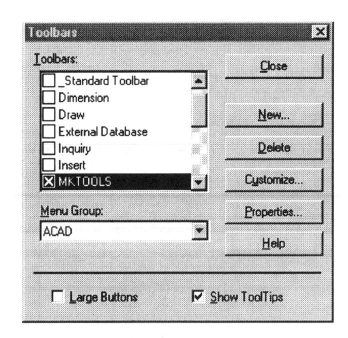

FIGURE 17–4
Move the New Toolbar to the Left Side of the Screen

Adding Tools to Toolbars

Add tools to your new toolbar from the Customize Toolbars dialog box (Figures 17–5, 17–6, 17–7, and 17–8):

Prompt	Response
The Toolbars dialog box:	CLICK: **Customize...**
The Customize Toolbars dialog box (Figure 17–5) appears:	CLICK: **the down arrow** to display the list of categories
	CLICK: **Draw** from the list of categories
The tools on the Draw toolbar appear:	**Copy the Line tool from the Draw category to your toolbar by moving the cursor so it is over the Line tool, then press the click button and hold it down while you drag the Line tool and release it inside your new toolbar.**
Your new toolbar now contains the Line tool:	**Copy the Polyline, Donut, and Dtext icons to your toolbar as shown in Figure 17–6.** (You will have to click the scroll bar to find the Dtext icon.)
	CLICK: **the down arrow in the Categories: list box**
	CLICK: **the Modify category** (Figure 17–7)

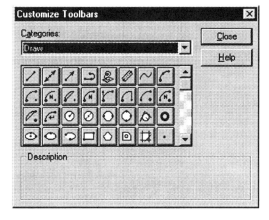

FIGURE 17–5
Customize Toolbars Dialog Box with Draw Category

FIGURE 17–6
New Toolbar with Line, Polyline, Donut, and Dtext Tools

FIGURE 17–7
Select Tools from the Modify Category

 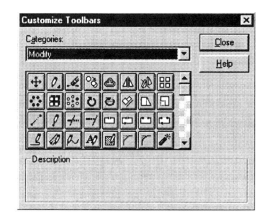

FIGURE 17-8
Select Tools from the Dimensioning Category

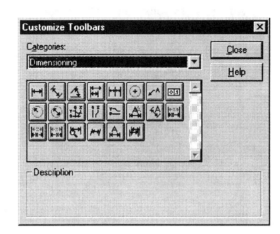

Prompt	Response
	Copy the Move, Copy, Mirror, Offset, Chamfer, and Fillet tools to your toolbar as shown in Figure 17-7
	CLICK: the down arrow in the Categories: list box
	CLICK: the Dimensioning category (Figure 17-8)
	Copy the Linear and Radius tools to your toolbar as shown in Figure 17-8.
	CLICK: **Close**
The Toolbars dialog box appears:	CLICK: **Close**

Deleting Tools from Toolbars

Delete the dimensioning tools from your new toolbar (Figure 17-9):

Prompt	Response
Command:	Toolbars... (or CLICK: any tool with the RETURN button of your mouse)
The Toolbars dialog box appears:	CLICK: **Customize...**
The Customize Toolbars dialog box (Figure 17-9) appears:	CLICK: the Linear Dimensioning tool on your toolbar by moving the cursor over the Linear Dimensioning tool and holding down the click button. Continue holding down the click button and drop the tool into the Customize Toolbars dialog box.
	Delete the Radius Dimensioning tool in a similar manner.
	CLICK: **Close**
The Toolbars dialog box appears:	CLICK: **Close**

FIGURE 17–9
Customize Toolbars Dialog Box

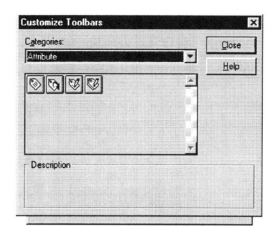

If you accidentally delete a standard tool from a toolbar, you can replace it from the Customize Toolbars dialog box. If you delete a tool you have customized, you cannot retrieve it.

Displaying Toolbars

You can display all toolbars (and eliminate your drawing area) or only the ones you use often.

Display all toolbars:

Prompt	Response
Command:	TYPE:**-TOOLBAR<enter>** (Be sure to include the hyphen.)
Toolbar name (or ALL):	TYPE: **ALL<enter>**
Show/Hide:	TYPE: **S<enter>**

On Your Own

Hide all toolbars. Follow the same procedure but substitute **H<enter>** for **S<enter>.**

Display your new toolbar and the Inquiry toolbar (Figure 17–10):

Prompt	Response
Command:	**Toolbars...**
The Toolbars dialog box appears:	**Check the Inquiry and (your initials)-TOOLS toolbars to display them as shown in Figure 17–10.**
	CLICK: **Close**

FIGURE 17–10
Display the Inquiry and (your initials)TOOLS Toolbars

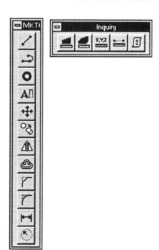

FIGURE 17–11
Copying and Moving Tools

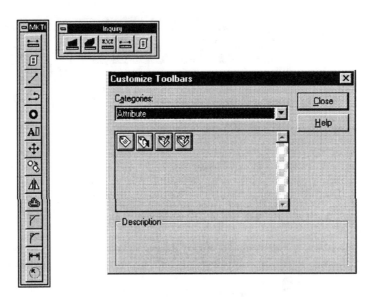

Moving Tools from One Toolbar to Another

Move the Distance icon from the Inquiry toolbar to your new toolbar (Figure 17–11):

Prompt	Response
Command:	**Toolbars...** (or CLICK: **any tool with the RETURN button of your mouse**)
The Toolbars dialog box appears:	CLICK: **Customize...**
The Customize Toolbars dialog box appears:	**Hold down the click button over the Distance icon on the Inquiry toolbar and drop it onto your new toolbar (Figure 17–11).**

When the Customize Toolbars dialog box is displayed, you can move or copy a tool from one toolbar to another.

Copying Tools from One Toolbar to Another

Copy the Distance icon from your new toolbar back to the Inquiry toolbar (Figure 17–11):

Prompt	Response
With the Customize Toolbars dialog box still displayed:	**Press and hold the Ctrl key while you hold down the click button over the Distance icon on your new menu and drop it onto the Inquiry toolbar (Figure 17–11).**

On Your Own

1. Copy (not move) the List icon from the Inquiry toolbar to your new toolbar.
2. Close the Toolbars dialog box.

Making New Toolbars and Letting AutoCAD Name Them

You can also make new toolbars by choosing Customize in the Toolbars dialog box and dragging an icon off the dialog box and dropping it anywhere but onto another toolbar.

Make two new toolbars and let AutoCAD name them for you (Figure 17–12):

FIGURE 17-12
Creating Two New Toolbars, Toolbar1 and Toolbar2

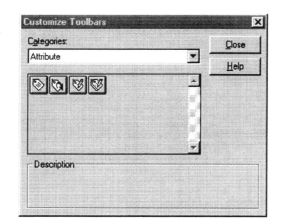

Prompt	Response
Command:	**Toolbars...** (or CLICK: **any tool with the RETURN button of your mouse**)
The Toolbars dialog box appears:	CLICK: **Customize...**
The Customize Toolbars dialog box appears with Attribute in the Categories: box	**Hold down the click button over any of the icons on the Attribute toolbar (any toolbar category will do) and drop it onto an open area off the Customize Toolbars dialog box (Figure 17–12).**
	Repeat the preceding procedure so you have the two toolbars as shown in Figure 17–12.
	CLICK: **Close**

You could now proceed to load tools onto these toolbars as described previously.

Deleting Toolbars

You may delete toolbars from the Toolbars dialog box. AutoCAD will ask you if you really want to delete the toolbar because you cannot undo this action. If you delete one of the major toolbars such as the Draw toolbar, you can recreate it by making a new toolbar, naming it the Draw toolbar and dragging tools onto it from the Draw Category after clicking Customize on the Toolbars dialog box. You can also reload the acad.mnu file from Preferences on the Tools menu on the menu bar. To reload the acad.mnu DOUBLE CLICK: **Menu, Help,** then **Browse...,** then DOUBLE CLICK: **Menu File,** then DOUBLE CLICK: **C:\program files\autocadr14\support\acad.mnu file,** then CLICK: the **acad.mnu** file, then CLICK: **OK**. When the warning appears, CLICK: **Yes**. You will replace any customizing you have done with the standard ACAD menu.

Delete the two new toolbars that AutoCAD named for you:

Prompt	Response
With the Toolbars dialog box displayed:	**Use the scroll bars in the Toolbars: list box to locate Toolbar1, and use the click button to highlight it.**
	CLICK: **Delete**
The AutoCAD warning appears —Delete toolbar ACAD.Toolbar1?	CLICK: **Yes**
	Delete Toolbar2 in a similar manner.
	CLICK: **Close**

Changing the Shape of a Floating Toolbar

You can change the shape, name, and appearance of a floating toolbar, move it, dock it, float a docked toolbar, reposition tools on a toolbar, and add space between tools.

Let's start with a relatively uncluttered screen.

Hide all toolbars:

Prompt	Response
Command:	TYPE: **-TOOLBAR<enter>**
Toolbar name (or ALL):	TYPE: **ALL<enter>**
Show/Hide:	TYPE: **H<enter>**

Display the (your initials)TOOLS Toolbar:

Prompt	Response
Command:	**Toolbars . . .**
The Toolbars dialog box appears:	**Check the (your initials)TOOLS check box**
	CLICK: **Close**

The floating (your initials)TOOLS toolbar appears:

A floating toolbar can be reshaped from vertical to horizontal or somewhere in between. The horizontal toolbar can also be reshaped to vertical. Docked toolbars cannot be reshaped.

Change the shape of the floating (your initials)TOOLS toolbar:

If your toolbar is horizontal:

Note: You can also CLICK: the top border, hold down the click button, and move your mouse down.

Prompt	Response
Command:	**Click the bottom border so that the cursor changes to a double arrow and hold down the click button while you move your mouse up.** (You will have to move it over halfway before a change occurs.)

If your toolbar is vertical:

Prompt	Response
	Click a side border so that the cursor changes to a double arrow and hold down the click button while you move your mouse to the left or right

Renaming a Toolbar

There will be a time when you will need to change the name of a toolbar. This is how to do it.

Rename the (your initials)TOOLS toolbar (Figure 17–13):

Prompt	Response
Command:	**Toolbars...**
The Toolbars dialog box appears:	**Locate (your initials)TOOLS in the Toolbars list box and highlight it as shown in Figure 17–13.**
	CLICK: **Properties...**

Prompt	Response
The Toolbar Properties dialog box appears with the word (your initials)TOOLS highlighted:	TYPE: **MY TOOLBAR** CLICK: **Apply** CLICK: **the - in the extreme upper left corner to close.**
The Toolbars dialog box appears:	CLICK: **Close**

The (your initials)TOOLS toolbar is now renamed MY TOOLBAR.

On Your Own

Rename the MY TOOLBAR to the (your initials)TOOLS toolbar.

Changing the Appearance of the Toolbar

The Toolbars dialog box allows you to change the size of the tools on the toolbar, whether toolbars are displayed in color or black and white, or whether tooltips (the text that appears when you hold the cursor over the tool) are displayed.

Change the appearance to large buttons (Figure 17–14):

Prompt	Response
Command:	**Toolbars...**
The Toolbars dialog box appears:	**Check Large Buttons as shown in Figure 17–14.** CLICK: **Close**

The (your initials)TOOLS toolbar now has large tools.

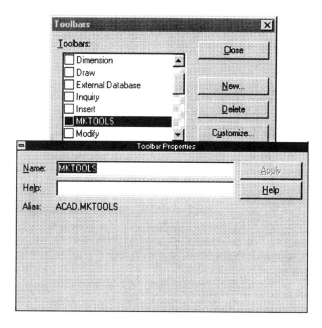

FIGURE 17–13
Selecting the (your initials)TOOLS Toolbar and Renaming It

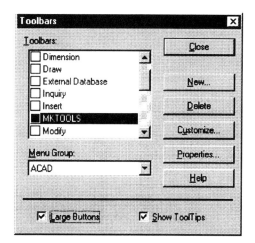

FIGURE 17–14
Check Large Buttons

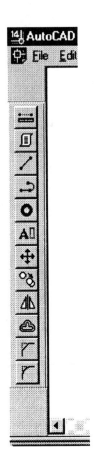

FIGURE 17-15
A Docked Toolbar

FIGURE 17-16
(your initials)TOOLS Toolbar with
List Tool Position Changed

Moving Toolbars

You can move toolbars by clicking the toolbar name area and holding down the click button while dragging the toolbar. You can also move toolbars by clicking the area between the outside border of the toolbar and the squares surrounding the tools, holding down the click button, and moving the toolbar where you want it.

Move the (your initials)TOOLS toolbar:

Prompt	Response
Command:	**Click the area between the outside border of the (your initials)TOOLS toolbar and the squares surrounding the tools, hold down the click button, and move the toolbar to another area**

Docking a Toolbar

It is sometimes helpful to get the toolbars out of the drawing area. They can be placed on the outside edges of the screen in what is known as a *docked position*, as shown in Figure 17–15.

On Your Own (Figure 17–15)

1. Change the icons back to small buttons.
2. Dock the (your initials)TOOLS toolbar on the left side of the screen by moving it as you did previously, except move it to the extreme left side so it appears as shown in Figure 17–15.

Floating a Docked Toolbar

Toolbars can be removed from their docked position by clicking the area between the tool squares and the toolbar border, holding down the click button, and moving the toolbar.

On Your Own

Float the (your initials)TOOLS toolbar.

Repositioning the Tools on a Toolbar

You can change the position of tools on a toolbar from the Customize Toolbars dialog box. When you click the tool and move it, you must drag the tool more than halfway across the tool that already exists in the new location.

Reposition a tool on the (your initials)TOOLS toolbar (Figure 17–16):

Prompt	Response
Command:	**Toolbars...**
The Toolbars dialog box appears:	CLICK: **Customize...**
	Position your cursor over the List tool, hold down the click button, and move the List tool so it is a little more than halfway past the Distance tool.

The (your initials)TOOLS toolbar appears as shown in Figure 17–16.

Adding Space between Tools on a Toolbar

If you prefer to have a little space between tools on the toolbar, you can change the spacing from the Toolbars dialog box.

Add space between tools on the (your initials)TOOLS toolbar (Figure 17–17):

FIGURE 17–17
Adding Space between Tool Icons

Prompt	Response
The Customize Toolbars dialog box	**Position your cursor over the List tool, hold down the click button, and move the List tool to the right or left or down but not more than half the distance of the next tool.**
	Repeat the preceding steps for all tools on the (your initials)TOOLS toolbar so it appears as shown in Figure 17–17, then return them to their original position.
	Close the Toolbars dialog box.

Basic Keystrokes Used to Modify Tool Macros

You can create your own tools by modifying or combining the tools that are supplied with AutoCAD.

AutoCAD recognizes commands in a macro (a command line) as if they were typed from the keyboard. The following keystrokes represent pressing the Enter key, an operator response, canceling a command, a transparent command, and international versions:

;	The semicolon is the same as pressing Enter.
\	The backslash tells AutoCAD to wait for the operator to do something.
^C^C	Two Ctrl-Cs cancel a previous command and any option of that command.
'	An apostrophe preceding the command allows it to be used transparently.
_	An underscore enables commands to work on international versions of AutoCAD.

The best way to understand how these work is to create a tool using some of these keystrokes.

Creating Tools

Create a tool (Figures 17–18 and 17–19):

Prompt	Response
Command:	**Place your cursor over the Donut tool on the (your initials)TOOLS toolbar and press the RETURN button on your mouse.**
The Toolbars dialog box appears:	**Place your cursor over the Donut tool on the (your initials)TOOLS toolbar and press the RETURN button on your mouse again.**
The Button Properties dialog box (Figure 17–18) appears:	**Change the information in the Name: box, the Help box, and the Macro: box as shown in Figure 17–19.** (The line in the Macro: box should read: ^C^C_donut;0;.125;\)

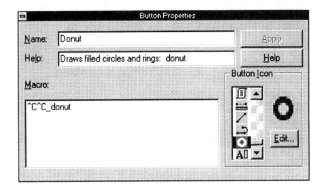

FIGURE 17–18
Button Properties Dialog Box

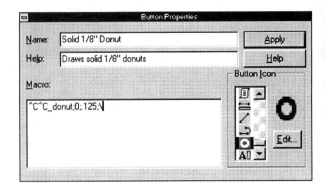

FIGURE 17–19
Button Properties Dialog Box for Solid ⅛″ Donut

Let's look at the elements of this line:

^C^C_donut   This is already here and it means that you are canceling previous commands (^C^C), making the command available to international versions (_), and activating the donut command (donut).

;   This acts as <enter>, as if you had typed DONUT and then pressed <enter>.

The donut command then asks you for an inside diameter.

0;   This tells AutoCAD you want an inside diameter of 0, as if you had typed 0 and pressed <enter>.

The donut command then asks you for an outside diameter.

.125;   This tells AutoCAD you want an outside diameter of .125, as if you had typed .125 and pressed <enter>.

The donut command then asks you to pick (or type coordinates for) the Center of the donut.

****   The backslash tells AutoCAD you will pick the center or type coordinates—an operator response.

Changing or Making Tool Icons

When you create a new command, AutoCAD allows you to change an existing icon or create an entirely new one with the Button Editor. When you open the Button Editor (Figure 17–20), you have an abbreviated paint program available to you. The four tools at the top of the editor from left to right are:

FIGURE 17–20
Button Editor

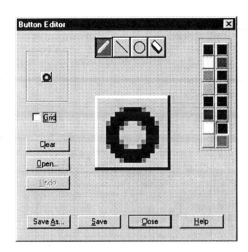

Pencil tool	Changes one pixel at a time.
Line tool	Draws lines in a selected color.
Circle tool	Draws circles in a selected color. Hold down the click button on your mouse to select the center of the circle; continue to hold the click button as you drag the circle to the desired radius.
Erase tool	Erases pixels as you move the cursor with the click button depressed over the area you want to erase.

The color bar to the right allows you to select from 16 colors by selecting one with the click button.

The **Grid** button gives you a grid.
The **Clear** button clears the image.
The **Open** button opens images you have saved previously.
The **Undo** button undoes the previous single action.

SaveAs... , Save, Close, and Help perform the standard functions for the tool icons.

Change the new tool icon to a solid circle (Figures 17–21 and 17–22):

Prompt	Response
With the Button Properties dialog box displayed:	CLICK: **Edit... in the Button Icon area**
The Button Editor dialog box appears:	**Click the same color in the color bar as the donut image if it is not already selected.**
	Use the Pencil tool to color all pixels of the inside of the donut as shown in Figure 17–21. (Hold down the click button with the Pencil tool selected and move it across the area.)

You could now save this icon to a file but you do not need to at this time.

Prompt	Response
Button Editor dialog box appears:	CLICK: **Close**
Would you like to save the changes made to your button?	CLICK: **Yes**
The Button Properties dialog box appears:	CLICK: **Apply**
	CLICK: **the - in the extreme upper left corner of the Button Properties to close**

FIGURE 17–21
Color the Inside of the Donut Icon

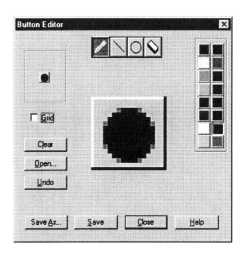

FIGURE 17–22
(your initials)TOOLS Toolbar with
Solid Donut Tool

FIGURE 17–23
(your initials)TOOLS Toolbar with
the Donut Tool Added

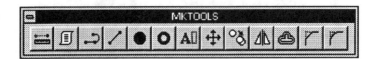

Your (your initials)TOOLS toolbar should now look like Figure 17–22. When you hold the cursor over the new tool, its tooltip now reads Solid $\frac{1}{8}''$ Donut.

On Your Own (Figure 17–23)

1. Add the original donut command to the (your initials)TOOLS toolbar (from the Draw Category) so it appears as shown in Figure 17–23.
2. Close the Customize Toolbars and the Toolbars dialog boxes.

Creating a Flyout

Making a flyout requires that you make a toolbar containing all the tools you want on that flyout before you make the flyout itself. The flyout can then be placed on any toolbar you choose.

Make a toolbar for the flyout (Figures 17–24 and 17–25):

Prompt	Response
Command:	**Toolbars...** (or CLICK: **any tool with the RETURN button of your mouse**)
The Toolbars dialog box appears:	CLICK: **New...**
The New Toolbar dialog box appears:	TYPE: **Tiedots** in the Toolbar Name: box
	CLICK: **OK**
The Toolbars dialog box appears:	CLICK: **Customize...**
The Customize Toolbars dialog box appears:	**Move the Tiedots toolbar into an open area as shown in Figure 17–24.**
	Copy the Solid $\frac{1}{8}''$ Donut from the (your initials)TOOLS toolbar onto the Tiedots toolbar.
	Copy the Solid $\frac{1}{8}''$ Donut from the (your initials)TOOLS toolbar onto the Tiedots toolbar again so you have two Solid $\frac{1}{8}''$ Donut tools on the Tiedots toolbar.

FIGURE 17–24
The Tiedots Toolbar

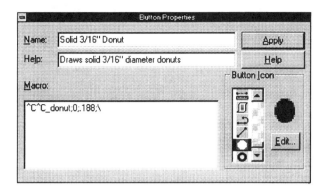

FIGURE 17–25
Button Properties Dialog Box for Solid $\frac{3}{16}''$ Donut

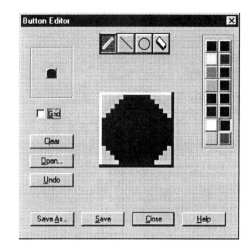

FIGURE 17–26
Enlarged Tool Icon

Prompt	Response
	Hold the cursor over one of the Solid $\frac{1}{8}''$ Donut tools and press the RETURN button on your mouse.
The Button Properties dialog box (Figure 17–25) appears:	Change the Name: to Solid $\frac{3}{16}''$ Donut, Help: to Draws solid $\frac{3}{16}''$ diameter donuts, Macro: to ^C^C_donut;0; .188;\ as shown in Figure 17–25.
	CLICK: **Edit...** in the Button Icon area
	Enlarge the icon using the Circle and Pencil tools as shown in Figure 17–26.
	CLICK: **Close**
Would you like to save the changes made to your button?	CLICK: **Yes**
The Button Properties dialog box appears:	CLICK: **Apply**
	Close the Button Properties dialog box.
The Customize Toolbars dialog box appears:	

Create a flyout (Figures 17–27 and 17–28):

Prompt	Response
With the Customize Toolbars dialog box displayed:	CLICK: **Custom** in the Categories: list box
The display shown in Figure 17–27 appears:	Click the square with the small triangle in the lower right, hold down the click button, and drop the flyout in an open area.
A new toolbar with the flyout is created:	Hold your cursor over the blank flyout on the new toolbar and press the RETURN button on your mouse.
The Flyout Properties dialog box (Figure 17–28) appears:	TYPE: **Dots** in the Name: box, **Draws $\frac{1}{8}''$ and $\frac{3}{16}''$ tiedots** in the Help: box

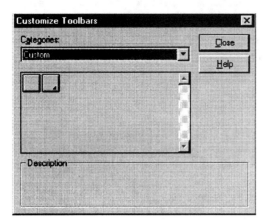

FIGURE 17–27
The Custom Category

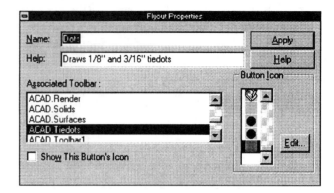

FIGURE 17–28
Flyout Properties Dialog Box

Prompt	Response
	CLICK: **ACAD.Tiedots** in the Associated Toolbar: list box
	CLICK: **Apply**
	CLICK: **-** in the upper left corner to close the Flyout Properties box
The Customize Toolbars dialog box appears:	CLICK: **Close**
The Toolbars dialog box appears:	CLICK: **Close**

On Your Own (Figures 17–29 and 17–30)

1. Test your flyout by selecting both solid donuts and drawing donuts with them as shown in Figure 17–29.

2. Move the toolbar containing your flyout to an area near the (your initials)TOOLS toolbar.

3. Select Customize... from the toolbars dialog box and move your flyout onto the (your initials)TOOLS toolbar as shown in Figure 17–30.

4. Delete Toolbar1. Do not delete the Tiedots toolbar or your flyout will not work because there is no toolbar associated with it.

Save

When you have completed Exercise 17–1, save your work.

FIGURE 17–29
Testing the Flyout

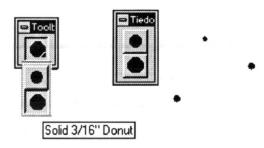

FIGURE 17–30
The Final Toolbar with Tiedots Flyout

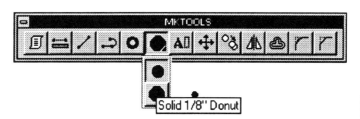

EXERCISE 17–2
Customizing Menus

The structure of the AutoCAD menu makes it easy to customize by rearranging commands on the menus, adding new commands, rearranging the menus, and creating keyboard aliases. Sometimes having fewer menus on the menu bar is better than having the full menu. If you occasionally need a command that is no longer on the menu bar, you can type it from the keyboard or access it from a toolbar. Exercise 17–2 will assume that you need a menu bar that has only the File, Edit, View, Insert, Format, Tools, Draw, and Modify menus. Your final menu will look similar to the one shown in Figure 17–31. Turn on the computer and start AutoCAD. The Start Up dialog box is displayed.

Removing and Replacing Menus from the Menu Bar

1. CLICK: **Use a Wizard**
2. CLICK: **Quick Setup**
   CLICK: **OK**
3. Set Drawing Units: **Architectural**
   CLICK: **Done**
4. **Use SaveAs... to save the drawing on the hard drive with the name CH17-2.**

Remove the File and Edit menus from the menu bar (Figure 17–32):

Prompt	Response
Command:	**Customize Menus...**
The Menu Customization dialog box appears:	CLICK: **Menu Bar tab**
The Menu Bar page appears:	CLICK: **File** in the Menu Bar: list as shown in Figure 17–32
	CLICK: << **Remove**
File is removed from the Menu Bar list:	CLICK: **Edit** in the Menu Bar: list
	CLICK: << **Remove**

Edit is removed from the Menu bar list.

Replace the File and Edit Menus on the menu bar (Figure 17–33):

Prompt	Response
Menu Customization dialog box:	With **View** highlighted on the Menu Bar: list, CLICK: **File** in the Menus: list as shown in Figure 17–33.

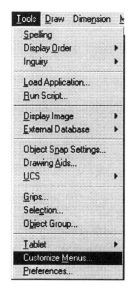

FIGURE 17–31
Shortened Menu Bar

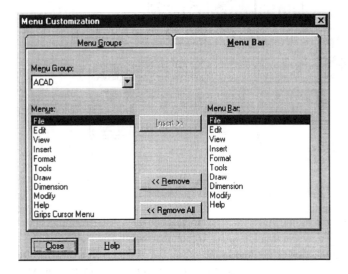

FIGURE 17–32
CLICK: File in the Menu Bar: List to Remove

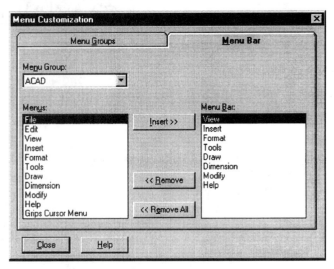

FIGURE 17–33
CLICK: File in the Menus: List to Insert

FIGURE 17–34
Your New Menu Bar

Prompt	Response
	CLICK: **Insert>>**
File appears in the menu bar list:	With **View** highlighted on the Menu Bar: list, CLICK: **Edit** in the Menus: list
	CLICK: **Insert>>**
Edit appears in the menu bar list.	

On Your Own

1. Remove the Dimension and Help menus from the menu bar.

2. Your menu bar appears as shown in Figure 17–34.

Exercise 17–2 is now complete. Continue with Exercise 17–3.

EXERCISE 17–3
Making a New Menu File

Returning the Complete Menu Bar

On Your Own (Figure 17–35)

1. Exercise 17–3 requires that the complete menu bar be present, so begin by returning all menus to their original location as shown in Figure 17–35 using Customize Menus... . You will have to remove and insert some menus twice to get the correct location.

2. Close the Menu Customization dialog box.

In Exercise 17–3 you will make a new menu file that contains new macros that you add to menus on the menu bar. Commands in the new menu file are also rearranged, deleted, and copied. To do that you must begin by copying the standard AutoCAD menu file under another name.

FIGURE 17–35
Original Menu Bar: Arrangement

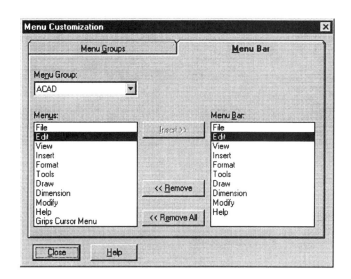

Locating the File Containing the Standard AutoCAD Menu (acad.mnu)

Find out where the acad.mnu file is located so you can copy it to a floppy disk under the name menu1.mnu (Figure 17–36):

Prompt	Response
Command:	**Preferences...**
The Preferences dialog box appears:	CLICK: **Files tab**
The Files tab appears as shown in Figure 17–36:	DOUBLE CLICK: **Menu, Help, Log, and Miscellaneous File Names**
	DOUBLE CLICK: **Menu File**
	Make a note of the drive, directory, and subdirectory where the Menu File is located. In this case: C:\program files\autocad r14\ support\acad
	CLICK: **OK**

FIGURE 17–36
Locating the Menu File

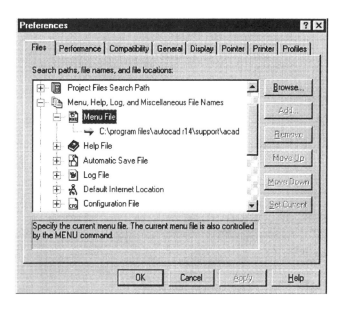

FIGURE 17–37
Start Windows Explorer

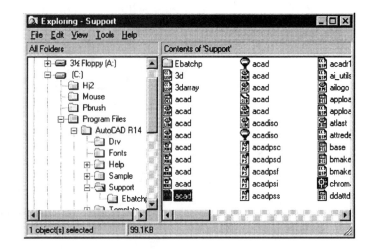

FIGURE 17–38
CLICK: the acad.mnu File

Copying the acad.mnu File to an Empty Floppy Disk in the A or B Drive

Copy the acad.mnu file to a floppy disk (Figures 17–37, 17–38 and 17–39):

Prompt	Response
	Place an empty floppy disk in the A drive.
Command:	CLICK: **Start**
	CLICK: **Programs**
	CLICK: **Windows Explorer** (Figure 17–37)
The Exploring dialog box appears:	CLICK: **Program Files folder**
The contents of the Program Files folder are displayed:	DOUBLE CLICK: **AutoCAD R14 folder**
The contents of the AutoCAD R14 folder are displayed:	DOUBLE CLICK: **Support folder**
The Support files are displayed:	CLICK: **the acad.mnu file** (Figure 17–38)
	CLICK: **File- Send To 3½ Floppy [A:]** or to whichever drive contains your floppy disk (Figure 17–39)
The copying From "SUPPORT to A:" message appears.	

Renaming the acad.mnu File

Rename the acad.mnu file on the floppy disk to Menu1.mnu (Figures 17–40 and 17–41):

Prompt	Response
	CLICK: **the vertical scroll bar in the All Folders box and scroll up to the floppy drive containing the copied acad.mnu file**
	CLICK: **the floppy drive**

FIGURE 17–39
Send the File to a Floppy Disk

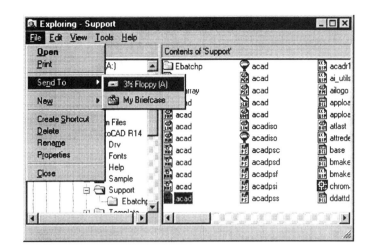

FIGURE 17–40
Rename the acad.mnu File
Menu1.mnu

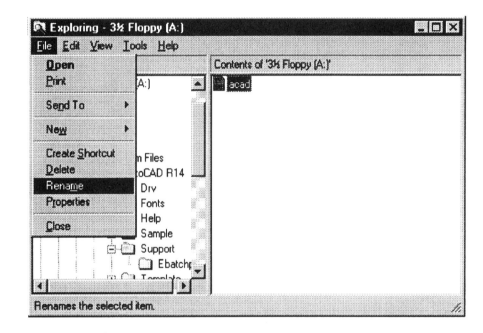

FIGURE 17–41
TYPE: Menu1 to Rename the
acad.mnu File

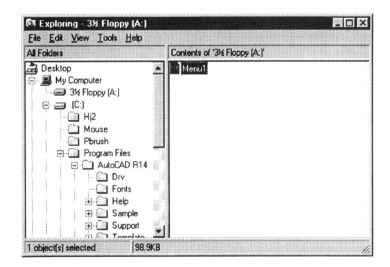

FIGURE 17–42
Open the Menu1.mnu File

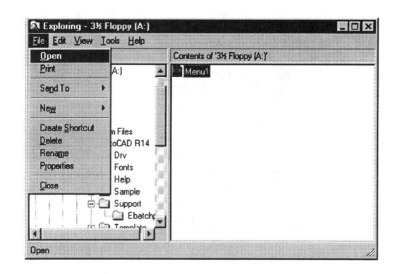

Prompt	Response
The Contents of the Floppy drive are displayed in the right panel:	CLICK: **the acad.mnu file** CLICK: **File-Rename** (Figure 17–40)
The acad.mnu file is highlighted:	TYPE: **Menu1.mnu** (Figure 17–41)

Opening the Menu1.mnu File So You Can Modify the Menu

Open the Menu1.mnu file on the floppy disk (Figure 17–42):

Prompt	Response
	CLICK: **File-Open** (Figure 17–42)
The Menu1.mnu file is displayed:	**Maximize the display.**

Relabeling the MENUGROUP

Relabel the MENUGROUP so AutoCAD will recognize this as a menu different from the original (Figure 17–43):

FIGURE 17–43
Change ***MENUGROUP =
ACAD to ***MENUGROUP =
MENU1

```
Menu1 - Notepad
File  Edit  Search  Help
//       (Rights in Technical Data and Computer Software), as applicable.
//
//
//       NOTE:  AutoCAD looks for an ".mnl" (Menu Lisp) file whose name is
//              the same as that of the menu file, and loads it if
//              found.  If you modify this menu and change its name, you
//              should copy acad.mnl to <yourname>.mnl, since the menu
//              relies on AutoLISP routines found there.
//


//
//       Default AutoCAD NAMESPACE declaration:
//
***MENUGROUP=MENU1


//
//    Begin AutoCAD Digitizer Button Menus
//
***BUTTONS1
// Simple + button
// if a grip is hot bring up the Grips Cursor Menu (POP 17), else send a car
$M=$(if,$(eq,$(substr,$(getvar,cmdnames),1,5),GRIP_),$P0=ACAD.GRIPS $P0=*);
$P0=SNAP $p0=*
^c^c
^B
^0
```

Prompt	Response
The Menu1.mnu file is displayed:	**Scroll down to the label ***MENUGROUP = ACAD and change ACAD to MENU1** (Figure 17–43).

On Your Own

1. Scroll down through the menu through the AutoCAD Button Menus (PRESS: the down arrow) so you become familiar with what the menu looks like.

2. Locate the line "Begin AutoCAD Pull-down Menus."

Deleting Commands from a Menu on the Menu Bar

You will now find the menus on the menu bar labeled ***POP1 through ***POP10. Begin modifying this menu by deleting some commands on ***POP7 that are not used a great deal.

Locate the ***POP7 pull-down menu:

Prompt	Response
	CLICK: **Find...**
The Find dialog box appears:	TYPE: ***POP7 in the Find what: text box
	CLICK: **Find Next**
	Close the Find dialog box by clicking the X in the upper right corner.

Delete the following commands from the ***POP7 menu:

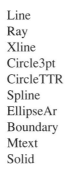

Line
Ray
Xline
Circle3pt
CircleTTR
Spline
EllipseAr
Boundary
Mtext
Solid

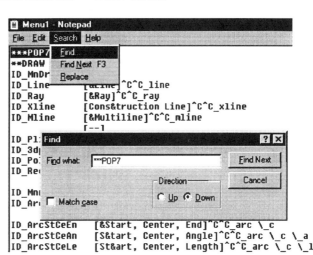

To delete a line of text, move your cursor to one end of the line, hold down the click button on your mouse, drag the cursor across the line to highlight the text, and press the Delete key. PRESS: **Backspace** to delete the space between lines.

If you make a mistake, CLICK: Undo from the Edit menu.

Adding Macros to a Menu on the Menu Bar

Adding macros to a menu requires that you know what the command is going to ask, and what response is required. For example, the Insert command when typed from the keyboard asks:

Block name (or ?) <default>:	Your response is to type the block name and press <enter>.
Insertion point:	Your response is to click a point with your mouse or type X and Y coordinates and press <enter>. The symbol in a macro that requires an operator response is the backslash (\).
X scale factor <1>/Corner/XYZ:	If you want the X scale factor to be 1, the correct response is to press <enter>. The symbol in a macro that represents <enter> is the semicolon (;).
Y scale factor (default = X):	If you want the Y scale factor to be the same as the X scale factor, the correct response is to press <enter>. The symbol in a macro that represents <enter> is the semicolon (;).
Rotation angle <0>:	If you want the rotation angle to be the same as the original block orientation, the correct response is to press <enter>. If you want to change the rotation angle often, leave this semicolon off the end of the macro.

In this exercise you will add four macros to the Draw pull-down menu. The first macro when clicked will execute the Insert command, insert a drawing named BLOCK1 (which you will have to make and save on a floppy disk in the A drive), insert it at an X scale factor of 1, Y scale factor of X, and it will ask you for a rotation angle. The other three macros will do the same thing for BLOCK2, BLOCK3, and BLOCK4.

Now add the macros to ***POP7 on the menu bar.

Type the four lines at the top of the ***POP7 menu as shown in Figure 17–44:

Give careful attention to the arrangement of the text and the exact position of each character. If you make even the slightest change, it will most likely be reflected in your menu.

FIGURE 17–44
Four Macros at the Top of
***POP7

```
ID_TabletCal    [&Ca&librate]^C^C_tablet _cal
ID_TabletCfg    [<-Co&nfigure]^C^C_tablet _cfg
ID_Menuload     [Customize &Menus...]^C^C_menuload
ID_Preferenc    [&Preferences...]^C^C_preferences

***POP7
**DRAW
ID_MnDraw       [&Draw]
ID_BLOCK1       [BLOCK1]^C^C_INSERT;A:BLOCK1;\;;
ID_BLOCK2       [BLOCK2]^C^C_INSERT;A:BLOCK2;\;;
ID_BLOCK3       [BLOCK3]^C^C_INSERT;A:BLOCK3;\;;
ID_BLOCK4       [BLOCK4]^C^C_INSERT;A:BLOCK4;\;;
ID_Mline        [&Multiline]^C^C_mline
                [--]
ID_Pline        [&Polyline]^C^C_pline
ID_3dpoly       [&3D Polyline]^C^C_3dpoly
ID_Polygon      [Pol&ygon]^C^C_polygon
ID_Rectang      [Rectan&gle]^C^C_rectang
                [--]
ID_MnArc        [->&Arc]
ID_Arc3point     [3 &Points]^C^C_arc
                 [--]
;
ID_MnCircle     [->&Circle]
ID_CircleRad     [Center, &Radius]^C^C_circle
ID_CircleDia     [Center, &Diameter]^C^C_circle \_d
```

Moving Commands from One Position to Another

Commands are easily moved from one position to another. Now that you have deleted several commands the arrangement of the commands on the Draw menu does not follow any particular pattern. Move the commands so that they are in alphabetical order. Begin by moving the Arc commands to the top of the menu.

Move the Arc commands to the top of the menu (Figures 17–45 and 17–46):

Prompt	Response
Command:	**Position your cursor at the beginning of the Arc commands, hold down the click button, and drag the cursor so that the lines are highlighted as shown in Figure 17–45.**

FIGURE 17–45

Highlight the Arc Commands and Cut Them to the Windows Clipboard

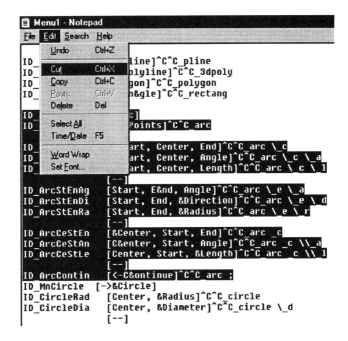

FIGURE 17–46

Arc Commands Are Moved

Prompt	Response
	CLICK: **Cut**
	Position your cursor to the left of ID_BLOCK1.
	CLICK: **Paste**

The menu appears as shown in Figure 17–46.

Copying Commands from One Menu to Another

You may decide that you would like to have other commands from other menus on the Draw menu. You can copy them from other menus using the Copy command found on the Edit menu of Notepad, then use Paste to place the copy in the correct locations.

Saving Menu1.mnu and Returning to AutoCAD

On Your Own

1. Save your Menu1.mnu file to your floppy disk using the Save command from the Notepad File menu.

2. Exit Notepad and Explorer.

3. Activate AutoCAD.

4. Make four drawings of items you often use and WBLOCK or save them on the floppy disk in the A drive with the names BLOCK1, BLOCK2, BLOCK3, and BLOCK4.

Loading a Menu

Menus are loaded with the MENULOAD command. You can TYPE: **MENULOAD <enter>** from the keyboard, or CLICK: **Customize Menus...** from Tools on the AutoCAD menu bar. When the menu is loaded, it then displays the commands in the new menu arrangement. You must also CLICK: the menu file from Preferences on the Tools menu on the menu bar. To provide a shortcut for loading the menu go directly to Preferences.

Load Menu1.mnu from the floppy disk in the A drive (Figures 17–47, 17–48, and 17–49):

Prompt	Response
Command:	**Preferences...**
The Preferences dialog box with the Files tab is displayed:	DOUBLE CLICK: **Menu, etc.**

FIGURE 17–47
Select the Menu1.mnu File on the Floppy Disk

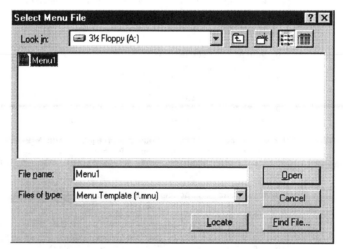

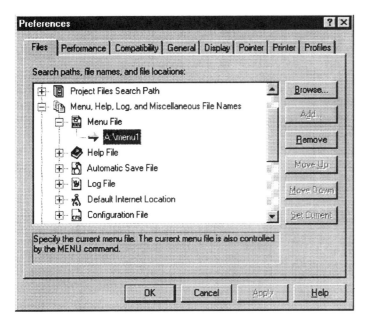

FIGURE 17–48
Preferences Dialog Box with A:\menu1 As the Menu File

FIGURE 17–49
***POP7 on the Menu1 Menu

Prompt	Response
	DOUBLE CLICK: **Menu File**
	Highlight: **the location of the Menu File**
	CLICK: **Browse**
	CLICK: **3½ Floppy [A:] or whichever drive contains your floppy disk with the Menu1.mnu file on it.**
	CLICK: **Menu Template (*.mnu) in the Files of type: box**
	CLICK: **Menu1.mnu so the name appears in the File name: box as shown in Figure 17–47.**
	CLICK: **Open**
The Preferences dialog box (Figure 17–48) appears with A:\menu1 highlighted:	CLICK: **OK**
The AutoCAD customization warning appears:	CLICK: **Yes**
The Menu1.mnu file loads:	CLICK: **OK**
	CLICK: **Draw on the menu bar**

Your menu should appear as shown in Figure 17–49.

If you have any errors, CLICK: Menu1.mnu at the bottom of the screen to return to Notepad and the Menu1.mnu file. Make any necessary changes and return to AutoCAD.

Because you loaded the Menu1.mnu file previously, you will get the "Error loading menu file" message when you try to load the file again. You will have to unload the Menu1.mnu file before you can load your new version of it again.

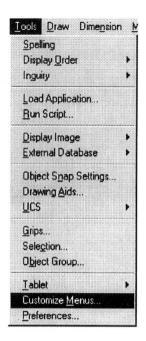

Note: If you lose the Menu Bar, TYPE: MENU<enter> and open the acad.mnu file or the acad.mnc to reload it.

Unloading, Reloading, and Saving a Menu

To unload a menu, CLICK: **Customize Menus...**, then CLICK: **Unload** to unload the Menu1.mnu file, since it will be the one highlighted. Then CLICK: **Browse** and locate the Menu1.mnu file on your floppy disk again to reload it.

On Your Own

1. When your menu is correct, use Notepad SaveAs... to save it on two floppy disks.
2. Return to AutoCAD and load the acad.mnu file.
3. Exit AutoCAD.

EXERCISE 17–4
Making a New Toolbar

Make a toolbar named My Blocks containing four of your most commonly used blocks.

1. Make four drawings of items you use often or call them up from an old drawing.
2. Wblock each drawing onto a floppy disk in the A drive using the names A:BLOCK1, A:BLOCK2, A:BLOCK3, and A:BLOCK4 or any other names you want.
3. Make a new toolbar named My Blocks.
4. Create four tools using icons that you will recognize as tools that insert your blocks. Name and describe them as you choose. Use the following as the Macro: for BLOCK1:

   ^C^C_insert;A:BLOCK1;
   Repeat the Macro: for BLOCK2, BLOCK3, and BLOCK4.

   Place the four tools on the new toolbar My Blocks.

EXERCISE 17–5
Modifying a Menu File

Modify Menu1 in the following manner:

1. Move the Properties... command from the Edit menu on the menu bar to the Modify menu on the menu bar.

2. Rearrange the Modify menu on the menu bar so that all commands are in alphabetical order.

3. Leave the flyouts as they are but put the flyout labels in alphabetical order.

REVIEW QUESTIONS

1. To make a new toolbar, CLICK: Toolbars..., and *Select:*
   a. New
   b. Delete
   c. Customize
   d. Custom
   e. File

2. When you delete a standard tool from a toolbox you cannot retrieve it.
   a. True   b. False

3. To display all toolbars, TYPE: -TOOLBAR **<enter>**, then TYPE: ALL **<enter>**, then TYPE:
   a. **S <enter>**
   b. **D <enter>**
   c. **H <enter>**
   d. **A <enter>**
   e. **T <enter>**

4. To copy a tool from one toolbar to another, CLICK: the tool and drag it to the other toolbar while holding down which key?
   a. Shift
   b. Alt
   c. Ctrl
   d. Esc
   e. F1

5. AutoCAD will make a new toolbar and name it for you when you CLICK: Customize... from the Toolbars dialog box, CLICK: any tool from any category, and
   a. PRESS: New
   b. Drop it on an existing toolbar
   c. Drop it in an open area
   d. PRESS: Ctrl
   e. PRESS: Esc

6. The standard AutoCAD menu file is named
   a. aclt
   b. Menu1
   c. acad
   d. AutoCAD
   e. lt

7. The Windows program used to copy and rename the AutoCAD menu file in this chapter is
   a. WordPad
   b. Files
   c. Windows Explorer
   d. Notepad
   e. StartUp

8. The item that was changed to allow AutoCAD to recognize the Menu1 menu file as different from the standard AutoCAD menu file is
   a. MENU1
   b. The File menu on the menu bar
   c. ***POP0
   d. ***MENUGROUP=
   e. The Button menu

9. The first response AutoCAD asks from you when the Insert command is activated is
   a. Insertion point:
   b. X scale factor
   c. Y scale factor
   d. Block name
   e. Rotation angle:

10. Which of the following displays the macro command and name on the menu?
    a. [BLOCK1]
    b. _BLOCK1
    c. BLOCK1<enter>
    d. BLOCK1
    e. (BLOCK1)

Complete.

11. To change tools to large buttons, which dialog box is used?

    _____

12. List the areas where toolbars can be docked.

    _____

13. Describe how to move a tool from one position on a toolbar to another position.

    _____

    _____

14. Describe what the ; character is used for in making macros.

    _____

15. Describe what ^C^C is used for in making macros.

    _____

16. Write a macro to draw a donut with a .125 inside diameter and a .250 outside diameter.

    _____

17. What do you pick from the Button Properties dialog box to change a tools icon?

    _____

18. Which command do you use to load a menu?

    _____

19. List the name of the menu that is numbered ***POP2.

    _____

20. List the name and the extension of the standard AutoCAD menu file.

    _____

PART IV THREE-DIMENSIONAL AUTOCAD

18 Basic Three-Dimensional Models

OBJECTIVES

After completing this chapter, you will be able to

☐ Describe the differences between working in 2D and 3D.
☐ Use Elevation, Thickness, UCS, and Viewports to create 3D objects in space.
☐ Use 3D Viewpoint to display different views of the same object.
☐ Change the location and orientation of the UCS while creating 3D models.
☐ Correctly use the following commands and settings:

Properties...	Mview
2D Solid	UCS
Elevation	Plan
Thickness	3D Viewpoint
Hide	Pspace
Mspace	Viewports
Tilemode	

INTRODUCTION

While creating the drawings in previous chapters you have been working in two-dimensional AutoCAD and making two-dimensional drawings of objects. This chapter introduces you to drawing in three dimensions; now you will be creating models. Although all the AutoCAD Draw and Modify commands work in 3D, your concept of what you are drawing must now change. You are creating models, not drawing pictures.

EXERCISE 18–1, PART 1
Creating 3D Models Using Elevation and Thickness

When you have completed Exercise 18–1, Part 1, your drawing will look similar to Figure 18–1. In Figure 18–1, four viewports display different viewpoints of a 3D model containing several shapes of varying heights. These heights are called *thicknesses*. Until now you have worked in only the X and Y directions. The Z dimension will now be added to give thickness (vertical shape) to your models. Creating the model in Exercise 18–1, Part

423

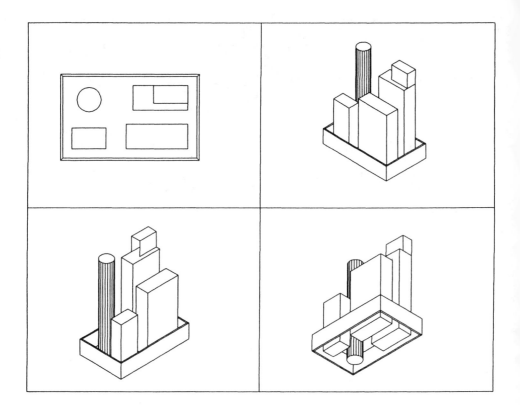

1, demonstrates drawing in 3D using the command ELEV (Elevation) and thickness. When you have finished drawing the model, you will use the VPORTS and VPOINT commands to create the four-viewport display.

To begin Exercise 18–1, Part 1, turn on the computer and start AutoCAD. The Start Up dialog box is displayed.

1. CLICK: **Use a Wizard**
2. CLICK: **Quick Setup**
   CLICK: **OK**
3. Set drawing Units: **Architectural**
   CLICK: **Next>>**
4. Set drawing Width: **60′** × Length: **60′**
   CLICK: **Done**
5. **Use SaveAs... to save the drawing on the hard drive with the name CH18-EX1.**
6. Set Grid: **12″**
7. Set Snap: **6″**
8. Create the following Layers:

LAYER NAME	COLOR	LINETYPE
3d-r	Red	Continuous
3d-b	Blue	Continuous
3d-g	Green	Continuous

The dimensions of the model are shown in Figures 18–2 and 18–3.

FIGURE 18–2
Front Elevation Dimensions

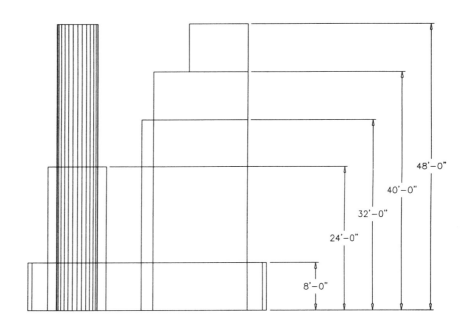

FIGURE 18–3
Plan View Dimensions

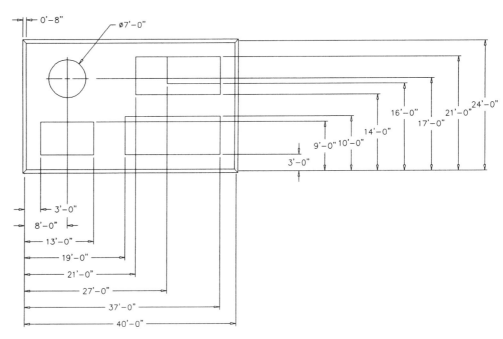

ELEV

Set the elevation and thickness for the outside wall (Figure 18–2):

Prompt	Response
Command:	TYPE: **ELEV<enter>**
New current elevation <0'-0">:	**<enter>**
New current thickness <0'-0">:	TYPE: **8'<enter>**

Note: The plan view of an object has a viewpoint of 0,0,1, meaning that you are above the object looking straight down on it.

Now everything you draw will be at elevation 0'-0" (the ground level for this model) with a thickness of 8'. Don't be concerned when you don't see any thickness for your shapes when you draw them in the following part of this exercise. Remember, you are looking directly down on the plan view of the model (0,0,1 coordinates). You will see the thickness of the model shapes when you change the viewpoint of the model later in the exercise.

On Your Own

Set Layer 3d-r current.

Draw the outside wall (Figure 18–3):

Prompt	Response
Command:	**Polyline** (or TYPE: **PL<enter>**)
From point:	TYPE: **10′,32′<enter>**
Current line-width is 0′-0″ Arc/Close/Halfwidth/Length/Undo/Width/ <Endpoint of line>:	TYPE: **W<enter>**
Starting width <0′-0″>:	TYPE: **8<enter>**
Ending width <0′-8″>:	**<enter>**
Arc/Close/Halfwidth/Length/Undo/Width/ <Endpoint of line>:	**With Ortho on, move the mouse to the right** and TYPE: **40′<enter>**
Arc/Close/Halfwidth/Length/Undo/Width/ <Endpoint of line>:	**Move the mouse down** and TYPE: **24′<enter>**
Arc/Close/Halfwidth/Length/Undo/Width/ <Endpoint of line>:	**Move the mouse to the left** and TYPE: **40′<enter>**
Arc/Close/Halfwidth/Length/Undo/Width/ <Endpoint of line>:	TYPE: **C<enter>**

The outside wall is complete. Setting the UCS origin to the lower left corner of the polyline (outside wall) will simplify drawing.

Set the UCS origin to the lower left corner of the polyline:

Prompt	Response
Command:	TYPE: **UCS<enter>**
Origin/ZAxis/3point/OBject/View/X/Y/Z/ Prev/Restore/Save/Del?<World>:	TYPE: **O<enter>**
Origin point <0,0,0>:	**Osnap-Intersection**
	Click the lower left corner of the Polyline.
Command:	TYPE: **UCSICON<enter>**
ON/OFF/All/Noorigin/ORigin <ON>	TYPE: **OR<enter>**

Set the elevation and thickness for the cylinder (Figure 18–2):

Prompt	Response
Command:	TYPE: **ELEV<enter>**
New current elevation <0′-0″>:	**<enter>**
New current thickness <8′-0″>:	TYPE: **48′<enter>**

Now everything you draw will be at elevation 0 with a thickness of 48′.

On Your Own

Set Layer 3d-b current.

Draw the cylinder (Figure 18–3):

Prompt	Response
Command:	**Circle-Center,Diameter**

Prompt	Response
3P/2P/TTR/<Center point>:	TYPE: **8′,17′<enter>**
Diameter:	TYPE: **7′<enter>**

The circle is complete. Next, the rectangle shape in front of the circle is drawn. Don't change the elevation or thickness. Draw the rectangle with a thickness of 48′, instead of 24′ as Figure 18–2 shows. Later in this exercise, the Properties... command will be used to change the thickness to the correct 24′.

Using the 2D Solid command, draw the rectangle shape in front of the circle (Figure 18–3):

Prompt	Response
Command:	**2D Solid** (or TYPE: **SO<enter>**)
First point:	TYPE: **3′,3′<enter>**
Second point:	TYPE: **13′,3′<enter>**
Third point:	TYPE: **3′,9′<enter>**
Fourth point:	TYPE: **13′,9′<enter>**
Third point:	**<enter>**

Set the elevation and thickness for the front right rectangle shape (Figure 18–2):

Prompt	Response
Command:	TYPE: **ELEV<enter>**
New current elevation <0′-0″>:	**<enter>**
New current thickness <48′-0″>:	TYPE: **32′<enter>**

Using the 2D Solid command, draw the front right rectangle shape (Figure 18–3):

Prompt	Response
Command:	**2D Solid** (or TYPE: **SO<enter>**)
First point:	TYPE: **19′,3′<enter>**
Second point:	TYPE: **37′,3′<enter>**
Third point:	TYPE: **19′,10′<enter>**
Fourth point:	TYPE: **37′,10′<enter>**
Third point:	**<enter>**

Set the elevation and thickness for the bottom rear right rectangle shape (Figure 18–2):

Prompt	Response
Command:	TYPE: **ELEV<enter>**
ELEV New current elevation <0′-0″>:	**<enter>**
New current thickness <32′-0″>:	TYPE: **40′<enter>**

Using the 2D Solid command, draw the bottom rear right rectangle shape (Figure 18–3):

Prompt	Response
Command:	**2D Solid** (or TYPE: **SO<enter>**)
First point:	TYPE: **21′,14′<enter>**
Second point:	TYPE: **37′,14′<enter>**
Third point:	TYPE: **21′,21′<enter>**
Fourth point:	TYPE: **37′,21′<enter>**
Third point:	**<enter>**

The smallest rectangle shape is sitting on top of the shape you just created, so its *elevation* will be the *thickness* of the previous solid. You can set that now.

Set the elevation and thickness for the smallest rectangle shape (Figure 18–2):

Prompt	Response
Command:	TYPE: **ELEV\<enter\>**
New current elevation <0'-0">:	TYPE: **40'\<enter\>**
New current thickness <40'-0">:	TYPE: **8'\<enter\>**

Note: The values of both the Elevation and Thickness settings can be positive or negative.

Now everything you draw will be at elevation 40' (the top of the 40' tall solid) with a thickness of 8'.

On Your Own

Set Layer 3d-g current.

Draw the smallest rectangle shape (Figure 18–3):

Prompt	Response
Command:	**2D Solid** (or TYPE: **SO\<enter\>**)
First point:	TYPE: **27',16'\<enter\>**
Second point:	TYPE: **37',16'\<enter\>**
Third point:	TYPE: **27',21'\<enter\>**
Fourth point:	TYPE: **37',21'\<enter\>**
Third point:	**\<enter\>**

The AutoCAD System Variables ELEVATION and THICKNESS can also be used to set elevation and thickness. They are described in Exercise 18–2.

Tiled Viewports (VPORTS)

Use the Tiled Viewports command to divide the screen into four viewports:

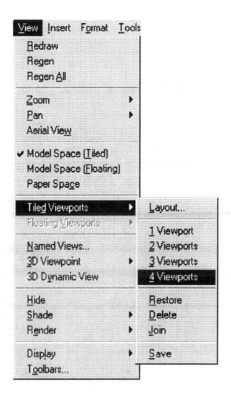

Prompt	Response
Command:	TYPE: **VPORTS<enter>** or
	CLICK: **Tiled Viewports-4 Viewports**
Save/Restore/Delete/Join/SIngle/?/2/<3>/4:	TYPE: **4<enter>**

The display area is now divided into four viewports. The active viewport, outlined with a solid line, displays the lines of the cursor when the cursor is moved into the active viewport.

3D VIEWPOINT (VPOINT) Command Line Options

Now let's take a look at the model you have drawn. 3D Viewpoint is the command used in this chapter for viewing 3D models. There are three means of selecting a viewing point (the location of the eye that is looking at your model) when you TYPE: **VPOINT <enter>**.

<View point> Using this option, you may type the X, Y, and Z coordinates of the view-point from the keyboard, and press enter.

axes Press the enter key at the VPOINT prompt. The AutoCAD compass and axis tri-pod appear. You can select a viewpoint by picking a point on the AutoCAD compass.

rotate The "rotate" option allows you to specify the viewpoint by entering two angles—one determines the angle in the X–Y plane from the X axis and the other determines the Z angle from the X–Y plane.

On Your Own

1. TYPE: **FILL<enter>**, then TYPE: **OFF<enter>** to save regeneration time.

2. Use Regen All to regenerate all viewports.

3. Select the upper right viewport as the current viewport by moving the cursor to any point in that viewport and picking it.

4. Set ELEVATION and THICKNESS to 0.

Next, the 3D Viewpoint command is used to select different viewpoints for the model in each viewport.

Select the viewpoint for the upper right viewport by typing the X, Y, and Z coordinates of the viewpoint (Figure 18–4):

Prompt	Response
Command:	TYPE: **VPOINT<enter>**
Rotate/<View point>	
<0'-0",0'-0",0'-1">:	TYPE: **1,-1,1<enter>**

Figure 18–4 shows the view that appears. Figure 18–5 shows the results of typing other coordinates:

☐ The upper left viewport is the plan view (0,0,1).

☐ The upper right viewport shows the viewpoint 1,-1,1. This means that the viewing eye has been moved one unit to the right, one unit in front, and one unit above the object.

☐ The lower left viewport (-1,-1,1) shows that the viewing eye has been moved one unit to the left, one unit in front, and one unit above the object.

☐ The lower right viewport (1,-1,-1) shows the view resulting from moving the viewing eye one unit to the right, one unit in front, and one unit below the object.

Note: Using the VPOINT command always causes a regeneration of the model drawing and displays the drawing as Zoom Extents.

Note: If a display in any viewport is off center, use Pan to center the display. If it is too large, use Zoom-Dynamic to reduce the size and to center the display in the viewport.

On Your Own

1. Experiment with typing different viewpoints if you like.

2. Return to the arrangement shown in Figure 18–4. TYPE: **Plan<enter>,** then **<enter>** again, or TYPE: **0,0,1** for the X, Y, and Z coordinates to return to the plan view.

3. Click the lower right viewport to make it active.

FIGURE 18–4
Four Viewports with One 3D
Viewpoint

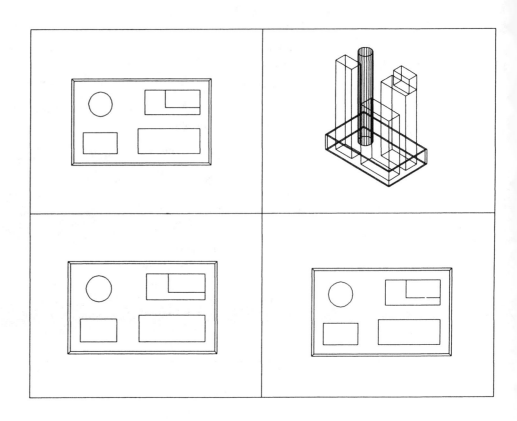

FIGURE 18–5
Standard Viewpoints

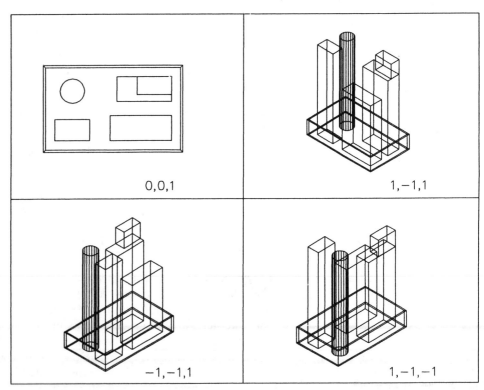

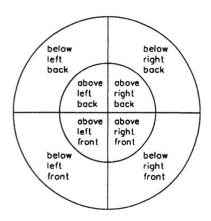

FIGURE 18–6
The AutoCAD Compass

Use the VPOINT command to view the AutoCAD compass (Figure 18–6):

Prompt	Response
Command:	TYPE: **VPOINT<enter>**
	(The AutoCAD tripod may also be selected from the View menu on the menu bar.)
Rotate/<View point>	
<0'-0",0'-0",0'-1">:	**<enter>**

The AutoCAD compass (Figure 18–6) and axis tripod appear. As you move the cursor inside the circles, the tripod with its X, Y, and Z axes moves to give you an idea of what the resulting display will be. When the tripod appears to have the desired orientation, pick that spot inside the compass to produce the desired viewpoint.

Study Figure 18–6 for a few moments to obtain an understanding of what each area on the compass signifies. Any point selected within the four parts of the smaller, inner circle is a viewpoint above the object. Any point selected within the four parts of the larger outer circle is a viewpoint below the object. Any point above the horizontal line is a viewpoint behind the object. Any point below the horizontal line is a viewpoint in front of the object. Any point to the right of the vertical line is looking at the right side of the object; any point to the left of the vertical line is the left side. Figure 18–7 shows examples of eight different clicks on the compass.

Warning: 3D Viewpoint is only a point from which the view is taken. Nothing is moved; nor are multiple objects displayed. This is all the same model, so if you do anything to move or alter the model itself in one view, you are doing it to all views. Keep in mind the distinction between viewing and creating a model.

Select the viewpoint for the lower right viewport by clicking a point on the AutoCAD compass (Figure 18–5):

Prompt	Response
The AutoCAD compass is visible.	**Click a point below the horizontal line and to the right of the vertical line, in between the inner circle line and the outer circle line, to create a view similar to the view shown in Figure 18–5.**

3D Viewpoint Menu Options

Select... The Viewpoint Presets dialog box, Figure 18–8, appears when 3D Viewpoint-Select... is clicked from the View menu in the menu bar.

Absolute to WCS—When this button is selected, the resulting viewpoint is relative to the World UCS.

Relative to UCS—When this button is selected, the resulting viewpoint is relative to the UCS that is current in the drawing at the time.

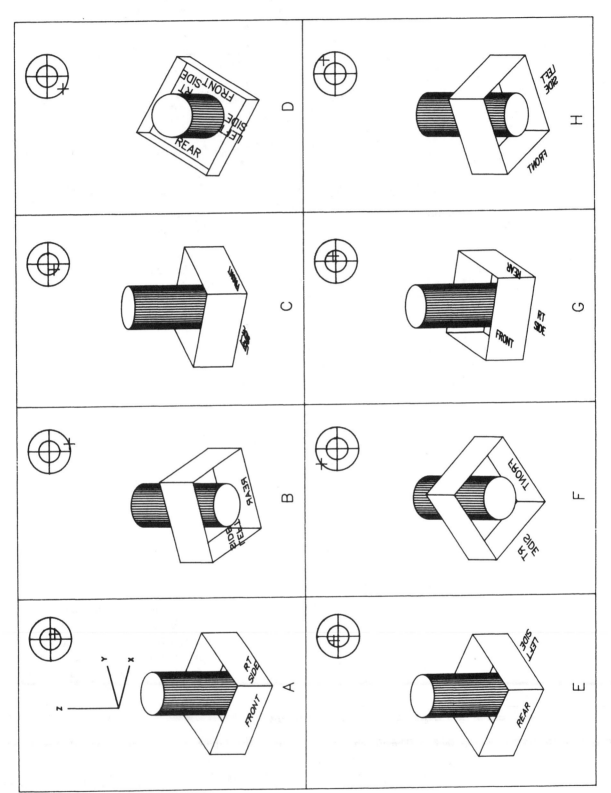

FIGURE 18-7
Compass Viewpoints

432

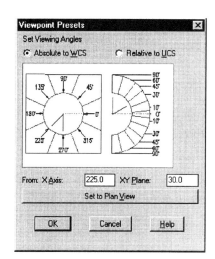

FIGURE 18-8
Viewpoint Presets Dialog Box

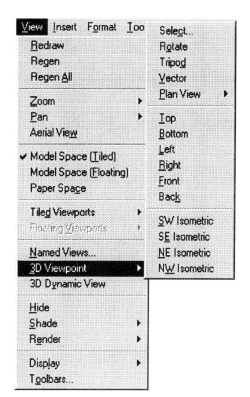

From X Axis: Button and Chart—Specifies the viewing angle from the X axis. The button allows you to type the angle; the chart above it allows you to specify a new angle by clicking the inner region on the circle. The red arm indicates the current angle; the black arm, the new angle. The chart, consisting of a square with a circle in it, may be thought of as a viewpoint looking down on the top of an object:

270	Places your view directly in front of the object.
315	Places your view to the right and in front of the object.
0	Places your view on the right side of the object.
45	Places your view to the right and behind the object.
90	Places your view behind the object.
135	Places your view to the left and behind the object.
180	Places your view on the left side of the object.
225	Places your view to the left and in front of the object.

From XY Plane: Button and Chart—Specifies the viewing angle from the X-Y plane. The button allows you to type the angle, and the chart above it allows you to specify a new angle by clicking the inner region on the half circle. Consisting of two semicircles, the chart allows you to specify whether the viewpoint is to be above or below the object:

0	Places your view directly perpendicular to the chosen angle. For example, a view of 270 on the left chart and 0 on the right chart places the viewpoint directly in front of the object.
10 to 60	Places your view above the object.
90	Places your view perpendicular to the top view of the chosen angle.
−10 to −60	Places your view below the object.
−90	Places your view perpendicular to the bottom view of the chosen angle.

Set to Plan View—Sets the viewing angles to plan view (270,90) relative to the selected UCS.

Now, look at other 3D viewpoint options:

Rotate   This option is the same as the "rotate" option when VPOINT is typed.
Tripod   The AutoCAD compass and Axis tripod appear.
Vector   This option is the same as the <View point> option when VPOINT is typed.
Plan View   Allows you to select the plan view of the current UCS, the World UCS, or a saved and named UCS.
Top   Gives you the top view of the model.
Bottom   Gives you the bottom view of the model.
Left   Gives you the left side view of the model.
Right   Gives you the right side view of the model.
Front   Gives you the front view of the model.
Back   Gives you the back view of the model.
SW Isometric   Gives you an isometric view from the front, to the left, above.
SE Isometric   Gives you an isometric view from the front, to the right, above.
NE Isometric   Gives you an isometric view from the back, to the right, above.
NW Isometric   Gives you an isometric view from the back, to the left, above.

Note: The front view is a 90° clockwise rotation of the plan view of the object looking straight into it. Left side, right side, and rear views are also 90° rotations.

On Your Own (Figure 18–8)

1. Click the lower left viewport to make it current.

2. Use the Viewport Presets dialog box to set the viewpoint of the lower left viewport; click the 225° angle in the left chart, and the 30° angle in the right chart as shown in Figure 18–8.

Your view should now look similar to the view in Figure 18–5.

Study the different methods for selecting viewpoints in 3D until you find the one or two methods you feel most comfortable with.

Next, let's correct the height of the rectangle shape that is in front of the cylinder.

To Change the Thickness of Part of a Model

The Properties... or CHPROP command can be used to change to 24′ the thickness of the solid (the rectangle shape in front of the circle) that is presently 48′. Any viewport may be current; it may be easiest to use the plan view.

Use the Properties... command to change the thickness of the solid in front of the circle:

Prompt	Response
Command:	**Properties...** (or TYPE: **MO<enter>**)
Select objects:	**Click the rectangle shape in front of the circle.**
Select objects:	**<enter>**
The Modify Solid dialog box appears:	DOUBLE CLICK: **the 48′ in the Thickness box** and TYPE: **24′**
	CLICK: **OK**

Note: Single Line Text (DTEXT) does not accept a THICKNESS setting. You can, however, change the thickness of some text fonts from 0 to any positive value. Use the Properties... command to change text thickness.

To Change the Elevation of Part of a Model

Elevation is not changed in the same manner. To change elevation, use the Move command and use relative coordinates to move any object in the Z direction. (For example, @0,0,48′ moves the object 48′ upward; @0,0,-48′ moves the object 48′ downward.) You may also change the elevation by typing **CHANGE<enter>** and then select Properties by typing **P<enter>** and the Elevation option by typing **E<enter>**.

HIDE

When you use the Hide command, the drawing is regenerated and all lines of the model that are covered by surfaces in front of them are suppressed. The next time the drawing is regenerated, all lines of the model become visible again.

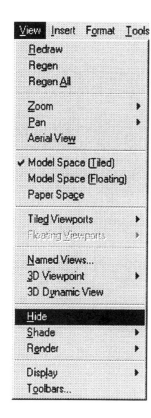

On Your Own

Select the upper right viewport to make it current.

Use the Hide command to hide surfaces that are behind other surfaces (Figure 18–9):

Prompt	Response
Command:	**Hide** (or TYPE: **HI<enter>**)

The resulting display in the upper right viewport is shown in Figure 18–9. Sometimes when surfaces touch, the Hide command produces incorrect results. If your display does not show the bottom line of the top block as a solid line, as in Figure 18–10, the following section will help you correct it.

FIGURE 18–9
Correct Result of the Hide
Command

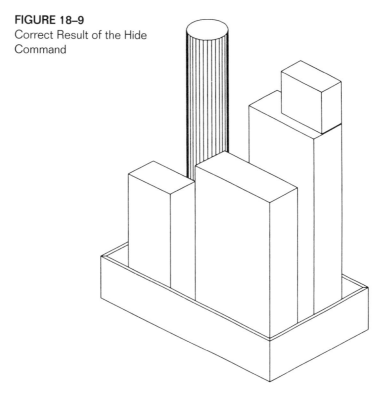

Incorrect Results of the Hide Command

The bottom line of the top solid does not show (Figure 18–10). When surfaces touch, the Hide command displays unpredictable results. To correct the display, either move the top box up a little or make the supporting box a little shorter (less thick).

Correct the display (Figure 18–11):

Prompt	Response
Command:	TYPE: **CHPROP<enter>**
Select objects:	**D1** (click the lower box)
Select objects:	**<enter>**
Change what property (Color/LAyer/LType/ ltScale/Thickness)?	TYPE: **T<enter>**
New thickness <40'-0">:	TYPE: **39'11<enter>**
Change what property (Color/LAyer/LType/ ltScale/Thickness)?	**<enter>**
Command:	TYPE: **HI<enter>**

The display now looks like Figure 18–9.

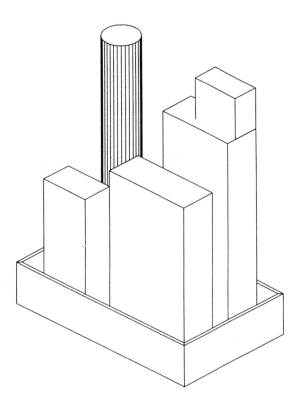

FIGURE 18–10
Incorrect Results of the Hide Command

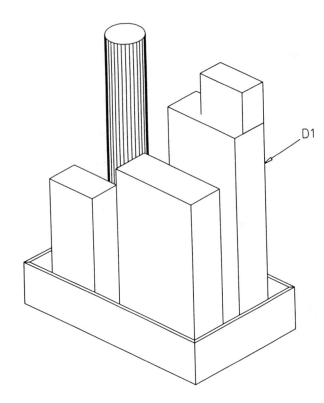

FIGURE 18–11
Correcting Incorrect Results of the Hide Command

You may solve in a similar manner other problems that you encounter. Cylinders inside other cylinders, such as a vertical support inside of a circular base, may produce lines that do not hide correctly. To correct the problem, increase the distance between the cylinder and the base by making the hole slightly bigger or the cylinder slightly smaller. A little experimentation will be required.

When you have corrected your hiding problem (if you had one) the drawing is complete.

Saving the Viewport Configuration and Restoring It in Paper Space

You have been working in model space. Next, the current viewport configuration (four viewports) is saved and restored in paper space. In paper space all four viewports can be plotted.

Save the current viewport configuration:

Prompt	Response
Command:	**Tiled Viewports-Save** (or TYPE: **VPORTS<enter>** then **S<enter>**)
?/Name for new viewport configuration:	TYPE: **VP1<enter>**

Restore the viewport configuration in paper space:

Prompt	Response
Command:	**Model Space [Floating]** (or CLICK: **Tile** to set Tilemode off, and TYPE: **MV<enter>**)
ON/OFF/Hideplot/Fit/2/3/4/Restore/ <First Point>:	TYPE: **R<enter>**

Note: As discussed in Chapter 16, all construction for 2D and 3D is done in model space, as you have done in all previous chapters. Paper space allows you to plot all your viewports at once and permits annotation within and across viewports. Paper space also allows viewports to overlap, creating a varied and flexible drawing space. These viewports may be erased, moved, or otherwise edited. Model space does not allow viewports to overlap, and only one model space viewport may be plotted at a time.

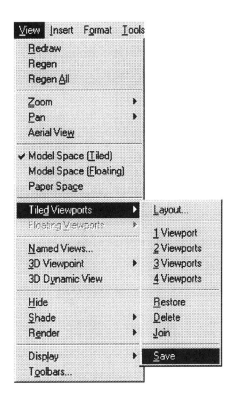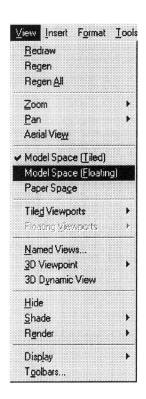

Prompt	Response
?/Name of window configuration to insert <*ACTIVE>:	TYPE: **VP1\<enter>**
Fit/\<First Point>:	TYPE: **0,0\<enter>**
Second point:	TYPE: **11,8-1/2\<enter>**

Use the Hideplot option of MVIEW (Floating Viewports) to remove hidden lines in a selected viewport when the drawing is plotted:

Prompt	Response
Command:	**Floating Viewports-Hideplot**
ON/OFF/Hideplot/Fit/2/3/4/Restore/ \<First Point>:	TYPE: **H\<enter>**
ON/OFF:	TYPE: **ON\<enter>**
Select objects:	**Pick the boundary of the upper right viewport.**
	\<enter>

You may now plot all viewports at the same time; on the plot Full Preview the upper right viewport displays a view with hidden lines removed, as shown in Figure 18–12.

SAVE

When you have completed Exercise 18–1, save your work in at least two places.

PLOT

Plot Exercise 18–1 on an $11'' \times 8\frac{1}{2}''$ sheet. Make sure you are in paper space with limits set at $11'' \times 8\frac{1}{2}''$ and use a plotting ratio based on the paper space limits.

Use the Hideplot option of the MVIEW (Floating Viewports) command to select all three-dimensional viewports and produce a plot similar to Figure 18–13.

FIGURE 18–12
Hideplot in Paper Space

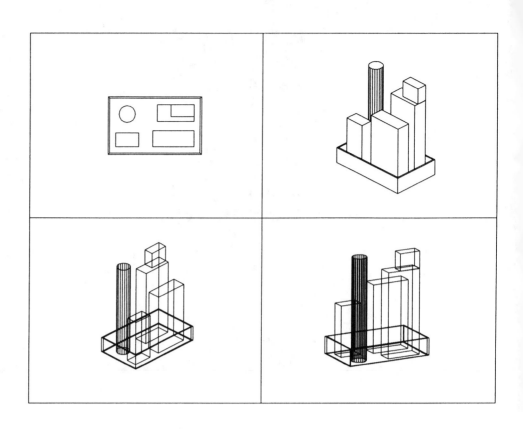

FIGURE 18–13
Print or Plot Exercise 18–1, Part 1

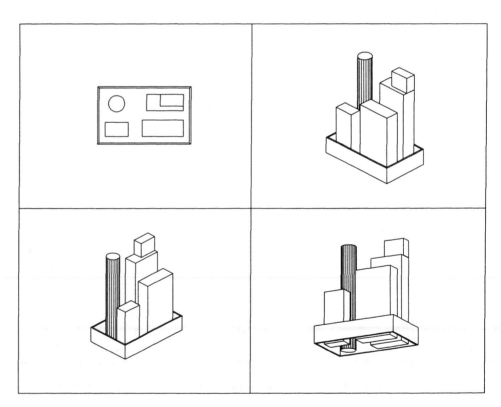

FIGURE 18–14
3D Objects

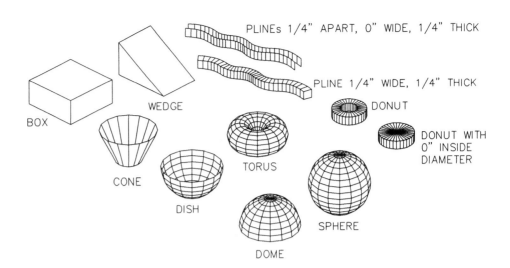

EXERCISE 18–1, PART 2
3D Shapes

Note: Although many of the Draw commands can be extruded to create 3D objects, the Hide command treats differently the objects drawn with the various commands. For example, a cube drawn with the Line command (extruded using THICKNESS) is treated as a square cube with no top or bottom; a cube drawn with the 2D Solid command (extruded using THICKNESS) is treated as a solid object with four sides, a top, and a bottom; a polyline with width has a top and bottom; a polyline with 0 width is treated as a line, with no top or bottom.

Note: Practice using Osnap modifiers to snap to 3D objects created with different commands. Each edge of a 3D object drawn with the 2D Solid command is treated as a separate line entity. Osnap snaps to the center of a wide 3D polyline.

In Exercise 18–1, Part 2, you can practice drawing 3D objects and using 3D Viewpoint to look at them. You may erase or plot this practice session. Some of the 3D objects are shown in Figure 18–14.

On Your Own

1. Return to model space.
2. Return to a single viewport.

Experiment with Extruded Objects

You can draw 3D objects by setting the THICKNESS and using the Arc, Circle, Donut, Ellipse, Line, Pline, Polygon, and 2D Solid commands. The objects are extruded because they have thickness. Return the viewport to plan view, and practice using these Draw commands with different ELEVATION and THICKNESS settings to create 3D objects. Then practice using 3D Viewpoint to select different viewpoints. Try drawing some 3D objects while you are in a viewpoint different from the plan view.

3D Objects

AutoCAD provides some 3D object shapes—box, cone, dish, dome, mesh, pyramid, sphere, torus, and wedge—that can be selected from the menu bar with a single click. AutoCAD then provides you with prompts to draw the object. Objects such as box and wedge ask for a rotation angle about the Z axis, allowing you to rotate the object in the plan view. Be aware that these are surface models, not solids. Solid modeling is covered in Chapter 18. You cannot use surface models with solids commands.

Draw the 3D object torus (Figure 18–15):

Prompt	Response
Command:	**3D Surfaces...**
The 3D Objects dialog box (Figure 18–15) appears:	**CLICK: Torus**
	CLICK: OK
Center of torus:	**Click a point on the screen.**
Diameter/<radius> of torus:	**Click a point to indicate the radius** or TYPE: **the radius size.**

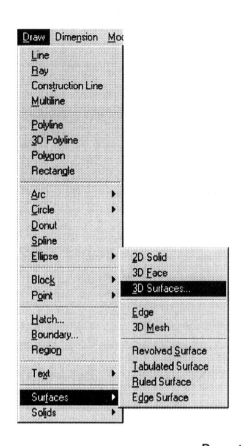

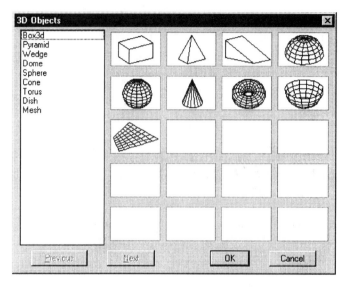

FIGURE 17–15
3D Objects Dialog Box

Prompt	Response
Diameter/<radius> of tube:	**Click a point** or TYPE: **the radius size.** (the DIAMETER of the tube—the inside circle—must be less than the RADIUS of the torus—the outside circle) **If you wish to use diameter, TYPE: D<enter> and then the diameter.**
Segments around tube circumference <16>:	**<enter>** (You may specify more or fewer segments than the default: more makes the object look more round but Hide takes longer; fewer looks less round and Hide is shorter)
Segments around torus circumference <16>:	**<enter>**

On Your Own

Experiment with 3D objects for a while. Use 3D Viewpoint to select different viewpoints. Then erase or plot this practice session.

EXERCISE 18–2
Create a 3D Model of the Tenant Space Reception Desk

To begin Exercise 18–2, turn on the computer and start AutoCAD. The Start Up dialog box is displayed.

1. CLICK: **Use a Wizard**
2. CLICK: **Quick Setup**

CLICK: **OK**

3. Set drawing Units: **Architectural**

   CLICK: **Next>>**

4. Set drawing Width: **24′** × Length: **15′**

   CLICK: **Done**

5. **Use SaveAs... to save the drawing on the hard drive with the name CH18-EX2.**

6. Set Grid: **2″**

7. Set Snap: **1″**

8. Create the following Layers:

LAYER NAME	COLOR	LINETYPE
3d-dr1-3	Blue	Continuous
3d-dr2	White	Continuous
3d-kick	White	Continuous
3d-panel	Red	Continuous
3d-sp	Blue	Continuous
3d-ws1	White	Continuous
3d-ws2	Green	Continuous

On Your Own

1. Create a 3D model of the tenant space reception desk using the dimensions shown in Figure 18–16.

2. Set the different layers as needed.

3. Use the correct elevation and thickness and the following commands:

□ *Kickplates*—Layer 3d-kick, Polyline, 2″ width, 0 elevation, 3″ thickness. Use a continuous polyline. Don't forget to draw the kickplate in front and on the inside of the smaller pedestals.

□ *Panels*—Layer 3d-panel, Polyline, 2″ width, 3″ elevation, 35″ thickness. Draw a separate polyline section for each panel. (A continuous polyline draws a diagonal line in the corners—which you don't want.) Draw the 66″ polyline to extend to the top of the 24″ polyline and to the bottom of the 96″ polyline.

□ *Work Surface 1*—Layer 3d-ws1, 2D Solid, $27\frac{1}{2}$″ elevation, $1\frac{1}{2}$″ thickness.

□ *Work Surface 2 (2 each)*—Layer 3d-ws2, 2D Solid, 25″ elevation, $1\frac{1}{2}$″ thickness.

□ *Spacer (2 each)*—Layer 3d-sp, Polyline, 2″ width, $26\frac{1}{2}$″ elevation, 1″ thickness.

□ *Drawer Pedestal (2 each)*—2D Solid
   Drawer 1: Layer 3d-dr1-3, 3″ elevation, 12″ thickness.
   Drawer 2: Layer 3d-dr2, 15″ elevation, 5″ thickness.
   Drawer 3: Layer 3d-dr1-3, 20″ elevation, 5″ thickness.

Note: When drawing in 3D, use as many different layer colors as needed to help you see the various pieces of the model while you are drawing.

Note: When you are drawing in Basic 3D, it does not matter in what order the parts of the model are drawn. In solid modeling order can make a difference.

Note: When using a wide polyline to draw an object, remember that the starting and ending points are the middle of the polyline.

Your model should closely resemble Figure 18–17 when you select a viewpoint of 1,1,1 and use the Hide command. In the next part of this exercise, the drawer handles are drawn by relocating the UCS.

Controlling UCS in Three Dimensions

Thus far, you have been using ELEVATION (ELEV) to locate the base and construction plane of the parts of the 3D models. This exercise shows you how to locate the construction plane by moving the UCS to the desired elevation and orientation.

   Understanding and controlling the UCS is extremely important in creating three-dimensional models. The UCS is the *location and orientation* of the origin of the X, Y,

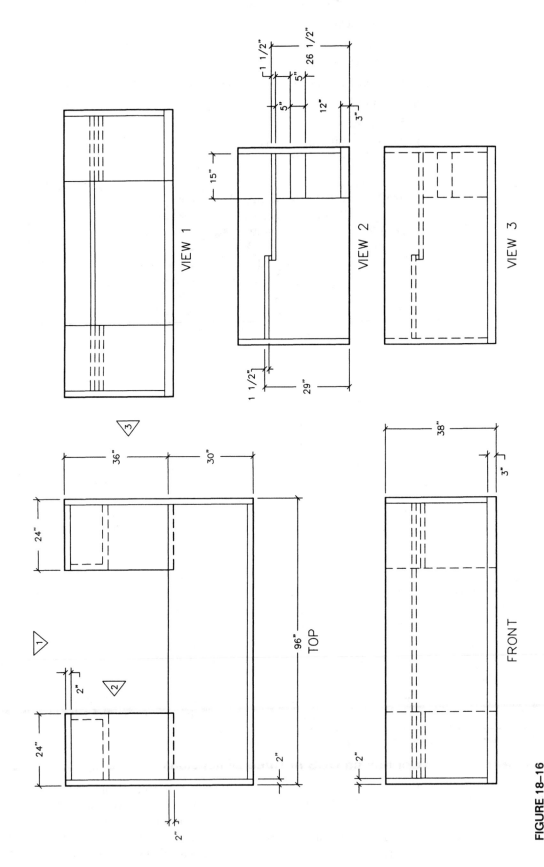

FIGURE 18-16

Exercise 18–2: Tenant Space Reception Desk Dimensions

VIEW 1

VIEW 2

VIEW 3

1 1/2"

26 1/2"

5"

5"

12"

3"

15"

1 1/2"

29"

36"

30"

24"

96"

TOP

24"

2"

2"

38"

3"

2"

2"

FRONT

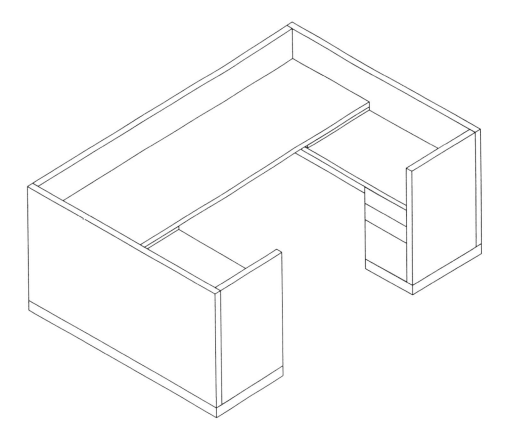

and Z axes. If you are going to draw parts of a 3D model on a slanted surface, you can create a slanted UCS. If you are going to draw a 3D object, such as the handles on the drawer pedestal, you can locate your UCS so that it is flush with the front plane of the pedestal. Thickness is then taken from that construction plane, and the handles can be easily created in the correct location.

The UCS command prompt is "Origin/ZAxis/3point/OBject/View/X/Y/Z/Prev/Restore/Save/Del/?/<World>:". The UCS command options Origin, OBject, Previous, Restore, Save, Delete, World, and ? were described in Chapter 11. The options described in this chapter are Origin, ZAxis, 3point, OBject, View, and X/Y/Z. All these options can be selected directly from the menu bar or the UCS toolbar.

On Your Own

In the following part of this exercise, you will practice with the UCS command options to define new UCS origin locations and orientations. Before continuing with the UCS options:

1. Return the ELEVATION and THICKNESS settings to 0. This avoids having the ELE-VATION setting affect the position of a model created in a new UCS. The construction plane is controlled by using the UCS command in the following part of this exercise.

2. Return to the plan view with the world UCS visible in the lower left corner.

3. Enter a viewpoint of 1,1,1, and use Hide. Notice how the World UCS is located on the drawing.

4. Set UCSICON (not UCS) to Origin; with this setting, the UCS icon is displayed at the origin of any new UCS coordinate system you create.

Origin

This UCS command option allows you to define a new UCS by shifting the origin of the current UCS, leaving the direction of its X, Y, and Z axes unchanged.

FIGURE 18–18
Use UCS Origin to Define a New
UCS

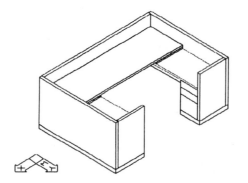
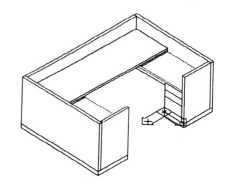

Use UCS Origin to define a new UCS (Figure 18–18):

Prompt	Response
Command:	TYPE: **UCS<enter>** (or select from the menu bar or the UCS toolbar)
Origin/ZAxis/3point/OBject/View/X/Y/Z/ Prev/Restore/Save/Del/?/<World>:	TYPE: **O<enter>**
Origin point <0,0,0>:	**Osnap-Intersection**
	Click the lower left corner of the largest drawer, where it intersects with the kickplate.

Note: When creating a new UCS, make sure the ELEVATION setting is set to 0.

The origin of the World UCS is shifted to the corner of the drawer, but the direction of its X, Y, and Z axes remained unchanged.

ZAxis

The ZAxis option allows you to change the direction of the Z axis. On the basis of a new Z axis, AutoCAD determines the direction of the X and Y axes. Before continuing, use the UCS command to return to the World UCS location, as follows.

Use UCS World to return to the World UCS location:

Prompt	Response
Command:	TYPE: **UCS<enter>**
Origin/ZAxis/3point/OBject/View/X/Y/Z/ Prev/Restore/Save/Del/?/<World>:	**<enter>**

The World UCS returns.

Use UCS ZAxis to define a new UCS (Figure 18–19):

Prompt	Response
Command:	TYPE: **UCS<enter>**
Origin/ZAxis/3point/OBject/View/X/Y/Z/ Prev/Restore/Save/Del/?/<World>:	TYPE: **ZA<enter>**
Origin point <0,0,0>:	**Osnap-Intersection**

FIGURE 18–19
Use UCS ZAxis to Define a New
UCS

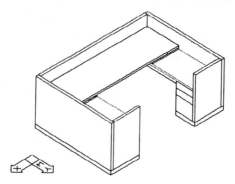
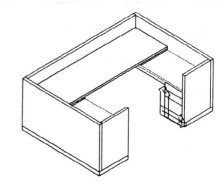

Prompt	Response
	Click the lower left corner of the largest drawer where it intersects with the kickplate.
Point on positive portion of Z-axis <default>:	**Use the crosshairs of the pointer to reorient the Z axis so it comes "out" from the lower left corner of the pedestal, and click a point** (with ORTHO and SNAP on).

The origin of the current UCS is moved to the corner of the drawer, and when the direction of the Z axis is changed, the X and Y axes follow.

X/Y/Z

These options allow you to rotate the User Coordinate System about any of the three axes. Keep the UCS just created and use the X/Y/Z option in the following exercises to rotate the UCS about the three axes.

Use UCS Y to define a new UCS by rotating the UCS about the Y axis (Figure 18–20):

Prompt	Response
Command:	TYPE: **UCS<enter>**
Origin/ZAxis/3point/OBject/View/X/Y/Z/ Prev/Restore/Save/Del?<World>:	TYPE: **Y<enter>**
Rotation angle about Y axis <0>:	TYPE: **60<enter>**
(The UCS rotates 60° counterclockwise around the Y axis to appear as in Figure 18–20.)	
Command:	TYPE: **U<enter>** (to return to the UCS created using the ZAxis option)

FIGURE 18–20
Use UCS Y to Define a New
UCS

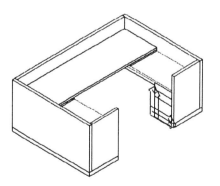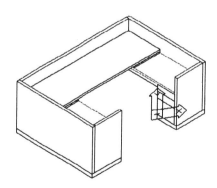

Use UCS Z to define a new UCS by rotating the UCS about the Z axis (Figure 18–21):

Prompt	Response
Command:	TYPE: **UCS<enter>**
Origin/ZAxis/3point/OBject/View/X/Y/Z/ Prev/Restore/Save/Del?<World>:	TYPE: **Z<enter>**
Rotation angle about Z axis <0>:	TYPE: **60<enter>**
(The UCS rotates 60° counterclockwise around the Z axis to appear as in Figure 18–21.)	
Command:	TYPE: **U<enter>** (to return to the UCS created by the ZAxis option)

FIGURE 18–21
Use UCS Z to Define a New
UCS

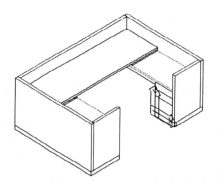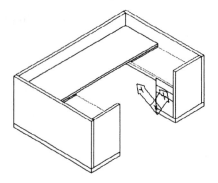

FIGURE 18–22
Use UCS X to Define a New
UCS

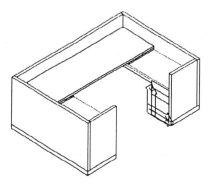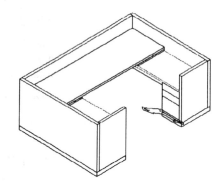

Use UCS X to define a new UCS by rotating the UCS about the X axis (Figure 18–22):

Prompt	Response
Command:	TYPE: **UCS<enter>**
Origin/ZAxis/3point/OBject/View/X/Y/Z/ Prev/Restore/Save/Del?<World>:	TYPE: **X<enter>**
Rotation angle about X axis <0>:	TYPE: **60<enter>**
(The UCS rotates 60° counterclockwise around the X axis to appear as in Figure 18–22.)	
Command:	<enter>

Use UCS World to return to the World UCS coordinate system:

Prompt	Response
Origin/ZAxis/3point/OBject/View/X/Y/Z/ Prev/Restore/Save/Del?<World>:	<enter>

The UCS returns to the World coordinate system.

View

This option creates a new coordinate system whose X–Y plane is parallel to the display screen. This is the UCS that must be used when a 2D format (border) is to be placed around a 3D drawing. A good way to combine the 3D drawing and the 2D format is to arrange the 3D drawing as you wish it to appear, set the UCS to View, and insert a previously drawn format around it. Also use the View option when you want to add text to your drawing; when "View" is used, you can enter text parallel to the screen while in a 3D viewpoint.

On Your Own

Create a text style with a Roman Simplex font.

Use UCS View to define a UCS parallel to the screen, and annotate the drawing (Figure 18–23):

FIGURE 18–23
Use UCS View to Define a New
UCS Parallel to the Screen

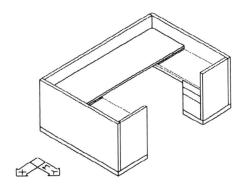
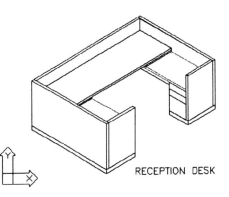

RECEPTION DESK

Prompt	Response
Command:	TYPE: **UCS\<enter\>**
Origin/ZAxis/3point/OBject/View/X/Y/Z/ Prev/Restore/Save/Del?\<World\>:	TYPE: **V\<enter\>**
(The UCS is parallel to your screen.)	
Command:	**Single Line Text** (or TYPE: **DT\<enter\>**)
Justify/Style/\<Start point\>:	**Click a point below the desk. Allow enough room for 4″ text** (see Figure 18–23).
Height \<default\>:	TYPE: **4\<enter\>**
Rotation angle \<0\>:	**\<enter\>**
Text:	TYPE: **RECEPTION DESK\<enter\>**
Text:	**\<enter\>**
(The 3D model of the reception desk is annotated.)	

On Your Own

Erase the text "RECEPTION DESK" from the drawing, and return to the World UCS.

OBject

The OBject option allows you to define a UCS by pointing to any object except a 3D polyline or polygon mesh. The Y axis of the UCS created with OBject has the same extrusion direction as the object that is selected.

Use UCS OBject to define a new UCS (Figure 18–24):

Prompt	Response
Command:	TYPE: **UCS\<enter\>**
Origin/ZAxis/3point/OBject/View/X/Y/Z/ Prev/Restore/Save/Del?\<World\>:	TYPE: **OB\<enter\>**
Select object to align UCS:	**Click any point on the largest work surface.**

FIGURE 18–24
Use UCS Entity to Define a New
UCS

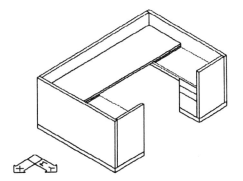
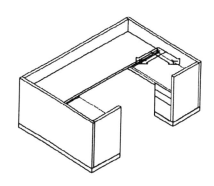

The work surface was drawn by using the 2D Solid command. The position of the UCS shown in Figure 18–24 may vary from the position of your UCS, because the first point of the solid (when drawn) determines the new UCS origin. The new X axis lies along the line between the first two points of the solid.

See the *AutoCAD Command Reference* for a description of how each entity—arc, circle, dimension, line, point, 2D Polyline, solid, 3D face, text, insert, attribute, and attribute definition—determines the position of the UCS origin when the OBject option is used.

3point

This option allows you to change the origin of a new UCS by specifying a new direction for the X and Y axes; the Z axis follows. In the next part of this exercise, you create a new UCS using the 3point option. This UCS will be used to draw the hardware on the drawers of the left pedestal.

On Your Own

Return to the World UCS.

Use UCS 3point to define a new UCS (Figure 18–25):

FIGURE 18–25
Use UCS 3point to Define a New UCS

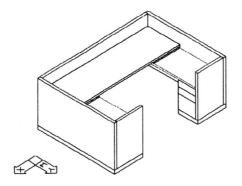

Prompt	Response
Command:	TYPE: **UCS\<enter>**
Origin/ZAxis/3point/OBject/View/X/Y/Z/ Prev/Restore/Save/Del?\<World>:	TYPE: **3\<enter>**
Origin point \<0,0,0>:	**Osnap-Intersection**
	Click the lower left corner of the largest drawer, where it intersects with the kickplate.
Point on positive portion of the X-axis < >:	**Osnap-Intersection**
	Click the lower right corner of the largest drawer, where it intersects with the kickplate.
Point on positive-Y portion of the UCS X-Y plane < >:	**Osnap-Intersection**
	Click the upper left corner of the largest drawer, where it intersects with the drawer above it.

The newly created UCS appears.

Thickness (System Variable)

When the UCS coordinate system is used to define the construction plane, the ELEVATION setting must be 0. Otherwise, the ELEVATION defines the construction plane from the current UCS.

You may also set ELEVATION and THICKNESS using the ELEVATION and THICKNESS system variables. The entire word—ELEVATION or TH for THICKNESS—must be typed and entered to set the system variable. Thickness may also be selected from Format on the menu bar.

Use the THICKNESS (system variable) to set the thickness for the drawer handles:

Prompt	Response
Command:	**Thickness** (or TYPE: **TH<enter>**)
New value for THICKNESS <default>:	TYPE: **1/2<enter>**

Drawing in 3D

In the following part of this exercise, the UCS created using the 3point option is used to add the drawer hardware to the drawers of both pedestals. The dimensions for the locations of the drawer hardware are shown in Figure 18–26.

Draw the drawer hardware on the left pedestal using the Polyline command:

Prompt	Response
Command:	**Polyline** (or TYPE: **PL<enter>**)
From point:	TYPE: **5,10<enter>**
Arc/Close/Halfwidth/Length/Undo/Width/ <Endpoint of line>:	TYPE: **W<enter>**
Starting width <default>:	TYPE: **1<enter>**
Ending width <0'-1">:	**<enter>**
Arc/Close/Halfwidth/Length/Undo/Width/ <Endpoint of line>:	TYPE: **10,10<enter>**
Arc/Close/Halfwidth/Length/Undo/Width/ <Endpoint of line>:	**<enter>**

The first drawer handle is complete.

On Your Own

1. Use the dimensions in Figure 18–26 to complete the drawer handles on the left pedestal.

2. Return to the World UCS.

3. Select a viewpoint of -1,1,1.

4. Use UCS 3point to create a UCS to draw the drawer handles on the right pedestal.

5. Using the same dimensions as you used on the left pedestal, draw the handles of the right pedestal drawers.

Note: If the UCS Icon origin is off screen, or if it is clipped at the viewport edges, it is displayed at the lower left corner of the viewport.

Note: When the UCS Icon appears as a broken pencil, that means that the view direction is edge-on at the current UCS. If the broken pencil is displayed, use another viewport, with a different view of the object, as a guide when using Draw and Modify commands.

Warning: When you are working in 3D, you absolutely must use OSNAP to Move or Insert objects as blocks. An object that appears to be placed on the Endpoint of a line, for example, may be in front, behind, below, or above where it appears to be unless OSNAP is used to designate the Endpoint of the line.

FIGURE 18–26
Drawer Hardware Dimensions

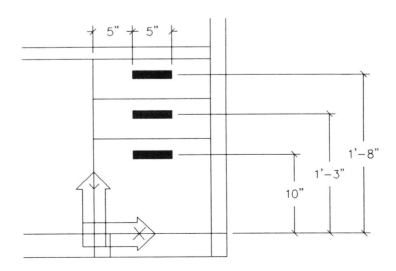

FIGURE 18–27
Reception Desk, Viewpoint 1,1,1

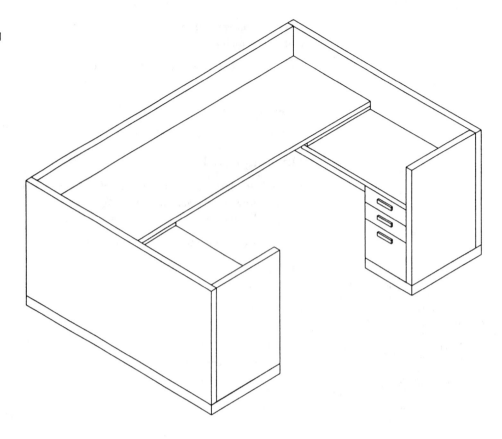

FIGURE 18–28
Reception Desk, Viewpoint -1,1,1

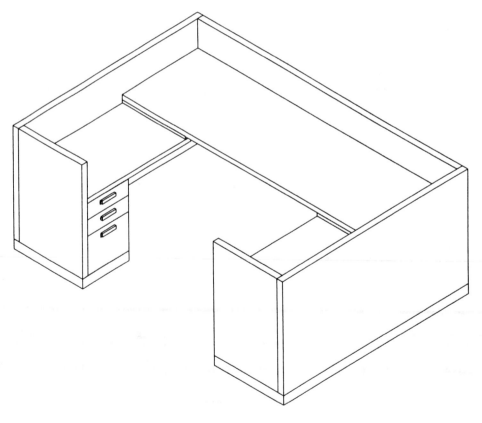

If you have done everything correctly, your drawing is complete. Figure 18–27 shows the model with a viewpoint of 1,1,1. Figure 18–28 shows the model with a viewpoint of -1,1,1.

If you find any errors, correct them at this time. You can use the Move command to correct location errors by noting the X, Y, and Z coordinates of the current UCS and moving objects using relative coordinates. For example, the response **@1,0,0** to the "Second point of displacement:" prompt of the Move command moves an object 1″ in the positive X direction. (You may select any point as the base point.)

PLAN

When you TYPE: **PLAN<enter>**, the prompt is "<Current UCS>/Ucs/World:". All these options may be selected from the menu bar.

<Current UCS>

When the Current UCS option is entered, the display is returned to the plan view (VPOINT 0,0,1) with respect to the current UCS.

Ucs (Named UCS)

This option prompts for the "?/Name of UCS:" and returns the display to the plan view for the named UCS.

World

This option returns the display to the plan view for the World Coordinate System.

UCSFOLLOW

The UCSFOLLOW system variable may be set so that when a new UCS is created, the display automatically goes to the plan view of the new UCS in the active viewport.

When you TYPE: **UCSFOLLOW<enter>**, the prompt is "New value for UCSFOLLOW <0>:". When UCSFOLLOW is set to 1, any UCS change automatically causes the screen to return to the plan view of the new UCS. When UCSFOLLOW is set to 0, a UCS change does not affect the display. You can set UCSFOLLOW separately for each viewport.

When part of a 3D model is viewed in plan view, be aware that you are viewing the entire model, *including* any part of it that is in front of the current UCS. For example, when the UCS is on the same plane as the pedestals, the *viewpoint* is from outside the

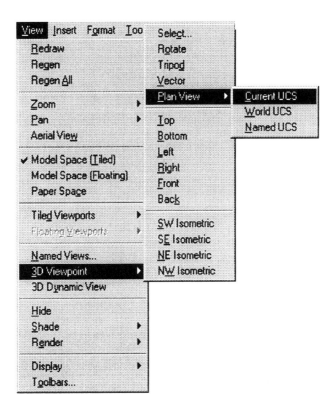

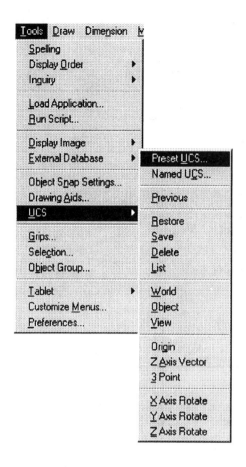

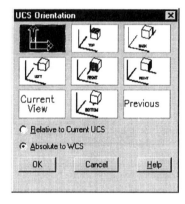

FIGURE 18–29
UCS Orientation Dialog Box

entire reception desk. Therefore, if you perform a Hide operation while the UCS is in this location, the entire pedestal will be hidden by the outside panel of the desk. That is because the pedestals are inside the model. Clipping planes, as described in the *AutoCAD Command Reference,* can be used to remedy this situation if it is a problem.

Otherwise, draw anything that is inside a model while the model in a 3D view, as you drew the drawer hardware.

UCS Orientation Dialog Box

You can also click Preset UCS... to obtain the UCS Orientation dialog box. The desired UCS coordinate system option can be selected from the UCS Orientation dialog box (Figure 18–29), and the Origin point is entered at the prompt. When UCSFOLLOW is set to 1, the plan view of the coordinate system automatically appears on the screen; otherwise, TYPE: **PLAN<enter>** to see the plan view. It is easiest to keep your orientation by returning to the plan view of the World UCS before you select a new UCS option from the dialog box.

It is important to understand the difference between the UCS option of Front and the Viewpoint option of Front. You may draw directly on the Front UCS option plan view and know exactly where you are drawing. If you draw on the Viewpoint option of Front and your UCS has not been located correctly on the front of the 3D model, you don't know where you are drawing.

SAVE

When you have completed Exercise 18–2, save your work in at least two places.

PLOT

Plot Exercise 18–2 at a scale of $\frac{1}{2}'' = 1'\text{-}0''$, Viewpoint 1,1,1, as shown in Figure 18–27.

EXERCISE 18–3
Create a 3D Model of the Tenant Space Reception Seating Area

Create a 3D model from the views and dimensions given in Figure 18–30. Plot a single view of the model to scale so that it fits on an $11'' \times 8\frac{1}{2}''$ sheet and still fills most of the sheet.

EXERCISE 18–4
Create a 3D Model of the Tenant Space Conference Room Cabinets

Create a 3D model from the views and dimensions given in Figures 18–31A and 18–31B. Plot a single view of the model to scale so that it fits on an $11'' \times 8\frac{1}{2}''$ sheet and still fills most of the sheet.

FIGURE 18–30

Exercise 18–3: Tenant Space Reception Seating Area Dimensions (Scale: $\frac{3}{8}'' = 1'\text{-}0''$)

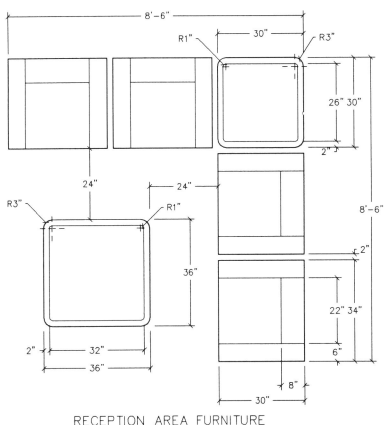

RECEPTION AREA FURNITURE
PLAN VIEW

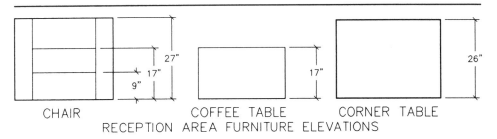

CHAIR   COFFEE TABLE   CORNER TABLE
RECEPTION AREA FURNITURE ELEVATIONS

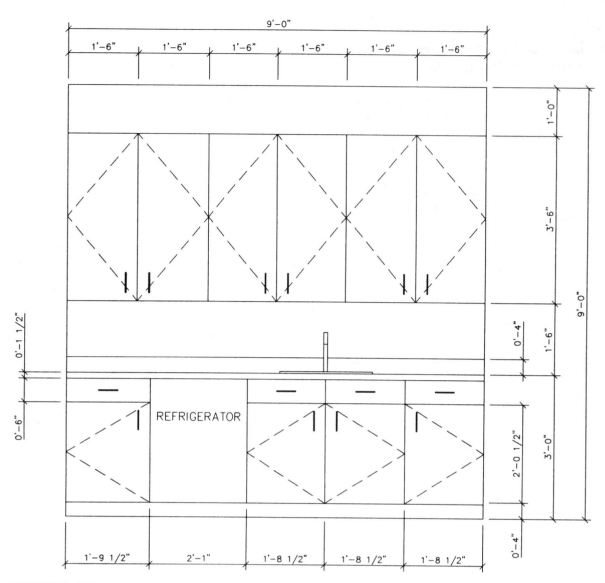

FIGURE 18–31A
Exercise 18–4: Tenant Space Conference Room Cabinets Dimensions (Scale: $\frac{1}{2}'' = 1'-0''$)

EXERCISE 18–5
Create a 3D Model of the Tenant Space Conference Room Chair

Create a 3D model from the views and dimensions given in Figure 18–32. Plot a paper space drawing containing four 3D views of the model on an $11'' \times 8\frac{1}{2}''$ sheet. The four viewpoints should be:

☐ Above, in front, and to the right
☐ Above, in front, and to the left
☐ Above, behind, and to the right
☐ Above, behind, and to the left

FIGURE 18-31B

Exercise 18-4: Tenant Space
Conference Room Cabinets
Dimensions (Scale: $\frac{1}{2}'' = 1'\text{-}0''$)

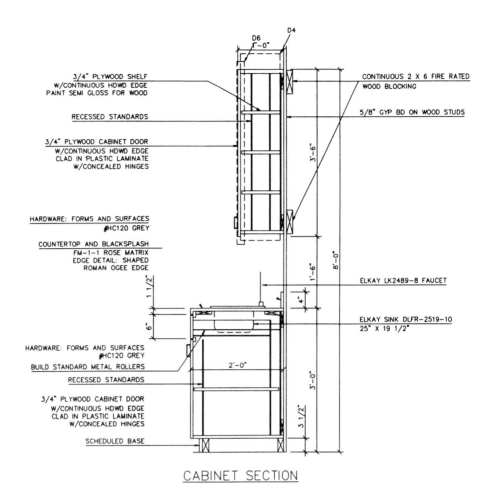

3/4" PLYWOOD SHELF
W/CONTINUOUS HDWD EDGE
PAINT SEMI GLOSS FOR WOOD

RECESSED STANDARDS

3/4" PLYWOOD CABINET DOOR
W/CONTINUOUS HDWD EDGE
CLAD IN PLASTIC LAMINATE
W/CONCEALED HINGES

HARDWARE: FORMS AND SURFACES
#HC120 GREY

COUNTERTOP AND BLACKSPLASH
FM-1-1 ROSE MATRIX
EDGE DETAIL: SHAPED
ROMAN OGEE EDGE

HARDWARE: FORMS AND SURFACES
#HC120 GREY
BUILD STANDARD METAL ROLLERS
RECESSED STANDARDS

3/4" PLYWOOD CABINET DOOR
W/CONTINUOUS HDWD EDGE
CLAD IN PLASTIC LAMINATE
W/CONCEALED HINGES

SCHEDULED BASE

CONTINUOUS 2 X 6 FIRE RATED
WOOD BLOCKING

5/8" GYP BD ON WOOD STUDS

ELKAY LK2489-8 FAUCET

ELKAY SINK DLFR-2519-10
25" X 19 1/2"

CABINET SECTION

FIGURE 18-32

Exercise 18-5: Tenant Space
Conference Room Chair
Dimensions (Scale: $\frac{1}{2}'' = 1'\text{-}0''$)

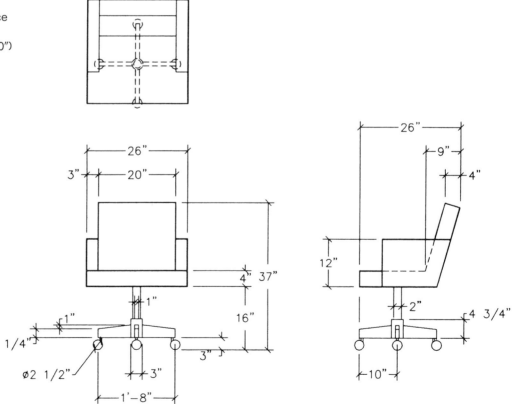

Chapter 18: Basic Three-Dimensional Models

REVIEW QUESTIONS

1. Drawing in three dimensions requires the same concepts of space as drawing in two dimensions.
   a. True
   b. False

2. Thickness values may be set with the use of which of the following commands?
   a. LAYER
   b. TILEMODE
   c. VPORTS
   d. ELEV
   e. VPOINT

3. 3D objects may be selected from which of the following pull-down menus in the menu bar?
   a. View
   b. Tools
   c. Draw
   d. Format
   c. Modify

4. Which of the following viewpoints displays a view to the right in front and above the object?
   a. 1,-1,1
   b. -1,-1,1
   c. -1,1,1
   d. 1,1,-1
   e. 0,0,1

5. Which of the following viewpoints displays a view one unit to the left, one unit in front, and one unit above the object?
   a. 1,-1,1
   b. -1,-1,1
   c. -1,1,1
   d. 1,1,-1
   e. 0,0,1

6. Which is the correct setting to use with the 2D Solid command, to create a 3D object that is 3′ from the floor and 5′ tall?
   a. Elevation 3′, thickness 5′
   b. Elevation 0, thickness 8′
   c. Elevation 5′, thickness 3′
   d. Elevation 8′, thickness -3′
   e. Elevation 0, thickness 5′

7. The Plan View command is found on which of the following menus on the View menu of the menu bar?
   a. 3D Viewpoint
   b. Tiled Viewports
   c. Named Views
   d. 3D Dynamic View
   e. Display

8. When PLAN<enter> is typed and the default option is selected by pressing <enter> again, Auto-CAD
   a. Displays a plan view of the current UCS
   b. Displays a plan view of the object
   c. Displays a plan view of the World UCS
   d. Displays a plan view of all named UCSs
   e. All the above

9. When the Viewpoint Presets dialog box is used, which of the following angles from the X–Y plane will provide a viewpoint from below the object?
   a. 60
   b. 30
   c. 0
   d. -30
   e. None of these angles can be used.

10. Clicking a point on the AutoCAD compass within the larger outer circle, above the horizontal line and to the left of the vertical line, produces which of the following views?
   a. Behind, below, and to the left of the object
   b. In front, below, and to the left of the object
   c. Behind, above, and to the left of the object
   d. In front, above, and to the left of the object
   e. Behind, below, and to the right of the object

11. Write the command described in this chapter that allows you to view an object in three dimensions.

   _____

12. Write the command that splits the active viewport into two, three, or four areas.

   _____

13. Write the command that allows you to restore a viewport configuration saved in model space to a display in paper space.

   _____

14. Describe the two different ways to set ELEVATION and THICKNESS.

   _____

   _____

15. Write the command that allows you to change the thickness of an existing entity.

   _____

16. Write the command that allows you to change the elevation of an existing entity.

   _____

17. Describe the uses of model space and paper space in constructing and plotting 3D models.

   Model space _____

   _____

   Paper space _____

   _____

18. List five 3D objects that can be created from the 3D Objects dialog box.

   _____   _____

   _____   _____

   _____

19. Describe how to activate the AutoCAD compass from the VPOINT prompt "Rotate/<View point><default>:".

   _____

20. Describe the view obtained with a viewpoint to the right side of a 3D object, at a -45° angle from the X–Y plane.

   _____

OBJECTIVES

When you have completed this chapter, you will be able to

☐ Draw the following primitive solids: box, sphere, wedge, cone, cylinder, torus.
☐ Make settings to display solids smoothly.
☐ Draw extruded solids.
☐ Draw revolved solids.
☐ Rotate solids about the X, Y, or Z axis.
☐ Form chamfers and fillets on solid edges.
☐ Join two or more solids.
☐ Subtract one or more solids from another solid.
☐ Form a solid model from the common volume of two intersecting solids.
☐ Obtain a perspective view of a complex solid model.

INTRODUCTION

AutoCAD provides three means of creating 3D models: basic 3D using elevation and thickness, surface modeling, and solid modeling. The previous chapter covered basic 3D. Surface modeling uses commands similar to those used in solid modeling but requires a wire frame on which surfaces are placed to give the illusion of a solid model. Models cannot be subtracted from other models when surface modeling is used, nor can they be joined to form a composite model. Surface modeling is not covered in this book. Solid modeling creates solids that are much more useful and easier to modify than surface models. A solid may be a single object called a *primitive,* or it may be a combination of objects called a *composite.*

SOLIDS Commands Used to Create Basic Shapes

A primitive solid is a single solid shape that has had nothing added to or subtracted from it. There are six solid primitives (box, sphere, wedge, cone, cylinder, torus) that are the basic shapes often used in solid modeling. They are drawn by using six commands:

    Box
    Cone
    Cylinder
    Sphere
    Torus
    Wedge

AutoCAD also allows you to form solids by extruding (adding height) and revolving (rotating about an axis) two-dimensional drawing entities such as polylines, circles, ellipses, rectangles, polygons, and donuts. The commands that extrude and revolve drawing entities to form solids are:

    Extrude
    Revolve

SOLIDS Commands Used to Create Composite Solids

Composite solids are formed by joining primitive solids, other solids, or a combination of the two. These combinations may also be added to or subtracted from other solids to form the composite model needed. The following commands used to create composite solids are described in this chapter:

Union Allows you to join several solids to form a single solid.

Intersect Allows you to create composite solids from the intersection of two or more solids. Intersect creates a new solid by calculating the common volume of two or more existing solids.

Subtract Allows you to subtract solids from other solids.

Interfere Does the same thing as Intersect except it retains the original objects.

SOLIDS Commands Used to Edit Solids

Slice Used to create a new solid by cutting the existing solid into two pieces and removing or retaining either or both pieces.

Section Used to create the cross-sectional area of a solid. That area may then be hatched using the Hatch or Bhatch commands with any pattern you choose. Be sure the section is parallel with the current UCS when you hatch the area.

Other Commands That Can Be Used to Edit Solids

Rotate 3D Used to rotate solids about X, Y, or Z axes.

Mirror3D Used to create mirror images of solids about a plane specified by three points.

Trim Used to trim lines, polylines and similar entities in 3D space, but this command will not trim a solid shape.

Extend Used to extend lines, polylines and similar entities in 3D space, but this command will not extend a solid shape.

Fillet Used to create fillets and rounds. Specify the radius for the fillet and then click the edge or edges to be filleted.

Chamfer Used to create chamfers. Specify the distances for the chamfer and then click the edge or edges to be chamfered.

Align Used to move a solid so that a selected plane on the first solid is aligned with a selected plane on a second solid.

Explode Used to explode a solid into regions or planes. (Example: An exploded solid box becomes six regions: four sides, a top, and a bottom.) Use care with Explode. When you explode a solid you destroy it as a solid shape.

All the following commands may be used to edit or view solids in the same manner as you have used them previously:

Move	Dview
Chprop	Vpoint
Erase	Mview
Scale	Zoom
UCS	Pan

Settings That Control How the Solid Is Displayed

FACETRES Used to make shaded solids and those with hidden lines removed appear smoother. Values range from 0.01 to 10.0. The default value is 0.5. Higher values take longer to regenerate but look better. If you change this value, you can update the solid to the new value by using the Shade or Hide command again.

ISOLINES Sets the number of lines per surface on solids. Values range from 0 to 2047. The default value is 4. Ten is a good middle ground. If you change this value, you can update the solid to the new value by regenerating the drawing.

FIGURE 19-1
Exercise 19-1 Complete

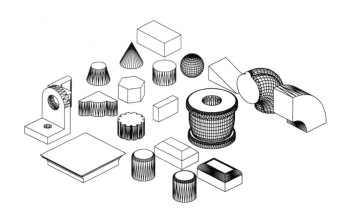

Changing AME Models from Previous Versions of AutoCAD to R14

Ameconvert   Used to convert AME solid models to AutoCAD solid objects. The solids selected must be AME Release 2 or 2.1 regions or solids. AutoCAD ignores all other objects.

Exercise 19–1, Parts 1 through 6, provides step-by-step instructions for using the solid commands just described. These basic commands will also be used to create complex solid models in Exercise 19–2. Upon completion of this chapter, and mastery of the commands included in the chapter, you will have a sound foundation for learning solid modeling.

When you have completed Exercise 19–1, Parts 1 through 6, your drawing will look similar to Figure 19–1.

EXERCISE 19–1, PART 1
Drawing Primitive Solids

In Part 1 of this exercise you will set FACETRES and ISOLINES and use Box, Sphere, Wedge, Cone, Cylinder, and Torus to draw primitive solids. Turn on the computer and start AutoCAD. The Start Up dialog box is displayed.

1. CLICK: **Use a Wizard**
2. CLICK: **Quick Setup**
   CLICK: **OK**
3. Set Drawing Units: **Architectural**
   CLICK: **Next>>**
4. Set drawing Width: **11″** × Length: **8$\frac{1}{2}$″**
   CLICK: **Done**
5. **Use SaveAs... to save the drawing on the hard drive with the name CH19-EX1.**
6. Set Grid: $\frac{1}{2}$
7. Set Snap: $\frac{1}{16}$
8. Create the following Layers:

LAYER NAME	COLOR	LINETYPE
3d-w	White	CONTINUOUS
3d-r	Red	CONTINUOUS
3d-g	Green	CONTINUOUS

9. Set Layer 3d-w current.

10. Use the Vports command to make two vertical viewports. Zoom-All in both viewports to start, then Zoom in closer so your view is similar to the figures shown. Either viewport may be active as you draw. You will need to Zoom-All occasionally in both viewports to see the entire drawing.

11. Use the Vpoint command to set a 1,-1,1 viewpoint for the right viewport.

FACETRES and ISOLINES

Set the FACETRES and ISOLINES variables:

Prompt	Response
Command:	TYPE: **FACETRES\<enter>**
New value for FACETRES <0.5000>:	TYPE: **2\<enter>**
Command:	TYPE: **ISOLINES\<enter>**
New value for ISOLINES <4>:	TYPE: **10\<enter>**

BOX

Draw a solid box, 1.2 × .8 × .5 height (Figure 19–2):

Prompt	Response
Command:	**Box** (or TYPE: **BOX \<enter>**)
Center/<Corner of box> <0,0,0>:	TYPE: **1/2,7-1/2 \<enter>**
Cube/Length/<Other corner>:	TYPE: **1-3/4,8-1/4 \<enter>**
Height:	TYPE: **1/2 \<enter>**

Center   Allows you to draw a box by first locating its center.
Cube   Allows you to draw a cube by specifying the length of one side.
Length   Allows you to draw a box by specifying its length (X), width (Y), and height (Z).

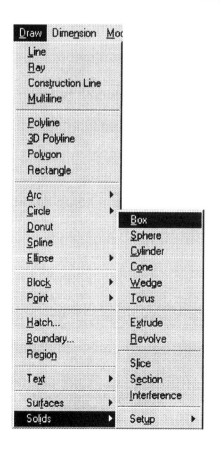

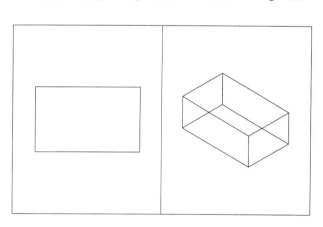

FIGURE 19–2
Draw a Solid Box

FIGURE 19–3
Draw a Solid Sphere

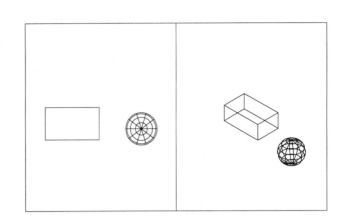

SPHERE

Draw a solid sphere, $\frac{3}{8}$ radius (Figure 19–3):

Prompt	Response
Command:	**Sphere** (or TYPE: **SPHERE <enter>**)
Center of sphere> <0,0,0>:	TYPE: **2-3/4,7-3/4<enter>**
Diameter/<Radius> of sphere:	TYPE: **3/8<enter>**

WEDGE

Draw a solid wedge, $\frac{3}{4} \times 1\frac{1}{4} \times \frac{1}{2}$ height (Figure 19–4):

Prompt	Response
Command:	**Wedge** (or TYPE: **WEDGE <enter>**)
Center/<Corner of wedge> <0,0,0>:	TYPE: **3-3/4,7-1/2<enter>**
Cube/Length/<other corner>:	TYPE: **5,8-1/4<enter>**
Height:	TYPE: **1/2<enter>**

CONE

Draw a solid cone, $\frac{3}{8}$ radius, $\frac{3}{4}$ height (Figure 19–5):

Prompt	Response
Command:	**Cone** (or TYPE: **CONE <enter>**)
Elliptical/<center point> <0,0,0>:	TYPE: **1-1/4,6-1/2<enter>**
Diameter/<Radius>:	TYPE: **3/8<enter>**
Apex/<Height>:	TYPE: **3/4<enter>**

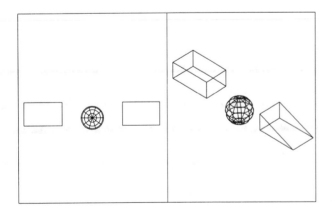

FIGURE 19–4
Draw a Solid Wedge

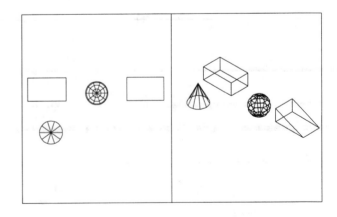

FIGURE 19–5
Draw a Solid Cone

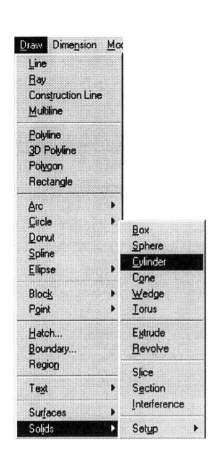

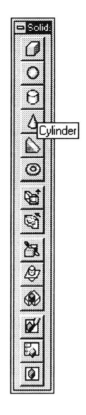

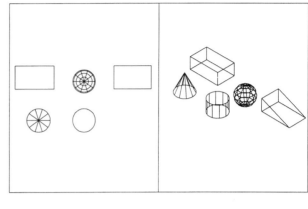

FIGURE 19–6
Draw a Solid Cylinder

CYLINDER

Draw a solid cylinder, $\frac{3}{8}$ radius, $\frac{1}{2}$ height (Figure 19–6):

Prompt	Response
Command:	**Cylinder** (or TYPE: **CYLINDER <enter>**)
Elliptical/<Center point> <0,0,0>:	TYPE: **2-3/4,6-1/2<enter>**
Diameter/<Radius>:	TYPE: **3/8<enter>**
Center of other end/<Height>:	TYPE: **1/2<enter>**

TORUS

Draw a solid torus (a 3D donut), $\frac{3}{8}$ torus radius, $\frac{1}{4}$ tube radius (Figure 19–7):

FIGURE 19–7
Draw a Solid Torus

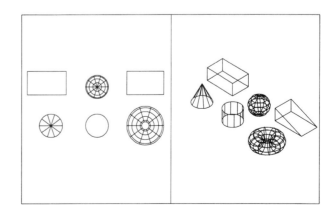

FIGURE 19–8

Radius of the Tube and Radius of
the Torus

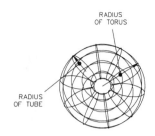

Prompt	Response
Command:	**Torus** (or TYPE: **TORUS\<enter>**)
Center of torus> <0,0,0>:	TYPE: **4-3/8,6-1/2\<enter>**
Diameter/<Radius> of torus:	TYPE: **3/8\<enter>**
Diameter/<Radius> of tube:	TYPE: **1/4\<enter>**

The radius of the torus is the distance from the center of the 3D donut to the center of the tube that forms the donut. The radius of the tube is the radius of the tube forming the donut (Figure 19–8).

EXERCISE 19–1, PART 2
Using Extrude to Draw Extruded Solids

Draw an Extruded Circle

Draw a circle (Figure 19–9):

Prompt	Response
Command:	TYPE: **C\<enter>**
3P/2P/TTR/<Center point>:	TYPE: **1-1/4,5\<enter>**
Diameter/<Radius>:	TYPE: **3/8\<enter>**

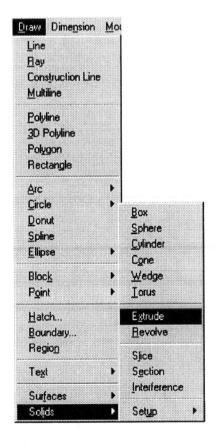

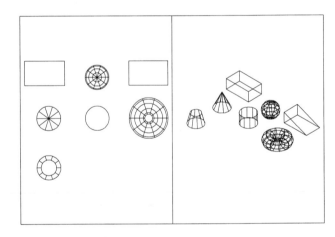

FIGURE 19–9

Extruding and Tapering a Circle

Extrude the circle, $\frac{1}{2}$ height, 15° extrusion taper angle (Figure 19–9):

Prompt	Response
Command:	**Extrude**
	(or TYPE: **EXT<enter>**)
Select objects:	**Click the circle.**
Select objects:	**<enter>**
Path/<Height of extrusion>:	TYPE: **1/2<enter>**
Extrusion taper angle <0>:	**15<enter>**

Draw an Extruded Polygon

Draw a polygon (Figure 19–10):

FIGURE 19–10
Extruding a Polygon

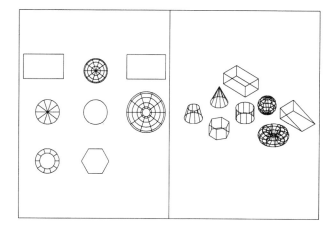

Prompt	Response
Command:	**Polygon**
	(or TYPE: **POL<enter>**)
Number of sides <4>:	TYPE: **6<enter>**
Edge/<Center of polygon>:	TYPE: **2-3/4,5<enter>**
Inscribed in circle/Circumscribed about circle (I/C)<I>:	TYPE: **C<enter>**
Radius of circle:	TYPE: **3/8<enter>**

Extrude the polygon, $\frac{1}{2}$ height, 0° extrusion taper angle (Figure 19–10):

Prompt	Response
Command:	**Extrude**
Select objects:	**Click the hexagon.**
Select objects:	**<enter>**
Path/<Height of extrusion>:	TYPE: **1/2<enter>**
Extrusion taper angle <0>:	**<enter>**

Draw an Extruded Rectangle

Draw a rectangle (Figure 19–11):

Prompt	Response
Command:	**Rectangle (or TYPE: REC<enter>)**
Chamfer/Elevation/Fillet/Thickness/ Width/<First corner>:	TYPE: **4-1/4,4-1/2<enter>**
Other corner:	TYPE: **4-1/2,5-3/8<enter>**

FIGURE 19–11
Extruding a Rectangle

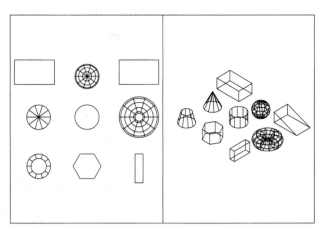

Extrude the rectangle, $\frac{1}{2}$ height, 0° extrusion taper angle (Figure 19–11):

Prompt	Response
Command:	**Extrude**
Select objects:	**Click the rectangle.**
Select objects:	**<enter>**
Path/<Height of extrusion>:	TYPE: **1/2<enter>**
Extrusion taper angle <0>:	**<enter>**

Draw an Extruded Structural Angle

Draw the outline of the cross section of a structural angle (Figure 19–12):

Prompt	Response
Command:	TYPE: **L<enter>**
From point:	TYPE: **1,3<enter>**
To point:	TYPE: **@7/8,0<enter>**
To point:	TYPE: **@0,1/4<enter>**
To point:	TYPE: **@–5/8,0<enter>**
To point:	TYPE: **@0,5/8<enter>**
To point:	TYPE: **@–1/4,0<enter>**
To point:	TYPE: **C<enter>**

Add a $\frac{1}{8}$ radius fillet to the outline (Figure 19–12):

Prompt	Response
Command:	**Fillet**
	(or TYPE: **F<enter>**)

FIGURE 19–12
Extruding a Structural Steel Angle

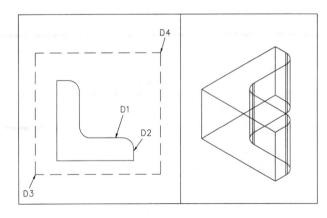

Prompt	Response
(TRIM mode) Current fillet radius = 0'-0" Polyline/Radius/Trim/	
<Select first object>:	TYPE: **R<enter>**
Enter fillet radius <0'-0">:	TYPE: **1/8<enter>**
Command:	**<enter>**
(TRIM mode) Current fillet radius = 0'-0 1/8" Polyline/Radius/Trim/	
<Select first object>:	**D1** (Use the Zoom-Window command if needed to allow you to pick the necessary lines.)
Select second object:	**D2**
Command:	**<enter>**

On Your Own (Figure 19–12)

Draw $\frac{1}{8}$ radius fillets at the other two intersections shown.

Use Edit Polyline (Pedit) to combine all the lines and fillets into a single entity (Figure 19–12):

Prompt	Response
Command:	**Edit Polyline**
	(or TYPE: **PE<enter>**)
Select polyline:	**Click one of the lines forming the structural angle.**
Select objects: 1 found	
Object selected is not a polyline Do you want to turn it into one?<Y>	**<enter>**
Close/Join/Width/Edit vertex/Fit/ Spline/Decurve/Ltype gen/Undo/eXit <X>:	TYPE: **J<enter>** (to select the Join option)
Select objects:	**D3**
Other corner:	**D4**
Select objects:	**<enter>**
8 segments added to polyline Open/Join/Width/Edit vertex/Fit/ Spline/Decurve/Ltype gen/Undo/eXit <X>:	**<enter>** (to exit from the Pedit command)

Extrude the cross section of the structural angle, $\frac{1}{2}$ height, 0° extrusion taper angle (Figure 19–12):

Prompt	Response
Command:	**Extrude**
Select objects:	**Click the polyline.**
Select objects:	**<enter>**
Path/<Height of extrusion>:	TYPE: **1/2<enter>**
Extrusion taper angle <0>:	**<enter>**

FIGURE 19-13
Extruding a Molding Shape

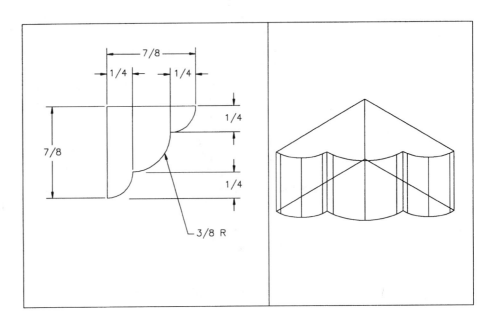

FIGURE 19-14
Extruding a Knurled Knob

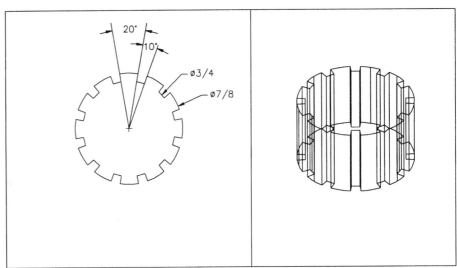

Draw Two Extruded Shapes

On Your Own (Figures 19-13 and 19-14)

1. Draw the two shapes shown as Figures 19-13 and 19-14 in the approximate locations shown in Figure 19-1. Draw one section of the knurled knob, Figure 19-14, and then create a polar array using the Array command. When you draw the section, be sure that you draw only what is needed. If you draw extra lines, the Edit Polyline command cannot join the lines into a single polyline.

2. Use the Edit Polyline command to join all entities of each figure into a single polyline.

3. Extrude each figure to a height of $\frac{1}{2}$.

EXERCISE 19-1, PART 3
Using Revolve to Draw Revolved Solids; Using Rotate
3D to Rotate Solids about the X,Y, and Z Axes

Draw Revolved Shape 1

Draw two circles (Figure 19-15A):

FIGURE 19–15
Revolving a Shape 90°

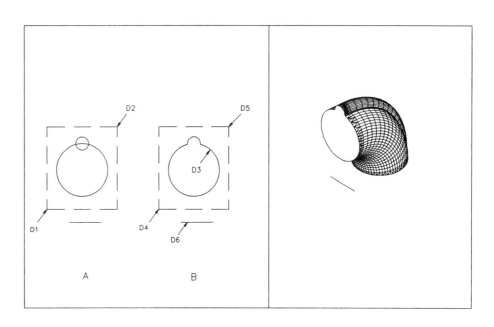

Prompt	Response
Command:	TYPE: **C<enter>**
3P/2P/TTR/<Center point>:	TYPE: **6-1/4,7-3/4<enter>**
Diameter/<Radius>:	TYPE: **1/2<enter>**
Command:	**<enter>**
3P/2P/TTR/<Center point>:	TYPE: **6-1/4,8-1/4<enter>**
Diameter/<Radius>:	TYPE: **1/8<enter>**

Use the Trim command to trim parts of both circles (Figures 19–15A and 19–15B):

Prompt	Response
Command:	**Trim** (or TYPE: **TR<enter>**)
Select cutting edges: (Projmode = UCS, Edgemode = No extend) Select objects:	**D1** (first corner of a window)
Other corner:	**D2** (second corner of a window)
Select objects:	**<enter>**
<Select object to trim>/ Project/Edge/Undo:	**Trim the circles as shown in Figure 19–15B.** (Zoom-Window to get in closer if needed.)

Join all segments of the circles into one polyline (Figure 19–15B):

Prompt	Response
Command:	**Edit Polyline** (or TYPE: **PE<enter>**)
Select objects:	**D3<enter>**
Object selected is not a polyline Do you want to turn it into one? <Y>	**<enter>**
Close/Join/Width/Edit vertex/Fit/ Spline/Decurve/Ltype gen/Undo/eXit <X>:	TYPE: **J<enter>**

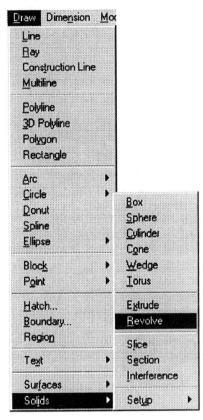

Select objects:	**D4**
Other corner:	**D5**
Select objects:	**<enter>**

1 segment added to polyline
Open/Join/Width/Edit vertex/Fit/
Spline/Decurve/Ltype gen/Undo/eXit <X>:   **<enter>** (to exit from the Edit Polyline
command)

Draw the axis of revolution (Figure 19–15B):

Prompt	Response
Command:	**Line** (or Type: **L<enter>**)
From point:	TYPE: **6,6-3/4<enter>**
To point:	TYPE: **@5/8<0<enter>**
To point:	**<enter>**

**Use Revolve to form a revolved solid created by revolving a single polyline 90°
counterclockwise about an axis (Figure 19–15B):**

Prompt	Response
Command:	**Revolve**
	(or TYPE: **REV<enter>**)
Select objects:	**D3**
Select objects:	**<enter>**
Axis of revolution - Object/X/Y/	
<Start point of axis>:	TYPE: **O<enter>**
Select an object:	**D6** (Be sure to click the left end of the line for counterclockwise rotation.)
Angle of revolution <full circle>:	TYPE: **90<enter>**

Draw a Revolved Rectangle

Draw a rectangle (Figure 19–16):

Prompt	Response
Command:	**Rectangle**
	(or TYPE: **REC<enter>**)
First corner:	TYPE: **7-3/8,7-3/8<enter>**
Other corner:	TYPE: **8-1/4,8-1/8<enter>**

Draw the axis of revolution (Figure 19–16):

Prompt	Response
Command:	TYPE: **L<enter>**
From point:	TYPE: **7-3/8,6-3/4<enter>**
To point:	TYPE: **@3/4<0<enter>**
To point:	**<enter>**

**Use the Revolve command to form a revolved solid created by revolving the
rectangle 90° counterclockwise about an axis (Figure 19–16):**

Prompt	Response
Command:	**Revolve**
Select objects:	**D1<enter>**

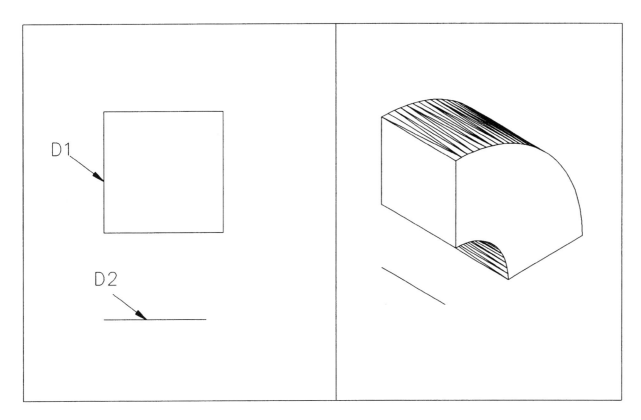

FIGURE 19–16
Revolving a Rectangle

Prompt	Response
Select objects:	**<enter>**
Axis of revolution - Object/X/Y/ <Start point of axis>:	TYPE: **O<enter>**
Pick entity to revolve around:	**D2**
	(Click the left end of the line.)
Angle of revolution <full circle>:	TYPE: **90<enter>**

Draw a Revolved Paper Clip Holder

On Your Own (Figures 19–17 and 19–18)

1. Draw the cross-sectional shape of the object shown in Figure 19–17 using the Line and Arc commands in the approximate locations shown in Figure 19–1.

2. Use the Edit Polyline command to join all entities of the shape into a single closed polyline.

3. Locate the axis of rotation for the shape in the position shown.

4. Use Revolve to revolve the shape full circle about the axis.

Rotate 3D

Use Rotate 3D to rotate the paper clip holder 90° about the X axis so that it assumes the position shown in Figure 19–18:

Prompt	Response
Command:	**Rotate 3D**
	(or TYPE: **ROTATE3D<enter>**)

471

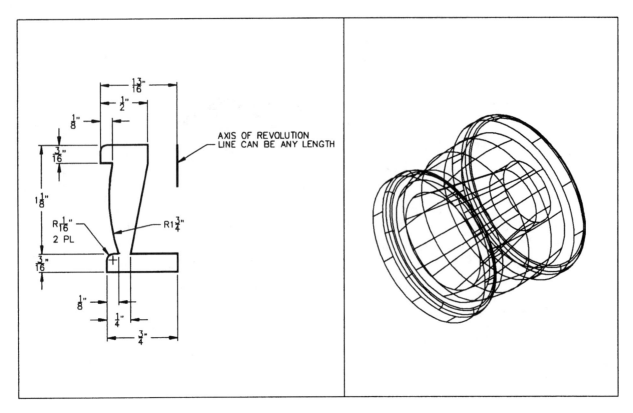

FIGURE 19–17
Revolving a Paper Clip Holder

Prompt	Response
Select objects:	Click: **the paper clip holder**
Select objects:	**<enter>**
Axis by Object/Last/View/Xaxis/Yaxis/	
Zaxis/<2points>:	TYPE: **X<enter>**
Point on X axis <0,0,0>:	TYPE: **CEN<enter>**
of	**D1**
<Rotation angle>/Reference:	TYPE: **90<enter>**

FIGURE 19–18
Rotating an Object about
the X Axis

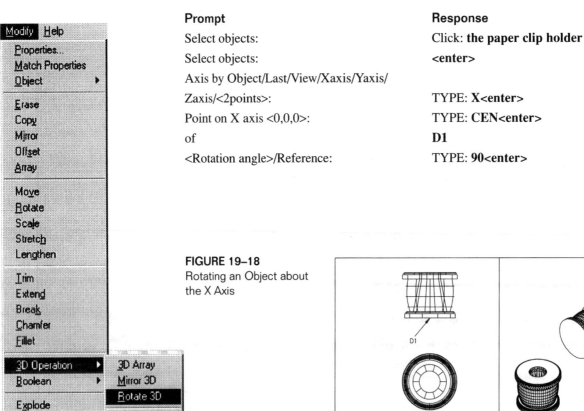

FIGURE 19–19
Chamfering and Filleting Solid
Edges

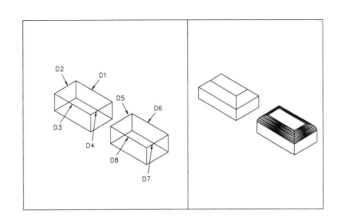

EXERCISE 19–1, PART 4
Using Chamfer and Fillet to Draw Chamfers and Fillets on Solid Edges

Chamfer and Fillet the Top Four Edges of Two Separate Boxes

On Your Own (Figure 19–1)

Use Box to draw two boxes measuring $1\frac{1}{4} \times \frac{3}{4} \times \frac{1}{2}$ H. each, in the approximate locations shown in Figure 19–1.

Chamfer the top four edges of the first box (Figure 19–19):

Prompt	Response
Command:	**Chamfer** (or Type: **CHA\<enter>**)
(TRIM mode) Current chamfer Dist1 = 0′-0″, Dist2 = 0′-0″ Polyline/Distance/Angle/Trim/Method/ \<Select first line>:	TYPE: **D\<enter>**
Enter first chamfer distance <0′-0″>:	TYPE: **3/16\<enter>**
Enter second chamfer distance <0′-0 3/16″>:	**\<enter>**
Command:	**\<enter>**
(TRIM mode) Current chamfer Dist1 = 0′-0 3/16″, Dist2 = 0′-0 3/16″ Polyline/Distance/Angle/Trim/Method/ \<Select first line>:	**D1** (Figure 19–19)
Select base surface:	
Next/\<OK>:	

If the top surface of the box turns dotted, showing it as the selected surface, continue. If one of the side surfaces is selected, TYPE: **N\<enter>** until the top surface is selected.

Prompt	Response
Select base surface:	
Next/\<OK>:	**\<enter>**
Enter base surface distance <0′-0 3/16″>:	**\<enter>**
Enter other surface distance <0′-0 3/16″>:	**\<enter>**
Loop/\<Select edge>:	**D1, D2, D3, D4**
Loop/\<Select edge>:	**\<enter>**

FIGURE 19–20

Chamfering and Filleting Cylinders

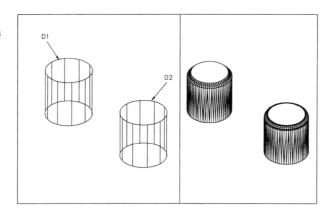

Fillet the top four edges of the second box (Figure 19–19):

Prompt	Response
Command:	**Fillet**
	(or Type: **F<enter>**)
(TRIM mode) Current fillet radius = 0'-0"	
Polyline/Radius/Trim/	
<Select first object>:	**D5** (Figure 19–19)
Enter radius <0'-0">:	TYPE: **3/16<enter>**
Chain/Radius/<Select edge>:	**D6,D7,D8**
Chain/Radius/<Select edge>:	**<enter>**

Chamfer and Fillet on the Top Edge of Two Separate Cylinders

On Your Own (Figure 19–20)

1. Draw two cylinders using Cylinder with a radius of $\frac{3}{8}$ and a height of $\frac{3}{4}$ in the approximate location shown in Figure 19–1.

2. Chamfer the top edge of the first cylinder (Figure 19–20) using chamfer distances of $\frac{1}{16}$. CLICK: **D1** when you select edges to be chamfered.

3. Fillet the top edge of the second cylinder (Figure 19–20) using a fillet radius of $\frac{1}{16}$. Click **D2** when you select edges to be filleted.

The edges of the cylinders should appear as shown in Figure 19–20.

EXERCISE 19–1, PART 5
Using Union to Join Two Solids; Using Subtract to Subtract Solids From Other Solids

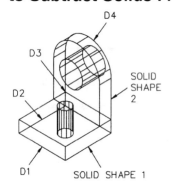

FIGURE 19–21

Drawing a Composite Solid

Draw Solid Shape 1

Draw solid shape 1 (the base of the shape), and a cylinder that will be the hole in the base (Figure 19–21):

Prompt	Response
Command:	**Box**
Center/<Corner of box> <0,0,0>:	TYPE: **4-1/2,3/4<enter>**
Cube/Length/<Other corner>:	TYPE: **@1,1<enter>**
Height:	TYPE: **1/4<enter>**
Command:	**Cylinder**
	(or TYPE: **CYLINDER<enter>**)

Prompt	Response
Elliptical/<center point><0,0,0>:	TYPE: **.X<enter>**
of	TYPE: **MID<enter>**
of	**D1**
(need YZ):	TYPE: **MID<enter>**
of	**D2**
Diameter/<Radius>:	TYPE: **1/8<enter>**
Center of other end/<Height>:	TYPE: **1/2<enter>** (Make the height of the hole tall enough so you can be sure it goes through the model.)

Draw Solid Shape 2

On Your Own

Set the UCS Icon command to ORigin so you will be able to see the ucsicon move when the origin is relocated. (TYPE: **UCSICON<enter>**, then **OR<enter>**)

Rotate the UCS 90° about the X axis, and move the origin of the UCS to the upper left rear corner of the box (Figure 19–21):

Prompt	Response
Command:	**UCS**
Origin/ZAxis/3point/OBject/View/X/Y/Z/ Prev/Restore/Save/Del/?/<World>:	TYPE: **X<enter>**
Rotation angle about X axis <0>:	TYPE: **90<enter>**
Command:	**<enter>** (to repeat the last command)
Origin/ZAxis/3point/OBject/View/X/Y/Z/ Prev/Restore/Save/Del/?/<World>:	TYPE: **O<enter>**
Origin point <0,0,0>:	TYPE: **END<enter>**
of	**D3**

Draw solid shape 2 (the vertical solid), and a cylinder that will be the hole in the vertical solid (Figure 19–21):

Prompt	Response
Command:	**Polyline** (or TYPE: **PL<enter>**)
From point:	TYPE: **0,0<enter>**
Arc/Close/Halfwidth/Length/Undo/ Width/<Endpoint of line>:	TYPE: **@1<0<enter>**
Arc/Close/Halfwidth/Length/Undo/ Width/<Endpoint of line>:	TYPE: **@3/4<90<enter>**
Arc/Close/Halfwidth/Length/Undo/ Width/<Endpoint of line>:	TYPE: **A<enter>**
<Endpoint of arc>:	TYPE: **@1<180<enter>**
<Endpoint of arc>:	TYPE: **CL <enter>**
Command:	**Extrude** (or TYPE: **EXT<enter>**)
Select objects:	**Click the polyline just drawn.**
Select objects:	**<enter>**
Path <Height of extrusion>:	TYPE: **1/4<enter>**
Extrusion taper angle <0>:	**<enter>**
Command:	**Cylinder**

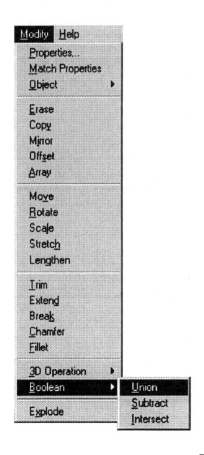

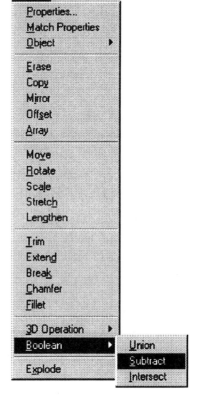

Elliptical/	
<center point><0,0,0>:	TYPE: **CEN<enter>**
of	**D4**
Diameter/<Radius>:	TYPE: **1/4<enter>**
Center of other end/<Height>:	TYPE: **1/2<enter>**

The cylinder is longer than the thickness of the upright piece so you can be sure that the hole goes all the way through it.

Make sure the base of the cylinder is located on the back surface of the upright piece. If the cylinder is located on the front surface of the upright piece, move the cylinder $\frac{3}{8}$ in the negative Z direction.

Union

Join the base and the vertical shape together to form one model:

Prompt	Response
Command:	**Union**
	(or TYPE: **UNION<enter>**)
Select objects:	**Click the base (shape 1) and the vertical solid (shape 2).**
Select objects:	**<enter>**

Subtract

Subtract the holes from the model:

Prompt	Response
Command:	**Subtract**
	(or TYPE: **SU<enter>**)

FIGURE 19–22
The Completed Model after a Hide

Prompt	Response
Select solids and regions to subtract from...	
Select objects:	**Click any point on the model.**
Select objects:	**<enter>**
Select solids and regions to subtract...	
Select objects:	**Click the two holes.**
Select objects:	**<enter>**

Hide

Perform a Hide to be sure the model is correct (Figure 19–22):

Prompt	Response
Command:	**Hide** (or TYPE: **HI<enter>**)

The model should appear as shown in Figure 19–22.

On Your Own

Return the UCS to the World origin.

EXERCISE 19–1, PART 6
Using Intersection to Form a Solid Model
from the Common Volume of Two Intersecting Solids

Drawing the solid model in Exercise 19–1, Part 6, demonstrates some powerful tools that can be used to form complex models.

In this exercise two separate solid shapes are drawn (in this case the same shape is copied and rotated so the two shapes are at right angles to each other) and moved so that they intersect. Intersection is used to combine the shapes to form one solid model from the common volume of the two intersecting solids. Figure 19–23 shows the two separate solid shapes, and the solid model that is formed from the common volume of the two solid shapes.

This shape will also be used in Exercise 19–3 to form the cornices at the top of the columns (Figure 19–43).

FIGURE 19–23
Two Shapes and the Shape Formed from the Intersected Volume of the Two Shapes

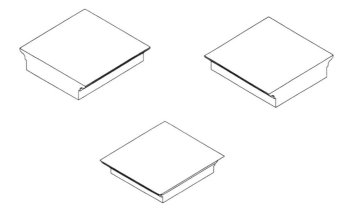

Draw Two Extruded Shapes at Right Angles to Each Other

On Your Own

1. Zoom out so you can draw the full size shape shown in Figure 19–24 (Zoom .5X) in the left viewport. In an open area of the screen draw Figure 19–24 using line and arc or circle commands.

2. Use Edit Polyline to join all parts of Figure 19–24 to form a single polyline.

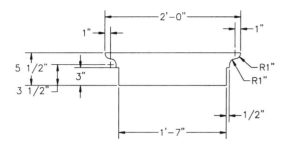

FIGURE 19–24
Dimensions for the Extruded Shapes

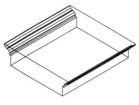

FIGURE 19–26
Both Shapes Extruded

FIGURE 19–25
Two Shapes Rotated 90° to Each
Other

3. Use the Scale command to scale the polyline to $\frac{1}{12}$ its size. (This a scale of $1'' = 1'$. In Exercise 19–3 you will scale this model to its original size.)

4. In the right viewport, copy the shape and and use Rotate 3D to rotate both shapes 90° about the X axis.

5. Use Rotate 3D to rotate the shape on the right 90° about the Z axis (Figure 19–25).

6. Rotate the UCS 90° about the X axis and extrude the shape on the left 2″ with a 0 taper angle (Figure 19–26).

7. Rotate the UCS 90° about the Y axis and extrude the shape on the right 2″ with a 0 taper angle.

Move One Solid to Intersect with the Other Solid

Use the Move command to move the solid on the left to intersect with the other solid (Figure 19–27):

Prompt	Response
Command:	**Move**
Select objects:	**Click the shape on the left.**
Select objects:	**<enter>**
Base point or displacement:	TYPE: **END<enter>**
of	**D1**
Second point of displacement:	TYPE: **END<enter>**
of	**D2**

Intersect

Use Intersect to form a solid model from the common volume of the two intersecting solids (Figure 19–28):

Prompt	Response
Command:	**Intersect**

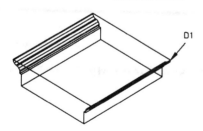

FIGURE 19–27
Moving One Shape to Intersect with the Other

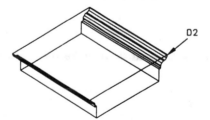

FIGURE 19–28
The Shape Formed from the Intersected Shapes

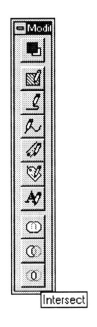

Intersect

Prompt	Response
	(or TYPE: INTERSECT<enter>)
Select objects:	**Click both shapes.**
2 solids intersected	

The display should appear as shown in Figure 19–28.

Perform a Hide to be sure the solid model is correct (Figure 19–29):

Prompt	Response
Command:	**Hide** (or TYPE: **HI<enter>**)

The display should appear as shown in Figure 19–29.

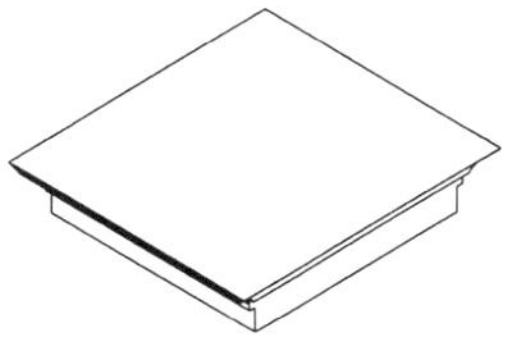

Wblock the Intersected Model

You should now Wblock the intersected model so you can use it in Exercise 19–3 to form the cornices at the tops of the columns (see Figure 19–43).

On Your Own

Return the UCS to World so you will not be surprised at the position the model will assume when it is inserted.

Use Wblock to save the model to a floppy disk (Figure 19–30):

Prompt	Response
Command:	TYPE: **WBLOCK<enter>**
The Create Drawing File dialog box appears:	**Locate the $3\frac{1}{2}$ Floppy [A:].**
	TYPE: **19-3** in the File name: as shown in Figure 19–30
	CLICK: **Save**
Block name:	**<enter>**
Insertion base point:	TYPE: **END<enter>**
of	**Click the bottom corner of the intersected shape using Osnap-Endpoint. It will be the lowest point on the display.**
Select objects:	**Click the intersected shape.**

FIGURE 19–29
The Intersected Solid after a Hide

FIGURE 19–30
Wblocking the Intersected Shape

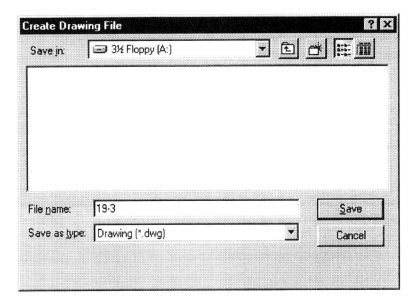

Prompt	Response
Select objects:	<enter>
Command:	**Undo**
	(or TYPE: **U<enter>**)

The shape now exists on your floppy disk as 19-3.dwg, and it is also on the current drawing.

Complete Exercise 19–1

On Your Own

1. Use the Move command to move the intersected shape to the approximate location shown in Figure 19–1.
2. Use the Vports command to return to a single viewport of the 3D viewport (Figure 19–1).
3. Set the UCS to View, and add your name to the lower right corner of the drawing.

PLOT

Plot the 3D viewport on a standard size sheet of paper. Be sure to pick the Hide Lines box in the Plot Configuration dialog box so the final plot appears as shown in Figure 19–1.

SAVE

Save the drawing in two places.

EXERCISE 19–2
Creating a Solid Model of a Chair

FIGURE 19–31
Exercise 19–2 Complete

In this exercise you will create a solid model of a chair (Figure 19–31). This chair will be inserted into the structure that you will create in Exercise 19–3. The Prompt/Response format will not be used in this exercise. The steps will be listed with suggested commands for creating this model. Turn on the computer and start AutoCAD. The Start Up dialog box is displayed.

1. CLICK: **Use a Wizard**
2. CLICK: **Quick Setup**
3. Set Drawing Units: **Architectural**
   CLICK: **Next>>**
4. Set drawing Width: **5′** × Length: **5′**
   CLICK: **Done**
5. **Use SaveAs... to save the drawing on the hard drive with the name CH19-EX2.**
6. Set Grid: **1**
7. Set Snap: $\frac{1}{4}$
8. Create the following Layers:

LAYER NAME	COLOR	LINETYPE
3d-m	Magenta	CONTINUOUS
3d-g	Green	CONTINUOUS

9. Set Layer 3d-m current.
10. Use the Vports command to make two vertical viewports. Zoom-All in both viewports to start, then Zoom in closer as needed. You will find it easier to draw in the left viewport and use the right viewport to determine if the model is proceeding as it should.
11. Use the Vpoint command to set a 1,-1,1 viewpoint for the right viewport.
12. Set FACETRES to 2; set ISOLINES to 10.

FIGURE 19–32
Dimensions for the Chair

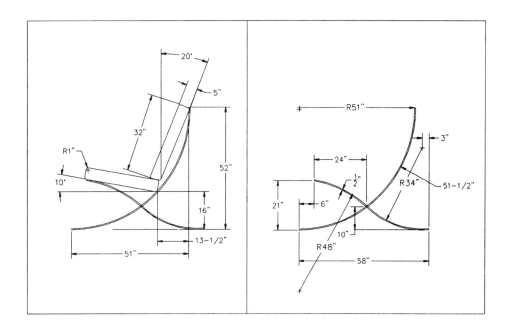

Draw Two 32″ × 5″ Cushions

1. Draw the cushions in vertical and horizontal positions and rotate them to the positions shown using the dimensions from Figure 19–32. (Both cushions are the same size.)

2. Draw a temporary construction line to locate the bottom of the chair legs.

3. Use Rectangle to draw the bottom cushion in a horizontal position 16″ above the temporary construction line. Use the Polyline option of the Fillet command to create the 1″ fillet on all four corners at the same time.

4. Use Rotate to rotate the bottom cushion −10° as shown.

5. Use Rectangle to draw the back cushion in a vertical position, and fillet all four corners.

6. Use Rotate to rotate the back cushion −20°.

7. Use Stretch to form the bottom of the back cushion so it fits flush against the bottom cushion.

Draw Chair Legs and Back Support

1. Set Layer 3d-g current.

2. Draw temporary construction lines as needed to locate the beginning and ending points of the three arcs.

3. Use Arc, Start-End-Radius to draw the three arcs. Be sure to use the Endpoint of the arc with the 48″ radius as the starting point of the arc with the 34″ radius so the two can be joined together to form a single polyline.

4. Use Edit Polyline to join the arcs with the 34″ and 48″ radii.

5. Use Offset to offset the joined arcs $\frac{1}{2}$″ down.

6. Use Offset to offset the arc with the 51″ radius $\frac{1}{2}$″ to the right.

7. Use the Line command to draw lines at the ends of all arcs so that the two metal legs have a thickness.

8. Use Edit Polyline to join all parts of each leg so they can be extruded.

Draw Chair Supports

1. Draw the three supports in Figure 19–33 in the locations shown.

2. Use the Rectangle command to draw the 2″ × $\frac{1}{2}$″ supports in either a vertical or horizontal position as needed.

3. Use the Rotate and Move commands to locate the supports in the positions shown.

FIGURE 19–33
Chair Supports Measuring 2″ × $\frac{1}{2}$″

Extrude Cushions, Legs, and Supports

1. Use the Extrude command to extrude the two cushions 36″ in the positive Z direction with a 0 taper angle.

2. Use the Extrude command to extrude the polylines forming the legs $2\frac{1}{2}$″ in the positive Z direction with a 0 taper angle.

3. Use the Extrude command to extrude the supports 31″ in the positive Z direction with a 0 taper angle.

Move Supports So They Sit on Top of the Legs

Use the Move command to move the three supports $2\frac{1}{2}$″ in the positive Z direction (second point of displacement will be @0,0,2-1/2).

Join Extruded Legs to Form a Single Piece

Use the Union command to join the two extruded legs to form a single piece.

Add the Other Set of Legs

Use the Copy command to copy the legs $33\frac{1}{2}$″ in the positive Z direction.

Rotate Chair to the Upright and Forward Position

1. Use the Rotate 3D command to rotate the chair 90° about the X axis. Click one of the lowest points of the end of one of the chair legs as the Point on X axis.

2. Use the Rotate 3D command to rotate the chair 90° about the Z axis. Click one of the lowest points of the end of one of the chair legs as the Point on Z axis.

Remove Hidden Lines

Use the Hide command to remove hidden lines so the chair appears as shown in Figure 19–31.

Save the Drawing as a Wblock

1. Use the Wblock command to save the drawing on a floppy disk with the name EX19-2. Use the bottom of the front of the left leg as the insertion point.

2. Undo the Wblock so you can plot the drawing.

3. Save the drawing as CH19-EX2.

PLOT

1. Plot the drawing at a scale of 1=24 in the center of an $8\frac{1}{2}$″ × 11″ sheet.

2. Do not use Single Line Text to place your name on the drawing. Write your name on this drawing so you can use the drawing in Exercise 19–3.

EXERCISE 19–3
Create a Solid Model of a Patio

In this exercise you will create a solid model of an elaborate patio area and insert your chair into it (Figure 19–34). The Prompt–Response format will not be used in this exercise. The steps will be listed with suggested commands for creating this model. Turn on the computer and start AutoCAD. The Start Up dialog box is displayed.

1. CLICK: **Use a Wizard**
2. CLICK: **Quick Setup**
3. Set Drawing Units: **Architectural**
   CLICK: **Next**

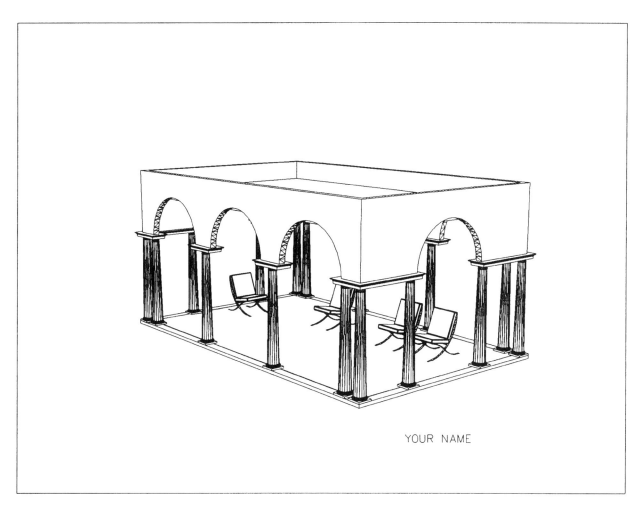

FIGURE 19–34
Exercise 19–3 Complete

4. Set drawing Width: **50′** × Length: **40′**
   CLICK: **Done**
5. **Use SaveAs... to save the drawing on the hard drive with the name CH19-EX3.**
6. Set Grid: **2′**
7. Set Snap: **6″**
8. Create the following Layers:

LAYER NAME	COLOR	LINETYPE
3d-m	Magenta	CONTINUOUS
3d-c	Cyan	CONTINUOUS

9. Set Layer 3d-m current.
10. Use the Vports command to make two vertical viewports. Zoom-All in both viewports to start, then Zoom in closer as needed. You will find it easier to draw in the left viewport and use the right viewport to determine if the model is proceeding as it should.
11. Use the Vpoint command to set a 1,-1,1 viewpoint for the right viewport.
12. Set FACETRES to 2; set ISOLINES to 10.

Let's begin at the bottom and work up.

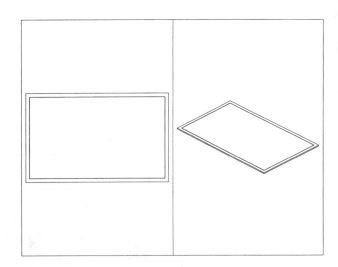

FIGURE 19–35
The Concrete Pad with a 1'
Border

Draw the Concrete Pad with a Border Around It

The concrete pad and the border have to be two separate objects extruded to a height of 4″. Draw the outside edge of the border and extrude it, then draw the inside edge, extrude it, and subtract it from the outside edge. Finally, draw the pad and extrude it (Figure 19–35):

1. Use the Rectangle command to draw a rectangle measuring 39′ × 24′. Start the first corner at absolute coordinates 6′,8′.

2. Use the Rectangle command to draw a rectangle measuring 37′ × 22′. Start the first corner at absolute coordinates 7′,9′.

3. Use the Offset command to offset the 37′ × 22′ rectangle 1/2″ to the inside to form the concrete pad with a $\frac{1}{2}″$ space between it and the border.

4. Use the Extrude command to extrude all three rectangles 4″ in the positive Z direction, 0 taper angle.

5. Use the Subtract command to subtract the inside of the border (the 37′ × 22′ extruded rectangle) from the outside of the border. You will have to Zoom a window so you can get close enough to pick the correct rectangle to subtract.

Draw the Base of the Columns

Draw the base of the columns on the lower left corner of the drawing. They will be copied after the columns are placed on them (Figure 19–36):

FIGURE 19–36
Draw the Base of the Column

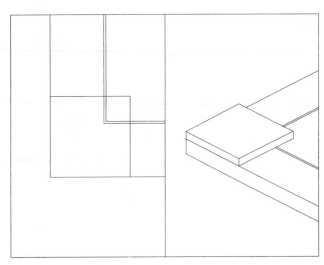

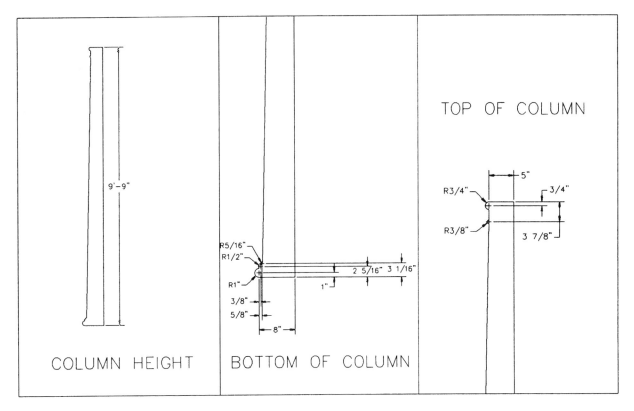

FIGURE 19–37
Dimensions for Drawing the Column

1. Zoom in on the lower left corner of the drawing as shown in Figure 19–36 in both viewports.
2. Use Box to draw the column base. The box measures 18″ × 18″ × 2″ height. Locate the "Corner of box" on the lower left corner of the border as shown. Use Osnap-Endpoint to click the first corner, then @18,18 to specify the other corner.

Draw the Columns

Draw the column and rotate it so it sits on top of the base (Figures 19–37, 19–38, 19–39, 19–40, and 19–41):

1. Use the dimensions in Figure 19–37 to draw the column in an open area of your drawing. Use the Line and Arc or Circle commands to draw this figure. It may be easier to

FIGURE 19–38
The Column Revolved

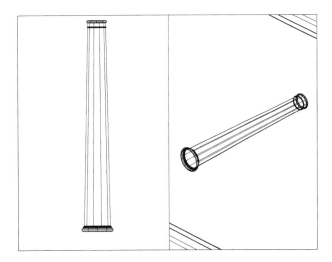

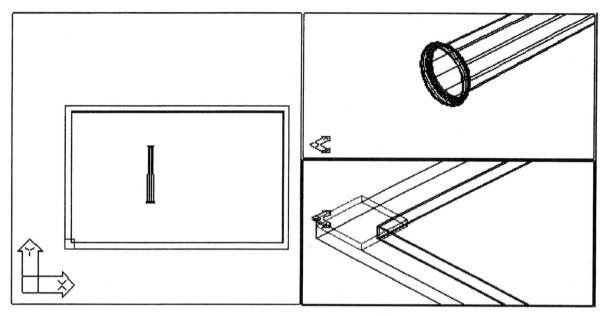

FIGURE 19–39
Move the UCS to the Top Lower Left Corner of the Base

FIGURE 19–40
Move the Column to the Center of the Base

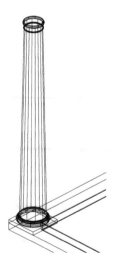

FIGURE 19–41
Rotate the Column to Its Upright Position

use Circle and Trim to draw the arcs on the bottom and top of the column instead of the Arc command.

2. Use Edit Polyline to join all the parts of Figure 19–37 into a single polyline.

3. Use the Revolve command to create the solid column as shown in Figure 19–38. Select both ends of the vertical line using Osnap-Endpoint as the Axis of revolution.

4. Use the VPORTS command to split the right viewport into two horizontal viewports and Zoom in on the bottom of the column and the box you drew as the column base, as shown in Figure 19–39.

5. Use the UCS command to move your UCS to the lower left corner of the top plane of the base as shown in Figure 19–39.

6. Use the Move command to move the column to the center of the base as shown in Figure 19–40. Use Osnap-Center as the Base point, and click the extreme bottom circular center of the column in the upper right viewport. TYPE: **9,9** as the second point of displacement to move the column to the center of the base.

7. Use the VPORTS command to return the display to two vertical viewports. Make the lower right viewport active, and use the join option of the VPORTS command to return the display to two vertical viewports.

8. Use the Rotate 3D command to rotate the column 90° about the X axis as shown in Figure 19–41.

Add the Cornice at the Top of the Column

Insert drawing 19–3 to form the cornice at the top of the column (Figures 19–42 and 19–43):

1. Use the Origin option of the UCS command to move the UCS to the extreme top of the column as shown in Figure 19–42. Use Osnap-Center to locate the UCS at that point.

2. Use the DDInsert command to insert drawing 19–3 onto the top of the column (Figure 19–43). Use the following:

Insertion point: 9-1/2,−9-1/2 (The bottom of the cornice drawing measures 19″, as shown in Figure 19–24. Because you picked the endpoint of the lower corner as the insertion point when you Wblocked the shape, 9-1/2,−9-1/2 will place the center of

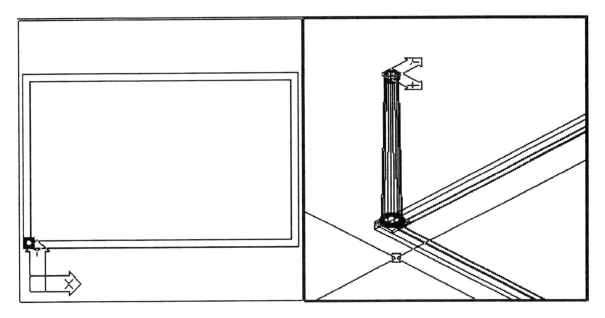

FIGURE 19–42
Move the UCS to the Center of the Top of the Column

FIGURE 19–43
Inserting the Cornice

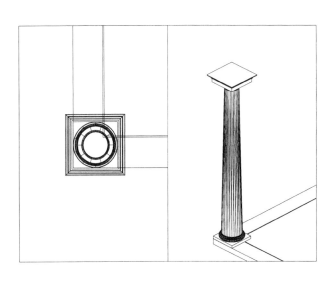

Tip: Be sure the insertion point is positive 9-1/2, negative −9-1/2.

the shape at the center of the column top. The shape must measure 24″ × 24″ when it is inserted. The arithmetic requires you to subtract 5″ from both measurements and divide by 2.)

After you have typed the insertion point and pressed <enter>, TYPE: **12<enter>** at the "X scale factor <1>/Corner/XYZ" prompt.

(The shape measures 2″ square, so an X scale factor of 12 will make the shape 24″ long.)

Y scale factor (default = X): PRESS: **<enter>** at this prompt (The shape must be 24″ in the Y direction also.)

The Z scale factor will also be X, even though you are not prompted to enter it. (The height of the original shape was reduced to $\frac{1}{12}$ of the $5\frac{1}{2}″$ dimension shown in Figure 19–24, so a scale factor of 12 will make it $5\frac{1}{2}″$ in this drawing.)

Rotation angle <0>: PRESS: **<enter>** at this prompt also.

3. Use the Explode command to explode the inserted cornice so it can be joined to form longer cornices. Explode it only once. If you explode it more than once, you destroy it as a solid.

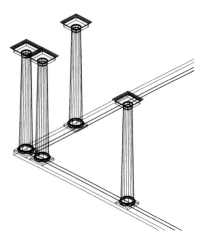

FIGURE 19–44
Copy the Base, Column, and Cornice Twice in the X Direction and Once in the Y Direction

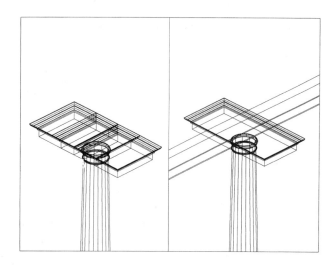

FIGURE 19–45
Copy the Cornice in the Positive X Direction and the Negative X Direction and Union of the Three Cornice Shapes

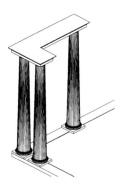

FIGURE 19–46
The L-Shaped Cornice after Using the Union and Hide Commands

Draw the Columns and Cornices at the Center and One Corner of the Structure

Copy the column and cornice to create supports at the center of the structure (Figures 19–44 and 19–45):

1. With Ortho ON use the Multiple option of the Copy command and direct distance entry to copy the column, its base, and cornice three times: 2′ and 12′9″ in the positive X direction, and once 6′2″ in the positive Y direction (Figure 19–44).

2. With Ortho ON use the Multiple option of the Copy command and direct distance entry to copy the cornice on the column that is to the far right 12″ in the positive X direction and 12″ in the negative X direction so that the cornice on this column will measure 48″ when the three are joined.

3. Use Union to join the cornice and the two copies to form a single cornice that is 48″ long (Figure 19–45).

Copy the cornice and join all the cornice shapes on the three corner columns to create the L-shaped cornice at the corner of the structure (Figure 19–46):

1. With Ortho ON use the Multiple option of the Copy command and direct distance entry to copy the cornice on the corner column six times: 12″ in the positive X direction and 12″, 24″, 36″, 48″, and 60″ in the positive Y direction so that the cornice on the three corner columns will measure 48″ in the X direction and 96″ in the Y direction when all these shapes are joined.

2. Use Union to join all the cornice shapes on the three corner columns to form a single L-shaped cornice, Figure 19–46.

Draw All the Remaining Columns

Mirror the existing columns twice to form the remaining columns (Figure 19–47):

1. Use the UCS command to return to the World UCS.

2. With Ortho ON use the Mirror command to form the columns on the right side of the structure. Select all existing columns, bases, and cornices. PRESS: **<enter>**, then using Osnap-midpoint, CLICK: **D1** (Figure 19–47) as the first point of the mirror line, then click any point directly above or below D1. Do not delete old objects.

3. With Ortho ON use the Mirror command to form the columns on the back side of the structure. Select all existing columns, bases, and cornices. PRESS: **<enter>**, then using Osnap-midpoint, CLICK: **D2** (Figure 19–47) as the first point of the mirror line, then click any point directly to the left or right of D2. Do not delete old objects.

FIGURE 19–47
Copying the Columns Using the
Mirror Command

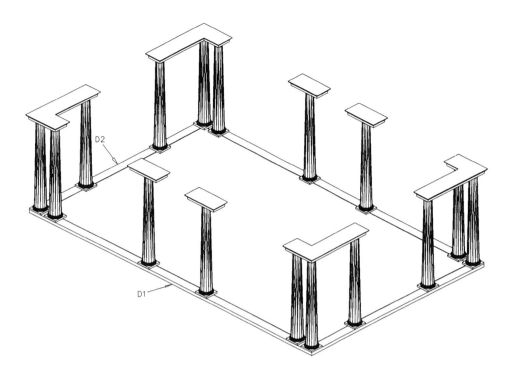

Draw the Upper Part of the Structure

Draw the front and rear elevations of the upper structure (Figure 19–48):

1. Use the UCS command to rotate the UCS 90° about the X axis.

2. Draw the upper part of the structure in an open area. You will move it to its correct location after it is completed.

3. Use the dimensions from Figure 19–48 to draw that shape with the Line and Arc or Circle commands.

4. Use Edit Polyline to join all the parts of the figure into a single polyline.

5. Use the Extrude command to extrude the polyline 8″ in the positive Z direction.

6. Use the Copy command to copy this shape 22′-6″ in the negative Z direction (Base point—click any point, Second point of displacement—@0,0,-22′6<enter>).

FIGURE 19–48
Dimensions for the Front and
Rear Elevations of the Upper
Structure

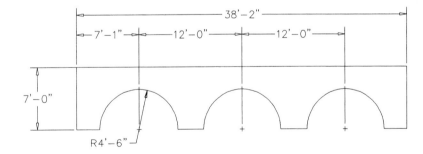

Draw the left and right elevations of the upper structure (Figures 19–49 and 19–50):

1. Use the UCS command to rotate the UCS 90° about the Y axis.

2. Use the dimensions from Figure 19–49 to draw that shape with the Line and Arc or Circle commands.

3. Draw the right side of the structure on the right ends of the front and rear planes (Figure 19–50).

4. Use Edit Polyline to join all the parts of the figure into a single polyline.

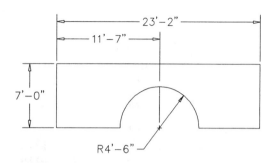

FIGURE 19–49
Dimensions for the Left and Right Elevations of the Upper Structure

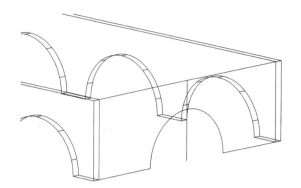

FIGURE 19–50
Draw the Right Elevation on the Right Ends of the Front and Rear Planes

5. Use the Extrude command to extrude the polyline 8″ in the negative Z direction.

6. Use the Copy command to copy this shape 37′-6″ in the negative Z direction (Base point - click any point, Second point of displacement - @0,0,−37′6<enter>).

Draw the roof and complete the upper part of the structure (Figures 19–51, 19–52, 19–53, and 19–54):

1. Make the 3d-c layer current.

2. Use the UCS command to return to the World UCS.

3. Use the Rectangle command to draw a rectangle to form the flat roof inside the upper part of the structure (Figure 19–51):

   First corner—D1
   Other corner—D2

4. Use the Extrude command to extrude the rectangle 8″ in the negative Z direction.

5. Use the Move command to move the extruded rectangle 18″ in the negative Z direction (Second point of displacement - @0,0,-18<enter>).

6. Use the Union command to join all parts of the upper structure into a single unit.

7. Use the Hide command to make sure your model is OK (Figure 19–52).

8. Use the UCS command to move the origin of the UCS to the endpoint of the lower left cornice (Figure 19–53).

9. Use the Move command to move the endpoint, D1 (Figure 19–54), of the lower right corner of the upper part of the structure to absolute coordinates 8,8,0. Be sure you do not put the @ symbol in front of the coordinates.

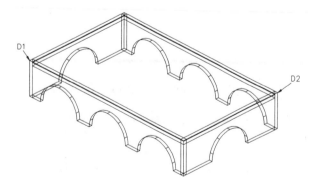

FIGURE 19–51
Draw a Rectangle to Form the Roof

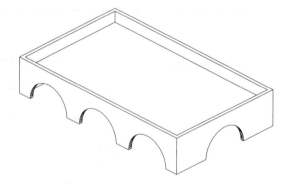

FIGURE 19–52
The Completed Upper Structure

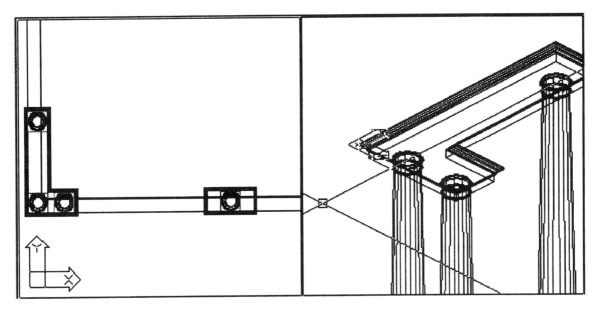

FIGURE 19–53
Move the UCS to the Top of the Cornice Corner

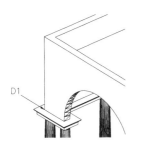

FIGURE 19–54
Move the Upper Structure into
Position

Insert Chairs to Complete the Model

Insert a chair at the correct elevation, copy it, rotate it, and complete Exercise 19–3 (Figures 19–55 and 19–56):

1. Use the UCS command to move the origin of the UCS to the top of the border surrounding the concrete pad, D1 (Figure 19–55).

2. Use the Insert command to insert the chair drawing, A:EX19-2, at absolute coordinates 18′,14′,0.

3. With Ortho ON use the Copy command to copy the chair three times to the approximate locations shown in Figure 19–56.

4. Use the Rotate command to rotate the chair on the far left 90°.

5. Use the 3Dviewpoint-Select... command to select a viewpoint of 315, 10.

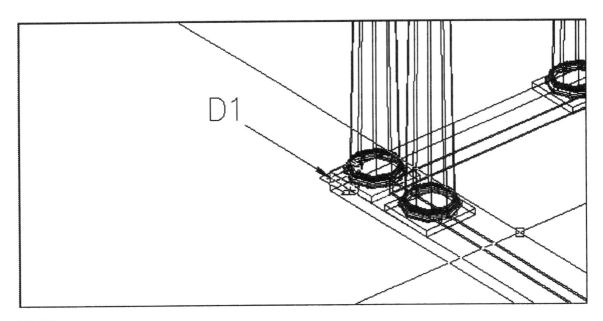

FIGURE 19–55
Move the UCS to the Top of the Border Surrounding the Pad

FIGURE 19–56
Locating the Chairs

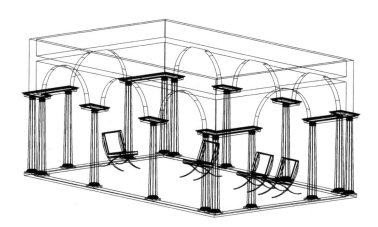

6. Use the Distance option of the Dview command. TYPE: **DV<enter>**, select the model, then TYPE: **D<enter>**, then TYPE: **100′** to select a viewing distance of 100′.

7. With the right viewport active, use the SIngle option of the VPORTS command to return the display to a single viewport.

8. Use the VPORTS command to save this view with the name VP1.

9. Set Tilemode to 0 or CLICK: **TILE** at the bottom of your display.

10. Use the Mview command (Floating Viewports) and restore VP1 in paper space. Use .5,.5 as the first point and 10.5,8 as the second point.

11. Use the Hideplot option of Mview to remove hidden lines when you plot. Turn Hideplot ON and click the outside edge of the viewport when you are prompted to select objects.

12. Use the Single Line Text command (TYPE: **DT<enter>**) to place your name in the lower right corner $\frac{1}{8}''$ high in the simplex font. Your final drawing should appear as shown in Figure 19–34.

SAVE

Use the SaveAs command to save your drawing in two places.

PLOT

Plot the drawing at a scale of 1=1.

EXERCISE 19–4
Drawing Solid Models of Eight Objects

1. Draw solid models of the eight objects shown in Figure 19–57. Use the dimensions shown in the top and front views of A through H:

   Draw the top view, join it to form a continuous polyline, and extrude it to the height shown in the front view.

   Rotate the UCS 90° about the X axis, draw a rectangle at the angle shown in the front view, extrude it, move it in the Z direction so it covers the area of the extruded top view that must be removed, and subtract it from the extruded top view.

2. Arrange the objects so that they are well spaced on the page and take up most of a 9″ × 7″ area on an 11″ × $8\frac{1}{2}''$ sheet.

3. Your final drawing should show eight solid objects in a viewpoint similar to Exercise 19–1.

4. Use UCS-View to place your name in the lower right corner in 1/8″ letters, and plot the drawing on an 11″ × $8\frac{1}{2}''$ sheet at a scale of 1=1.

5. Save your drawing in two places with the name EX19-4.

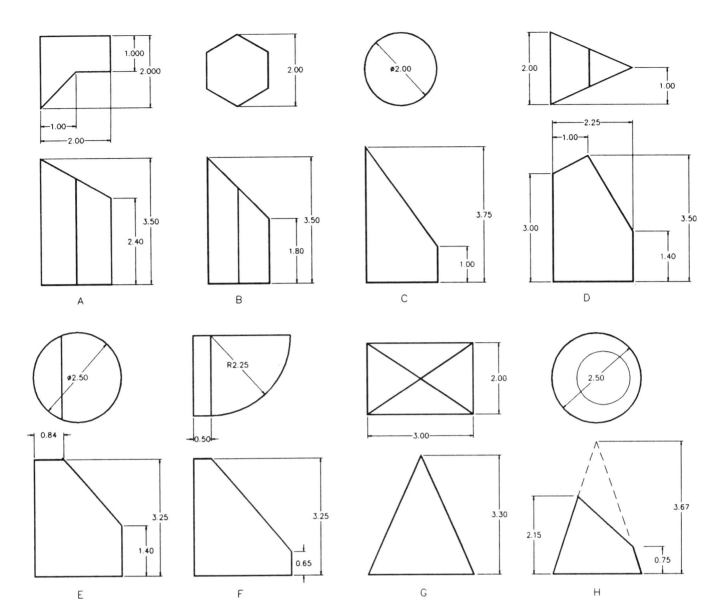

FIGURE 19–57
Exercise 19–4: Draw Solid Models of Eight Objects

EXERCISE 19–5
Drawing a Solid Model of a Lamp Table

1. Draw a solid model of the lamp table shown in Figure 19–58. Scale the top and front views using a scale of 1"=1'-0" to obtain the correct measurements for the model.

2. Use Revolve for the table pedestal. Use Polyline and Extrude for one table leg, and duplicate it with Polar Array. The table top can be an extruded circle or a solid cylinder.

3. Use the Distance option of the Dview command to obtain a perspective view of your final model and insert it into paper space before you plot.

4. Place your name in the lower right corner in $\frac{1}{8}''$ letters using simplex or an architectural font.

5. Plot the drawing at a scale of 1=1 on an 11" × $8\frac{1}{2}''$ sheet. Be sure to use the Hideplot option of the Mview command before plotting.

6. Return to model space with Tilemode ON (World UCS current) and Wblock the lamp table to a floppy disk with the name TABLE.

7. Save your drawing with the name EX19-5.

FIGURE 19–58
Exercise 19–5: Create a Solid
Model of a Table
(Scale: 1″ = 1′-0″)

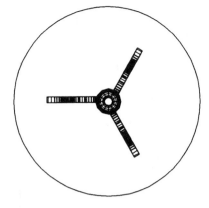

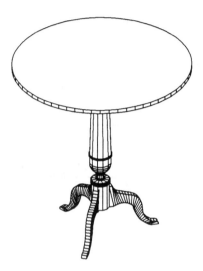

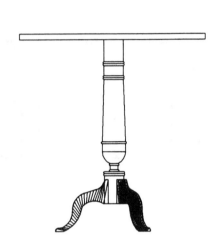

EXERCISE 19–6
Drawing a Solid Model of a One-Story House

1. Draw a solid model from the elevations and floor plan shown in Figure 19–59.

2. Draw only the exterior walls. It is not necessary to show brick, but you can if you like. You will have to experiment with a hatch pattern of brick and move it a fraction of an inch off the solid surface for it to show.

3. Measure the drawing at a scale of $\frac{1}{8}″=1′$ to get any dimensions not shown, and draw the model full scale.

4. You will have to use a hatch pattern such as AR-RSHKE on the roof. You may want to draw the roof, extrude it 1″, place your hatch pattern on it, and rotate it into place.

5. Use the Distance option of the Dview command to obtain a perspective veiw of your final model, and insert it into paper space before you plot.

6. Place your name in the lower right corner in 1″ letters using simplex or an architectural font.

7. Plot the drawing at a scale of $\frac{1}{8}″=1′-0″$ on an 11″ × $8\frac{1}{2}″$ sheet. Be sure to use the Hideplot option of the Mview command before plotting.

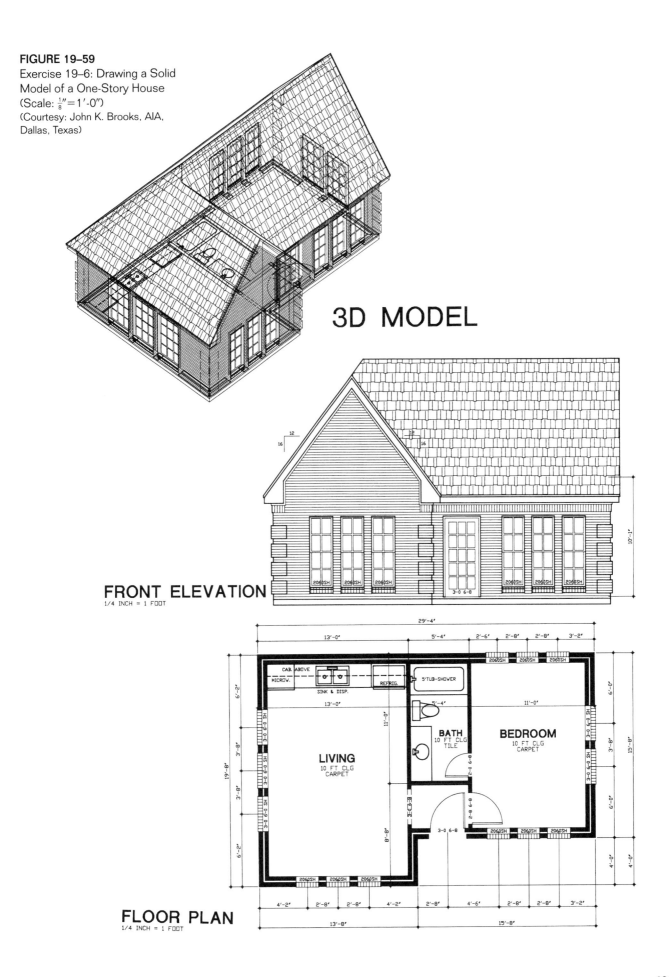

FIGURE 19–59

Exercise 19–6: Drawing a Solid
Model of a One-Story House
(Scale: $\frac{1}{8}''=1'\text{-}0''$)
(Courtesy: John K. Brooks, AIA,
Dallas, Texas)

3D MODEL

FRONT ELEVATION
1/4 INCH = 1 FOOT

FLOOR PLAN
1/4 INCH = 1 FOOT

EXERCISE 19–7
Drawing a Solid Model of a Two-Story House: Elevation I

1. Draw a solid model from the elevations and floor plan shown in Figure 19–60.

2. Draw only the exterior walls. It is not necessary to show brick, but you can if you like. You will have to experiment with a hatch pattern of brick and move it a fraction of an inch off the solid surface for it to show.

3. Measure the drawing at a scale of $\frac{1}{16}''=1'$, and draw the model full scale.

4. You will have to use a hatch pattern such as AR-RSHKE on the roof. You may want to draw the roof, extrude it 1", place your hatch pattern on it, and rotate it into place.

5. Use the Distance option of the Dview command to obtain a perspective view of your final model, and insert it into paper space before you plot.

6. Place your name in the lower right corner in 3" letters using simplex or an architectural font.

7. Plot the drawing at a scale of $\frac{1}{8}''=1'$-$0''$ on an $11'' \times 8\frac{1}{2}''$ sheet. Be sure to use the Hideplot option of the Mview command before plotting.

EXERCISE 19–8
Drawing a Solid Model of a Two-Story House: Elevation II

1. Draw a solid model from the elevations and floor plan shown in Figure 19–61.

2. Draw only the exterior walls. It is not necessary to show brick, but you can if you like. You will have to experiment with a hatch pattern of brick and move it a fraction of an inch off the solid surface for it to show.

3. Measure the drawing at a scale of $\frac{1}{16}''=1'$, and draw the model full scale.

4. You will have to use a hatch pattern such as AR-RSHKE on the roof. You may want to draw the roof, extrude it 1", place your hatch pattern on it, and rotate it into place.

5. Use the Distance option of the Dview command to obtain a perspective view of your final model, and insert it into paper space before you plot.

6. Place your name in the lower right corner in 3" letters using simplex or an architectural font.

7. Plot the drawing at a scale of $\frac{1}{8}''=1'$-$0''$ on an $11'' \times 8\frac{1}{2}''$ sheet. Be sure to use the Hideplot option of the Mview command before plotting.

FIGURE 19–60

Exercise 19–7: Drawing a Solid
Model of a Two-Story House: Ele-
vation I (Scale: $\frac{1}{16}'' = 1'-0''$)
(Courtesy: AmeriCAD, Inc., Plano,
Texas)

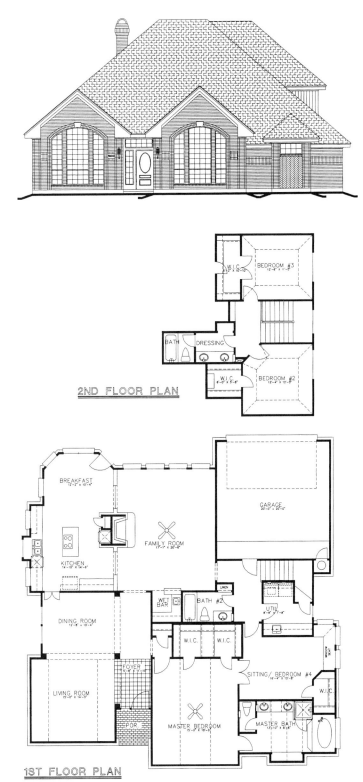

2ND FLOOR PLAN

1ST FLOOR PLAN

FIGURE 19–61

Exercise 19–8: Drawing a Solid Model of a Two-Story House: Elevation II (Scale: $\frac{1}{16}''=1'-0''$) (Courtesy: AmeriCAD, Inc., Plano, Texas)

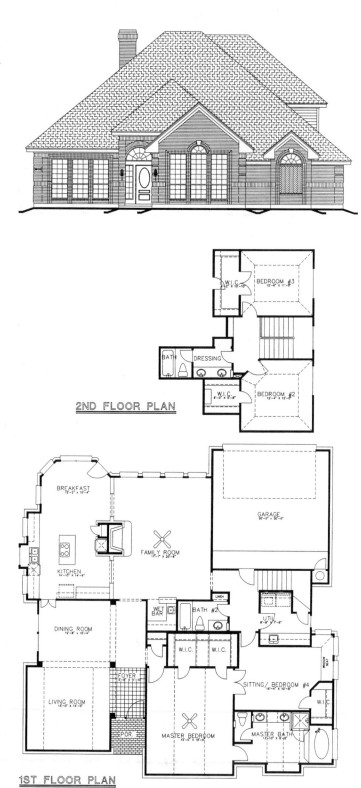

2ND FLOOR PLAN

1ST FLOOR PLAN

REVIEW QUESTIONS

1. Which of the following is *not* a SOLIDS command used to draw solid primitives?
   a. Box
   b. Cylinder
   c. Rectangle
   d. Wedge
   e. Sphere
2. Which of the following is used to make a rounded corners on a solid box?
   a. Chamfer
   b. Extrude
   c. Intersection
   d. Round
   e. Fillet
3. Which is the last dimension called for when the Box command is activated?
   a. Height
   b. Width
   c. Length
   d. First corner of box
   e. Other corner
4. Which is the first dimension called for when the Sphere command is activated?
   a. Segments in Y direction
   b. Segments in X direction
   c. Radius
   d. Center of sphere
   e. Diameter
5. Which of the following cannot be extruded?
   a. Polylines
   b. Circles
   c. Regions
   d. Polygons
   e. Solids
6. Which of the following commands is used to join several polylines into a single entity?
   a. Edit Polyline
   b. Offset
   c. Union
   d. Intersection
   e. Extrude
7. Which of the following is used to make a solid by revolving a polyline about an axis?
   a. Revolve
   b. Extrude
   c. Intersection
   d. Round
   e. Fillet
8. Which of the following adjusts the smoothness of objects rendered with the Hide command?
   a. SURFTAB1
   b. MESH
   c. SEGS
   d. WIRE
   e. FACETRES and ISOLINES
9. Which of the following allows you to rotate an object around X,Y, or Z axes?
   a. Rotate
   b. Rotate 3D
   c. Extrude
   d. Solrot
   e. Offset
10. Which of the following sets the number of lines on rounded surfaces of solids?
    a. FACETRES
    b. ISOLINES
    c. Union
    d. Fillet
    e. Interfere

11. List the six Solids commands used to make solid primitives.

_____   _____   _____

_____   _____   _____

12. List the Solids command used to extrude a polyline into a solid.

_____

13. List the Solids command used to create a new solid by cutting the existing solid into two pieces and removing or retaining either or both pieces.

_____

14. List the Solids command that allows you to join several solids into a single object.

_____

15. List the Solids command used to subtract solids from other solids.

_____

16. List the command and its option that is used to move the ucsicon so that it is displayed at the origin of the current coordinate system.

_____   _____
command   option

17. List the Solids command used to create a cross-sectional area of a solid.

_____

18. List the command and its option that allows you to view a solid model in perspective mode.

_____   _____
command   option

19. List the command and the rotation angle that may be used to rotate an object 90° clockwise about the Z axis.

_____   _____
command   rotation angle

20. List the Solids command used to create an object from the common volume of two intersecting solids.

_____

Glossary

Absolute coordinates The location of a point in terms of distances and/or angles from a fixed origin point.

Alias Two names for the same command (Example: L is an alias for LINE).

Ambient light The background light in a scene for rendering. It comes from no particular light source and does not create shadows.

ANSI American National Standards Institute; sets drafting standards.

Array A rectangular or circular pattern of graphical objects.

ASCII American Standard Code for Information Interchange; a standard set of 128 binary numbers representing keyboard information such as letters, numerals, and punctuation.

Associative dimensions Dimensions that automatically update their values when the associated geometry is modified.

Associative hatching Hatching of an area that changes as the size and shape of the area changes.

Attribute Textual information associated with CAD geometry. Attributes can be assigned to drawing objects and extracted from the drawing database. Applications include creating bills of material.

AUI Advanced User Interface; a user-interface enhancement that includes on-screen dialog boxes, a menu bar that can be customized, pull-down menus, and icon menus.

AutoCAD Development System (ADS) A C programming language used to create programs to run with AutoCAD.

Autodesk Device Interface (ADI) A system of developing device drivers needed for peripherals such as printers, digitizers, and monitors to work with the AutoCAD program.

AutoLISP A programming language contained within the AutoCAD program that is used for writing macros for graphics applications.

B-spline curve A blended piecewise polynomial curve passing near a given set of control points. The blending functions are the type that provide more local control, as opposed to other curves like Bezier.

Baseline dimensioning A dimension relative to a fixed horizontal or vertical datum or reference.

Baud rate See *bps*.

Binary The numerical base, base 2, by which computers operate. The electrical circuitry of a computer is designed to recognize only two states, high and low, which easily translate to logical and arithmetic values of 1 and 0. For example, the binary number 11101 represents the decimal number 29.

Bit (binary digit) The smallest unit of computer data.

Bitmap A picture made up of dots or pixels instead of vectors.

Blips Temporary screen markers displayed on the AutoCAD screen when you digitize or specify a point.

Block One or more AutoCAD objects grouped to create a single object.

Board (printed circuit board) Board onto which components are soldered and connected via etched circuits on the board.

Boot To turn the computer on and start a program.

bps (bits per second) A unit of transmission; also called baud rate.

Buffer An intermediate storage device (hardware or software) between data handling units.

Busy lamp Indicator on the front of a disk drive that lights when the drive is writing or reading a disk.

Byblock A condition whereby the object inherits the color or linetype of any block containing it.

Bylayer A condition whereby the object inherits the color or linetype associated with its layer.

Byte A string of 8 bits representing 256 different binary values. A kilobyte (Kbyte) is 1024 bytes.

CAD Computer-aided design; the use of graphics-oriented computer software for designing and drafting applications.

Chamfer A beveled edge or corner between two otherwise intersecting lines or surfaces.

Chip (integrated circuit) A miniature circuit made by etching electronic components on a silicon wafer.

Clipping The process of setting the display boundaries of graphical items.

Clock Electronic timer used to synchronize computer operations. A clock is an indication of the speed of the computer operations.

Cold boot Starting the computer by turning it off and then on again.

Command A word used to initiate a task.

COM port A communications port allowing data to flow into and out of the computer. Most communication ports are serial ports. Digitizers and most plotters are connected to communication ports. Most COM ports have pins rather than holes.

Composite region A single 2D object resulting from the intersection, union, or subtraction of two or more regions.

Composite solid A single 3D solid object resulting from the intersection, union, or subtraction of two or more solids.

Configuration A particular grouping of computer hardware as a functional unit. It may also include the allocation of hardware resources and sometimes refers to software parameter settings.

Coons patch A bicubic surface patch interpolated between four adjoining general space curves.

Coordinate filters An AutoCAD feature (also called XYZ point filters) that allows a user to extract individual X, Y, and Z coordinate values from different points in order to create a new, composite point.

CPU Central processing unit; it is responsible for arithmetic computations, logic operations, memory addresses, and data and control signal traffic in a computer.

Crosshairs A cursor usually made up of two perpendicular lines on the display screen used to select coordinate locations.

CRT Cathode-ray tube; the video display tube used with computers.

Cursor An indicator on the display screen that shows where the next entered data will appear.

Database Related information organized and stored so that it can be easily retrieved and, typically, used in multiple applications. A noncomputer example of a database is the telephone directory.

Default A parameter or variable that remains in effect until changed. It is what a computer program assumes in the absence of specific user instructions.

Dimension style A named group of settings for each dimensioning variable affecting the appearance of a dimension. Also called a dimstyle in AutoCAD.

Directory Groups of files identified by a directory name.

Disk or diskette A thin, flexible platter coated with a magnetic material for storing information.

Disk or diskette drive A magnetic device that writes on and retrieves data from a disk.

Display resolution The number of horizontal and vertical rows of pixels that can be displayed by a particular graphics controller or monitor. For example, 640 columns and 350 rows of pixels can be displayed by a standard EGA graphics controller and color monitor.

Display screen A video-display tube or CRT used to transmit graphical information.

DOS Disk operating system; software that controls the operation of disk drives, memory usage, and I/O in a computer.

Dragging Dynamically moving the virtual image of a graphical entity across the display screen to a new location using a mouse.

Drawing file A collection of graphical data stored as a set (file) in a computer.

Drive A device used to read or write information on a disk or diskette.

DXF Drawing interchange file; a file format used to produce an ASCII description of an AutoCAD drawing file.

Edit To modify existing data.

Endpoint The exact location on a line or curve where it terminates.

Enter key (↵) Sometimes called the Return key; it signals the computer to execute a command or terminate a line of text.

Expansion slot Location inside the system unit for the connection of an optional printed circuit board. Expansion slots for optional boards are available in many computers.

Expansion option Add-on hardware that expands power and versatility.

External reference A drawing file that is linked (or attached) to another drawing. Also called an XREF in AutoCAD.

Extrusion In AutoCAD, the process of assigning a thickness property to a given entity. The direction of the extrusion is always parallel to the Z axis of the UCS in effect when the entity was created.

Face A bounded section of the surface of a modeled object.

Fence A line that selects objects it passes through.

File Information stored by a computer.

Fill Solid coloring covering an area bounded by lines and/or curves.

Fillet A curved surface of constant radius blending two otherwise intersecting surfaces; a 2D representation of the preceding involving two lines or curves and an arc.

Finite Element Analysis (FEA) Numerical technique of approximately determining field variables such as displacements or stresses in a domain. This is done by breaking down the domain into a finite number of "pieces," also called "elements," and solving for the unknowns in those elements.

Finite Element Modeling (FEM) Process of breaking down a geometric model into a mesh, called the finite element mesh model, that is used for finite element analysis.

Floppy disk A circular plastic disk coated with magnetic material mounted in a square cardboard or plastic holder. It is used by a computer to store information for use later. It can be inserted or removed from a floppy disk drive at will. It is also called a diskette.

Folder A group of files identified by a folder name.

Font A distinctive text typeface, usually named and recognized by the aesthetic appearance of its characters.

Formatting Preparing a disk to accept data.

Function key A key on the keyboard that can be assigned to perform a task. A function key is typically used as a shortcut to a lengthy string of keystrokes.

Grid An area on the graphics display covered with regularly spaced dots used as a drawing aid.

Hard copy A paper printout of information stored in a computer.

Hard disk A rigid magnetic storage device that provides fast access to stored data.

Hardware The electronic and mechanical parts of a computer.

Hatching A regular pattern of line segments covering an area bounded by lines and/or curves.

High-density The storage capacity of a disk or disk drive that uses high-capacity disks.

Hz (hertz) A unit of frequency equal to one cycle per second.

Icon A graphical symbol typically used to convey a message or represent a command on the display screen.

IGES Initial Graphics Exchange Specification: a file format for the exchange of information between CAD (and CAM) systems.

Interface A connection that allows two devices to communicate.

I/O Input/output; a mechanism by which a computer accepts or distributes information to peripheral devices such as plotters, printers, disk drives, and modems.

ISO An abbreviation for isometric, a view or drawing of an object where the projections of the X, Y, and Z axes are spaced 120° apart and the projection of the Z axis is vertical.

KB (kilobyte) 1024 bytes.

Layer A logical separation of data to be viewed individually or in combination. Similar in concept to transparent acetate overlays.

Linetype Sometimes called line font, it represents the appearance of a line. For example, a continuous line has a different linetype than a dashed line.

Load Enter a program into the computer's memory from a storage device.

Load lever Lever on the front of a disk drive that locks the disk in place.

Macro A single command made up of a string of commands.

MB (megabyte) One million bytes.

Memory   An electronic part of a computer that stores information.

Menu   A display of programs or tasks.

MHz (megahertz)   One thousand hertz.

Microprocessor   An integrated circuit "chip" (or set of chips) that acts as the CPU of a computer.

Mirror   To create the reverse image of selected graphical items.

Mode   A software setting or operational state.

Model   A 2- or 3D representation of an object.

Model space   Space in which model geometry is created and maintained. Typically, you draw entities in model space to scale of the design feature. Model space is the complement of paper space. See *paper space*.

Modem (modulator-demodulator)   A device that links computers over a telephone.

Monochrome   A video display that features different shades of a single color.

Motherboard   The main printed circuit board in a computer to which all other boards are connected.

Mouse   A hand-operated, relative-motion device used to position the cursor on a computer display screen.

Network   An electronic linking of computers for communication.

Numerical control (NC)   Programmable automation of machine tools.

Operating system   Also called the disk operating system; software that manages computer resources and allows a user access and control.

Origin   The intersection point of the axes in a coordinate system. For example, the origin of a Cartesian coordinate system is the point at which the X, Y, and Z axes meet, (0, 0, 0).

Orthographic projection   The 2D representation of a 3D object without perspective. In drafting, it is typically the front, top, and right-side views of an object.

Ortho mode   An AutoCAD setting that permits only horizontal or vertical input from the graphical pointing device (mouse, puck, or stylus).

Osnap   Object snap, an AutoCAD setting that allows the user to specify point locations based on existing geometry. This allows for the graphic selection of the precise location of midpoints and endpoints of lines, center points and tangent points of circles and arcs, etc.

Overwrite   Storing information at a location where information is already stored, thus destroying the original information.

Pan   Redefines the display boundaries without changing magnification. It is analogous to panning a camera.

Paper space   Space in which documentation graphics such as title blocks, some annotation, or borders could reside. Typically, you create entities in paper space to the scale at which they will be plotted. Some 3D features also work in paper space. Working in paper space allows you to work with non-tiled viewports. See *model space*.

Parallel interface   Interface that communicates 8, 16, or 32 bits at a time.

Parallel port   A connector on the back of the computer that usually has holes rather than pins. This connector always has 25 connections. Most printers are connected to parallel ports.

Parallel printer   A printer with a parallel interface.

Peripheral   An input or output device not under direct computer control.

Perspective projection   The simulation of distance by representing parallel lines converging at a vanishing point.

Pixels (picture elements)   Tiny dots that make up a screen image.

Plotter   A computer-controlled device that produces text and images on paper or acetate by electrostatic, thermal, or mechanical means (with a pen).

Point light   A single point source that emits beams of light.

Polar coordinate   A coordinate specified by a distance and angle from an origin.

Polyline   An AutoCAD geometric entity composed of one or more connected segments treated as a single entity. Polylines can be converted into curves.

Port   A connection on a computer where a peripheral device can be connected.

Primitive   A basic geometric model from which more complex models are constructed. Primitives are points and lines in wire-frame models and simple shapes such as blocks, cones, and cylinders in solid models.

Processor   A computer on a chip.

Program   A detailed list of instructions that will be quickly, precisely, and blindly followed by a computer.

Prompt   A message from the computer software requesting a response from the user.

RAM (random-access memory)   Temporary read/write memory that stores information only when the computer is on.

Read   To extract data from a storage device such as a floppy disk or hard disk.

Region primitive   A closed 2D area created by solidifying objects such as polylines, arcs, and circles.

Relative coordinates   Coordinates specified by differences in distances and/or angles measured from a previous set of coordinates rather than from the origin point.

Rendering   The application of color, light, and shading to a 2- or 3D model.

Right-hand rule   Using the fingers of the right hand to remember the relative directions of the positive X, Y, and Z axes of a Cartesian coordinate system. It is particularly useful in Auto-CAD in visualizing UCS orientations.

ROM (read-only memory)   Permanent computer memory that cannot be written to.

RS-232C   Standard interface cable for serial devices.

Save   To store data on a disk.

Selection set   One or more entities selected for processing with a command.

Serial interface   An interface that communicates information one bit at a time.

Serial port   A connector on the back of the computer that has pins rather than holes. This connector may have either 9 pins or 25 pins.

Serial printer   A printer with a serial interface (receives information one bit at a time).

Slide   A file that contains a raster image or snapshot of the display on the graphics screen. It has the extension .sld.

Slide library   A collection of slide files organized for convenient retrieval and display.

Software   Computer programs.

Solid model   A computer representation of a fully enclosed 3D shape. Solid models define the space a real object occupies in addition to the surface that bounds the object.

Spotlight   A light source that emits a directional cone of light.

Structured Query Language (SQL)   A language that AutoCAD uses to communicate with external databases.

Surface model A 3D representation of an object made of a wire frame on which surfaces are attached. A surface model is hollow. A solid model is solid.

Surface of revolution A surface generated by revolving a profile curve around an axis.

System board The main printed circuit board inside the system unit, into which other boards are connected.

System unit The component that contains the computer parts, disk drives, and option boards.

Tiling Approximation of all of an object's surfaces with planar facets, or tiles. A tiling engine automatically generates pixel data for an array of tiles for use in a color-shaded display or plot.

TILEMODE An AutoCAD system variable that controls whether viewports are tiled or nontiled when created.

Toolbar Icons that initiate commands grouped together for the convenience of the operator.

Transparent command A command started while another is in progress. If you choose to type a transparent command while another command is in process, precede the command name with an apostrophe.

Unit A user-defined distance. It may be inches, meters, miles, etc.

User coordinate system A movable, user-defined coordinate system used for convenient placement of geometry. It is frequently referred to as the UCS.

Vector A mathematical entity with a precise direction and length (but no specific location).

View A graphical representation of a 2D drawing or 3D model from a specific location (viewpoint) in space.

Viewpoint A location in 3D model space from which a model is viewed.

Viewport A bounded area on a display screen that might contain a view. If a viewport is created when TILEMODE is set to 1, then it is tiled. When TILEMODE is set to 0, viewports are created with the Mview command. They are nontiled or model space viewports and reside in paper space. See *model space* and *paper space*.

Wireframe model A 2D or 3D representation of an object consisting of boundary lines or edges of an object.

World Coordinate System (WCS) A coordinate system used as the basis for defining all objects and other coordinate systems.

Write To record or store information in a storage device.

Write-enable notch Slot on the side of a floppy disk that when uncovered permits the disk to be written on.

Write-protecting Covering a floppy disk write-enable notch, thus preventing writing on the disk.

Zoom The process of reducing or increasing the magnification of graphics on the display screen.

Index

D

E

Menu commands, 415
Menu Customization dialog box, 410
Menu files, 410–419
  copying, 412
  loading, 418
  making new, 410–19
  menugroup, 414
  renaming, 412
  saving, 420
  unloading, 420
Menugroup, 414
MENULOAD command, 418
Mhz (Megahertz), 503
Microprocessor, 503
Microsoft Windows, 12
Midpoint Osnap mode, 89, 91
Minsert command, 177
Mirror command, 233, 234, 503
Mirroring objects, 233, 234
Mirroring text (*See* MIRRTEXT system variable)
Mirror 3D command, 459
MIRRTEXT system variable, 233
Mledit command, 164, 165
Mline command, 161–64
Mlstyle command, 158, 161
Mode, 503
Model, 503
Model space, 366, 503
Model space (floating), 372, 436
  Hideplot, 437
Model space icon, 232
Modem, 503
Modify-attribute-global, 281
Modify-attribute-single, 279
Modify menu, 17
Modify-object-text, 216
Monitors, 11
Motherboard, 503
Mouse, 12, 503
Move command, 58–61
Moving objects, 58–61
Mslide command, 395
Mspace command, 366
Mtext command, 125
Multiline command, 161–64
Multiline style command, 158–61
Multiline text command, 125, 135, 136
Mview command, 372, 373
  Fit, 373
  Hideplot, 373, 437
  Off, 373
  On, 373
  Restore, 350, 373
Mvsetup command, 379
  align, 384
  create, 384
    options, 384
    scale viewports, 384
    title block, 384
    undo, 384

N

Nearest Osnap mode, 42
Network, 503
New command, 28, 76, 156
NEWTEXT command, 216
New Toolbar dialog box, 394
Node, 88, 89
Node Osnap mode, 89, 91
None Osnap mode, 89, 91
Non-tiled viewports, 372
Notepad, Windows, 414
Numerical control, 503
Numeric keys, 11

O

Object Properties toolbar, 46
Object Snap modes, 89, 91, 92
Oblique dimensioning, 214
Offset command, 78, 79
Offsetting objects, 78, 79
Oops command, 48, 171
Open a drawing, 28, 46
Open traverse, 324–27
Operating system, 503
Ordinate dimensioning, 188
Origin, UCS, 503
Origin for plotting/printing, 146, 503
ORTHO mode, 47
Osnap modes, 89, 91, 92
Osnap tracking, 84
Outlet plan, 314
Overscore text, 133

P

Pan command, 57, 503
  realtime, 57
  scroll bars, 57
Paper size and orientation for plotting, 146, 147, 152
Paper space, 366, 379, 503
Paper space icon, 366, 379
Paragraph text, 125, 135, 136
Parallel interface, 503
Parallel lines, 78, 79
Parallel port, 503
Parallel printer, 503

T

Tangent Osnap mode, 92
Tangents, drawing, 92
Telephone legend, 307, 308, 314, 317
Templates, 39
Tenant space floor plan, 156–78
Tenant space reception area, 3D, 440–51
Text, 125, 128–35, 136
   changing properties, 136–38
   line, 125, 128–35
   paragraph, 135–36
Text Fill (Print/Plot Configuration dialog box), 145, 151
Text fonts, 126
Text style, 125
Text Style dialog box, 127
Thawing layers, 36, 374–76
Thickness, 425–28, 448
3D, 8
3D Blocks, 479
3D coordinates, 445–56
3D Dynamic View, 395
3D Models, 8
3D Objects, 439
3D Surfaces, 439
3D Viewpoint, 429–33
3D Viewpoint Select dialog box, 391, 429
Tick marks, 190
Tiff file, 113
Tiled Viewports, 367, 372, 429
   delete, 370
   join, 370
   restore, 370
   save, 367, 436
   single, 370
   2, 3, 4, 370
Tilemode command, 372, 504
Tiling, 504
Title block, 379
Toggle to isoplanes, 342
Toolbar command, 19–21
Toolbars, 19, 46, 504, 393–413
   changing the appearance, 401
   changing the shape, 20, 400
   closing, 21, 28
   customizing, 22, 393–408
   deleting, 399, 408
   displaying, 19, 20, 397
   docked, 21, 22
   floating, 19
   flyouts, 406–8
   moving, 402
   naming, 394–96, 398
   new, 394–96, 398
   renaming, 400
   top level, 19
Toolbars dialog box, 19
Tools:
   adding space between, 400
   adding to toolbars, 395
   buttons, large, 21
   copying, 398
   creating, 403
   deleting, 396
   icons, making, 404, 405
   macros, 403, 404
   moving, 398
   repositioning, 402
   resizing, 21
Tools menu, 16
Tooltips, 17
Torus, 439, 440, 447
Tracking Osnap mode, 84
Transparent commands, 57
Traverse:
   closed, 327–30
   open, 324–27
Trim command, 81
2D coordinates, 49, 50
2D drawings, 2–9
2D Solid, 68, 69, 158, 427

U

U command, 48
UCS command, 231, 237, 242
   and 3D Viewpoint, 447
   Delete, 231
   Named, 242
   Object, 231, 447
   Origin, 231, 426, 444
   Restoring, 231
   Rotating, 445, 446
   Save, 237
   3-Point, 231, 448
   View, 446
   World, 231, 444
   XYZ, 445
   Z-axis, 444
UCS control dialog box, 243
UCSFOLLOW command, 451
Ucs Icon command, 232, 443
Ucs Orientation dialog box, 452
Underlining text, 133
Underscore, 133
Undo command, 48, 61–63
Union command, 459, 474–76
Unit, 29, 504